THE CINEMATIC CENTURY

THE CINEMATIC CENTURY

An Intimate Diary of America's Affair with the Movies

HARRY HAUN

APPLAUSE

NEW YORK • LONDON

An Applause Original

THE CINEMATIC CENTURY

By Harry Haun

Copyright © 2000 Applause Books

ISBN 1-55783-400-8 (trade paperback)

Supervising Editor and Publisher: Glenn Young
Managing Editor and Interior Design: Greg Collins
Cover Design: Angela Lidderdale
Production Director: Paul Sugarman
Publicity Director: Kay Radtke

PHOTOGRAPHS COURTESY OF PHOTOFEST

Photo Research and assistance
by John Cocchi

Library of Congress Cataloging-In-Publication Data

Library of Congress Card Number: 99-068812

British Library Catalogue in Publication Data
A catalogue record for this book is available from the British Library

APPLAUSE BOOKS

1841 Broadway # 1100
New York, NY 10023
Phone (212) 765-7880
Fax: (212) 765-7875

Combined Book Services Ltd.
Units I/K Paddock Wood Distribution Centre
Paddock Wood, Tonbridge, Kent TN12 6UU
Phone: (44) 01892 837171
Fax (44) 01892 837272

10   9   8   7   6   5   4   3   2   1

This book is dedicated to

The World's Greatest Movie Fan,

wherever he is . . .

. . . and to the people who helped it happen. Here are some: Richard Adelson, Monty Arnold, Jean Bach, Bob Balaban, Roger Blunck, David Blum, Michael Buckley, John Cocchi, Greg Collins, Lauren B. Cramer, Scott Dunn, Bob Edison, Julius J. Epstein, Bruce Feld, Lucy Lee Flippen, Joe Frazzetta, John Fricke, David Grambs, Jim Haspiel, Edward Hibbert, Jim Hitt, Don Humphreys, Kelly Keele, Bill Kenly, Jane Klain, Nancy Kolomitz, Kevin Lally, Dick Lemon, Kevin Lewis, Lillian Lewis, Howard Mandelbaum, Howard McMillin, Wilson Morales, Charles Nelson, Joanna Ney, Brent Oldham, Robert Osborne, Bob Porter, Robert Rosterman, Mervyn Rothstein, Vinnie Sassone, Shirley Sealy, Daniel Mayer Selznick, Cathy Smith, Eric Spilker, John Springer, Sam Staggs, George Stevens Jr., Paul Sugarman, Tabitha Rivera, Jim Watters, Phil Weinstock and Beverly Wright.

IN PRAISE OF MOVIE MYOPIA

Of course Mama Rose knows a Depression is going on. She reads Variety, doesn't she?

And, yes—to the professional showfolks who inhabit the world of *All About Eve* and try out plays out of town—New Haven is "a short stretch of sidewalk between the Shubert Theater and the Taft Hotel, surrounded by what looks very much like a small city."

It's all a question of focus orientation—selective seeing. The 20th century is the first century to provide, from beginning to end, an unreal world-view—an attractive alternative to a world too much with us. Some call it film. Some call it movies. Some call it cinema.

The picture that moves—movies—was just flickering into existence in fits and starts when the century rounded the bend from the 19th to the 20th, and, by the time it took that turn again, it had grown immeasurably. Some films now tower to skyscraper-size. Some gain a dimension beyond the flat screen. Some smell bad, on purpose. Almost all utilize every color of the rainbow. And many of them are endowed with great emotional depth.

Inevitably, psychic inroads have been made from screen to soul. Movies are now a part of the fabric of our lives, illusion weaving into reality weaving into illusion. How well they do at the box office is legitimate news in most papers and play alongside harsher realities.

In the early '60s, when the U.S. and the U.S.S.R. were "eyeball to eyeball" and waving destructive missiles at each other, President Kennedy took a break from the terrible tension and, for 119 minutes, wrapped himself around the easy enchantment of *Roman Holiday*. And, when he was struck down by an assassin's bullet in Dallas, Audrey Hepburn was inside an English coach on the Burbank backlot, filming *My Fair Lady*.

When the wall separating East and West Germany went up, it created a great human crisis, the least of which was the conflict it caused Billy Wilder (he was there shooting *One Two Three* and had to build his own Brandenburg Gate on a studio set). When the wall came down, it instantly neutralized a Cold War thriller Nicholas Meyer was shooting there.

In spring of 1939, when all of Europe was going to hell in a handbasket, Louella Parsons led off her syndicated column with an impressive disregard for the world she lived in. "The deadly dullness of the last week," she said, "was lifted today when Darryl Zanuck admitted he had bought all rights to Maurice Maeterlinck's *The Blue Bird* for Shirley Temple."

Here, then, is a history book for the reality-challenged—events small and smaller, viewed through the wrong end of the telescope, missing The Big Picture a country mile to swim contentedly in the movie minutiae. It is not intended to trivialize the real world—just keep it at bay. It is an entertainment, nothing more and hopefully nothing less.

Harry Haun
October, 1999

AN UNDULATING DAME: Garbo as *Two-Faced Woman*.
AN INDECISIVE DANE: Olivier as *Hamlet*.
AN AIDS FATALITY: Ron Vawter, Jason Robards and Tom Hanks in *Philadelphia*.

1

1942: Critics, on this day, start tearing at *Two-Faced Woman* like a dog with a rag. This misguided attempt (albeit by **George Cukor**) to Americanize the enigmatic **Garbo** produced a weird spectacle: The sight of The Swedish Sphinx skiing, swimming and undulating a wicked rumba, scoffed *Time*, "is almost as shocking as seeing your mother drunk." *But nobody meant for her to go away forever!* "In this hard new world, there is no place for me anymore," sighed Two-Faced Woman. Then, Garbo lived it—and made a permanent screen exit.

1947: The New Year's Honors List posted today proclaims a new Bachelor Knight of the Theater: **Ralph Richardson** — and the buzz begins, "Can **Laurence Olivier** be far behind?" As it happened, Olivier was a mere seven months and seven days away; he spent this New Year's Day cinching his knighthood by phoning Zurich to inform his financier, **Filippo Del Giudice**, he was nixing one soon-to-be-Oscared title role (Cyrano de Bergerac) so he could do another (his Hamlet).

1950: The grand plan to return **Garbo** to films after eight years is history. Only the day before, **Walter Wanger** gave MCA his proposition to produce her comeback abroad, but he did this without any supporting documents, allowing agent **Jules Stein** the legal lever to call the whole thing off. Garbo's long-promised comeback never got beyond some ravishing test footage shot by designated cameraman **James Wong Howe**. (The magic was still there.)

1960: The man who threw color on the silver screen — **Dr. Herbert T. Kalmus**, 78 — retires from the company he had founded 45 years before: Technicolor.

1969: "The only Indian I haven't played is Pocahontas," **Burt Reynolds** memos his agent (**Dick Clayton**) on this day. "I'm tired of shaving my arms — it's easy to get the left, but when you shave the right with your left, you cut yourself to ribbons." Two years after this S.O.S., he was delivered *Deliverance*, his best flick. Director **John Boorman** opted for Reynolds not from screening his films but from watching him sub for **Johnny Carson** on *The Tonight Show*.

1995: *The New York Times* reports that, of the 53 actors in 1993's *Philadelphia* who had AIDS or were H.I.V. positive, all but ten have died — including **Ron Vawter**, the gay actor playing **Tom Hanks**' straight colleague who sounded the lone note of compassion among Hanks' homophobic fellow attorneys.

THE MONSTER, THE MASTER AND THE MRS.: From left, Boris Karloff, director James Whale, and Elsa Lanchester, working on *Bride of Frankenstein*.
STARS PASSING: Dick Powell and Jack Carson finally crossing professional paths for a television show 18 months before their deaths.

1930: *Such Men Are Dangerous*, a bromidic drama in which a rich and ugly **Warner Baxter** remedies his love life with plastic surgery (administered by a benign **Bela Lugosi**!), proves tragically well-titled on this day when two film-crew planes collide in midair over the Pacific, killing 10 (including director **Kenneth Hawks**, husband of **Mary Astor** and brother of **Howard Hawks**). The incident still stands in *The Guinness Book of Records* as Hollywood's worst accident.

1935: Director **James Whale** begins on this day the impossible chore he has been ducking for four years — a sequel that will be superior to his original *Frankenstein* — and, to the minds of many, he succeeds brilliantly with *Bride of Frankenstein*. In a career cluttered with colorful and eccentric characters, the title performance remains **Elsa Lanchester**'s most memorable. Ironically, she was identified only as playing The Monster's literary creator, Mary Wollstonecraft Shelley, in the film's prologue (the credits claimed "The Monster's Mate" was played by "?"). Few documentaries on horror films resist clipping Lanchester's love-at-first-screech reaction to The Monster of her dreams (**Boris Karloff**).

1940: Dentist **Petter Lindstrom** sees his actress-wife and their **Pia** off to a new life on this day as the *Rex* sails out of Genoa. Producer **David O. Selznick**, fearing World War II would keep her in Sweden, summoned his *Intermezzo* star — **Ingrid Bergman** — even though he had no vehicle waiting for her. **Shaw**'s *Saint Joan*, a part she coveted, he nixed—wrongly (**Maxwell Anderson**'s rewrite of that role landed her a Tony award in 1947 and an Oscar nomination in 1948). When two shots at co-starring with **Fredric March** (*Victory* and *So Ends Our Night*) went by the boards and the American remake of her own Swedish hit, *A Woman's Face*, went to **Joan Crawford** — Selznick, just to keep Bergman busy, let her do Broadway (Julie to **Burgess Meredith**'s Liliom); stalling for more time, the mogul leased her out to Columbia (for *Adam Had Four Sons*) and MGM (for *Rage in Heaven* and the **Spencer Tracy** *Dr. Jekyll and Mr. Hyde*). Then — hallelujah! — came *Casablanca*. . .

1963: Two former Warner contractees who were real-life neighbors die of cancer on this day — within five hours of each other: **Jack Carson**, 52, and **Dick Powell**, 58.

1974: A heart attack silences singing cowboy **Tex Ritter**, 67, on this day. The star of some 80 B-grade shoot-'em-ups (*Arizona Days*, *Roll, Wagons, Roll*, etc.), had only one A-film credit — and that was invisible: in 1952, mournfully wailing **Dimitri Tiomkin**'s Oscar-winning "High Noon (Do Not Forsake Me, Oh My Darlin')" while **Gary Cooper** manfully strode out to meet the Miller gang.

1931: Sweden's **Warner Oland**, following two Japanese actors (**George Kuwa** and **Kamiyama Sojin**) and an English one (**E.L. Park**) into the role of **Earl Derr Biggers**' aphorism-spouting Chinese sleuth, carries on accordingly in *Charlie Chan Carries On*, commencing on this day a characterization that carried him through 16 Chan chapters to his death in 1938. The part then went to a Scot (**Sidney Toler**), an American (**Roland Winters**) and a Brit (**Peter Sellers**).

1948: On this day, **Darryl F. Zanuck** memos Fox prexy **Spyros Skouras** some Monday-morning-quarter-backing about how poor titling scuttled *Nightmare Alley*, *Kiss of Death*, *The Late George Apley* and *The Ghost and Mrs. Muir*. "A classical example of stupidity on all of our parts," mourned DFZ, was the switching of *Summer Lightning* to *Scudda-Hoo! Scudda-Hay!* The boys in advertising didn't know what to make of that title so they "freely translated" it as "a cry that stirs young hearts to love." No such thing, countered *New York Times* critic **Bosley Crowther**: "It is simply what a driver says to mules when he wants them to 'gid-dap.' There is no evidence that it stirs anything to love."

1949: Warners signs **Alfred Hitchcock** on this day for four pictures. They became *Stage Fright*, *Strangers on a Train*, *I Confess* and *Dial M for Murder*.

1961: The movie version of *The Music Man* checks in its Marian the Librarian on this day: **Shirley Jones**. She was promised the same leading man she was promised for *Carousel* — **Frank Sinatra** — and, again, it didn't happen. **Cary Grant** handed the title role back to **Jack L. Warner**, declaring not only would he not do the movie, he wouldn't even see it if anyone other than **Robert Preston** was cast. Preston, the Tony-winning original, had, at 44, totally reinvented himself as a musical comedy star. Warner only succumbed to the obvious when the show's author (**Meredith Willson**) and director (**Morton Da Costa**) personally went to him and pitched Preston for the part.

A KNIGHT IN AMERICA: Alfred Hitchcock and George Sanders in a cut scene from *Rebecca*.
A WARNING SHUSH: Shirley Jones in *The Music Man*.
A BARN STORM: Walter Brennan, Robert Karnes, June Haver and Lon McCallister in *Scudda-Hoo! Scudda-Hay!*

1967: A former Roosevelt New Deal Democrat-turned-conservative Republican, **Ronald Reagan** puts in the first full day of his two terms as California's 33d governor. When ex-boss **Jack L. Warner** heard Reagan had entered this race, he responded in character: "No, no! **JIMMY STEWART** for governor — Reagan for best friend."

1980: The British consul visits Universal Studios on this day and confers belated knighthood on **Alfred Hitchcock**, the screen's peerless master of suspense who spent 60 of his 80 years in the film industry (almost all of it in Hollywood, since his Oscar-winning *Rebecca* in 1940). When he died almost four months later, Hitch was the best-known movie director in the world.

4

1941: In a beautiful display of bitchery, **Hedda Hopper** phones her rival's boss on this day about a film she has just seen. "Mr. **Hearst**," she cooed, "I don't know why **Louella** hasn't told you this picture is about you." Such was the shove that got the negative ball rolling for *Citizen Kane*. The embarrassed **Parsons** never pardoned its creator, **Orson Welles**, and rarely dropped his name in print.

1941: A daughter is born to **Dorothy Comingore** on this day, two and a half months after completing her claim-to-fame role: Susan Alexander, Citizen Kane's second wife. She was pregnant when she signed aboard, but subtle shadows and clever camera-angles by cinematographer **Gregg Toland** kept her secret — till she had to stand up and walk out on the title character; then, a strategically placed muff took it from there.

1957: *Collier's* magazine hits stands for the final time on this day, going out in style with the world's only Oscar-winning princess gracing its last cover — **Grace (Kelly) Rainier**.

1960: "This is the most pornographic script I have ever read," **Elizabeth Taylor** complained to MGM about the film she starts on this day in a dank, dusty studio on New York's West Side. "I've been here for 17 years, and I was never asked to play such a horrible role as Gloria Wandrous. She's a sick nymphomaniac. I won't do it for anything." But she did — for her regular $125,000 salary, concluding her contractual commitment to MGM so she could do a million-dollar *Cleopatra*. She also got **Helen Rose** for costumes, **Sydney Guilaroff** for hairdos, hubby **Eddie Fisher** for co-star — and, making the best of this bad-girl thing (*Butterfield 8*), the Oscar as 1960's Best Actress. (A well-timed tracheotomy, performed while the Academy was voting, helped.)

1998: *L.A. Confidential* wins the Best Picture and Best Director (**Curtis Hanson**) nods from the National Society of Film Critics on this day, marking the first time the top five major voting critics groups ever agreed in these categories. (The New York Film Critics Circle, the Los Angeles Film Critics, the Boston Film Critics and the National Board of Review had earlier singled the film out for that double distinction.) Not that this cut any ice with Academy Award voters; up against the *Titanic* juggernaut, *L.A. Confidential* only mustered Oscars for Best Supporting Actress (**Kim Basinger**) and Best Adapted Screenplay (**Brian Helgeland** and Hanson).

OSCAR'S CALL GIRLS: From left: Kim Basinger in *L.A. Confidential* and Elizabeth Taylor in *Butterfield 8*. **BEMUDDIED & BEMUSED:** Orson Welles and Dorothy Comingore in *Citizen Kane*.

5

1930: Universal puts into general release on this day its first all-sound outdoor picture: *Hell's Heroes*, which **John Ford** had directed before (as 1919's *Marked Men*) and would direct again (as 1948's *Three Godfathers*). This time the helmsman went unmentioned in *The New York Times* review and was called "Wilbur Wylans" by *Variety*. Eventually, the world got it right: **William Wyler**.

1939: Playing what critic **Frank S. Nugent** called "the founder of the wrong-number industry," **Don Ameche** on this day begins the picture for which he is best-known, if not synonymous: *The Story of Alexander Graham Bell*. So marked was Ameche by the title role that comics began referring to the phone as "the Ameche." (**Barbara Stanwyck**, as the slang-spouting chanteuse in 1941's *Ball of Fire*, called the telephone "the Ameche" because, she said, "he invented it.")

1941: On this day, **Garbo** and **Chaplin** are conspicuous no-shows for The New York Film Critics Circle's annual award-giving at Radio City's Rainbow Room. She was scared away by autograph hounds baying at the entranceway, and he shrugged off their Best Actor citation (for *The Great Dictator*). At least **Katharine Hepburn** (the Best Actress winner for *The Philadelphia Story*) was nice enough to phone in her thanks from Dallas, where she was giving the same performance on stage.

1946: Oscar-winning Annie Hall, **Diane Keaton**, is born Dianne Hall.

1959: "I'm here to make a film about the end of the world, and this sure is the place for it," cracks **Ava Gardner** at a press conference on this day when she arrives in Melbourne for *On the Beach*. (That didn't endear her to the Aussies.)

1970: *Z* finishes first with The National Society of Film Critics as its Best Picture of 1969 on this day. A month later **Costa-Gavras**' controversial political thriller became the first movie ever Oscar-nominated for both Best Picture *and* Best Foreign Language Film. The Algerian entry won the latter — plus an Oscar for **Francoise Bonnot**'s editing. The only other movie Oscar-nominated for both Best Picture and Best Foreign Language Film is Italy's 1998 *Life Is Beautiful*, and it too won the latter — plus Oscars for **Roberto Benigni**'s acting and **Nicola Piovani**'s music. Four foreign language films have Oscar-contended for Best Picture (1938's *Grand Illusion*, 1972's *The Emigrants*, 1973's *Cries and Whispers* and 1995's *The Postman*).

1998: Pop star-turned-politician **Sonny Bono**, 62, dies on this day in a skiing accident on the slopes of the Heavenly Ski Resort in South Lake Tahoe — a mishap eerily echoing one that claimed a **Kennedy** (**Michael**) six days earlier.

AN INVENTIVE *BELL*-RINGER: Don Ameche in *The Story of Alexander Graham Bell*. LA-DE-DAHLING: Diane Keaton in *Annie Hall*. OSCAR FOREIGNERS, FROM *LIFE* TO *Z*: From left: Roberto Benigni in *Life Is Beautiful* and Yves Montand in *Z*.

6

SINGED SURVIVORS: Alice Brady and Tyrone Power in *In Old Chicago*.
FIRE*BRAND 451*: Ian Charleson in *Chariots of Fire*.
CARY & KATE & COACH: Grant and Hepburn and Walter Catlett in *Bringing Up Baby*.

1938: The madcap capper of screwball comedies calls it a wrap on this day, and the whole set sighs with relief. For all its frantic fun, *Bringing Up Baby* was fiercely dangerous to film, "Baby" being an unpredictable eight-year-old leopard who was falling for the fall of **Katharine Hepburn**'s skirt and about to get playful. Kate's other cat was **Walter Catlett**, a Ziegfeld comic hired to keep her from pushing too hard for laughs. (Grateful Kate got him a part in the film — Constable Slocum — so he'd be around to coach her.)

1938: The Chicago fire of 1871 lights up Manhattan skies as *In Old Chicago* premieres at the Astor. A $2-million four-alarmer intended as 20th Century-Fox's retort to MGM's San Francisco earth-shaker, this disaster epic pitted **Tyrone Power** against **Don Ameche** over **Alice Faye**—a routine the trio reprised to **Irving Berlin**'s music eight months later in *Alexander's Ragtime Band*. Off-setting this fictional friction: **Alice Brady**'s hearty, Oscar-winning work as the widow O'Leary (the one with the cow).

1960: The War of the Noses officially begins on this day as moviegoers get their first whiff of *Scent of Mystery*, a whodunit filmed in Smell-O-Vision bowing at Chicago's Todd Cinestage Theater. **Elizabeth Taylor** halted her Oscar-winning acting in *Butterfield 8* to come in from New York to launch the film, for which she contributed a cameo as a courtesy to the producer (her ex stepson-in-law, **Michael Todd Jr.**). *Scent of Mystery* lost the dubious distinction of being "the first movie that ever smelled on purpose" by only 29 days: On Dec. 9, 1959, New York's DeMille Theater uncorked a process called AromaRama, dispensing some 30 scents through the air-conditioning system, for *Behind the Great Wall*, a documentary travelogue of China. Neither gimmick rang box-office bells, so the threat of a third cinematic "smellie" — *The Scent of New Mown Hay*, a drama produced by **Aubrey Schenck** and **Howard Koch** — evaporated.

1990: AIDS claims **Ian Charleson**, 40, on this day, shortly after his heroic, much-applauded Hamlet at London's National Theatre. His finest film performance: **Eric Liddell**, the Scottish-missionary runner who at the 1924 Olympics declined to compete on the Sabbath, in 1981's Oscar-winning *Chariots of Fire*.

1998: Distributing his annual Felix Awards for dubious achievements on this day, *Village Voice* columnist **Michael Musto** discovers two worthies on the MTV Video Music Awards show: "Low Point of Modern History: **The Spice Girls**' poignant tribute to **Princess Di** — She had girl power" and "Penultimate Low Point: **Madonna**, who's made the world her gynecologist, chastising mankind for caring too much about scandal and gossip."

7

1867: The future prexy of Universal Pictures, **Carl Laemmle**, is born — as is (in 1873) the future prexy of Paramount Pictures, **Adolph Zukor**.

1935: David O. Selznick memos **Greta Garbo** he's cool about producing her *Anna Karenina* and wonders if she'd rather do *Dark Victory*. No vay! Garbo stuck to her Tolstoy, which was more than she did in 1927 when she first filmed that property — with a modern setting and a happy ending; even the title had to go — to accommodate the ad copy (i.e., "Garbo and **Gilbert** in *Love*!"). Her redemptive second shot at *Anna Karenina* won Best Actress honors from The New York Film Critics — but no votes from her Vronsky, **Fredric March**, who suffered frostbite after she rebuffed his obligatory pass-at-the-leading-lady. "Co-starring with Garbo," he sniffed, "hardly constituted an introduction."

1942: The Warner Bros. Hollywood News Press Service posts *Casablanca*'s first casting announcement on this day: **Ronald Reagan** and **Ann Sheridan**, fresh from *Angels Wash Their Faces* and *Juke Girl*, will triangulate with **Dennis Morgan**. This "bulletin" provoked such high-decibel denials in the corridors of power that the service rescinded the whole thing the next day: Supposedly, the project had been put on hold — hours after the announcement, apparently — and, instead, the trio would star in *Shadow of Their Wings* (eventually released as *Wings for the Eagle*, with **Jack Carson** replacing Reagan). When the trades next broached the subject of *Casablanca* casting — on April 10 — **Humphrey Bogart** had succeeded the Army Reserve-bound Reagan, and the only Morgan mentioned was France's **Michele Morgan** for leading lady — a ploy intended to speed up secret negotiations then going on with **David O. Selznick** for **Ingrid Bergman**. (It worked.)

1955: The formation of Marilyn Monroe Productions is announced. Because of the erratic deportment of its president and star, the company collapsed after its first — and only — production: *The Prince and the Showgirl*.

1966: Irked that he won't be directing **Frank Sinatra** in *In Cold Blood* because Irving Lazar sold the screen rights to **Truman Capote**'s book to **Richard Brooks** for $500,000 without entertaining any other offers, **Otto Preminger** begins baiting the offending agent with Sinatra threats on this day at the "21" Club. Lazar, sometimes called Swifty, swiftly crowned his taunter with a drinking glass, sending Preminger staggering for the exit with not-so-cold blood streaming from his bald pate. "This is not the first time Swifty Lazar has drawn blood from a producer," noted one scribe. "He does it every time he negotiates. This is merely the first time he used a deadly weapon." Preminger hit back with a felonious assault charge but later dropped it when Lazar sent a letter of apology.

A-TEAM TRIANGLE: Paul Henreid, Ingrid Bergman and Humphrey Bogart in *Casablanca*. B-TEAM TRIANGLE: Dennis Morgan, Ann Sheridan and Jack Carson in *Wings for the Eagle*. LEO THE LION'S TOLSTOY: From left: Garbo and Gilbert in *Love*; Garbo and March in *Anna Karenina*.

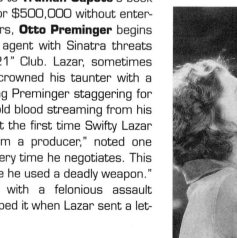

8

1946: When **James Stewart** turns down doing Doc Holliday to **Henry Fonda**'s Wyatt Earp in *My Darling Clementine*, a relieved **Darryl F. Zanuck** agrees — in writing, on this day — with director **John Ford** to fill the part "in house" (via Fox contract player **Victor Mature**); however, Zanuck believed the title role of Holliday's sweetheart too slight for **Jeanne Crain**'s star-power and threw **Cathy Downs** to Ford instead. In 1964, for a sequence in *Cheyenne Autumn*, Ford picked Stewart to play Earp (to **Arthur Kennedy**'s Holliday).

1947: *The Man Who Fell to Earth* — **David Bowie** — is born in London.

1967: Poland's best-known film star — a physical and emotional carbon-copy of **James Dean** named **Zbigniew Cybulski** — meets a sudden, tragic, Dean-like end when, trying to board a late-night train at Wroclaw, he falls under its moving wheels. *The Train* and *The Night Train* just happened to be among 40-odd films he did during the last dozen of his 40-odd years. "The Dean thing," consciously culled from *Rebel Without a Cause* and set to shining in **Andrzej Wajda**'s 1958 classic *Ashes and Diamonds*, continued posthumously.

1973: On his 38th birthday **Elvis Presley** records "Separate Ways," then goes single himself, suing his wife of six years, **Priscilla**, for divorce.

1990: Gap-tooth madcap **Terry-Thomas**, 71, loses his 19-year bout with Parkinson's disease, dying nearly penniless at a nursing home in England.

1992: It's a girl — the daughter kind — for **Warren Beatty**, 54. Mother and co-star (**Annette Bening**, 33) doing fine. The *Bugsy* duo wedded a few weeks later. Neither would say where or when — they value their privacy — and the only wedding guest was **Kathlyn Bening Beatty**, who wasn't talking (yet). A son was produced Aug. 23, 1994, by *Love Affair* (their first film as husband and wife, ironically). Hey, guys, there are easier ways to keep track!

1993: The U.S. Post Office does its largest commemorative-stamp issue ever (500 million), marking what would have been **Elvis Presley**'s 58th birthday with a stamp for The King of Rock 'n' Roll. For the first time, the public voted on the stamp likeness they preferred (Young Elvis won over Old Elvis). The stamp's first abuse: letters to nonexistent addresses so the stamp would boomerang back with the title of Presley's big hit, "Return to Sender."

TIN-STARRED IN TOMBSTONE: Henry Fonda in *My Darling Clementine*.
A PICK OF PRESLEYS: Postmaster General Anthony Frank giving the public a choice of Elvis stamps.
POLAND'S JAMES DEAN: Zbigniew Cybulski in *Ashes and Diamonds*.

1931: "Mother of mercy, is this the end of Rico?" No, it's the start of **Edward G. Robinson**, laying siege to the Strand today in his first starring film role, *Little Caesar*. (Actually, the line Rico went out on was "Mother of God, is this the end of Rico?" — but it was altered to avoid objections from the United Council of Churches.) Then-congressman **Fiorello H. LaGuardia** created a stink about the character being Italian, but the movie's grosses shattered house records and triggered the gangster genre.

1936: A heart attack, brought on by heavy boozing, finishes off the talkies' greatest casualty, **John Gilbert**, 36, on this day —one day after **Gary Cooper** was announced for *Desire*, a **Marlene Dietrich** movie Gilbert was to do. Dietrich had nursed Gilbert back from an earlier heart attack but flew to Coop when she found Gilbert begging **Garbo** to resume their affair. Double-struck with grief and guilt, Dietrich almost collapsed in the church aisle at Gilbert's funeral.

1939: *Tarzan Finds a Son!* (the same place he was found: in a jungle plane-crash), as 8-year-old **John(ny) Sheffield** begins filming his half of the title bill. "Finds" was the operative word, since Tarzan and his Jane lived together in a jungle tree-house without benefit of clergy — a point of concern to literal-minded bluenoses. Their new-found son — designated "Boy" by Tarzan — was a part Sheffield perpetuated seven times before becoming his own "(Bomba the Jungle) Boy" for 12 low-budget installments. Sheffield's father was **Reginald Sheffield**, the British actor who was the screen's first David Copperfield.

1953: Taking a sharp right from hunger to *Eternity*, **Frank Sinatra** signs up for a supporting role. Bored watching bride **Ava Gardner** support him as she filmed *Mogambo* in Africa, Sinatra struck out for Columbia — Pictures, on Gower St., in Hollywood — over a single weekend, making a 27,000-mile round-trip at his own expense (Ava's, actually) to do a two-scene, 15-minute test for the supporting role of Angelo Maggio in *From Here to Eternity*. Studio chief **Harry Cohn** favored **Eli Wallach** for the part, but Sinatra's asking price ($8,000) made more cents than Wallach's ($20,000). At the end of Sinatra's comeback trail 14 months later, Gardner was up for an Oscar, too (for the only time in her career, for *Mogambo*), but, by then, the marriage was over.

1976: *Rocky*, starring its screenwriter (**Sylvester Stallone**, a hard-headed holdout who'd have it no other way), starts lensing at last on this day. That big Sly move paid off in stardom and an Oscar (for Best Picture, if not for writing or acting) — and a series was born: *Rocky* went four more film rounds.

GAMBLING A *FORTUNE*: Walter Matthau in *The Fortune Cookie*.
HEARST-CURSED: Joseph Cotten, Orson Welles and Everett Sloane in *Citizen Kane*.
LOVE FINDS MR. CHIPPING: Robert Donat and Greer Garson in *Goodbye, Mr. Chips*.

1936: Director **Rene Clair** wanted **Olivier** and producer **Alexander Korda** wanted **Laughton**, but the apparition materializing at the Rivoli in *The Ghost Goes West this particular day* is **Robert Donat**.

1938: The *Hollywood Reporter* reiterates its earlier error that **Charles Laughton** has a lock on the title role in *Goodbye, Mr. Chips*. Apparently, the lock was on the doors of the Notre Dame cathedral (where Laughton was then enjoying sanctuary as RKO's Quasimodo) because the chap who brought Chips to the screen 18 months later was the one who'd been squire to Laughton's Oscar-winning Henry VIII: **Robert Donat**. Now, it was his time to graduate into the Oscar elite.

1941: *Daily Variety*'s front page screams "HEARST BANS RKO FROM PAPERS," under a story about a *Kitty Foyle* review being yanked from yesterday's late editions of the Los Angeles *Examiner*. More RKO releases might rate the same slighting, the story said, now that the veil of secrecy surrounding the studio's *Citizen Kane* was starting to lift and reveal **Orson Welles**' warts-and-all portrait of a ruthless newspaper magnate to be **William Randolph Hearst**. *Variety* predicted other studios would suffer for the sins of Welles as well, but two weeks later the ban was lifted for everything except the mention of *Citizen Kane* itself. Nevertheless, plots to stop the picture continued on high: MGM's all-powerful **Louis B. Mayer** suggested studios take up a fund, buy the *Kane* negative and convert it into guitar picks, but RKO chief **George Schaefer** stood his ground and premiered the picture May 1 to a packed Palace in New York. Said Welles, who maintained all along his Charles Foster Kane was fiction: "When I get *Citizen Kane* off my mind, I'm going to work on an idea for a great picture based on the life of William Randolph Hearst."

1965: A reformed compulsive-gambler, **Walter Matthau** backslides, makes a bet, lies to his wife about it and suffers a heart attack. ("I haven't bet since. What do I need, cancer?") He was the second star in a row to be stricken with a heart attack on a Sunday while making a **Billy Wilder** movie, causing Wilder to quip to collaborator **I.A.L. Diamond**, "I wonder if it isn't a mistake to give actors a day off. They always get in trouble on Sundays." At least Matthau got a chance to finish *The Fortune Cookie* — and win an Oscar for it — but **Peter Sellers**' heart attack during *Kiss Me Stupid* the year before forced Wilder to scrap the footage and start all over again with **Ray Walston**.

1922: *Foolish Wives* — which holds the *Guinness Book of Records* title for Longest Commercially-Made American Movie To Be Released Uncut — is unleashed in relatively short form, weighing in at *only* 24 reels and running past midnight at New York's Central Theater. It got shorter — 12 reels for its roadshow run, and 10 reels for its general release — but lucky Latin America got the whole enchilada: 32 reels amassed by director **Erich von Stroheim** from July 12, 1920, to June 18, 1921 (filming only concluded when the cameras were confiscated). During this 49-week shoot, Universal's **Carl Laemmle** kept the public posted on the film's soaring expenses with a giant Broadway bulletin board where the budget blazed in golden Mazda bulbs which were changed on Wednesdays with much fanfare by the New York Fire Brigade.

1933: The world's biggest cinema, Radio City Music Hall, opens for film biz on this day — by serving *The Bitter Tea of General Yen*, with **Barbara Stanwyck**.

1937: *Make Way for Tomorrow*, a trail-blazing tear-jerker (possibly the first film to address the touchy subject of what to do with elderly parents), begins filming on this day. **Leo McCarey** directed — from the heart — and, when he won the Oscar 14 months later for *The Awful Truth*, he couldn't resist telling the wonderful truth: "Thanks, but you gave it to me for the wrong picture."

WHOA WHOA WHOA, MRS. ROBINSON: Anne Bancroft and Dustin Hoffman in *The Graduate*.
ROVING MONOCLE: Erich von Stroheim in *Foolish Wives*.
NO *LAUGH-IN* SKIT: Beulah Bondi and Victor Moore in *Make Way for Tomorrow*.

1940: *His Girl Friday*, a replate of *The Front Page*, debuts at Radio City Music Hall, testing director **Howard Hawks**' theory that **Charles MacArthur** and **Ben Hecht**'s mythic comedy about Chicago newspapermen was really a cleverly disguised love story: Here, duking it out as Machiavellian managing editor and star reporter — filmed nine years earlier by **Adolphe Menjou** and **Pat O'Brien** — were ex-marrieds (**Cary Grant** and **Rosalind Russell**). *Vive la difference*, as they say in the City Room.

1967: Producer **Joseph E. Levine** announces a month-long search for a male Star of Tomorrow, age 19 to 23, to play the title role in *The Graduate*. He and director **Mike Nichols** discovered two likely contenders — but both were 29. The younger (by ten days), they let go, figuring **Robert Redford** was too good-looking to have trouble getting a girl; with **Dustin Hoffman**, however, that might well be a problem. That casting decision got Nichols the Oscar, Hoffman a career and Levine a cult hit that spoke to a whole generation — and the faces of future leading men in film were finally free to be flawed.

12

J A N U A R Y

THE EXCESSES OF ERICH: ZaSu Pitts, Gibson Gowland and Hughie Mack in *Greed*.
SO LONG, *SAYONARA*: Marlon Brando in *Sayonara*.
RESTLESS SOULS: Charles Laughton, Bela Lugosi and Richard Arlen in *Island of Lost Souls*.

1915: Whenever the subject of *The Stain* came up, she'd always snap, "I started out a star and remained a star" so, accordingly, **Theda Bara** today hits the screen for the first time — a full-blown, un-*Stained* star — in *A Fool There Was*. She held to that line her whole career, modifying it only in the 40s by calling *The Stain* her "screen test" for *A Fool There Was*. **Frank Powell**, who directed both films, made her a face in the crowd in *The Stain* to see how she'd photograph. Liking what he saw, A Star There Was.

1924: Some nine hours of *Greed* (42 reels) unravel on this day before an audience for the first — and last — time. In that state, it got the Guinness nod for "Hollywood's longest-ever film in its original form," but only the small coterie of friends **Erich von Stroheim** invited to this screening at MGM could ever attest to the magnificence of his almost-line-for-line cinemazation of **Frank Norris**' 1899 novel, *McTeague: A Story of San Francisco*. One who did was **Idwal Jones**, the San Francisco *Daily News* drama critic who got the word out in his next Saturday column, then railed against the studio butchery required to make the film exhibitable. With tears, von Stroheim trimmed it to 24 reels; a friend, fellow director **Rex Ingram**, took it down to 18; the *coup de grace* was administered by **Irving Thalberg**, who pared the picture down to 10 reels. The result, when released, was ignored. Its true merit emerged, after 34 years of marinating, when it placed sixth (after *Potemkin*, *The Bicycle Thief*, *The Gold Rush*, *The Passion of Joan of Arc* and *La Grande Illusion*) in a 1958 poll the Cinematheque de Belgique conducted for the Brussels International Exposition on The 12 Greatest Films of All Time.

1933: "They are restless tonight," **Charles Laughton** says of the natives at a tense dinner-party in his island fortress — introducing a new catch phrase to the world — in *Island of Lost Souls*, premiering at NYC's Rialto.

1957: **Marlon Brando** arrives in Tokyo to film his new, "improved" version of **James A. Michener**'s established bestseller, *Sayonara*. At the star's insistence, Michener's *Madame Butterfly* finale was replaced with a happy ending that cast a then-hardline vote for miscegenation (and made the title pointless!). That change assured box-office success and got Oscar nominations for Brando and for the credited screenwriter (playwright **Paul Osborn**); it also worked Oscar-winning wonders for **Red Buttons** and **Miyoshi Umeki**, who inherited the tragic *Butterfly* business Brando discarded.

13

TWO *ACCUSED*, ONE OSCARED: Loretta Young (with Douglas Dick) in 1949; Jodie Foster in 1989.
NO 'WAR' IN *CAMELOT*: Vanessa Redgrave in *Camelot*.

1939: To get the Scarlett O'Hara role, **Vivien Leigh** signs a seven-year contract with **David O. Selznick** — without informing fiancé **Laurence Olivier**, who, sure enough, objects. Selznick then reminded him of the fate that befell the former Mrs. Olivier: The actor had yanked her back to England, forcing her to surrender the star-making role which Selznick had extended to her (which was why **Katharine Hepburn**, and not **Jill Esmond**, filled *A Bill of Divorcement*).

1942: **W.C. Fields** checks into 20th Century-Fox for the first and only time in his career. During the next five days — for $50,000, at least twice the salary of any other player in the picture — he filmed a 20-minute vignette for *Tales of Manhattan*, an all-star, multi-episode saga hung by the frayed thread of a tail coat from creation to scarecrow finish; its wearing wove a tattering trail from an actor (**Charles Boyer**) to a bridegroom (**Henry Fonda**) to a conductor (**Charles Laughton**) to a hobo (**Edward G. Robinson**) to a bogus temperance-lecturer looped on spiked coconut milk (Fields) to a backwoods black (**Paul Robeson**). The Fields segment, abetted by **Margaret Dumont** and **Phil Silvers**,

went down great with previewers in May, and there were rumors of rewarding Fields with top billing — but, just prior to the movie's release, the sequence was cut. Hilarity "interrupted the flow of the film" (overlong, anyway), and the eminently trimmable Fields diversion got left at the starting gate. Happily, it was restored for the video release.

1949: In the title role of a rape victim in *The Accused*, says *The New York Times* on this day, **Loretta Young** "brings a high degree of conviction to her portrayal." There was no Oscar for this. That came 40 years later to **Jodie Foster**, also in the title role of a rape victim — in another Paramount picture called *The Accused*.

1991: Via an ad in *The New York Times*, **Vanessa Redgrave** attempts to clarify her stance against U.S. forces in the Persian Gulf: She was just being anti-war, she said — not pro-Iraq. Her objection to war was always total — so total she couldn't bring herself to utter that three-letter obscenity in *Camelot*; accordingly, **Alan Jay Lerner** came up with another lyric.

1995: After three months of nail-biting and navel-plumbing, **Steven Spielberg**, **Jeffrey Katzenberg** and **David Geffen** announce the name they've dreamed up for their new movie-production company: DreamWorks SKG.

14

1896: The first public screening ever held in Britain takes place at the London headquarters of the Royal Photographic Society. Its bill of fare consisted of five short films photographed by **Birt Acres**: *The Derby, Rough Seas at Dover, Boxers, Three Skirt Dancers* and *The Opening of Kiel Canal*. The last — considered the first news film — was shot by Acres on June 20, 1895, as **Kaiser Wilhelm II** presided over the canal opening and reviewed his troops.

1932: L.A. newspapers chronicle two unique occurrences: Snow falls on Hollywood, and **John Barrymore** meets **Greta Garbo** on the *Grand Hotel* set. Barrymore's arrival in the role of the nobleman thief was MGM's kiss-off to Garbo's ex-lover, **John Gilbert**, whose three talkie-floppies-in-a-row suddenly rendered him "unsuitable" for the part. The other Barrymore brother, **Lionel**, stepped into a role that could have carried another silent-screen star farther into talkies: **Buster Keaton** tested for the part of the dying bookkeeper, but **Irving Thalberg** opted instead to go with the more experienced dramatic actor.

1935: A shooting, a stabbing and a skyscraper swan-dive (by a screaming **Wini Shaw**) violently counterpoint "Lullaby of Broadway" — **Busby Berkeley**'s personal favorite of all his musical sequences — from *Gold Diggers of 1935*, which he finishes mining on this day. The song won **Harry Warren** and **Al Dubin** the Oscar, but Buzz's dance direction lost the award to **David Gould**'s less flashy work on "I've Got a Feelin' You're Foolin'" in *Broadway Melody of 1936*. (No foolin'.)

1954: In a civil ceremony at San Francisco's City Hall, **Marilyn Monroe** marries **Joe DiMaggio**. As a wedding present, 20th Century-Fox ended her one-month suspension for not reporting to work on *Pink Tights* with **Frank Sinatra**, **Van Johnson**, **Mitzi Gaynor** and **Dan Dailey**. (MM had been miffed about salary discrepancies — Sinatra's $5,000-a-week vs. her $1,500 — forcing Fox to recast the part with **Terry Moore**, who quickly passed it to new-girl-on-the-lot **Sheree North**). Eventually, the project just went away, but North came in handy when Monroe picked suspension over *How To Be Very, Very Popular.*

1957: At 2:30 a.m. — 20 minutes after **Humphrey Bogart**, 57, has died from throat cancer — widow **Lauren Bacall** tearfully telephones the news to journalist **Joe Hyams**, Bogie's buddy and later his Boswell. "It was the last story he could give you," Bacall said, "and he wanted you to have it first."

1919: "So the lunatics have taken charge of the asylum," smugly observes Metro Pictures president **Richard A. Rowland**, when he learns that artists have united to form United Artists. The studio was officially created on this day when **Mary Pickford** added her mark to the articles of agreement already signed by **Charles Chaplin**, **D.W. Griffith** and Pickford's soon-to-be-husband, **Douglas Fairbanks**.

1937: The youngest — and last — star sent into the MGM firmament by **W.S. Van Dyke II** is born on this day: **Margaret O'Brien**. The daughter of circus performers, she had lost her real father four months before her birth, so Van Dyke became something of a surrogate father for her, steering her through *Journey for Margaret* to stardom. On Feb. 5, 1943 — a couple of months after the release of that picture, his 81st and final film — the 53-year-old veteran director died.

1947: **Darryl F. Zanuck** alerts executive assistant **Lew Schreiber** to secure necessary clearances so 20th Century-Fox can film a fact-based thriller about a Chicago newsman who answers a scrubwoman's want-ad to prove her incarcerated son is no cop-killer. The result, *Call Northside 777*, rescued **James Stewart**'s postwar career from floundering after two financial flops in a row (*It's a Wonderful Life* and *Magic Town*).

1955: Directors **Gene Kelly** and **Stanley Donen** and scripters/lyricists **Betty Comden** and **Adolph Green** call it a collaboration as filming ends on their third, and last, team effort. *It's Always Fair Weather* was a long way from their blissfully sunny *Singin' in the Rain*, beginning as a peacetime postscript to their *On the Town*, updating the lives of those three gobs-on-leave (**Frank Sinatra**, Kelly and **Jules Munshin**). The glitch: Sinatra had long since sworn off sailor suits and was, in fact, on the next soundstage, infiltrating *High Society* — so the plot became the reunion of a new trio of Army buddies (**Dan Dailey**, Kelly and **Michael Kidd**) on a live *This Is Your Life*-like TV show.

1974: Hitting Harvard Square like Normandy in an armored personnel carrier, **John Wayne** arrives to claim *Harvard Crimson*'s "Brass Balls" award.

1987: The last of the Yellow Brick Road gang — indeed, the last of *The Wizard of Oz* stars: beloved Scarecrow **Ray Bolger**, 83 — succumbs to cancer.

1988: The critical advice about *Rent-a-Cop*, in multiple openings around New York on this day, is: Wait, and rent-a-copy. Ten negative reviews vs. a lonely positive one pointed to a short shelf-life for this second screen-teaming of **Burt Reynolds** and **Liza Minnelli**. Obviously, their *Lady Luck* was still holding.

A *JOURNEY* BEGINS: Laraine Day, Margaret O'Brien, William Severn and Robert Young in *Journey for Margaret*.
ARTISTS UNITED: The four founders of United Artists: Mary Pickford, D.W. Griffith, Charles Chaplin and Douglas Fairbanks.
PICKUP ON YELLOW BRICK ROAD: Judy Garland and Ray Bolger in *The Wizard of Oz*.

15

16

BEAU AND HIS BROS:
Robert Preston, Ray Milland and Gary Cooper in *Beau Geste*.
HELL IN *VEGAS*: Elisabeth Shue and Nicolas Cage in *Leaving Las Vegas*.
001 FOR 007: Sean Connery and Joseph Wiseman in *Dr. No*.

1914: On this day — and for the next three — **Charles Chaplin** performs in his first film, a Mack Sennett one-reeler called *Making a Living*.

1939: Director **William A. Wellman** starts shooting the first remake of *Beau Geste* on this day, 19 miles West of Yuma at the same set that foresighted Paramount built 13 years previously for the silent *Beau Geste*. **Gary Cooper**, **Ray Milland** and **Robert Preston** manfully filled the brother-Legionnaire boots earlier occupied by **Ronald Colman**, **Neil Hamilton** and **Ralph Forbes**, but the villains still had the best roles (**J. Carrol Naish** and an Oscar-nominated **Brian Donlevy** now; **William Powell** and **Noah Beery Sr**. then).

1942: Plane or train? A flip of the coin this day decides **Carole Lombard**'s fate. She opted for the former and won — overruling her mother (**Mrs. Elizabeth Peters**) and publicist (**Otto Winkler**), both of whom perished with her when the plane returning them for an Indianapolis war-bond rally crashed into Table Rock Mountain 30 miles southwest of Las Vegas. Mrs. Peters, an experienced numerologist, computed the flight data and came up with a fatal number, but Lombard insisted — because she was jealous, having left hubby **Clark Gable** literally in the arms of his *Honky Tonk* co-star, **Lana Turner**, as they toiled so over a re-teaming, *Somewhere I'll Find You*.

1958: Director **Fred Zinnemann** and crew hop a 14-hour flight from London to Stanleyville to film the Belgian Congo portion of *The Nun's Story*.

1962: A new screen stalwart swaggers into view —"Bond. James Bond." — as Pan American Flight 323 pulls into the Palisadoes Airport in Kingston, Jamaica, to start *Dr. No*, the first of 19 (to date) films featuring **Ian Fleming**'s intrepid British Agent 007. The whole day's shooting produced only 116 seconds of completed screen time, but in it **Sean Connery** stepped off the plane into international stardom as the civilized superspy who battled title villain **Joseph Wiseman**. Neither actor was first choice for their respective roles: **Richard Burton** passed on Bond, and **Noel Coward** nixed *No*, wittily, with "Dear Ian, The answer to *Dr. No* is No! No! No! No!.

1996: The best and worst of 1995 films boast Vegas backdrops, according to lists posted simultaneously in The New York *Daily News*: *Leaving Las Vegas*, an oddly comic dirge about a town drunk, led the nominees for the Independent Feature Project's 11th annual Independent Spirit Awards, while the Boring Institute's 11th annual list of cinematic under-achievers gave *Showgirls* a special category all of its own — "Most Boring Sex Film."

1931: After the miseries and maladies of a seven-month shoot in Africa — then divorce proceedings for philandering with the leading lady (**Edwina Booth**) — more woe visits **Duncan Renaldo**, a mere 18 days before his star-making performance in *Trader Horn* bows in NYC: He is arrested on charges of entering the U.S. illegally and sentenced to two years in federal prison. President **Franklin Roosevelt** eventually pardoned him, enabling Renaldo to leave the country, then re-enter it legally and become a citizen of America where he labored as a high-profile actor — occasionally rising to "A" films like *For Whom the Bell Tolls*, but mostly remembered as the big-screen's last — and small-screen's first — Cisco Kid.

1938: **Bette Davis** finishes filming her Southern-fried *Jezebel*, and the Academy Award it brings her 13 months later comes as a consolation prize for not winning the Scarlett O'Hara role; nevertheless, she did give **Vivien Leigh**'s Scarlett a good run for the Oscar gold anyway with the best Bette of 'em all — the doomed heiress in *Dark Victory*, a property Warners purchased for $27,500 from the temporarily distracted producer of *Gone With the Wind*, **David O. Selznick** (who'd tried in vain to get it off the ground variously with **Janet Gaynor**, **Greta Garbo**, **Carole Lombard** and **Merle Oberon**).

1964: *The Incredible Mr. Limpet*, in which **Don Knotts** and an animated fish share the title role of America's secret World War II weapon (don't ask), rates a subterranean send-off on this day, as more than 100 national movie scribes are shoehorned into a tank and taken to the bottom of Weeki Wachee Springs for the film's official underwater unreeling. Its Technicolor tended to, er, wash out.

1992: *Juice*, the nine-years-in-the-making directing debut of **Ernest Dickerson** (cinematographer on **Spike Lee** movies), opens with a bang — sadly, several of them: Five people were injured, and one was killed, at theaters playing the film. "We do not feel that it is in any way incendiary," Paramount exec **Barry London** had said on the eve of the tragedy, responding to the charge of a NYPD gang officer (**Jay St. John**) that the studio's ad campaign was "irresponsible" and "exploitive," especially in view of the bloody bows of *Boyz N the Hood* and *New Jack City*. The film's original one-sheets showed four shadowy youths against a graffiti-cluttered background, and one of them (**Tupac Shakur**) packed a gun; later versions of that same ad "disarmed" him by having the gun painted out.

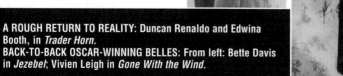

A ROUGH RETURN TO REALITY: Duncan Renaldo and Edwina Booth, in *Trader Horn*.
BACK-TO-BACK OSCAR-WINNING BELLES: From left: Bette Davis in *Jezebel*; Vivien Leigh in *Gone With the Wind*.

17

18

THE *FALCON* FOUR:
Humphrey Bogart,
Sydney Greenstreet,
Peter Lorre and Mary
Astor in *The Maltese
Falcon*.
LOST IDEAL: Wallace
Reid.
GOOD IDEA, THAT:
Monroe and Montand
in *Let's Make Love*.

1923: "It was the ideals back of that handsome face, corresponding so completely with the beauty and fineness of his outward being, that earned him the love of his fans," wrote **Adela Rogers St. John** of **Wallace Reid** after his death on this day at age 31, one of the first movie-star victims of drug addiction. For 12 years in 177 films, he projected the ideal American youth — and lived that ideal, marrying a beautiful co-star (**Dorothy Davenport**, daughter of character actor **Harry Davenport**) and settling in a lavish home (L.A.'s first with a swimming pool). All that changed in 1919 when a train carrying him through the High Sierras to film *Valley of the Giants* crashed. Reid emerged from the wreckage with a head injury and blinding headaches. The company's doctor freely prescribed morphine, and the resulting drug-dependency showed on screen, his last three years of films chronicling his declining health. Finally he collapsed on the set of *30 Days* and was institutionalized. Shortly after his funeral (which was attended by 10,000), his widow walked up to the mike at a Hollywood banquet radio-broadcast and declared with pride: "Hello, everybody. This is Mrs. Wallace Reid" — providing the factual basis for a famous last line in films (see Jan. 25).

1954: "Mary dear, hold my hand, tell me I won't make an ass of meself," **Sydney Greenstreet** asided to **Mary Astor** right before plunging into a long monologue about The Black Bird — his very first scene in a 23-film career that ran from 1941's *The Maltese Falcon* to 1950's *Mayala*. In the summer of '41, at age 61, after 41 years on the stage, the 285-pound Brit made his move into movies, and Oscar welcomed him with a nomination for *Falcon*'s "fat man," Kasper Gutman. He meant to rejoin **The Lunts** on their tour of *There Shall Be No Night*, but Warners kept films flying at him so fast he forgot about the stage. Throughout his too-brief second career, Greenstreet was one of the heaviest of movie heavies — until his death on this day, at 74.

1960: *Let's Make Love* begins lensing today — and, quickly, its two (married) stars start doing just that. The movie began as *The Billionaire*, then *The Millionaire*, emphasizing a rich man wooing a showgirl; **Norman Krasna** made the role resemble **Howard Hughes** and wrote it for **Yul Brynner**, who passed the part on to **Gregory Peck**. When **Marilyn Monroe**'s overqualified hubby, **Arthur Miller**, beefed up her showgirl part, Peck balked and walked. **Rock Hudson**, **William Holden**, **Charlton Heston**, **Cary Grant** and **James Stewart** similarly declined. Finally, Miller saved the day (if not his marriage) by suggesting **Yves Montand**.

1940: Going into general release is *You Nazty Spy*, giving **Moe Howard**'s two-reel take-off of Hitler (the madman of Moronica) a nine-month jump on **Charles Chaplin**'s feature-length one (the tyrant of Ptomania, a.k.a. *The Great Dictator*). Of all the shorts done by **The Three Stooges**, this was Moe's personal favorite.

1940: A little *Red Dust* is sprinkled on *Maisie* — and *voila*! Chapter Two in the movie series goes into general release as *Congo Maisie*. This foray into MGM's deepest, darkest backlot returned **Ann Sothern** to the title role (a part that had been originally earmarked for *Red Dust* star **Jean Harlow**) and paired her with a passably Gablesque Great White Hunter (the mustachioed **John Carroll**). When *Red Dust* was recycled again — as *Mogambo* — **Gable** took on his original role and **Ava Gardner**.

1960: The New York Times reports **Otto Preminger** has hired the blacklisted **Dalton Trumbo** to script **Leon Uris**'s bestseller, *Exodus* — prompting Universal to give Trumbo screen credit first (for the *Spartacus* he'd authored in secret). Earlier, Uris had submitted his own *Exodus* screenplay to Preminger, who scrapped it on the ludicrous grounds that the novelist "didn't have the proper feel for the material."

1973: Too ill to do the Oscar-winning role that had finally come his way (**John Houseman**'s in *The Paper Chase*), **Edward G. Robinson** learns — one week before his death — he's to receive an honorary Oscar. His appreciation of this long-overdue award was read by his widow on Oscar night: "It couldn't have come at a better time in a man's life. Had it come earlier, it would have aroused deep feelings in me, still not so deep as now. I'm so very grateful to my rich, warm, creative, talented, intimate colleagues who have been my life's association. How much richer can you be?"

BEATING CHAPLIN TO THE PUNCH: Curly Joe Howard, Florine Dickson, Larry Fine and Moe Howard in *You Nazty Spy*.
URIS *TSORIS:* Otto Preminger directing *Exodus*.
TROPICAL FEVERS: *Congo Maisie* (Ann Sothern) and John Carroll flanked by two Gables — 1932's *Red Dust* with Jean Harlow, and 1953's *Mogambo* with Ava Gardner.

1929: The first "outdoor talking film" comes out shootin' at New York's Roxy. *In Old Arizona*, filmed in old Utah, had **Raoul Walsh** for star and director — till he found it too outdoorsy: A jackrabbit crashed into his car windshield, costing him an eye, an Oscar and an acting career. **Warner Baxter** got the Oscar when he inherited the role — The Cisco Kid, a part he reprised in lesser films for a decade. **Irving Cummings** took over the direction, but Walsh's contribution can still be heard (if not seen): in hoofbeats, gunshots and other unheard-of wonders of the new talkies.

1934: The first of five proposed *George White's Scandals* for the Fox Film Corporation finishes production. **White**, a producer-director-writer who'd been turning out stage musical revues under that title since 1919, stopped his screen series at Installment Two — *George White's 1935 Scandals* — but he left the studio with two major assets: Just before shooting started, he fired leading lady **Lilian Harvey** and hired a singer from his 11th Broadway *Scandal*. The film-debuting **Alice Faye** quickly found a future at Fox, as did the cutie-pie who came out for the casting call and wasn't hired (but still caught the attention of enough Fox execs): **Shirley Temple**.

1978: The Broadway musical hit *Annie* hits a new high for screen rights: $9.5 million.

1984: The Tarzan of Tarzans — **Johnny Weissmuller**, 79 — dies of lung blockage at his Acapulco home. As he requested, burial was in Acapulco (where he lensed *Tarzan and the Mermaids*, his last Tarzan), and a recording of his trademark Tarzan yell sounded as his coffin was lowered into the grave. The actor, who took up swimming to overcome childhood polio and pursued it vigorously enough to win five Olympic Gold Medals, was left an invalid by a series of strokes and spent his last seven years looking out at a Pacific Ocean he couldn't swim in.

1990: President **George Bush** names "Conan the Republican" (a.k.a. **Arnold Schwarzenegger**) Chairman of his Council on Physical Fitness and Sports.

1996: It's a happy 100th birthday for **George Burns** on this day, and his wish is for **Sharon Stone**. The next night, Stone got *her* wish: a Golden Globe for *Casino* ("Okay, it's a miracle," she cracked, getting a handle on Incredible). Sadly, Burns lived only seven weeks more and did not see the Best Actress Oscar go to another S.S.—**Susan Sarandon** for *Dead Man Walking*.

20

ONE EYE, ONE OSCAR: From left: director Raoul Walsh; Warner Baxter in *In Old Arizona*.
BUSH-LEAGUER: Arnold Schwarzenegger in *Conan the Barbarian*.
A *SCANDALOUS* START: Alice Faye in *George White's Scandals*.
THE TARZAN OF TARZANS: Johnny Weissmuller.

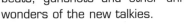

1929: Following **Erich von Stroheim**'s detailed direction, **Tully Marshall** today takes **Gloria Swanson**'s hand and dribbles tobacco juice on it to slip a ring on her finger for a scene in *Queen Kelly*. Furious (and, fresh from breakfast, nauseous), Swanson fled the set and phoned her lover/producing partner in Florida, **Joseph P. Kennedy**, who fired the author-director instantly — "the single most damaging blow to von Stroheim's career," opined biographer **Richard Koszarski**. Swanson bought the existing footage and assembled a kind of closure — with a rare directorial assist from **Irving Thalberg** (who'd twice shot "Von" down — at Universal and MGM). The resulting *Queen Kelly* only played abroad because von Stroheim wouldn't permit U.S. showings — until, ironically, he himself flipped the switch of a projector as Swanson's butler in *Sunset Boulevard* two decades later and showed a tantalizing morsel.

KING DISCO AND *QUEEN KELLY*: From left: John Travolta in *Saturday Night Fever*, Gloria Swanson in *Queen Kelly*. *UNCLE WIGGILY WENT THATAWAY*: Susan Hayward and Dana Andrews in *My Foolish Heart*.

1950: "Uncle Wiggily in Connecticut," the only **J.D. Salinger** yarn ever filmed, goes into general release — as *My Foolish Heart*, replete with an Oscar-nominated song (by **Victor Young** and **Ned Washington**) and an Oscar-nominated **Susan Hayward**. The screenwriting **Epstein** twins provided her a lover (**Dana Andrews**), even though his character never appeared in the original story.

1950: Ignoring **George Stevens**' eventually Oscared direction, **Montgomery Clift** spends the last day of shooting *A Place in the Sun* walking the last mile of his last scene to the electric chair, preferring to go out numb and resigned rather than terrified as Stevens wants.

1978: The *Saturday Night Fever* soundtrack boogies to the top of the music charts where it stays for 24 weeks. Not only was it the biggest-selling album before **Michael Jackson**'s *Thriller* in 1983 and the biggest-selling movie soundtrack of all time, it also spawned four singles, won four Grammys and made disco kings of its authors, **The Bee Gees** (Barry, Robin and Maurice Gibb). Inexplicably, none of the above impressed Academy voters, who failed to include any of the film's top-ten hits among the ten Best Song semifinalists! The whole score was similarly slighted. **Robert Stigwood**, the film's stunned producer, quite rightly requested a recount, and, not getting one, had his spokesman complain to *People* magazine that the Academy's music branch was made up of "retired violinists who probably still play 78s on their Victrolas."

22

1875: The father of film, **D.W.** (David Wark) **Griffith**, is born today in La Grange, KY. Southern roots accounted for his pro-KKK stance in *The Birth of a Nation*.

1940: Actors and actual veterans of *The Fighting 69th* attend the picture's New York preview, presided over by one of the **Warner** Bros., **Jack**, and by **Col. John J. Mangan**, commander of the 165th Infantry (formerly the 69th). The real **Father Francis Duffy** came face to face with his reel counterpart, **Pat O'Brien** (who might have been **Spencer Tracy** had 20th Century-Fox not bowed to Warners and abandoned its *Father Duffy of the Fighting 69th*).

1948: With *T-Men* taking over New York's Criterion, director **Anthony Mann** steps out of the B-movie league and into the A-film arena. Crisscrossing film noir with a semidocumentary look, he and cameraman **John Alton** created some brooding realism and got off one of the more memorable murders in movie history: the steambath rubout of **Wallace Ford**, executed by one of the killers of *The Killers* (**Charles McGraw**).

1962: **Richard Burton** does his first scene with **Elizabeth Taylor** in *Cleopatra* — a love-at-first-sight encounter — and it's no stretch for them. Groggy from a nightlong bender, he got to the set unshaven and shaking; she giggled at his condition, then administered coffee till he came around. "There comes a time during a movie when the actors become the characters they play — that happened today," producer **Walter Wanger** wrote in his diary. "You could almost feel the electricity between them."

1985: *Variety* reports that the firing of **Eric Stoltz** midway through 12 weeks of shooting has *Back to the Future* backed up to Square One. "A good actor in the wrong role," Stoltz was giving a performance that "wasn't consistent with the original concept," said the filmmakers, who chose instead to use **Michael J. Fox** (when he wasn't tied up with his weekly TV *Family Ties*). The gamble paid off big-time: The concept got to market as planned, the film was a smash requiring two big-bucks follow-ups, and Fox became a star. The setback didn't stop Stoltz' star from ascending, either.

23

1925: The largest single order of body make-up to date — 600 gallons-plus for *Ben-Hur*'s throng — is completed by **Max Factor**. For *Noah's Ark* four years later, Max & Co met and mastered the challenge of making-up more than 2,000 extras before the day's shooting via "mass make-up" (i.e., adding a liquid solvent to the make-up, then spray-painting the mob).

1947: *Lady in the Lake* bows at NYC's Capitol, a decidedly different whodunit wherein the camera became the eyes of sleuth Philip Marlowe (played by director **Robert Montgomery** but visible only when he passed a mirror). In the cast-crawl lurked a clue: The title role of Chrystal Kingsby was credited to one **Ellay Mort,** but neither actress nor character showed up (because "Ellay Mort" is the phonetic spelling for the French "she's dead").

1957: At New York's Palace on this day, 1947's *Singapore* (**Fred MacMurray** and **Ava Garnder**) is recycled as 1957's *Istanbul* (**Errol Flynn** and **Cornell Borchers**). The remake's sole distinction occurred ten minutes into the picture when an eighth-billed **Nat King Cole** introduced "When I Fall in Love." (**Edward Heyman** supplied lyrics to a gorgeous melody composer **Victor Young** had squandered on *One Minute to Zero*, a routine Korean war opus of '52, with **Robert Mitchum** and **Ann Blyth**.) Young, 56, died of a heart attack Nov. 10, 1956, never knowing of the song's success or that he was four months away from the Oscar that always (after 22 nominations!) eluded him — for scoring *Around the World in 80 Days*.

1959: *Plunderers of Painted Flats* rides out into national release, the last of the homegrown Republic Pictures. With low-watt star-power (**Corinne Calvet**, **John Carroll**, **Skip Homeier**, **George Macready**, **Edmund Lowe**) and vague shades of *Shane* plottage (cattle baron vs. squatter farmers, with a gunslinger on the side), the movie made no ripples and no revenue. Like Republic, it went thataway . . .

1962: French filmmaker **Francois Truffaut** premieres in Paris a classic screen triangle: *Jules et Jim* and the lit-from-within **Jeanne Moreau**.

1981: Thinking characteristically big, **Francis Ford Coppola** rents Radio City Music Hall (for three days) to give proper size, scope and grandeur to his presentation of **Abel Gance**'s technically innovative widescreen epic of 1927, *Napoleon*. Coppola also hired his pop, **Carmine**, to compose and conduct a new musical score. At the end of the opening-night performance, a phone call was placed from the Music Hall stage to Paris so Gance could hear the audience cheering. When he died at age 92 later that year (Nov. 10), Gance was still planning to film *Christopher Columbus*.

24

BEGINNING A 39-YEAR REIGN: Audrey Hepburn in *Roman Holiday*.
KATE & COMPANY: Katharine Hepburn with her favorite (and most frequent) director, George Cukor, working on *Sylvia Scarlett*.
THAT'S EARLE, BROTHER!: Ida Lupino and Humphrey Bogart in *High Sierra*.

1924: **Darryl F. Zanuck** acquires his first Fox — in marriage: actress **Virginia** (no relation to **William Fox**, founder of Fox Film Corporation which merged with Zanuck and **Joseph M. Schenck**'s Twentieth Century Pictures in 1935 and made Mr. Z the Vice President in Charge of Production of 20th Century-Fox). For the man who invented "the casting couch" and produced "feature-length screen tests" for his favorites-of-the-moment (**Bella Darvi**, **Juliette Greco**, **Irina Demick**, **Genevieve Waite**), it was a rocky marriage, barely existing from 1956 to 1973 but kicking in again for his last six years.

1939: *Gunga Din* gets a gala launching in L.A., with its late **Rudyard Kipling** in tow (impersonated on screen, for about two months, by **Reginald Sheffield**). In March, when the film bowed in London, the author's widow requested all mention and likeness of him be removed from the film, contending his presence there was so incongruous people laughed. She was not around to object to **Christopher Plummer**'s brilliant Kipling cameo in **John Huston**'s 1975 Kipling caper, *The Man Who Would Be King*.

1941: *High Sierra* hits New York's Strand, bringing **Humphrey Bogart** to a permanent plateau of stardom. **Ida Lupino**, playing moll to Bogie's Roy "Mad Dog" Earle, also profited professionally from the picture, but the two didn't part friends and wouldn't reteam.

1974: **Larry Fine,** the middle man of **The Three Stooges**, succumbs to a stroke. **Moe Howard**, the last original Stooge survivor, died May 4, 1975.

1983: His best film was *The Women*; his favorite film was *Little Women*; then, there were *Two-Faced Woman, Tarnished Lady, My Fair Lady, Les Girls, Girls About Town, Sylvia Scarlett, Camille, Zaza, Justine, Romeo and Juliet, Pat and Mike, Susan and God, The Model and the Marriage Broker, Heller in Pink Tights, The Actress* — he was the ultimate Woman's Director, and his was the longest directing career in Hollywood. **George Cukor**, who helmed his 50th and last film (MGM's *Rich and Famous*) in 1981 at age 81 — dies on this date. For the record: the world's oldest director was Dutch filmmaker **Joris Ivens**, who made the Franco-Italian *Une Histoire de Vent* at 89 in 1988, a year before his death.

1993: In the Swiss hamlet of Tolochenaz (her home for the last 26 of her 63 years), **Audrey Hepburn** is laid to rest. Oscared 39 years earlier when she soared straight to stardom (and planets beyond) in *Roman Holiday*, she never lost her sweet lilt in the two dozen films that followed. Her passing left alive only one Oscar-winning Best Actress from the '50s: **Joanne Woodward**.

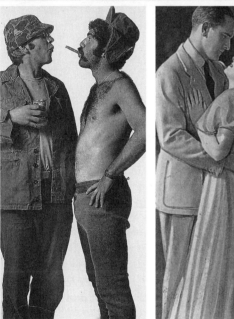

OKIE ODYSSEY: Dorris Bowden, Jane Darwell and Henry Fonda in *The Grapes of Wrath*.
THE FIRST *M*A*S*H*ERS AND MAINES: From left: Donald Sutherland and Elliott Gould in *M*A*S*H*; Fredric March and Janet Gaynor in *A Star Is Born*.

1937: Producer **David O. Selznick** memos director **William A. Wellman** a new curtain-line for *A Star Is Born* — "Hello, everybody. This is Mrs. Norman Maine" — guaranteeing them that big uplift they didn't get at the first preview. Thus, the last scene in the movie was the last to be shot, and it became one of the greatest tag-lines in film history — good enough for **Judy Garland** to reprise in the 1954 remake.

1940: "In the vast library where the celluloid literature of the screen is stored there is one small, uncrowded shelf devoted to the cinema's masterworks, to those films which by dignity of theme and excellence of treatment seem to be of enduring artistry, seem destined to be recalled not merely at the end of their particular year but whenever great motion pictures are mentioned," writes **Frank S. Nugent** in *The New York Times*, less than a month into 1940, assigning to that special shelf the film which director **John Ford**, producer **Darryl F. Zanuck** and adapter **Nunnally Johnson** made from **John Steinbeck**'s Pulitzer Prize-winning novel, *The Grapes of Wrath*.

1947: The male leads in *Easy To Wed* share the same wife for a day: Four hours after **Evie Abbott** divorces **Keenan Wynn**, she weds **Van Johnson**.

1970: "I always say *M*A*S*H* wasn't released — it escaped!" contends **Robert Altman** — so, today, his mad little movie "escapes" to NYC's Baronet. *M*A*S*H* began when its back-from-the-blacklist, about-to-be-Oscared adapter, **Ring Lardner Jr.**, alerted agent **Ingo Preminger** (yes, **Otto**'s brother) to **Richard Hooker**'s Korean War novel of the same initials (for "Mobile Army Surgical Hospital"), and Preminger was impressed enough to turn producer for it. Altman entered the picture only after **George Roy Hill**, **Sidney Lumet**, **Stanley Kramer**, **Bud Yorkin** and ten other Name directors declined, and even then, 20th Century-Fox drove a hard bargain: $75,000 flat and no points. Execs **Richard Zanuck** and **David Brown** were underwhelmed with the results, but they permitted the director's cut to prevail at previews, and instantly the flick clicked with audiences. *M*A*S*H* is the only one of Altman's 30-odd films to be a huge hit, although he never personally shared in the wealth; the only Altman to make money on *M*A*S*H* was son **Mike**, via his "Suicide Is Painless" lyrics to a jaunty melody later appropriated to jump-start the TV spinoff for 14 seasons. Preminger earned his money as Altman's buffer during filming — and never produced another film, or had to (because of *M*A*S*H*'s double-media smashes).

LET THE *WIND* BEGIN: "Maybelle Merriwether" (Mary Anderson) hoists the flag to start *Gone With the Wind*.
A TWIN-ANNIVERSARY PREMIERE: Gregory Peck in *Twelve O'Clock High*.
BOY, WERE THEY EVER!: Grant Withers and Loretta Young in *Too Young To Marry*.

26

1930: The stars of *The Second-Floor Mystery* (**Grant Withers**, 25, and **Loretta Young**, 17) elope this day to Yuma — but, before they can get to market with their second movie, *Too Young To Marry*, they've come to that very conclusion. By her count, the marriage lasted nine months. The hard-drinking Withers, who became a member of **John Ford**'s stock company and ODed on sleeping pills at age 55, left Young with the label that has lasted a lifetime: "The Steel Butterfly."

1939: Signaling the start of shooting on *Gone With the Wind*, actress **Mary Anderson** — the film's "Maybelle Merriwether" — runs the Confederate stars and bars up a flagpole on the front lawn of Selznick International.

1950: *Twelve O'Clock High* world-premieres at NYC's Roxy, commemorating not only the eighth birthday of the 8th Air Force but also the seventh anniversary of the first daylight precision bombing raid on Germany at Wilhelmshanen.

1960: The marquee at the Sands Hotel in Las Vegas posts the three-week gig of **Frank Sinatra**, **Dean Martin**, **Sammy Davis Jr.**, **Peter Lawford** and **Joey Bishop** there while they toil around town on their day job (*Ocean's 11*).

1995: Pneumonia claims **Pat Welsh**, 80, the Marin County housewife whose two-pack-a-day habit produced one of sound cinema's most famous voices. **Debra Winger** pitched it a little vocal gravel of her own, but Welsh did most of the appealingly screechy speaking for E.T. **George Lucas**' sound designer, **Ben Burtt**, who overheard the retired elocution teacher screeching in a local camera store, persuaded her to remove her dentures and deliver all of E.T.'s dialogue into the microphone toothlessly. Welsh's "15 minutes of fame" lasted nine and a half hours and netted her $380.

FIT TO BE TY'S: Linda Christian, shown at the left, helping Van Heflin administer to Lana Turner in *Green Dolphin Street*, was less helpful in real life (above), swiping and marrying Lana's big love, Tyrone Power.
SOMEONE WHO'S *SOMEONE*: Marlon Brando in *The Godfather*.

1937: Born Merle Johnson Jr. on this day, **Troy Donahue** played a Merle Johnson in the only Oscar-winning film he was ever involved with — *The Godfather Part II* — passing through it ever-so-briefly as one of **Talia Shire**'s several spouses.

1938: "It might be better to make the Communists the 'Heavies,'" writes The Hays Office's **Joseph Breen** to MGM's **Louis B. Mayer**, suggesting a possible scapegoat so the Nazis in *Three Comrades* wouldn't look as nasty as they did in **Erich Maria Remarque**'s novel of that name. Goaded on by the German Consul General (**Dr. George Gyssling**), the meddlesome Breen did manage to get cut out a reference to **Felix Mendelssohn**, the Jewish composer whose music was banned in Germany under the Nazi regime. Also: bookburning was deleted, swastikas were scrapped and **Henry Hull**'s "We are Jews" speech was squelched.

1949: **Lana Turner** today loses the all-time "love of my life" (**Tyrone Power**) — and to the 11th-billed starlet playing her maid in *Green Dolphin Street* (**Linda Christian**), at that! — a "degradation" not many stars of her stature have had to endure in public: At the medieval Church of Santa Francesca Romana near the Forum in Rome occurs what conservative Fox flacks called "The Wedding of the Century." The Power-Christian sparks started when they crossed paths (waaaay off Turner's backlot turf, in the wilds of Mexico) filming, respectively, *Captain From Castile* and *Tarzan and the Mermaids*. The Marriage of the Century, it wasn't — ending after five years but producing two daughters who had brief acting careers, **Romina** and **Taryn**.

1966: Stranded without a movie career or a monied hubby, **Hedy Lamarr** is arrested for shoplifting in a Wilshire Boulevard store. Oh, Delilah!

1971: "NO STARS FOR *GODFATHER* CAST — JUST SOMEONE NAMED **BRANDO**" is *Variety*'s dry headline for the big story Paramount makes public.

1974: The overlooked star of **Martin Scorsese**'s *Mean Streets*, **Harvey Keitel**, attends The New York Film Critics awards ceremony at Sardi's — as guest of the guy who stole his picture and won the critics' award for Best Supporting Actor of 1973, **Robert De Niro**. During dinner, the wife of *Saturday Review*'s **Hollis Alpert** started strangling on a piece of steak and collapsed — to the helpless horror of Alpert, De Niro and the one card-carrying hero in the room, **Paul Newman** — but not to Keitel and not to **Bill Crist**, husband of *New York* magazine's **Judith Crist**: They rushed forth, dislodged the meat in a pre-Heimlich maneuver of their own and saved her life. The next day's press reported Mrs. Alpert had been saved by De Niro.

THE FIRST LORD OF THE JUNGLE: Elmo Lincoln in *Tarzan of the Apes*.
BOUNCER BY NIGHT, *E.T.* BY DAY: Henry Thomas and Pat Bilon in *E.T.*
BULLDOG'S VELVET BARK: Ronald Colman in *Bulldog Drummond*.

1918: *The New York Times* salutes the arrival of an eight-reel *Tarzan of the Apes* at the Broadway Theater. A stocky ukulele player named **Winslow Wilson** began that title role but, in a burst of patriotism, bolted to enlist when World War I broke out a few days later. **Elmo Lincoln**, a barrel-chested brute who'd served **D.W. Griffith** as "White Arm Joe" in *The Birth of a Nation* and "The Mighty Man of Valor" in *Intolerance*, took over the part—*aggressively:* During a scene where a lion menaced the heroine, Lincoln yanked the beast by the mane, and the animal (though old and drugged) attacked in earnest, only to be stabbed to death by the actor and wind up a lobby display at the film's opening.

1929: One of the glories of talkies sounds today: the incomparable voice of **Ronald Colman**, starting a seductive spell of almost 30 years by dispensing deductions as **Sapper**'s *Bulldog Drummond*. "What **Chaplin** is to silent film, Colman will be to sound!" declared his boss, **Samuel Goldwyn**.

1935: *The Case of the Curious Bride*, the second of **Warren William**'s three outings as Perry Mason, starts shooting, bringing **Errol Flynn** into Hollywood films D.O.A.—as a corpse. After another wasted Warner effort (*Don't Bet on Blondes*), Flynn suddenly leapt to real stardom as *Captain Blood*.

1942: A mere 52 days after the Day of Infamy, *A Yank on the Burma Road* comes marching to market (New York's Criterion) as the first film fiction—albeit a "B" from MGM—to include Pearl Harbor in its plotline.

1948: *You Were Meant for Me*, some vintage song-and-dance bowing at the Roxy with **Jeanne Crain** and **Dan Dailey**, is dismissed by critic **James Agee** in less words than can be found in its title: "That's what you think."

1950: A movie name is created by a Baptist minister in Fort Worth, joining a pregnant **Vera Jayne Palmer** in holy matrimony with **Paul J. Mansfield**.

1983: The world's only nightclub bouncer measuring 2ft. 10ins. high and **Steven Spielberg**'s main (little) man for *E.T.*—**Pat Bilon**—dies from pneumonia complications in his hometown of Youngstown, OH. Bilon executed most of the alien's running, walking and stumbling activities in the film, with an occasional assist from two standby human extra-terrestrials (**Tamara de Treaux** and **Matthew de Merritt**). He was the same age as Spielberg: 35.

1925: "MAE – VON SIGN PEACE," blares the front page of the Los Angeles *Record*, shoving aside world events to announce accord has been struck — at midnight, in the MGM offices of **Louis B. Mayer** — between *The Merry Widow* (**Mae Murray** and her director, **Erich von Stroheim**): *He* will direct, it is decided. Mayer's right-hand man, **Irving Thalberg**, detested "Mae" and "Von" equally, and teaming them was his demonic idea — but Murray was never better showcased, the movie became a hit, and a pre-Oscar polling of critics found von Stroheim to be Best Director — and *The Merry Widow* Best Picture — of 1925 (which, up against **Charles Chaplin**'s *The Gold Rush* and **King Vidor**'s *The Big Parade*, was saying Something).

1937: Today at Wilshire and San Vicente Blvd., a 50-foot replica of **Pearl Buck**'s Pulitzer Prize-winning novel, *The Good Earth*, points the way to the picture's world premiere at L.A.'s Carthay Circle Theater. It was the first film launching covered by a national network (the Mutual System) and only the second time the name of MGM's late, great Boy Wonder appeared on screen; following Leo the Lion's welcoming roar was a loving foreword: "To the memory of **Irving Grant Thalberg**, we dedicate this picture — his last great achievement." The modest mogul personally supervised the studio's most prestigious product but always contended, "If you are in a position to give credit, you don't need it."

1945: **Gloria Swanson** enters the shortest of her six marriages, No. 5: to investment broker **William N. Davey** — history after 44 days.

1958: Starting their first film together (*The Long, Hot Summer*), **Paul Newman** and **Joanne Woodward** decide to co-star in real life as well and, at Hotel El Rancho Vegas in Las Vegas, wed. Aside from **Laurence Olivier** and **Vivien Leigh** (who eventually divorced), the Newmans are the screen's only Academy Award-winning acting couple — a distinction that was a long time in coming: Specifically, it took Newman seven nominations and 29 years to match the 1957 Oscar that Woodward won with her first nomination.

1990: Life imitates art: **Ava Gardner**, 67, of Hollywood, Madrid and London is laid to rest at Sunset Memorial Park in her hometown — Smithfield, NC — while almost 500 mourners stand around under umbrellas in the miserable drizzle, echoing the send-off she got 36 years before as *The Barefoot Contesa*.

29

1931: "A Comedy Romance in Pantomime Written and Directed by **Charles Chaplin**," trumpets the first title card of *City Lights*, premiering this day in L.A. almost three and a half years after **Al Jolson** said, "You ain't heard nothin' yet." Bucking the talkie trend, this last true silent gave off a lovely glow.

1946: After **Jean Arthur** turns him down to do Broadway's *Born Yesterday* (which she fled from on the road), director **Frank Capra** asks MGM on this day to borrow contractee **Donna Reed** to play **James Stewart**'s wife in *It's a Wonderful Life*. **Hedda Hopper** had rumored **Ginger Rogers** for the role, but it was Reed who came aboard — a big step up for the erstwhile studio starlet.

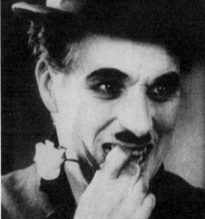

A DOOMSDAY PIE-FIGHT: Peter Bull vs. Peter Sellers in *Dr. Strangelove*.
SILENTS FADE OUT: Chaplin at the close of *City Lights*.
A CALL TO STARDOM: Donna Reed and James Stewart in *It's a Wonderful Life*.

1964: *Dr. Strangelove, Or How I Learned To Stop Worrying and Love the Bomb* lands at two different NYC theaters — minus its original finale. Director **Stanley Kubrick** had intended to end the world not with a bang but with a splat: a pre-apocalyptic custard-pie fight at the end of which the U.S. President (**Peter Sellers**) and the Soviet ambassador (**Peter Bull**) plop down and built "pie-castles" like children on a beach. "We threw a thousand pies a day for five days," recalled **George C. Scott**, who participated on Our Side (kinda) as General Buck Turgidson. "Stanley wouldn't let us clean them up. Every day, we'd walk into the War Room set, and rancid sugar and cream would be everywhere. Once, Peter Bull threw a pie at me. I ducked, and it hit Peter Sellers, who swooned into my arms. Then, I had the line, 'Gentlemen, our beloved President has been struck down in the prime of his life by a pie.' When **Kennedy** was killed, the whole sequence went. It was a helluvah scene, but it was untenable because of the circumstances."

1969: For 42 minutes, till the bobbies politely blow the whistle on it, **The Beatles** jam for the last time today — a lunchtime blast on the roof of their Apple Corps headquarters in London. Happily, somebody (**Michael Lindsay-Hogg**, the director-son of **Geraldine Fitzgerald**) remembered to bring the cameras, and half that swan song showed up in *Let It Be*, a rough-hewn documentary which surfaced in Manhattan theaters 16 months later. Eventually, it turned The Fab Four into better-late-than-never-bloomin' Oscar-winners: The following spring — on April 15, 1971, two years and three months after this sign-off gig — *Let It Be* won the group the Oscar for Best Original Song Score.

1921: **Mario Lanza** today enters the world — a little more than six months before **Enrico Caruso** leaves it, a coincidence not lost on the heir apparent and one that came harmoniously together May 10, 1951, when Lanza bowed as *The Great Caruso* at the Radio City Music Hall for a then-record run of 10 weeks, grossing $1.5 million. The film's soundtrack became the first operatic album to sell more than a million copies, but such success sent the singer's ego into self-destructive overdrive and (in less than two years' time) off a cliff.

1931: Signing in as "America's New Sweethearts," **Marie Dressler** and Wallie (i.e., **Wallace**) **Beery** leave their footprints in Grauman's Chinese cement in conjunction with their first screen-teaming, *Min and Bill*.

1936: "Indian Love Call" starts echoing through New York's Capitol Theater as *Rose Marie* debuts there, winning new fans for **Jeanette MacDonald** and **Nelson Eddy**. Their seasoned director, **W.S. Van Dyke**, did not count himself among the deeply enamored: "I've handled Indians, African natives, South Sea Islanders, rhinos, pygmies and Eskimos and made them act — but not Nelson Eddy."

1950: *The Greatest Show on Earth* gets rolling. The ultimate all-star Big Top spectacular was lorded over by producer-director-showman **Cecil B. DeMille**, who, his 69th time at bat, finally hit his homer: The result was not only C.B.'s best, it was also the Oscar-winning Best Picture of 1952.

1982: More than 200,000 volunteer extras rounded up through ads fall in today with 94,560 contracted players at Delhi's ceremonial mall, the Rajpath, to film the funeral scene for *Gandhi* — not accidentally, the 33rd anniversary of the actual funeral. In the finished 188-minute release, the sequence lasts only a minute and a half, but that's enough for *The Guinness Book of Records* to credit the turnout as the largest number of extras ever in a film.

1987: *The Cure for Insomnia*, the *Guinness* title-holder for The Longest Movie Ever Made, starts unspooling in its entirety at its premiere at the Art Institute of Chicago, ending 85 hours later on Feb. 3. Its 4,080-page title poem was read by author **L.D. Groban**, punctuated by the rock sounds of **J.T.4** and **Cosmic Lightning** and five hours of optional "X-rated footage."

LIKE FATHER, LIKE SON: Johnny Ray, Mitzi Gaynor, Dan Dailey, Ethel Merman, Donald O'Connor and Marilyn Monroe in *There's No Business Like Show Business*.

1887: En route to the Los Angeles County offices to register the 120 acres he has acquired, Kansas real-estate entrepreneur **Harvey Wilcox** asks his wife what he should call the property. **Daeida Wilcox** suggested the name of a summer estate she once overheard, from a stranger on a train: Hollywood.

1937: A surprise birthday party (his 36th) awaits **Clark Gable** when he and fiancee **Carole Lombard** return from lunch to the set of his most miscast star-assignment, *Parnell*. Greeting them, atop an upright piano was a teenage **Judy Garland**, who then proceeded to serenade him with "You Made Me Love You" (touched up with a special fan-letter intro, "Dear Mr. Gable," lyricked by **Roger Edens**). The singer and the sung-to both teared up, and the assembled big-brass insisted she reprise it in *Broadway Melody of 1938*—which, in turn, turned her into star stuff herself.

1939: The role that forever defined **Clara Blandick** falls to her on this day (after **May Robson** waved it away as insignificant and undemanding, after **Janet Beecher** proved too patrician and after **Sarah Padden** flunked her screen test): Auntie Em in *The Wizard of Oz*. **Harlan Briggs** was hired the same day to play Uncle Henry, then fired when first choice **Charley Grapewin** became available.

1966: Two of the last-known visitors to Norma Desmond's musty manse on Sunset Boulevard—columnist **Hedda Hopper**, 75, and comedian **Buster Keaton**, 70—cash in their chips. Keaton succumbed to lung cancer at his Woodland Hills home, and Hopper died of pneumonia at Cedars of Lebanon in Hollywood.

1967: The so-called Spaghetti Western starts unspooling on these shores via *A Fistful of Dollars*, served en masse at 75 theaters in the New York area. Critics came out, guns a-blazin'—but the movie (a Westernization of **Akira Kurosawa**'s *Yojimbo*, set in Mexico, filmed in Spain, financed by Germans and directed by Italy's **Sergio Leone**) had already made a mint abroad and had spawned two equally hot sequels. Its success surprised its star, **Clint Eastwood**, who did it for $15,000 and the free trip to Europe during his hiatus from TV's *Rawhide* three years earlier when the film was called *The Magnificent Stranger*. Suddenly his salary jumped to $250,000 — clearly, a Clint well-spent.

TOTO ANNIHILATION: Clara Blandick, Judy Garland, Toto, Margaret Hamilton and Charley Grapewin in *The Wizard of Oz*.
A WHOLE CAREER IN *POLTERGEIST*S: Heather O'Rourke.
EAST MEETS WESTERN: From left: Toshiro Mifune in *Yojimbo*, and Clint Eastwood in *A Fistful of Dollars*.

1988: Twelve-year-old **Heather O'Rourke**, the blonde moppet best-known for uttering the spooky pronouncement "They're baaack!" in *Poltergeist*, dies of complications from a congenital disorder during emergency surgery at San Diego's Children's Hospital —just before the third installment in that series is released. This trio of films constituted her entire big-screen career.

1939: The longest, and strongest, director-actor collaboration in screen history gets underway on this day as *Stagecoach* reaches Los Angeles. Director **John Ford** overrode producer **Walter Wanger** 's choice of star (**Gary Cooper**) in favor of an old poker-playing crony who'd been his "third assistant prop man" in silent films. He pulled **John Wayne** up by the bootstraps from B-grade shoot-'em-ups to the A-team big-time, suckering him into the film by handing him the *Stagecoach* script and asking him for ideas on casting The Ringo Kid. Wayne suggested **Lloyd Nolan**. The intrigue dragged on until Ford finally said flat-out, "Dammit, Duke, I want you to play The Ringo Kid"— and for the same $3,000 Wayne made on Poverty Row—but the director badgered, bullied and berated him into a believable performance. Pleased with the results, Ford doubled back and reshot Wayne's memorable star entrance in *Stagecoach*, stopping the stage while twirling his rifle—underlining the moment. From that moment on, the two Johns were joined at the hip, and they reteamed 13 more times. Years later, when asked what had set him apart from **Bob Steele**, **Tim McCoy**, **Tex Ritter**, **Roy Rogers**, **Gene Autry** and the rest of that cowboy herd, Wayne said: "John Ford."

1949: Producer **Stanley Kramer** swears cast and crew (some 600 strong) to silence as something called *High Noon* commences two weeks of rehearsals prior to its 17-day shoot. The title, which he and screenwriter **Carl Foreman** concocted (and would later use again), camouflaged the fact they were secretly filming *Home of the Brave*, **Arthur Laurents**'s award-winning play about race prejudice in World War II. On stage, the issue had been anti-Semitism; on screen, it was anti-black—and the first such film to address that subject. **James Edwards**, a **Poitier** precursor, made the most of his opportunity here. The shooting was executed without incident, and the results were much praised by critics. Even Laurents approved of the new color scheme, telling Kramer he'd originally written the lead role as a black rather than as a Jew (hence, the film's seamless switch).

1950: *Volcano*—the movie that **Anna Magnani** made in artistic vengeance after her lover, director **Roberto Rossellini**, gave his heart (and her *Stromboli*) to **Ingrid Bergman**—spews forth at its premiere in Rome's Fiamma Cinema *up to a point*: Midway through, news reached the audience that the Rossellini-Bergman love child had been born across town, and reporters fell all over themselves getting to the exit. Then, the projector bulb broke (considering the mess on the screen, some thought this too was an act of God). When Magnani died Sept. 26, 1973, at her side were her son—and Rossellini.

STAGECOACH TO STARDOM: George Bancroft, John Wayne and Louise Platt in *Stagecoach*.
HOW TO STOP LAVA IN ITS TRACKS: Geraldine Brooks and Anna Magnani in *Volcano*.
PICK A PREJUDICE: Jeff Corey and James Edwards in *Home of the Brave*.

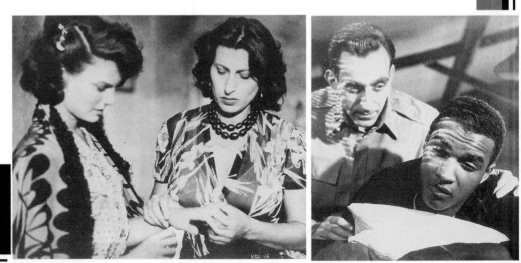

1959: The **Ritchie Valens** Story (*La Bamba*) and *The Buddy Holly Story* both come to their tragic real-life conclusions on this day —"the day the music died," as **Don McLean** (then 13) would later call it—when a tiny Beechcraft plane chartered by Holly crashes into a snow-covered cornfield outside Ames, IA. Both rockers and **The Big Bopper** (J.P. Richardson) perished, along with pilot **Roger Peterson**, who, unknown to them, was not certified to fly by instruments and, misreading them, crashed the plane eight minutes after takeoff. **Waylon Jennings** had relinquished his seat on the plane to Richardson at the last moment, and Valens won his from **Tommy Allsup** in a coin toss.

1959: A pregnant **Audrey Hepburn** is flown from Durango to L.A. with four vertebrae in her back fractured from a fall from her horse, Diabolo, while filming *The Unforgiven*. Shooting stopped for three weeks while she recouped, tended by **Marie-Louise Habets**, whose life she had just filmed as *The Nun's Story*. When Hepburn returned to Mexico, she got back on Diabolo and finished the film, but in July she miscarried. The whole experience left her so saddened and shaken she was ill-prepared for her next assignment : to star with **Laurence Harvey** in **Alfred Hitchcock**'s *No Bail for the Judge*—as a London barrister who uses a crook to get evidence proving her father (an Old Bailey judge) didn't murder a prostitute. **Samuel Taylor**'s script called for her to be brutally raped, and her abhorrence of violence caused her to bail out of *No Bail*. Hitch canceled the film rather than recast it—and never forgave her.

1970: British bobbies pinch **Andy Warhol**'s *Flesh*, confiscating the film and projector at London's "avant garde" Open Space Theater. But the bust brought criticism from Britain's film censor, **John Trevelyan**, who found no problem with the picture being seen by "a specialized audience" in a film club. Both film and projector were sheepishly returned in less than a month—*plus* the *London Times* critic *liked* this crude character-study of a male hustler married-with-child (**Joe Dallesandro**). Aside from this brouhaha, the movie's other distinction is that Warhol just produced and left the directing-writing-lensing to protege **Paul Morrissey**.

**RIDING FOR A FALL: Audrey and Audie in *The Unforgiven*.
A STYLE OF HIS OWN: John Cassavetes directing the Mrs. (Gena Rowlands) as *Gloria*.
THE SAME SAD END: From left: Gary Busey as Buddy Holly in *The Buddy Holly Story*, and Lou Diamond Phillips as Ritchie Valens in *La Bamba*.**

1989: The Oscar-nominated member of *The Dirty Dozen*—**John Cassavetes**, 59—dies of cirrhosis of the liver. That was his only time up as an actor, but, as an independent filmmaker of rough-hewn dramas, he put others in the Oscar running—from **Seymour Cassel** and **Lynn Carlin** (1968's *Faces*) to his own wife, **Gena Rowlands** (1974's *A Woman Under the Influence* and 1980's *Gloria*). Cassavetes ran as well, for original screenplay (*Faces*) and directing (*A Woman Under the Influence*).

4

1912: The so-billed "first movie stuntman" does his stuff on this day: **Frederick Law** jumps (with parachute) from the torch of the Statue of Liberty.

1935: **Ernst Lubitsch** becomes the first director anointed head of production at a major studio. Paramount kept him tied up in executive red tape till Feb. 7, 1936, when he learned (from the studio barber, he said, but it was actually from **Louella O. Parsons**) he had been replaced by **William LeBaron**.

1937: *The Hollywood Reporter* reports on this day the return of the *High, Wide and Handsome* company (**Irene Dunne, Randolph Scott, Dorothy Lamour, Charles Bickford**, et al.) to Chino, CA, for additional location scenes under the direction of **Mitchell Leisen**—instead of the credited **Rouben Mamoulian**. (Orchard heater smoke and influenza had halted shooting in mid-January.)

1944: Director **Clarence Brown** fires the starting gun for *National Velvet*, triggering stardom for **Elizabeth Taylor**. To land the title role, she promised to cut her hair for the scene where she must pass for a male jockey—but reneged and later sent Brown a note of apology for breaking her word.

1947: Producer **Darryl F. Zanuck** wires director **Elia Kazan** that their *Gentleman's Agreement* adapter, **Moss Hart**, is holding off on scripting **Laura Z. Hobson**'s controversial bestseller till the three can huddle and hear Hart's take on it— a half-Harted take, in the long run: The playwright, in one of his infrequent film flings, preferred the polite approach to anti-Semitism, letting the theme "sneak up" on the audience, and, although the result was daring for its day, this timid attack dated as times toughened. Kazan's Oscar-winning direction of it particularly paled beside his Oscar-winning direction of *On the Waterfront*. Signs of the times: Both movies won Best Picture Oscars.

1952: At the Snow Ranch in Calabasas, CA, **William Holden** gets down to some serious, Oscar-winning work: playing the P.O.W. conman of *Stalag 17*. **Charlton Heston** and **Kirk Douglas** were originally considered for the role, and Holden himself was cool about doing it (having walked out after the first act of the stage version), but adapter-director **Billy Wilder**—as he did with *Sunset Boulevard*—talked him into doing the right thing and doing it *well*.

1959: In the *Photoplay* poll for "Most Popular Actress of 1958" made public, **Elizabeth Taylor** is unseated by somebody younger—33 days younger: **Debbie Reynolds**. Fifteen days later, Reynolds divorced **Eddie Fisher** but declined to identify her former "best friend" who stole him away from her.

TOO *GENTLEMANLY:* Gregory Peck, Dorothy McGuire, John Garfield and Celeste Holm in *Gentleman's Agreement.*
FUDGING THE BUZZ CUT: Mickey Rooney and Elizabeth Taylor in *National Velvet.*
CIGS FOR SIG: Sig Rumann and William Holden in *Stalag 17.*

1927: "'It,' hell! She had *Those*," sniped **Dorothy Parker** about **Clara Bow**, who today (and forevermore) becomes "The 'It' Girl," via the New York premiere of *It*. The title was the euphemism for animal magnetism, and *It*'s author-inventor was the writing rage of the day, **Elinor Glyn**, a self-styled high priestess of sex who did a slow pan of Hollywood and decreed that only Clara Bow and **Antonio Moreno** had "It." Paramount, happily having both under contract, commissioned Glyn to say *It* again as a novel, paid her $50,000 for the movie rights and filmed *It*. Upshot: the public flocked to this double-blast of "It," the one about the lingerie salesgirl who nabs the department store owner on a direct line — "I'll take the snap out of your garters!".

1939: *Mother Goose Goes Hollywood* garners an Oscar nomination as 1938's Best Cartoon on this day. This Disney short marked the first screen-teaming of **Spencer Tracy** and **Katharine Hepburn**: For a "Rub-a-Dub Dub" episode, a pantalooned Little Bo Peep (Hepburn) sails by three men in a shaky tub (Tracy and **Freddie Bartholomew** as their *Captains Courageous* characters, Manuel and Harvey, and **Charles Laughton** as Captain Bligh). Three years later, on this day, Tracy and Hepburn bowed as a live-action act at Radio City Music Hall in *Woman of the Year*. The producer of that film and the man who introduced Tracy to Hepburn—**Joseph L. Mankiewciz**, 83—died on this day in 1993.

1943: Proflic **W.S. Van Dyke**, 53, dies. He was known as "One Take Woody" because of his fast filming style — *too* fast, thought some. In the sardonic assessment of producer **Joseph L. Mankiewicz**, Van Dyke "shot *San Francisco* in 46 days, and there were 54 days of retakes."

IT FLIES!: Clara Bow in *It*.
OSCAR'S ODD COUPLE: Barry Fitzgerald and Bing Crosby in *Going My Way*.
THEY MET IN A CARTOON: Spencer Tracy and Katharine Hepburn in *Woman of the Year*.

1945: **Barry Fitzgerald** becomes the only person to win *two* competitive Oscar nominations—for Best Actor and Best Supporting Actor—for *one* performance: the elderly priest in *Going My Way*. Fitzgerald got the New York Film Critics' nod for Best Actor but settled for a supporting Academy Award and let his parish sparring-partner, **Bing Crosby**, take the Best Actor Oscar. Actually, Fitzgerald *did* wind up with two Oscars. He accidentally decapitated the one he got, practicing his golf swing around the house, and Paramount forked over $10 for a spare. (Oscars during the war years were made of plastic and painted gold.)

1955: **Dan Dailey** weds **Gwen O'Connor**, the ex of **Donald**, who'd just played his son in *There's No Business Like Show Business*. That's show business!

6

1957: *The Pajama Game* completes production on this day, with almost all its original Broadway cast repeating their roles on film—a rarity for Hollywood. **Doris Day**, the most conspicuous Hollywood touch, favored **Dean Martin** or **Gordon MacRae** for a leading man. Warners wanted **Frank Sinatra**. Co-director **George Abbott** voted for **Marlon Brando**, then **Stephen Douglass** (the Joe Hardy of his *Damn Yankees*). **Bing Crosby** priced himself out of the running. **Howard Keel** came close but had incurred co-director **Stanley Donen**'s wrath for trying to have him replaced on *Seven Brides for Seven Brothers*. Almost by default, *The Pajama Game*'s male lead went to the Broadway original. It was **John Raitt**'s only star turn in films, and it cost him Broadway's *Bells Are Ringing*—plus, he had to do it for only $25,000 (a tenth of what Day got and $5,000 less than Tony-winning supporting player **Carol Haney**).

1962: The critical cheering commences on this day for the new **Dirk Bogarde**, who just arrived at New York's Forum and Murray Hill theaters in the title role of *Victim*. At age 40, after 34 films and 14 years as a top Rank star, Bogarde celebrated his contractual liberation with a role his studio would never have allowed him to do: a closeted gay battling blackmailers. (Homosexuality was, then, still a criminal offense in England.) The film helped change attitudes and established Bogarde as something more than a matinee idol—an actor.

1964: What **Sam Peckinpah** darkly envisioned as the antithesis of a **John Ford** cavalry Western—a "*Moby Dick*-on-horseback"—goes before the cameras in Durango, Mexico. What emerged on the screen of Hollywood's Egyptian Theater, one day short of a year later, was anybody's guess. **Charlton Heston**, **James Coburn** and others from the cast and crew joined Peckinpah in the back row to witness the mess made of their *Major Dundee*. Producer **Jerry Bresler** took the director's cut of 156 minutes and trimmed it to 124 minutes, ripping "holes the size of soundstages in the narrative" and leaving $500,000 in production values on the cutting-room floor. "We came out of the Egyptian, and Sam was absolutely rigid," recalled Coburn. "He reached in his pocket for this pint of whiskey, and he was shaking so much he dropped it and broke it on the sidewalk." Five years later, after the success of *The Wild Bunch*, Peckinpah got the last laugh: Columbia invited him to rework and reedit the film back into his original vision, but by then he was too busy. "Like **Von Stroheim**'s *Greed* and **Welles**' *Magnificent Ambersons*," wrote Peckinpah biographer **David Weddle**, "*Major Dundee* became one of the cinema's legendary lost masterpieces."

THE ORIGINAL *GAME* PLAYERS: John Raitt and Carol Haney in *The Pajama Game*.
DIRK IN THE DARK: Dirk Bogarde in *Victim*.
DUD *DUNDEE*: Charlton Heston and Senta Berger in *Major Dundee*.

7

1919: One of the more notable examples of a stuntman making the grade as a leading man, **Jock Mahoney** becomes the second screen Tarzan to be born on this day: **Buster Crabbe** beat him there by a good 11 or 12 years. (Mahoney was also **Sally Field**'s real-life stepfather.)

1946: *Adventure* lands with a legendary thud at Radio City Music Hall, returning **Clark Gable** to the post-World War II screen in one big belly-flop of a flick. The ad copy was also the stuff of legend: "Gable's Back and **Garson**'s Got Him"—and that was the second choice. Originally, the copy read: "Gable's the guy that put the arson in Garson," but Greer demurred. "Why not say 'Garson's the dame that put the able in Gable'?" Score one for the redhead, who, like another one [**Jeanette MacDonald** during the *San Francisco* filming), was cold-shouldered by "The King" when the cameras weren't turning. His tastes ran more to the blonde in the third corner of *Adventure*'s triangle: "Well," said third-billed **Joan Blondell**, "*she* may have gotten him on-screen, but beyond that I will say no more." Actually, she did say more—to *Village Voice*'s **Arthur Bell**. According to his "Bell Tells" column of Jan. 21, 1980, what she got from Gable was a marriage proposal. "You've always reminded me of **Carole Lombard**," he supposedly told Blondell about his late actress-wife. "You're the only woman I know who could replace Carole in my life." Blondell chose to be a friend over a replacement—and remained one until Gable's death.

1958: A heart attack kills **Walter Kingsford**, 76. In his prolific career as a character actor, he achieved his most recognition presiding over 14 Kildare/Gillespie outings as the chief of Blair General, Dr. Walter Carewe.

1972: *The Getaway* gets underway inside the penitentiary at Huntsville, TX, where **Steve McQueen** tries to pass himself off as just one of the cons. At least the guard dogs were convinced and gave chase when he split away from the other prisoners after the scene was shot. Much like bloodhounds snappin' at his rear end was a scene in which he was to shower with the other convicts. Only homosexuals volunteered for it, freaking McQueen. Things took a decidedly heterosexual turn when **Ali MacGraw** arrived to play his bank-robbin' other half in the picture. Before long, they were playing marrieds so well it wrecked their respective real-life marriages and created a new one of their own. Understandably, this "development" also wrecked the plans her husband, producer **Robert Evans**, had to reteam them in a remake of *The Great Gatsby*.

1915: *The Clansman* rides roughshod into Clune's Auditorium in Los Angeles on this day, changing forever the face of film. When the picture premiered March 3 at New York's Liberty Theater, it was wearing a more even-keeled, epic-sounding title: *The Birth of a Nation.*

1946: A new, improved version of *The Big Sleep* is successfully sneaked. The film was finished Jan. 12, 1945, and ready for release two months later—but, because Warners needed to work off its easily dated war-movie slate before World War II ended, *The Big Sleep* was put to bed in the studio's vault. During the year and a half it languished there at the bottom of the heap, *Confidential Agent*—the film **Lauren Bacall** did after her spectacular debut in *To Have and Have Not*—came out, and the star plummeted from critical favor. Fearing more bad reviews for her, agent **Charles K. Feldman** persuaded **Jack L. Warner** to roust *The Big Sleep* for extensive retakes. The star *was* saved, but the thread of the narrative remained hopelessly knotted in the process.

1953: After a decade of 20th Century-Fox froth, **June Haver** signs off the lot as *The Girl Next Door* and signs in with the Sisters of Charity Convent in Xavier, KS, with the avowed desire to become one of them. Almost eight weeks later, however, she checked out of the convent—ill—with the hope of regaining her strength in the outside world so she could return and fulfill her wish to become a nun. Instead, she re-met widower **Fred MacMurray**. Their marriage lasted till his death November 5, 1991.

1989: The second coming of *Lawrence of Arabia* (newly restored to 216 minutes) bows on this day at New York's Ziegfeld, and the restoration boasts at least one subtle change. The original director, **David Lean**, discovered when he was reworking the picture that an entire reel had been accidentally flopped in transferring the film from its original 70mm to 35mm. For 20 years, the camels had been moving in the wrong direction—*and nobody noticed!*

RIDING ROUGHSHOD INTO HISTORY: *The Birth of a Nation* debuts. WRONG-WAY O'TOOLE: Peter O'Toole in *Lawrence of Arabia.* SHE GOT TO A NUNNERY: June Haver in *The Girl Next Door.*

1939: Seasoned (sometimes, *overly* seasoned) character actor **Charley Grapewin** takes down his retirement notice, delaying it a week to play **Judy Garland**'s Uncle Henry in *The Wizard of Oz*—but that dovetailed into his two greatest film roles—Grampa Joad in *The Grapes of Wrath* and Jeeter Lester in *Tobacco Road*—and kept him toiling before the cameras another decade.

1945: A Goldwyn Girl graduates to leading lady—a title(d) role, at that!—via *The Princess and the Pirate*, the **Bob Hope** antic bowing on this day at New York's Astor. **Virginia Mayo** had been slotted for the role **Constance Dowling** played in **Danny Kaye**'s first film, *Up in Arms*, but mogul **Samuel Goldwyn** got shouted down by his minions and had to slip her in among the three dozen girls constituting his studio chorus-line. Immediately, he ordered acting lessons while she simmered on the sidelines a year. Then, after *Princess*, when a second Kaye flick (*Wonder Man*) came along, she became his leading lady—and remained so for the rest of their Goldwyn days (*The Kid From Brooklyn*, *The Secret Life of Walter Mitty* and *A Song Is Born*). When they left Sam's shop, Kaye and Mayo went to Warners—but, alas, never worked together again.

1969: Shaggy sagebrusher **George "Gabby" Hayes**, 83, who sidekicked with the best of 'em (**Roy Rogers**, **William Boyd**'s Hopalong Cassidy, **John Wayne**, **Wild Bill Elliott**, **Buck Jones**, **Rex Bell**, **Hoot Gibson**, et al), succumbs to a heart ailment. A surprisingly cultivated cuss off-camera, he played the opposite—spending most of his career in the movie West, bewhiskered and toothless, spitting out "Consarn it!" or "You're durn tootin'" when the occasion called for it—but he also popped up (billed as "George F. Hayes") in **Frank Capra**'s 1936 *Mr. Deeds Goes to Town*, practically clean-shaven, speaking for impoverished farmers and making an impassioned plea to *nouveau riche* Everyman **Gary Cooper**, Mr. Good Deeds himself.

1979: Two veterans from *The Fall of the Roman Empire* conspire to cause the fall of Jack the Ripper in *Murder by Decree*, opening at New York's Ziegfeld: **Christopher Plummer** and **James Mason** as, respectively, Sherlock Holmes and Dr. Watson. The role of Holmes came naturally to Plummer: His second cousin was **Nigel Bruce**, the Watson to **Basil Rathbone**'s Holmes.

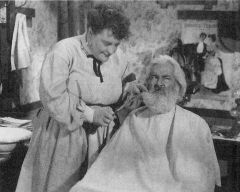

A CO-STAR FROM THE CHORUS LINE: Danny Kaye, Virginia Mayo and Dinah Shore in *Up in Arms*.
THE GRAPEWIN OF *WRATH*: Slim Summerville, Marjorie Rambeau, Charley Grapewin, Elizabeth Patterson, William Tracy and Gene Tierney in *Tobacco Road*.
HE SHAVED FOR *MR. DEEDS*: Jody Gilbert and George "Gabby" Hayes in *Albuquerque*.

10

1939: *Made for Each Other* goes into general release on this day, with ads declaring "Carole Cries!" (to compete with, and kid, *Ninotchka*'s "Garbo Laughs!"). This attempt to make audiences forget **Carole Lombard**'s past as a screwball comedienne and accept her as a tragedienne didn't jerk a single tear from previewers, so producer **David O. Selznick** recalled the picture for major script surgery—prompted by his own recent past: When his brother-agent **Myron** fell ill from lobar pneumonia and lapsed into a coma, Selznick saved his life by chartering a TWA to transport the needed serum from NYC to L.A. Once the crisis passed, the producer told his staff, "This is too good to waste on Myron—let's put it in the picture," so an elongated climax was tacked on in which a serum is flown to Lombard's dying child. It may have worked wonders on Myron, but it didn't do a damn thing for the picture.

1955: *The Desperate Hours*, **Joseph Hayes**' Tony-winning stage thriller in which escaped convict **Paul Newman** laid seige to **Karl Malden**'s suburban home, starts ticking away its six-month run on Broadway. *Already*, the movie version is in the can. Director **William Wyler** had wanted **Marlon Brando** or **James Dean** vs. **Gary Cooper** or **Henry Fonda**, but all declined. Then he offered the family-man role to **Humphrey Bogart**, and Bogie bit—but preferred the escaped-con part. **Fredric March** took up the family-man job—which weighed a ton the first day and a half of filming: The exacting director spent that long retaking a good 50 times the simple opening scene where March comes out of his home, kisses wife **Martha Scott** goodbye and leaves for the office. Wyler reshot it till March stopped "acting" and trudged wearily off to work as he should. "If **Erich von Stroheim** was the man you loved to hate, Wyler must be the man you hate to love but must," March remarked, meaning it kindly (kinda).

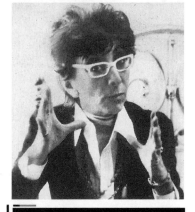

FAMILY STRIFE: From left: Dewey Martin, Mary Murphy, Fredric March, Martha Scott, Richard Eyer, and Humphrey Bogart in *The Desperate Hours*; Carole Lombard, Jackie Taylor and James Stewart in *Made for Each Other*.
WELCOME TO THE CLUB: Lina Wertmuller.

1977: **Lina Wertmuller** becomes the first woman ever to be Oscar-nominated for Best Director (for *Seven Beauties*). **Jane Campion** joined her in that category (for *The Piano*) 17 years later. Like Wertmuller, she was also nominated for Best Screenplay and, unlike Wertmuller, won for the latter work.

1998: The little old lady who lives directly across from the condo where **Nicole Brown Simpson** and **Ron Goldman** were murdered—**Gloria Stuart**, 87—becomes the oldest Oscar nominee of all time for her supporting performance in *Titanic*. **Kate Winslet**, up for Best Actress, starred as a younger version of the same character, making them the first two performers to be Oscar-nominated for playing the same role in the same movie.

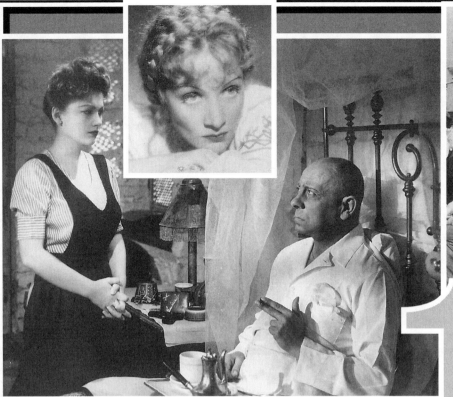

1932: Director **Ernst Lubitsch** on this day adds a new ending to *One Hour With You*—on the opposite coast from where the rest of this froufrou was filmed: To accommodate the schedule of his star—**Maurice Chevalier**, then in concert in New York—the re-shoot was done at Paramount's Astoria studios.

1935: The saga of an Irish Judas named Gypo Nolan—*The Informer*—begins three weeks of filming. **Victor McLaglen**'s title performance was said to be a **John Ford** manipulation—but, late in life, the director dispelled notions he'd gotten McLaglen drunk, thrown him into the interrogation scene with a hangover, redone dialogue at the last moment—anything to keep him off-balance and stumbling through the part. Whatever, it worked—and won Oscars for *both* of them.

1936: In response to **Ernst Lubitsch** being booted off the Paramount mountain, **Marlene Dietrich** and **Charles Boyer** vacate *Hotel Imperial*. That **Pola Negri** silent they were remaking (first as *Invitation to Happiness*, then as *I Loved a Soldier*) was 28 days and $900,000 into production, but, without Lubitsch to keep her in line, Dietrich found herself legally free to leave—and *did* when director **Henry Hathaway** suggested deglamorizing her. (She and Boyer beat a path to *The Garden of Allah*—hardly sanctuary.) Reverting to its original shingle, *Hotel Imperial* re-opened for business with **Margaret Sullavan**, but she fell and broke her left forearm three days into filming, and the S.O.S. went out to **Bette Davis, Claudette Colbert** and **Elissa Landi**. All passed on the property, which by now was known as "Paramount's million-dollar jinx." *Hotel Imperial* remained empty for three years, till **Isa Miranda** checked in (unmemorably, save for her uncanny resemblance to Dietrich). Only when director **Billy Wilder** and his scripting collaborator, **Charles Brackett**, upholstered *Hotel Imperial* and put it down in World War II's North Africa did the material work—as *Five Graves to Cairo*.

1955: For whom the Belle Watling told: Despondent over her career stall, **Ona Munson**, 55, dies of a barbiturate overdose, leaving behind a poignant note for her husband that said, "This is the only way I know to be free again."

1991: In *The New Yorker*, **Pauline Kael** reviews her last and retires. Few critics addressed films with as much unbridled brilliance and passion.

HOTEL IMPERIAL **GOT WILDER: From top: Marlene Dietrich in** *I Loved a Soldier* **(briefly), and Anne Baxter and Erich von Stroheim in** *Five Graves to Cairo*.
A BELIEVABLE BENDER: Victor McLaglen in *The Informer*.
BELLES ON HER EARS: Ona Munson as Belle Watling in *Gone With the Wind*.

1912: *Der Toten Tanz*, starring **Asta Nielsen**, goes before the cameras, inaugurating what *The Guinness Book of Records* calls "the oldest film studio still operating"—East Berlin's Babelsberg Film Studio (a.k.a. DEFA in its Communist era and UFA in the '20s and '30s). **Fritz Lang**'s *Metropolis* and **Josef von Sternberg**'s *The Blue Angel* were two of the 7,700 films made there.

1945: Screenwriter-producer **Joseph L. Mankiewicz** finds his true niche on this day —directing—as he starts shooting *Dragonwyck*. The immediate results were undistinguished, but six years later on this day his writing and directing of *All About Eve* produced a record number of Oscar nominations—14—and this stayed intact until Feb. 10, 1998, when *Titanic* sailed away with the same number. (Ironically, the 1997 *Titanic* was not nominated in one category for which the 1953 *Titanic* won: writing.) On March 23, 1998, *Titanic* created a second tie by equaling *Ben-Hur*'s all-time record of 11 Oscar wins.

1955: A director is born —**Fraser Clarke Heston**—"precocious enough to secure employment at the moment of his birth," as his dad later noted. "CONGRATULATIONS. HE'S CAST IN THE PART. **CECIL B. DEMILLE**," read the wire Fraser's parents received while he was getting his first breakfast. DeMille had promised **Lydia** and **Charlton Heston** if their first-born were a boy-child he'd use him as Baby Moses in *The Ten Commandments*. Three months later, the infant played his first (and last) scene with **Judith Anderson**, **Nina Foch** and **Martha Scott** in the bulrushes of Paramount's backlot. He retired with that performance "and put his salary into Paramount stock, where it has multiplied, like the Children of Israel." Fraser subsequently directed his pop in *The Mountain Men* and *Alaska*.

A DIRECTOR IS BORN: Judith Anderson, Fraser Heston and Nina Foch in *The Ten Commandments*. REBELS WITH A CURSE: Sal Mineo, James Dean and Natalie Wood in *Rebel Without a Cause*. TO THE VICTOR: Bette Davis, Gary Merrill, Anne Baxter and George Sanders in *All About Eve*.

12

1976: Like **James Dean** and **Natalie Wood** (his co-stars in *Rebel Without a Cause*), 37-year-old **Sal Mineo** comes to a senselessly early end. Returning home from rehearsing the L.A. edition of *P.S. Your Cat Is Dead*, he was fatally stabbed in the heart. The killer made himself known two years later, bragging to a Michigan cellmate he'd murdered Mineo and it'd been easy. **Lionel Ray Williams** is now serving a 51-years-to-life sentence.

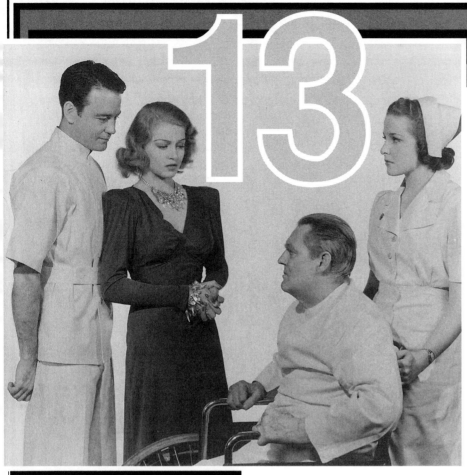

13

1939: Despite a sexy smokescreen from false-hearted gun-moll **Lana Turner**, love finds James Kildare (**Lew Ayres**)—in the form of the nurse right beside him, Mary Lamont (**Laraine Day**)—as *Calling Dr. Kildare* starts filming on this day. Their romance perked along for seven more series installments—right up to 1941's *Dr. Kildare's Wedding Day* when she was struck and crushed by a truck.

1980: **David Janssen**, 49, dies of a heart attack at his Malibu home—before he could loop his last performance: a cynical war correspondent in *Inchon*. There were plans to redo his voice with mimic **Rich Little** (who had dubbed **David Niven**'s last two performances), but it took so long to line up a U.S. distributor that the entire press-corps subplot featuring Janssen and **Rex Reed** was cut to camouflage the fact the film spent three years on the shelf.

LOVE WALKED IN: Lew & Lana & Lionel & Laraine in *Calling Dr. Kildare*.
INCHON INCHED ON: David Janssen, Ben Gazarra and Rex Reed in a scene cut from *Inchon*.
MASSIMO'S EFFORT: Massimo Troisi in *The Postman*.

1995: "It's so ironic that one of Italy's most successful comics—and a very talented filmmaker—will have his first film released in the U.S. after his death," laments Museum of Modern Art film curator **Adrienne Mancia** to *Variety*. Her MoMA homage to the late **Massimo Troisi** was crowned by the first U.S. glimpse of his 12th film, *The Postman (Il Postino)*. Troisi not only co-scripted the flick but also rounded up a British friend, **Michael Radford**, to direct him in the title role—a fisherman's son who is hired to deliver mail every day to exiled Nobel Prize-winning Chilean poet **Pablo Neruda** and is transformed into a romantic by the experience. Born with congenital heart problems, Troisi collapsed shortly after filming began and was told by doctors he needed a transplant immediately. Rather than hold up production, he pressed on, putting in an hour a day until the film was done. Radford not only rewrote scenes to allow Troisi to be seated as much as possible but also rehearsed **Philippe Noiret**, who played Neruda, with a stand-in so all would be in readiness for Troisi, who rarely did more than one take per scene. On June 4, 1994—eleven hours after wrapping the film at Rome's Cinecitta studios—the 41-year-old Troisi went to sleep at his sister's house and never woke up. Exactly one year after the *Variety* item—on Feb. 13, 1996—Troisi become the fourth person (after **James Dean**, **Spencer Tracy** and **Peter Finch**) to be posthumously Oscar-nominated for Best Actor. *The Postman* rang four other times—for 1995's Best Picture, Best Director, Best Adapted Screenplay and Best Original Dramatic Score, winning the award for the last.

1938: Out to break up a movie monolopy, **Louis B. Mayer** and other moguls deliver a venomous Valentine to columnist **Louella O. Parsons**: They start her ex-tipster, **Hedda Hopper**, running barefoot across Lolly's formerly exclusive turf—via a showbiz column of her own in the *Los Angeles Times*.

1943: Having directed Round One of **Bette Davis** vs. **Miriam Hopkins** (*The Old Maid*), **Edmund Goulding** got elected to referee the rematch (*Old Acquaintance*), but the prospect produced a heart attack, so into the fray marched **Vincent Sherman**, who finishes the film —on Valentine's Day, ironically. One could safely say *lots* of love was lost along the way. In fact, the showdown where Davis gave Hopkins a good shaking drew a record number of set visitors, packing the soundstage as if a prizefight were going on (and it was, too).

A TOAST TO NEVER RETEAMING: Davis and Hopkins in *Old Acquaintance*.
ALL THAT JAZZ: The *Esquire* photograph that prompted *A Great Day in Harlem*.

1948: In this day's edition of *The Nation*, critic **James Agee** delivers a prickly Valentine to *Tycoon*, a **John Wayne** action romp: "Several tons of dynamite are set off in this movie—none of it under the right people."

1995: A first film (by **Jean Bach**) about a first photograph (by **Art Kane**) for an art director (**Robert Benton**) putting out his first issue of *Esquire* magazine makes the Oscar running for Best Documentary Feature of 1994. *A Great Day in Harlem* recalled the euphoric morning in the summer of 1958 when the *creme de la creme* of New York jazz suddenly converged at 10 a.m. and spilled across the stoops of a Harlem tenement for a fabled photo op—legends like **Dizzy Gillespie, Gerry Mulligan, Count Basie, Marian McPartland, Mary Lou Williams, Thelonious Monk, Charles Mingus, Art Blakely, Hank Jones, Coleman Hawkins, Willie (The Lion) Smith, Sonny Rollins, Milt Hinton, Lester Young**—59 in all. No one connected with the shoot remembered the specific date—indeed, no one expected so many nightlife stars to come out at such an ungodly hour. "Most of them," said a startled eyewitness (ad exec **Steve Frankfurt**), "didn't realize there were two 10 o'clocks in the same day." The photo, which *Esquire* published in its January 1959 issue, was the first feather in the cap for Benton, who went on to become the Oscar-winning writer-director of 1979's *Kramer vs. Kramer*. To take that historic picture, Benton prevailed on his art teacher, Kane, who was not at the time a photographer but who was hep to jazz. Kane's lifelong manic-depressive condition made the shot happen. On the upswing, he suggested this grandiose shot of jazz giants; on the downside, it caused his death: A week after the film was Oscar-nominated, the 69-year-old Kane went into an emotional slump and committed suicide.

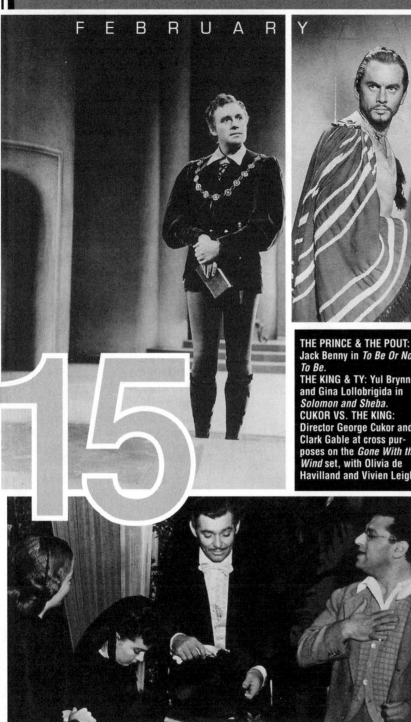

15

THE PRINCE & THE POUT: Jack Benny in *To Be Or Not To Be*.
THE KING & TY: Yul Brynner and Gina Lollobrigida in *Solomon and Sheba*.
CUKOR VS. THE KING: Director George Cukor and Clark Gable at cross purposes on the *Gone With the Wind* set, with Olivia de Havilland and Vivien Leigh.

1939: On this day, **George Cukor** finishes directing the scene in which Scarlett presents Ashley with a sash for his uniform—and then departs from *Gone With the Wind* (after two years of elaborate pre-production work). The reason for his dismissal: bad blood between him and **Clark Gable**. His successor, **Victor Fleming** (freshly extricated from *The Wizard of Oz*), pressed on until he toppled and had to withdraw from the production (April 27-May 18). During that interval, **Sam Wood** manned the megaphone—and kept it up even after Fleming's return to the set. Whenever possible, two scenes would be shot simultaneously. The sole directorial credit—and, subsequently, the Oscar—went to Fleming.

1942: *To Be Or Not To Be*—**Ernst Lubitsch**'s brave, rule-breaking attempt to mine laughs in Nazi-occupied Warsaw—goes into general release, sobered considerably by the plane-crash death of its star, **Carole Lombard**, only a month before. "To say it is callous and macabre is understating the case," huffed *The New York Times*' **Bosley Crowther**. In time, however, the sorrow passed and the fun of her final film came into focus. Today, it looks a lot like the finest hour for all hands. The title, amusingly, was Lombard's signal to a member of the audience (boyish bombardier **Robert Stack**) to leave his seat and join her backstage for a little tryst while Hamlet's soliloquy is savored on stage by her hambone husband (**Jack Benny** at his most vainglorious, as "that great, great actor, Joseph Tura"). As one Nazi critic put it: "What he did to Shakespeare, we are now doing to Poland."

1959: As per his contract stipulation, **Yul Brynner**'s 10-week emergency reign as replacement king for the late **Tyrone Power** in *Solomon and Sheba* comes to a close on this day. For double the $300,000 salary Power got, Brynner was glad to oblige, but he insisted on his own interpretation. Coaxed into a black wig (in the hopes of salvaging some expensive spectacle footage with Power), he still clung to a more macho monarch than Power had envisioned, and this was discernible in every movement and gesture— "even in the long shots"—forcing the producers to scrap all the Power footage. "It was a perfectly valid conception," director **King Vidor** grudgingly agreed—just not what was wanted or needed. "Ty was a more thoughtful actor in his approach to the role, while Brynner was more 'attack.' The differences could not be concealed."

1961: During a 20-minute total eclipse of the sun, director **Richard Fleischer** successfully stages *Barabbas*' dramatically stunning Crucifixion scene in the village of Roccastrada some 120 miles north of Rome. It's the only time a real eclipse has been utilized in a feature film.

1944: When **Jack L. Warner** carps about an error of omission in *The Sullivans* (ignoring the Jewish ancestry of the mother of the five Irish Catholic brothers who went down on the same ship in World War II), non-Jewish **Darryl F. Zanuck** returns fire, writing that this non-issue never came up in the movie's many story conferences and that, if it had, he would have "done everything in my power to keep it out of the story. I can imagine nothing that could be more harmful, in the present Jewish situation, than to have a scene in a typical Irish Catholic story, where you bring up any problem of race or creed. Audiences throughout the world, not knowing the true facts in the case, would immediately accuse the so-called 'Jewish producers in Hollywood again trying to stuff propaganda down their throats.'" In closing, Zanuck confessed credit for creating the Jewish sergeant (**Sam Levene**) in *The Purple Heart*—to say nothing of producing *The House of Rothschild!*—and added a final fillip: "P.S. Did you know that Sergeant **Alvin York**'s great-grandfather was Jewish?"

1955: Driving one of two truck-loads of nitroglycerine over treacherously rocky terrain to a raging South American oil-well fire, **Yves Montand** finds his career taking an abrupt turn—from cabaret singing to dramatic acting—via *The Wages of Fear*, a French palm-sweater pulling into New York's Paris Theater. Credit for this radical change of direction went to **Henri-Georges Clouzot**, who thought Montand looked more like a truck driver than a saloon entertainer and directed him so that he convinced audiences of the same thing.

1986: **Howard da Silva**, 76, dies of lymphoma—three weeks before **Ray Milland**, 81, succumbs to cancer. In *The Lost Weekend*, da Silva played the bartender who fueled Milland's greatest performance (still the yardstick against which Oscar measures its tanked-up award contenders). In private life, Milland professed to being a teetotaler—which was not exactly on-the-money correct, but for him to claim otherwise would undercut his accomplishment.

1996: A heart attack befalls *M*A*S*H*'s befogged commander, Lt. Col. Henry Blake—*for two days running*: **Roger Bowen**, 63, who originated the role in the ground-breaking 1970 movie, dies on this day —only one day after the death of **McLean Stevenson**, 66, who played the part for three years (1972-1975) on the television series. (Before taking up acting, the latter worked on the losing Presidential campaign of his cousin and next-door neighbor, **Adlai Stevenson**).

BROTHERS IN WAR: Edward Ryan, George Offerman Jr., James Cardwell, John Alvin and John Campbell as *The Sullivans.*
***M*A*S*H* BLAKES:** From left: Roger Bowen and McLean Stevenson.
TAVERN PALAVER: Yves Montand and Vera Clouzot in *Wages of Fear*, Howard da Silva and Ray Milland in *The Lost Weekend.*

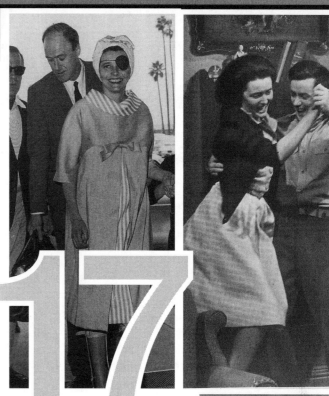

1914: *The Squaw Man* is tradeshown at NYC's Longacre —less than two months from the first day of shooting—and, in a glance, it's clear producer-director-creator **Cecil B. DeMille** has bought himself a great bill of goods from **Max Factor**. The man who got Mr. DeMille ready for his closeups carved out a cosmetic kingdom for himself by convincing DeMille to accept no substitutes for genuine Grade-A human hair in wigs. The clumsy substitutes—straw, excelsior, Spanish moss, wool, tobacco leaves—just weren't cutting it in the closeups. DeMille wouldn't buy the expensive wigs but did *rent* them—a factor Factor hadn't considered but one which quickly made him rich.

1947: "I never wanted to be a dancer—it's true!—I wanted to be a shortstop for the Pittsburgh Pirates," once confessed **Gene Kelly**, who on this day gets only as far as *The Pirate* as that swashbuckler-with-**Cole Porter**-songs begins production. Still percolating: his idea for a baseball musical, which ultimately becomes *Take Me Out to the Ball Game.*

1964: Nineteen going out for "Sixteen Going on Seventeen" (Liesl von Trapp in *The Sound of Music*), **Mia Farrow** puts in the last of three unsuccessful readings for the role. Director **Robert Wise** thought she lacked energy and dancing skills and therefore passed on her—as well as on **Sharon Tate**, **Teri Garr**, **Geraldine Chaplin**, **Shelley Fabares**, **Lesley Ann Warren**— in favor of **Charmian Carr**. Other also-rans for the Von Trapp kids ranged from a former Oscar winner (**Patty Duke**) to a future one (**Richard Dreyfuss**) and included **Victoria Tennant**, **Kurt Russell**, **Ann Jillian** and **Paul Petersen**.

1965: A pregnant **Patricia Neal**, 39, spends this day—her fourth on **John Ford**'s last film, *Seven Women*—riding a donkey across the *Good Earth* sets of the MGM backlot, and, in the evening, she suffers a series of three strokes that will keep her off screen for the next three years—until her Oscar-nominated comeback in *The Subject Was Roses* in 1968. Two days after her hospitalization, her role in *Seven Women* was taken over by an old friend, **Anne Bancroft**, who had co-starred with Neal in the original Broadway production of *The Miracle Worker.*

1976: During lunch with **Carol Kane** at the Russian Tea Room, **Sylvia Miles** excuses herself to call her agent and gets the word her *Farewell, My Lovely* cameo got her Oscar-nominated for Best Supporting Actress. Her return to her table was out of *Aida*—a triumphant march, jubilant commotion on all sides, congratulations from Kane and everybody. In time, when the uproar subsided, Miles turned to Kane and said, "Oh, I forgot to tell you. You were nominated, too" (for Best Actress, for her starring role in *Hester Street*).

A PUBLIC COMEBACK: From left: Patricia Neal on the mend with then-husband, Roald Dahl, and fully recovered with Martin Sheen in *The Subject Was Roses.*
MORE SWASHBUCKLED THAN BASEBALL: Gene Kelly in *The Pirate.*
AN OVERSLIGHT: Sylvia Miles and Robert Mitchum in *Farewell, My Lovely.*

1929: An announcement made casually (and suspenselessly!) on the back page of the Academy Bulletin declares **Janet Gaynor** the first person to win the Oscar for Best Actress. To this day, she remains the only person to win that award for three different performances in the same year (for *Seventh Heaven*, *Street Angel* and *Sunrise*). Her next (and only other) nominated performance—the original Esther Blodgett/Vicki Lester of 1937's *A Star Is Born*—was less blessed, but it (and **Fredric March**'s performance of her actor-husband, Norman Maine) were the first portrayals of Oscar winners ever given by actual Oscar winners.

1938: *Test Pilot*, the *Top Gun* of its time, concludes production with **Clark Gable**, **Myrna Loy** and **Spencer Tracy**. One morning a month into filming, Gable fans mobbed MGM's gateway for autographs and created a star-studded gridlock—including the totally ignored Tracy, who stood up in his car, threw Gable a mock bow and hailed, "Long live the king!" The prop department carried the gag another revolution, creating a cardboard crown with rabbit's fur and crowning Gable in the studio commissary. These antics made the papers and prompted columnist **Ed Sullivan** to poll his readers for real about a King and Queen of Hollywood. The results legitimized Gable's royalty, and Loy was elected Queen. Tracy's "consolation prizes" started rolling in three months later: back-to-back Best Actor Oscars for 1937's *Captains Courageous* and 1938's *Boys Town*.

1957: *Giant*, like *East of Eden* the year before, earns **James Dean** a special place among the Best Actor nominees. His singularly unique niche in Oscar history is that he's the only performer posthumously nominated *twice*.

1957: "This just proves what we've known all along—that the **Bowery Boys** series couldn't have lasted this long if not for the fine writers," cracks Allied Artists prexy **Steve Broidy** when **Elwood Ullman** and **Edward Bernds** are Oscar-nominated for Best Motion Picture Story for their *High Society*. The intended nominee was **John Patrick** for the other 1956 movie called *High Society*, but, since that was hardly an original screenplay (coming from *The Philadelphia Story*, a play and a film), the Academy at first tried saving face by saying they *had* meant the Bowery Boys film—but, mercifully, the nominated writers bowed out rather than compete with **Jean Paul Sartre** (for France's *The Proud and the Beautiful*) or risk a prank victory that would embarrass the Academy. "The biggest boo-boo in Academy nomination history," *Variety* called it—and that was *before* this category was won by a nonexistent **Robert Rich** (i.e., blacklisted **Dalton Trumbo**, who wrote *The Brave One* under that pseudonym.)

1934: One of show business' longest-running marriages begins in Erie, PA, on this day as songstress **Dolores Reade** weds **Bob Hope** (of Broadway's *Roberta*).

1940: *Andy Hardy Meets Debutante*—in real life, a little late: By the time filming begins on this day on Installment Nine in the screen series, title players **Mickey Rooney** and **Diana Lewis** are no longer the item they once were. Indeed, for more than a month, she had been the bride of **William Powell**. "Mr. Powell's more suave than I am," shrugged The Mick, masterfully understating the case. The 24-year-old starlet and 47-year-old Powell met when MGM borrowed his pool for some studio-ordered cheesecake shots of her. The lord of the manor (unmarried since his divorce from **Carole Lombard** and uninterested since the death of his fiancee, **Jean Harlow**) looked out of his bedroom window at the poolside posing and said to himself, "I'm going to marry that girl"—and he *did*, a few weeks later. She retired from films in 1943 (soon after she and **Lana Turner** studied sociology together in *Johnny Eager*), and he retired in 1955. Their marriage lasted 44 years — till his death March 5, 1984, at age 91.

1942: *Johnny Eager* bows at New York's Capitol, with a famous ad-copy come-on ("TNT—Taylor 'n' Turner—Together They're Terrific"), but its Oscar went to **Robert Taylor**'s besotted, Bard-spouting sidekick: **Van Heflin**. Backhanded compliment from the *New York World-Telegram* critic: "Any film which has sense of humor enough, if not sense of humor at least temerity enough, to offer **Lana Turner** as a student of sociology deserves to be treated kindly."

1974: With more than a little help from a previous winner in this category (**Mercedes McCambridge**, who, in nine days of redubbing, did *all* the devilish vocality for the role), **Linda Blair** emerges among 1973's Oscar-nominated Best Supporting Actresses as *The Exorcist*'s demonically possessed teen.

1992: At 24, **John Singleton** betters—by two years—a distinction **Orson Welles** held a full half-century, since *Citizen Kane*: for *Boyz N the Hood*, he becomes the youngest person to contend for the Best Director Oscar.

1999: Two performers in two different pictures are Oscar-nominated for playing the same character—Queen Elizabeth I: **Cate Blanchett** was cited for Best Actress in, and as, *Elizabeth*; **Judi Dench** emerged among the Best Supporting Actresses for *Shakespeare in Love*. The latter, winning her category for her solid-gold cameo, admitted modestly, "I feel for eight minutes on the screen I should only get a little of him." (Only **Beatrice Straight** in 1976's *Network* turned in a shorter Oscar-winning performance.)

TWO OSCAR-NOMINATED ELIZA-BETHS: From left: Cate Blanchett in *Elizabeth*, and Judi Dench in *Shakespeare in Love*.
WELLES DONE: Ice Cube, Redge Green, Dedrick D. Gobert, director John Singleton and Cuba Gooding Jr. filming *Boyz N the Hood*.
THE SHORT MAN BEFORE 'THE THIN MAN': Mickey Rooney and Diana Lewis in *Andy Hardy Meets Debutante*.

20

1947:

The century's two most famous Americans-in-wheelchairs miss their date with destiny—at **Eleanor Roosevelt**'s *insistence*—on this day, as the saga of the atomic bomb (titled after **Truman**'s words: *The Beginning or the End*) bows at New York's Capitol, with **Godfrey Tearle** (not **Lionel Barrymore**) playing **FDR**. The President's widow objected to private remarks Barrymore purportedly made about her husband during the 1944 Presidential campaign when he was in **Thomas Dewey**'s camp. The actor wrote her disavowing any unrecorded verbal attacks, but she *still* objected to his playing the President so he gallantly bowed out.

1951:

"What did you get that for, bowling?" cracks **Jose Ferrer** when **Gloria Swanson** flashes him an Oscar in their Broadway revival of the **Hecht-MacArthur** *Twentieth Century*—and nightly, now, it brings the house down: Both are up for said award (he for *Cyrano de Bergerac*, she for *Sunset Boulevard*). He won, but Swanson lost to **Judy Holliday** of *Born Yesterday*. For the performance of a lifetime (and one of the great Hollywood comebacks), Swanson garnered only the Golden Globe. It's hard to imagine anyone as regally deranged as her silent-screen queen, Norma Desmond, but in truth she was the fourth actress to whom writer-director **Billy Wilder** pitched the part (**Mae West, Mary Pickford** and **Pola Negri** preceded her). Ironically, the director of Holliday's Oscar-winning performance—**George Cukor**—was the person who had suggested Swanson to Wilder.

1967:

Everybody with a speaking part in *Who's Afraid of Virginia Woolf?* makes the Oscar running — **Richard Burton, Elizabeth Taylor, George Segal** and **Sandy Dennis**—and the women wound up winners seven weeks later. The only other films to get Oscar nominations for their entire casts are *Give 'Em Hell, Harry* (**James Whitmore**'s one-man show on **Harry Truman**) and *Sleuth* (a two-man show with **Michael Caine** and **Laurence Olivier** in a multi-disguised star-duel).

1974:

I Got You Babe—*NOT*: **Cher** files for divorce from **Sonny Bono**.

1992:

A strapping Indiana lad waylaid by bad health in Hollywood, 63-year-old **Dick York** dies in Rockford, MI, where he had been confined to his home for years with emphysema and a degenerative spinal condition. His chronic back problems started with the arduous filming of 1959's *They Came to Cordura*, and in ten years' time it finally forced him into retirement and out of his best-known role: Darrin Stephens, befuddled hubby to **Elizabeth Montgomery** on TV's *Bewitched*. A fair physical facsimile, **Dick Sargent**, took over the part, and the series perked merrily along for Seasons 6 through 9. York's best-known role on the *big* screen: *Inherit the Wind*'s forgotten man—an accused Darwinist dwarfed by the courtroom histrionics of **Spencer Tracy**-versus-**Fredric March**.

21

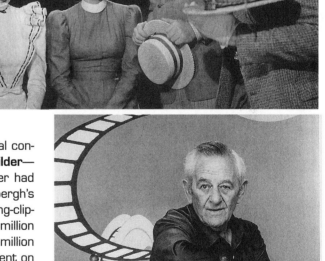

1941: *The Strawberry Blonde* strolls into New York's Strand, making a star of **Rita Hayworth**, who stepped into that title role when "Oomph Girl" **Ann Sheridan** said uh-uh. Hayworth was underappreciated back home at Columbia Pictures, thrown away on B's and programmers (*Blondie on a Budget*, *Angels Over Broadway*) or imported to Fox (*Blood and Sand*, *My Gal Sal*), MGM (*Susan and God*) and Warners (*Affectionately Yours*). But after Columbia cast her in a couple of **Fred Astaire** musicals and *Cover Girl*, her stardom firmly took hold, and "Lady Loan-Out" never left the lot again—till **Prince Aly Kahn** came along and claimed her for his princess.

1957: *The Spirit of St. Louis* lifts off in the cavernous Radio City Music Hall on this day with a gala benefit. At the controls, as 25-year-old **Charles A. Lindbergh**, was 47-year-old **James Stewart**, chosen over more logical contenders (**John Kerr**, **Peter Graves**)—teased his director, **Billy Wilder**—because he "had a pilot's license." The critics, while conceding Wilder had triumphed over some major storytelling obstacles in recreating Lindbergh's 33 1/2-hour solo flight from New York to Paris, still came with wing-clippers, and the film nosedived at the box office, earning back only $2.6 million of its original $6 million investment. A sixth of that was the first million shelled out for the film rights of a book. The first seven-figure sum spent on a *play* was also for a Stewart vehicle, **Mary Chase**'s Pulitzer Prize-winning *Harvey*—**Garson Kanin**'s *Born Yesterday* fetched the same amount the same year (1950)—and both properties paid back in Academy Awards for their leading females: the latter's **Judy Holliday** and the former's **Josephine Hull**, both JH's recreating their original Broadway performances.

1966: *The Collector* completes **William Wyler**'s collection of Best Director Oscar-bids: an even dozen—the all-time record for this category.

1966: **Laurence Olivier**'s title portrayal in *Othello* becomes the only performance of a black man by a white man to get Oscar-nominated. **Ronald Colman** won an Oscar playing an actor who played Othello (*A Double Life*), and **Albert Finney** nabbed an Oscar nomination for doing the same (*The Dresser*).

THE FIRST MILLION-DOLLAR PLAYS: From left: Judy Holliday and Broderick Crawford in *Born Yesterday*; James Stewart and Josephine Hull in *Harvey*.
COLUMBIA GRADUATE: Rita Hayworth, Olivia de Havilland, James Cagney and Jack Carson in *The Strawberry Blonde*.
OSCAR'S MOST NOMINATED DIRECTOR: William Wyler.

22

1934: In *It Happened One Night*, slipping into Radio City Music Hall on this day, **Clark Gable** removes his shirt and reveals a bare torso—sending men's undershirts to the cellar in sales.

1934: Shooting starts on *Twentieth Century*, which, according to *The New York Times*' **Vincent Canby** some 60 years later (June 30, 1995), "may be the best comedy ever made by anybody, anywhere, at any time." **John Barrymore**, in his last great comic performance, and **Carole Lombard**, in her first, sparred spectacularly as an overripe theatrical impresario and his diva discovery, Lily Garland (the former Mildred Plotka).

1940: Go figure: Radio City Music Hall celebrates Washington's birthday by unveiling **Raymond Massey** as *Abe Lincoln in Illinois*.

1962: The seventh and last child of **John Wayne** is born on this day and named after a favorite role of his (Ethan Edwards in *The Searchers*). "I love it," Wayne said. "**John Ethan Wayne**. J.E.W. We'll have our own little Jew in the family." The birth caught Wayne between cameos in his most financially successful films: He got $250,000 to work four days on *The Longest Day* (eight scenes, totaling 12 minutes and 15 seconds of screen time) and $25,000 to work six days on *How the West Was Won* (one scene, totaling 3.5 minutes). The discrepancy in pay had to do with some sweet vengeance Wayne was extracting from **Darryl F. Zanuck**, who'd sounded off in print that Wayne had no "right" to produce, direct *and* star in *The Alamo*. "That had to be the most expensive interview a movie producer ever gave," chortled Wayne on his way to the bank. As DFZ came to realize: what would World War II—or the West—be without John Wayne?

1971: "The Best Picture of 1944," as one critic labeled *Airport*, winds up on this day among the Oscar contenders for Best Picture of 1970. It also led off *Variety*'s list of top rental earnings for the year at $37,650,000 and unleashed a new screen genre: The Disaster Flick, full of churning chaos and famous-face droppings (*The Towering Inferno*, *The Swarm*, *Earthquake*, *The Poseidon Adventure*, etc.). Producer **Ross Hunter** piled the all-stars on high and mighty. **Maureen Stapleton**, who swore off planes in real life, did the best work of those on land (**Burt Lancaster**, **Jean Seberg**, **George Kennedy**, **Dana Wynter**, **Lloyd Nolan**, **Barbara Hale**), as the wife of the mad bomber on board (**Van Heflin**). Handling the in-flight frights: **Jacqueline Bisset**, an Oscar-winning **Helen Hayes**, **Barry Nelson**. Despite the drunk jokes, **Dean Martin** donned the pilot's cap and took 10% of the film's profits, earning so much he only dabbled in movies after that.

1939: Pressured by MGM and much against his will, **Spencer Tracy** tuxes up and attends the Oscar offerings, making history-of-a-kind by becoming the first person ever to win the Oscar for Best Actor two years in a row (for 1937's *Captains Courageous* and, now, 1938's *Boys Town*)—a distinction only slightly diminished by the fact that his opposite number in the Best Actress category is likewise a repeat winner: **Bette Davis** (for 1935's *Dangerous* and 1938's *Jezebel*). Nevertheless, his back-to-back Best Actor victory stood for 56 years—till March 27, 1995, when it was finally matched by **Tom Hanks** (for 1993's *Philadelphia* and 1994's *Forrest Gump*)—and, *again*, an actress came forth to collect her second Oscar, this time in the supporting ranks: **Dianne Wiest** (for 1986's *Hannah and Her Sisters* and 1994's *Bullets Over Broadway*). There was never a consecutive winner for Best Supporting Actress, but there was one for Best Supporting Actor—**Jason Robards** (for 1976's *All the President's Men* and 1977's *Julia*)—and two for Best Actress: **Luise Rainer** (for 1936's *The Great Ziegfeld* and for 1937's *The Good Earth*) and **Katharine Hepburn** (for 1967's *Guess Who's Coming to Dinner* and for 1968's *The Lion in Winter*).

23

DOUBLING THEIR PLEASURE: Spencer Tracy and Bette Davis at the '38 Oscars.
BOUND & BONDING: Sidney Poitier and Tony Curtis in *The Defiant Ones*.
IT BEGAN WITH A BELCH: Gary Cooper, Henry Slate and Charles Bronson in *You're in the Navy Now*.

1951: *U.S.S. Teakettle*, a service farce about a shipload of 90-day wonders, steams into New York's Roxy —and sinks like a rock, despite a comedy-of-the-year rave from *The New York Times*' **Bosley Crowther**. Raised from the depths and renamed *You're in the Navy Now*, the film finished its run to better business. It marked **Gary Cooper**'s first film for 20th Century-Fox since 1925 when he rode as an extra with **Tom Mix** in *The Lucky Horseshoe*. It also marked the first film ever of two tough-guys who were among the five survivors in *The Dirty Dozen*: **Lee Marvin** and **Charles Bronson**. The latter (then billed as Buchinski) always said he got his first role because he could belch on cue.

1959: An uglied-up **Tony Curtis** and a super-charged **Sidney Poitier**—a.k.a. *The Defiant Ones*—continue their chained life as rivals for the same Best Actor Oscar, both eventually losing to the *Separate Tables* contender, **David Niven**. Curtis got this—his one and only Oscar shot, he got it because his cracker-convict role was nixed by **Marlon Brando**, **Kirk Douglas**, **Gregory Peck**, **Frank Sinatra**, **Richard Widmark**, **Burt Lancaster**, **Lee Marvin** and **Anthony Quinn**.

1965: On this day expires Arthur Stanley Jefferson, 74. The world knew him as **Stan Laurel**.

1968: In New Orleans, **Peter Fonda** turns 28 *and* producer on this day as he and his co-star director, **Dennis Hopper**, rev up and get rolling with *Easy Rider*.

BEFORE & BEHIND THE CAMERA: From left: John Huston acting in *The Cardinal*; David Lean directing *Ryan's Daughter*.
MIDLIFE CRISES: Ruth Chatterton and Walter Huston in *Dodsworth*.
BIKING BEATLES: Ringo Starr, Paul McCartney, John Lennon and George Harrison in *Help!*

1934: *Dodsworth* debuts at New York's Shubert, bringing **Walter Huston** his longest Broadway run—and, eventually, the movie version. **Sidney Howard**, who adapted **Sinclair Lewis'** novel for the stage, had suggested **Samuel Goldwyn** buy the book for $20,000 years earlier when he was scripting Lewis' *Arrowsmith* for Goldwyn, but the filmmaker refused, forcing Howard to retaliate with the stage hit. When Goldwyn came calling again for the screen rights, he learned the asking price had leapt to $160,000. Fine with Sam: "This way, I buy a successful play. Before, it was just a novel." Alas, the movie was not the hit that the play and novel had been. Goldwyn believed it was because the people weren't attractive enough and always hoped to remedy that with a **Clark Gable** remake. Beyond the TV version done by **Fredric March** and **Claire Trevor** in the 1950s, the closest *Dodsworth* came to a remake was in the '80s when **Gregory Peck** commissioned an updated screenplay that would star him; scripters ranged from **Julius J. Epstein** to **Jon Robin Baitz** to **Alfred Uhry**; co-stars varied from **Elizabeth Taylor** to **Faye Dunaway**, but financing wasn't forthcoming, and Peck overgrew the role.

1964: Oscar-winning writer-director **John Huston** cracks a new category —Best Supporting Actor—earning an Oscar nomination for *The Cardinal* and opening up the possibility of more acting assignments (25, in fact, followed).

1965: *Help!* is finally on the way, as **The Beatles** begin Film 2.

1969: An Oscar nomination goes to **Jule Styne** and **Bob Merrill**'s supposedly original title tune for the movie version of their *Funny Girl*. (It was a number they had dropped on the road to Broadway.) Less lucky was "Maybe This Time," a non-show song which **John Kander** and **Fred Ebb** wrote in 1963 and inserted briefly into their Broadway-bound *Cabaret*: When it surfaced again in 1972 in the *Cabaret* film, it was ruled ineligible for Oscar consideration; six years earlier, **Liza Minnelli** had used "Maybe This Time" to audition for the show's director, **Harold Prince**, who turned her down—for **Jill Haworth**. Of course, Liza had the last laugh, landing the movie version *and* the Oscar.

1970: "Working with **David Lean** is like being made to build the Taj Mahal out of toothpicks," said **Robert Mitchum**, whose one brush with the director—*Ryan's Daughter*—wraps 52 weeks of exasperatingly painstaking filmmaking.

1939: A month into filming, *Gone With the Wind* suffers its first fatality: **Robert Gleckler**—who was playing Tara's evil overseer, Jonas Wilkerson—dies of uremic poisoning. The scene he did with **Barbara O'Neil** was reshot March 3 with **Victor Jory**, who outlived all the film's principal males.

1957: On this day in Clovis, NM, **Buddy Holly and The Crickets** record their first hit—"That'll Be the Day"—titled after a recurring line of derision **John Wayne** muttered to various pioneer pip-squeaks in *The Searchers*.

1963: For the second time in Oscar history, a performer enters Best Actress contention as a fictional character named Jane Hudson—in this case, *Baby* Jane Hudson: **Bette Davis** in *What Ever Happened to Baby Jane?* Just plain Jane Hudson was **Katharine Hepburn**'s nominated ticket in *Summertime*.

WHAT EVER HAPPENED TO FAIR PLAY?: Joan Crawford and Bette Davis in *What Ever Happened to Baby Jane?* WHAT EVER HAPPENED TO JOAN CRAWFORD?: Olivia de Havilland and Bette Davis in *Hush . . . Hush, Sweet Charlotte?* WHAT EVER HAPPENED TO SPINSTER JANE?: Rossano Brazzi and Katharine Hepburn in *Summertime.* WHAT EVER HAPPENED TO JONAS WILKERSON?: Robert Gleckler, left, and Victor Jory.

1963: Miffed she didn't make the nomination sheets for *What Ever Happened to Baby Jane?* and co-star **Bette Davis** did, **Joan Crawford** starts plotting vengeance: She cut a deal to accept the Oscar for *any* Best Actress contender absent from the ceremony—and did just that, with uncommon joy, when **Anne Bancroft** won for *The Miracle Worker*—beaming among the winners in the morning papers and incurring the everlasting wrath of Davis, who got the last laugh when producer-director **Robert Aldrich** tried to reteam the two divas in *Hush . . . Hush, Sweet Charlotte*. In no time, Davis had Crawford on the ropes, in the hospital and out of the picture. **Barbara Stanwyck** and **Loretta Young** were asked to replace her but declined for friendship's sake, and **Vivien Leigh** was personally vetoed by Davis herself (still smarting from having lost Scarlett O'Hara to Leigh 26 years before). When filming finally resumed, Davis had an old friend—**Olivia de Havilland**—in Crawford's part, and the two of them gleefully clinked their Coke bottles over the exit of the Pepsi queen. Fade forward 18 years: Bancroft was to have played Crawford in *Mommie Dearest*, till **Faye Dunaway** ran away with the role—a spectacle that couldn't have delighted Davis, who found Dunaway as loathsome to work with as Crawford.

26

1942: At the first Oscar-giving after Pearl Harbor, show folks rub elbows with political figures (notably, Chinese Ambassador **Dr. Hu Shih** and the most recent Republican also-ran for President, **Wendell Willkie**)—very strange bedfellows, indeed! When Willkie was leaving New York, he informed the press he was going to "speak at the movie banquet where they award those—you know, those little Okies." And **Cecil B. DeMille** seconded that motion when he stepped to the podium to name the Best Director winner and admitted, "Some of the people who spoke before me have stolen the thunder, like Mr. Willkie and the Jap—I mean, Chinese—ambassador." During the long silent limo ride home, DeMille's wife delivered the haymaker: "Well, Cecil, at last you have done something that Hollywood will remember."

1942: "I would have preferred getting my Oscar for Brigid rather than for Sandra," **Mary Astor** reflected years later in her autobiography about her Best Supporting Actress victory on this day. Of her two fine performances in 1941, playing "the other woman" to **Bette Davis** (in *The Great Lie*) impressed Academy nominators more than playing femme fatale to **Humphrey Bogart** (in *The Maltese Falcon*). In the long run, the latter mattered more. The headline accompanying her obituary in *The New York Times* would have pleased her: Mary Astor, 81, Is Dead; Star of 'Maltese Falcon.'

1942: Sisters compete for the Best Actress Oscar for the first time on this day: **Olivia de Havilland** for *Hold Back the Dawn* versus **Joan Fontaine** for *Suspicion*. The latter won, but the former matched her four years later (for 1946's *To Each His Own*) and topped her three years after that (for 1949's *The Heiress*). They are the only pair of sisters who are Oscar-winning actresses. (And, no, they don't speak to each other.)

1950: A kid from Texas (**Audie Murphy**) premieres *The Kid from Texas* (the movie) in Dallas—despite the slight historical fact that the kid in question (Billy the Kid, a.k.a. **William Bonney**) was born in NYC and not, as the film made out, in El Paso. Two dozen more Universal Pictures followed for Murphy. "I made the same Western 30 times," he liked to say, "with different horses."

1985: After ten years and eight months, *Emmanuelle* calls it a run at Paris' Paramount City. *The Guinness Book of Records* called it "the longest continuous run of any film at one cinema." It was seen by 3,268,874 patrons.

1987: *One Flew Over the Cuckoo's Nest* rounds off its 11-year run in Stockholm. It was figured that the film, during these 573 straight weeks, had been seen by 2 million Swedes (approximately one fourth of Sweden).

1935: *It Happened One Night*, on *this* night, becomes the first film to sweep clean the top five Oscar shelves: Best Picture, Best Actor (**Clark Gable**), Best Actress (**Claudette Colbert**), Best Director (**Frank Capra**) and Best Screenplay (**Robert Riskin**)—pretty good hittin' in light of the fact that MGM had "sentenced" Gable to a second-rate studio as disciplinary action to keep him in line! This remarkable victory has been equaled only twice: by 1975's *One Flew Over the Cuckoo's Nest* and 1991's *The Silence of the Lambs*.

1941: *The Philadelphia Story* produces two Oscar-winning Stewarts: Best Actor (**James Stewart**) and Best Adapter (**Donald Ogden Stewart**, who actually *improved* on **Philip Barry**'s play with a little uncredited scripting assist from producer **Joseph L. Mankiewicz**). Cracked the latter Stewart, refreshingly: "There has been so much niceness here tonight that I am happy to say that I am entirely—and solely—responsible for the success of *The Philadelphia Story*."

1980: Cancer claims character comedian **George Tobias**, 78, in Hollywood—or, as he put it when he played the Bronx subway guard who expired in combat in the arms of **Gary Cooper**'s *Sergeant York*, "This is where we change cars, Alvin—the end of the line." Tobias got his last laugh posthumously, and that too involved car-changing: As his remains were being transported in a station wagon from the hospital to the mortuary, the mortuary's driver was involved in a minor traffic mishap on Sunset Boulevard, and, while he was exchanging information with the other driver, two boys made off with the station wagon. Their joy ride came to a screeching halt three blocks later when they discovered the body on a gurney in the back under a blanket and fled the vehicle screaming, leaving the motor running and the doors ajar. The body was recovered safely and sent to New York for burial without further incident or indignity.

1993: **Lillian Gish** dies at 99—"the same age as film," her manager, **James E. Frasher**, noted: "They both came into the world in 1893." Gish began acting on stage, at 5, as "Baby Lillian" with her sister, **Dorothy**; they film-debuted together as extras in **D.W. Griffith**'s 1912 *An Unseen Enemy* and eventually became his *Orphans of the Storm*—but Lillian toiled too for modern directors like **Robert Altman** (1978's *A Wedding*) and **Lindsay Anderson** (1987's *The Whales of August*). When a reporter reminded her in her dotage that her 75-year career got her *Guinness*' title as "most enduring actress of the large screen," she paused a thoughtful beat, then said, "I made a movie with him once"—and the interview careened to West Africa, **Sir Alec** and *The Comedians*.

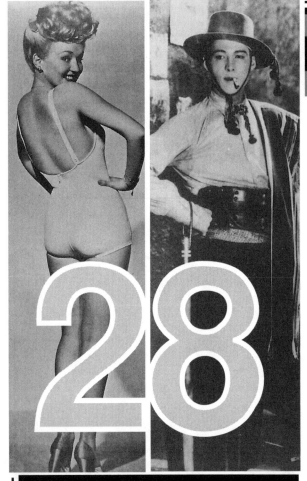

28

1930: "I've got two reasons for success, and I'm standing on both of them," declared **Betty Grable** the realist. At 13, she heeded her first call for chorines—a newspaper ad placed by director **H. Bruce Humberstone**—and, out of the 500 auditioning, won a Fox contract. First stop, arriving at the Roxy on this day: an early song-and-dancer prophetically tagged *Let's Go Places*, in which she was (sometimes in blackface) one of the (63) ladies of the chorus.

1936: Filming begins on *The Good Earth* without the all-Chinese cast **Irving Thalberg** had envisioned. When that plan was abandoned (for lack of "enough suitable Chinese actors"), **Charles Boyer**, **Katharine Cornell**, **Nils Asther** and **Barbara Stanwyck** were among the non-Asians considered for the lead couple, "Wang" and "O-Lan." The roles went to **Paul Muni** and **Luise Rainer**, both of whom were coming off of Oscar-winning performances (he for *The Story of Louis Pasteur*, she for *The Great Ziegfeld*), but otherwise it would be difficult to imagine a more incompatible pair. Their work methods and acting styles collided constantly. Muni was quite vocal about his unhappiness with her, and Rainer shrewdly used his disapproval to the betterment of her performance, which earned her a second Oscar (while Muni had to content himself with only a nomination—for *The Life of Emile Zola*).

1984: The "Lady in Black" who for more than half a century visited **Rudolph Valentino**'s grave every August 23 to mourn his passing—**Ditra Flame**, 78—is herself buried in San Jacinto, CA, in the black dress, shawl and veil that had become her trademark during the pilgrimages. When she was 14 and near death, the famous screen lover visited her in the hospital as a favor to her mother, put a red rose on her bed and told her, "You are not going to die. You are going to live forever. But one thing for sure: If you die before I do, you will come to stay by me because I don't want to be alone either."

1993: Cancer claims **Ruby Keeler**, 83. In her first feature fling—1933's *42nd Street*—she was the sweet-faced embodiment of Broadway's favorite myth: "a raw kid from the chorus," tapped to replace the big star on opening night, then terrorized into stardom by a tyrannical director, **Warner Baxter** ("Sawyer, you're going out a youngster, but you've got to come back a star!"). Keeler kept that illusion alive in eight other toe-tappers cranked out during **Busby Berkeley**'s boom at Warners—*Gold Diggers of 1933*, *Footlight Parade*, *Flirtation Walk*, *Go Into Your Dance* (her only opus with her then-husband, **Al Jolson**), *Dames*, *Colleen*, *Shipmates Forever* and *Ready, Willing and Able*.

. . . AND STANDING TALL: Betty Grable.
A FLICKERING FLAME: Rudolph Valentino in *The 4 Horsemen of the Apocalypse*.
BADGERED INTO AN OSCAR: Luise Rainer and Paul Muni in *The Good Earth*.
LYING THIS ONE OUT: Eddie Kane, Al Jolson, Nick Copeland, Henry Kolker and Ruby Keeler in *Go Into Your Dance*.

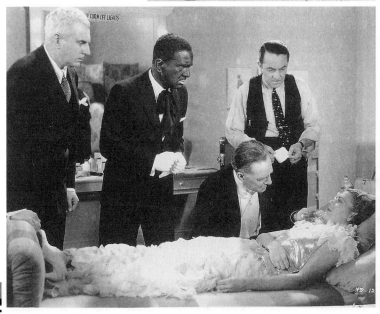

29

1940: One of the few *unnominated* leading players in *Gone With the Wind*, **Thomas Mitchell** nevertheless wins his category (Best Supporting Actor) via a different vehicle—**John Ford**'s *Stagecoach*—playing the drunken comic-relief on board, Doc Boone. During the filming, Mitchell was ridden unmercifully by Ford—till the designated "whipping boy" brilliantly returned the serve: "Remember, Mr. Ford: I saw your *Mary of Scotland*." Suddenly, it was all quiet on the Western front.

1940: Seated at the back by the kitchen, **Hattie McDaniel** becomes (1) the first black person to attend the Academy Awards ceremonies and (2) the first of her race to win an Oscar. Her award for Best Supporting Actress was one of eight given *Gone With the Wind*. (On top of everything else, it was the first color film to win Best Picture.) "Isn't it wonderful, this benefit for **David O. Selznick**?" quipped Oscar emcee **Bob Hope**.

1968: *The Killing of Sister George*, a lesbian triangle (**Beryl Reid**, **Susannah York** and **Coral Browne**) tipping the very heavy hand of director **Robert Aldrich**, is banned in Boston —primarily because of an explicit sex-scene elaborated on (for five minutes!) from a single sentence in **Lukas Heller**'s screenplay. (The scene didn't exist at all in the **Frank Marcus** play which won Reid the Tony.) Stoking the embers of controversy: the film's X rating and its controversial logo which, depending on how you look at it, is either a curiously coiffed feminine face or a nude female draped across a woman's head.

1974: **Rex Reed** becomes the first (and, to date, only) critic to have his film review written into the Congressional record—a rhapsody to *Hearts and Minds*, **Peter Davis**' subsequently Oscared documentary on Vietnam when the war was a raging controversy. Reed's own paper, the New York *Daily News*, opted *not* to publish the notice—and missed a free ride into history.

1996: The talking heads of *My Dinner With Andre* (**Wallace Shawn** and **Andre Gregory**) and the Oscar-nominated author of *Atlantic City* (**John Guare**) lead the eulogies for their director, France's **Louis Malle** on this day, at a memorial service at the New Victory Theater. One anecdote concerned his controversial 1971 *Murmur of the Heart*, which miraculously got away with an approving look at incest between a woman and her teenage son. It had been filmed at a resort frequented by the Malle family when he was growing up, but the opening-night audience in Paris didn't know that, and some were shocked when Malle's mother swooped across the lobby after the screening, shouting enthusiastically, "It was just like the old days."

DANCING TO DIFFERENT DIRECTORS: Jennifer Jones and Gregory Peck in *Duel in the Sun*.

1933: To staff his first film at MGM (*Dinner at Eight*), producer **David O. Selznick** merely memos his father-in-law, **Louis B. Mayer**, on this day for a dream cast: **Marie Dressler, Clark Gable, John** and **Lionel Barrymore, Wallace Beery, Jean Harlow, Lee Tracy** and **Louise Closser Hale**. Mayer reneged only on Gable, believing The King would be wasted as Harlow's passive lover; **Edmund Lowe** was given the part, and Mayer threw in **Madge Evans, Jean Hersholt, Phillips Holmes, May Robson, Karen Morley** and **Elizabeth Patterson** for extra garnishment. The role of the dinner's airhead hostess went to **Billie Burke** (over seasoned scatterbrain **Alice Brady**), and she did such a dandy job of daffy it became her permanent screen persona; privately, the widow **Ziegfeld** was still in mourning for the showman husband she'd lost eight months earlier.

1936: Shangri-La, which runs 1,000 feet long and 500 feet wide, starts going up on this day at the Columbia ranch in Burbank, CA. It took 150 workers two months to complete the lamasery set for **Frank Capra**'s elaborate *Lost Horizon*.

1936: On this day, **Don Ameche** hits Hollywood–and four months later is hitting movie screens in *Sins of Man*, the first of his star-run for 20th Century-Fox. He stuck with it until he got his big breakdance number in Fox's *Cocoon*–and that in turn brought him, 50 years to the month after his arrival, the Oscar.

1945: *The Picture of Dorian Gray* reaches the Capitol screen in New York on this day, bringing **Hurd Hatfield** his full 15 minutes of fame as **Oscar Wilde**'s notorious narcissist who has a portrait in the attic wear his years and moral decay for him. The title role was originally, if incredibly, meant for **Garbo**.

1971: Among the souvenirs 20th Century-Fox puts up for auction on this day is **Elizabeth Taylor**'s *Cleopatra* throne. One unsuccessful bidder: **Debbie Reynolds**.

1997: A record price of $410,000–four times its estimated value–is shelled out by collector **Dennis Schnagel** on this day at Sotheby's for a 1932 movie poster by **Karoly Grosz** depicting **Boris Karloff** tightly wrapped as *The Mummy*.

BACKLOT PARADISE: Jane Wyatt and Ronald Colman in *Lost Horizon*.
HOSTESS WITH THE MOSTEST STARS: Billie Burke in *Dinner at Eight*.
RE GRETA?: Lowell Gilmore, Hurd Hatfield and George Sanders in *The Picture of Dorian Gray*.

2

1933: "The eighth wonder of the world" goes public on this day: *King Kong* world-premieres at Radio City Music Hall–*and* the Roxy (the only movie to play both theaters simultaneously). Rejecting all the various readings given the film over the years (racial, Freudian, etc.), producer **Merian Cooper** bothered to reiterate late in his life: "*King Kong* was never intended to be anything more than the best damned adventure picture ever made. Which it is; and that's all it is."

1943: *Saratoga Trunk* starts shooting on this day, with that together-again duo from *For Whom the Bell Tolls*, **Gary Cooper** and **Ingrid Bergman**. Coop had come in first in a poll *Cosmopolitan* conducted on who should play the leads in the film version of **Edna Ferber**'s saga, but Bergman placed 26th. Readers had a better idea for the shady heroine than the miscast St. Ingrid: **Vivien Leigh**. (This — after *Gaslight* — was the second-role-in-a-row Bergman had snatched from **Hedy Lamarr**, whose unavailability for *Casablanca* created Bergman's star base.)

1944: On this day–her 25th birthday–**Jennifer Jones** gets a solid-gold gift from her Hollywood peers: the Oscar (for *The Song of Bernadette*). Came the cruel dawn, she initiated divorce action against **Robert Walker** with whom she'd just done some difficult, emotionally draining love scenes for *Since You Went Away* – scenes not made easier by the fact they were reciting romantic lines scripted by her current love and future husband, producer **David O. Selznick**.

1953: From Here to Eternity commences filming in Hollywood on this day, and not at all with the cast originally intended: **Robert Mitchum, Joan Crawford, Aldo Ray, Eli Wallach** and **Julie Harris**. Instead, the film starred **Burt Lancaster, Deborah Kerr, Montgomery Clift, Frank Sinatra** and **Donna Reed**–and, 50 weeks later, all five of the players were rewarded with Oscar nominations.

1967: Two of the three Grammys **Frank Sinatra** wins on this day–Record of the Year and Best Vocal Performance, Male–is for a catchy ditty **Melina Mercouri** introduced in *A Man Could Get Killed*. "Strangers in the Night," with English lyrics by **Charles Singleton** and **Eddie Snyder** added to German composer **Bert Kaempfert**'s theme, subsequently became Sinatra's biggest chartmaker single–but it stayed strangers to Oscar nominators who instead saw fit to cite "My Wishing Doll" from *Hawaii* and "A Time for Love" from *An American Dream*; the eventual Best Song winner: **John Barry** and **Don Black**'s *Born Free* title tune.

EX-WRAY VISION: *King Kong.*
THE *BELL TOLLS* AGAIN: Gary Cooper and Ingrid Bergman in *Saratoga Trunk.*
PERMANENT PARTING: Robert Walker and Jennifer Jones in *Since You Went Away.*

1935: A surprise 24th birthday party is thrown **Jean Harlow** on the *China Seas* set on this day. Conspicuously absent was her co-star, **Wallace Beery**, who didn't have to act his animosity for her doing *Dinner at Eight*. Their real friction somehow sparked the movie's best scenes. They were a screen team who truly hated each other. "He's a mean old son-of-a-bitch whose grave I'd love to piss on," she said—but never got the chance, dying of uremic poisoning almost a dozen years before him.

1940: While vacationing in Sun Valley on this day, 20th Century-Fox's **Darryl F. Zanuck** memos executive assistant **William Goetz** that novelist **John O'Hara**'s script-attempt at turning 1938's *Kentucky* into *Down Argentine Way* is a no-go. (Eventually, **Darrell Ware** and **Karl Tunberg** penned the piece.) An appendicitis forced **Alice Faye** out of — and **Betty Grable** into — the star spot, where she stayed longer than any other Fox(y) lady. In fact, Grable's presence among the top ten money-making stars from 1942 to 1951 remains a record unequaled by any other female star. **Carmen Miranda** also checked in, for the first of 10 Fox flicks, debuting with some specialty spots filmed in NYC between her Waldorf-Astoria shows.

1944: "Not since **Greta Garbo** made her cinematic bow has there been anything so terrific as the inimitable **Danny**," rules **Frank Quinn** on this day in the New York *Daily Mirror* about the **Kaye**niption fit just thrown into Radio City Music Hall, *Up in Arms*. "Up" was right, too. The other critics came out to greet Danny Kaye with palm leaves, too, and he was off and running (amok) in movies.

> **SCREAM TEAM:** From left: Beery & Harlow in *Dinner at Eight* and *China Seas*.
> **DESIGN FOR STARDOM:** Lee Remick, Eve Arden and James Stewart in *Anatomy of a Murder*.
> **SPANISH AYES:** Carmen Miranda in *Down Argentine Way*.

1959: Director **Otto Preminger** and **Lana Turner** collide over who'll wear the pants in *Anatomy of a Murder* and split before the cameras can turn a single revolution, tattles **Louella O. Parsons** on this day. When handed slacks right off the rack to play a second lieutenant's wife, Turner balked–and walked. Only **Jean Louis** designed for her, she huffed, hitting the door. Her side of it was that Preminger's arrogance (and expletives) prompted her departure. "God forbid that I should ever be so hungry that I would ever think of working for Mr. Preminger," she was saying as late as 1975–but Preminger had a last laugh: He got **Lee Remick** for the part, and she slinked her way to major stardom–in non-designer slacks.

1987: *The Court Jester* of movies–**Danny Kaye**, 74–dies on this day at Los Angeles' Cedars-Sinai Medical Center of a heart attack brought on by internal bleeding and post-transfusion hepatitis. The carrot-topped comedian made a specialty of sprinting lickety-split through a maze of tongue-twisting lyrics (usually the witty work of his spouse of 47 years, **Sylvia Fine**).

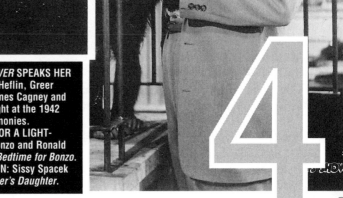

MRS. MINIVER SPEAKS HER MIND: Van Heflin, Greer Garson, James Cagney and Teresa Wright at the 1942 Oscar ceremonies.
REQUIEM FOR A LIGHTWEIGHT: Bonzo and Ronald Reagan in *Bedtime for Bonzo*.
IN LIKE LYNN: Sissy Spacek in *Coal Miner's Daughter*.

1942: On this day, **Billy Wilder** turns director via *The Major and the Minor*—a gamy scene with **Ginger Rogers** in **Robert Benchley**'s apartment ("No matter what the weather is, I always say — why don't you get out of that wet coat and into a dry martini?")—only he doesn't get a single foot of usable film the whole day, due to the rooting-section **Ernst Lubitsch** recruited to put Wilder at ease (**William Wyler, Preston Sturges, Michael Curtiz, William Dieterle** and other top directors welcoming him to their club). And a major addition he was, too!

1943: *Mrs. Miniver* rakes in half a dozen Oscars on this day. The thank-yous of title-player **Greer Garson** were said to tip the scales at about five and a half minutes–although myth made it more like an hour (either way, that *still* is the record for Oscar filibustering). Her Oscar-winning director, **William Wyler**, was otherwise engaged–embroiled in bombing missions over Germany.

1951: Fire sweeps through the animal dorm of Universal's backlot on this day when a heater ignites the quonset hut where the title chimp in *Bedtime for Bonzo* and all his stand-ins are caged between pictures. Firemen got the four out alive, but all died of smoke suffocation. The day Bonzo was to host the SPCA's first annual Patsy Awards for animal performers at Hollywood's Carthay Circle, his death was announced. He had just returned from a successful string of personal appearances to launch the film. Although his death represented a direct loss of $50,000, it was easy to feel $5 million had gone up in smoke.

1952: With **William Holden** and wife **Brenda Marshall** for best man and matron of honor, **Nancy Davis** becomes the second Mrs. **Ronald Reagan** on this day. The union went considerably beyond *Hellcats of the Navy*, their one screen-teaming.

1954: Producer **Samuel Goldwyn** plops down on this day $1 million for screen rights to *Guys and Dolls*, then spends $4.5 million on a production directed and adapted by **Joseph L. Mankiewicz**, who, himself a writer of Oscar-winning note (*A Letter to Three Wives, All About Eve*), couldn't resist the temptation to tinker with **Jo Swerling** and **Abe Burrows'** Tony-winning script. **Orson Welles** informed Burrows that "they put a tiny turd on every one of your lines."

1974: *People* magazine hits the stands for the first time on this day, with **Mia Farrow** as cover girl, plugging "the year's next big movie"–*The Great Gatsby*.

1980: On this day, **Sissy Spacek**'s soon-to-be-Oscared portrayal of *Coal Miner's Daughter* (country-music star **Loretta Lynn**) bows on Lynn's hometurf, Nashville.

1936: Pioneer director **D.W. Griffith** provokes the first standing ovation at an Academy Awards function when he shows up on this day to receive a special Oscar. Later, he posed for photographs with the evening's golden girl, **Bette Davis**. A spontaneous, but unsuccessful, write-in nominee the year before (for her breakthrough work in *Of Human Bondage*), Davis nailed the Oscar this time out–for a much less stunning job in *Dangerous* –and accepted the award as a delayed Academy reaction. (Privately, she always felt that specific Oscar belonged to **Katharine Hepburn**'s *Alice Adams*). Years later, she couldn't remember if **Archie Mayo** or **Alfred E. Green** had directed *Dangerous*. (Alfred E. Green had.)

1936: The fact that *Mutiny on the Bounty* produces the greatest number of Oscar contenders for Best Actor ever– three: **Clark Gable, Charles Laughton** and **Franchot Tone**–proves to be its undoing on this day, fragmenting the vote and assuring a win for the category's only other nominee: **Victor McLaglen** for *The Informer*. Indeed, when the runner-up was announced (as it was in those days), it was none of the above but a write-in candidate: **Paul Muni** for *Black Fury*. A write-in candidate even won that year–**Hal Mohr** (for Best Cinematography: *A Midsummer Night's Dream*); phoning Mohr at home, the Academy told him to join the party and pick up his prize. Thereafter, write-in votes were prohibited.

1936: Oscar's Best Actor and Best Actress of 1935 go on no-speaking terms on this day when he (**Victor McLaglen**), looking spiffy if improbable in a tux, drinks in her painfully dowdy attire and whispers to her (**Bette Davis**), "You musta decided to come as a housewife." Three years later, when she stepped to the stage to collect her second Academy Award [for *Jezebel*], she "wore feathers and went partly uncovered. Nobody complained, and I'm sure Mr. McLaglen was by then wishing that he was getting roles as good as I was."

1960: On this day, **Elvis Presley** gets his Army discharge and begins the biggest homecoming for any soldier this side of **General Douglas MacArthur**.

1982: At the Chateau Marmont on this day, **John Belushi** is discovered dead from drug overdose. His tragedy as an artist was that his comic potential was left dangling, like a participle. Others have tried to fill the void. The best perhaps was **Bill Murray**, who stepped into Belushi's *Ghostbusters* boots.

D.W. AND THE *DANGEROUS* LADY: D.W. Griffith and Bette Davis at the 1935 Oscar ceremonies.
BETTE'S PICK FOR BEST ACTRESS OF 1935: Ann Shoemaker, Fred MacMurray, Hattie McDaniel, Katharine Hepburn and Fred Stone in *Alice Adams*.
THE GANG'S *NOT* ALL HERE: Ernie Hudson, Dan Aykroyd, Bill Murray and Harold Ramis in *Ghostbusters*.

1934: *Hollywood Revue of 1933*, a sequel to *Hollywood Revue of 1929*, is redubbed *Star Spangled Banquet*–according to a *Daily Variety* item on this day–but what comes out three months later is *Hollywood Party*. The talent roster deflated, too. Among the all-star no-shows: **Joan Crawford** (as a light-skinned black passing for white in "Black Diamond," a musical imitation of the then-topical *Imitation of Life*), **Marie Dressler**, **Johnny Weissmuller** (in a swimming chorus), **Lee Tracy**, **Buddy Rogers**, **Frank Morgan**, **Nils Asther**, **Ed Wynn** and (as a hotel night operator singing a **Rodgers** and **Hart** song called "Prayer") **Jean Harlow**. Lorenz Hart jazzed up the lyrics of the latter and used it later as "The Bad in Ev'ry Man" in *Manhattan Melodrama*; when he did it again, it was "Blue Moon."

1937: On this day, principal photography begins on *They Won't Forget*, and what they don't forget is **Lana Turner**'s famous walk to stardom. By outfitting her in a tight sweater and skirt and then following her with a long, 75-foot tracking shot, director **Mervyn LeRoy** extracted the desired "flesh impact" that conveyed (without the actual use of the words) a rape-murder in the offing.

1939: Instead of *On Your Toes* with **James Cagney** at Warners, **Ginger Rogers** winds up in *Bachelor Mother* on her homelot of RKO on this day. Sulking over these priorities, she opted for suspension–while she held out, her leading men changed from **Cary Grant** to **James Ellison** to **Douglas Fairbanks Jr.** to **David Niven**–but eventually exec **Pandro Berman** strong-armed Rogers into the picture, and it became a big hit. She *still* hated it–but, even in 1991, she could recite her favorite line from the film (really **Charles Coburn**'s: "I don't care who the father is. I'm the grandfather!").

1986: While chasing **Burt Lancaster** and **Kirk Douglas** in *Tough Guys*, **Adolph Caesar**, 52, suffers a fatal heart attack on this day. (His role was taken over by **Eli Wallach**.) A major career had started to open up for Caesar with parts in the film versions of two Pulitzer Prize-winning works: *The Color Purple* and *A Soldier's Story*. His complex portrayal of a black-hating black in the latter won him acclaim on stage and an Oscar shot on screen.

1995: The video version of *The Lion King* sold in excess of 20 million copies its first week of release, roars Disney on this day. Its first-day sales, in fact, were greater than the combined one-day consumer sales of *Snow White and the Seven Dwarfs*, *Aladdin* and *Beauty and the Beast* (which at the time were the industry's first, second and third best-sellers respectively).

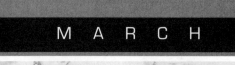

1955: "Did the wrong figure go to **Jane Russell**'s head?" wonders *Life* magazine on this day about a case of body-doubling that just surfaced in the courts. **Lyn Jones**, 21, filed suit for $100,000 worth of mental anguish because her body was attached to Russell's face in the *Underwater!* ads. Some truth, however, could be argued in the copy that accompanied the image of the Jones girl's torso: It promised "Jane Russell as you've never seen her before."

1957: Artistic differences between Hecht-Hill-Lancaster and director-star **Laurence Olivier** scuttle a film version of **Terence Rattigan**'s *Separate Tables* on this day. He'd have co-starred with *That Hamilton Woman*, wife **Vivien Leigh**. Producer **James Hill** gave her role to his wife-to-be, **Rita Hayworth**, and **Burt Lancaster** assigned himself Olivier's; the other stars—**Deborah Kerr**, **David Niven** and **Wendy Hiller**—rated the Oscar once-over, and the latter two won.

1986: The producing-directing team of **Ismail Merchant** and **James Ivory** on this day takes *A Room With a View* at New York's Paris Theater—for 7.5 months, as it happily turned out. Their most successful team-effort (nearly $25 million) was also their most sumptuous—the sort of classy read of a classic that has become synonymous with "A Merchant Ivory Production" (in this case, **E.M. Forster**'s witty yarn about some uptight Edwardian Brits misspent in Florence).

1988: *Pink Flamingos*' 300-pound transvestite star—**Harris Glenn Milstead**, 42 (reel name: **Divine**)—dies of natural causes due to an enlarged heart, on the eve of his big mainstream breakthrough: **John Waters**' *Hairspray*. The only part he didn't play in a dress was the villain in *Trouble in Mind*.

1996: Director and *Hamlet* **Kenneth Branagh** on this day goes into his "To be or not to be" soliloquy, complicating matters with mirror tricks and reflections.

1999: The **J.D. Salinger** of filmmakers—to some, "the world's greatest working director"—brilliant, elusive, painfully prosaic and complex **Stanley Kubrick**, 70, dies in his sleep of a heart attack on this day at his English estate, Childwickbury Manor. In 46 years, he did only 13 features. Most were critic-labeled "great."

BREASTS OF THE WEST: Divine and Lainie Kazan in *Lust in the Dust*.
FIELD OF DREAMS: Julian Sands and Helena Bonham Carter in *A Room With a View*.
TORSO MORE SO: The controversial *Underwater* ad.
MIRROR MONOLOGUE: Kenneth Branagh in *Hamlet*.

1931: In the shoot-'em-up pulling into New York's Hippodrome on this day, two citified guys who say they can ride a horse (and, of course, can't) square off in *The Painted Desert*, the film as well as the locale outside Flagstaff. Good-guy **William Boyd** didn't bother with horses until he had to—and he *did* have to four years later when he hit his Hopalong Cassidy stride—but bad-guy **Clark Gable** took lessons at Griffith Park Riding Academy so he'd not look like a total tenderfoot. *The Painted Desert* proved to be Gable's launching pad for a meteoric ascent into films. Snarling out a persuasive villain in his sound debut, the fourth-billed Gable was hitting the screen for the first of 12 times during 1931. Nine of his next 11 films were for MGM. By year's end, he was a Star putting out white heat to **Garbo**, **Shearer**, **Crawford** and **Harlow**.

BEWITCHING HOUR: John Barrymore, Hedda Hopper, Don Ameche, Mary Astor, Francis Lederer, Claudette Colbert, and Elaine Barrie (Barrymore) in *Midnight*.
LOST & FOUND: Philip Terry, Jane Wyman and Ray Milland in *The Lost Weekend*.
BEFORE THEY WERE CASSIDY AND "THE KING": William Boyd, James Dolan, and Clark Gable in *The Painted Desert*.

1939: Made amid much acrimony between the director (**Mitchell Leisen**) and the screenwriters (**Billy Wilder** and **Charles Brackett**), *Midnight* emerges at an industry screening on this day "just about the best light comedy ever caught by a camera"—or so says *Motion Picture Daily*.

1946: Driving onto the Paramount lot on this day—hours after winning Oscars for directing and co-scripting *The Lost Weekend*—**Billy Wilder** finds a sweeter salute awaiting him: a bottle of booze dangling on a string from every window in the Writers' Building, an allusion to the picture's first and last shots.

1947: At Ciro's in Hollywood on this day, **Frank Sinatra** punches out *New York Mirror* amusements editor **Lee Mortimer** for suggesting that the singer was too chummy with Cuban mobsters. In terms of legal expenses and compensation, that blow cost Sinatra $25,000—but, insisted the singer, "it was worth it."

1983: At Patriotic Hall in downtown L.A. on this day, a 19-year-old Yale freshman-turning-actress named **Jennifer Beals** goes into "her" famous *Flashdance* audition—a dazzling display of gymnastic leaps, bounds and whirls actually executed by at least six dance doubles (including one male who specialized in head-spinning). Most of the dance-doubling was done by French-born **Marine Jahan**, 24, the ex of **Kevin Bacon**'s *Footloose* double, **Peter Tramm**.

1986: On this day, for the first time in its history, The Directors Guild of America selects for its Best Director of the Year somebody who is *not* in the running for Oscar honors: **Steven Spielberg**. Had he been nominated, *The Color Purple* would have emerged two weeks later even blacker and bluer from its Oscar race—surpassing, instead of merely equaling, the unenviable record set by *The Turning Point* back in 1977: 11 losses out of 11 nominations. In 1994, Spielberg got his second Guild award—and first Oscar—for *Schindler's List*. The only other director to get the DGA nod without an Oscar nomination was **Ron Howard** for 1995's *Apollo 13*.

1935: *A Midsummer Night's Dream,* which brought out the stars of Warner Bros. (**James Cagney**, **Dick Powell**, **Joe E. Brown**, **Jean Muir**, **Frank McHugh**, **Hugh Herbert**, et al), comes to an end on this day. It was the only Hollywood movie–and talkie–made by **Max Reinhardt**, the European stage producer-director.

1944: *The Purple Heart*, a flag-waver as stirring as they came in World War II, is saluted by **Bosley Crowther** in his *Times* review on this day. The film was supposedly based on "a Japanese announcement" about U.S. fliers, downed during the Tokyo raid of 1942, being executed after "investigation and confession."

1948: The only studio other than 20th Century-Fox to have **Marilyn Monroe** under contract – Columbia Pictures–gives the girl a whirl, starting on this day. Save for 11 days as one of the *Ladies of the Chorus* (daughter of the burlesque headliner, **Adele Jergens**), she served her whole six months idle after declining an intimate weekend with Columbia chief **Harry Cohn**. For her only other Columbia credit (*Riders of the Whistling Pines*), she didn't even have to show up: **Gene Autry** serenaded a photograph of a rancher's dead wife (a glossy of MM). A year after leaving Columbia, Monroe found fame, and Cohn caught a ride, squeezing one last penny from her pointless employment: In 1952's *Okinawa*, rowdy GIs watch her prance through the musical highlight of *Ladies of the Chorus*–"Every Baby Needs a Da-da-daddy."

1953: "It was like a burlesque show," a "horrified" **Joan Crawford** tells columnist **Bob Thomas** after **Marilyn Monroe** hip-waves her way to the winner's circle to collect *Photoplay*'s prize for "Fastest Rising Star of 1952" on this day. The following March, MM strode the podium to accept the magazine's award for Best *Actress* of 1953 for *Gentlemen Prefer Blondes* and *How To Marry a Millionaire*. This award–and the Golden Globe *Some Like It Hot* won her seven years later for "Best Actress in a Comedy"–were the only awards Monroe ever got in this country for her acting. Abroad, her work in *The Prince and the Showgirl* won the equivalent of Oscars in France and Italy, but back home she never netted one Oscar nomination.

1955: *East of Eden* premieres on this day at the Astor, and a star is born–only to die in a car-crash six and a half months later. All told, from that premiere to his death, **James Dean** enjoyed just 206 days as a star.

1981: *Blade Runner* is put into production on this day by director **Ridley Scott**. When released 15 months later, this futuristic *film noir* (based on **Phillip K. Dick**'s novel, *Do Androids Dream of Electric Sheep?*) found its cult following–but the director's cut didn't arrive for another decade.

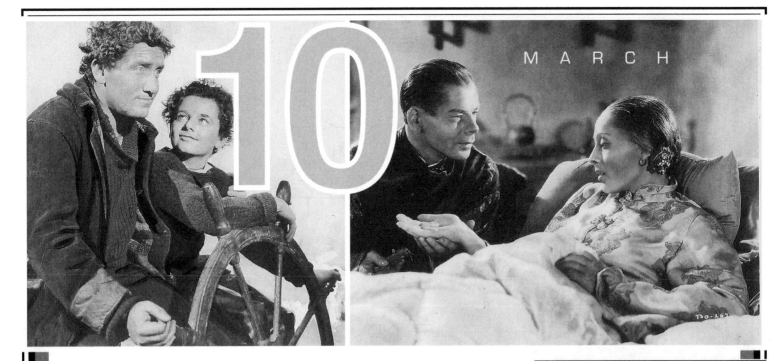

10

1933: Hollywood reverberates on this day from the rumblings of a killer quake rattling up from Long Beach, plunging "The Shadow Waltz" (which **Busby Berkeley** was staging for *Gold Diggers of 1933* at Warners) into pitch-blackness–save for 100 neon-lit violins, wielded by 100 short-circuiting chorines. Even more bizarre was the scene on the top floor of the Hollywood Roosevelt Hotel where **Jack L. Warner**, **Darryl F. Zanuck**, **Louis B. Mayer**, **B.P. Schulberg**, **Harry Cohn** and **Merian Cooper**–all the studio kingpins assembled in one room, shouting about belt-tightening for the Depression–were suddenly shaken into stunned silence by God; reason bolted back to the negotiating table, and, after a weekend of sober reflection, producers and unions compromised on salary cuts.

1938: Imported as a threat to **Garbo** by MGM, **Luise Rainer** proves to be Just That on this day: Her portrayal of O-Lan in *The Good Earth* wins the Oscar over Garbo's *Camille*! To achieve this unthinkable feat meant that Rainer had set two Academy Award precedents: A Best Actress winner the year before (for *The Great Ziegfeld*), she became the first performer to (1) win two Oscars and (2) win them consecutively, which was history-making the hard way! The downside of her glory night: Rainer arrived at the ceremony in hysterics–browbeaten by her insecure then-husband, **Clifford Odets**, for even attending the affair–and had to be walked around the block a couple of times to regain her composure.

1938: Finding it no fun to lose the Oscar (as he had the year before for *San Francisco*), **Spencer Tracy** skips the whole affair on this day via some shrewdly scheduled surgery–which is just as well since the Oscar he winds up winning this time (for *Captains Courageous*) is inadvertently engraved to "Dick Tracy."

1962: In *The New York Times* on this day, critic **Bosley Crowther** goes after MGM's second set of *The 4 Horsemen of the Apocalypse* like ducks in a row, with the obvious starting-point being **Glenn Ford** (glaringly miscast in the shadow of The Sheik himself, **Rudolph Valentino**): "Mr. Ford as the gay hidalgo from the pampas who hits the boulevards [of Paris] wearing a gray fedora, black gloves and swinging an ebony cane is about as convincingly Argentine and possessed of urbanity as a high-school football coach from Kansas who has never been out of the state." Crowther's only relief from the performance came in love scenes with Sweden's **Ingrid Thulin** where he could focus on how her "voice and lip movements do not match." (Otherwise, the substitution of **Angela Lansbury**'s voice for Thulin's was, for a few years, a secret.)

11

1937: Taking off at Radio City Music Hall on this day is *Wings of the Morning*. The title was the name of the race-horse romantically linking a Frenchwoman-playing-Spanish (**Annabella**) and an American-playing-Canadian (**Henry Fonda**, just off *The Trail of the Lonesome Pine*, the first outdoor Technicolor film made stateside). Fonda was a walking color-tester back then: This was the first three-strip Technicolor feature produced in England (indeed, in Europe), and one of its camera operators became the great color cinematographer of 1947's *Black Narcissus*, 1948's *The Red Shoes* and 1956's *War and Peace*: **Jack Cardiff**.

1957: A scene that didn't occur in **Pierre Boulle**'s original novel and was invented wholly for the movie version–the blowing-up of *The Bridge on the River Kwai*–is spectacularly executed on this day by director **David Lean**. It was his second stab at the shot. The day before, Lean called the whole thing off at the last second when one of the five photographers covering the action failed to signal back that he was safely in the trenches. Unfortunately, this quick call couldn't stop the locomotive full of dummy Japanese soldiers from barreling across the bridge at top speed into the sand drag and colliding with a generator. Miraculously, everything was repairable and operative for a retake the next day. As shot, the sequence was a stunner–but it still fell short of Lean's vision: "I had wanted to blow up the piles on one side of the bridge only so that the whole bridge and the train would fall into the water"–a notion which so rattled **Sam Spiegel** that the skittish producer insisted on explosives under every pile "so the bridge just sank. It looked good enough, but it would have been wonderful to see the whole bloody thing keel over with a moving train on top of it."

1979: On this day–five days after fellow character actor **Charles Wagenheim**, 84, was fatally bludgeoned in his apartment only a mile away–87-year-old **Victor Kilian** suffers identically the same fate from burglars who break into *his* Hollywood apartment. Wagenheim's most famous cinematic turn was as the assassin in **Hitchcock**'s 1940 *Foreign Correspondent*; Kilian specialized in grizzled sheriffs and fire-snorting parsons and was lanky enough to get away with Lincoln, which he did once (in *Virginia City*, granting **Errol Flynn** an eleventh-hour reprieve), but he didn't play Abe in *The Tall Target*, the Lincoln-assassination plot toward the end of his run in features -some 130 films, from 1932 to 1951. (The blacklist got 'im, bumping him off the big screen, but he did stumble into some small-screen fame late in life, as the grandfather on *Mary Hartman,*

VIOLENT ENDS: From left: Charles Wagenheim (with Joel McCrea and Albert Basserman) in *Foreign Correspondent*, and Victor Kilian. NOT MADE TO LAST: Alec Guinness in *The Bridge on the River Kwai*. TECHNICOLOR TRAIL-BLAZING: Henry Fonda (with Annabella) in *Wings of the Morning*.

Mary Hartman: Raymond Larkin, a.k.a. "The Fernwood Flasher").

12

1935: Stage actress **Helen Gahagan** begins her screen career on this day, playing **H. Rider Haggard**'s enigmatic exotic, *She*. The adventure film lost $180,000 at the box office, and Gahagan never went back for seconds, content to leave the acting to her hubby, **Melvyn Douglas**— but she did enter California politics and in 1950 was defeated in a run for Congress by **Richard Nixon**.

1943: *Forever and a Day*, with credits to match, makes its bow on this day at New York's Rivoli Theater. A British war effort of a movie, it gainfully employed the services of seven directors and producers, 21 writers and 79 English players—all of them chronicling the history of a London house and its inhabitants from 1804 to World War II when it was turned into a public air-raid shelter and struck by a Nazi bomb. *The Guinness Book of Records* lists this episodic saga as the film with the greatest number of credited co-writers.

1953: CinemaScope is officially in full flower at 20th Century-Fox on this day, as per the edict **Darryl F. Zanuck** issues to all his producers and execs. "For the time being, intimate comedies or small scale, domestic stories should be put aside and no further monies expended on their development," decreed DFZ. Instead, the studio "will concentrate exclusively on subjects suitable for CinemaScope." The studio's best example of such scenic concentration, *Three Coins in the Fountain*, lost the next Best Picture Oscar to a film Fox turned down because it didn't meet its elongated criterion: *On the Waterfront*.

1969: "Mrs. Robinson," a catchy little catcall that a predatory **Anne Bancroft** inspired **Paul Simon** and **Art Garfunkel** to compose and perform in/for *The Graduate*, collects Grammys on this day for Record of the Year and Best Group Vocals, eventually becoming BMI's ninth most-performed song of all time (two notches beneath S&G's "Bridge Over Troubled Waters"). In contrast, the tin-eared Motion Picture Academy ignored *all* the songs from *The Graduate*, Oscaring instead a **Leslie Bricusse** ditty from *Doctor Dolittle*, "Talk to the Animals."

1979: A fine actor on the brink of a brilliant career — **John Cazale**, 42 — is cut down by cancer on this day at New York's Sloan-Kettering, with fiancee **Meryl Streep** at his side. He only did five films—*The Conversation*, *Dog Day Afternoon*, *The Godfather*, *The Godfather Part II* and *The Deer Hunter*—but all contended for Oscar honors as Best Picture, and the last three actually won.

FOUNTAIN WAS NO *WATERFRONT*: Clifton Webb, Dorothy McGuire, Louis Jourdan, Maggie McNamara, Rosanno Brazzi and Jean Peters in *Three Coins in the Fountain*.
ONE-SHOT *SHE*: Helen Gahagan.
A CAREER IN BEST PICTURE CONTENDERS: John Cazale (with Al Pacino) in *Dog Day Afternoon*.

1934: Getting a two-day jump on the Ides of March, *Cleopatra* barges down **DeMille** Stream on this day, with **Claudette Colbert** the title-role centerpiece for two months of studio-shot screen spectacle. When in Rome, in 1961-62, this same story took almost a year to film (but there were extenuating triangles).

1939: Republic Pictures wraps on this day its most expensive film to date: *Man of Conquest*–by any other name, Sam Houston, twice president of the Republic of Texas; **Richard Dix** played the part. **Robert Barrat**, **Victor Jory**, **Robert Armstrong** and **C. Henry Gordon** did Davy Crockett, William B. Travis, James Bowie and Santa Anna–roles Republic later (1955) gave to **Arthur Hunnicutt**, **Richard Carlson**, **Sterling Hayden** and **J. Carrol Naish** for *The Last Command*, its epic attempt to spite **John Wayne** and derail his dream of filming *The Alamo*.

1940: *Road to Singapore*, the first of seven **Crosby-Hope-Lamour** *Road* shows, reaches the screen of the Paramount in New York on this day, after a couple of crucial detours. The antic started out as a **Burns** and **Allen** vehicle called *Beach of Dreams*, and, when they turned it down, it was turned into *Road to Mandalay* for **Fred MacMurray** and **Jack Oakie**, both of whom nixed it. Then, the third time proved the charm: Crosby and Hope ran with it, with gag-writers on the set at all times, throwing them ad-libs to fuel their rapid-fire rapport.

1947: Freshly elected to his first Presidency–of the Screen Actors Guild (edging out **Gene Kelly** and **George Murphy** for the office)–**Ronald Reagan** tries out this new role in public on this day at the 19th annual Academy Awards by narrating the "Parade of Stars," a silent compilation of Oscar-winning films. Unfortunately, the footage that came out of the projector came out upside down and backwards and ran its course on the ceiling rather than on a screen as Reagan, oblivious to the snafu, solemnly intoned, "This picture embodies the glories of our past, the memories of our present and the inspiration of our future." So who said the road to the White House was going to be easy, anyway?

1947: *The Best Years of Our Lives* wins Oscars on this day for producer **Samuel Goldwyn** and director **William Wyler** — but the two aren't speaking by this point.

THE "QUICKIE" CLEO: Henry Wilcoxon and Claudette Colbert in *Cleopatra*.
PLAY IT AGAIN, REPUBLIC: Richard Dix and Joan Fontaine in *Man of Conquest*.
THREE FOR THE *ROAD*S: Dorothy Lamour, Bing Crosby and Bob Hope in *Road to Singapore*.

BOND-BANNED *DE BERGERAC:* Jose Ferrer as an Oscar-winning *Cyrano.*
BAR ORDER & 'BAR NOTHING': From left: Greta as *Anna Christie*; Rita as *Gilda.*
THE *HOUSE* THAT GEORGE BUILT: Florence Arliss, George Arliss, Loretta Young, Robert Young, and C. Aubrey Smith in *The House of Rothschild.*

1930: In *Anna Christie*, bowing at the Capitol, **Garbo** talks—a husky voice barking "Gimme a visky, ginger ale on the side, an don' be stingy, babee" to waterfront bartender **Lee Phelps**. Sound merely deepened her mystery.

1934: *The House of Rothschild* opens for business at New York's Astor—totally a let-**George Arliss**-do-it project. The star found the unproduced play on which the film was based, saw in it two characters he could play (one of whom—**Mayer Rothschild**, the founder of the firm—wasn't in the play) and had two studios acquire the rights for him. His tenacity paid off not only in one of his best screen vehicles but also in an Oscar-contending Best Picture of 1934.

1944: The era of The Star As Studio Slave officially ends when a Los Angeles Superior Court judge returns the precedent-setting decision that Warner Bros. can no longer add suspension time onto **Olivia de Havilland**'s contract. Her attorney, **Martin Gang**, invoked California's ancient antipeonage law (which limited to seven calendar years the time an employer could enforce a contract against an employee) and won the case with it. An artist could at last exert control over his or her career.

1946: **Rita Hayworth** slinks into Radio City Music Hall in the most celebrated role of her career: *Gilda.* She didn't put all her blame on Mame, either. "If I were a ranch," ran one of her more breathtakingly self-deprecatory lines, "they would have named me the 'Bar Nothing.'"

1951: According to *Daily Variety*, **Ward Bond** talked the California Teachers Association out of giving **Jose Ferrer** an award for *Cyrano de Bergerac* because of Ferrer's "subversive" contacts. But the old Red-witchhunter didn't cut much ice with the Motion Picture Academy with that line because, 15 days later, Ferrer copped the Best Actor of 1950 Oscar for said *Cyrano.*

1957: The stunning opening-shot that jump-starts *Touch of Evil* into existence (and cult acclaim) is photographed on this day by director **Orson Welles** and one of his *Magnificent Ambersons* lensmen, **Russell Metty**—a three-minute sequence shot with a 22-foot crane in one take along three people-packed blocks of Venice, CA. Starting in close-up on a car-bomb timer, the camera swept by poster-peeling buildings before plunging into the crowd, picking up on two pages of dialogue among protagonists and victims alike, ending with a car explosion as **Charlton Heston** and **Janet Leigh** kiss. *WHEW!*

14

15

1933: *Secrets*, which starts unraveling at the Rivoli this "Ides" day, brings the feature career of **Mary Pickford** to its 194th, and last, stop. "Say anything you like," groused her rival in flickers, **Mabel Normand**, "but don't say I love to work–that sounds like Mary Pickford, the prissy bitch!"

1945: Even without Oscars for *King Kong* OR *Gone With the Wind*, **Max Steiner** becomes on this day the first composer to write three Oscar-winning Best Original Scores (*The Informer*, *Now, Voyager* and, now, *Since You Went Away*). His record was subsequently matched by **Dimitri Tiomkin** (*High Noon*, *The High and the Mighty*, *The Old Man and the Sea*), **Miklos Rozsa** (*Spellbound*, *A Double Life*, *Ben-Hur*), **Maurice Jarre** (*Lawrence of Arabia*, *Doctor Zhivago*, *Passage to India*) and **Alan Menken** (*The Little Mermaid*, *Beauty and the Beast*, *Aladdin*)–and topped by two who've written four original Oscar-winning scores: **John Barry** (*Born Free*, *The Lion in Winter*, *Out of Africa*, *Dances With Wolves*) and **John Williams** (*Jaws*, *Star Wars*, *E.T.*, *Schindler's List*).

1945: "Tomorrow I go to work in a picture with Bing and Mr. McCarey, and I'm afraid if I didn't have an Oscar, too, they wouldn't speak to me," kids **Ingrid Bergman**, getting her *Gaslight* Oscar the same night **Bing Crosby** and **Leo McCarey** got theirs for *Going My Way*. Their picture-in-progress, *The Bells of St. Mary's*, put all three winners back in the Oscar running 51 weeks later — but this time no gold-band cigar.

1950: At New York's Paramount on this day, **Chill Wills** takes up talking for Francis the talking Army mule — his first dubbing assignment since he lent his down-home basso to **Stan Laurel** for a rare musical moment with **Ollie** ("In the Blue Ridge Mountains of Virginia" from 1937's *Way Out West*). The box-office success of the *Francis* farce inspired six more installments and earned the mule not only the first Patsy Award for animal-acting but also more fan mail than co-star **Donald O'Connor,** who endured that indignity by doing his best work (*Singin' in the Rain*, *Call Me Madam*) at other studios. Two years passed before a second Francis flick was called for, and by then the mule was 250 pounds over-oated; to keep the part, he shed 150 pounds with exercise and a specially built steam cabinet. O'Connor and Wills checked out of the series with Episode 6, letting **Mickey Rooney** and the voice of **Paul Frees** finish it off with 1956's *Francis in the Haunted House*. **Arthur Lubin**, who helmed the first six outings, went to TV and created *Mister Ed* (with **Allan "Rocky" Lane**'s voice).

16

DISTORTED VIEW: Dirk Bogarde and James Fox in *The Servant*.
BLAZING BOX-OFFICE: Wilder and Little in *Blazing Saddles*.
OSCAR ACQUIRES AN ENGLISH ACCENT: Charles Laughton in *The Private Life of Henry VIII*.

1934: To align themselves with the regular calendar year, Academy members are allowed–on this day only–to vote on 17 months of movies (Aug. 1, 1932-Dec. 31, 1933). The practice of announcing runners-up (discontinued when Price Waterhouse & Company entered the picture) was still in effect: **Paul Muni** and **Leslie Howard** trailed **Charles Laughton**'s winning work in *The Private Life of Henry VIII* (the first time a performance *not* filmed in Hollywood was Oscared).

1934: "Come up and get it, Frank," **Will Rogers** beckons to the Oscar-winning Best Director on this day, and **Frank Capra** charges forth, getting halfway to the dais before realizing the winner is **Frank Lloyd** for *Cavalcade*. Paralyzed with mortification, Capra returned to his table in slow-motion–"the longest, saddest, most shattering walk in my life"–but a year later he won Best Director for real (for *It Happened One Night*) and repeated that victory two years later (for *Mr. Deeds Goes to Town*) and, again, two years after that (for *You Can't Take It With You*). He was king of the category–the screen's most Oscared director–till **John Ford** came along to match him in 1942 and top him in 1953, .

1971: Born-again Christian **James Fox** tells the world on this day he's leaving acting for a higher calling: He joined a Colorado-based evangelical movement, the Navigators, which steered him into a decade of vocational Christian service in England, working with university students in the Yorkshiretown of Leeds. (There, he met and married **Mary Piper**, a nurse, and they produced five children.) "My life as an actor without Christ was something of a mess," he confessed. In 1977, he started easing back into acting with a small part in a film financed by the Billy Graham Organization, *No Longer Alone*. While still regarding himself as "a committed Christian," he didn't feel his "gifts lay in the line of church leader." Several TV series followed before he hit his feature-length stride again (*Greystoke*, *A Passage to India*). Fox, who first found fame as the weak master dominated by *The Servant* (an insidious **Dirk Bogarde**), finally returned as lord of the manor (served by **Anthony Hopkins** in *The Remains of the Day*).

1974: *Blazing Saddles* comes out shooting on this day, eventually becoming the top-grossing Western of all time. **Richard Pryor** (who scripted the flick with **Andrew Bergman**, director **Mel Brooks**, **Norman Steinberg** and **Alan Uger**) was to do the lead–Black Bart, town sheriff–but backed out and left it to **Cleavon Little**, a more benign spoofer. **Gig Young**, assigned the role of Black Bart's drunken-gunfighter sidekick, got canned when Brooks took his hyperventilation for inebriation; **Dan Dailey**, who replaced him, ducked out hours before he was to start, and the part fell–fortunately–to **Gene Wilder**.

1937: On this day, *I, Claudius* pages **Claudette Colbert** to replace **Merle Oberon** (injured the day before in a London car crash)–but she declines, prompting **Alexander Korda** to cancel the film and collect from Lloyds of London. In truth, in light of the terrible title-performance director **Josef von Sternberg** was torturing out of **Charles Laughton**, the accident was a godsend. The Korda-Laughton reign, begun with *The Private Life of Henry VIII*, died here.

DIRECTING & EXTERMINATING: From left: Barbra Streisand and Arnold Schwarzenegger.
'BYE, *CLAUDIUS*: Charles Laughton and Flora Robson in the aborted *I, Claudius*.

1953: In great mental disarray, **Vivien Leigh** arrives in Hollywood on this day from Ceylon where she has been filming *Elephant Walk* with **Dana Andrews** and **Peter Finch**. One week later, husband **Laurence Olivier** flew in to fetch her and escort her to an asylum in England. ("I'm not Scarlett O'Hara" she screamed at a psychiatric aide carting her away, "I'm Blanche DuBois." Sadly, she *was* both–and Oscared for both–the Oscar for Blanche coming this very week only a year before. In moments of extreme angst, she'd lapse into Blanche's lines and speech patterns.) Leigh lingers on in *Elephant Walk* in long shots but otherwise was replaced by **Elizabeth Taylor**, who, though 18 years younger, turned out to be an apt choice: Not only did Taylor also go on to become a screen Cleopatra and win two Oscars like Leigh, a decade later she again stood in for her (in a fictitious sense): **Terence Rattigan**, a friend and frequent playwright of Leigh's, was prompted to write *The V.I.P.'s* by an incident in which Leigh left Olivier for Finch, only to change her mind during the long wait when their plane was grounded by London fog.

1992: Left out of the Oscar running for Best Director (*again!*), **Barbra Streisand** surfaces gamely on this day at the annual Nominees Luncheon tossed by the Academy in Beverly Hills–as producer of *The Prince of Tides*, a Best Picture contender.

1992: Oscar, Schmoscar–**Arnold Schwarzenegger** on this day collects the *real* award: the Best Picture prize presented to his *Terminator 2–Judgment Day* at the 18th annual People's Choice Awards. If anything, it was a tad redundant after the action flick raked in an estimated $52.8 million in its weekend debut. And Schwarzenegger didn't do badly himself: He was paid $14 million to reprise his title portrayal of a do-good cyborg. With 700 words of dialogue, that came out to $20,000 per word. And, in the Academy Award race, ironically–because of its killing in the technical categories (Sound, Sound Effects Editing, Visual Effects, Makeup)–*T-2* wound up as 1991's second most honored film (after the Best Picture Oscar winner, *The Silence of the Lambs*).

18

1937: *Maytime*, the third and most popular of the eight **Jeanette MacDonald-Nelson Eddy** film duets, blossoms at the Capitol on this day and becomes MGM's top-grossing attraction of the year.

1940: The second of three film versions of *Waterloo Bridge*, based on **Robert E. Sherwood**'s sentimental play about war-crossed lovers, wraps on this day. It was **Vivien Leigh**'s first Hollywood outing after *Gone With the Wind*, and she wanted fiance **Laurence Olivier** opposite her–but got instead **Robert Taylor**, who'd known her as a fourth-billed dalliance in *A Yank at Oxford*. This time, she got billing over Taylor.

1941: Warner Bros. places **Humphrey Bogart** on suspension on this day for not saddling up and playing Cole Younger in *Bad Men of Missouri*–a chore he considered disciplinary action because of his allegedly boorish behavior to **Ida Lupino** and **George Raft**. (Lupino refused to do *Out of the Fog* with him, and Raft wouldn't co-star with him in *Manpower*.) The last laugh was Bogie's: He was taken off suspension to do *The Maltese Falcon* when Raft rejected it.

1954: For a mere $23,489,478 and some change–twice the net worth of his crippled company–**Howard Hughes** buys all the outstanding stock from astonished RKO stockholders, thereby becoming on this day the first individual ever to wholly own a major motion picture company. Many folks assumed from this brash, bizarre act that he had really rounded the bend; however, on July 18, 1955, Hughes sold the studio and its film backlog to General Teleradio–at a profit.

1959: *The Diary of Anne Frank*, an emotional epic-in-an-attic thoughtfully wrought by producer-director **George Stevens** from the prize-winning play, opens on a reserved-seat basis at New York's Palace on this day.

1959: Feathers, Stumpy, Colorado and Dude–in the respective, disparate forms of **Angie Dickinson**, **Walter Brennan**, **Ricky Nelson** and **Dean Martin**–rally 'round John T. Chance (**John Wayne**), a sheriff besieged by badguys, in *Rio Bravo*, bowing on this day at NYC's Roxy. Director **Howard Hawks** made the movie as a right-wing response to *High Noon*: "**Gary Cooper** ran around trying to get help and no one would give him any, and that's a rather silly thing for a man to do so I said, we'll do just the opposite and take a real professional viewpoint."

1975: With a blast of "Quintaphonic Sound," **The Who**'s rock opera *Tommy* arrives as a film on this day at New York's Ziegfeld. **Ann-Margret**, **Elton John**, **Tina Turner** and **Pete Townshend** were among the 600 who, after that world-premiere unreeling, descended into the 57th Street subway station which had been transformed into a three-block-long fantasy of flora, fauna, flowers and food.

BRAVA, TOO!: John Wayne, Dean Martin, Ricky Nelson and Angie Dickinson in *Rio Bravo*.
RAYS OF HOPE: Joseph Schildkraut, Gusti Huber, Lou Jacobi, Millie Perkins, Shelley Winters, Richard Beymer and Diane Baker in *The Diary of Anne Frank*.
LOVE IN BLOOM: Nelson Eddy and Jeanette MacDonald in *Maytime*.

19

1939: As an answer-of-sorts to MGM's Andy Hardy, Paramount activates on this day Henry Aldrich–via its film version of **Clifford Goldsmith**'s Broadway hit, *What a Life*. **Ezra Stone**, who originated the role on stage and perpetuated it on radio, was deemed too "unphotogenic" to play the character on film so **Jackie Cooper** got the part–and repeated it in a sequel. Then **Jimmy Lydon** took over the role and brought it up to series speed, from 1941 to 1944, with nine more screen installments.

1948: "If he doesn't receive an Oscar, I shall stand up tomorrow night and tell the world the whole disgraceful story," vows **Jean Hersholt** on this day, arguing till 4 a.m. in favor of an honorary Oscar for **James Baskett** in *Song of the South*. In opposition were certain members of the Academy board who either objected to the fact Baskett had played a slave or felt "Negroes should play only doctors, lawyers and scientists," but they caved in with this threat, and **Ingrid Bergman** presented Baskett his Special Oscar the following night for "his able and heart-warming characterization of Uncle Remus, friend and storyteller to the children of the world." A regular of radio's *Amos 'n' Andy Show*, he stepped into the Uncle Remus role when "De Lawd" of *The Green Pastures* (**Rex Ingram**) declined. On July 9, 1948–less than four months after he got the award–the 44-year-old actor died of a heart ailment.

1953: On this day, **Katherine DeMille Quinn** is twice-blessed with Oscars: Her dad, producer-director **Cecil B. DeMille**, lands Best Picture (for *The Greatest Show on Earth*), and her then-husband, **Anthony Quinn**, is named Best Supporting Actor (for *Viva Zapata!*). Quinn's win put him one up on his movie brother–the merely-nominated title-player, **Marlon Brando**, who got (Quinn thought) favored treatment during the film from **Elia Kazan**. The director, who'd actually picked Quinn to replace Brando in the Broadway *Streetcar Named Desire*, wickedly encouraged the idea and told each of them–just before filming their big knockdown drag-out fight–that the other was jealous about being the second-best Stanley Kowalski and was using the fight to work off the rage. Another thing: Quinn has always claimed the wheezy voice Brando affected for Don Vito Corleone in *The Godfather* he "borrowed" from Quinn's Mountain Rivera in *Requiem for a Heavyweight*.

1958: *South Pacific* reaches New York's Criterion on this day. **Elizabeth Taylor, Doris Day** and **Audrey Hepburn** were considered for the Little Rock nurse who's "as corny as Kansas in August," but the part went to a Chicago-born descendant from Balkan aristocracy, **Francesca Mitzi Marlene de Charney von Gerber** (also known as **Mitzi Gaynor**).

20

1928: *The Trail of '98*, a Klondike Gold Rush saga filmed along the Great Divide outside Denver at an elevation of 11,600 feet amid temperatures as low as 60 below, premieres at New York's Astor on this day—and gets a chilly reception from the audience. The difficulties defeated the film, which (according to director **Clarence Brown**) cost at least five lives. Among the lucky survivors was a stunt double who managed to pass for the ravishing **Dolores Del Rio** in the long shots: **Lou Costello**, working solo and in drag.

1948: On this day, in an (obviously!) early edition of the *Los Angeles Times*, a headline declares "**ROZ RUSSELL** WINS OSCAR." Her win for *Mourning Becomes Electra* was considered a foregone conclusion on Oscar eve, and the actress herself was even rising out of her seat to accept the award when the words "**Loretta Young**" connected with her consciousness. When they did, she continued her rise and, sportingly, led the applause for her successful rival. *Variety*'s "Rambling Reporter" couldn't resist pointing out that Young's winning ticket, *The Farmer's Daughter*, was supposedly turned down by **Ingrid Bergman, Olivia de Havilland**—and Russell.

1952: Creating the most costumes (32,000) for a single movie (*Quo Vadis*) earns **Herschel McCoy** a niche in *The Guinness Book of Records* but not an Oscar: On this day, the prize for Best Costume Design of 1951 goes to **Orry-Kelly**, **Walter Plunkett** and **Irene Sharaff** for *An American in Paris*. Twelve years later, La Sharaff—along with **Vittorio Nino Novarese** and **Renie**—got the Oscar *and* the *Guinness* mention for designing the most costumes ever worn by an individual in a single film: 65 frocks, all of which were rustled up at a cost of $130,000 for **Elizabeth Taylor**'s *Cleopatra*. Both of these *Guinness* records toppled on Christmas Day 1996 when **Madonna**'s *Evita* flounced into release, wearing *85* costumes and accessorized to excess (39 hats, 45 pairs of shoes, 56 pairs of earrings and 42 different hair styles). Costume designer **Penny Rose**, working with a staff of 72 in three countries, took care of the extras, too—40,000 of them, outfitting them in '40s and '50s frocks from 20 different costume houses in London, San Francisco, Paris, Los Angeles, Buenos Aires, New York, Budapest and Rome—and none of this extravagant stitching netted a single Oscar nomination.

1956: *Marty* becomes on this day the first–and only–Best Picture Oscar-winner to come from "enemy country" (i.e., television). Seconding that motion: **Paddy Chayefsky** earned the Oscar for turning his teleplay into a screenplay, **Delbert Mann** for Best Director and title player **Ernest Borgnine** for Best Actor.

1965: With children **Lorna** and **Joey** at her side, **Judy Garland** reaches L.A. on this day to begin work on *Harlow* and walks right into a photo op, replete with **Barry Sullivan** (who'll play her husband in the film) brandishing ads for this quickie flick, to be filmed in seven or eight days in Electronovision. It, of course, was not to be. She bolted in four days' time, replaced by the star who'd stepped in for her in *The Barkleys of Broadway*: **Ginger Rogers**. This indignity and her abbreviated trek into *Valley of the Dolls* two years later were Garland's final flings at a film career (which had ended in 1963 with *I Could Go On Singing*).

1989: *The Thin Blue Line*, **Errol Morris**' film investigation of unjust incarceration–which won awards for Best Documentary of 1988 from The New York Film Critics and The National Board of Review–wins an even greater prize on this day: freedom for its subject, **Randall Dale Adams**. As a result of the film's extraordinary reportage, the courts overturned Adams' 1977 conviction of killing a Dallas policeman and ordered his release. One of Adams' first acts as a freshly freed man was to sue Morris for film rights to his own life.

1994: *Schindler's List* becomes, on this day, the first black-and-white film in 33 years — since *The Apartment* in 1961 — to win the Best Picture of 1993 Oscar.

1999: A movie critic finally rates a mention on the Oscar show: Chicago's **Gene Siskel**, 53, who died Feb. 20, nine months after having brain surgery.

THE *LIST* OF LIFE: Liam Neeson and Ben Kingsley in *Schindler's List*.
LONELYHEARTS: Ernest Borgnine and Betsy Blair in *Marty*.
IT LOOKED GOOD ON THE DRAWING BOARD: Barry Sullivan, Lorna Luft, Judy Garland and Joey Luft.
...BUT GINGER DID THE ROLE: Rogers (with Sullivan and Carol Lynley) in *Harlow*.

1937: Replacing **Bert Glennon**, cinematographer **James Wong Howe** enters *The Prisoner of Zenda* picture on this day, three weeks late–but just in time to catch the coronation scene where commoner **Ronald Colman** accepts the crown for his kidnapped, lookalike cousin (also Colman).

1939: Fox chief **Darryl F. Zanuck** sends, on this day, director **John Ford** a cautionary note about the *Young Mr. Lincoln* rushes, suggesting a quicker tempo for characters other than the title one essayed by **Henry Fonda** ("I don't mean that we should speed up Fonda, as it is the slowness and deliberate character that you have given him that make his performance swell") and recommending low-angle camera shots for the character exclusively ("Not only does it give him height, which is essential, but when you look up at him, for some reason or other, he looks exactly like Lincoln and not Fonda"). And, too, it couldn't hurt to shove that lock of hair a tad to the right to avoid the shadow on Fonda's forehead . . .

1951: MGM's *Show Boat* drops anchor at Pacific Palisades' Bay Theater on this day for its first preview, and those attending are the only audience to hear **Ava Gardner** sing Julie La Verne. **Annette Warren** was dubbed in afterward, but Gardner's throaty renderings of "Can't Help Lovin' That Man" and "Bill" did survive on the soundtrack album. The third contender for the role after **Judy Garland** and **Dinah Shore**, Gardner felt Julie's two songs required as much acting ability as vocal skill and was determined to sing them herself, even though she'd tested with the singing voice of **Lena Horne** (the ideal Julie). Gardner's reaction to this dubbing betrayal was ballistic, but MGM didn't hear till April 1954 when she was asked to play singer **Ruth Etting** in *Love Me or Leave Me*. "What in Christ's name are you trying to do to me? I stand there mouthing words like a goddamn goldfish while you're piping in some goddamn dubbed voice?" she shrieked by way of saying no. MGM had to rent **Doris Day** from Warners for $200,000, but the resulting performance–Day's best–was worth it. "We made a big mistake," Gardner later said to **George Cukor**, who'd turned down the Etting assignment, too. "Dear, if you and I had done it," the director said, "it wouldn't have been so good."

1958: Producer **Mike Todd** and his biographer, screenwriter **Art Cohn**, perish on this day when Todd's chartered aircraft–The Lucky Liz–crashes into a mountain near Albuquerque in a blinding rainstorm. Considering the lowly status of writers in Hollywood, fellow scripter **Harry Kurnitz** envisioned the headline: "MIKE TODD KILLED IN PLANE CRASH. Additional death by Art Cohn."

23

1950: "I just want to say to all beginning actresses," declares the Best Supporting Actress of 1949, waving her *All the King's Men* Oscar high in the air: "don't ever get discouraged. Hold on. Just look — look what can happen!" One week short of 13 years later, **Mercedes McCambridge** tried overdosing on sleeping pills and was rushed to Santa Monica Hospital in time.

1958: "Producer" **Joseph L. Mankiewicz** is believed to have been aboard The Lucky Liz with **Mike Todd** and **Art Cohn** when it crashed in Nevada, according to an early edition of *The New York Times* on this day. "It really pissed me off they called me a producer," Mankiewicz lived to grumble. The famous writer-director was indeed set to catch that doomed plane to huddle with Todd about a forthcoming *Don Quixote* film, but his justifiably hysterical sister-in-law talked him into canceling because of the turbulent weather. The *true* Lucky Liz — Todd's wife, **Elizabeth Taylor** — missed the flight only because she was bedridden with raging pneumonia and a 102-degree fever. She and Mankiewicz survived and filmed *Suddenly, Last Summer* (1959) and *Cleopatra* (1963).

1959: On this day, **Otto Preminger** begins his best movie with his most inspired casting—**Joseph N. Welch** introducing himself to jurors and lawyers (and movie audiences) as the presiding judge–in the first scene shot for *Anatomy of a Murder* at the county courthouse of Marquette, MI. Now it can be told: That incredible performance was entirely read from cue-cards out of camera range.

1998: The sole Yank among the Brits up for 1997 Best Actress honors — *As Good As It Gets*' **Helen Hunt** — becomes the third leading lady to win an Oscar while playing opposite an Oscar-winning **Jack Nicholson**. (The others: **Louise Fletcher** in *One Flew Over the Cuckoo's Nest* and **Shirley MacLaine** in *Terms of Endearment*). Hunt's win also made her the first star to earn an Oscar while still starring in a television series, *Mad About You*. (In the supporting ranks, **Cloris Leachman** got her Oscar for *The Last Picture Show* while still playing Phyllis on *The Mary Tyler Moore Show*.) Hours before her win, Hunt and her TV co-star **Paul Reiser** re-signed their contracts for a reported $1 million an episode. Her next job: playing Shakespeare's man-masquerading Viola in *Twelfth Night* at Lincoln Center–for scale. (**Gwyneth Paltrow**'s first career move after winning the Best Actress Oscar a year later was to play Shakespeare's man-masquerading Rosalind in *As You Like It* at the Williamstown Theater Festival–for scale.)

ON THE BENCH: James Stewart, Joseph N. Welch, Lee Remick and George C. Scott in *Anatomy of a Murder*.
VALIDATING A DREAM: John Ireland and Mercedes McCambridge in *All the King's Men*.
SOME CROSSDRESSING SHAKESPEARE FOR OSCAR ATONEMENT: From left: Helen Hunt in *As Good As It Gets*, and Gwyneth Paltrow in *Shakespeare in Love*.

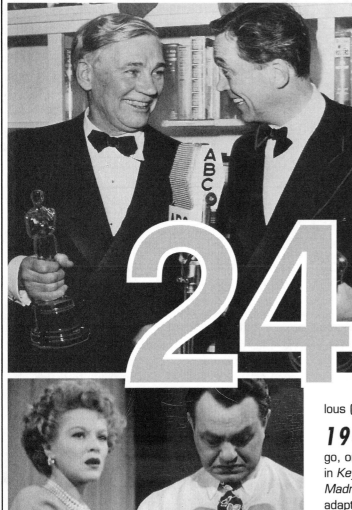

24

_1949:_ The first non-Hollywood production–and _only_ Shakespearean film–ever Oscared for Best Picture of the Year is announced on this day: _Hamlet_. Ironically, the announcement was made by **Ethel Barrymore**, whose brother **John** was considered by many the greatest Hamlet of all. The film's title player, **Laurence Olivier**, became the first person to direct himself (officially) to a Best Actor Oscar–a distinction that stood for half a century until March 21, 1999, when it slipped from the sublime to the ridiculous (**Roberto Benigni** for _Life Is Beautiful_).

_1949:_ Both of the 1948 Oscars for supporting performances go, on this day, to performances **John Huston** directed–**Claire Trevor** in _Key Largo_ and his own father, **Walter**, in _The Treasure of the Sierra Madre_–and he picks up a pair of prizes himself for directing and adapting the latter; 37 years later–to the day!–Huston directed his own daughter, **Anjelica**, to a supporting Oscar (for _Prizzi's Honor_), making the Hustons the only three-generation Oscar family.

_1974:_ "Before **Richard Burton** fell over backward into a camellia bush," begins a report in the _San Francisco Chronicle_ on this day, "he had been talking about his wife **Elizabeth** and the 'desperate nothingness' he felt in her absence." Such was the sound of the coming-apart of the most celebrated couple of their time nine days past a full decade of turbulent togetherness. Marriage No. 1 (of 2) for the Burtons came down in vodka-fumed flames in the northern California berg of Oroville (Gold City), which was trying to pass for Alabama while he was trying to pass (between Shakespearean slip-ups) for a Southern aristocrat. The movie was called _The Klansman_, and all its drama occurred off-camera, including a 17-martini showdown with co-star **Lee Marvin**. Visiting-press vultures converged the day after La Taylor departed (in a huff, about him giving a $450 ring to an 18-year-old waitress at Sambo's Coffee Shop), and Burton blurred through the rest of the shoot on three bottles a day, winding it up with an alarmingly real death scene. Promptly admitted to Santa Monica's St. John's Hospital, he was told he was two weeks away from death himself. It was sobering news: He straightened up and flew relatively right for another ten years.

LIKE FATHER, LIKE SON, LIKE GRANDDAUGHTER: From left: Walter Huston and John Huston for _The Treasure of the Sierra Madre_, and Anjelica Huston (with Jack Nicholson) for _Prizzi's Honor_.
ANOTHER _KEY_ HUSTON PLAYER: Claire Trevor (with Edward G. Robinson) in _Key Largo_.
A COUPLE OF HUSTON CONTENDERS: From left: Sam Jaffe in _The Asphalt Jungle_, and William Hickey in _Prizzi's Honor_.

_1984:_ Cancer claims **Sam Jaffe** on this day, two weeks before his 93d birthday. Active to the end, he was looking forward to working again with **John Huston**, the only person to direct him to an Oscar nomination (for 1950's _The Asphalt Jungle_). **William Hickey** inherited the role intended for Jaffe–the old don in _Prizzi's Honor_–and got the Oscar nomination that went along with it.

1954: On this day, **Mel Ferrer**'s fiancee, **Audrey Hepburn**, wins the Oscar for Best Actress of 1953 (for *Roman Holiday*)—over his co-star in *Lili*, **Leslie Caron**—and picks up the prize in New York where she and Ferrer are appearing in *Ondine*. Afterwards, they celebrated with drinks at the Persian Room of The Plaza with her most serious Oscar rival, *From Here to Eternity*'s **Deborah Kerr**, who was also on Broadway at the time in *Tea and Sympathy*. A scant three days later, Kerr suffered a second major award loss to Hepburn: The Tony.

1965: *John Goldfarb, Please Come Home* takes a merciless drumming from the New York critics on this day, but something of value does emerge from this film fiasco: It enabled the screenwriter, **William Peter Blatty**, to cross professional paths with British director **J. Lee Thompson** and actress-producer **Shirley MacLaine**, both of whom became the basis of fictional characters in a novel he would start writing four years later. The result, *The Exorcist*, rode the bestseller list for 60 weeks and became a supersuccessful flick that won Blatty the Oscar for 1973's Best Screenplay. Not only was MacLaine the origin of his Chris MacNeil character, Blatty used the French couple who ran her house and put a photo he took of MacLaine's daughter, **Sachi**, on the cover of the book. **Ellen Burstyn** and **Linda Blair** got Oscar-nominated as the Shirley & Sachi facsimiles, and Thompson came very close to impersonating his alter-ego, Burke Dennings, himself. When he backed out, **Jack MacGowran** stepped in and delivered his final film performance; he died at age 54 Jan. 31, 1973, right after doing the role.

1976: As *Star Wars* starts shooting in Tunisia on this day, **George Lucas** makes one slight (but right!) last-minute switch in his script—the name of his hero/alter-ego: Luke Starkiller becomes, more pacifistically, Luke Skywalker. Otherwise, The Force was not entirely with the movie's writer-director Lucas. The first day's filming had its technical glitches—namely, C-3PO (See-Threepio) and R2-D2 (Artoo-Detoo); both refused to budge across the Sahara, and their electronic devices only picked up Tunisian radio signals. (*Actors!*)

1991: Broadway tunesmith **Stephen Sondheim** wins the Best Song Oscar on this day for a *Dick Tracy* ditty that he wrote for **Madonna**, "Sooner Or Later." (It's the second Disney song with that title; the other was done by **Hattie McDaniel** in 1947's *Song of the South*, and that was overshadowed by *its* Oscar-winning number, "Zip-a-Dee-Doo-Dah.") Sondheim, sidelined with a leg injury, skipped the ceremony but hosted an Oscar party at his home in Connecticut. Guests say, when Madonna came out to sing the number, Sondheim turned his back to the television set.

ANOTHER KIND OF CHANNELING: Linda Blair, director William Friedkin and Ellen Burstyn in *The Exorcist*.
THE SONG NOT THE SINGER: Madonna and Al Pacino in *Dick Tracy*.
LILI OF THE FIELD: Leslie Caron in *Lili*.
OFF TO A SANDY STOP: R2-D2 and C3PO in *Star Wars*.

26

1958: On this day, **Joanne Woodward**'s flashy, triple-strength emoting in *The Three Faces of Eve* earns her the Oscar for Best Actress of 1957, but this is not a distinction which she has particularly cherished over the years: In fact, "If I had an infinite amount of respect for the people who think I gave the greatest performance," Woodward once remarked, "then it would matter."

1964: The man who spent 24 nights staging the burning of Rome for *Quo Vadis*, hoping to direct the whole thing (alas, **Mervyn LeRoy** got the job)–**Anthony Mann** finally gets to finish what he started 13 years earlier via *The Fall of the Roman Empire*, coming down at New York's DeMille Theater on this day.

1975: Far-out director **Ken Russell** lets fly with his *Tommy*, bowing in London on this day. In three weeks time, its soundtrack became the *third* version of **Pete Townshend**'s rock opera showing on the same music charts, joining **The Who**'s original recording and a classic rendering by The London Symphony.

1990: *Driving Miss Daisy* presumably drives itself into the Oscar winner's circle for Best Picture of 1989 on this day, its designated director (**Bruce Beresford**) totally overlooked and unnominated. This dubious distinction is shared by only two other unnominated directors: **William A. Wellman** for the Best Picture of 1927-1928 (*Wings*) and **Edmund Goulding** for the Best Picture of 1931-1932 (*Grand Hotel*).

1990: On this day, **Howard Ashman**, who wrote the first X-rated lyrics ever Oscar-nominated ("Mean Green Mother from Outer Space," a new number added to the 1987 film of his Off-Broadway *Little Shop of Horrors*), steps up with composer **Alan Menken** to collect the Oscar for Best Song of 1989 ("Under the Sea" from *The Little Mermaid*). The next day Ashman informed his partner he had AIDS, and, 13 days short of a year later, at age 40, he died. He continued to make Oscar history, however: In 1991, he became the first person nominated posthumously for four Oscars—one as producer of the first cartoon feature to be nominated for Best Picture (*Beauty and the Beast*), and the rest for being the first wordsmith to have three Best Songs nominees from the same film; one of these numbers, the title tune, won. A fifth posthumous nomination followed in 1992 for the last song he did with Menken ("Friend Like Me" from *Aladdin*).

THE DRIVER-LESS *MISS DAISY*: Jessica Tandy and Morgan Freeman in *Driving Miss Daisy*.
ONE THIRD OF *EVE*: Joanne Woodward in *The Three Faces of Eve*.
THE WHO DONE IT: Ann-Margret and Roger Daltrey in *Tommy*.

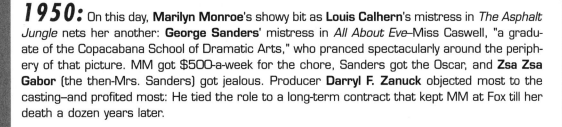

1950: On this day, **Marilyn Monroe**'s showy bit as **Louis Calhern**'s mistress in *The Asphalt Jungle* nets her another: **George Sanders**' mistress in *All About Eve*–Miss Caswell, "a graduate of the Copacabana School of Dramatic Arts," who pranced spectacularly around the periphery of that picture. MM got $500-a-week for the chore, Sanders got the Oscar, and **Zsa Zsa Gabor** (the then-Mrs. Sanders) got jealous. Producer **Darryl F. Zanuck** objected most to the casting–and profited most: He tied the role to a long-term contract that kept MM at Fox till her death a dozen years later.

1957: Director **George Stevens** on this day wins his second Academy Award for his second **Elizabeth Taylor** movie (*Giant*, which lost the Best Picture prize to *Around the World in 80 Days*, an epic produced by Taylor's then-husband, **Michael Todd**). Stevens' first Taylor-made Oscar came for *A Place in the Sun* five years earlier, and it too lost the Best Picture Oscar (to *An American in Paris*).

1973: On this day, **Charles Chaplin** wins his only competitive Oscar–two decades after the fact–for the musical score of 1952's *Limelight*. (Somehow, it took the flick 20 years to get around to playing its Oscar-qualifying week in L.A.). Interestingly, Chaplin contended that the music was the movie's prime mover. "I will do this film to the musical score, like a ballet," he said. "It is all choreographed in my mind. All that remains is to film it."

1977: Two weeks into filming *Saturday Night Fever*, **John Travolta** learns on this day that cancer has claimed **Diana Hyland**. Eighteen years his senior, she had played his mother in a TV-movie (*The Boy in the Plastic Bubble*), and the two had become lovers in real life. Somehow he transposed his devastation into work, which paid off in superstardom and an Oscar nomination for Best Actor. "The pain was on every inch of his body," recalled director **John Badham**. "Some of the best scenes in the picture were done in that advanced stage of grief."

1977: Taxiing for takeoff on a fog-covered runway in the Canary Islands, a Pan Am 747 from L.A. bound for Tenerife is struck by a KLM jet barreling in at top speed, creating on this day the worst aviation disaster in history. Among the 574 fatalities was a pin-up pioneer, **Eve Meyer**, ex (and exec producer) of **Russ Meyer**, the cheesecake lensman who glorified the American girlie. She not only produced his 1959 film-directing debut, *The Immoral Mr. Teas*– the first "nudie movie" to become a mainstream hit–she also starred in his *Eve and the Handyman*.

HOSTESS & MISTRESS: Bette Davis, Marilyn Monroe and George Sanders in *All About Eve*. OSCAR'S LONGEST DELAYED REACTION: Charles Chaplin in *Limelight*.

28

1932: Lensing ends on *Letty Lynton* —
what **Edith Head** (herself the Academy's most honored woman, with eight Oscars to her credit) would later label "the single most important influence on fashion in film history." **Adrian** decided **Joan Crawford**'s broad, mannish shoulders *were* assets and accentuated them with padding and puffed sleeves. Later, the designer admitted: "I never thought my career would rest on Joan Crawford's shoulders."

1940: *Broadway Melody of 1940* bows at New York's Capitol on this day, bringing **Fred Astaire** into the MGM fold and pairing him with **Eleanor Powell** for a beguiling "Begin the Beguine."

1957: *Funny Face* is plastered all over Radio City Music Hall on this day, and the word "choreography" surfaces for the very first time in the credits of a **Fred Astaire** film. **Eugene Loring**, a ballet choreographer who'd put him through his paces in *Yolanda and the Thief*, came before Astaire in the choreography billing.

1979: "*The China Syndrome*," intoned Columbia Pictures' "tease-by-TV" ad campaign. "It's not about China. It's about choices. Between honesty and ambition, career and conscience, responsibility and profit. *The China Syndrome*. Today, only a handful of people know what it means. On March 16, so will you." And on this day—with the near-meltdown at the Three Mile Island nuclear plant in PA, a dozen days into the film's release—the planet knows.

29

AN UNBROKEN STRING OF M.S. WINNERS: From left: Maureen Stapleton, Mary Steenburgen, Meryl Streep and Maggie Smith.
A MEETING OF MINDS: Woody Allen directs a young alter-ego, Jonathan Munk, in *Annie Hall*.

1934: *The Girl From Missouri* goes before the cameras on this day, the first **Jean Harlow** flick to come within the jurisdiction of the movies' newly adopted "Production Code." Censors started with the name of the film and reached this tepid title by whittling it down from *Eadie Was a Lady* (as per a popular song of the day), then *Born To Be Kissed* and even the immaculate *100% Pure*.

1955: The premature arrival of **Joseph Wiley ("Joey") Luft** on this day prevents his nominated mom, **Judy Garland**, from attending the Oscarcast the next night. A television crew waited outside her hospital room in case she won (for *A Star Is Born*). She didn't, and, as the crew started to disperse, Garland was treated to some poetry from hubby **Sid Luft**: "Fuck the Academy Awards—you've got yours in the incubator."

1978: "I couldn't let down the guys," **Woody Allen** explains to the inquiring press when he shows on this day—like every Monday—at Michael's Pub for his regular gig: playing clarinet with the New Orleans Funeral and Ragtime Orchestra. He returned home at midnight, read himself to sleep with *Conversations With Carl Jung* and learned the next morning in *The New York Times* his *Annie Hall* had won Oscar's Triple Crown (Best Picture, Best Director, Best Screenplay).

1982: For the fourth year in a row, an Academy Award goes to an M.S. for Best Supporting Actress: to **Maureen Stapleton** of 1981's *Reds* (following **Mary Steenburgen** of 1980's *Melvin and Howard*, **Meryl Streep** of 1979's *Kramer vs. Kramer* and **Maggie Smith** of 1978's *California Suite*).

1989: Simultaneously contending for 1988's Best Actress (*Gorillas in the Mist*) AND Best Supporting Actress (*Working Girl*), **Sigourney Weaver** earns on this day the dubious niche of being the first person ever to strike out in both categories—an "honor" matched in 1994 by **Emma Thompson**'s "distinguished" double loss for both starring (*The Remains of the Day*) and supporting (*In the Name of the Father*) categories. All of the double nominees prior to "The Sigourney Shut-Out"—**Fay Bainter** in 1938, **Teresa Wright** in 1942, **Barry Fitzgerald** in 1944 and **Jessica Lange** in 1982—took home the supporting prize. **Geena Davis** in *The Accidental Tourist*, winning over Weaver, rewrote that rule.

1992: Twice "blessed" by The Golden Raspberry Foundation on this day, **Sean Young** hogs its female categories with both of her performances of twins in *A Kiss Before Dying*: The sister not killed by **Matt Dillon** earned her Worst Actress (dis)honors; the one who *was* got her Worst Supporting Actress. Her *No Way Out* co-star, **Kevin Costner**, was declared Worst Actor for *Robin Hood: Prince of Thieves*, and *Hudson Hawk* swept up Worst Picture/Script/Director.

1962: Shrugging off the warning signs printed big in the morning papers (photos of his wife and her Marc Antony, in bathrobes, kissing openly on the set), **Eddie Fisher** throws a classic press conference on this day at the Hotel Pierre. When denials didn't wash, he impulsively phoned Rome where **Elizabeth Taylor** was filming *Cleopatra* and asked her to lay to rest The Story that she and **Richard Burton** were committing The Big A. Lay to rest, the lady does–in her blisteringly honest fashion: "Well, Eddie," sez Liz, within earshot of the press, "I can't actually do that because there is, you see, some truth in the rumors." Eyes shining, cheeks drawn, he turned back to the yelping horde with egg-on-his-face and diluted even *that*: "Elizabeth has no statement to make." **Louis Nizer**'s law firm made the statement the day after April Fool's Day: "Elizabeth and Eddie Fisher announce that they have mutually agreed to part. Divorce proceedings will be instituted soon." L.A.'s nightspot, The Loser, threw his name on its marquee as Loser of the Week, and soon even he was going with the flow, leading off his act with "Arrivederci, Roma." Asked why, he snapped, "What did you expect me to sing–'Take Me Out to the Ball Game'?"

1987: The Oscar-winning Best Actor of 1985 (**William Hurt** for *Kiss of the Spider Woman*) announces on this day 1986's Best Actress winner–in sign language: his *Children of a Lesser God* co-star and girlfriend, **Marlee Matlin**. A dozen years later, Matlin told the downside of that day to a women's group in New Brunswick. After running the paparazzi gauntlet, she settled into the backseat of a limo with Hurt, who'd lost in his category. He looked at her new Oscar and said, "Just because you have that little man sitting next to you, do you really think you deserve it?" *Bummer!* "I can't remember anything else that happened the entire evening after that," Matlin admitted.

1987: On this day, **Paul Newman**'s seventh Oscar nomination–for *The Color of Money*, playing a latter-day version of his Oscar-nominated Fast Eddie Felson from *The Hustler*–finally brings home the gold; present to lose on all six previous occasions, he skipped the ceremonies this time–and somehow won.

1990: *Teenage Mutant Ninja Turtles* pounces on 2,006 screens on this day and soon becomes the highest-grossing independent feature of all time.

ONLY WHEN IT'S HURT'S: William Hurt and Marlee Matlin in *Children of a Lesser God*.
THE MAGNIFICENT FOUR: *Teenage Mutant Ninja Turtles*.
"FAST EDDIE" FOR A QUARTER OF A CENTURY: From left: Paul Newman with Jackie Gleason in *The Hustler* and with Tom Cruise in *The Color of Money*.

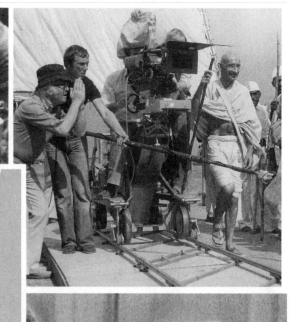

ACTORS OSCARED AS DIRECTORS: Robert Redford (with Mary Tyler Moore) for *Ordinary People*, Warren Beatty (with Diane Keaton) for *Reds* and Richard Attenborough (with Ben Kingsley) for *Gandhi*.
MR. PRESIDENT, MEET MR. DIRECTOR: President Richard Nixon honors director John Ford.

31

1937: On this day, **Paul Muni** delivers—*really delivers*—his big courtroom speech in *The Life of Emile Zola*, provoking instant praise from Warner Bros. executive producer **Hal B. Wallis**—and, at year's end, Best Actor honors from The New York Film Critics. The same group named *Zola* Best Picture of 1937—as did Oscar the following spring; even better, it turned into the studio's top moneymaker that year—which was rarely the way with the Warners historicals that followed Muni's Oscar-winning outing of '36, *The Story of Louis Pasteur*.

1952: In a "personal and confidential" letter to **David O. Selznick** on this day, **Darryl F. Zanuck** patiently explains how inappropriate Mrs. Selznick (**Jennifer Jones**) would be for *My Cousin Rachel*—not being (1) English or, more importantly, (2) 40: Preserving the age gap between **Daphne du Maurier**'s enigmatic heroine and her 25-year-old lover was essential to keep the story unique. The film's original director, **George Cukor**, in fact, harbored hopes of luring his old *Camille* out of retirement for the title role, but **Garbo** wanted to be alone. **Henry Koster** replaced Cukor and settled for 36-year-old **Olivia de Havilland**, who didn't duplicate the success her sister (**Joan Fontaine**) had in du Maurier's *Rebecca*; and, too, she was less than receptive to the randy, 27-year-old **Richard Burton**, in an upstaging, Oscar-nominated American film debut.

1973: On this day—exactly five months before his death—director **John Ford**, 78, is presented the Medal of Freedom by **President Nixon** and honored with the first Life Achievement Award ever presented by the American Film Institute.

1981: The Oscars are a little late this year—having been called off the day before because of the assassination attempt on **President Reagan**. Press greet the Best Actor winner, **Robert De Niro** (for *Raging Bull*), with the embarrassing news that his five-year-old *Taxi Driver* example may have triggered the gunman.

1981: On this day, via *Ordinary People*, **Robert Redford** begins a three-year run of established actors winning Oscars as Best Directors. He was followed by **Warren Beatty** for *Reds* in 1982 and **Richard Attenborogh** for *Gandhi* in 1983.

1993: About a week from completing *The Crow*, **Brandon Lee** is fatally shot doing an action sequence in Wilmington, N.C. A gun that was supposed to hold a blank instead fired part of a dummy bullet that struck and killed the 28-year-old son of martial arts master **Bruce Lee**, himself a mid-film fatality. Computer animation and a double finished *The Crow*, which soared to considerable box-office success. As a murdered rock star in this mystical adventure, Brandon was impervious to the barrage of bullets shot at him—but the one that actually killed him was refilmed and converted into a tasteful stabbing.

THE UNLUCKIEST IN LOVE:
Hedy Lamarr, Judy Garland and
Lana Turner in *Ziegfeld Girl*.

1929: *The Wild Party* begins at New York's Rialto on this day, marking **Clara Bow**'s bow in talkies. Unhappily, her gum-smacking, nasal Brooklynese was out of sync with her jazz-baby *joie de vivre*. Before sound technology could catch up with her, too many wild parties in real life took their physical and mental toll. She retired early (*very*: it was all over at 26).

1939: An elaborate studio junket launches *Dodge City* on its namesake turf on this day. The town swelled tenfold from all the promotional commotion caused by a chartered 16-car train importing celebs to the premiere festivities. An estimated 70,000 turned up to ogle **Errol Flynn**, **Olivia de Havilland**, et al.

1950: *Times* critic **Bosley Crowther** finds **Clifton Webb** on this day heavily disguised as a patriarch (*of 12*)–and still playing Belvedere–in *Cheaper by the Dozen*.

1962: Director **Stanley Donen** and screenwriter **Peter Stone** get together in London on this day and commence the *Charade* that finally unites **Cary Grant** with **Audrey Hepburn**. Initially, Grant gave the script a cursory read and opted instead to do *Man's Favorite Sport?* so *Charade* was rechanneled for (then lovebirds) **Warren Beatty** and **Natalie Wood**. Then, Columbia wouldn't cough up enough cash, and the project was about to go under when Grant boarded it again and Hepburn quickly fell into place. **Billy Wilder** tried twice to get these two together, and both times Grant bolted, leaving Wilder with less felicitous alternatives (**Humphrey Bogart** in *Sabrina* and **Gary Cooper** in *Love in the Afternoon*). The closest Grant came to being in a Wilder film was via the phony English accent **Tony Curtis** affected to fool **Marilyn Monroe** in *Some Like It Hot*. When Wilder screened that picture for the actor, Grant turned to him and said — *exactly* the way Tony Curtis did it — "I don't talk like that."

1968: Composer **Alex North**, who scored **Stanley Kubrick**'s *Spartacus*, sits down to the premiere of their *2001: A Space Odyssey* at the Loews Capitol in New York on this day–and finds his score has been supplanted by classical pieces Kubrick played while editing the picture (**Richard Strauss'** "Thus Spake Zarathustra," **Johann Strauss'** "The Blue Danube," etc.). Another soundtrack switch: **Douglas Rain** replaced **Martin Balsam** as the voice of that "human" computer, HAL-9000.

NOTHING TO SHOUT ABOUT: Clara Bow's talkie bow, *The Wild Party*.
DADDY BELVEDERE: Sara Allgood, Clifton Webb, Myrna Loy and brood (Jeanne Crain, Barbara Bates, et al.) in *Cheaper by the Dozen*.
CITY TREKKERS: Errol Flynn and Olivia de Havilland in *Dodge City*.
THE THIRD TIME'S THE CHARM: Cary Grant and Audrey Hepburn in *Charade*.

1936: Selznick International Pictures' premiere presentation becomes Radio City Music Hall's Easter holiday offering on this day: *Little Lord Fauntleroy*, starring **Selznick**'s *David Copperfield*, **Freddie Bartholomew**. It was up to his studio motto ("In the Tradition of Quality")—although Selznick's longtime scripter, **Ben Hecht**, took a dim view of this childhood favorite as movie material. "The trouble with you, David," he said, "is that you did all your reading before you were 12."

1942: When **Julius J.** and **Philip G. Epstein** turn in the first third of their *Casablanca* script on this day, producer **Hal B. Wallis** instructs them to tell the story to **David O. Selznick** in the hopes of securing the services of **Ingrid Bergman**. "*What* story?" they asked. "Wing it," Wallis shot back. Which they did, while Selznick lunched in his suite at New York's Hotel Carlyle, slurping soup, not looking up as the two dutifully tap-danced out their tangled yarn of intrigue and letters of transit. Not till they reduced their labors to "a lot of crap like *Algiers*" did Selznick look up and nod. At that moment, they knew Bergman was *Casablanca*-bound—and, 23 months later, that "crap" made the Epsteins the first Oscar-winning set of twins in screen history.

1955: Unable to talk his *Shane* (**Alan Ladd**) into the *Giant* role of Jett Rink, **George Stevens** gives in on this day to the earnest lobbying of new-star-on-the-lot **James Dean**. Both lived long enough to regret it: By August 1, Dean had amassed a list of 16 infractions in which the actor's tardiness or total absence caused production delays. Maybe he was annoyed to be pulling down the same salary as some of the pricy I-got-the-Fix-in bit players (i.e., $1,500 a week for **Paul Fix**'s fleeting Dr. Lynnton). In any event, the director assured the actor they'd never work together again.

STARTING *LITTLE*: Freddie Bartholomew and C. Aubrey Smith in *Little Lord Fauntleroy*.
THINK RINK: James Dean being directed by George Stevens in *Giant*.
SCHELL'S GAME: Maximilian Schell and Marlon Brando in *The Young Lions*.

1958: New York's freshly refurbished Paramount on this day throws open its doors to a freshly refurbished film version of *The Young Lions*—this one dictated by **Marlon Brando**. Christian, the evil-Nazi soldier Brando played, came across so soft-focused on film he seemed halo-lit. The upshot of this character-reconstruction? **Maximilian Schell**, in a career-making Hollywood debut, stole all Brando's thunder—*playing an evil Nazi!* **Montgomery Clift** fared well, too—but got cheated out of the death scene his character had in the book because Brando insisted on taking the last-reel fall himself, dying the death of The Good German, felled by an American bullet. However, when Brando suggested his dead body fall spread-eagled like the Crucifixion, Clift threatened to walk off the film, causing Brando to agree to a less saintly exit. "When Clift's around," cracked a wag, "there's only room for one Jesus Christ."

3

1924: On this day, a few hours apart, **Doris Day** and **Marlon Brando** are born.

1939: *Maisie* clocks in as an MGM series on this day, as filming begins on the first of ten screen outings for a brassy, blonde Miss Fix-It. The title role, intended for **Jean Harlow**, went to **Ann Sothern**.

1943: While playing golf at a Hollywood club on this day, 50-year-old **Conrad Veidt** dies of a heart attack. One of the screen's most hissable heavies, he *insisted* on typecasting and, at the time of his death, was three years into an MGM contract which specified he do only villains. It was an early calling (Cesare the somnambulist in 1919's *The Cabinet of Dr. Caligari*), and it was a gift that worked equally well in English (the wicked Grand Vizier in *The Thief of Bagdad*), but true fame came with his next-to-last movie role: *Casablanca*'s Major Strasser.

1953: *TV Guide* is born on this day–for 15 cents a copy–and on its cover is television's other new baby: **Desi Arnaz Jr.**, born Jan. 19, 1953, with two-thirds of the nation's TV viewers in attendance during the regularly scheduled broadcast of *I Love Lucy*. The show's writers had bet **Lucille Ball** would have a boy–and scripted the episode accordingly–and, although Junior didn't take over that role on the series, he did grow up to become an actor and, completing a cycle of sorts, played his pop in *The Mambo Kings*.

1981: Well after his prime screen time, **John Gavin** garners his first nomination–from **President Reagan** (to become U.S. Ambassdor to Mexico).

1989: After putting in a hard day on the set directing *Impulse*, **Sondra Locke** is informed by **Clint Eastwood** on this day their 13-year-old thrill is gone. A week later, Locke found herself locked out of their home. Her palimony suit, filed before month's end (April 26), was settled outside of public view. In 1997, she told all in her tell-all, *The Good, the Bad and the Very Ugly*.

PERMISSSSIBLE TO BE HISSSSSABLE: Claude Rains and Conrad Veidt in *Casablanca*.
DAY OF THE STARS: Doris Day and Marlon Brando.
THE BITTER END: Clint Eastwood and Sondra Locke in *The Gauntlet*.

4

1923: A certificate of incorporation filed in Delaware on this day turns the Brothers Warner–Harry, Albert, Jack and Sam–into Warner Bros. Pictures. In its first year of operation, the company ground out 14 films–including *The Little Church Around the Corner*, *Main Street* and an adaptation of F. Scott Fitzgerald's *The Beautiful and Damned*. A picture a week soon became the norm.

1946: The trades report on this day that DeMille's King of Kings, H.B. Warner, will be "delighted" to play the drunken druggist in *It's a Wonderful Life*, cracking the Christ typecasting at last (thanks to director Frank Capra).

1947: Almost four years since his last film (*This Is the Army*), Ronald Reagan returns to the screen–leastways, the Strand's in NYC on this day–riding down *Stallion Road* on his own horse ("Baby," playing "Tar Baby"). The role of a dedicated vet who halts an outbreak of anthrax was to have been assigned to Errol Flynn and adapted by William Faulkner, but booze got them both booted off the project. A week before filming began, Humphrey Bogart and *his* "Baby" (Lauren Bacall) bowed out of the picture–which was then instantly downgraded from Technicolor to black and white–and their roles were thrown to Zachary Scott and Alexis Smith. The free ride into postwar cinema which Reagan was expecting from the popularity of the Bogarts didn't happen. Indeed, *Stallion Road* went nowhere. Bacall took a studio suspension rather than do the picture, and, when MGM tried to borrow her from Warners for Spencer Tracy's *Cass Timberlane*, her miffed bosses declined. It was, she reminisced almost half a century later on Tom Snyder's TV show, her only shot at co-starring with either actor. She regretted missing Tracy but bore up quite well about Reagan.

1960: After two years of angry silence, Gregory Peck and director William Wyler resume speaking when they meet backstage the night of Wyler's *Ben-Hur* Oscar triumph. They fell out over the buckboard-razzing scene in *The Big Country*. Peck felt he came off "a cretin" in all that horseback-roughhousing and wanted it reshot; when Wyler refused, the actor (forgetting he was also co-producing the film with Wyler) walked off his own picture in disgust.

A "CRETIN" GOES *COUNTRY*: Gregory Peck in *The Big Country*.
"CHIRST" BEHIND THE COUNTER: James Stewart and H.B. Warner in *It's a Wonderful Life*.
BOGIE & "BABY" BOWED OUT: Zachary Scott, Ronald Reagan, Patti Brady and Alexis Smith in *Stallion Road*.

1916: With only one Oscar for acting on his mantle, **Gregory Peck** still has something to shoot for: He shares the same birthday as three two-time Oscar winners: **Spencer Tracy** (1900), **Melvyn Douglas** (1901) and **Bette Davis** (1908).

1949: On this, the second day of shooting *Annie Get Your Gun*, **Howard Keel**'s horse falls on him, shattering the actor's ankle and forcing him out of the film for six weeks. When production resumed, it's six *months* later–with a new crew: **George Sidney**, **Betty Hutton**, **Benay Venuta** and **Louis Calhern** replacing **Busby Berkeley**, **Judy Garland**, **Geraldine Wall** and the late **Frank Morgan**.

BIRTHDAZE: From left: Bette Davis and Spencer Tracy in *20,000 Years in Sing Sing*; Gregory Peck and Melvyn Douglas (with Ava Gardner) in *The Great Sinner*.
A PROPHETIC EXIT LINE: Barbara Stanwyck and Walter Huston in *The Furies*.
THERE'VE BEEN SOME CHANGES MADE: Betty Hutton, Howard Keel, Louis Calhern, Benay Venuta, J. Carrol Naish, Keenan Wynn and Edward Arnold in *Annie Get Your Gun*.

1950: Delayed two days in New York by the death of **Kurt Weill** (who composed his signature song, "September Song"), **Walter Huston** checks in at 20th Century-Fox on this day to be fitted and tested for a title role he's to start shooting in five days–a genial counterfeiter of one-dollar bills, *Old 880* (subsequently retitled *Mister 880* and retailored for **Edmund Gwenn**)–but the next day, Huston fell ill and skipped his 66th birthday party thrown by his writer-director son, **John**, at Romanoff's. During the night, he suffered an aneurysm and died the following morning. On April 11, what would have been his second day as *Old 880*, the actor was accorded a star-packed memorial service at Hollywood's Academy Theater (where the Hustons won father-and-son Oscars for *The Treasure of the Sierra Madre* only 54 weeks before). The eulogies were eloquent, but Walter Huston himself delivered his own epitaph— five months later, with the release of his 48th and final film, *The Furies*: Dying in the arms of daughter **Barbara Stanwyck**, he uttered his last words on screen, "And don't go naming my grandson T.C. It's too big a bag for him to carry. He'll have too much to live up to 'cause there'll never be another like me."

1941: In *Men of Boys Town*, a tame sequel bowing at New York's Capitol on this day, **Spencer Tracy** and **Mickey Rooney** return to their Oscar-winning roots—Tracy took 1938's Best Actor prize, Rooney made off with an honorary—both fresh from 1940 performances of **Thomas Alva Edison**: Rooney as *Young Tom Edison*, Tracy as *Edison the Man*.

1954: *Prince Valiant*, a lackey in King Arthur's court hoping for more heroic chores, moves from funny papers to the Roxy's big screen on this day in the form of **Robert Wagner**, wearing earnest expressions, medieval garb and black bangs ("my imitation of **Jane Wyman**," he called it).

1959: Nominated for the wrong performance (the determined fisherman in *The Old Man and the Sea* instead of the political kingpin in *The Last Hurrah*), **Spencer Tracy** loses the Oscar on this day to **David Niven**—in a role Tracy almost did (the blustery major in *Separate Tables*). **Laurence Olivier** pitched him the part when he was thinking of directing *Separate Tables*, but the project fell apart. They almost co-starred again in *Judgment at Nuremberg*, but Olivier bowed out at the last minute. **Burt Lancaster** filled both vacancies. Tracy once told **Roderick Mann** of the *London Sunday Express* his biggest regret was never working with Olivier.

1964: "What do you mean, heart attack? You've got to have a heart before you can have an attack," a dry-eyed **Billy Wilder** supposedly cracks on this day when told his *Kiss Me, Stupid* star had suffered a mild heart attack and was in Cedars of Lebanon Hospital for observation. At 4:32 a.m. the next day, a blood clot from the initial attack brought on a massive coronary. **Peter Sellers'** heart suddenly stopped beating for 90 seconds and had to be manually restarted by the heart specialist in attendance. Seven more heart attacks followed that day, and at one point he was technically dead. His full recovery would (and did) require six months—which effectively kissed *Kiss Me, Stupid* goodbye. A month of wonderful Sellers footage was junked, and Wilder took it from the top again. **Tony Randall**, **Bob Hope**, **Danny Kaye** and **Tom Ewell** lined up as replacement possibilities, but Wilder picked **Ray Walston**. In the fallout that followed, a second Sellers-Wilder film — *The Private Life of Sherlock Holmes*, with **Peter O'Toole** co-starring was delayed until 1970 when Wilder did it with **Robert Stephens** and **Colin Blakely**.

1997: Despite the picture of domestic bliss they presented at the Academy Awards eight days earlier when he won one Oscar for writing *Sling Blade* and lost another for enacting it, **Billy Bob Thompson** and wife **Pietra** call the marriage off on this day.

POST-OSCAR GROUPINGS: *Young Tom Edison* (Mickey Rooney, here with George Bancroft) and *Edison the Man* (Spencer Tracy, with George Meader) turn into *Men of Boys Town* (with Bobs Watson).
POST-JANE BANGS: Robert Wagner and Janet Leigh in *Prince Valiant*.
POST-OSCAR SCRAPPING: Billy Bob Thompson in *Sling Blade*.

A CLEAN OSCAR SWEEP — AND THEN SOME: Maurice Chevalier, Leslie Caron and Louis Jourdan in *Gigi*. **DEFYING DULLNESS:** Shirley Temple in *The Blue Bird*. **WYLER'S CAST FOR FORD'S VALLEY:** Donald Crisp, Roddy McDowall and Sara Allgood in *How Green Was My Valley*.

1938: The movie that left a 17-year-old **Lana Turner** lightly "marked for life" lands in Radio City Music Hall on this day: To get the bit role of the Eurasian cupcake courted by **Alan Hale** (!) in *The Adventures of Marco Polo*, the teenage Turner allowed her eyebrows to be shaved—and they never grew back.

1939: "The deadly dullness of the last week was lifted today when **Darryl Zanuck** admitted he had bought all rights to **Maurice Maeterlinck**'s *The Blue Bird* for **Shirley Temple**," trills **Louella O. Parsons**, leading off her popular syndicated column on this day–right after the Fascist sacking of Albania.

1941: Exhilarated to have *How Green Was My Valley* back on production track, **Darryl F. Zanuck** bombards his new director with casting suggestions: **Martha Scott** or **Geraldine Fitzgerald** for Bronwyn, **Gene Tierney** for Angharad, **Ray Milland** or **George Brent** for the preacher. **John Ford**, however, stuck with the casting **William Wyler** came up with before moving on to *The Little Foxes*: **Anna Lee**, **Maureen O'Hara** and **Walter Pidgeon**. (It was also Wyler who set **Roddy McDowall**, **Donald Crisp** and **Sara Allgood** for roles that couldn't possibly be cast better.) Playing the cast he was dealt, Ford got the Oscar for Best Director–plus an Oscar showing from supporting actor Crisp. The Best Picture prize Zanuck picked up was particularly well-placed since he got *Valley* green-lighted again after 20th Century-Fox's nervous moneybags in New York refused funds because of Wyler's well-earned reputation for slow-moving perfection.

1959: Telephone operators at Metro-Goldwyn-Mayer answer the phone "M-*Gigi*-M" on this day, the day after **Lerner**-and-**Loewe**'s musical made *more* than merely a clean Oscar sweep (nine for nine–plus an honorary for **Maurice Chevalier**). This set the new record for the most Academy Awards, and it was not duplicated until 1988 when another multi-nominated clean-sweeper came along–also nine for nine, and also with nary an acting nomination: *The Last Emperor*, the first Western production made about modern China with the full cooperation of that nation's government. Three other films have earned more Oscars–1959's *Ben-Hur* and 1997's *Titanic* both with 11, and 1961's *West Side Story* with 10–but their respective sweeps weren't 100%.

1970: Well-cast on this day as the Oscar presenter for Special Visual Effects, **Raquel Welch** steps to the mike and says, "There are two of them," referring (the world gradually realizes) to the nominees. The winner was *Marooned*, an expensive lost-in-space saga that anticipated the Apollo 13 mishap by five months; needless to add, its prize-winning tricks dated fast and were quaintly hokey compared to the state-of-the-art machinery in *Apollo 13* 25 years later.

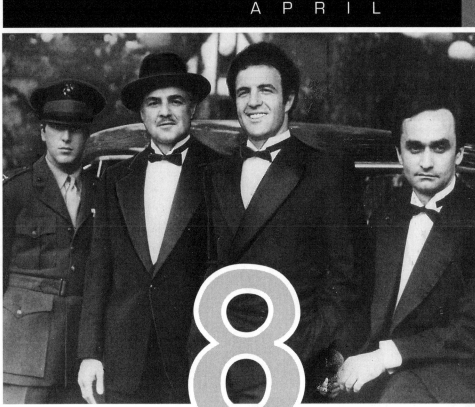

8

OSCARS FOR THE PATRIARCH: From left: Robert De Niro (with Francesca DeSapio and their brood) in *The Godfather Part II*, and Marlon Brando (with Al Pacino, James Caan and John Cazale) in *The Godfather*.

1935: On this day, **Spencer Tracy**'s career takes a hairpin turn: In the morning, the Fox Film Corporation announced he and the studio were parting after almost five years. By afternoon–without losing a day's pay–he was installed at MGM for the next 25 years. Tracy's benders had accelerated in direct ratio to the decline in quality of his Fox scripts. The month before, wound up from the windup of *It's a Small World*, he got busted in Yuma, made headlines and did major structural damage. Fox, for punishment, assigned him to support (menace, actually) **Janet Gaynor** and the film-debuting **Henry Fonda** in *The Farmer Takes a Wife*. Rather than endure this demotion, Tracy was direct: "Just fire me." They did. "They" had their days numbered as well: Three months after he split, the Fox regime folded, fading into Twentieth Century Pictures and becoming 20th Century-Fox.

1937: "Girl Discovered At Soda Fountain Gets Film Career" declares the headline of a *United Press* filler on this day — datelined, of course, Hollywood. In January of 1936, one month before her 15th birthday, a transplanted beauty from Wallace, ID–**Julia Jean Turner**, soon to be redubbed **Lana**–cut her typewriting class at Hollywood High and skipped across Sunset Boulevard to grab a nickel drink at Top's Cafe (not Schwab's, as myth would have it). **Billy Wilkerson**, publisher of *The Hollywood Reporter*, spotted her on the stool and hooked her up with the **Zeppo Marx** Agency, which pointed her toward the movies. First stop was the prophetically titled *A Star Is Born*, in which she and **Carole Landis** were among the extras milling about the Santa Anita racetrack bar after the **Fredric March-Lionel Stander** brawl. Incredibly, the camera never caught her face–but it caught everything when she made her celebrated 75-foot stroll to stardom, in a snug-fitting sweater, in **Mervyn LeRoy**'s *They Won't Forget*. After that, it was nonstop.

1970: On this day——the day after he won the Oscar for playing the one-eyed lawman of *True Grit* ("If I had known that, I would have put that eyepatch on 35 years earlier") — **John Wayne** returns to Tucson to resume filming *Rio Lobo* and is greeted by a mass of eyepatches worn by cast and crew–even his horse.

1975: On this day, **Robert De Niro** becomes the first performer to beat his own acting teacher (**Lee Strasberg**) out of an Oscar. De Niro's winning support to *The Godfather Part II* also made his role–Don Vito Corleone–the only character to trigger Oscar-winning portrayals from *two* different actors. **Marlon Brando** set the pace as the older version of Vito in 1972's *The Godfather*, and De Niro went to elaborate lengths to reprise Brando's mannerisms at a younger age.

9

1962: The first Oscar ever accorded a performance in a foreign-language film is awarded on this day–to **Sophia Loren** for *Two Women*. The second occurred March 21, 1999, when **Roberto Benigni** was named Best Actor for the equally Italian *Life Is Beautiful*. (The only other foreign-language performance favored with an Oscar was **Robert De Niro**'s support–all of it in Sicilian, save for nine words in English–in *The Godfather Part II*). The first phonetically learned performance to win the Oscar was **Anna Magnani**'s Italian-into-English one for 1955's *The Rose Tattoo*.

1979: A radically gaunt **John Wayne** makes his final public appearance on this day–two months before his death of cancer–giving the Best Picture Oscar to **Michael Cimino**'s anti-war saga, *The Deer Hunter*. (Duke called him "Chipino.")

1979: The only Oscar-winning portrait of an Oscar loser is announced on this day: **Maggie Smith**'s in *California Suite*. The way it usually works is that stars *lose* Oscars playing Oscar winners: **Janet Gaynor**, **Fredric March**, **Judy Garland** and **James Mason** were Oscar-losing Oscar winners in various versions of *A Star Is Born*. Ditto **Kirk Douglas** in *The Bad and the Beautiful* and **Bette Davis** in *The Star*.

1984: On this day, **Linda Hunt** wins the only Oscar ever given for playing someone of the opposite gender (in *The Year of Living Dangerously*). Nine years later, **Jaye Davidson** reversed that particular procedure and got a nomination for Best Supporting Actor, playing a transvestite in *The Crying Game*.

1992: *The New York Times* reports on this day that a *Casablanca* bash at the Museum of Modern Art marking the film's 50th anniversary drew a crowd of 700, including the son of **Humphrey Bogart** and the daughters of **Ingrid Bergman**. One of the latter, **Pia Lindstrom**, read a message from an ex-actor once considered for the role of Rick–**Ronald Reagan**, who, she noted dryly, "went on to get top billing in another production." And that, said *The Times*, slipping a refined pun into "All the News That's Fit to Print," was "a different *casa blanca*."

1999: Basking in cushy retirement in Palm Springs, [**Jiggs**] **Cheetah** observes his 67th birthday on this day. The chimp was born the same year **Johnny Weissmuller** took to the vine and was one of four chimpanzees who played Tarzan's pal over the years. Not only did he survive the other three, he seeks the *Guinness Book of Records* title of world's oldest chimpanzee. Honored with a spot on the "Walk of Stars" in his new hometown, he is also seeking his own star on the Hollywood Walk of Fame.

WEDDING IN PENNSYLVANIA: Robert De Niro, John Savage, John Cazale, Rutanya Alda and Christopher Walken in *The Deer Hunter*.
WAR IN INDONESIA: Mel Gibson and Linda Hunt in *The Year of Living Dangerously*.
OSCAR IN ITALIANO: From left: Anna Magnani in *The Rose Tattoo*, Sophia Loren (with Eleanora Brown) in *Two Women* and Roberto Benigni (with Giorgio Cantarini) in *Life Is Beautiful*.

1952: On this day, in secret session with the House Un-American Activities Committee, **Elia Kazan** names the names of people he knows to be members of the Communist Party. Two days later, he took an ad in *The New York Times* explaining his position. Pressing his point farther, he made two fact-based features: *Man on a Tightrope*, about a circus fleeing Communist-ruled Czechoslovakia, and *On the Waterfront*, about a corrupt harbor union toppled by a single "cheese-eater." **Marlon Brando**, who played this informer, at first shunned the project but (out of respect for the man who had directed him brilliantly in *A Streetcar Named Desire* and *Viva Zapata!*) took it on and gave a great, powerful, redemptive performance that capped both their careers. Many people remain enraged about Kazan's actions on this day, and they were very vocal in the spring of '99 when he was voted an honorary Oscar for his lifetime achievement.

1953: The career of **Vincent Price** takes a sharp right (or is it wrong?) turn on this day as his 3-D *House of Wax* opens for (very big) business at New York's Paramount. What Price gory? He chose to do this film instead of heeding actor/director **Jose Ferrer**'s call to return to Broadway in *My Three Angels* (filmed as *We're No Angels*). This may have been the low road, but it carried Price to wealth and established him with an unshakable movie-monster persona.

1967: On this day, **Elizabeth Taylor** snaps up a second Oscar for appearing opposite a husband-of-the-moment (**Richard Burton** in *Who's Afraid of Virginia Woolf?* this time; **Eddie Fisher** in *Butterfield 8* six years earlier).

1968: For the first time since the costume-design Oscar began in 1948, **Edith Head** breathes easily on this day: She's *not* nominated. In her 1,000-film career, she nabbed 35 nominations and eight Oscars (an industry record).

1972: On this day—a real make-nice day for **Charles Chaplin** from the town that had denied and abandoned him 20 years before—he receives belatedly 1) his own star in The Hollywood Walk of Fame and 2) a new honorary Oscar. (His first, "for versatility and genius in writing, acting, directing and producing *The Circus*," came May 16, 1929, at the very first Academy Awards presentation.)

1935: Production begins on this day on *A Tale of Two Cities*, with **Ronald Colman** heading an impeccable cast. Researcher **Val Lewton** was prodded to get his aunt, the great (**Alla**) **Nazimova**, to audition for the evil Madame Defarge by producer **David O. Selznick**. She recommended **Blanche Yurka** instead. Yurka, the 67th and last person seen for the part, landed the job. Another reluctantly arrived-at perfect casting: **Isabel Jewell** as the timid seamstress who goes to guillotine right before Colman. Well-aware of her wisecracking persona, director **Jack Conway** wouldn't test her so she went over the top to Selznick and badgered him till she got the role. Both portrayals are classic.

1949: With only 40 pages completed on their script (and *that* innocuously mislabeled *A Can of Beans* to mislead prying executives who might pull the plug on their warts-and-all take on Hollywood), director **Billy Wilder** and producer **Charles Brackett** lunge into filming their last team-effort on this day: *Sunset Boulevard*. The start was a stumbling one because their star attraction (**Montgomery Clift**) fell out of the picture two weeks earlier, contending he couldn't convincingly play the love object of a woman 22 years older than he (**Gloria Swanson**)—even though, at the time, he was involved with a woman *20* years older than he ('20s torch singer **Libby Holman**, 48 to his 28). The *real* reason: Holman, believing the movie's older woman-younger man plot-angle was a crude parody of their private life, threatened suicide if he did the film. Frantically, Wilder began casting about for a replacement, pitching the part first to his *Double Indemnity* star (**Fred MacMurray**, who turned it down on moral grounds) and then to Broadway's original *Pal Joey* (**Gene Kelly**, who couldn't be freed from MGM). As a last resort, Wilder forced into the role a reluctant **William Holden**, who feared he couldn't deliver. He did, though, bounding out of his bland "Smiling Jim" role-rut and into the Oscar running for the first time in his career.

1957: *Hellcats of the Navy* splashes down at San Diego's Spreckles Theater on this day, with both stars attending. Not only was it the *first* screen-teaming of **Ronald Reagan** and **Nancy Davis**, it was also their *last* feature (although he *did* do a 1964 TV-movie remake of *The Killers* that was so violent it had to be released theatrically). Needless to add, the future President and First Lady never knew that the "Raymond T. Marcus" credited with the *Hellcats* script was the necessary *nom de plume* of **Bernard Gordon**, a screenwriter blacklisted because he didn't cooperate with the House Un-American Activities Committee.

FROM *HELL* TO WHITE HOUSE: Ronald Reagan and Nancy Davis in *Hellcats of the Navy*.
GUILLOTINING A JEWELL: Isabel Jewell and Ronald Colman in *A Tale of Two Cities*.
WELCOME TO THE DARK SIDE: William Holden and Gloria Swanson in *Sunset Boulevard*.

1932: *Grand Hotel* opens for business at New York City's Astor Theater on this day, and a genre is born: the all-star opus. **Garbo**, The Brothers **Barrymore** (**John** and **Lionel**), **Wallace Beery, Jean Hersholt, Lewis Stone** and the most treacherous scene-thief of them all, **Joan Crawford**, drew lavish praise—but nary a one of them copped an acting nomination. Fact is, the film mustered only *one* Oscar bid, but it was for Best Picture of 1931-1932--and it won!

1951: Oscar-winning Mrs. Miniver (**Greer Garson**) becomes American on this day.

1954: At the Pythian Temple Studio in NYC on this day, **Bill Haley and the Comets** record two songs for Decca— "Thirteen Women" and "(We're Gonna) Rock Around the Clock." Not only did the latter become Haley's all-time topper when it found itself at the beginning and end of *Blackboard Jungle* the following spring, it also became the first rock-and-roll song featured in a film.

1958: In response to the chief criticism of his most recent picture–i.e., that he looked too old to make *Love in the Afternoon* with **Audrey Hepburn**–an obliging **Gary Cooper** gives in to the inevitable on this day: a facelift. Reviewers and audiences alike gulped over the age-gap between these *Afternoon* lovers. Even she quipped (kidding on the square): "It would have made more sense for Gary Cooper to have played my father and **Maurice Chevalier** my lover." A sprightly 68, Chevalier ran rings around Cooper, a frazzled 56. Indeed, if writer-director **Billy Wilder** wasn't drenching Cooper in ravishing shadows, he was removing the lubricious twinkle in the Frenchman's eye. The latter had a lot to be happy about: This brought him back to movies big-time, giving him a second wind that kept him knee-deep in films his last decade.

1961: Director **Henry Koster** takes the helm of *Mr. Hobbs Takes a Vacation* on this day, replacing the ailing **Leo McCarey**, and signs up **Maureen O'Hara** for Mrs. Hobbs. Almost immediately, second thoughts set in, and he started casting around for a less fiery, more domesticated housewife–like, say, **Loretta Young, Lucille Ball, Olivia de Havilland, Ginger Rogers, Rosalind Russell, Polly Bergen**- but all of the above proved otherwise engaged, forcing Koster and producer **Jerry Wald** to crawl back to O'Hara and sweettalk her back aboard.

1961: "Theme from *A Summer Place*" earns **Percy Faith** a 1960 Grammy for Record of the Year on this day, but its composer, **Max Steiner,** loses the song-writer's award to **Ernest Gold** for another instrumental hit, "Theme from *Exodus*." Faith's recording was the rock era's most successful instrumental, but the Oscar nominators totally overlooked the tune for Best Song and Best Score.

CUTTING CLASS: Vic Morrow and Glenn Ford in *Blackboard Jungle*.
GRAND DAME: Joan Crawford, Wallace Beery and Lionel Barrymore in *Grand Hotel*.
A FULL-SERVICE LAIR: The Gypsies, Gary Cooper and Audrey Hepburn in *Love in the Afternoon*.

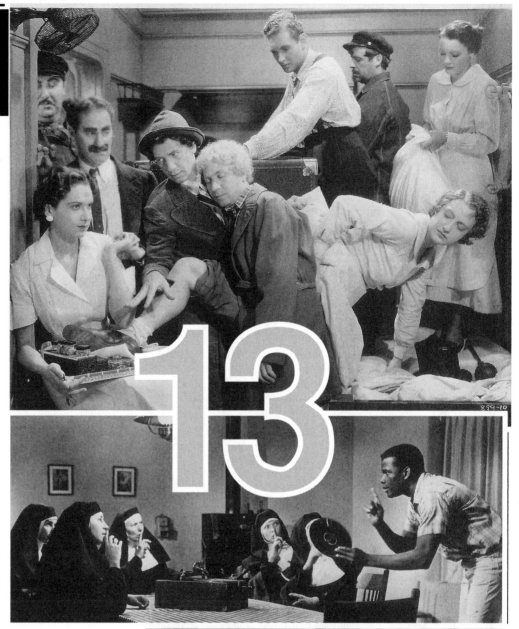

1935: A mini-tour in which **The Marx Brothers** try-out and fine-tune the jokes they'll film for *A Night at the Opera* starts on this day at Salt Lake City's Orpheum. The stateroom scene, which was considerably less than shipshape on stage, was included in the movie version only at **Irving Thalberg**'s insistence. Instinctual Irving was right again: It's the ultimate Marx Bros. sequence (but its architect, gagster **Al Boasberg**, inexplicably missed out on screen credit).

1952: Exploring "the new Hollywood" on this day, *See It Now* becomes the first TV program to do a feature on the making of a movie: *Hans Christian Andersen*.

1964: "It has been a long journey to this moment," says **Sidney Poitier**, the first black Oscar-winning Best Actor (for *Lilies of the Field*), on this day.

1975: A heart attack kills **Larry Parks**, 60, on this day—one day before cancer claims the actor who got the Oscar that had Parks' name on it: **Fredric March** (for 1946's *The Best Years of Our Lives*). Parks' bid, *The Jolson Story*—and its 1949 sequel, *Jolson Sings Again*—were the twin peaks in his career. His comet came through the backdoor of Columbia's B-movies, soared high with the **Al Jolson** bios and sank fast in the ugly glare of the House Un-American Activities Committee. As the first out of the chute before HUAC, Parks more or less did as he was asked and *literally* never worked in that town again—except as a real estater; his only films after that were made in England (1955's *Tiger by the Tail*) or Germany (1962's *Freud*). Columbia trotted out a 70mm-stereophonic sound print of *The Jolson Story* a few months after his death. A buffet supper at The Friars Club, which Jolson helped found, followed its Beverly Hills re-premiere; guests included two of its stars (**Evelyn Keyes** and **William Demarest**), its "lucky one-shot" producer (columnist **Sidney Skolsky**), Parks' widow (**Betty Garrett**) and their sons (**Garrett** and **Andrew**).

14

1934: Surrounding himself in his dingy flat with clippings, contracts and reviews from glory days not so long-gone, **Karl Dane** ends it all with a gun on this day. *The Big Parade* of 1925 brought him into MGM front-ranks, but the emerging talkies took him back. Dane's tangled Danish proved impenetrable, and, in the space of a single year, he slid from five of MGM's top 1930 flicks (*Navy Blues*, *Montana Moon*, *Free and Easy*, *The Big House*, *Billy the Kid*) to running a hot-dog stand near the studio entrance.

1948: A star is born as a direct consequence of **Betty Hutton** giving birth to a second daughter, **Lindsay Briskin**, on this day: Her pregancy prevented her from doing (on a loan-out from Paramount) *Romance on the High Seas* and forced Warners into film-debuting **Doris Day**. "It's Magic," as Doris would sing.

1960: The screen's first million-dollar performance hits NYC's Astor and Plaza theaters: **Marlon Brando**'s in *The Fugitive Kind*. It was worth less than that to his leading ladies: **Anna Magnani** wanted her lover-at-the-time (**Anthony Franciosa**) in the part, and **Joanne Woodward** later said, "After that picture, the only way I'd work with Marlon Brando is if he were in rear projection."

1969: It falls to **Ingrid Bergman** on this day to announce the first Oscar tie for Best Actress: a first Oscar to **Barbra Streisand** (for *Funny Lady*) and a third Oscar to **Katharine Hepburn** (for *The Lion in Winter*). During her lifetime, Bergman managed to match Hepburn's three Oscars and came close to a fourth with her final film performance (in 1978's *Autumn Sonata*). Hepburn knocked off the tie-breaking No. 4 (with 1981's *On Golden Pond*). These two were personal rivals as well, stemming from the fact that **Spencer Tracy** had gone from an affair/film with Bergman (*Dr. Jekyll and Mr. Hyde*) directly into an affair/film with Hepburn (*Woman of the Year*). Affair One soon faded, but Affair Two endured to the day of Tracy's death. Hepburn's only mention of Bergman in her autobiography, *Me*, was a bitchy two-line throwaway about *Dr. Jekyll and Mr. Hyde*: "Ingrid Bergman played the whore; she won an award, I think."

1986: On this day, about the same time **President Ronald Reagan** is ordering a deadly air strike against Libya, TBS-TV is airing his last outing as an actor–a particularly vicious crime czar in 1964's *The Killers*.

A FAST FALL FROM GLORY: Karl Dane.
A RILED REAGAN: Ronald Reagan and Angie Dickinson in *The Killers*.
THE FIRST MILLION-DOLLAR MAN AND SOME SMALLER CHANGE: Anna Magnani, Marlon Brando and Joanne Woodward in *The Fugitive Kind*.
THE FIRST DAY: Doris Day in *Romance on the High Seas*.

15

1950: Bitchiness is already in the air as cameras begin rolling on *All About Eve* on this day, on location at San Francisco's Curran Theater: **Bette Davis** learned from co-star (and future husband) **Gary Merrill** that on the flight to Frisco **Celeste Holm** was heard to wonder aloud what it would be like working with Diva Davis. Imagining malice in the remark, La Davis lay in wait for Holm, and one morning when the latter arrived on the set and chirped a cheery "Good morning" to her, The Star snapped back, "Oh, shit! Good manners." It was the last exchange to pass between the two when the cameras weren't turning, but, being pros, both mustered Oscar-nominated illusions of bosom buddies.

1957: Producer **Jerry Wald**, who talked **Joan Crawford** into playing the mother of a teenager (i.e., her Oscar-winning *Mildred Pierce*), has persuaded **Lana Turner**, 36, to bite the bullet and do the same in *Peyton Place*, reports **Louella O. Parsons** on this day. This "premature" motherhood (of an 18-year-old) got Turner her one shot at the Oscar. When she came home from the awards March 26–Oscarless but still dripping in diamonds–she was beaten by beau **Johnny Stompanato** for not asking him to escort her there. This abuse ended nine days later when her 14-year-old daughter, **Cheryl Christina Crane**, fatally stabbed Stompanato with a nine-inch butcher's knife as the couple quarreled. On April 11, six days short of a year from this original casting announcement, Turner found herself in identically the same position as her *Peyton Place* character: breaking down on the witness stand while testifying about a teenage girl driven to murder.

1980: "A fiery horse, with the speed of light and a cloud of dust, a hearty 'Hi-Yo, Silver'"–yep, The Lone Ranger rides again as cameras start turning on this day on *The Legend of The Lone Ranger*. Squandered on the title role was a total unknown trying to turn actor and doing so badly his dialogue had to be done over by **James Stacy**. He couldn't even sit a horse convincingly, and his deportment off-camera–nocturnal boozing and brawling–got him barred from local bars during the Santa Fe filming. So who, you might rightly ask, was that masked (and dubbed) man? For the record–**Klinton Spilsbury**, who, after this single shot at stardom, returned to his earlier, truer callings: fashion photography and modeling. He did a little of both–plus TV commercials in Europe. By the end of the decade, after some humbling hard-times, he resurfaced in Hollywood–resume in hand–and told the *Los Angeles Times* he'd been doing waiter work "even at a Subway sandwich place."

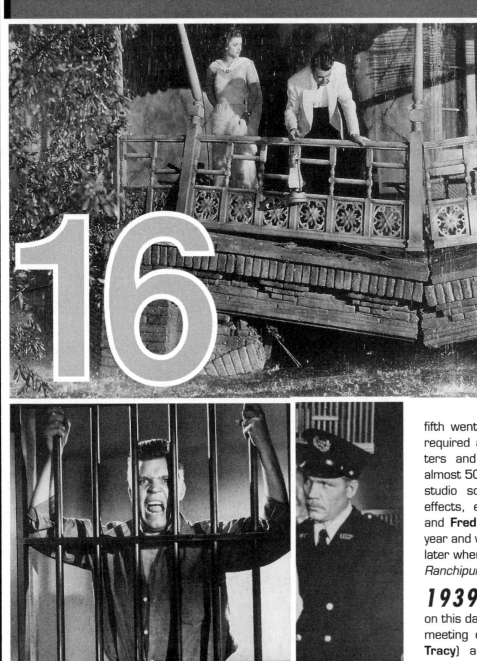

16

1932: Piano-hauling to **Billy Gilbert**'s hilltop home, **Stan Laurel** and **Oliver Hardy** put in three reels of their only Oscar-winning work (*The Music Box*, 1932's Best Live Action Comedy Short Subject), and it goes into general release on this day. Laurel always considered it the finest of their shorter films.

1939: *The Rains Came* commences production on this day, with **Tyrone Power** and **Myrna Loy** in roles originally intended for **Ronald Colman** and **Marlene Dietrich** and California's Balboa Park passing for a soggy, simulated India. A fifth of the film's $2.5-million budget went for sets that would be swept away, and another fifth went for flood and earthquake scenes which required a month's work from 350 grips, carpenters and assorted laborers. A tank containing almost 50,000 gallons of water was erected on the studio soundstage for the deluge. The special effects, executed by **E.H. Hansen** (photography) and **Fred Sersen** (sound), copped the Oscar that year and were good enough to be reprised 16 years later when the rains came again — as *The Rains of Ranchipur*.

1939: *Stanley and Livingstone* finishes filming on this day. The hardest scene was the momentous meeting of newsman Henry M. Stanley (**Spencer Tracy**) and lost African missionary Dr. David Livingstone (**Sir Cedric Hardwicke**). Tracy just couldn't, without cracking up, get out the line "Dr. Livingstone, I presume?" Far easier for him was an impassioned 640-word speech which he knocked off in a single take. This was Tracy's lone loan-out from MGM, and it got MGM **Tyrone Power** (for *Marie Antoinette*) in *his* lone loan-out from Fox. Scheduling prevented Power from appearing in *Stanley and Livingstone*, and the part went to **Richard Greene**.

1979: One full week from his Oscar glory for *The Deer Hunter*, director **Michael Cimino** today starts tailspinning into the *Heaven's Gate* filming.

1992: World War II's fourth most decorated soldier–who, like the first (**Audie Murphy**), went into movies–dies of emphysema on this day at age 71. Gun in hand, **Neville Brand** made his screen entrance in *D.O.A.*, the 1950 *film noir* classic, and spent most of the next 40 years behind bars or barbed wire (*Riot in Cell Block 11*, *Bird Man of Alcatraz*, *Stalag 17*).

THE WASHED, THE UNWASHED & THE HEAVILY WASHED: Myrna Loy and George Brent in *The Rains Came*.
BEHIND BARS & IN FRONT OF THEM: From left: Neville Brand in *Riot in Cell Block 11* and *Bird Man of Alcatraz*.
PRESUMING TOO MUCH: Spencer Tracy and Cedric Hardwicke in *Stanley and Livingstone*.

17

1942: Fresh from France and ready for wartime Hollywood films, **Jean-Pierre Aumont** gets tested on this day by one of Warners' in-house directors (**Vincent Sherman**) for the third corner of the *Casablanca* triangle, resistance fighter Victor Laszlo. Verdict: too young. **Philip Dorn** proved too busy (with *Random Harvest*) and **Joseph Cotten** too costly (to rent from **David O. Selznick**), so **Paul Henreid** had to be talked into the role. He'd turned it down initially, finding it patently absurd that an underground leader would parade around in a white tropical suit, chatting up Nazis. Only when Warners promised to beef up his part and billing (to equal that of **Bogart** and **Bergman**) did he change his mind.

1943: Producer **David O. Selznick** puts the word out on this day, via the gossip grapevine, that **Ingrid Bergman** would *not* be available for any *Casablanca* sequel. One such project *was* in the works, and (fleeting) thought was given to recasting **Geraldine Fitzgerald** as Ilsa before reason reigned: "Without Bergman, why bother?" The sequel, titled *Brazzaville*, never got beyond a ten-page outline which followed up the Free French work of Rick and Renault and returned Ilsa to their lives–in fresh, new, form-fitting "widow's weeds."

1951: On this day, **Arlene Dahl** weds **Lex Barker**, then writes a movie-mag piece about why their marriage will last. Well, it lasted till Oct. 15, 1953–to be specific. By then, **Lana Turner** had finished with **Fernando Lamas** so Dahl married him, while Turner tied the knot with Barker. You needed a scorecard.

1961: "I lost to a tracheotomy!" carps *The Apartment*'s Oscar-losing contender, **Shirley MacLaine**, on this day, referring to the sympathy vote that followed **Elizabeth Taylor**'s well-timed, life-saving operation. Liz's personal opinion of *Butterfield 8*, the film that won her Oscar No. One, was unprintable.

1970: Thanks to an honorary Ph.D. conferred during a filming break on this day by nearby Pima College in Tuscon, AZ, *Rio Lobo* now stars a **Dr. John Wayne**.

1980: Lunch at Lutece on this day leads to a 12-year union, on and off screen, for **Woody Allen** and his most-used actress, **Mia Farrow**. She needlepointed the date on a sampler that hung on his bedroom wall at least until Aug. 13, 1992, when their private life exploded into a public media-circus.

1991: On this day–two days after he begins shooting his *JFK* in Dallas' Dealey Plaza–director **Oliver Stone** gets the okay from Texas School Book Depository officials to shoot in its historic building. The hitch: He has to use the seventh floor to film the assassination scene, since the sixth (where **Lee Harvey Oswald** shot President **John Kennedy**) has been turned into a museum.

1938: *Four Daughters*, starring three **Lane** Sisters (**Priscilla**, **Rosemary** and **Lola**) and **Gale Page**, begins lensing on this day–an Oscar-nominated adaptation of **Fannie Hurst**'s short story, "Sister Act"–but it was the male among them who gave the film distinction: **John Garfield**, in an upstaging star-turn that earned him an Oscar nomination for "support." He was not the upcoming New York theater actor intended for the role: Written with **Van Heflin** in mind but offered to **Burgess Meredith** (who proved unavailable), the part nevertheless provided Garfield with an image for his whole career: Society's whipping boy.

1945: A Japanese machine gun on this day writes "–30–" to the life and career of foxhole correspondent **Ernie Pyle**, 44, who in daily newspaper dispatches from the trenches glorified the

"little man" winning World War II. At the time of his death, Hollywood was filming his story–*The Story of G.I. Joe*. **Fred Astaire**, of all people, was first choice to play Pyle, but the part went to **Burgess Meredith**, who managed a fair physical approximation of Pyle (thanks to the skimpiest wig ever prepared by Max Factor: only 2,000 hairs).

1946: As a milquetoasty milkman-turned-boxer–*The Kid from Brooklyn*, bowing on this day at New York's Astor–**Danny Kaye** goes the same route, virtually scene for scene, that **Harold Lloyd** did a decade earlier in *The Milky Way*. Among the new sightings Kaye encountered was the first ever on film of **Kay Thompson**, a vocal coach content behind the camera. Her only other film appearance 11 years later was more memorable than the milkmaid she played here: In *Funny Face*, she was a fashion editor patterned after **Diana Vreeland** right down to the buzz word "bizzazz." The movie introduced the term to the masses who, somewhere along the line, turned it into "pizzazz"–an improvement, ruled Vreeland. "I wish I had said 'pizzazz,'" she later told *Funny Face* scripter **Leonard Gershe**.

1966: "Heaven is small enough compensation for sitting through this atrocity, so studiously saccharine that one feels that one has tumbled into the hold of a tanker bringing molasses from the Caribbean," wrote critic **Stanley Kauffmann** of *The Sound of Music*, which, on this day, goes blithely on to win five Oscars (including Best Picture) and become the "All-Time Box Office Champion" from 1966 to 1972. The film's premiere gig at New York's Rivoli Theater ran an unprecedented 93 weeks, and its initial U.S. release lasted four-and-a-half years. It remains, Mr. Kauffmann, the most popular movie musical ever made.

A PRINCESS FOR REAL & FOR REEL: Grace Kelly wedding Prince Rainier; and whetting Alec Guinness (in *The Swan*).
TOO FREE WITH HIS FISTS: Bruce Cabot, Joanne Tree, and Paul Kelly in *Girls Under 21*.
RESUMING WAR'S HORRORS: Dennis Hopper, Martin Sheen and Frederic Forrest in *Apocalypse Now*.

1927: Screen tough-guy **Paul Kelly**, 27, goes into a faint on this day when charged with murdering stage hoofer **Ray Raymond**, 33, who died a few days after their drunken donnybrook over the latter's wife (actress **Dorothy Mackaye**, 28). Although the two men supposedly met and made up in the interim and the inquest ruled that the cause of death was kidney trouble and cerebral hemorrhage (induced by acute alcoholism, not fisticuffs), Kelly was convicted of manslaughter and sentenced to one to ten years in San Quentin, and Mackaye drew one to three in the same prison for conspiring to conceal facts about her husband's death. She organized a drama club there, did plays—one all-killer production toplined hammer murderess **Clara Phillips** and "jazz slayer" **Dorothy Ellington**—and dramatized her observations in 1932 as *Women in Prison*; Warners

filmed her play twice, once in 1933 as *Ladies They Talk About* with **Barbara Stanwyck** and **Lillian Roth** and again in 1942 as *Lady Gangster* with **Faye Emerson** and **Julie Bishop**. Model prisoners both, Mackaye was out in a year and Kelly in 25 months. Their marriage in 1931 lasted till her car-crash death in 1940. Kelly copped a Tony playing the hard-boiled general in 1947's *Command Decision* and scored another Broadway triumph as the alcoholic actor in 1950's *The Country Girl*—roles that went respectively to **Clark Gable** and **Bing Crosby** for the movie versions—but the screen kept him confined to key supporting roles (*The Roaring Twenties*, *Crossfire*, *The High and the Mighty*, *Ziegfeld Girl*, *Flying Tigers*); he even played the warden of the pen he did time in, **Clinton Duffy**, twice—in *Duffy of San Quentin* and its sequel, *The Steel Cage*.

1934: *Stand Up and Cheer* opens on this day at Radio City Music Hall, and that's just what audiences do for a pint-sized scene-stealer four days away from her sixth birthday. The picture proved to be little **Shirley Temple**'s breakthrough into The Big Time: 20th Century-Fox immediately signed her up for seven years, set her age back a year and braced for the big box office ahead.

1956: Prince Rainier III of Monaco weds **Grace Kelly** of MGM, and the pictures were ready in a week — picture, really: *The Swan* (where she weds Prince **Alec Guinness**) sailed serenely into Radio City Music Hall on April 26.

1977: Felled by a near-fatal heart attack exactly seven weeks earlier, **Martin Sheen** resumes filming *Apocalypse Now* on this day, returning to work to shoot his arrival by boat at the jungle compound. Waiting for him there were two brand-new horrors for the film's already-harried director, **Francis Coppola**, to contend with: a spaced-out **Dennis Hopper** and an obscenely obese **Marlon Brando**.

19

1940: The book that bumped **Margaret Mitchell**'s *Gone With the Wind* off the top of the bestseller lists–**Rachel Field**'s *All This, and Heaven Too*–finishes filming on this day. Warners braced for a similar reaction, but it didn't happen. "I'll tell you what was wrong with the picture–*Gone With the Wind* was wrong with it," confessed director **Anatole Litvak** from the comfortable vantage point of several decades of hindsight. "My picture was overproduced. You couldn't see the actors for the candelabra, and the whole thing became a victory for matter over mind. **Bette Davis** was the world's most expensively costumed governess."

1942: On this day, **Louella O. Parsons** falls for a fabrication from Warners Publicity and syndicates the myth verbatim that previewers of *The Gay Sisters* were so impressed with the guy **Geraldine Fitzgerald** and **Nancy Coleman** have their tug-of-war over that audiences now refer to him by his character's name–so, hereafter, **Bryant Fleming/Bryon Barr** will be known as **Gig Young**. "Those were the days," Young later cracked, "when you could say the name of the picture and not get a laugh." Other performers who changed names in mid-screen to the names of the characters they played include Dawn O'Day (**Anne Shirley** from *Anne of Green Gables*) and Justus E. McQueen (**L.Q. Jones** from *Battle Cry*).

1945: *The Horn Blows at Midnight*, a not-half-bad fantasy in which **Jack Benny** dreams he's an angel sent to earth to announce Doomsday with a blast from Gabriel's horn, sounds off at the Strand on this day, supplying him with years of undeserved self-deprecating humor on radio and TV. All it ended was his movie run, save for sometime cameos (*Gypsy*, *A Guide for the Married Man*, etc.).

1967: UPI issues a series of photographs on this day capturing the frantic state of **Judy Garland** as she enters the filmmaking fray for the final time to play the **Merman**esque monster star, Helen Lawson. After ten days of filming and nothing usable in the can, Fox fired her and hired **Susan Hayward**. The ejected, dejected Garland took her case to *Dolls* author **Jacqueline Susann** (who'd created her Neely O'Hara character out of Garland fact-and-fiction), complaining nobody at the studio returned her calls. "I'm a star, aren't I?"

1989: *Field of Dreams*, **Burt Lancaster**'s last theatrical feature, world-premieres on this day in Dubuque, IA. It permitted the seasoned screen veteran a poignant, almost mythic exit: As his character heads for the cornfield (and oblivion), shaking hands with the ballplayers along the way as he goes, the legendary Shoeless Joe Jackson yells after him, "Hey, rookie, you were good." The camera takes a last look at Lancaster, who then vanishes into the stalks.

END OF THE WORLD & BENNY: Alexis Smith, Jack Benny and Guy Kibbee in *The Horn Blows at Midnight*.
A *WINDY* **HEAVEN:** Charles Boyer and Bette Davis in *All This, and Heaven Too*.
EXITING VIA *VALLEY* **&** *FIELD:* From left: Judy Garland reporting for *Valley of the Dolls*, and Burt Lancaster filming *Field of Dreams*.

21

1916: *The Good Bad Man* (**Douglas Fairbanks**, playing a no-name Westerner known only as Passin' Through) becomes the first to, er, pass through the portals of "the temple of the motion picture" as New York's Rialto debuts.

1933: *Morning Glory* starts to flower as a film, one of the few shot in the same sequence as its script. The only setback: **Mary Pickford** and **Douglas Fairbanks Sr.** visiting the set the day **Doug Jr.** and **Katharine Hepburn** did the balcony scene in *Romeo and Juliet* in costume — it rattled the actors so much the scene was cut from the finished film and exists now only as stills.

1937: *A Star Is Born* opens where it actually ends: at Grauman's Chinese. This mother-lode of Tinseltown folklore was itself based on film (1932's *What Price Hollywood?*) as well as fact (the sad marital seesaw of fading **John Gilbert** and rising **Virginia Bruce**). When **John Barrymore** proved to be too busy *living* the part of a boozed-up, washed-out movie star to play one by the name of Norman Maine, **Fredric March** wound up with the Maine chance and made the most of it. **Janet Gaynor** nosed **Elisabeth Bergner** and **Margaret Sullavan** out of the title role, and both leads landed Oscar bids—as did **James Mason** and **Judy Garland** in the same roles 17 years later; **Kris Kristofferson** and **Barbra Streisand** went unnominated for the '76 remake, but Babs was Oscared for composing (to **Paul Williams**' lyrics) the year's Best Song: "Evergreen."

1941: You can scratch **Thomas Mitchell** as "Mr. Scratch": A buggy spill on this day during the filming of *The Devil and Daniel Webster* left him with a concussion, forcing him to relinquish this devilishly good role to **Walter Huston** (who made the Oscar running with it).

1952: The King (**Clark Gable**) and his fourth queen, the titled **Lady Sylvia Ashley**—and the widow of **Douglas Fairbanks Sr.**—divorce on this day.

1955: **Samuel Goldwyn** outbids his former business partner, **Mary Pickford**, and acquires the old United Artists studio.

MRS. NORMAN MAINE ARRIVES AT GRAUMAN'S CHINESE: May Robson, Andy Devine, Janet Gaynor and Adolphe Menjou in 1937's *A Star Is Born*.
MULTIPLE BIRTHS: From top: Lowell Sherman and Constance Bennett in 1932's *What Price Hollywood?*; James Mason and Judy Garland in 1954's *A Star Is Born*, and Kris Kristofferson and Barbra Streisand in 1976's *A Star Is Born*.

1938: An idyllic *Holiday* comes to the end of filming. At the wrap party, director **George Cukor** surprised his star, **Katharine Hepburn**, by showing the screen test that had won her *A Bill of Divorcement* and a contract with RKO Radio: It was a scene from *Holiday*. She had understudied **Hope Williams** in the original Broadway production and was still doing theater when the 1930 movie version came out starring **Ann Harding**. Happily, Columbia kingpin **Harry Cohn** agreed to a remake only eight years later; happier still, the results pleased the playwright, **Philip Barry**, so much he tossed Hepburn a couple of career-restoring life-savers just when she needed them most—*The Philadelphia Story* and *Without Love*—both of which she did to great effect on stage and screen.

1947: A pregnant **Bette Davis** receives from one of her favorite producers (**Henry Blake**) a script of *The African Queen* and the promise of **James Mason** for co-star. She had rejected the project in 1938 when it was first proposed to her with **David Niven**—mainly because of the arduous location-shooting required. That factor (compounded by the birth of her **Barbara Davis Sherry** nine days later) scuttled this new endeavor. Eventually, she came to realize the role would be worth the physical sacrifice and actively sought it before and after she left Warners—but, by that late date (1949), **Katharine Hepburn**'s antenna had shot up, and she was already doggedly on the case.

1952: Throwing himself "on the mercy of the court," **Walter Wanger** draws a four-month sentence at Castaic Honor Farm for shooting an agent (**Jennings Lang**) he thought was having an affair with the then-Mrs. Wanger (**Joan Bennett**). He emerged from behind bars Sept. 5, 1952—98 days into the sentence—with a clear idea of what to produce next: *Riot in Cell Block 11*.

1991: The 31-year-old *Spartacus* charges back into the marketplace on this day, restored to its original glory. Title player **Kirk Douglas**, on the mend from a helicopter crash, was conspicuously missing from its national launching the night before at New York's Ziegfeld Theater, but co-stars **Jean Simmons** and **Tony Curtis** gave the occasion sufficient glitter. Although much was made at the time of the film's original release that its script was the work of the no-longer-blacklisted **Dalton Trumbo**, this second-coming gala brought the news that **Charles Laughton** wouldn't utter the lines assigned him and his scenes with **Peter Ustinov** were rewritten by Ustinov, who gave himself enough witty asides (or ad-libbed them on the spot) to win a supporting Oscar.

ANOTHER NUN'S STORY: Julie Andrews and a nun escort in *The Sound of Music*.
A CLAIR CASE: Raymond Cordy in *A Nous la Liberta*.
A PROTESTING POP: James Stewart, Sandra Dee and Philippe Forquet in *Take Her, She's Mine*.

1937: Filmes Sonores Tobis, a French film company, files a plagiarism suit on this day, claiming **Charles Chaplin** stole his *Modern Times* conveyor-belt scene from another classic machine-age spoof, **Rene Clair**'s 1931 *A Nous la Liberte*. Clair declared he was flattered, if such were the case, since he'd borrowed plenty from Chaplin. Given that attitude, the suit was sheepishly withdrawn.

1941: On this day, **Shirley Temple** enters her teens–unexpectedly. She woke up believing this was her 12th birthday, but her mother informed her otherwise: A year was shaved off her true age in 1933 when Temple was signed up by Fox.

1944: Filming on *I'll Be Seeing You* is put on hold for an hour on this day so producer **David O. Selznick** can throw a sweet-16 birthday party for contractee **Shirley Temple** on the *Since You Went Away* set that she previously inhabited. The whole bash set big-spender Selznick back $46.11 (cake, $24; five gallons of vanilla ice cream, $17.50; three boxes of candy, $4.61). Temple's loot included roses (cast and crew), a silver bracelet (Selznick) and gag gifts from her current co-stars, **Ginger Rogers** and **Joseph Cotten**. A beau gave her a fake newspaper, headlined "Shirley Temple Will Be 65 in 1993." (She was, too.)

1963: After a nine-month shutdown necessitated by the bankrupting woes of *Cleopatra*, 20th Century-Fox gets back into production on this day. First film before the camera: *Take Her, She's Mine* with **James Stewart** and **Sandra Dee**.

1964: Some 600 Salzburg extras fill Mondsee Cathedral on this day to watch **Christopher Plummer** and **Julie Andrews** wed in *The Sound of Music*. The romantic spell had some spillage off-camera as well. **Dan Truhitte**, the film's Rolf (the telegram boy smitten with Liesl) met **Gabriele Henning** standing-in for Liesl on that day, and they embarked on a 20-year marriage. The feeling of kismet was hard to resist, Truhitte admitted: "Gabriele's parents were named Liesl and Rolf."

1964: Inspector Jacques Clouseau, the screen's second most successful serial sleuth (after 007) gets down to comedy cases on this day as *The Pink Panther* prowls into Radio City Music Hall. **Peter Ustinov** was set to play the bumbling French bloodhound but bowed out (because **Ava Gardner** wasn't cast opposite him, reportedly), and **Peter Sellers** bowed in–with **Capucine**.

1986: Composer **Harold Arlen**, 81, dies in his Manhattan apartment on this day. He won a 1939 Oscar for "Over the Rainbow," but his bumper crop of evergreens came in 1943 when three were nominated ("That Old Black Magic," "Happiness Is a Thing Called Joe" and "My Shining Hour"), two weren't ("One for My Baby" and "Hit the Road to Dreamland")–and he *still* lost, to "You'll Never Know."

A VIRAL "FREAK-OUT": Margot Kidder in *Superman*.
HARDLY A PARTY: Tom Hanks in *The Bonfire of the Vanities*.
A FALL FROM LOVE'S PERCH: Lana Turner in *Ziegfeld Girl*.

1941: *Ziegfeld Girl* opens at New York's Capitol on this day, and **Lana Turner** is heard to wonder: "Why can't the men you want have the things you want?" The story of her life! At the time, her marriage to **Artie Shaw** was falling apart, and she would go back to the altar seven more times. Her co-star in *Love Finds Andy Hardy*, **Mickey Rooney**, equaled her eight-is-enough marital record—as did, more recently, Mick's *National Velvet*, **Elizabeth Taylor**. When her biography came out in 1982, Turner was claiming celibacy since 1969.

1991: *The Bonfire of the Vanities*, the **Tom Wolfe** bestseller which cost Warner Bros. $5 million (the most ever paid for the film rights to a novel)—only to be miserably miscast and botched badly by director **Brian De Palma**, goes to video on this day at the height of the Gulf War. If we run out of ammo in the Persian Gulf, suggested **Billy Crystal**, we can drop videocassettes of *Vanities*.

1996: Disheveled, disoriented, missing her dental work and wearing dirty clothes she got from a vagrant, **Margot Kidder** on this day emerges from a Glendale woodpile and what she later called "the most public freak-out in history." The thing that had pushed her manic-depressive buttons was a computer virus which caused her laptop to swallow three years of work on her autobiography. (The book was called, correctly, *Calamities*.) When a data retrieval company said her files were unsalvageable, "that's when I went from really distressed to absolute delusion." Paranoia set in, and she spent four dark days trying to out-run it before she was found. A computer whiz recovered much of the missing material while Kidder was in therapy, herself recovering.

1997: Two 89-year-old Hollywood luminaries—**Julius J. Epstein** and the widow of **Robert Riskin** (a.k.a. **Fay Wray**)—charge Washington's Capitol Hill on this day to lobby for a change in the copyright laws to give older screenwriters a portion of the payments for replaying their movies. Epstein and his twin brother, **Philip**, and **Howard Koch** each received $15,208 (and later the Oscar) for writing *Casablanca*—and not a dime more for a picture that has practically been in perpetual replay ever since. Riskin, who was writing *his* Oscar-winning ticket (*It Happened One Night*) while his wife was filming *King Kong*, had a stroke in 1950 and spent his final five years in the Motion Picture Country Home. The pair came to Washington to "put a human face" on a copyright bill which Congress was considering that would extend payments to copyright holders for 20 years to bring American law into line with European copyright law.

1939: On this day—exactly seven weeks after getting fired from *Gone With the Wind*—**George Cukor** begins *The Women*. The ultimate "woman's director" corralled the largest all-female cast ever assembled for a single film (true to its ads: "135 women with men on their minds"). Even the animals used in the opening credits to suggest each character's true analogous natures were female: fawn (**Norma Shearer**), leopard (**Joan Crawford**), panther (**Rosalind Russell**), chimpanzee (**Mary Boland**), fox (**Paulette Goddard**), lamb (**Joan Fontaine**), owl (**Lucile Watson**), doe (**Virginia Weidler**), cow (**Phyllis Povah**) and donkey (**Marjorie Main**). When not directing/refereeing *The Women*, Cukor kept coaching **Vivien Leigh** and **Olivia de Havilland** on the Q.T. in their *GWTW* roles.

1940: With the arrival of *Strange Cargo* at New York's Capitol on this day, the *on*-cameras amours of **Clark Gable** and **Joan Crawford** officially end with this, their eighth romantic pairing in as many years.

1953: America dons 3-D glasses to see the special in-your-face horrors of *House of Wax*, which goes into national release on this day. Ironically in charge of this first (and best) three-dimensional thriller was **Andre de Toth**, a one-eyed director who physically couldn't appreciate the film's visual effects.

1955: At three in the morning on this day, **Susan Hayward** comes across a line on page 61 of a script she's studying that saves her life—an exchange in *I'll Cry Tomorrow* in which **Lillian Roth**'s mother frets about her daughter's boozing and is told by the singer: "Relax, Max. I'll always be able to support you." Hayward circled the line in red and phoned her own mother, informing her groggily, "Don't worry, Mother, you'll be taken care of." Deducing her daughter was OD-ing on sleeping pills, **Ellen Marrener** phoned LAPD who got the actress to a stomach pump in time. Hayward left Cedars of Lebanon three days later and started the movie on schedule, delivering one of her best performances.

1972: "Dear World: I am leaving because I am bored. I am leaving you with your worries in this sweet cesspool," writes **George Sanders**, 65, on this day, just before downing five vials of Nembutal in a Barcelona hotel room. It hardly seemed like a boring life. Two of his four wives were **Gabor**s, **Zsa Zsa** *and* **Magda**, and he still found time to walk his brittle, urbane demeanor through 111 pictures — from 1934's *Life, Love and Laughter* to 1972's *Psychomania*. His lasting image is his Oscar-winning one: the acerbic theater critic in 1950's *All About Eve*, Addison De Witt--an instant archetype, that.

EIGHT WAS ENOUGH: Clark Gable and Joan Crawford in *Strange Cargo*.
WHO'S FAKING THE SENSATION?: Vincent Price, Phyllis Kirk, and Andre de Toth promoting the 3-D *House of Wax*.
BRIGHT LIGHTS, DARK DAY: George Sanders and Susan Hayward in *I Can Get It for You Wholesale*.

26

1924: Employees from three different movie companies gather on the lawn outside Goldwyn Studios at Culver City on this day, joining hands–and hyphens–to inaugurate Metro-Goldwyn-Mayer. "If there is one thing I insist upon, it is quality," promised/threatened the first vice president, **Louis B. Mayer**, seconding that motion with something in Latin: *Ars Gratia Artis* ("Art for Art's Sake"), the new company's motto which would adorn every MGM movie.

1940: *Forty Little Mothers* is released on this day, with a brief glimpse of things to come: During filming, the star (**Eddie Cantor**) blew his celebrated stack when a bit player (**Constance Keane**) upstaged him by letting her long, blonde tresses drop and droop over her right eye. The actress changed her name but not her hair style for her next picture, *I Wanted Wings*, and–*voila!* **Veronica Lake**'s "peekaboo" hairdo became a staple of war-years fashion (as well as a working hazard for female factory-workers emulating the Lake look.)

1986: The stars of Oscar-winning Best Pictures two decades apart die on this day: **Bessie Love**, 87, of 1929's *The Broadway Melody* and **Broderick Crawford**, 74, of 1949's *All the King's Men*–she in London, he in Rancho Mirage, CA.

1986: The **Kennedy** clan gathers on this day at Hyannis to watch one of their number–**JFK**'s niece, **Maria Shriver**–wed a Republican: **Arnold Schwarzenegger**.

1989: A Lucy to love, **Lucille Ball**, dies on this day.

1995: The headline occupying all six columns of the obituary page in *The New York Times* on this day says it all: "**Ginger Rogers**, Who Danced With **Astaire** and Won an Oscar for Drama, Dies at 83." The night that the versatile performer copped her Academy Award for the songless *Kitty Foyle*–Feb. 27, 1941–her dancing partner wired her a single word of congratulations: *"OUCH!"*

THE GREAT LEVELER: From left: Top-hatted Bessie Love (with Mary Doran, Anita Page and Charles King) in *The Broadway Melody* and Broderick Crawford (with Mercedes McCambridge) in *All the King's Men*.
STAGE DOOR ALUMS: Lucille Ball and Ginger Rogers.
NOT KEEN ON KEANE: Bonita Granville, Martha O'Driscoll, Eddie Cantor, Baby Quintanilla, Charlotte Munier and Louise Seidel in *Forty Little Mothers*.

27

1934: Fast-filming director **W.S. Van Dyke** (a.k.a. "One Take Woody") strikes again on this day, finishing his finest flick in 16 days flat! He, *The Thin Man* and the actor most people take for the title character (**William Powell**) all made the Oscar running that year for time well-spent. The movie domesticated the detective genre, giving it a much-needed second wind, and the quality of amiable matrimony Powell and **Myrna Loy** projected as Nick and Nora Charles--between equal measures of smooching and sleuthing--was one of the merriest in movies. They kept this up for five sequels and 13 years. **Edward Ellis** did *not* make the additional romps. *He* had the title role--an inventor pursued by the Charleses--and he didn't live through Installment One.

1950: Unceremoniously, **Louis B. Mayer** cans **Frank Sinatra** on this day over a crack Sinatra made in the studio commissary about the mogul and his mistress-of-the-moment. On hearing that Mayer was in a total body cast after falling off a horse, Sinatra shot back, "Naw, he fell off **Ginny Simms**." Mayer was not amused. In fact, said Sinatra, "He has no sense of humor."

1954: "My mother-in-law and I are very friendly. She is letting me stay at her place until I can rent suitable quarters," **Rod Cameron** tells AP on this day by way of announcing that his marriage to **Angela Alves Lico** is over. In seven years' time, this living arrangement had solidified to such an extent that Cameron eloped with **Dorothy Alves Lico**, but they kept it quiet for a year. "It happened some time ago," reported her daughter, the first Mrs. Cameron. "I talk to my mother occasionally, but we never discuss Rod."

1996: The 25th anniversary "director's cut" of *The Last Picture Show* has its U.S. theatrical premiere on this day at NYC's Angelika 57. "[Director **Peter**] Bogdanovich improves on perfection!" opted the *New York Post*'s **Larry Worth**, noting seven new R-rated minutes (mostly, some pooltable sex-play between **Clu Gulager** and **Cybill Shepherd**). The revival gained something else, too--poignancy from the passing, 19 days earlier, of **Ben Johnson**, who served as its Sam the Lion, the poolhall and movie "palace" proprietor. It was a part which he repeatedly declined--and only did when the cuss words were cut--but one, he later allowed, that "changed my life. Everybody thought I knew something after I won that old Oscar. All of them wanted to give me a new job and more money."

1996: The stars of 1990's *State of Grace*--**Sean Penn**, 35, and **Robin Wright**, 29--achieve some on this day, wedding after eight years of turbulent togetherness and two children (**Dylan**, 5, and **Hopper**, 2).

SAM THE LION AND HIS CUBS: Ben Johnson and the Bottom brothers, Timothy and Sam, in *The Last Picture Show*.
STATE OF THEIR UNION: Robin Wright and Sean Penn in *State of Grace*.
HIS FILMS WERE NUMBERED: Edward Ellis and Natalie Moorhead in *The Thin Man*.

1937: At Warner's Beverly Hills Theater on this day, previewers got their first peek at *Kid Galahad*, a sandy-headed bellhop-turned-prizefighter played by **Wayne Morris** (who got only $66 a week, for a total of $396, for his best-known, star-making performance). The real battling occurred behind the scenes between the higher priced help: a $50,000 **Edward G. Robinson** vs. a $18,400 **Bette Davis**. When Davis started weeping copious tears all over his big death scene, Robinson stopped the action and asked director **Michael Curtiz**, "Don't you think Bette is crying too much?" Years later, in his autobiographical *All My Yesterdays*, Robinson wrote: "Miss Davis was, and is, every inch a lady–polite, mannerly, gracious, even self-effacing–but, by today's standards, she could never have gotten a job in a high school production of *East Lynne*. I know it's goatish of me to say it, but Miss Davis was, when I played with her, not a very gifted amateur and employed any number of jarring mannerisms that she used to form an image. In her early period, Miss Davis played the image, and not herself, and certainly not the character provided by the author."

1939: On this day, **Bette Davis** informs **Jack L. Warner** that she will not do *The Private Lives of Elizabeth and Essex* (then called, terribly, *The Knight and the Lady*) unless she is assured top billing over **Errol Flynn**. (Come to that, she'd prefer **Laurence Olivier** do Essex.) Good Queen-of-the-Lot Bette got her way on billing, and, years later, watching the film on TV, she came to the better-late-than-never conclusion Flynn wasn't such a shabby Essex after all.

1946: *It's a Wonderful Life* pauses in filming on this day to celebrate a crotchety life: **Lionel Barrymore** turned 68 on the set, playing the villain of the piece, Old Man Potter–the closest he ever came to a screen Scrooge (his traditional Yuletide radio role). To disinfect Barrymore's long-standing image of a lovable curmudgeon, director **Frank Capra** ordered him made up like **Grant Wood**'s "American Gothic," and the trick must have worked: Potter was one of a precious few film heavies from that Production Code-restricted period to pull off a crime (i.e., stealing **James Stewart**'s $8,000) and go unpunished–a fretful fact that drew more mail from viewers than anything else in the movie.

1956: On this day, after a whirlwind courtship, **Peggy Lee** weds the second of her four husbands, actor **Dewey Martin**. "I don't want to go into the problems of that marriage," she said later about their subsequently stormy union, "but I will say my doctor told me I should either get a divorce or a crash helmet."

28

1935: Filmdom's top tap star, **Eleanor Powell**, hits her big-time stride on this day as *Broadway Melody of 1936* goes into production. Her dance partners in the "Sing Before Breakfast" number– **Buddy Ebsen** and sis **Vilma**–made double debuts.

1937: **Louis B. Mayer** practically does a leaflet drop on New York's Capitol, disowning the MGM movie arriving there today (*Night Must Fall*, based on **Emlyn Williams**' stage thriller about a literal lady-killer)–but critics drown him out with high praise. In fact, **Robert Montgomery**'s uncanny carbon-copy of Williams' stage performance and **Dame May Whitty**'s screen reprise of her own got Oscar-nominated.

1976: An on-set union craftsman who in January of 1972 turned actor for a day becomes, on this day, the first actor to be federally prosecuted for his work (**Lenny Bruce** was prosecuted in a local court). Herbert Streicher–a.k.a. **Harry Reems**, the star of *Deep Throat*–relinquished all further rights to that Miami-made movie for the $100 he was paid for that day's work as "Dr. Young," but two and a half years later–when he was performing with the National Shakespeare Company in New York–he was arrested and extradited to Memphis where a 12-week, $4-million trial found him and 10 others guilty of "national conspiracy to transport interstate an obscene motion picture." A year later, all charges of obscenity were dropped against the accused by the new U.S. District Attorney in Memphis, **Mike Cody**, when Federal Judge **Harry Wellford** ordered a new trial based on "a shift in obscenity standards."

1992: On this day dies **Mae Clarke**, 81, remembered for the 15 seconds of fame that kept her typecast. In *The Public Enemy*, she caught a faceful of grapefruit from **James Cagney** who, after the thrust and the squash, gave it a deft, contemptuous twist. "This was, and remains," in the view of critic **Bosley Crowther**, "one of the cruelest, most startling acts ever committed on film–not because it is especially painful (except to the woman's smidge of pride), but because it shows such a hideous debasement of regard for another human being." Most of the men behind the scenes of this film lined up to claim responsibility for this monstrous "bit of business": producer **Darryl F. Zanuck** contended he thought it up in a story conference; scripters **John Bright** and **Kubec Glasmon** cited the omelet antic that an actual petty-gangster named **Hymie Weiss** pulled on his girlfriend, and director **William A. Wellman** confessed to harboring such thoughts about his wife at breakfast–but it was Clarke who, ultimately, took the fall. Cagney had it tough, too: He gave up dining out because some joker would always have a complimentary half-grapefruit sent over to the actor's table as a gag.

WHAT WOULD EMLYN DO?: Dame May Whitty, Rosalind Russell and Robert Montgomery in *Night Must Fall*. A MORNING MASSAGE: Mae Clarke and James Cagney in *The Public Enemy*.
A MORNING DANCE: Vilma Ebsen, Eleanor Powell and Buddy Ebsen in *Broadway Melody of 1936*.

30

PULL TOGETHER

1927: The first official cement signing-in ceremony at Grauman's Chinese occurs on this day. Fittingly, founder **Sid Grauman** kicked off the custom with the royal couple of Hollywood–**Mary Pickford** and **Douglas Fairbanks**–dunking their paws in the gray goo of his theater forecourt. **Norma Talmadge** soon followed suit so three different sets of star prints were on view when the theater lifted off May 18, 1927, with its premiere of *The King of Kings*. The concept of such quirky immortalization came to Grauman on April 15, 1927, when he had the three stars over to his theater construction site and Talmadge accidentally alighted from her automobile into the wet cement of the curb. Grauman saw the handwriting in the cement instantly and joined the trio in putting the idea to a concrete test; alas, their impressions were so faint there had to be retakes. Grauman's chief cement mason, **Jean Klossner**, whipped up some cement from his own special personal formula (as closely guarded as Coca-Cola's), and a tradition was born. Pickford was only too happy to be Grauman's first cemented celebrity because his father, **D.J. Grauman**, had been the first to spell out "America's Sweetheart" in electric lights when her *Tess of the Storm Country* played his movie theater in San Francisco in 1914.

1940: Via inter-office communication on this day, **Hal B. Wallis** tells director **Lloyd Bacon** the locker-room pep-talks **Pat O'Brien** is delivering with gung-ho gusto in *Knute Rockne — All American* have to be brought down a notch or two.

1942: The door-slamming commotion accompanying the opening of *Twin Beds* on this day obscures the screen reunion of two old adversarial co-stars — Almira Gulch (**Margaret Hamilton**) and Toto (**Terry** the terrier) — and at the same site (New York's Capitol Theater) as their first famous encounter (*The Wizard of Oz*).

1948: *State of the Union* goes into general release on this day, the most unplanned and unexpected of all **Spencer Tracy-Katharine Hepburn** pairings. Hepburn, who'd rejected **Howard Lindsay** and **Russel Crouse**'s Pulitzer Prize-winner as a Broadway vehicle, was helping Tracy with his lines for the movie version when–three days before shooting began–director **Frank Capra** asked her to step in for **Claudette Colbert**. It seems, on the Friday before the Monday start, the aging Colbert informed Capra her doctor and her agent (read: her husband and her brother) didn't want her filming after five o'clock. Feeling vaguely held up, Capra contacted Tracy, who brought Hepburn along to the first day of filming (in her own clothes, until a wardrobe could be created), and the picture stayed on schedule. Colbert and Capra, who had won Oscars for *It Happened One Night* 14 years before, didn't speak again for 34 years–till he personally asked her to appear in his 1982 American Film Institute salute.

RAH RAH *SOTTO VOCE*: George Reeves and Pat O'Brien in *Knute Rockne — All American*.
KATE CAME LATE: Spencer Tracy and Katharine Hepburn in *State of the Union*.

1946: His first day on a movie soundstage, **Burt Lancaster** comes out swinging, literally, filming "The Swede's" last boxing bout in *The Killers*.

1948: *A Letter to Four Wives*, the script **Joseph L. Mankiewicz** has made of a **John Klempner** novel called *A Letter to Five Wives*, comes under the editing-conscious scrutiny of **Darryl F. Zanuck**, who, in a memo to Mankiewicz on this day, pinpoints the problem precisely. The problem, as Zanuck saw it, was with Martha and Roger: "They have no real problem"–or, if they did, certainly one that paled in comparison to those of the other couples. Zanuck suggested shelving the whole sequence so whatever conflict an ex-President's daughter might have had and whatever nuance **Anne Baxter** could have brought to it flew out the window. Upshot: *A Letter to Three Wives* won two Oscars for Mankiewicz (one for 1949's Best Screenplay and the other for Best Director).

1959: **Eleanor Powell** observes hubby **Glenn Ford**'s 43d birthday by filing for divorce, demanding $3,000 a month alimony and custody of their son.

1967: **Elvis Presley** and **Priscilla Beaulieu** wed at the Aladdin Hotel in Las Vegas. Nine months-to-the-day later, daughter **Lisa Marie** is born.

1974: *The Lords of Flatbush*, a nostalgic comedy about the leather-jacketed Brooklyn teenagers of 1957, swaggers into Manhattan's Baronet on this day, foreshadowing good things ahead for two of its title players: The one who assisted on the script was two years away from *Rocky* (**Sylvester Stallone**), and the one playing "Butchey" was really doing a dry-run of his soon-to-be-famous "Fonzie," a character he was preparing for TV's *Happy Days* (**Henry Winkler**).

1995: A clash of **Kevin**s who had worked profitably and compatibly on *Robin Hood: Prince of Thieves* (producer-star **Costner** vs. director **Reynolds**) erupts with some fire and finality on this day. Their Waterloo? *Waterworld*. When Costner took over the editing, Reynolds took off, grumbling "In the future, Costner should only appear in pictures he directs himself. That way, he can always be working with his favorite actor and his favorite director."

1997: Sweden's second-most significant filmmaker (after **Ingmar Bergman**) dies on this day in Angelholm, Sweden, after a long illness: **Bo Widerberg**, 66. *Elvira Madigan*, a romantic tragedy bathed in Mozart's Piano Concerto No. 21 and lyrical shampoo-commercial photography, put him on the moviemaking map in 1967 (if not in the Oscar running for Best Foreign Language Film–this, he made for 1996's *All Things Fair*, 1969's *Adalen '31* and 1964's *Raven's End*). The latter, about Sweden's urban poor in the 1930s, was named The Best Swedish Movie Ever Made in a 1995 poll conducted by a Stockholm arts publication.

FOUR FRIENDS: Sylvester Stallone, Perry King, Paul Mace and Henry Winkler in *The Lords of Flatbush*.
THREE WIVES: Ann Sothern, Linda Darnell and Jeanne Crain in *A Letter to Three Wives*.
TWO LOVERS: Pia Degermark and Thommy Berggren in *Elvira Madigan*.

1926: Tomorrow's Superstar comes on as Saturday's Hero on this day as *Brown of Harvard* charges into NYC's Capitol. Morrison of USC–a randy freshman later named **John Wayne**–racked up a secret screen debut by doubling for **Francis X. Bushman Jr.** in a touchdown run. *Brown* of the title was **William Haines**, one of the first cinema stars to fall from studio favor for being gay.

1938: On this day, shooting starts on *Suez*, a $2,000,000 "courtship" for **Tyrone Power** (as canal architect Ferdinand de Lesseps) and **Annabella** (as his fictional dalliance). The course of true love never runs smoothly, but theirs ran smack into a spectacular sandstorm. Real sand was not used–it would have cut the skin off the cast–so ground cereal was thrown in front of 24 plane prop fans manned by **Lou Witte** and **Fred Sersen**, the two who had torched 1937's *In Old Chicago*. Man-made Mother Nature gave both stars a going-over, and, at one point, Annabella was flown like a kite, a wire her only contact with Earth. Two months into the shoot, Power proposed marrying–and they did April 23, 1939. The divorce came almost a decade after their first meeting–on Jan. 26, 1948.

1946: *The Postman Always Rings Twice,* bowing on this day at New York's Capitol, finds **Lana Turner** convincingly vamping out a deadly adulteress in white-hot get-ups. These clashed with **Joel McCrea**'s white-hat image so he declined being her partner-in-crime, saying it would smutty-up his good-guy rep. **Cameron Mitchell**, on the basis of a terrific test, seemed the most likely to succeed–till **John Garfield** got invalidated out of the service and into Turner's arms. Their subsequent sparks were memorable.

1960: With **Marlon Brando** and **Shirley MacLaine** standing vigil outside San Quentin protesting his execution, convicted rapist **Caryl Chessman** walks The Last Mile to the gas chamber on this day–a one-way trip he'd spent years legally avoiding. During his long wait, he wrote several books and even witnessed a B-grade, as-far-as-it-goes film biography (1955's *Cell 2455, Death Row,* starring **William Campbell**). Brando lobbied to do another: When he first sat down with the designated director of *Mutiny on the Bounty,* **Sir Carol Reed**, he seriously suggested they mutiny and, instead, do Chessman's life.

1999: "I think he probably went the way he would have wished," says **Glenda Jackson** of her hell-raising co-star in *The Devils* and *Women in Love,* **Oliver Reed**, 61, who dies of a heart attack on this day shortly after collapsing in a bar in Valetta. He was on the Mediterranean island of Malta filming *The Gladiators* for director **Ridley Scott**. His best-known role was the brutish Bill Sikes in the *Oliver!* musical directed by his Oscar-winning uncle, **Sir Carol Reed**.

ROUNDING OFF A TRIANGLE: Cecil Kellaway, John Garfield and Lana Turner in *The Postman Always Rings Twice.*
LOVE & SAND: Annabella and Tyrone Power in *Suez.*
REQUIEM FOR A ROWDY: Olivier Reed and Glenda Jackson in *Women in Love.*

DOOLEY DOOD IT: Humphrey Bogart and Dooley Wilson in *Casablanca*.
STANLEY STEALER: Marilyn Monroe and Don Murray in *Bus Stop*.
DOE IN THE FREEZER: Barbara Stanwyck and Gary Cooper in *Meet John Doe*.

1938: In a trade-ad diatribe on this day, Independent Theater Owners of America president **Harry Brandt** posts a list of low-grossing stars, shaking their very pedestals, costing them prestige and, in some cases, contracts. Among those indicted as "box-office poison" were **Garbo**, **Dietrich**, **Edward Arnold**, **Bette Davis**, **Fred Astaire**, **Joan Crawford**, **Kay Francis**, **Mae West** and **Katharine Hepburn**. The latter led the list. "They say I'm a has-been," she shrugged at the label. "If I weren't laughing so hard, I might cry." Hepburn's bosses at RKO Radio were less amused and assigned her *Mother Carey's Chickens* to do that same day. Within hours, they had her check for $200,000 to cover the last two films on her contract. Turning on her heels, she never worked for RKO again.

1941: *Meet John Doe* meets the people on this day as the picture goes into national release. Director **Frank Capra** started shooting without an ending—one that would spare **Gary Cooper** his sacrificial suicide (i.e., leaping to his death from the top of City Hall on Christmas Eve to protest all the injustices done the "little man" in America)—which meant the cast had to shiver through filming four different endings, all shot in an ice house in downtown L.A.

1942: Through an interoffice snafu on this day, **Dooley Wilson** is accidentally assigned the role of Sam, the gregarious ivory-tickler of Rick's Cafe Americain in *Casablanca*. Two days earlier, producer **Hal B. Wallis** had instructed an underling to hire **Clarence Muse** for the part, but, for reasons never known, Wilson wound up with it, despite conspicuous shortcomings. His piano-playing had to be dubbed (by **Elliott Carpenter**), and serious consideration was given to dubbing his singing. (Needless to add, not being a piano player—much less the most famous one in movies—plagued his subsequent cabaret career.) For his role-of-a-lifetime, Wilson got $150 a week (while Paramount, the studio lending him to Warners, pulled in $500 a week). Of the 34 nationalities supposedly comprising the *Casablanca* company, Wilson was the only one who had actually *been* to Casablanca: He and his band, The Red Devils, performed there at a soiree honoring World War I hero **T.E. Lawrence**.

1956: Validation Day finally arrives for **Marilyn Monroe** on this day as she starts *Bus Stop*. Between her director (**Joshua Logan**) and her acting coach (**Paula Strasberg**), she came up with a Method-ical interpretation of a "chantoosie" on the loose—albeit a note-for-note, nuance-for-nuance, inflection-for-inflection carbon-copy of what **Kim Stanley** had brilliantly done in the Broadway edition of **William Inge**'s play. The following year, Stanley took up movies with a vengeance, debuting as *The Goddess* (a note-for-note, nuance-for-nuance, inflection-for-breathy-inflection carbon-copy of Monroe).

1934: *Manhattan Melodrama* bows at NYC's Capitol on this day, bringing into the MGM fold two major players: **Mickey Rooney**, as a kid version of "The King" (**Clark Gable**), and **William Powell**. Another start-of-something: The latter met his perfect-wife/foil, **Myrna Loy**, on camera. She leapt into a limo containing Powell, who, just out of camera range, arched his eyebrow and said, "Miss Loy, I presume." Their *next* movie, *The Thin Man*, seconded this motion, and their classy chemistry went on to fuel a dozen more screen pairings (1934-1947).

1937: *Dead End* begins filming on this day with a clang of egos typical of the push-pull partnership of producer **Samuel Goldwyn** and director **William Wyler**. Forward-thinking Wyler wanted to shoot it on location in New York, but Goldwyn chose expensively to build his own East River tenement ghetto on the backlot. The day before the lensing began, the producer inspected his magnificent set and found garbage everywhere. When he ordered an immediate clean-up, Wyler resigned rather than deal with an "immaculate slum." Adapter **Lillian Hellman**, a Wyler loyalist, quit too, and even Goldwyn's promise of **Lewis Milestone** to direct couldn't get her back. Only Wyler's reinstatement two days later would do–and did–the trick.

1940: Getting wind that **Paul Muni** nixed Roy "Mad Dog" Earle in *High Sierra*, **Humphrey Bogart** talks **George Raft** into giving it the go-by as well and, on this day, puts in *his* bid for the part–in writing–to Warners exec **Hal B. Wallis**. This was the breakthrough role that brought Bogie into the big time.

1944: *Gaslight*, **Ingrid Bergman**'s Oscar-winning mad-act, bows at New York's Capitol on this day a few Broadway blocks from where the play version of the film (*Angel Street*) continues its epic long-run. MGM took on the property under the provision that the negatives of the 1940 British film version (with **Anton Walbrook** and **Diana Wynyard**) be destroyed. Luckily, prints have survived.

1960: The most famous marriage of the '50s officially ends five months and four days into the '60s: On this day, **Lucille Ball** divorces **Desi Arnaz**.

LESS THAN *FOREVER*: Desi Arnaz and Lucille Ball in *Forever Darling*.
EYES FOR THE GOOD GUYS: From left: Clark Gable, Myrna Loy and William Powell in *Manhattan Melodrama*; Charles Boyer, Ingrid Bergman and Joseph Cotten in *Gaslight*.

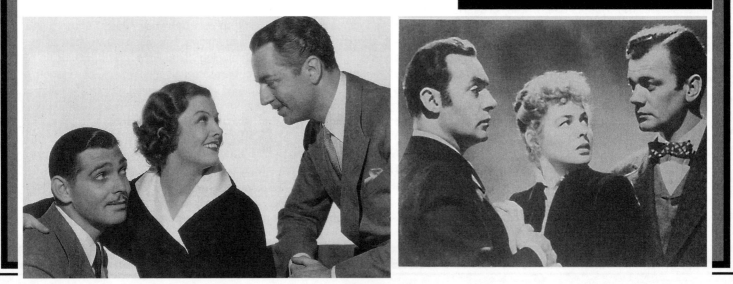

5

1935: A midshipman-uniform fitting at Western Costumers, slated on this day so he can play Tinker in the **Gable-Laughton** *Mutiny on the Bounty*, forces **Dick Winslow** out of a weekend dove-hunting expedition with two fellow child-stars (1930's *Tom Sawyer*, **Jackie Coogan**, and 1931's *Huckleberry Finn*, **Junior Durkin**) and playwright **Robert Horner**. That probably saved his life. Nearing home, the spiffy new Coogan coupe plunged over an embankment and tumbled end over end down a boulder-studded slope into a ravine, killing Horner and Durkin as well as Coogan's father, who was driving, and the ranch foreman. Coogan escaped injury, cushioned in the rumble seat by the weekend's kill: 350 dead doves. Durkin's next role–the kid-brother in *Ah, Wilderness!*–went by default to **Mickey Rooney**, who also followed him as the screen's next Huck.

1937: Dr. Kildare makes his first screen appearance on this day at New York's Paramount, and he's not who you think: **Joel McCrea** originated the role in *Internes Can't Take Money*. MGM didn't buy that title but did buy **Max Brand**'s original yarn from Paramount (plus any of his Kildare books that followed) and began a popular 15-film series the following year with *Young Dr. Kildare* (that's right: **Lew Ayres**).

1958: *Damn Yankees* begins batting out a 43-day production schedule on this day, with most of its cast recruited from the original Broadway show–from its trio of Tony winners (**Ray Walston**, **Gwen Verdon** and **Russ Brown**) on down. The principal Hollywood addition (**Tab Hunter**) does surprisingly well as the soul-selling Joe Hardy–a role Warners had planned for **James Dean**. The highlight: "Who's Got the Pain?" mamboed out by Verdon and hubby, choreographer **Bob Fosse** (their only screen dance together).

1968: Veteran **Albert Dekker**, 62, whose credits run from 1937's *The Great Garrick* to 1969's *The Wild Bunch*, is discovered dead on this day, chainlocked inside the bathroom of his Hollywood apartment. Clad in ladies' silk lingerie, with obscenities scrawled in lipstick across his body, he was bound and handcuffed, dangling from a rope tied to a shower rod. The coroner's ruling was "accidental death."

1990: Backstage at Radio City Music Hall's "Night of 100 Stars III" on this day, **Katharine Hepburn** and **Joseph L. Mankiewicz** embrace and speak to each other for the first time in 32 years. Their relationship had come to a shocking end in 1958 when she finished her final shot for his *Suddenly, Last Summer*. Believing him too tough on co-star **Montgomery Clift**, she spat in the director's face and walked away. (And *he* had introduced her to **Spencer Tracy**!)

A MOCK FIGHT MASKING THE REAL THING: Katharine Hepburn, Montgomery Clift, director Joseph L. Mankiewicz and Elizabeth Taylor on the set of *Suddenly, Last Summer*.
MAMBO MARRIEDS: Bob Fosse and Gwen Verdon in *Damn Yankees*.
YOUNGER DR. KILDARE: Barbara Stanwyck and Joel McCrea in *Internes Can't Take Money*.

6

1941: In following up a *Song of the Islands* story conference held five days earlier, **Darryl F. Zanuck** instructs its scripters on this day to (1) eliminate the plot angle pilfered from *Cafe Metropole*, (2) concentrate on the one swiped from *Second Honeymoon* and (3) add a dash of *He Married His Wife*–then, "we can get a *Philadelphia Story* type of picture out of this, in a Hawaiian setting."

1950: "I just love everything about getting married," gushes **Elizabeth Taylor Hilton Wilding Todd Fisher Burton Burton Warner Fortensky** on this day– her *first* wedding day–a big MGM production timed to the release of her *Father of the Bride*. **Helen Rose** designed both wedding dresses, and **Edith Head** did the going-away outfit. Most of MGM's galaxy filled pews of The Church of the Good Shepherd in Beverly Hills, with preferential seating accorded Taylor's past screen parents: **Walter Pidgeon** and **Greer Garson** (*Julia Misbehaves*), **Donald Crisp** and **Anne Revere** (*National Velvet*), **Leon Ames** and **Mary Astor** (*Little Women*) and **Spencer Tracy** and **Joan Bennett** (*Father of the Bride*). Her marriage to **Conrad "Nicky" Hilton** barely survived its three-month honeymoon. By year's end, she was making *Love Is Better Than Ever* with her new beau, director **Stanley Donen**.

1954: *Executive Suite*, an all-star arm-wrestle for control of a furniture company, sets up shop at Radio City Music Hall on this day. **Barbara Stanwyck**, billed third for one week's work, duked it out with **William Holden, Fredric March, Walter Pidgeon, Paul Douglas, Dean Jagger** and **Louis Calhern**. But it was the loyal secretary keeping the minutes–**Nina Foch**–who quietly stole scenes and made off with the movie's only Oscar nomination for acting.

1997: "Believe me, anytime Moses wants to make a statement, you let him," says **Wayne LaPierre Jr.**, the National Rifle Association's top gun, on this day as **Charlton Heston**, 72, is elected NRA's first VP. The deliverer of **DeMille**'s 1956 *Ten Commandments* found this victory more rewarding than leading a Presidential task force or the Screen Actors Guild: Neither "was concentrated on an agenda with nearly the iconic significance of the Bill of Rights."

AISLE ONE: Elizabeth Taylor and Spencer Tracy in *Father of the Bride*.
HOW FAR AWAY, PHILADELPHIA, PA: Betty Grable in *Song of the Islands*.
HIS ROD AND HIS STAFF: Charlton Heston in *The Ten Commandments*.
TRULY A SUPPORTING PLAYER: Louis Calhern, Paul Douglas, Dean Jagger, Fredric March, Barbara Stanwyck, William Holden and Nina Foch in *Executive Suite*.

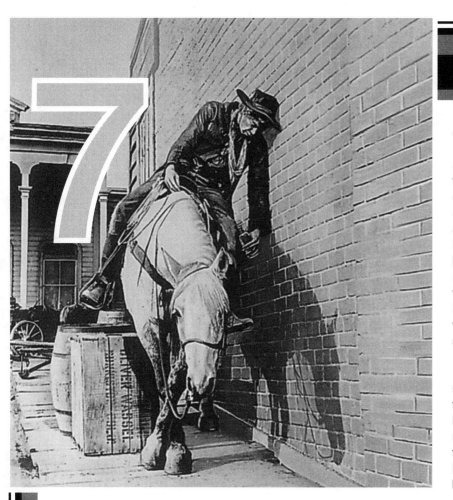

7

_1957:_ Midway through a _Gunsmoke_ shoot on this day, a heart attack fells **Charles King**, 57, a potbellied badguy who scowled, slugged and shot his way through two decades of indistinguishable Poverty Row shootouts. Regardless of who happened to be head heavy, King was always king of the henchmen, throwing hot lead and haymakers with unerring inaccuracy at **Ken Maynard, Buck Jones, Tex Ritter** and such. **Buster Crabbe**, himself a white-hatted hero never nicked by King, would tell nostalgia conventioneers about the time–not long after Monogram and PRC and Republic bit the dust–when an unemployed King opted to end it all by shooting himself. True to form, he missed!

_1958:_ Into New York's Capitol on this day swaggers **Glenn Ford** in a spoofy shoot-'em-up that triggers a ringing endorsement from critic **Bosley Crowther**–despite its desperately unpressing title: _The Sheepman_. MGM jacked that up to _Stranger With a Gun_ for the hinterland, and it did markedly better business. For Europe, it was all stops out: France called it _Powder Valley_, Latin America called it _Bloody Pastureland_, and Japan (possibly overstepping itself a bit) called it _One's Sphere of Influence in a Territory_.

_1965:_ _Cat Ballou_, a satiric sagebrusher filmed in 32 days, comes out of the chute at Denver's Centre Theater on this day, with **Lee Marvin** and title player **Jane Fonda** attending. In double harness as whisky-slinging gunslinger Tim Strawn and his silver-nosed evil twin Kid Shelleen, Marvin achieved the unique feat of shooting it out with himself at showdown time. Even more unique was the Academy Award that came for these _comedy_ performances 11 months later, the first Oscar-winning dual role since **Fredric March**'s _Dr. Jekyll and Mr. Hyde._ "I think," said Marvin, clutching his Oscar and recalling his loopy scene-stealing steed, "half of this belongs to a horse somewhere out in the Valley."

_1996:_ A New York State appeals court on this day upholds **Samuel L. Jackson**'s $540,000 award from the New York City Transit Authority for an old knee injury. In 1988, while still a struggling actor, he was dragged 300 feet on the station platform when his foot got caught in a subway door.

STINKO WITH STEED: Lee Marvin and his helpful horse in _Cat Ballou_.
KING OF THE HENCHMAN: Buck Connors and Charles King in _The Law Rides_.
ONE'S SPHERE ON A DANCEFLOOR: Shirley MacLaine and Glenn Ford in _The Sheepman_.

YOUNG & UN-OSCARED: Rich Ciulei and Connie Karcher in *Young Americans*. DUEL & DUAL: Mel Ferrer and Stewart Granger in *Scaramouche*; half of the Mauch twins (Bobby) and Errol Flynn in *The Prince and the Pauper*.

1937: *The Prince and the Pauper*, the **Twain** twin tale of mistaken royal identity, is tackled for once by real twins–the **Mauch** brothers, **Billy** and **Bobby**–in the fourth of seven screen tellings going into national release on this day. Until the brothers Mauch (and Warner) Bros. marched along, MGM was preparing to split-frame **Freddie Bartholomew** and do it there.

1948: "Screened *Casbah*," reads the entry in **Cecil B. DeMille**'s personal casting journals on this day. One week later, after a screening of *Black Bart*, he reached his decision on **Yvonne DeCarlo**–and it was written: "Doesn't have the right personality to play Delilah." **Hedy Lamarr**, DeMille decided, did.

1952: *Scaramouche* sweeps into Radio City Music Hall on this day, with title player **Stewart Granger** and suave villain **Mel Ferrer** indulging in Hollywood's longest swordfight–six and a half minutes of clanging steel. During one fencing sequence, Granger was almost killed when a huge iron chandelier crashed to the floor–not at all on cue.

1967: Hollywood greets **Barbra Streisand** with a resounding *Hello, Dolly!* on this day–her second day in Hollywood and her fourth in front of the *Funny Girl* cameras–as **Richard Zanuck** proclaims the 25-year-old new-girl-in-town 20th Century-Fox's musical matchmaker, Mrs. Dolly Levi. Among the hometown girls who'd hoped for the part: **Doris Day**, **Shirley MacLaine** and **Elizabeth Taylor**. The original musical Dolly, **Carol Channing**, got the bad news from *Daily Variety* at a Montreal high-rise where she was staying while doing the show at Expo '67. "I thought, 'Well, it wouldn't be any trouble at all to fling myself out that window,'" Channing recalled. But she didn't–and she was still touring *Dolly* successfully *decades* after Streisand's **Mae West** imitation of Dolly had faded from memory.

1969: For the only time in its existence, The Motion Picture Academy of Arts and Sciences on this day revokes an Academy Award, voiding the one given *Young Americans* as Best Documentary Feature of 1968. The film was found ineligible, having played a few dates in the Eastern and Southern United States in October of 1967, so the prize was recalled and given to the runner-up contender, *Journey Into Self*.

1999: One of Britain's best actors–**Sir Dirk Bogarde**, 78–dies of a heart attack on this day in his London home. The man who became England's top box-office star in 1955, 1957, 1958 and 1959–via *Doctor in the House* and its subsequent series installments–suffered a stroke in 1996 and spent the last year of his life under 24-hour nursing care.

9

1933: *Lady for a Day* begims filming on this day, and director **Frank Capra** gets down to some serious Oscar-questing, directing **May Robson** to a Best Actress shot in this Cinderella-by-**Runyon** yarn and earning a bid for himself–the first of his six. He won on half of those (*It Happened One Night*, *Mr. Deeds Goes to Town*, *You Can't Take It With You*), and, when time came to call it a career (1961), he did it by dusting off *Lady for a Day* and running it around the block again as *Pocketful of Miracles*–with **Bette Davis** as the Apple Annie of the hour.

1936: "If we'd known he was going to be an actor, we'd have given him a fancier name," said **Alice Finney**, who on this day gives birth to **Albert**. Another RADA grad of note also born on that same day: **Glenda Jackson**.

1939: Round One of an old Warners war (**Bette Davis** vs. **Miriam Hopkins**) ends on this day as *The Old Maid* wraps. The object of their respective affections, **Humphrey Bogart**, ducked out after two days' shooting and was replaced by **George Brent**. Left on the cutting-room floor: a film-bowing **Rod Cameron**. The Davis-Hopkins rematch–1943's *Old Acquaintance*–was equally calamitous.

SECOND FIDDLE TO A FULL MONTY: Davis and Woolley in *The Man Who Came to Dinner*.
STEEL SMILES: Crawford and Davis signing up for *What Ever Happened to Baby Jane?*
HOPKINS-MAD: From left: Miriam vs. Bette in *The Old Maid* and *Old Acquaintance*.

1941: On a set littered with idiot cards, **John Barrymore** puts in a desperate test for Sheridan Whiteside in *The Man Who Came to Dinner* on this day. Producer **Hal B. Wallis** toyed with the notion for ten days before giving up on it and letting the floodgates down for other applicants. **Fredric March** and **Charles Laughton** actually tested for it, **Orson Welles** and **Cary Grant** got to the deal-talking stage, and fleeting consideration was given to **Clifton Webb**, **Jack Benny**, **Bob Hope** and **Douglas Fairbanks Jr.** Eventually, Warners went with the Broadway original, **Monty Woolley**–after it had installed **Bette Davis**, for box-office insurance, in the secondary role of Whitehead's secretary.

1962: Round One of a *new* Warners war (**Bette Davis** vs. **Joan Crawford**) commences on this day as these two former queens-of-the-lot show up at a photo-op signing-up ceremony for *What Ever Happened to Baby Jane?* The smiles faded fast, and their rematch (*Hush . . . Hush, Sweet Charlotte*) died aborning, with Crawford scrambling for cover and being replaced by **Olivia de Havilland**.

1969: The much-married **Lana Turner** reaches her eight-is-enough limit on this day when she weds nightclub hypnotist **Ronald Dante**. By December, her head was clear, and they separated. He wanted $250,000 for a divorce, and the case dragged on until Jan. 26, 1972, when it was settled in Turner's favor. She never again married, preferring instead (according to her autobiography) a life of calming, uncomplicated chastity.

THE BIG PARADE: Robert Preston and his "boys band" in *The Music Man*.
STIRRED WELL: Burt Lancaster and Ava Gardner in *The Killers*.
ANNIE OOPS & *ANNIE* OAKLEY: From left: Judy Garland beginning, and Betty Hutton finishing, *Annie Get Your Gun*.

1937: Seasoned by small roles in British films, **George Sanders** begins his first American movie on this day–and **Gregory Ratoff** starts his first as a director. *Lancer Spy* was also to introduce **Germaine Aussey**, a French star signed by **Darryl F. Zanuck**, but she was suddenly replaced by **Dolores Del Rio** and never made a film here.

1946: On this day–his tenth day in movies–**Burt Lancaster** does his first scene with **Ava Gardner**, "easily one of the most beautiful women that ever lived," he called her. "And when I had to kiss her, I found myself deeply stirred. It took a form of some embarrassment." Co-star **Jeff Corey** confirmed that the sexual heat generated by these two rubbing together in *The Killers* was genuine: "I have reason to believe that they enjoyed kissing each other a great deal. They both had mentioned that to me."

1949: On this day, **Judy Garland** is fired from *Annie Get Your Gun*, and that role is waved in front of Republic's **Judy Canova**, Warners' **Doris Day** and MGM's **Betty Garrett** before it's finally snapped up by Paramount's **Betty Hutton**. She scored a bull's-eye with it.

1961: Although **Meredith Willson** was quite specific that "76 trombones led the big parade, with 110 cornets right behind," only 72 trombones and 30 cornets show up for the parade finale of *The Music Man*, which wraps its two-day shoot on this day. They were augmented by 24 clarinets, 6 piccolos, 6 French horns, 6 baritones, 6 euphoniums, 6 bassoons, 12 snare drums (military), 6 bass drums, 6 bass drum carriers, 6 glockenspiels, 6 sousaphones and 6 cymbals.

1971: Actor **Tom Tryon** officially turns into author Thomas Tryon on this day, with Knopf's publication of *The Other*. This gothic tale of tragedies caused by 12-year-old twin boys came to him while reading *Rosemary's Baby*. Tryon screen-adapted *The Other* himself but otherwise stayed a novelist till his death of cancer, at 65, on Sept. 4, 1991.

1977: San Antonio-born Lucille Fay LeSueur, 69, dies on this day alone in her Manhattan apartment. The world knew her as **Joan Crawford**. On the West Coast, on the same day, Crawford's co-star in *What Ever Happened to Baby Jane?*–**Bette Davis**–meets her escort of the evening, **Burt Reynolds**, running late but looking radiant. "Well, the bitch is dead!" Davis exclaimed on arrival. Heading off further discussion, Reynolds introduced the reporter beside him. Davis looked the newsman straight in the face and added, "She was always on time."

1888: The stage's best music man (**Irving Berlin**) is born in Russia on this day, a day after the screen's best music man (**Max Steiner**) is born in Austria.

1935: Director **George Stevens** signals **Fred Astaire** and **Ginger Rogers** to go into their *Swing Time* on this day. Of their ten films, it was Rogers' favorite. Why? "It gave me a bigger role than Mr. Astaire!"

1958: On this day, **Christian Devi Brando** is born — seven months to the day after **Marlon Brando** married **Anna Kashfi**–and named for a French actor who'd later direct him in *Candy*, **Christian Marquand**. Since Brando was between screen Christians—Christian Diestl in *The Young Lions* and Fletcher Christian in *Mutiny on the Bounty*–many assumed the name came from this. Indeed, when asked on TV's *Hollywood Squares* what screen role Brando named his first son after, **Paul Lynde**'s response was "either Desire . . . or . . . Waterfront."

1962: "An almost premiere" of *Mr. Hobbs Takes a Vacation* is staged by 20th Century-Fox on this day at the Fox Wilshire, and six of **James Stewart**'s leading ladies attend: **Rosalind Russell**, **Lee Remick**, **Ruth Hussey**, **Shirley Jones**, **Joanne Dru** and the current Mrs. Hobbs, **Maureen O'Hara**.

1966: On this day, **Charles Chaplin** directs his last scene ever, wrapping *A Countess From Hong Kong* with **Sophia Loren** and **Marlon Brando**. A week before, he performed for the camera for the final time–a brief stagger-on as a seasick steward.

1986: On this day, writer-director **Claude Lelouch** launches *A Man and a Woman: 20 Years Later* at Cannes where, 20 years and a day before, he launched *A Man and a Woman*. **Jean-Louis Trintignant** and **Anouk Aimee** resumed their title roles, making this the second-longest interval between a sequel and its original with the same stars. (The longest, by a full decade: 1968's *The Odd Couple* and 1998's *The Odd Couple II*, both starring **Jack Lemmon** and **Walter Matthau**.)

1998: "One of the few movie stars to walk away from stardom at the peak of her career" is how **Aljean Harmetz** characterizes **Alice Faye** in the star's *New York Times* obituary on this day. When Faye saw the way **Darryl F. Zanuck** edited, and sabotaged, her one dramatic shot (1945's *Fallen Angel*)–to keep her in musicals–she left 20th Century-Fox for a role that ran 54 years: Mrs. Phil Harris. In 1962, she returned to the screen for *State Fair*–for Fox, ironically.

1999: Pneumonia claims **Catherine McLeod**, 75, who starred in Republic's first Technicolor offering–an uncharacteristically lavish production called *I've Always Loved You*–but fame came from a 1963 Anacin commercial in which her headache-induced outburst ("Mother, *please*! I'd rather do it myself!") became a national catch-phrase.

1907: On this day, **Katharine Hepburn** is born–"despite," says *Me*, her autobiography, "everything I may have said to the contrary" (i.e. Nov. 8).

1933: After a week of rehearsals and 17 days of filming, **Katharine Hepburn** on this day finishes the first of her four Oscar-winning performances–an actress on the ascent playing one. Eva Lovelace in *Morning Glory* was the fictional facsimile of **Tallulah Bankhead**, fashioned by her friend, **Zoe Akins**, into an unproduced play Hepburn found (earmarked for **Constance Bennett**) on producer **Pandro Berman**'s desk. *She* demanded to play it so a radical rewrite replaced Eva's initial sarcasm with a starry-eyed idealism more compatible with Hepburn's persona. Hepburn later said she put some **Ruth Gordon** in Eva as well.

1949: In *The Stratton Story*, bowing at the Radio City Music Hall on this day, six-foot-three **James Stewart** finds his favorite film wife–five-foot-one **June Allyson**–and their movie marriage was repeated in *The Glenn Miller Story* and *Strategic Air Command*. Stewart was second choice to play Chicago White Sox pitcher Monty Stratton and only got the part because he could get the ball over the plate with more conviction than **Van Johnson** (who gracefully bowed out of the project, pleading "a motorcycle mishap").

1956: On this day, five weeks into filming *The Teahouse of the August Moon*, 61-year-old **Louis Calhern** is found dead of a heart attack in his Tokyo hotel room. His role of the flustered Colonel Purdy was reshot with the Broadway original, **Paul Ford**, who came into screen prominence with this performance.

1975: Five subversive Republicans break into Democratic headquarters in the Watergate complex, and guard **Frank Wills** catches them again–this time acting out his real-life role for the opening sequence of *All the President's Men*, which commences its 13-week location shoot in Washington D.C. on this day.

1987: A Congressional panel on this day hears about the evils of colorization from **Ginger Rogers** (who spent most of her film career in black and white) and from **Woody Allen** (for whom black and white is retro novelty). Allen also took a strong stand for film preservation. It was his avowed contention that "all film deserves to be saved–with the possible exception of the *Porky's* films."

THREE-TIMES MARRIED: From left: June and Jimmy in *The Stratton Story*, *The Glenn Miller Story* and *Strategic Air Command*.
NIX ON NIXON: Robert Redford in *All the President's Men*.
ALL ABOUT EVA: Douglas Fairbanks Jr. and Katharine Hepburn in *Morning Glory*.

1937: "*Shall We Dance*, which asks so rhetorical a question it does not even bother to add the interrogation point, is one of the best things the screen's premiere dance team has done," observes *Times* critic **Frank S. Nugent** about the **Astaire-Rogers** vehicle which sails into Radio City Music Hall on this day.

1954: The old **Ruby Keeler** myth comes true for **Shirley MacLaine** on this day: Four days into the run of *The Pajama Game*, **Carol Haney** broke her ankle, forcing MacLaine to go out there an understudy and come back a star. Two nights later, she came back a *movie* star when producer **Hal B. Wallis** caught her in action, set up a screen test and signed her to a seven-year contract.

1956: Negotiating the canyon road from **Elizabeth Taylor Wilding**'s home, **Montgomery Clift** suffers a near-fatal car-crash on this day. The film they were doing–*Raintree County*–halted for six weeks while he recovered and went through facial reconstruction (part of his face never regained full mobility). Taylor spent the break making a break of her own–accepting **Mike Todd**'s invitation for a weekend cruise (June 30), splitting from **Michael Wilding** (July 19), receiving Todd's impulsive pro-posal of marriage (July 20)–and returned to work July 21 changed as well.

1960: The already-complicated life of **Gloria Grahame** enters a new dimension on this day when she weds **Tony Ray**, son of her former husband, director **Nicholas Ray**. That made her ex her cur-rent father-in-law, and the son they had together, **Tim**, Tony's half-brother *and* stepson. Before divorc-ing (ten days short of their 14th anniversary), she and Tony had added a daughter to the mix.

1961: *Mad Dog Coll*, a cops-and-robbers caper that "belongs back in the pound" (according to critic **Howard Thompson** in this day's edition of *The New York Times*), finds **Telly Savalas** film-debut-ing on the side of Good. Previously, he was ABC's Senior Director of News and Specials and the man who shoved a mike at **Howard Cosell** when a sports announcer didn't show.

1972: Six-foot-four, 260-pound **Dan Blocker** dies of a pulmonary embolus following a gall blad-der operation on this day. The 43-year-old actor was about to play an impotent, alcoholic writer in *The Long Goodbye*, a caper helmed by an old *Bonanza* director, **Robert Altman**. Altman tried in vain to get Blocker cast as one of the *M*A*S*H* leads. This time, he had the role specifically written for him. **Sterling Hayden** inherited it.

1980: On this day–for the second time in less than three weeks–a singer **Susan Hayward** played to Oscar-nomi-nated effect dies: **Lillian Roth**, 69; **Jane Froman**, 72, died April 24. Their impersonator, 56, died first: March 14, 1975.

NO QUESTION: Fred Astaire, Ginger Rogers and a Ginger mask in *Shall We Dance*.
SING ME A BIO: From left: Susan Hayward as Lillian Roth in *I'll Cry Tomorrow* and as Jane Froman in *With a Song in My Heart*.

14

1936: With set visitor **D.W. Griffith** coerced into conducting the orchestra on this day–the last day of shooting *San Francisco*–**Jeanette MacDonald** goes into her third rendition of the title tune, cuing the walls (and everything else) to come crashing down in MGM's elaborate approximation of the great quake that shook the city at 5:30 a.m. April 18, 1906. Director **W.S. Van Dyke**, D.W.'s A.D. on *The Birth of a Nation*, took bows for the movie's 20-minute devastation, but most of it was executed by an uncredited special-effects genius, **James Basevi**, who went on to wreak additional havoc on *The Good Earth* and *The Hurricane*.

1946: While resting in director **Jules White**'s chair on this day waiting to do his last scene in *Half-Wits' Holiday*, **Curly Howard** suffers a stroke that permanently sidelines him as one of **The Three Stooges**. He died six years later on Jan. 18, 1952, at age 48. The Stooges series continued, with his brother **Shemp** carrying on for him. When *he* died Nov. 24, 1956, at age 60, the slot was filled by a couple of Joes (**Joe Besser**, 1956-1958, and **Joe DeRita**, 1958-1975).

1961: "HE LIVED AND DIED . . . AT HIGH NOON," goes the *Sunday News* headline on this day, reporting the death of **Gary Cooper** the day before (at 12:27 p.m., actually).

1985: *Mask* has two competing press conferences at Cannes on this day–Universal and **Cher** in one camp, **Peter Bogdanovich** and **Rusty Dennis** (the real-life character Cher played) in the other–and verbal missiles are fired back and forth. Miffed that the studio had cut two scenes totaling eight minutes and had swapped **Bob Seger** songs for **Bruce Springsteen** songs, the director turned down the Cannes trek, then paid his own way so he could upstage and counteract the company press conference. Cher's position was simple: Bogdanovich had nothing at all to do with her performance, and she would never work with him again.

1996: The on-screen lovers of *Two Much* — **Antonio Banderas**, 35, and a by-now-pregnant **Melanie Griffith**, 38 — tie the knot off screen on this day in London.

1998: A heart attack stills The Voice on this day as **Francis Albert Sinatra**, 82, dies at Los Angeles' Cedars-Sinai Hospital. "A talent like Sinatra comes along once in a lifetime — why did it have to be in my lifetime?" his first idol and closest competitor, **Bing Crosby**, once groused affectionately.

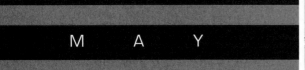
1931: *The Public Enemy* goes into general release on this day, proving how right director **William A. Wellman** was in the casting-switch he made three days into filming, having sidekick **James Cagney** and head hoodlum **Edward Woods** reverse roles. Production chief **Darryl F. Zanuck**, anxious to show up **Howard Hughes** for not casting Cagney as Hildy Johnson in *The Front Page*, okayed the change. And, *voila*! a star was born, one of the great ones.

1937: On this day–a month and a day into production–**Leslie Howard** gets a leading lady in *It's Love I'm After*, Reason for the delay: the thrashing-about of producer **Hal B. Wallis** to find a plausible alternative to Howard's first choice–a frightfully unphotogenic $25,000 freelancer named **Gertrude Lawrence**. He found her in his own Burbank backyard–$6,000 contractee **Bette Davis**. (Even the secondary lead, **Olivia de Havilland**, pulled down $8,615.) Howard who instigated the whole project–for Gertie–got $70,000.

1967: For the first time since she got off *The Marriage-Go-Round* almost seven years ago, **Susan Hayward** comes "home"–to 20th Century-Fox–on this day to put in two weeks' work (four scenes) for $50,000 and a special framed billing at the end of the cast list of *Valley of the Dolls*. "It's great to be here again," she told the press attending her home-coming. "As long as I know I can go home again." Edging out **Bette Davis**, **Jane Wyman** and **Tammy Grimes** to replace **Judy Garland** (away at play in the valley of the dolls herself), Hayward insisted Garland get full salary and whatever Garland got she would get double.

1994: Lean and Lincolnesque **Royal Dano**, 71, dies of heart failure on this day at his Santa Monica home. Debuting in 1950's *Undercover Girl*, he spent most of his movie career as scruffy Westerners. His one shot at greatness–the seriocomic death of The Tattered Man in **John Huston**'s *The Red Badge of Courage*–was praised on the screening-room circuit as the best scene in the film, if not one of the best of all time, but it didn't survive the "creative surgery" done in Huston's absence to "popularize" the film. Dano's breakthrough moment wound up on the cutting-room floor–and was promptly burned "to make sure nobody would know what a horrible mistake they made," he speculated. "It's like going in to take out the wrong kidney."

1996: For **Barton Heyman**, 59, who dies of heart failure on this day, acclaim came at the tail-end of a 30-year acting career–literally for the last three words he uttered on film. As captain of the prison guards in *Dead Man Walking*, he spoke those title words to clear the path for the execution-bound **Sean Penn**.

STARDOM SHOT DOWN: Edward Woods (with James Cagney) in *The Public Enemy*.
STARDOM SIDETRACK: Leslie Howard, Bette Davis and Olivia de Havilland in *It's Love I'm After*.
STARDOM STIFLED: Royal Dano.

1929: At a banquet in the Blossom Room of the Hollywood Roosevelt Hotel where Oscars are bestowed for the first time, **Emil Jannings** (the Best Actor winner for *The Last Command* and *The Way of All Flesh*) becomes on this day Oscar's first no-show. He'd picked his up in advance (making him also the first person ever to get an Oscar). He posed for a photograph with it, then left for Europe. The German actor feared he wasn't getting through to folks in his Hollywood films. One clue was a fan letter he got the year before: "Dear Miss Jannings, You are my favorite actress. I go to see all your pictures because I like the way you wear your clothes. To me you are the best best-dressed actress on the screen as well as the most beautiful. I try to imitate your clothes and your stylish way of wearing your hair."

1929: Oscar takes *Wings*, and vice versa, on this day–but its director, **William A. Wellman**, is in the studio "dog house" at the moment and barred from the ceremony. Not only was Paramount's pioneering aerial epic the first film to win the Best Picture Oscar, it was also the last silent work so honored. Sound had started to revolutionize the business, thanks to *The Jazz Singer*, which lost Oscars for writing and engineering effects but got an honorary award.

1957: A year after **Grace Kelly** moved from movies to Monaco, **Lauren Bacall** on this day steps up to the comedy plate at Radio City Music Hall in *Designing Woman*, some retailored fluff initially fitted for the Princess-to-be and her *Rear Window* co-star, **James Stewart**. Left Grace-less, Stewart dropped out of the picture, and an improbable but game **Gregory Peck** dropped in. The plot (the one about the fashion designer and the sportswriter) won **George Wells** the Oscar for Best *Original* Screenplay–just as it did 15 years earlier for **Michael Kanin** and **Ring Lardner Jr.** when they told essentially the same story with **Katharine Hepburn** and **Spencer Tracy** and called it *Woman of the Year* (the one about the international commentator and the sportswriter). In 1981, Bacall did *Woman of the Year* as a Broadway musical and *still* professed to see no similarities.

1986: *Top Gun* hits 1,028 screens on this day, scoring a box-office bull's-eye. In this hard-driving, high-tech approach to the peacetime military, old barracks cliches bit the dust, and new stars reached for the sky: **Tom Cruise, Val Kilmer, Kelly McGillis, Anthony Edwards, Tim Robbins, Meg Ryan, Rick Rossovich, John Stockwell, Barry Tubb, James Tolkan, Adrian Pasdar**. All that, and a soon-to-be-Oscared song, "Take My Breath Away." It did, too

OSCAR'S FIRST WINNER: From left: Emil Jannings in *The Way of All Flesh* and *The Last Command*. OSCAR'S AERIAL FAVORITES: From left: Clara Bow and Charles "Buddy" Rogers in *Wings*; Kelly McGillis and Tom Cruise in *Top Gun*. OSCAR'S IDEA OF AN "ORIGINAL" *WOMAN*: From left: Katharine Hepburn and Spencer Tracy in *Woman of the Year*; Gregory Peck and Lauren Bacall in *Designing Woman*.

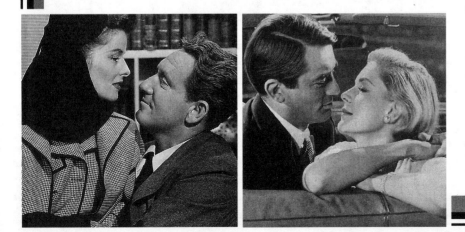

1944: *Cobra Woman* slithers into NYC's Criterion on this day, offering patrons two **Maria Montez**es for the price of one—an island beauty and her evil twin—"a rich puzzle, trying to guess which is which," meows *Films and Filming.* Costumes helped: sarongs for the former, ornate gowns for the latter. Half of the script was by **Richard Brooks** (before he got to *Blackboard Jungle*), and the direction was by **Robert Siodmak** (before he got to *The Spiral Staircase*).

1950: *In a Lonely Place* opens at New York's Paramount on this day—a pretty appropriate handle, considering that the marriage of director **Nicholas Ray** and leading lady **Gloria Grahame** went down for the count during its filming. They met and wed two years before doing *A Woman's Secret*, and it was only because she kept their bustup a secret that the studio didn't yank him off of *In a Lonely Place*. No one suspected, but in retrospect it's possible to see poignancy in the screenwriter's speech he had her do at the end: "I was born when you kissed me. I died when you left me. I lived a few days when you loved me."

1981: "Someday," croaked **Ronald Reagan** to **Pat O'Brien**'s *Knute Rockne–All American* in 1940, "when the team's up against it, breaks are beating the boys, ask them to go in there with all they've got. Win one for the Gipper." With those words, the future President made his most famous speech in films, playing Notre Dame's great football star, **George Gipp**, gasping his last from pneumonia. It didn't get him the Oscar (or anywhere near a nomination)—but, on this day, it gets him a honorary degree from Notre Dame when he shows up to deliver the commencement address. "Coach" O'Brien is on hand, too, beaming proudly from the sidelines. (If Reagan's big death scene doesn't ring a bell, that's right, also. The speech was originally written for a December 1938 "Cavalcade of America" radio program on Rockne. Warner Bros. purchased it and incorporated it into **Robert Buckner**'s otherwise-original screenplay, but, when the writer of the speech threatened a lawsuit, the studio cut a quick deal so the scene wouldn't be cut from the film's theatrical release. No provision was made for television, so it was deleted when the film passed on to TV in 1956—but Reagan's dying Gipp made a miraculous comeback for the video release.)

1990: The deaths of Mr. Wonderful and Kermit the Frog vie for the *New York Post*'s front page on this day: entertainer **Sammy Davis Jr.**, 64, and Muppet master **Jim Henson**, 53. Movies were only part of their respective big pictures.

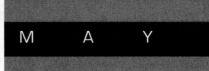

18

1927: No less than *The King of Kings* ushers Grauman's Chinese into opulent existence on this day. Present to partake of the new movie palace and The Gospel According to **DeMille** were luminaries like **Gary Cooper**, **Dolores Costello**, **Charles Farrell**, **Janet Gaynor** and **Gloria Swanson**—and all went on auxiliary batteries as the evening wore on, thanks to the gargantuan live-action curtain-raiser **Sid Grauman** concocted for the occasion. "The Glories of the Scriptures" was a DeMillian prologue that leafed, tableau-fashion, through such big Biblical moments as Daniel in the (drugged) lions' den, the flight into Egypt and on and on and on. At one in the morning when intermission was mercifully called, the audience did a mass exodus, leaving behind a loyal microcosm (mostly, relatives or staff of DeMille and Grauman). "Well, Cecil, there's only one thing left now," **Will Hays** asided to DeMille as he took his leave at 2 a.m., "and that is to get run over on the way home."

1934: At NYC's Roxy on this day, **Bela Lugosi** and **Boris Karloff** go out to meet their public as Vitus Verdegast and Hjalmar Poelzig in *The Black Cat*, a **Poe**-less but polished pairing (their first).

1986: Attention is paid on this day to a long-neglected legendary filmmaker as the Directors Guild of America presents its first posthumous award to **Oscar Micheaux**. The pioneering black director helmed the *Body and Soul* that brought **Paul Robeson** to the screen in 1924.

ARRIVING "GORGEOUS": Barbra Streisand in *Funny Girl*.
BELA & BORIS, ROUND ONE: Lugosi vs. Karloff in *The Black Cat*.
A THEATER FOR *KINGS*: Julia Faye and H.B. Warner in *The King of Kings*.

1995: The last surviving cast-member of *The Maltese Falcon* of 1941 expires on this day at a nursing home in Big Pine, CA: **Elisha Cook Jr.**, who played Wilmer the itchy-fingered gunsel for the sinister Kasper Gutman (**Sydney Greenstreet**).

1996: Obsessions R Us: **Barbra Streisand**'s first line on film (to a mirror, at the start of *Funny Girl*) and also her welcoming line to her Oscar—"Hello, Gorgeous!!"—is now the name of a store/shrine/museum in her honor, opening on this day in the Castro sector of San Francisco. For $2, patrons milled among the memorabilia which included dozens of photographs. For several hundred dollars more, the store provided a total Streisand makeover, replete with her signature unbobbed nose ($79 for the prosthesis) and a '60s-style wig (about $125). When nay-sayers tried to talk propriertor-founder **Ken Joachim** out of devoting an entire boutique to a single diva, he's said to have snapped back musically with "Don't Rain on My Parade." Nevertheless, the rains came and the store closed in two years.

DESERT DERRING-DON'TS: From left: John Wayne and Susan Hayward in *The Conqueror*; Warren Beatty and Dustin Hoffman in *Ishtar*.
IN STITCHES: MM at JFK's birthday party.

1942: Tragedy on this day puts the soaring career of **Orson Welles** into a lifelong nosedive. After *Citizen Kane* and *The Magnificent Ambersons*, the 27-year-old "Boy Wonder" opted to do *It's All True*, an ambitious but unwieldy documentary on South America. One segment tried reenacting an incident in which four fishermen from northern Brazil sailed, sans compass, 1,650 miles from Fortaleza to Rio to petition Brazil's president for social reforms in their poverty-ridden community. They got what they wanted and became national heroes–but, when the quartet re-created their Rio arrival for Welles' cameras, a large wave struck their raft, hurling the four overboard. Only three surfaced; **Manuel Olimpio Meira** (**"Jacare"**), leader of the expedition, drowned or was taken by a shark. Welles pressed on with a double for "Jacare" until RKO stopped the funding and the project was dropped, shelved almost forever. A month before Welles' death, 140,000 feet of the film's lost footage was found, but he refused to go near it, considering it "cursed"–if not the cause of his Hollywood downfall.

1953: An atom bomb is exploded on this day in Yucca Flats, NV, and a freak wind sweeps the radioactive fallout–subsequently known as "Dirty Harry"–137 miles away to Saint George, UT, where a year later *The Conqueror* was shot. Half the denizens of the town contracted cancer, as did 91 members of the film crew including producer **Howard Hughes**, director **Dick Powell, John Wayne, Susan Hayward, Pedro Armendariz, Agnes Moorehead, Thomas Gomez** and **Jeanne Gerson**.

1962: In a $12,000 **Jean Louis** nude-illusioned gown that had to be sewn onto her body, **Marilyn Monroe** vamps out a breathy "Happy birthday, Mr. President" to **JFK** on this day in a nationally televised celebration at Madison Square Garden. (Conspicuously absent: The First Lady.) The appearance, done in direct defiance of studio orders, triggered events leading to MM's firing and death.

1987: Another bad day for the desert: On this day–the same day that brought death, in 1935, to the real (**T.E.**) **Lawrence** of Arabia and, in 1958, to the *Beau Geste* of the silent screen (**Ronald Colman**)–*Ishtar* opens (D.O.A.). **Stewart Klein**, critic for WNYW-TV, dismissed the movie in two words: "*Ishtar*. Stinkar."

1989: "Lowe-down dirt" hits the fan on this day when the mother of an underage girl accuses **Rob Lowe** of videotaping sex with her daughter during the 1988 Democratic Convention in Atlanta. Exhibit A actually hit the access airways where *Midnight Blue* host **Al Goldstein** decreed Lowe could toil in pornography if acting didn't pan out. The actor's career did suffer discernibly, in point of fact, and he did put in some hours of community service (over jail time).

1944: On this day, **Fred Astaire** and **Gene Kelly** square off on Stage 21 for a dance duel: "The Babbitt and the Bromide," a segment for *Ziegfeld Follies*. Except for co-hosting *That's Entertainment: Part II*, it was the only time they appeared together on film. Kelly would have preferred doing "Pass That Peace Pipe," which **Roger Edens**, **Hugh Martin** and **Ralph Blane** had written expressly for them but which was deemed "not important enough" (although **Joan McCracken** and **Ray McDonald** did well with it when it found its way into *Good News*.) Uneasily teamed, Astaire and Kelly had the inevitable problem of who would lead. Said producer **Arthur Freed**: "When I'd talk to Fred alone, he'd say, 'Gene is wonderful, but why does he want everything his own way?' And, when I'd see Gene alone, he'd say, 'I admire Fred so much, but why does he want everything his own way?'"

1946: The starlet who finished second (to **Marilyn Monroe**) for the star-making role of **Louis Calhern**'s mistress in *The Asphalt Jungle*–**Georgia Holt**–gives birth on this day to a future Oscar winner: Cherilyn Sarkisian (a.k.a. **Cher**).

1956: The sleeper that established **Stanley Kubrick**–*The Killing*, an *Asphalt Jungle*-like heist replayed on a racetrack–slips into NYC's Mayfair on this day, with a budget of $320,000 and a cast of familiar character faces. His previous features were passion-driven independent efforts crudely executed *sans* stars or budget (the $13,000 *Fear and Desire* in 1953 and the $40,000 *Killer's Kiss*). After this *Killing*, Kubrick was king.

1991: New York's major film critics cram into Columbia's tiny screening room on this day and collectively hoot **Bruce Willis'** *Hudson Hawk* off the screen. Reviews were a turkey shoot: "No need to phone ahead," rat-a-tat-tatted *People*'s **Ralph Novak**. "This is the movie playing all the time on every screen of every theater in hell." The picture subsequently plummeted to a dubious perch in *The Guinness Book of Records*: the greatest loss incurred by a film–$57 million. The $65-million action-romp returned only $8 million in the United States (and hardly anything elsewhere).

21

LEOPOLD & LOEB FACSIMILES: From left: Dean Stockwell and Bradford Dillman in *Compulsion*; Farley Granger and John Dall in *Rope*.
OVERSHOOTING THE RUNWAY: John Cassavetes and Peter Falk in *Mikey and Nicky*.
FADING TO BLACKLIST: From top: Canada Lee and John Garfield in *Body and Soul*; Mady Christians and J. Edward Bromberg.

1924: A dental appointment on this day disrupts the daily routine of **Armand Deutsch**, 11, saving his life. The grandson of the chairman of the board of Sears, Roebuck and Co. was the intended target for teenage thrill-killers **Nathan Leopold** and **Richard Loeb**, but, when Deutsch didn't show, they settled for 14-year-old **Bobby Franks**, inviting him for a spin in their rented Willys-Knight automobile, then bludgeoning him to death just for the experience. This heinous crime was the inspiration for **Hitchcock**'s fictional *Rope*. A closer-to-the-truth version emerged in *Compulsion*, the 1956 novel, 1957 play and 1959 movie. Deutsch outlived his would-be killers and became a producer of some note at MGM (*Ambush*, *The Magnificent Yankee*, *Green Fire*, *Saddle the Wind*).

1952: On this day, **John Garfield** is discovered dead in bed in the apartment of an actress-friend, **Iris Whitney**. There was much speculation about what brought the 39-year-old star to a fatal heart attack, but he wasn't the first actor to die prematurely under the insistent glare of the House Un-American Activities Committee. **Canada Lee**, 45, who memorably played Garfield's punch-drunk sparring-partner in *Body and Soul*, had suffered the same fate 12 days before. So, too, in 1951 did **J. Edward Bromberg**, 47, and **Mady Christians**, 51.

1973: Paramount puts into production in Philadelphia on this day a picture that doesn't get released till Dec. 21, 1976–*Mikey and Nicky*. Reason: lawsuits and countersuits between the studio and director **Elaine May** over her eccentric shooting habits. Somehow, she exposed 1.4 million feet of film for a low-budget flick requiring only 10,000 feet–undoubtedly, the record ratio for film shot to film shown (140 to 1). During one early a.m. outdoor shoot, she blew her stack when the cameraman said "Cut!" simply because **Peter Falk** and **John Cassavetes** strolled out of camera range. "Yes," said May, allowing that point, "*but they might come back*!"

1988: Hollywood's Dick and Jane, **Dickie Moore** and **Jane Powell**, marry.

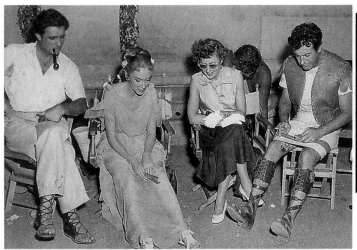

MAY

22

1950: "Well, there it is, boys—Rome," says centurion **Robert Taylor** in the opening line of *Quo Vadis*, which commences Cinecitta filming on this day. Off camera, Taylor partook of *la dolce vita* so conspicuously—mostly with a red-headed slave girl, **Lia de Leo**—wife **Barbara Stanwyck** trekked to Rome to save their marriage. She couldn't, and an idyllic Hollywood union crumbled after 12 years. As for his plywood work *on* camera—that won him Harvard Lampoon's vote for Worst Actor of 1951—but he never qualified for Worst Supporting Actor, keeping up alimony payments (15% of his earnings) to Stanwyck till he died June 8, 1969. She always said he was the only man she ever loved, and they remained friends, co-starring 12 years after the divorce in her final feature, 1965's *The Night Walker*.

1955: "The Fight Was for Blood—and They Got It," headlines the *Los Angeles Times* on this day, reporting on the previous day's *Rebel Without a Cause* shoot. Real switchblades were used for realism and, during a knife-fight with **Corey Allen**, produced real blood from The Star. Director **Nicholas Ray** yelled "Cut!" and rushed a first-aid man to **James Dean**, infuriating Mr. Method Acting. "What the hell are you doing?" he raged at Ray. "Can't you see I'm having a *real* moment? Don't you *ever* cut a scene while I'm having a real moment. What the fuck do you think I'm here for?"

1971: At the posh **Guggenheim** estate on Long Island Sound, **John Marley** (as studio mogul Jack Woltz in *The Godfather*) wakes up, on this day, to the grisly fact he's in bed with the head of his prize racehorse. Paramount had encouraged director **Francis Ford Copula** to use a fake horse's head, but the one the prop department came up with fooled no one so location scouts found a real horse set for slaughter at a New Jersey rendering plant. The head arrived in a metal container loaded with dry ice and placed on the bed beside Marley, who did the scene repeatedly, his silk pajamas soaked in Kara blood. Two weeks later, he told a friend he could still see the head.

1998: "Live fast, die young and leave a good-looking corpse" was the motto **John Derek** briefly lived by as the doomed delinquent of *Knock on Any Door*, his arrival film—but, in reality, he extended that to 71 years, dying of heart trouble on this day. Eventually, he gravitated to the other side of the camera—first as still photographer, then as movie director—playing Svengali to a succession of beautiful wives (**Patti Behrs**, **Ursula Andress**, **Linda Evans** and his *10* for 25 years, **Bo Derek**). All four attended his wake.

1949: *On the Town* resumes shooting on the Culver City backlot on this day after a daring little filming foray in NYC where **Gene Kelly, Frank Sinatra** and **Jules Munshin** hit the location high-spots singing the praises of "New York, New York." It was the first time a studio shot musical scenes on public sites in Manhattan, and the results were spectacular.

1955: At Warners' Burbank plant on this day, *Giant* begins lensing–without **James Dean**, who's winding things up on a neighboring soundstage. Three days later, he finished *Rebel Without a Cause* and went directly into makeup and wardrobe tests for *Giant*. "No one, not even Dean himself," noted biographer **Random Riese**, "realized how the rushed makeup job would hinder the impact of his performance. It was a fatal and unfortunate flaw in his final film."

1960: The Cannes Film Festival's Golden Palm on this day goes to **Federico Fellini**'s *La Dolce Vita*–and how *dolce* it is, what with bluenoses in an uproar, causing such a wonderful run on the box office! In time, the title became cynically synonymous with the jaded life of the fast-track Via Veneto set.

1962: "When the legend becomes a fact, print the legend," newsman **Carleton Young** says, deciding *not* to reveal *The Man Who Shot Liberty Valance* (**James Stewart** or **John Wayne**) at the end of the Western reaching NYC's Capitol on this day. Although he did four other films, this was the last great one from a director who had printed his share of legends ("My name is **John Ford**–I make Westerns," he'd say, undercutting his art a country mile).

1991: At 34, tough-guy thespian **Mickey Rourke** proves it's not just acting or attitude, making his boxing bow on this day in a Fort Lauderdale bout with **Steve Powell** and winning a unanimous decision. Eight more fights–and six more wins–followed over the next three years, but Rourke took a beating every time. In 1995, the *New York Post*'s **Bill Hoffmann** recounted–under the headline 'The only thing he can box is pizza'–Rourke's injuries: "a broken cheekbone, two fractured ribs, a broken toe, four broken knuckles, a split tongue and a disfigured nose." When the actor retired from the ring in 1994, said Hoffmann, it was "after a sparring partner whumped him so badly he needed seven hours of surgery." Visually, a new man returned to the screen.

1997: After 44 years, *Shane* does come back to the Grand Teton Valley where it was filmed–via a freshly refurbished print shown on this day at the Teton Theater in Jackson Hole, WY. **George Stevens**' 1953 classic Western, named to the National Film Registry in 1993, was screened as part of the NFR tour.

THE MARVELS OF MANHATTAN: Frank Sinatra, Jules Munshin and Gene Kelly in *On the Town*.
THE DUDS OF DEAN?: James Dean dressing for *Giant*.
THE WONDERS OF WYOMING: Alan Ladd, Jean Arthur and Van Heflin in *Shane*.

DFZ'S D-DAY: Producer Zanuck launching troops for *The Longest Day*.
THE LAST "RIGHT PLACE": James Mason and John Gielgud in *The Shooting Party*.
CANUTT'S CROWNING ACHIEVEMENT: The chariot race from *Ben-Hur*.

1961: On this day, **Darryl F. Zanuck** rushes to the rescue of his Normandy Invasion epic, *The Longest Day*, arguing four eloquent hours with 20th Century-Fox board-members trying to scrap the project weeks before lensing begins. DFZ won—and so did the studio a year later. The only cash that kept Fox afloat during the last costly days and delays of *Cleopatra* was the $18 million in roadshow rentals *Day* earned.

1966: The Old Guard caves in to The New Hollywood on this day as **Frank Capra** abandons *Marooned* after two years of preproduction and never again brightens a soundstage. **Mike Frankovich**, the Columbia president who entered the business with a radio-announcer bit in Capra's *Meet John Doe*, insisted unrealistically he bring in this NASA saga for $3 million. After Capra withdrew, Frankovich stepped down from Columbia's topper slot and produced the picture himself independently—for *$8 million*.

1985: "Life is so extraordinarily pleasant for those of us who are fortunate enough to have been born in the right place," says **James Mason** in the opening line of his last feature, *The Shooting Party*, bowing at NYC's Cinema I on this day. It seemed as much an epitaph for himself as it did a last gasp for the Old Guard he represented. A last-minute substitute for **Paul Scofield**, he gave a gracious final display of a doomed civility—then, darn if he didn't take it with him.

1986: The stuntman's stuntman—**Yakima Canutt**—dies a peaceful death (of natural causes, in his sleep) on this day at age 90. Such serenity came in sharp contrast to the history of hard knocks he sustained over the years doubling for **Errol Flynn**, **Tyrone Power**, **Henry Fonda**, **Roy Rogers**, **Randolph Scott** and, of course, **John Wayne**, with whom he also swapped punches in Poverty Row shootouts. An authentic cowboy from Washington state—even an award-winning one: *five times* the World's Champion All-Round Cowboy—Canutt entered films with the first silent Westerns of the '20s. Because his "voice came across like a hummingbird," he stayed silent and behind-the-scenes, pioneering as a stunt director of action scenes. In 1966 he got an honorary Oscar that credited him "with helping to create the stuntman profession and with developing safety devices used by stuntmen everywhere." His highest-profile work was in choreographing the chariot race for the 1959 *Ben-Hur* which his son, **Joe**, helped execute. His *own* favorite stunt—"the only stunt I created and did that's never been duplicated"—was in *Stagecoach* when, playing an attacking Indian, he leapt full-gallop from his own horse to the six-horse team pulling the coach; he then fell between the horses, dragged along the ground and lay motionless as the horses and coach sped over him.

1933: *The Emperor Jones*, **Eugene O'Neill**'s drama of a Pullman porter turned Caribbean kingpin, goes before the cameras on this day, with **Paul Robeson** in the title role he inherited from **Charles Gilpin** on Broadway. **Fredi Washington**, in her movie debut, drew double duty as Robeson's "high-yaller" mistress: Her footage had to be reshot because the producers feared audiences might think Robeson was romancing a white woman. The second time around, Washington wore thick, dark pancake makeup to discourage this notion. Of course, her light skin was an asset for her next–and best–role: the black daughter who tried to pass for white in the original 1934 *Imitation of Life*.

1938: *Marie Antoinette*'s filming in Culver City comes to an end on this day, and her Louis XVI (**Robert Morley**) hightails it back across The Big Pond, not to return to Hollywood again for another 25 years (to do *Take Her, She's Mine*). His first performance on film, Morley's Louis earned him his one and only Oscar nomination. The role became hotly contested when **Charles Laughton** bowed out--**John Gielgud**, **Peter Lorre**, **Oscar Homolka** were all dying to do it–but MGM went with Morley, the dark horse from the British stage.

1965: *Frankie and Johnny*, the triangle tragedy-turned-ballad, takes another turn on this day–into a film musical, with **Donna Douglas** and **Elvis Presley** playing the title duo **Helen Morgan** and **Chester Morris** essayed at Republic in 1936. **Ava Gardner** and **Frank Sinatra** pondered a replay at MGM in the '50s but didn't. The *Frankie and Johnny* of 1991–though superbly played by **Michelle Pfeiffer** and **Al Pacino**–was less than legend (a hash-house waitress and a short-order cook).

1969: The only X-rated film to win the Oscar for Best Picture opens on this day at New York's Coronet: *Midnight Cowboy*, director **John Schlesinger**'s shattering portrait of a hick hustler in Manhattan. (That rating dropped to an "R" in subsequent re-issues.)

1977: "A long time ago, in a galaxy far, far away. . .," *Star Wars* lifts off on this day. It was greeted so enthusiastically sequels soon followed. "Sometimes, I get the feeling that if I have any more success, it's going to be obscene," mused the series' creator, **George Lucas**. "I'm embarrassed by it."

1979: In *Alien*, which lunges onto the screen nationwide on this day, the freshly hatched title monstrosity made its startling entrance by bursting forth from the stomach of the well-named **John Hurt**. To heighten the horror of the scene, director **Ridley Scott** opted not to tell the rest of the cast who reacted with authentic terror. So did audiences. That one stomach-turning special effect spawned three sequels and a host of graphically grisly ripoffs.

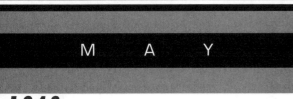

1943: "When I first saw **von Stroheim** at the wardrobe tests for his role as **Rommel**, I clicked my heels and said: 'Isn't it ridiculous, little me directing you? You were always ten years ahead of your time.' And he replied, 'Twenty.'" Thanks to director **Billy Wilder**'s *Five Graves to Cairo*, which opens at New York's Paramount on this day, Erich von Stroheim returned as an in-demand actor to a Hollywood that had discarded him as a director of excess. A hard habit to break, that: To do Rommel properly, he required *real* German field glasses and a *real* Leica camera *with real 35mm film inside* because "an audience always senses whether a prop is genuine or false."

1956: *The Searchers*, arguably **John Ford**'s best Western, goes into national release on this day, but few notice. The cult came later. Even the head-over-heart French were susceptible: **Jean-Luc Goddard** admitted, as much as he detested the reactionary politics of **John Wayne**, he could never help but be moved "by the emotion of the awesomely avuncular gesture in which Wayne gathers **Natalie Wood** in his arms."

1961: The Cinerama cameras start telling *How the West Was Won* on this day along the Ohio River around Battery Rock, Ill., as location lensing begins on "The Rivers" segment. **Henry Hathaway** directed this episode which starred **James Stewart, Carroll Baker, Walter Brennan, Agnes Moorehead, Debbie Reynolds** and **Karl Malden**.

1967: *The War Wagon* is rolled into Arlington, TX, for its world premiere by **John Wayne** on this day–his 60th birthday–and two days later he heads for Fort Benning, GA, to enter a reel war–one that he'll produce, direct and star in: *The Green Berets*. "Some people were asking if I'd like to direct him in *The Green Berets*," said **Burt Kennedy**, who'd spent most of his time in the director's seat of *The War Wagon* duking it out with The Duke. "I told them, other things being equal, I'd rather *join* the Green Berets!"

1989: "I'm sure all the rest have been destroyed," deadpans **Harrison Ford** on this day as he donates the rumpled leather jacket and the brown fedora he wore in all three of his Indiana Jones outings to the History of American Entertainment collection at the Smithsonian's National Museum of American History in Washington D.C. A museum spokesperson noted that the adventurer's get-up "influenced men's fashion in the 1980's." In truth, it was a look **Ronald Reagan** had pioneered, swaggering through *Hong Kong* and *Tropic Zone* in the early '50s. (Some industry-wise people thought, by calling attention to these two minor-league romps, **George Lucas**—co-author of the Indiana stories–was getting back at Reagan for dubbing the Presidential war toys *Star Wars*.)

REAGAN-REGULATION: From left: Harrison Ford in *Raiders of the Lost Ark*; Ronald Reagan, Danny Chang, and Rhonda Fleming in *Hong Kong*.
TRAIL'S BEGINNING & TRAIL'S END: From left: James Stewart, Mark Allen, Carroll Baker, Kim Charney, Brian Russell and Karl Malden in *How the West Was Won*; John Wayne and Natalie Wood in *The Searchers*.

26

27

LAUNCHING: Howard Hughes heralding *Hell's Angels*.
FLYING: Margot Kidder and Christopher Reeve in *Superman*.
SPEEDING: Keanu Reeves in *Speed*.

1930: *Hell's Angels* takes off at Grauman's Chinese on this day, with hundreds of searchlights sweeping the sky, catching squadrons of vintage planes in intricate formation over Hollywood. The absolute topper in cinematic send-offs at that time, the event alone cost $40,000–a hundredth of what the film itself cost (at $4.2 million, it rivaled the bloated budget of 1925's *Ben-Hur*)–but this extravagance produced aerial spectacle never seriously surpassed, and it established its 25-year-old producer-director as a major player in movies. **Howard Hughes** began filming the month *The Jazz Singer* debuted (October of 1927). When filming ended in May of 1929, he realized what was missing: sound–so he reshot the whole thing!

1932: *Red Headed Woman*, starring the screen's most famous platinum blonde, completes principal photography on this day. MGM got the property for **Garbo**, then dangled it before **Lillian Roth**, **Barbara Stanwyck** and **Clara Bow** before tossing it to goodtime-girl-in-residence **Jean Harlow**. When Glendale previewers were slow in picking up on the film's comic tone, **Irving Thalberg** ordered screenwriter **Anita Loos** back to the typewriter. Her new opening line not only eased Harlow into the title role and set the tone for lightweight things to come, it also contained three little words that made Loos lousy rich: "So gentlemen prefer blondes, do they? Yes, they do."

1949: The prince and the showgirl–**Aly Khan**, 36, and **Rita Hayworth**, 29–begin their short-lived storybook marriage on this day. Seven months later, **Princess Yasmin** made three. "Seven-month babies are common in the family," explained the prince.

1970: *Variety* on this day reports the passing of **Vinton J. Hayworth**, 64, a performer with several identities: a character actor who appeared in 60-plus pictures under the pseudonym of "Jack Arnold" (the name of a character he played for five years on the radio series, *Myrt and Marge*), a founder of AFRA (now AFTRA) who carried membership card No. 10–and the real-life uncle of **Fred Astaire**'s top two screen partners: **Ginger Rogers** and **Rita Hayworth**.

1995: "You'll believe a man can fly!"–the catch-phrase that made 1978's *Superman–The Movie* the most successful release in Warners history and the one that carried title-player **Christopher Reeve** to overnight stardom–becomes poignantly passé on this day when a horseback-riding spill in Virginia brings the 42-year-old actor tragically to earth, paralyzing him from the shoulders down. But, in two months time, he was driving his wheelchair by puffing air through a plastic tube, and, in five months' time, he was receiving a five-minute ovation in his first public appearance at a Creative Coalition dinner in NYC.

1996: *Speed* star **Keanu Reeves**, 31, crashes his motorcycle into a car on this day, landing in Hollywood Presbyterian Medical Center and requiring surgery.

28

1941: After three weeks of arduous filming with **Spencer Tracy**, **Anne Revere** and a young Atlantan named **Gene Eckman** in the insect-infested Florida Everglades, MGM announces on this day **King Vidor** will take over from **Victor Fleming** the direction of *The Yearling*. Alas, Vidor couldn't resume production immediately (which was essential given the rapid growth-rate of fawns being bred for the title role), so the project was scrapped at a loss of $500,000, flickering briefly to life again the following year when 14-year-old **Roddy McDowall** was tested for the lead. After the war, director **Clarence Brown** took on the project and made it his crowning achievement but vowed "Never again! You have to direct a deer or a stalk of corn to understand my problems." Still, *The Yearling* gave *The Best Years of Our Lives*, *It's a Wonderful Life*, *Henry V* and *The Razor's Edge* a good run for 1946's Best Picture Oscar. There were nominations for Brown, **Gregory Peck**, **Jane Wyman** and editor **Harold Kress** and actual awards for sets, cinematography and the teenage towhead Brown found in a Nashville classroom, **Claude Jarman Jr.**

1965: For the first time in the history of the Cannes Film Festival, a jury chooses on this day to give *both* acting prizes to the same picture. *The Collector*, billed as "a kind of love story," was a strange character-study of a kidnapper and his victim, and it was carefully cast by director **William Wyler**, who weeded through **Warren Beatty**, **Natalie Wood**, **Dean Stockwell**, **Sarah Miles** and **Anthony Perkins** before finding **Terence Stamp** and **Samantha Eggar**.

1983: Having just played a wrestler in his second film (*Hadley's Rebellion*), **Griffin O'Neal**, 18, decides to take down Father **Ryan**, 42, with a wrestling hold on this day. The older, taller, heavier O'Neal, who'd competed in the L.A. Golden Gloves of 1956 and 1957, instinctually responded by throwing a left punch that knocked out his son's two front teeth.

HELL TO DIRECT: Claude Jarman Jr., Gregory Peck and Jane Wyman in *The Yearling*.
A HAIR-CURLING DAY FOR SYDNEY: Norma Shearer in *Marie Antoinette*.
TWO CANNES DO: Samantha Eggar and Terence Stamp in *The Collector*.

1997: The first hairstylist to get screen credit (for 1937's *Camille*)–**Sydney Guilaroff**, 89–dies of pneumonia on this day at a Beverly Hills nursing home. He gave **Louise Brooks** her "shingle," **Claudette Colbert** her bangs, **Judy Garland** her *Wizard of Oz* braids, **Lucille Ball** her redheadedness and, in his 40-year reign as MGM's chief stylist during Hollywood's golden era, designed signature looks for **Greta Garbo**, **Marilyn Monroe**, **Greer Garson**, **Ann-Margret**, **Elizabeth Taylor**, **Debbie Reynolds**, **Lena Horne**, **Ava Gardner**, **Lana Turner**, **Hedy Lamarr**, **Grace Kelly**, **Nancy Davis Reagan**, **Natalie Wood**, **Shirley MacLaine**. His hardest film assignment: 1938's *Marie Antoinette*, which required 2,000 court wigs (some with actual birds in cages), lesser wigs for 3,000 extras and **Norma Shearer**'s monumental bejeweled and feathered artists' ball creation.

1942: As **Diana Barrymore** braces for the L.A. sneak of her first film (*Eagle Squadron*), Uncle **Lionel** summons her to Hollywood Presbyterian Hospital. "I can't possibly do it — I have a very important appointment," she said. "So has your father," he retorted. Indeed, just before 10 — before daughter Diana arrived from the screening — **John Barrymore** died of bronchial pneumonia.

1942: In *The Falcon Takes Over*, slipping into Manhattan's Rialto on this day, **Michael Arlen**'s Falcon (**George Sanders**) takes over a case **Raymond Chandler** originally assigned to Philip Marlowe. The plot was readdressed in 1944 as *Murder, My Sweet* (with **Dick Powell** as a crackerjack Marlowe) and, again, in 1975 under the novel's original name, *Farewell, My Lovely* (with **Robert Mitchum** as a believably battered Marlowe).

1949: A week behind in the rent, **Marilyn Monroe** commits a desperate, star-making act on this day: With an **Artie Shaw** record on the turntable and a sheet of red velvet on the floor, she posed nude while **Tom Kelley**'s eight-by-ten Deardorff View Camera clicked away for two hours. Only two of the two dozen poses were sold. One became known worldwide as the "Golden Dreams" calendar. A second calendar — named "A New Wrinkle" — was also issued. Three years later when the nude news broke, Monroe was doing *Don't Bother To Knock*. Advised to deny everything, she 'fessed up instead. There was no stopping her after that.

1962: "M-G-M's *How the West Was Won* has completed filming," reports the *New York Morning Telegraph* on this day, one year and three days after lensing began. The Cinerama shoot-'em-up entailed the services of 12,617 players, 3 directors, 1,200 buffaloes, 875 horses, 200 sheep, 160 mules and 24 stars. The last-named talent constituted the hugest hunk of the epic's epic $14,480,000 budget — $2,204,000 — and an additional $350,000 was spent on those five little words constituting the title (paid to **Bing Crosby**, who'd bought the handle from a *Life* magazine headline). The script lurking under that title cost less ($270,000) and took **James R. Webb** almost two years to write, but he struck Oscar gold with it, even though high-brow critics shrugged it off as "a great big old **Roy Rogers** Western."

1979: The Canadian who became "America's Sweetheart" — the first movie star to have her name spelled out in marquee lights, the first to have an international following, the first to be paid in the thousands of dollars a week–dies of a stroke on this day: **Mary Pickford**, 86.

1987: A Los Angeles jury on this day finds director **John Landis** and four assistants not guilty of involuntary manslaughter in the deaths of **Vic Morrow** and two Asian-American children while filming of *Twilight Zone: The Movie*.

1937: Makeup man **Bud Westmore** weds one of his subjects, **Martha Raye**, on this day. The union lasts two days short of four months, ending on Sept. 28, 1937.

1962: On this day, **Steve McQueen** leaves the States for front-rank stardom–for Munich to film *The Great Escape*. To spice up his stock role, he suggested escaping by bike and (contrary to the true World War II story being told) had written into the script a motorcycle chase to show off his bike-riding skill. German stuntmen couldn't match it, in fact, so McQueen did much of his own "doubling." But that 60-feet leap over a barbed-wire fence on the cycle was done by **Bud Ekins**, McQueen's bike teacher who, in 1968's *Bullitt*, took San Francisco's hills in airborne jumps, going 110 mph in a souped-up GT Mustang.

1967: One of the great velvet voices of cinema is stilled by death on this day. It never brought **Claude Rains** an Academy Award–he contended four times: *Mr. Smith Goes to Washington*, *Casablanca*, *Mr. Skeffington* and *Notorious*–but he did enjoy the admiration and respect of his peers. **Bette Davis** counted him her favorite playing partner, and when she was asked shortly before her death, what happened to her character in *Now, Voyager* after she and **Paul Henreid** finished their cigarettes, she responded with some certainty that Charlotte Vale continued her work with Dr. Jaquith (Rains) and, in time, married him.

1977: While lying on the Hawaiian beach on this day, musing about moviemaking, **Steven Spielberg** tells **George Lucas** he always wanted to do a 007 film with **Sean Connery**, sending Lucas into a swashbuckling talespin about a James Bond forerunner named Jones. Indiana Jones. Connery hitched up with the series on Installment 3–1989's *Indiana Jones and the Lost Crusade*–as Indy's dad.

1982: Actors Equity elects its first female prexy on this day: **Ellen Burstyn**.

1997: Great lines from *Twister*–"Get in the car! Get out of the car!" "Hold on!"–are ridiculed by **Mike Medavoy** and **Rob Reiner** on this day at a panel on megapic scripting at the Writers Guild Foundation's Words Into Pictures conference. The film's producer, **Kathleen Kennedy**, conceded special-effects spectacles afforded little chance for pungent prose–"It is a level of writing that often gets very little respect"–but said she was going full steam ahead with plans for a sequel. Reiner had a suggestion for the title: *Drizzle*.

30

THE WIND AND THE WORDS: Helen Hunt and Bill Paxton in *Twister*.
BIKE BREAK: Steve McQueen in *The Great Escape*.
GOING TO THE SOURCE: Steven Spielberg, Harrison Ford and Sean Connery working on *Indiana Jones and the Lost Crusade*.

31

1960: That "Perfect Wife" of the movies, **Myrna Loy**, sheds Hubby No. 4 (former Assistant Secretary of State **Howland H. Sargeant**) in a quicky Juarez divorce action on this day—and unofficially retires from the matrimonial ring, lest those headline-writers drag out her "Perfect Wife" tag again. "It's a title nobody could live up to, really," she said realistically (if a bit wistfully).

1971: A search party reaches the site on Brushy Mountain near Roanoke where a fog-and-rain-blinded twin-engined Aero-Commander had crashed four days earlier and discovers, thrown free of the wreckage but dead of "massive total body injuries," **Audie Murphy**. Murphy's screen career ran from one prophetic title (1948's *Beyond Glory*, after he had been named America's most decorated World War II hero) to another (1969's *A Time for Dying*, two years before his death at age 46). There was some irony in the fact the death of this war hero-turned-film actor occurred during Memorial Day weekend.

1977: The showman who gave the world Emergo (an illuminated skeleton floating over audiences of *House on Haunted Hill*) and Percepto (electrical shocks wired to theater seats for *The Tingler*) dies of a heart attack on this day at his Beverly Hills home. **William Castle**, 63, directed a mother lode of low-budget horrorshows, goosing them up with silly gimmicks—but his best film was one he only produced (and left the directing to **Roman Polanski**): *Rosemary's Baby*.

1994: *The Christian Science Monitor* on this day reports that *The Longest Day*—loudly touted in its time as the most expensive black-and-white film ever made (because **Darryl F. Zanuck** felt it better conveyed the gritty reality of World War II)—has been colorized by Fox Video for release on a new videocassette.

1994: A remark **Dennis Hopper** "lets slip" on *The Tonight Show* on this day—that he didn't cast **Rip Torn** in the **Jack Nicholson** role in *Easy Rider* because Torn pulled a knife on him—is ruled almost five years later (May 7, 1999) to be "made with malice" by a Los Angeles judge, who awards $475,000 in punitive damages to Torn—this, in addition to the $475,000 Torn received in January 1997 for "lost income . . . and emotional distress." Torn and witnesses said it was Hopper who pulled the knife. (oh)

1995: Learning nothing from the mistakes of **Dan Quayle**, Presidential contender **Bob Dole** indulges in some film criticism at a GOP fund-raiser in Century City on this day, tearing into *True Romance* and *Natural Born Killers*. **Oliver Stone**, who directed the latter, called the blast "a '90s form of McCarthyism." It later developed that Dole hadn't seen or heard much of what he had dissed.

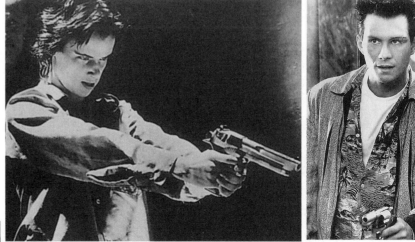

FOUR FACES WEST: John Wayne, Henry Fonda, John Agar & Shirley Temple in *Fort Apache*

A BIG DAY FOR BROADCASTING: From left: Cecil B. DeMille begins CBS's "Lux Radio Theater," and radio announcer Ronald Reagan turns Warners star in *Love Is on the Air* (with Eddie Acuff).
A LAST DAY FOR MARILYN: Wally Cox, MM and Dean Martin in the abandoned *Something's Got To Give*.

1936: With **Clark Gable** and **Marlene Dietrich** in/as *The Legionnaire and the Lady*, **Cecil B. DeMille** launches his legendary "Lux Radio Theater" on this day. As host and supposedly (but not really) director of the weekly series which dramatized successful films with their original casts whenever possible, DeMille became a household name and attained an annual salary of $100,000. All of that he gave up for $1 — or, rather, for *not* paying $1 (for a political assessment, levied by the American Federation of Radio Artists, which he did not believe was right) — and, on Jan. 22, 1945, after presenting *Tender Comrade* with **Olivia de Havilland** and **Dennis O'Keefe**, he did his goodbye to radio.

1937: Warners signs up a 26-year-old **Ronald Reagan** on this day — for seven years, at $200 a week — and, in a matter of days, he is starting at the top of the cast, starring in a B-movie called *Love Is on the Air*; radio announcer Reagan was kindly cast as one in this airwaves remake of **Paul Muni**'s 1934 newspaper saga, *Hi, Nellie!*. In Film Two — an "A" called *Hollywood Hotel* — he was a radio functionary on **Louella O. Parsons**' staff, but he got no billing. That start-stop aspect set the tone for his roller-coaster ride at Warners.

1943: **Leslie Howard**, 50, is killed when his plane is shot down over the waters of the Bay of Biscay by Germans believing that **Winston Churchill** is aboard.

1952: Turning 26 on this day and toppling **Betty Grable** as the queen of the lot, **Marilyn Monroe** learns that she'll be Lorelei Lee in the movie version of *Gentlemen Prefer Blondes*. It made a certain amount of cents for 20th Century-Fox to hire someone contractually bound to a maximum of $1,500 a week (which amounted to $18,000) instead of spending $150,000 to get Grable for the role.

1962: A scene for the sadly well-named *Something's Got to Give*, trying to convince **Dean Martin** that **Wally Cox** was the guy she sexlessly shared a desert island with, occupies **Marilyn Monroe** on this day — her 36th birthday *and* her last day before the movie cameras. Because of her many no-shows, 20th Century-Fox made it a full workday, then ended it with a strained birthday party for her (replete with cake). She never set foot in the studio again. On her way home, she performed a last act of charity, appearing at a muscular dystrophy benefit at Dodger Stadium in L.A. It proved to be her final public appearance. She was bedridden by a virus the next day and fired by Fox a week later.

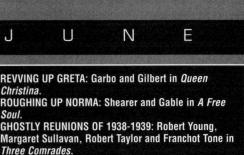

REVVING UP GRETA: Garbo and Gilbert in *Queen Christina*.
ROUGHING UP NORMA: Shearer and Gable in *A Free Soul*.
GHOSTLY REUNIONS OF 1938-1939: Robert Young, Margaret Sullavan, Robert Taylor and Franchot Tone in *Three Comrades*.

1931: Reluctantly, **Irving Thalberg** surrenders *A Free Soul* to the big screen of New York's Astor on this day. It was meant to be a vehicle for Mrs. Thalberg — **Norma Shearer** — but, when he saw the film with previewers, he realized all the good scenes had gone to **Lionel Barrymore**, in the flashier role of her drunken-lawyer father. To balance the act better, he put the film back into production, and new scenes were shot to generate some Shearer sympathy by having her hoodlum beau slap her around. Unfortunately, this was administered by a newcomer named **Clark Gable**, whose brutish behavior turned out to be a turn-on. The studio got swamped with fan mail for him, and this rough brand of manhandling became a screen constant with "The King" for the next 30 years.

1933: "Everyone in Hollywood of any importance has been tested for the part," reports *The Hollywood Reporter* on this day about Don Antonio Pimentelli de Parada, the Spanish envoy and lover of **Greta Garbo**'s *Queen Christina*. **Leslie Howard** was Garbo's first choice but declined, prompting the procession. "Just about everyone but **Ben Turpin**" applied before **Laurence Olivier** bounded over from Britain. Garbo okayed the casting herself, but their subsequent camera-clinches left her so cold director **Rouben Mamoulian** summoned to the set her old flame, **John Gilbert**, to get her up to the desired emotional pitch. Gilbert had been an early suggestion of hers, but **Louis B. Mayer** hated Gilbert and ranted her out of the notion. Twelve days into filming, she insisted he stay on in the part, and the movie began again. The dumped Olivier returned to England and avoided Hollywood for six years.

1938: The only film **F. Scott Fitzgerald** got onscreen credit for writing — *Three Comrades* — is unveiled on this day at New York's Capitol. Producer **Joseph L. Mankiewicz** later claimed he'd written it but couldn't recall who dreamed up the concluding shot — a superimposed montage allowing **Robert Taylor** and **Franchot Tone**, still among the living, to walk with the ghosts of **Margaret Sullavan** and **Robert Young** into a hopeful tomorrow — but that image inspired **Samuel Goldwyn** to raise Cathy and Heathcliff from the dead in *Wuthering Heights* (after a disastrous preview) and have them "cloud walk" to Heaven hand in hand. Director **William Wyler** refused to shoot it — and **Laurence Olivier** and **Merle Oberon** declined to play it — all three contending a "happy ending" would be out of place in light of what had gone before. Needlessly, Goldwyn had **H.C. Potter** run the camera over the stars' doubles heading from the moors to Heaven. When the new print was previewed in Santa Barbara, applause drowned out the closing music. "Well," grunted the contented producer, "they understood it."

THE CEILING'S THE LIMIT: Charlton Heston and Rex Harrison in *The Agony and the Ecstasy*.
WAYWARD HAYWARD: As Barbara Graham in *I Want Yo Live!*
ONE OSCAR, ONE TONY, ONE ROLE: Lila Kedrova for *Zorba*'s Madame Hortense.

1939: *Winter Carnival* — a flimsy campus romance barely held together by old school ties — wraps on fake backlot snow on this day. A Dartmouth dropout angling for an honorary doctorate from the college, producer **Walter Wanger** decided to feature it in a film and drafted a pair of disparate alums to do the script (a budding **Budd Schulberg**, 25, and a broken **F. Scott Fitzgerald**, 40), hauling them both to Hanover for the annual frozen fun 'n' games. The idea was to soak up atmosphere, but Fitzgerald instead soaked up most of the booze in town and proved such embarrassment to Wanger he was canned after one Hanover hangover too many. Schulberg subsequently fictionalized this lost weekend as a 1951 novel and a 1959 play, both called *The Disenchanted*. **George Grizzard** played Schulberg, and **Jason Robards** made a memorable, Tony-winning Fitzgerald.

1955: Convicted of murder, **Barbara Graham** is put to death in the gas chamber at San Quentin on this day. A film that begged to differ with that verdict and sentence came along three years later — **Robert Wise**'s *I Want To Live!* — providing Oscar-winning work for **Susan Hayward**, whose harrowing depiction of Graham's final hours was a heartbreaker.

1964: Preparing for *The Agony and the Ecstasy* ahead of him, **Charlton Heston** sets his Michelangelo makeup and peruses the painter's letters on this day. The next day he cased the real Sistine Chapel ceiling, which he'd "paint" for Pope **Rex Harrison** and director **Carol Reed**. So thorough was his research on Michelangelo that 30 years later he declined to contribute to *The Celluloid Closet*, a documentary on gays in movies, because he had come to conclusion that (despite irrefutable evidence to the contrary) Michelangelo was not homosexual.

1984: On this day, **Lila Kedrova** becomes the only person ever to win a Tony for the musical version of a performance that had already won her an Oscar: Madame Hortense, the (still) aging courtesan of *Zorba the Greek*.

1985: The June 10 issue of *New York* magazine hits the stands on this day, supplying just the right term for the eight New Faces of 1985 illuminated by *St. Elmo's Fire* (**Ally Sheedy, Emilio Estevez, Demi Moore**, an artless no-string scene-thief named **Andrew McCarthy, Andie McDowell, Judd Nelson, Mare Winningham** and **Rob Lowe**). The label-slinging press had worked itself into a lather trying to pigeon-hole this junior-league *Big Chill* ensemble — "The Little Chill," suggested **Lloyd Sachs** in the *Chicago Sun-Times*; **Michael Musto** of *The Village Voice* volunteered "*The Chapman Report*-for-the-MTV set" — but the winner in this category was *New York*'s **David Blum**, who, punning around with the **Sinatra** gang of 25 years earlier, dubbed them "Hollywood's Brat Pack."

4

CHRISTMAS IN JUNE: John Payne, Maureen O'Hara, Natalie Wood and Edmund Gwenn in *Miracle on 34th Street*.
PISTOL-PACKIN' JUDY: Horace (later Stephen) McNally, Judy Garland, and Angela Lansbury in *The Harvey Girls*.
GRANDSON AND *GODFATHER*: Anthony Gounaris and Marlon Brando in *The Godfather*.
FAN-MAGAZINE MARRIAGE: Tony Curtis and Janet Leigh in *The Black Shield of Falworth*

1942: Producer **Hal B. Wallis** instructs his *Casablanca* director **Michael Curtiz** on this day to muzzle the mugging **Leonid Kinsky** is doing as Sascha the bartender. Instead of retaking the scene or indeed reshooting it with **George Tobias**, Wallis went the less expensive route: minimizing the character and throwing scenes to his partner-in-comedy, Carl the headwaiter (cast 11 days later with the inestimable **S.Z. Sakall**). A bit of business in which Sascha innocently slipped a German officer a Mickey Finn fell by the wayside. Kinsky outlived just about every actor inhabiting *Casablanca*, dying Sept. 8, 1998, at age 95.

1945: *The Harvey Girls* comes to an end on this day — as does **Judy Garland**'s marriage to **David Rose**. Eleven days later, she began again with **Vincente Minnelli**.

1945: On this day — the day following their sixth wedding anniversary — **Merle Oberon** divorces the producer who put her in pictures, **Alexander Korda**.

1947: The ultimate Christmas cult-movie bows at the Roxy on this day, very out of season: *Miracle on 34th Street*. It was made only when adapter-director **George Seaton** promised 20th Century-Fox he would, in exchange, tend a turkey called *Chicken Every Sunday*. The Santa saga's big payoff came — again unseasonably — in spring when **Edmund Gwenn** got the Oscar for his Kris Kringle impersonation. "Now," said a grateful Gwenn, "I know there *IS* a Santa Claus."

1951: A marriage made in Hollywood (not to last) on this day: **Tony Curtis** and **Janet Leigh**. But it produced a pair of acting daughters: **Kelly** and **Jamie Lee Curtis**.

1958: *From Hell to Texas*, a **Don Murray** Western, rides into New York theaters on this day with one note of distinction — a grand-scale war-of-wills (Young Turk vs. Old Hollywood) that occurred during filming: **Dennis Hopper** required 15 hours and 86 takes for a simple 10-line scene before he did it to **Henry Hathaway**'s satisfaction. Then, director Hathaway vowed Hopper was through in films — and he *was*, save for a couple of inconsequential programmers, until Hathaway himself hired him for *The Sons of Katie Elder* in 1965.

1971: Trying to make friends with a three-year-old co-star who on this day will share one of his greatest scenes, **Marlon Brando** shoves an orange slice in his own mouth and growls. Instead of laughing, **Anthony Gounaris** cried — inspiring director **Francis Ford Coppola** to shoot the scene that way: Don Vito Corleone dying as a monster to his own grandchild in *The Godfather*, collapsing from a cardiac while romping with him in a tomato patch. "Sometimes," said the director, plainly proud of that moment, "you catch lightning in a bottle."

1926: A $50-a-week cowboy extra signs up on this day to be a background rider in *The Winning of Barbara Worth*, but fate rewrites that contract. In the right spot at the right time, **Gary Cooper** found himself in his first featured role, elevated to the film's central triangle with **Ronald Colman** and **Vilma Banky** by accident. **Harold Goodwin**, who was to do that part, was detained by **Ernst Lubitsch**'s ill-named *Honeymoon Express* — forcing director **Henry King** to use Coop, first from the back of the head only and then finally full-face when his big scene came off without a hitch. The scene: Cooper, having supposedly ridden 24 hours across the desert to deliver a message to Colman, was to knock, then fall exhausted into Colman's arms when the door opened. To achieve a convincing exhaustion, King kept Cooper walking for hours prior to the shot. **Samuel Goldwyn** bought the scene, but, before the producer could buy the actor (i.e., ink him to a contract), Coop had flown the coop, moseying over to the greener pastures of Paramount and the waiting arms of **Clara Bow**, who got him into stardom stride with three of her films (*It*, *Children of Divorce* and *Wings*). It took Goldwyn nine years to get him under contract, and then it cost the mogul more each week than it would have cost to have Coop for all of 1927.

1935: *Top Hat*, the topper in **Astaire-Rogers** pairings, finishes filming on this day. The idea of the title number, in which a tailcoated Astaire "mowed down" a chorus line of identically attired dancers with his cane, came to him at five in the morning after a fitful night's sleep.

1939: *On Your Toes* steps off into a screen production on this day, starring **Eddie Albert** and **Alan Hale** (instead of the previously promised, but otherwise engaged, **James Cagney** and **Adolphe Menjou**). The **Rodgers** and **Hart** score was reduced to background music, save for the **Balanchine**-choreographed, **Zorina**-executed "Slaughter on Tenth Avenue" ballet.

1944: Another two-star marriage — that of **Brian Aherne** and **Joan Fontaine** — goes down for the count on this day after four years, seven months and six days.

1967: The American Film Institute opens in Washington D.C. on this day.

1982: On this day, after serving 17 days for tax evasion, **Sophia Loren** is freed from Italian jail. (She had pleaded "crooked accountant" — to no avail.)

1999: The pregnant stars of *Cruel Intentions* — **Ryan Phillippe**, 24, and **Reese Witherspoon**, 23 — display some honorable ones on this day and wed in Charleston, SC.

6

1938: *Boys Town* begins filming on this day, bringing Oscars to two men: **Dore Schary**, who co-authored the original screenplay with **Eleanore Griffin**, and **Spencer Tracy**, who portrayed **Father Edward Flanagan**. In his autobiography (*Heyday*), Schary soft-pedaled the drinking problem that almost derailed Tracy's performance. Later when Schary succeeded **Louis B. Mayer** as head of MGM, he proved adept at manipulating the always recalcitrant actor into work — until Tracy finally had to be dropped permanently from the studio payroll because his deportment jeopardized the filming of *Tribute to a Badman*.

1944: Far removed from the deadly commotion of Normandy — an explosion rocks Camp Mackall, NC, and takes the hands of a sergeant preparing explosive charges with nitro-starch packages and blasting caps. A meat cutter in civilian life, **Harold Russell** referred to the accident as "an argument with a block of T.N.T. — and I lost. The score was two hands off about six inches above the wrist." The silver lining to his tragedy was actually golden: He became the only person to get two Oscars for one portrayal — Homer Parrish in *The Best Years of Our Lives*. Originally written as a spastic and assigned to **Farley Granger**, the role was revised to Russell's situation when director **William Wyler** recalled *Diary of a Sergeant*, an Army Pictorial Service documentary in which Russell demonstrated not only mastery of his steel-claw "hooks" but also acceptance of his disability. Nobody thought the scene-stealing veteran had a chance against the veteran scene-stealers up for Best Supporting Actor — **Charles Coburn**, **William Demarest**, **Claude Rains** and **Clifton Webb** — so, in a separate ceremony on Oscar eve, Russell received an honorary Oscar "for bringing hope and courage to his fellow veterans through his appearance in *The Best Years of Our Lives*." Then, the next night, he won the competitive Oscar. "I'll never forget coming off the stage for press pictures after being given my second award and having **Cary Grant** . . . lean over and whisper, 'Where can *I* get a stick of dynamite?'"

1968: On this (D-) day, open warfare erupts on location in Garrison, NY, between the two stars of *Hello, Dolly!*: "Cool it, baby," **Walter Matthau** warns **Barbra Streisand** (who's about as "baby" as the one in *Bringing Up Baby*). "You may be the singer in this picture, but I'm the *actor*." It seems Matthau had his fill of her directing his performance, circuitously slipping "suggestions" on how his part should be played to their lame-duck director, **Gene Kelly**. The Greatest Star reminded Matthau the name of the movie was not *Hello, Walter!* and exited for her dressing room. "Okay, baby," the unrepentant Matthau called after her, "but remember: **Betty Hutton** thought she was indispensable, too."

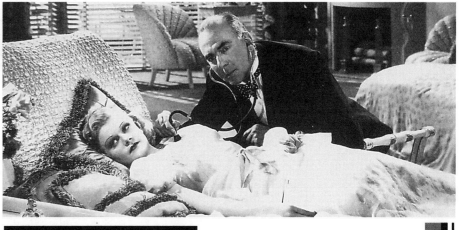

GABLE ARRIVES & HARLOW EXITS: From left: Clark Gable in *The Last Mile*; Jean Harlow (with George Zucco) in *Saratoga*. FOX TROTTED: Vivien Leigh and Marlon Brando in *A Streetcar Named Desire*. ONE HAT, ONE HORSE: James Stewart in *The Rare Breed*.

1930: "Killer Mears" goes West: The stage role that made a star of **Spencer Tracy** on the East Coast works the same wonders for **Clark Gable** on the West Coast when he comes out shootin' on this day in *The Last Mile* at L.A.'s Belasco. A flood of film-test invites followed. **Gloria Swanson** tested him for a film but realized at a glance he wasn't the white-tie-and-tails type. **Mervyn LeRoy** tested him for the sidekick slot opposite **Edward G. Robinson**'s *Little Caesar*, but **Darryl F. Zanuck** nixed the notion with a classic kiss-off: "His ears are too big. He looks like an ape." A fairer airing was had at MGM, where Gable was waved aboard by **Lionel Barrymore**, who'd starred in a play (*The Copperhead*) the inexperienced Gable had stumbled through. "I think you'd do better in motion pictures," Barrymore said at the time. Impressed with how far Gable had come in *The Last Mile*, Barrymore tested him for a film he was to direct called *Never the Twain Shall Meet*. **W.S. Van Dyke** eventually brought it to the screen when Barrymore returned to acting, but the test became legend — as practical jokes go: The mischievous Barrymore got Gable up as an Indian warrior wearing feathers, war paint and little else, then marched him around the backlot — to catcalls and wolf whistles at every corner. The mortified Gable wanted to rush back to his dressing room and get a top coat, but Barrymore wouldn't hear of it. "The hell with all of them," he huffed. "Haven't they ever seen feathers before?"

1937: On this day — two-thirds of the way filming through *Saratoga* — uremic poisoning claims **Jean Harlow**, 26. MGM announced the film would be reshot with **Rita Johnson**, but the public outcry was such the execs opted to rewrite the film, using all the Harlow footage — then, stand-in **Mary Dees** (in longshots).

1950: Riding into New York's Paramount on this day with his *Winchester '73* blazing, **James Stewart** breaks in the hat and horse that will serve him in Westerns for the next 20 years — through *The Cheyenne Social Club* in 1970. The hat was a battered, gray, sweat-stained affair; the horse, Pie, a "beautiful sorrel, sort of half quarter horse and half Arabian."

1950: On this day, **Darryl F. Zanuck** memos agent-turned-producer **Charles Feldman** that *A Streetcar Named Desire* was on 20th Century-Fox's tracks *before* Feldman acquired the screen rights but that he [Zanuck] had to renege on the deal because Fox prexy **Spyros Skouras**, fearing the censorship rows it would cause, threatened to resign if the company made the picture. In his reasoning, Skouras was right, but the prestige the film bought to Warner Bros. long outlasted its shock value.

1939: "Frankly, my dear, I don't care!" declares **Clark Gable** on this day as he begins filming his *Gone With the Wind* exit line — to satisfy censors. Two days later, Gable filmed it right — "Frankly, my dear, I don't give a damn!" — but that four-letter word cost $5,000. Rather than weaken the ending, producer **David O. Selznick** paid that much to the Producers Association for this on-screen "offense" — even though the word had come up before on screen: Both **Leslie Howard** and **Marie Lohr** had uttered it in 1938's *Pygmalion*, as had **Fred Stone** in 1935's *Alice Adams* and **Emma Dunn** in 1932's *Blessed Event*, and there were three "damns" in 1929's *Glorifying the American Girl*. By the time The Motion Picture Association of America began its ratings in 1968, the word was so commonplace that *GWTW* got a "G"-rating.

1944: On this day — her 23d birthday — **Alexis Smith** takes herself a husband: **Craig Stevens**, a fellow Warners contractee. Their marriage endured till her death by cancer in 1993 — the day after their 49th wedding anniversary.

1950: "That 'Asphalt Pavement' thing is full of nasty, ugly people doing nasty, ugly things — I wouldn't walk across the room to see a thing like that," groused studio chief **Louis B. Mayer** about *The Asphalt Jungle*, which bows at NYC's Capitol on this day — to the greater glory of MGM (much to his chagrin).

1960: "Much of the acting has all the subtlety of a hypodermic needle," hoots the *Variety* reviewer on this day about *Portrait in Black*. And that went double for twice-Oscared man-of-the-soil **Anthony Quinn**, clumsily miscast as a society doctor who prescribes adultery and murder for **Lana Turner**. "You're kidding," Quinn supposedly said when producer **Ross Hunter** first pitched him the part. No, alas, he wasn't — so the actor gamely charged forth with real bull-in-a-china-shop abandon, trying to mask his embarrassment. In his overreaching ardor during a love scene, he accidentally broke one of Turner's teeth by kissing her too violently.

RHETT SAILS INTO THE SUNSET: Vivien Leigh and Clark Gable in *Gone With the Wind*.
BACK IN THE GAME: Ralph Bellamy and Don Ameche in *Trading Places*.
SUBTLETY TAKES A HOLIDAY: Anthony Quinn and Lana Turner in *Portrait in Black*.
NOT MEMBERS OF L.B.'S CLUB: Clockwise: Sam Jaffe, Brad Dexter, Marilyn Monroe, Marc Lawrence, Sterling Hayden, Jean Hagen, and Louis Calhern of *The Asphalt Jungle*.

1983: *Trading Places*, in which preppie stockbroker **Dan Aykroyd** and street hustler **Eddie Murphy** do just that, goes into national release on this day, returning **Don Ameche** to the big screen for the first time since *The Boatniks* (1970). For all practical purposes retired, he pounced when paged to trade places with **Ray Milland**, who couldn't pass the studio's insurance physical. When (and only when) Paramount agreed to pay him what they'd offered Milland, Ameche raced to Philadelphia to join **Ralph Bellamy** as the elderly brothers who run a commodity brokerage and engineer the Aykroyd/Murphy switch. Before he could catch his breath and re-retire, Ameche went into *Cocoon*. That one got him the Oscar and made his final decade a productive one in pictures.

1934: Donald Duck debuts on this day with the release of a *Silly Symphony* short called *The Wise Little Hen*. It was just a bit, but it went over big, prompting 20 co-starring stints and, with *Donald's Ostrich* in 1937, true star status. He often functioned as a contrasting foil for **Walt Disney**'s calm, in-control firstborn, Mickey Mouse, coming into clear focus for Disney one night in 1932 when he happened to tune in an L.A. radio show, *The Merry Makers*, and heard a local milk-company spokesman, **Clarence Nash**, playing a tongue-tied duck reciting "Mary Had a Little Lamb." Nash was hired on the spot, and he played the quick-tempered quackster in 164 cartoons (including 1942's Oscar-winning *Der Fuehrer's Face*) and a few features like *The Three Caballeros*.

1948: "When I start out to make a fool of myself, there's very little can stop me," says **Orson Welles**, tempting the critical gods in the opening line of *The Lady From Shanghai*, bowing on this day at New York's Loews Criterion. The film that followed that disarmingly brave intro — directed, written, produced and performed by the Wonder Boy himself — was not entirely foolish, but it did effectively finish off his marriage to the leading lady (**Rita Hayworth**, gone abruptly blonde for the title role) and his directing career in Hollywood (save for *Touch of Evil* a decade later).

1958: A special goodbye to Mr. Chips: The brilliant **Robert Donat** dies of a respiratory ailment on this day in London, a few days after he finished dubbing a role he'd come out of a two-year retirement to play: the Mandarin who befriends China missionary **Gladys Aylward** in *The Inn of the Sixth Happiness*. In his final moments on film, he bids goodbye to Aylward (**Ingrid Bergman**), looking squarely into the camera and saying, in effect, to us: "We shall not see each other again, I think." At year's end, The National Board of Review remembered Donat with a special posthumous prize "for the valor of his last performance."

1980: While "freebasing" cocaine on this day, **Richard Pryor** suffers third-degree burns on most of his upper body when the mix of coke and booze suddenly ignites and explodes. Two months of painful skin-grafts followed, but he lived to tell the tale — film it, in fact (*Jo-Jo Dancer, Your Life Is Calling*, a 1986 quasi-autobiography which he wrote, acted and made his movie-directing debut).

1982: At auction on this day, **Steven Spielberg** shells out $60,500 for a sled — albeit one of the "Rosebud" sleds that survived the furnace in *Citizen Kane*.

HARDLY A FUN-HOUSE FILMING: Orson Welles and his then-blonde then-wife, Rita Hayworth, in *The Lady From Shanghai*.
HIS LAST *GOODBYE*: Robert Donat in *The Inn of the Sixth Happiness*.
A PRYOR LIFE: Richard Pryor in *Jo-Jo Dancer, Your Life Is Calling*.

10

1939:

O'Haras are be falling right and left all over the *Gone With the Wind* sets on this day: While director **Victor Fleming** steers **Vivien Leigh** and the A-team through Scarlett's staircase tumble, getting it right in two takes, production designer **William Cameron Menzies** commands the second-unit work covering the fatal horse-fall of Gerald O'Hara (**Earl Dobbins**, doubling for **Thomas Mitchell**). The beautiful white stallion used for the shot later galloped on to a measure of screen immortality as The Lone Ranger's Silver; its low point — sissified with a braided tail and pink satin bows as **Lucille Ball**'s carousel pony in the "Bring On the Beautiful Girls" opening number of 1946's *Ziegfeld Follies* — was so low the horse's trainer threatened a law suit.

1955:

Fed up with being a top-billed second-banana, **Dean Martin** heads for Hawaii with the wife and kids on this day, leaving **Jerry Lewis** to head for the Catskills alone to premiere *You're Never Too Young*, their 13th screen-team effort. It's an unlucky 13: That solo act was the first public signal of the schism to come. Barely able to speak to each other on camera, the disintegrating duo somehow managed to eke out two more movies — titled (irony intended and encouraged) *Pardners* and *Hollywood or Bust* — but "bust" it was Dec. 23, 1956, when the latter checked them into New York's Loews State, officially signing them out as a team. By then, they'd already taken off in opposite directions again — to launch separate (and quite successful!) careers.

1964:

"A major triumph" cheers *Variety*'s **"Rich"** from London on this day about the luminous star performance in *Seance on a Wet Afternoon*. Producer **Richard Attenborough**'s first choice to play his maladjusted medium of a missus — **Margaret Lockwood** — got mired in distributor red-tape, but he struck gold with his second: a rare and rewarding film portrayal from out of the blue (the U.S. stage, actually). **Kim Stanley**'s brilliant emoting made the Oscar running and was damned more serious work than what *did* win: Julie **Andrews'** *Mary Poppins*.

1967:

On this day — 15 days after he finished filming *Guess Who's Coming to Dinner* — **Spencer Tracy**, 67, dies of a heart attack in his little rented house on **George Cukor**'s property that he shared with **Katharine Hepburn**. His inability to get insurance kept him off the screen the final four years of his life. It was only because Hepburn and producer-director **Stanley Kramer** put their own salaries in escrow to compensate for the lack of insurance that he managed this last hurrah. *Guess Who's Coming to Dinner* was his ninth Oscar nomination and his ninth screen-pairing with Hepburn, who waltzed off with Best Actress honors (but knew better than anyone the Oscar was for Tracy).

1934: At the new Tanforan Race Track outside San Francisco on this day, producer-director **Frank Capra** cues the cameras to start rolling on *Broadway Bill* — and it turns out to be footage he'll recycle 16 years later in his **Bing Crosby** remake, *Riding High*, along with a fair share of its character-actor cast (**Clarence Muse**, **Ward Bond**, **Margaret Hamilton**, **Raymond Walburn**, **Frankie Darro**, **Irving Bacon**, **Douglass Dumbrille**, all continuing characterizations they began in 1934). Capra's Oscar-winning *It Happened One Night* was indeed a hard act to follow, and this wasn't made any easier by having **Warner Baxter** in a role that had been written for another *One Night* Oscar winner, **Clark Gable**. Thus, by default, it fell to Baxter to be the first to use the phrase "the little fella" in a Frank Capra film — this when telling off his rich father-in-law (**Walter Connolly**): "You're only interested in one thing — accumulating money, expanding the Higgins enterprises, and gobbling up the little fella."

1935: Because of **Robert Donat**'s precarious health, Warners decides to look elsewhere for its *Captain Blood*, starting with its own roster of contract players. On this day, **Hal Wallis** orders tests of **George Brent** and **Errol Flynn**.

1969: On this day, **Sidney Poitier**, **Barbra Streisand** and **Paul Newman** all join hands and form their own moviemaking company: the short-lived First Artists, Inc. Later on, **Steve McQueen** and **Dustin Hoffman** threw in their lot as well.

1979: A man of the Western, **John Wayne**, succumbs to cancer on this day at age 72 — or, as one Tokyo newspaper chose to announce it, "Mr. America passes on."

1991: On this day — only three days before she is to meet *Flatliners* co-star **Kiefer Sutherland** at the altar—**Julia Roberts** cancels the wedding and wings to Dublin with a friend of his (**Jackie Gleason**'s grandson, actor **Jason Patric**).

1996: German silent-screen star **Brigitte Helm**, 88, dies on this day in Ascona, Switzerland, where she had lived the past 30 years in virtual seclusion. Of the 35 films she did before retiring in 1935, the most famous was *Metropolis*, **Fritz Lang**'s groundbreaking futuristic epic. A mere teenager at the time, she became a kind of a cinematic icon playing the robotic seductress worshipped by worker slaves of a decadent ruling order. Apparently, she did Unapproachable Diva off-camera as well — like rejecting **Josef von Sternberg**'s offer to do *The Blue Angel*, turning down in effect the career that went to **Marlene Dietrich**.

12

1937: *Nothing Sacred* goes into production on this day with **Fredric March**, **Carole Lombard** and a classic script by **Ben Hecht** — but without a satisfactory ending. (*That* was sweated out later by **Ring Lardner Jr.** and the young **Budd Schulberg**.)

1938: According to *The New York Times* on this day, **Walt Disney** discarded 2,300 feet of the film on his forthcoming *Pinocchio* — roughly, five months of work — "because it had missed the feeling he had in mind." Fraught with missteps and false starts, the animated feature used only 300,000 of its two million drawings. The problem had to do with making the title puppet rounder, cuter, more audience-friendly. **Dick Jones** took over Pinocchio's voice from **Cliff Edwards**, who was reassigned the voice of Pinocchio's cricket/conscience, Jiminy. "I'm a Happy-Go-Lucky Fellow," a song Edwards recorded for *Pinocchio*, surfaced seven years later for Jiminy's cameo in *Fun and Fancy Free*. Gideon, the alley-cat sidekick of J. Worthington Foulfellow (the **Barrymore**sque fox played by **Walter Catlett**), was initially conceived as a motormouth, then recharacterized mute, and all that remained of the reams of dialogue **Mel Blanc** recorded was a couple of hiccups.

1957: The feuding **Dorseys** (or, as their 1947 film biography called them, *The Fabulous Dorseys*) are history on this day: Six and a half months after the death of trombonist **Tommy**, 51, cancer claims saxophonist **Jimmy**, 53.

1962: "Where were you in '62?" On this particular day, 18-year-old **George Lucas** is near death in Modesto City Hospital, the victim of a car crash that turns his Fiat into a metal pretzel. Exactly one decade and two weeks later, in nearby San Rafael, CA, Lucas started directing *American Graffiti*, cramming into 28 shooting days the four years he spent cruising up and down 10th Street in Modesto prior to that crash. Along for the ride were New Faces of 1972: **Richard Dreyfuss, Cindy Williams, Harrison Ford, Mackenzie Phillips, Ron Howard, Suzanne Somers, Paul LeMat, Candy Clark, Charles Martin Smith.**

1967: *Speedway*, another lap around the sports-car track with **Elvis**, starts lensing on this day — and premieres on this day a year later in Charlotte, NC. **Petula Clark** had declined the co-star shot, but **Nancy Sinatra** said *YES*. She'd met him March 3, 1960, as his official greeter when he deplaned from West Germany at McGuire Air Force Base.

1999: Considering what they've been through together — *Scream* and *Scream 2* (but who's counting?) — it is not entirely surprising that **Courteney Cox** and **David Arquette** would, on this day, wed.

13

1940: *Our Town*, **Thornton Wilder**'s stage portrait of life and death in small-town New England at the start of this century, reaches the screen at Radio City Music Hall on this day as a life and near-death experience. Producer **Sol Lesser** found it impossible to let the heroine die in childbirth as she had on stage and somehow prodded the play's Pulitzer Prize-winning author to the same conclusion. In the screenplay he himself adapted with **Harry Chandlee** and the play's narrator/"stage manager" (**Frank Craven**), Wilder spared her — at the expense of his eloquent third act. "Emily should live," he wrote, rationalizing this Lesser route as the difference between theater and film. "Insofar as the play is a generalized allegory, she dies-we die-they die; insofar as it's a concrete happening it's not important that she die; it is disproportionately cruel that she die. Let her live — the idea will have been imparted anyway." **Martha Scott**, Broadway's Emily Webb Gibbs, was eliminated from movie consideration because she'd tested poorly for *Gone With the Wind*'s Melanie. Only after scores of other actresses had tested for Emily did she get a shot at the role she'd originated. She made the Oscar running with it, her first film performance.

1941: "The Hays Office warned us that we couldn't show the heroine as a prostitute," director **Fritz Lang** recalled about his *Man Hunt*, bowing at the Roxy on this day. But there's, always, A Way: "We had to put a sewing machine in her apartment, so, in that way, she was not a whore but a seamstress."

1956: Oscar's two most-nominated (6) non-winning women — **Deborah Kerr** and **Thelma Ritter** — surface in the same picture: *The Proud and the Profane*, opening on this day at Manhattan's Astor Theater — and breaking nobody's tie. The film's director, **George Seaton**, discovered Ritter for his *Miracle on 34th Street* and steered **Helen Hayes** to an Oscar in what could only be called "a Thelma Ritter role": Ada Quonsett, the little-old-lady stowaway in *Airport*. (Ritter, 63, had died of a heart attack mere months before *Airport* filming began.)

1963: "All is monumental — but the people are not," declares **Judith Crist** in *The New York Herald Tribune* on this day, hailstoning the Rivoli arrival of the $40 million **Elizabeth Taylor-Richard Burton** *Cleopatra*. "The mountain of notoriety has produced a mouse." Incredibly, the critic and the film's co-writer and director, **Joseph L. Mankiewicz**, became great friends after that review. Mankiewicz tended to agree, primarily because 20th Century-Fox reneged on its promise to divide the picture into two feature-length halves. Burton told him he felt he did his best acting ever in footage the public never saw.

1922: On this day — Flag Day — **Harold Lloyd** celebrates in a flamboyant fashion quite apt for "The King of Daredevil Comedy": hanging from a flagpole 12 stories high for a classic stunt in *Safety Last*, the best of the "thrill comedies" he pioneered. The day's work also included an image that became his icon: dangling from the hands of a huge clock. No trick shots were used for the sequence, but mattress-laden scaffolding lurked under him out of camera range, in case (only, as he later remarked, "who wants to fall three stories?")

1945: *Night and Day*, a hokey bio where **Cary Grant** sits down at a piano and blithely pecks out the title tune in an inspirational surge, begins lensing on this day. As its Hungarian director, **Michael Curtiz**, said: "This man **Cole Porter**, he sticked to purpose of making good music, come hell or hayride." (It was common to find on the Warners lot signs promising: "Curtiz spoken here.")

1948: On this day, **Judy Garland** goes into rehearsals with **Fred Astaire** for *The Barkleys of Broadway* (then tagged *You Made Me Love You*), and, for three weeks, she finds herself in the same picture with **Oscar Levant** — an occasion, quipped Levant, that almost caused the pharmaceutical companies to declare a national holiday. Sure enough, the medication caught up with Garland, and, on July 19, she suddenly found herself replaced by Astaire's RKO partner, **Ginger Rogers** — but she did return to the set periodically to sulk, jeer and send Rogers to her trailer in tears.

1950: In a hastily composed wire on this day, director **William Wyler** heads off his Hurstwood (**Laurence Olivier**) before Olivier can rendezvous in London with their hoped-for *Carrie* (as in **Theodore Dreiser**'s *Sister Carrie*): **Elizabeth Taylor**, then 18 and five weeks into her first honeymoon. MGM was not too keen about loaning her out again to Paramount, where she'd just given her best performance-to-date — in *A Place in the Sun*, based on Dreiser's *An American Tragedy*. Taylor's unavailability (MGM wasted her on the routine *Love Is Better Than Ever*) prompted Paramount to page **Ava Gardner**, but it wound up being **Jennifer Jones** who *Carri*ed on.

1970: For the first time, an actor enters the House of Lords on this day — a milestone that turns **Sir Laurence Olivier** into **Lord Olivier**. The only other actors to become Lords: **Richard Attenborough** and **Bernard Miles**.

1980: On this day, **Mel Gibson** arrives on the Manhattan movie scene, burning rubber, pursuing the bikers who killed his son, in Round One of/as *Mad Max*.

HANGING BY THE HANDS OF TIME: Harold Lloyd in *Safety Last*.
TRUTHS ACCORDING TO WYLER & CURTIZ: From left: Basil Ruysdael and Laurence Olivier in *Carrie*; Selena Royle and Cary Grant in *Night and Day*.
ROAD RAGE: Mel Gibson in *Mad Max*.

1942: *Holiday Inn* goes into national release, and **Bing Crosby** starts dreaming unseasonably early of a "White Christmas." The most popular movie song of them all—indeed, the top-seller of all time until **Elton John**'s "Candle in the Wind '97"—debuted in this by-the-seasons songfest. A sad sidebar to this song is that it came from a man who lost his only son—25-day-old **Irving Berlin Jr.**—on Christmas Day of 1928.

1946: As the wish-I'd-never-been-born George Bailey of *It's a Wonderful Life*, **James Stewart** trudges down Main Street at RKO's Encino Ranch in the midst of a studio-created snowstorm—this, despite a California heat wave in the sweltering 90s.

1955: For the first time, **Susan Hayward** confronts the cameras of MGM, and gobs of stars wander over from adjacent sets to watch. Which was large of them, considering Hayward snatched *I'll Cry Tomorrow* away from a home-lot girl (**June Allyson**). In **Lillian Roth**'s gut-wrenching autobiography, Hayward saw a sure Oscar shot since it combined the lush/thrush elements that got her there before (*Smash-Up—The Story of a Woman*, *My Foolish Heart*, *With a Song in My Heart*). Keeping that thought, she picked **Daniel Mann** to direct since he had directed (to an Oscar) **Shirley Booth** in *Come Back, Little Sheba*. Unfortunately, he'd also just directed **Anna Magnani** in *The Rose Tattoo*—and well enough to win the Oscar over Hayward's efforts.

1967: One of the original survivors of *The Dirty Dozen*, arriving with much rat-a-tat-tat at the Loews Capitol in New York—**Richard Jaeckel**—dies of cancer one day short of that day 30 years later at the age of 70. *The Dirty Dozen* was the most distinguished of his many World War II engagements, which started in 1943 when he stepped out of the mail room at 20th Century-Fox into *Guadalcanal Diary*. That was followed by *Wing and a Prayer*, *Battleground*, *Sands of Iwo Jima*, *Fighting Coast Guard*, *Attack!*, *The Naked and the Dead*, *The Gallant Hours*, *The Devil's Brigade*, et al. His best work—a heartbreakingly protracted drowning scene in *Sometimes a Great Notion*—was Oscar-nominated.

1999: The skipper of *The African Queen* and his first-mate—**Humphrey Bogart** and **Katharine Hepburn**—finish first as the top American stars of the century in a poll conducted by AFI and announced in a CBS special. The nine following Bogie: **Cary Grant**, **James Stewart**, **Marlon Brando**, **Fred Astaire**, **Henry Fonda**, **Clark Gable**, **James Cagney**, **Spencer Tracy** and **Charles Chaplin**. The nine after Hepburn: **Bette Davis**, **Audrey Hepburn**, **Ingrid Bergman**, **Greta Garbo**, **Marilyn Monroe**, **Elizabeth Taylor**, **Judy Garland**, **Marlene Dietrich** and **Joan Crawford**. Only the stars of *Reflections in a Golden Eye*—Brando and Taylor—are still alive.

MOVIE ROYALTY RODE *THE AFRICAN QUEEN*: Katharine Hepburn and Humphrey Bogart.
MANN-MADE NOMINEE: Daniel Mann directing Susan Hayward in *I'll Cry Tomorrow*.
"WHITE CHRISTMAS" IN JUNE: From left: James Stewart in *It's a Wonderful Life*; Bing Crosby, Virginia Dale, Marjorie Reynolds and Fred Astaire in *Holiday Inn*.

16

1915: By the time she arrives as *The Devil's Daughter* on this day — six months and four films into an indelible screen persona — there's a word for the role **Theda Bara** has pioneered. It, and she, are called "vamp." That varied little in her 39-film, four-year career. She went the way of all flesh, leading upright men to rack and ruin — as Carmen, Cleopatra, Salome, Cigarette, Esmeralda, Juliet, etc. And that image was reinforced with a bio fabricated by publicists who claimed her name was an anagram for "Arab Death" when it actually was a contraction of her first name (**Theodosia Goodman**) and an extraction of her Swiss grandfather's name: **Francois Bar(r)anger de Coppet**. Her mystique, they said, was what comes of being born in the shadow of the Sphinx, daughter of a Mid-East potentate — but really she was born in Cincinnati, daughter of a Jewish tailor.

1937: With two screen lovers (**Nelson Eddy** and **Allan Jones**) in attendance, **Jeanette MacDonald** weds **Gene Raymond** in Beverly Hills' Wilshire Methodist Church on this day — but she reported to work on *The Firefly* the next day. Their union lasted till her death Jan. 14, 1965. Her dying words were to him: "I love you, Gene." (She left Eddy her print of *Rose Marie*.)

1959: The B-movie *Superman* of TV turns out *not* to be faster than a speeding bullet on this day: Despondent his series success prevented him from landing other roles, **George Reeves** dies of a gunshot wound, supposedly self-inflicted.

1967: The first major rock festival — The Monterey International Pop Festival, opening on this day in California — produces the first major rock concert film (*Monterey Pop*, premiering Dec. 26, 1968, at Lincoln Center's Philharmonic Hall). **Janis Joplin**'s "Ball and Chain" and **Jimi Hendrix**' "Wild Thing" stood out in a field that included **Otis Redding, Jefferson Airplane, The Who, The Mamas and the Papas** and **Ravi Shankar**. All worked for free, and the price of admission ranged from $3.50 to $6.50.

1980: In Chicago on this day, **John Belushi** and **Dan Aykroyd** start breaking in their *Blues Brothers*, stretching a skit-size act into a feature-length film.

1998: Three hours of prime CBS time on this day go to a roll call of the 100 greatest American movies, as determined by an American Film Institute poll. The champ: *Citizen Kane*, followed by *Casablanca, The Godfather, Gone With the Wind, Lawrence of Arabia, The Wizard of Oz, The Graduate, On the Waterfront, Schindler's List* and *Singin' in the Rain*. Only six of these top ten won Oscars for Best Picture in their respective years.

THE CENTURY'S CHAMP: Orson Welles in *Citizen Kane*.
CATCHING SOME STEAM: John Belushi, Steve Lawrence and Dan Aykroyd in *The Blues Brothers*.
A BRIDAL BLUSH, ON SCREEN AND OFF: From left: Jeanette MacDonald with Allan Jones in *The Firefly* and with husband Gene Raymond in real life.

1924: *He Who Gets Slapped* spanks life into a new studio on this day as the newly merged Metro-Goldwyn-Mayer gets rolling with its first feature — a Big Top triangle about a scientist-turned-clown (**Lon Chaney**) in love with a bareback rider (**Norma Shearer**) in love with her riding partner (**John Gilbert**).

1935: *Barbary Coast*, which was to have starred **Gary Cooper**, **Gloria Swanson** and **Paul Kelly** under **William A. Wellman**'s direction, goes into production on this day starring **Joel McCrea**, **Miriam Hopkins** and **Edward G. Robinson** under **Howard Hawks**' direction. A rowdy gold-rush romp of the 1850s, it boasted a colorful supporting cast (**Brian Donlevy**, **Harry Carey**, **Frank Craven**, **Walter Brennan**, **Donald Meek**) — plus an early **David Niven**, *very* much out of character as a boozed-up, mustache-drooping Cockney sailor who's hurled out of the window of a waterfront brothel and into the muddy streets of San Francisco. His one line — "'Orl rite — I'm goin'!" — was uttered as he sailed past the Madam; then — while his face stayed mired in several inches of mud — Hopkins, McCrea, Brennan, 30 vigilantes and some donkeys walked over the top of him. Happily for him, more civilized conduct lurked just around the corner.

1936: "Chronic illness" claims **Henry B. Walthall**, 58, on this day. The veteran character actor had six releases the year of his death and was up for a role that would have rivaled his most famous ("The Little Colonel" in *The Birth of a Nation*) — The High Lama in *Lost Horizon*. Walthall's other claim to fame: He was the first actor to wear make-up created specifically for motion picture use. Indeed, he modeled for the screen tests when the make-up was introduced.

1954: On this day, *The New York Times* reports **David O. Selznick**'s plans to film *War and Peace* — and suddenly the race was on to film **Tolstoy**'s tall story. By February, **Marshal Tito** was busily drafting the Yugoslav Army into the Battle of Borodino being staged by two other rival productions — one produced by **Mike Todd** and directed by **Fred Zinnemann** from a screenplay by **Robert E. Sherwood**, the other produced by **Carlo Ponti** and **Dino DeLaurentiis** and directed by **King Vidor** starring "**Gregory Peck**, **Jean Simmons** and either **Stewart Granger** or **Montgomery Clift**." The latter is the lone version that got into production, but the result unveiled on the Capitol screen two years and two months later starred **Henry Fonda**, **Audrey Hepburn**, **Mel Ferrer** — and the *Italian* army.

THE LITTLE COLONEL AND THE LITTLE CORPORAL: From left: Henry B. Walthall (with Mae Marsh) in *The Birth of a Nation*; Herbert Lom as Napoleon in *War and Peace*.
MGM *GETS SLAPPED* INTO LIFE: Norma Shearer and Lon Chaney in *He Who Gets Slapped*.
EXCUSE ME, YOU'RE STANDING ON A STAR: Miriam Hopkins and Joel McCrea in *Barbary Coast*.

1937: The Spanish Civil War finally reaches the U.S. screen on this day — but **Frank S. Nugent**, in his *New York Times* notice the next day, cautioned not to put much stock in *The Last Train From Madrid* that just pulled into the Criterion: By any other name, this was *Grand Hotel*-with-a-topical-update — the twinkling interplay of all-stars on the brink (**Dorothy Lamour**, **Lew Ayres**, **Gilbert Roland**, **Karen Morley**, **Lionel Atwill**, **Helen Mack**, **Robert Cummings**, **Anthony Quinn** and **Lee Bowman**). Location shooting ranged from Valencia, Spain, to **Cecil B. DeMille**'s Spanish-style bungalow on the Paramount backlot. Gamely, DeMille agreed to do a crowd scene.

1949: Mistaking newsreel photographers for studio cinematographers, Norma Desmond (**Gloria Swanson**) makes her staircase descent into madness on this day, as principal photography is completed on *Boulevard*. When director **Billy Wilder** yelled "Print it!" for the last time, Swanson broke into tears. The comeback that should have followed this magnificent performance didn't, but the experience did permit Swanson one last hurrah which somehow kept her star-lit the rest of her days. Unfortunately, Wilder's 12-year, 13-film scripting collaboration with producer **Charles Brackett** did not survive. After this crowning achievement, the two went separate ways.

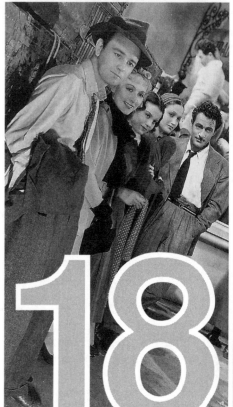

1951: *Singin' in the Rain* starts shootin' on the backlot on this day at MGM. Reviews, when the film debuts April 10, were uniformly favorable — and they keep getting better and better with every passing year. Now, it has reached a point where film scholars debate in all seriousness if it's the best or (after *The Band Wagon* a year later) just the second-best film musical of all time.

1959: Director **Fred Zinnemann**'s 18-month struggle to bring *The Nun's Story* to the screen ends on this day with its arrival at Radio City Music Hall. His battle began with getting line-by-line approval of **Robert Anderson**'s script from the Catholic Church, and it ended with a clash over the film's musical finale. Suspecting composer **Franz Waxman** of an anti-Catholic bias from the joyful noises he made at the end when **Audrey Hepburn** turned in her habit, Zinnemann insisted on noncommittal silence and took his case to **Jack L. Warner**, contending "If you have festive music, you are saying to the audience, 'Warner Bros. congratulates the nun on quitting the convent.'" This proved a convincing argument.

1992: Entertainer **Peter Allen**, 48, dies of an AIDS-related illness on this day. He became an Oscar winner simply by looking out of a plane window one night and noticing the moon against the Manhattan skyline — "caught between the moon and New York City," as it were — and that phrase found its way into **Marvin Hamlisch** and **Carole Bayer Sager**'s Oscar-winning song, "Arthur's Theme (Best That You Can Do).

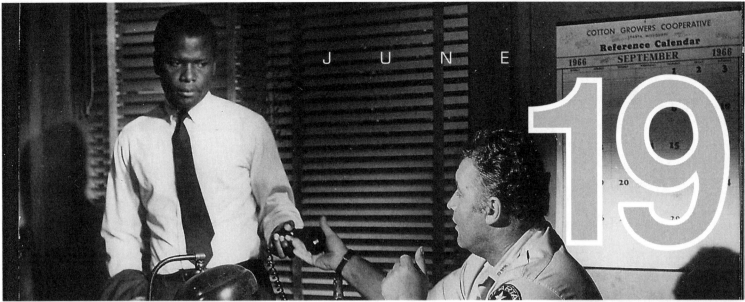

J U N E

19

1931: New York critics are not overly impressed on this day with *Smart Money*, what will be the only screen pairing of *Little Caesar* and *The Public Enemy* (i.e., **Edward G. Robinson** and **James Cagney**).

1935: *So Red the Rose*, predating Scarlett's debut on the best-seller lists by a good year, goes into production on this day — a million-dollar Civil War saga that paid the price for coming before its time. **Margaret Sullavan**, who played the belle/hellion of the manor, had to sit out the mad diva scramble for *GWTW* because of her film's bleak box office.

1942: *This Gun for Hire* is released on this day, and the bad-guy gets the good marks. The cold-blooded hit-man of the title was to be played by an 22-year-old unknown from Atlanta — **DeForest Kelley** — but, at the last moment, the part went to an equally unknown bit-player, who connected solidly with female fans and became a star. **Robert Preston**, **Veronica Lake** and **Laird Cregar** were billed above **Alan Ladd** the first time out, but, when the film was reissued in 1948, Ladd topped the bill — and Cregar was misspelled.

1962: Supposedly the largest gathering of Iowans *ever* — 125,000 strong — turns out on this day for the big parade bringing **Meredith Willson** back to his Mason City roots. He brought along a little film to premiere there, too — the film version of his Broadway hit, *The Music Man* — and title-player **Robert Preston**.

1965: *The New York Times* announces on this day the screen is acquiring its first black detective — Virgil Tibbs from the novels of **John Ball** — and he will be played by **Sidney Poitier**. Installment One wound up with the Oscar for Best Picture of 1967 — *In the Heat of the Night* — and produced a Best Actor Oscar for **Rod Steiger**, playing the redneck sheriff who became Tibbs' reluctant partner-in-crime-detection. A Poitier line from **Stirling Silliphant**'s Oscar-winning screen adaptation became the title of Film Chapter Two: 1970's *They Call Me MISTER Tibbs!* Detective Poitier retired after his third case (1971's *The Organization*), the law of diminishing returns being very much in effect.

1992: The returns of *Batman Returns* ($16.1 mil) set the opening-day record on this day, then top *that* the next day by setting the single-day record ($16.8 mil). Its phenomenal $44.55 million weekend became the industry's best since — well, since the first *Batman* bounded forth June 23-25, 1989 ($40,489,746). The third *Batman* did even better on June 16, 1995; via the simple ploy of playing in one out of every five theaters in the U.S., *Batman Forever* soared to the biggest opening ever: $58.2 mil. ('BATMAN' ROBBIN' RECORD BOOK, said *Variety*).

20

1941: *Bluebeard, Landru, The Ladykiller* and *The Life of Desire* are titles registered with the Motion Picture Producers' Association on this day, covering a screenplay **Orson Welles** has written for **Charles Chaplin**. On April 11, 1947, Chaplin comes to market with his own film on this subject, *Monsieur Verdoux* — careful to credit it's "based on an idea by Orson Welles."

1945: On this day — his 21st birthday — World War II's most decorated soldier, **Audie Murphy**, meets the Oscar-winning impersonator of World War I hero **Alvin York**. "I should have on stilts to talk to you," quipped the kid who'd someday be called the "pint-sized **Gary Cooper**" when he met his movie idol in Dallas, drumbeating for *Along Came Jones*. Coop asked if Murphy would like to hear how York had captured 132 Germans, but Murphy declined, saying he'd rather hear how Cooper was able to gobble like a turkey (as per that little trick in *Sergeant York* that got the Germans to poke their heads up from the trenches).

1961: The two heads of a new producing unit called Eon ("Everything or Nothing") — **Albert R. Broccoli** and **Harry Saltzman** — huddled on this day with **Arthur Krim**, President of United Artists — and, in less than an hour, form a deal to finance the first James Bond flick for $1 million. *Thunderball* was to start the series, but, because of an impending legal battle over that particular property (which was eventually filmed twice: as *Thunderball* and as *Never Say Never Again*), it was decided to go with *Dr. No*, even though its title created confusion in some corners of the globe. "When *Dr. No* went to Japan," **Sean Connery** once recalled, "they translated it as *No Need for Any Doctors*."

1969: As the Lion Rorys: **Lita Baron** sues **Rory Calhoun** for divorce on this day, charging him with adultery and naming **Betty Grable** — along with 78 other women.

1984: A heart attack claims character actress **Estelle Winwood**, 101, on this day at the Motion Picture and Television Country Hospital. Birdlike and British-born, she started acting on stage at 5 and was still doing it on television at 100. In between were choice feature-film assignments like fairy godmother to **Leslie Caron** in *The Glass Slipper* and easy-mark investor to **Zero Mostel** in *The Producers*. Her final big-screen outing was *Murder by Death*, which she played in a wheelchair she didn't actually need. In her last year, she admitted to tippling Gallo cream sherry, smoking three packs of cigarettes a day and playing bridge three times a week.

1991: Side-by-side obits of two stars once wed to producer **Frank Ross** are run by *The New York Times* on this day: **Joan Caulfield**, 69, and **Jean Arthur**, 90/85.

WHAT PRICE INVESTMENT?: Estelle Winwood and Zero Mostel in *The Producers.*
THE LITERAL LADYKILLER: Charles Chaplin in *Monsieur Verdoux.*
THE WIVES OF FRANK ROSS: From left: Jean Arthur and Joan Caulfield.
LITA RESTS HER CASE: Betty Grable and Rory Calhoun in *How To Marry a Millionaire.*

21

"MR. SMITH" GOES TO COURT: Paul Stanton, Irene Dunne, Skippy and Cary Grant in *The Awful Truth*.
ROGERS AND OUT: Will Rogers and Anne Shirley in his last, *Steamboat Round the Bend*.
THOROUGHLY MODERN MARY: Pickford in *Coquette*.
"COOP" COUPLING: From left: Gary Cooper with Barbara Stanwyck in *Ball of Fire*, and with Patricia Neal in *The Fountainhead*.

1928: "The most famous head of hair since Medusa's" — **Mary Pickford**'s cascading curls — is sacrificed to the scissors of **Charles Bock**'s salon on East 57th, while New York press cameras click away. The ringlets had become a strangling synonym for Pickford, stunting her growth as an actress. Now, streamlined and bobbed, she took on the talkies — and won an Oscar her first time at bat, playing the small-town *Coquette*.

1935: *Steamboat Round the Bend* (replete with a title tune composed by, of all unlikely people, **Oscar Levant**) is skippered to a stopping point by director **John Ford** on this day — which also happens to be **Will Rogers**' last day on a movie set *ever*. Less than two months later (Aug. 15), he was killed in a plane crash in Alaska. Quality-wise, *Steamboat* streamrolled right over Rogers' previous film (*In Old Kentucky*) and went into posthumous release first. Its closing shot — Rogers waving goodbye to the character played by **Irvin S. Cobb** — was eliminated (over Cobb's objections) by a super-sensitive studio fearing this sight would send audiences away in tears.

1937: The efforts of **Cary Grant** and **Irene Dunne** to change partners and divorce comprise *The Awful Truth*, a dizzy marriage-go-round which starts spinning on this day under **Leo McCarey**'s Oscar-winning direction. Product of their broken home: a feisty wire-haired terrier named "Mr. Smith," played by **Skippy** (a.k.a. *The Thin Man*'s Asta). The antic got near the top of the screwball-comedy heap.

1948: In the morning papers on this day, **Barbara Stanwyck** sees **Patricia Neal** will star in *The Fountainhead* — a property Stanwyck found, brought to Warners' attention and had the studio buy for her — so, bitterly disappointed, she wires **Jack Warner** for immediate release from her contract, which he permits. He felt Stanwyck lacked the necessary sex appeal for the part, and the subsequent sparks Neal generated with **Gary Cooper** proved authentic enough to start a long affair that jeopardized Cooper's marriage.

22

1943: Paramount's all-star salute to the ten brave American nurses who survived the bloody defeats of both Bataan and Corregidor — *So Proudly We Hail* — premieres on this day at Radio City Music Hall with all flags waving. Off-camera, "So Loudly We Rail" was more like it! When a reporter asked **Paulette Goddard** which co-star she liked better — **Claudette Colbert** or **Veronica Lake** — Paulette picked the latter, purring a wickedly tactless (and wrong) postscript: "After all, we *are* closer in age." (In truth, she was two years closer to Colbert's age than to Lake's.) The remark steamed Colbert, who was already quite exasperated with the number of retakes that were required for Goddard's line-fluffing. The upshot of this Claudette-vs.-Paulette catfight came in February when Goddard garnered the movie's single acting nomination.

1951: **Dore Schary** replaces **Louis B. Mayer** as MGM's top lion. Fourteen years later on this day, Mayer's famous former son-in-law — **David O. Selznick** — dies of acute coronary occlusion at Hollywood's Mt. Sinai Hospital; it was death in the afternoon — 2:22 p.m. — for the man who created what was in its time the longest movie ever made (the 222-minute-long *Gone With the Wind*). The following day, the inevitable headline that the 63-year-old producer had always predicted for himself finally saw print: "Producer of *GWTW* Dies."

1987: On this day –18 years to the day following the death of his *Easter Parade* co-star, **Judy Garland**, 47 — **Fred Astaire**, 88, dies in the arms of his wife, the onetime star jockey **Robyn Smith**. Two days later, poignantly on what would have been their seventh wedding anniversary, Mrs. Astaire buried him.

1988: "Stay tooned," trumpet the ads announcing the New York opening of *Who Framed Roger Rabbit*, a splashy, magnificent mix of live action and animation.

1990: Carolco plunks down a record auction-bid of $3 mil on this day for the **Joe Eszterhas**-scripted *Basic Instinct*, a movie remembered not for its writing but for a sliver of a second (albeit, a star-making one) in which **Sharon Stone** uncrossed and crossed her legs during a police quizzing. The next Eszterhas-Stone outing, rightly named *Sliver*, was nowhere as interesting as the game of musical beds accompanying its creation: Stone lured co-producer **Bill Macdonald** from his new bride, **Naomi**, who, in turn, lured Eszterhas away from *his* wife.

SO PROUDLY WE MEOW: Claudette and Paulette and Veronica in *So Proudly We Hail.*
PASSING *PARADE*: Judy and Fred in *Easter Parade.*
WRITING HAD NOTHING TO DO WITH IT: Sharon in *Basic Instinct.*

23

1946: Grim-faced, iron-jawed **William S. Hart**, 80, dies of a stroke on this day. During his 11 years on the screen (1914-1925), he set the standard for strong-and-silent types at a time when that was all a Western hero *could* be. His portrayals were more rough-hewn and realistic than movie audiences were used to — the "good-bad-man" was a specialty — and he carried the genre a giant step forward with classics like *Hell's Hinges* and *The Return of Draw Egan*. When Paramount threatened to put him out to pasture unless he streamlined his sagebrushers the way **Tom Mix** and **Buck Jones** did, Hart went peacefully out of the picture business — uncompromised and content — personally producing a major Western to ride out on: *Tumbleweeds*. Alas, it was thrown away by a vindictive distributor — and not really appreciated until 1939 when it was reissued with an added musical score and an eight-minute prologue in which Mr. Strong-and-Silent not only spoke to the audience but spoke *beautifully*, in a startlingly stage-trained voice. This man of the movie West turned out to have been born back East — in New York state — and done Shakespeare on Broadway. When he had his first brush with horses, they came attached to chariots: He created the role of *Ben-Hur*'s villainous Messala and played it for two years on stage.

FORD IN OVERDRIVE: Harrison Ford in *Raiders of the Lost Ark*.
HOLLYWOOD'S VERSION OF "WINO WILLIE": Marlon Brando in *The Wild One*.
HART OF THE WEST: William S. Hart.
HOPELESSLY DEVOTED: Olivia Newton-John and John Travolta in *Grease*.

1977: At the Paramount plant on this day, **John Travolta** and **Olivia Newton-John** start cooking with *Grease*. Counting its 20th anniversary reissue in 1998, it would become the highest-grossing musical ever ($179.9 million).

1980: *Raiders of the Lost Ark* begins filming on this day in the French coastal city of La Rochelle at the limestone submarine pens housing a duplicate World War II German U-boat (the same sub that was used in *Das Boot*). The preferred Indiana Jones didn't make this trip because CBS refused to delay the start of his *Magnum P.I.* series. As it turned out, an actors' strike did that, and **Tom Selleck** *could* have done both. "When I lost *Raiders*, through no fault of my own, I thought, 'Well, that was my shot. From now on, I'm a TV actor,'" Selleck shrugged sadly. "I felt entitled to get something out of it and kept telling people, 'That was *my* part, you know.' Now I've seen the film, it's hard to imagine anyone being better than **Harrison Ford**. He was quite . . . wonderful."

1997: The real-life version of **Marlon Brando** in *The Wild One* — **William "Wino Willie" Forkner**, 76 — dies of a ruptured aortic aneurysm on this day. He led the Boozefighters, a South Central Los Angeles biker gang, in a rowdy raid on Hollister, a town near Monterey. The raid was the factual basis for that film.

1930: With the bow of *The Big House* at New York's Astor on this day, **Wallace Beery** officially sets up shop in MGM's Dream Factory. When cancer claimed **Lon Chaney** before he could play that film's "Machine Gun" Butch Schmidt, Beery spun out of a career skid, nabbing not only the role and the Oscar nomination that went with it but also a studio contract that lasted the rest of his days.

1938: Presidential aide **James T. Early** greets **Shirley Temple** on this day as she arrives — early — at the White House to meet her most famous fan. Alas, **President Franklin Roosevelt** was otherwise engaged at a ceremonial signing of the Black-Connery Bill — an irony not lost on Temple, who'd write in her autobiography: "Borrowed from the English law, which had ruined **George Bernard Shaw**'s offer to bring me to the London stage, FDR's law prohibited people my age from working at all. During congressional debate, however, an amendment had been attached which exempted all child performers in movies from the age limitation. Without inclusion of the so-called Shirley Temple amendment, a stroke from the President's pen would have put me out of work that morning."

1948: *Fort Apache* lays siege to New York's Capitol on this day, the first of director **John Ford**'s famous "cavalry trilogy." *She Wore a Yellow Ribbon* rode out the following year and *Rio Grande* the year after that — but neither quite stirred up the critical dust as much as the first. Contrary to the superimposed still for lobby displays, **John Wayne** did *not* make the last stand of hard-headed martinet **Henry Fonda** but instead lived to eulogize his fallen comrades.

1962: Shaking the desert sand from his boots, director **David Lean** begins lensing on this day the fatal motorcycle ride that starts *Lawrence of Arabia*.

1971: Critic **Pauline Kael**'s idea of "a beautiful pipedream of a movie — a fleeting, almost diaphanous vision of what frontier life might have been" — opens wide at selected theaters in New York on this day: **Robert Altman**'s *McCabe & Mrs. Miller*, in which **Warren Beatty** and **Julie Christie** ride out a bordello bonanza in the wild 'n' unruly North. It came perilously close to going into release with the bizarre title, *The Presbyterian Church Wager*.

J U N E

1931: For $60,000, **Alfred Lunt** and **Lynn Fontanne** — Broadway's most legendary couple — turn into MGM stars on this day and stay in that state for 21 days, during which time they preserve (with Oscar-nominated film performances) their greatest stage success: **Ferenc Molnar**'s 1924 farce, *The Guardsman*. Lunt shunned the "rushes" like the plague during the three-week lensing — but sent Fontanne on reconnaissance. "It seems to be going well," she reported back. "In fact, you're wonderful, Alfred. Your voice, your manner, your timing — they all register beautifully. Of course, you could use a little more makeup to define your mouth — you look as if you have no lips — but that's a trivial matter. You have such flair, such panache, it's just wonderful. But, oh, Alfred, I am dreadful. I look scared to death, very plain and haggard with awful lines under my eyes — no shine in my hair — I look as if I'd been buried and dug up again. It's terribly disappointing. No, if the film succeeds, it will be your doing, there's no doubt about it." Then, according to the story popularized by **Samuel Marx** and/or **Alexander Woollcott**, Lunt absorbed all of the above silently, ran his finger across his mouth and said, "No lips, eh?"

BEYOND SMITH & WESSON: Smith and Jones in *Men in Black*.
BROADWAY UNBOUND: Alfred Lunt and Lynn Fontanne in *The Guardsman*.
NO *BADMAN* FINISH: Robert Francis.

1943: On a 90-day leave to put together a two-reel feature documentary, director **William Wyler** returns from World War II on this day. When he set eyes on his wife, **Talli**, it was at opposite ends of a long hallway leading to their room at the Hampshire House on NYC's Central Park South — and they raced to embrace. It was a dry run (if not a dry-eyed run) at the emotional reunion of **Fredric March** and **Myrna Loy** in *The Best Years of Our Lives*. "When I did the same thing for the movie, it was no great invention," Wyler admitted.

1955: Twenty years of distinguished MGM service comes to a blunt end on this day for **Spencer Tracy** when director **Robert Wise** unceremoniously boots him out of *Tribute to a Badman* for being AWOL on location. A stunned Tracy broke down and sobbed, believing this was the end of his career. It wasn't, but it was the end of **Robert Francis**'. The 25-year-old actor, who shot most of his scenes during Tracy's absence, took up flying lessons when the production shut down until **James Cagney** could take over Tracy's part and, on July 3, was killed when the trainer plane he was piloting crashed. His role went to **Don Dubbins**.

1997: Columbia rolls out the black carpet at Hollywood's Cinerama Dome on this day to launch *Men in Black*. Emulating the dress code of title players **Smith** & **Jones** (a.k.a. **Will** & **Tommy Lee**), first-nighters donned the dark sunglasses.

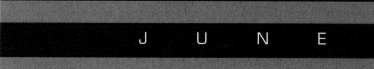

1937: On this day, an 11-year-old **Norma Jeane Baker** leaves the Los Angeles Orphans Home Society where, from her bedroom window, she could see the RKO Studios water tower. Eight years later on this day, under her married name of **Norma Jeane Dougherty**, she dons a sweater and poses for Army photographer **David Conover**, who takes the first professional photos of her (one of which winds up on the cover of *Yank* magazine). In 1953 on this day, now known as **Marilyn Monroe**, she and **Jane Russell** ballyhoo their new movie (*Gentlemen Prefer Blondes*) by leaving their hand- and footprints in cement in the courtyard of Grauman's Chinese Theater — a former haunt of Norma Jeane Baker who liked to step into the famous footprints left by **Valentino**, **Harlow**, et al.

1938: *The Young in Heart* finishes filming on this day, and **Janet Gaynor** retires from pictures — till 1957's *Bernardine* — to wed costumer **(Gilbert) Adrian**. The movie's other distinction: the two screen newcomers scene-stealing from the all-stars (Gaynor, **Douglas Fairbanks Jr.**, **Paulette Goddard**, **Roland Young**, **Billie Burke**, et al) — debuting **Richard Carlson** and stage veteran **Minnie Dupree**. Dupree was third choice to play "Miss Fortune," a kindly little old lady who reforms a family of scoundrels; producer **David O. Selznick** tried to talk two legendary ladies of the theater into the talkies — **Maude Adams** and **Laurette Taylor** — and even tested them in the role, but no dice and no diva.

1941: *Blossoms in the Dust* takes root at Radio City Music Hall on this day, and so does a new screen team: **Greer Garson** picked for her leading man the gentleman who consented to appear with her in her screen test, **Walter Pidgeon**. It was chemistry at second sight, and the compatibility was real. "I did nine pictures with that gal," he said, "and we never had a bad word between us." They also never had (at least discernible to the camera's eye) a real sexual current between them. The *Blossoms* that began their screen-teamwork was the biography of **Mrs. Edna Gladney**, who founded a home for Texas foundlings, and the *Scandal at Scourie* that ended it 12 years later found them bringing a foundling into their own home. Theirs was the comfortable-shoe, old-marrieds kind of togetherness. "Somebody said we were like ham and eggs," she recalled. "I sent him a telegram asking him what to make of it — and signed it 'Eggs.'"

ONE ENTRANCE, ONE EXIT: Ronald Young, Janet Gaynor, Billie Burke, Douglas Fairbanks Jr. and Minnie Dupree in *The Young at Heart*. Inset: Maude Adams.
THE CEMENT SIGN-IN: Marilyn Monroe and Jane Russell at Grauman's Chinese.
A TEAM TAKES OFF: Greer Garson and Walter Pidgeon in *Blossoms in the Dust*.

26

27

1944: Amply filling the title role of *Bathing Beauty*, **Esther Williams** plunges into the star ranks her third film out. (Mercifully, the title was switched at the last moment from *Sing Or Swim.*) It bows on this day at the Astor, and 11 years of splashy stardom follow. The lack of depth didn't faze the "Million Dollar Mermaid," who, in cynical wetrospect, would later quip: "All they ever did for me at MGM was to change my leading men and the water in the pool."

1960: The second movie in a single week recounting **Oscar Wilde**'s libel suit against the **Marquis of Queensberry** surfaces on this day in New York, at the Paris: *The Trials of Oscar Wilde* with **Peter Finch**, telling identically the same story *Oscar Wilde* did seven days earlier with **Robert Morley**. The *deja vu* proved self-destructive: Neither entry exactly set the box-office woods afire.

1964: Fire and water (**Ernest Borgnine**, 47, and **Ethel Merman**, 55) are mixed maritally on this day, prompting one wit to quip: "I want the pick of the litter." Alas, the 38-day marriage barely survived the honeymoon. A full blank page is spent on this odd coupling in The Merm's autobiography, which was just as well: Only a **Walter** (*A Night To Remember*) **Lord** could really do it justice!

1969: "JUDY'S PEOPLE DIDN'T FORGET" and "AN ALL-NIGHT VIGIL FOR JUDY" shout the front pages of different editions of New York's *Daily News* on this day. Shortly before midnight on the day **Judy Garland** was buried at Ferncliff Cemetery in Hartsdale, NY, police conducted a routine raid on the Stonewall Inn, a gay bar on Christopher Street in the heart of Greenwich Village, and in the melee that followed (2,000 gay men and lesbians vs. 400 club-wielding riot police), Gay Liberation was born. The rioting ran till dawn and resumed the following day. It was, according to historian **John D'Emilio**, "the first gay riot in history" (or, as the gay Mattachine Society newsletter campily concluded, "The Hairpin Drop Heard Round the World"). Within a month of The Stonewall Rebellion, the Gay Liberation Front was established, and, within a year, dozens of gay liberation organizations had been formed across the U.S.

1994: In that paradise called Hawaii, on this Day of Infamy for Universal Pictures, production begins on a subterranean sci-fi saga that'll soon set the high-water-mark for Most Expensive Movie: *Waterworld*. What sloshed to market, bloated and waterlogged, a year and a day later weighed in at somewhere between $185 million and $200 million. Volatile weather took the blame for the spiraling cost, but **Albert Brooks** advanced a better theory: "They used Evian."

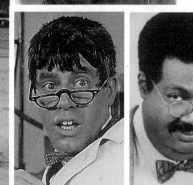

28

1933: Having departed RKO with producer **David O. Selznick** for the dreamier pastures of MGM and *Dinner at Eight*, director **George Cukor** returns to his home studio on this day to finish off his contract there with one last picture — his personal favorite: *Little Women*. When Selznick decided to remake the property 13 years later with wife **Jennifer Jones** as Jo March, he tried coaxing Cukor into directing it, but Cukor declined, contending that **Katharine Hepburn** was the definitive Jo. **June Allyson** wound up doing the role in 1949 for director **Mervyn LeRoy**.

1954: The stars of 1945's *Where Do We Go from Here?* — **Fred MacMurray**, 45, and **June Haver**, 28 — answer that question by marrying in Ojai on this day.

1978: Borrowing the title of a 1943 **Don Ameche** movie (*Heaven Can Wait*) to remake a 1941 **Robert Montgomery** movie (*Here Comes Mr. Jordan*), **Warren Beatty** bows at NYC theaters on this day as an angel-before-his-time. The following February, that film earned him Oscar nominations as actor, co-director, co-screenwriter and producer — bettering (by one) the record set in 1977 by "**Diane Keaton**'s other boyfriend" (**Woody Allen** for *Annie Hall*) and tying **Orson Welles'** record for *Citizen Kane*.

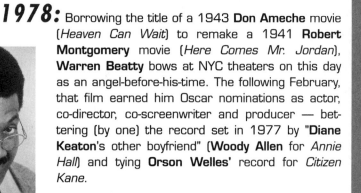

1986: Sotheby's in New York rings up $275,000 on this day for the Aston Martin DB5 James Bond (**Sean Connery**) tooled through *Goldfinger* — the *Guinness* record-holder for the highest price paid at auction for a movie prop.

1996: In a $40-million remake of **Jerry Lewis**' acknowledged masterpiece, **Eddie Murphy** weighs in on this day as 400-pound Sherman Klump, *The Nutty Professor* — and comes to the exact *opposite* conclusion. As **Jack Mathews** noted in his *Newsday* review: "Lewis' chemistry professor was an extension of all the nerds and geeks Lewis did as **Dean Martin**'s sidekick. The alter ego waiting to escape from inside him was . . . Martin, with slicked-back hair, a cigarette and a drink in his hands, an insouciant swagger and a tendency to lean on a piano and croon." The lean, mean ladykiller emerging in the new version (Murphy without makeup) was less loving and lovable than the corpulent Klump, the Jekyll-and-Hyde formula subtly turning into *Beauty and the Obese*. Not only did the results get Murphy back on the right box-office track, "now," said *Entertainment Weekly*, "the words Eddie Murphy and Oscar are being mentioned in the same sentence for the first time." Even more bizarre than that Oscar notion, the National Society of Film Critics pick Murphy its Best Actor of 1996.

1999: "The dean of special-effects artists" — **John Stears**, who fathered *Star Wars*' R2-D2 and C-3PO and 007's Aston Martin DB5 — dies of a stroke on this day at age 64.

A SIGHT FOR SHAW EYES: Claude Rains and Vivien Leigh as his *Caesar and Cleopatra*.
MEDIA-CIRCUS RINGMASTER: Kirk Douglas in *The Big Carnival*.
A CUSTER WHO BECAME PRESIDENT: William Lundigan, George Haywood, William Marshall, Ronald Reagan, Errol Flynn, David Bruce, Frank Wilcox and Van Heflin in *Santa Fe Trail*.

29

1944: "When it is finished, it will lick creation," pronounces **George Bernard Shaw** on this day, apparently pleased with the progress being made as he visits the set of his *Caesar and Cleopatra* — but the sight of hundreds of seemingly idle people milling about sat none too well with him: "Were they all on the payroll?" he asked. (No, they'd come to see him.) The Great One couldn't coax **John Gielgud** before the cameras to play his Caesar but settled instead (nicely and surprisingly) for **Claude Rains**, and he *did* succeed in borrowing "Scarlett O'Hara" from producer **David O. Selznick** to portray the Queen of the Nile.

1951: *The Human Interest Story* reaches the screen (New York's Globe) on this day under the title of *Ace in the Hole* — but even that soon changes, when the grosses don't come in, to *The Big Carnival*. Ironically, the film was about none of the above — not human interest, not gambling, not carnivals. It was a modernization of the **Floyd Collins** tragedy in which a media circus exploited a trapped, doomed miner. **Kirk Douglas**, who played the principal exploiter and newshound, feared that he was snarling out too vicious a characterization and asked writer-director **Billy Wilder** for permission to bring it down a notch or two. Nothing doing, said Wilder: "Kirk, give it both knees. Both knees."

1978: On this day, **Bob Crane** is discovered bludgeoned to death in his apartment in Scottsdale, AZ, where he is doing summer stock at the time. The murder was never solved, although a pal who participated in Crane's videotaped sexual adventures with young women — **John Henry Carpenter** — was brought to trial 16 years later, accused of fatally clubbing Crane with a tripod when the actor threatened to end the friendship (and the easy access to women). A jury in Phoenix deliberated 2 1/2 days before acquitting Carpenter.

1980: Friends and foes alike are having a field day frolicking in the film past of Presidential contender **Ronald Reagan**, says a Sunday piece by **Danielle Morton** in *The New York Times* on this day. The article, headlined "Ronald Reagan: Bookings for *Bonzo*," noted that both camps clamoring for *Bedtime for Bonzo* made it the most popular of the actor's 53 flicks. **Ray Ettore**, renting United Artists films to schools, felt more than liberals and collegiates were shelling out the standard $45 rental fee to see Reagan as General Custer in *Santa Fe Trail*, denouncing dishonesty in public office. And **Tom Bates**, running for his third term as Berkeley's Democratic Assemblyman, promised two pre-election benefit screenings of *That Hagen Girl*, just for the perverse pleasure of watching Reagan running for the Senate — as a character named Tom Bates.

1936: *Lost Horizon* finally finds its 200-year-old High Lama on this day: **Sam Jaffe**. Director **Frank Capra** had tested **A.E. Anson**, a 90-year-old ex-stage star recruited by **C. Aubrey Smith**, and, on learning the part was his, Anson died — smiling. **Henry B. Walthall** was next in line, but he died, too — before he could test.

1948: What director **Billy Wilder** and producer **Charles Brackett** began as *Operation Candybar* is unwrapped at New York's Paramount on this day as *A Foreign Affair* — an indication their inspection of Occupied Berlin leaned heavily along fraternization lines. **Jean Arthur**, **John Lund** and **Marlene Dietrich** occupied the central triangle. An expert farceur underused in films, Lund died May 10, 1992, at 81 — and even in death he was eclipsed by Dietrich, who died four days earlier, at 90, and grabbed all the newspaper space.

1949: *Any Number Can Play* (except **Scotty Beckett**, evidently) opens on this day at New York's Capitol. Just before filming began, Beckett was arrested on a drunk-driving charge and fired from the picture; **Darryl Hickman** replaced him as **Clark Gable**'s teenage son, but nobody replaced the photograph of Beckett on Gable's fireplace mantle. This firing signaled the start of Beckett's dizzying decline. The child star who had played young versions of Anthony Adverse and **Al Jolson** (and, as a teenager, Oogie Pringle in *A Date With Judy*) was busted in 1954 for carrying a concealed weapon and in 1957 for drug-possession. In 1960, he got a 180-day suspended sentence for hitting his stepdaughter with a crutch. On May 10, 1968, he died from an overdose of sleeping pills.

1995: In a *Times* piece on MoMA's retrospective of filmed plays on this day, **Vincent Canby** calls **William Wyler**'s *The Little Foxes* (1941) "possibly the most satisfying and esthetically successful adaptation of a Broadway play ever done in Hollywood. With the exception of **Elia Kazan**'s *Streetcar Named Desire* (1951), no adaptations of **Tennessee Williams** or **Arthur Miller** come anywhere near it, although **Mike Nichols**' screen version of **Edward Albee**'s *Who's Afraid of Virginia Woolf* (1966) is a runner-up." According to Canby, Wyler and his cinematographer (*Citizen Kane*'s **Gregg Toland**) made "glorious use of deep-focus shots that allow characters in the foreground and background to be seen with equal clarity. Note especially **Herbert Marshall**'s heart attack scene. As Wyler frames it, it's one of cinema's blessed achievements." *And* shrewdest: Because Marshall had a wooden leg in real life and couldn't climb the stairs required for his death scene, the shot is set up so Marshall could fall out of camera range for an instant and a stunt man could lunge back to complete the scene.

A HIGH LAMA WHO LIVES TO TELL THE TALE: Ronald Colman, Sam Jaffe and Frank Capra on the *Lost Horizon* set.
LAUGHS AMONG THE RUINS: Jean Arthur, John Lund and Marlene Dietrich in *A Foreign Affair*.
JUST BEFORE THE FALL: Scotty Beckett (with Elizabeth Taylor) in *A Date With Judy*.
THE OLD STAIRCASE TRICK: Bette Davis and Herbert Marshall in *The Little Foxes*.

1939: Principal photography on *Gone With the Wind* ends on its 449,512th foot of film on this day — **Olivia de Havilland**'s 23d birthday, which she spends doing retakes on the birthday party of her screen husband, Ashley Wilkes (**Leslie Howard**). Other celebs celebrating births on this day:

Dan	Aykroyd	(1952),
Karen	Black	(1942),
Genevieve	Bujold	(1942),
Leslie	Caron	(1931),
Madge	Evans	(1909),
Jamie	Farr	(1934),
Constance	Ford	(1929),
Farley	Granger	(1925),
Charles	Laughton	(1899),
Jean	Marsh	(1934),
Murray	Matheson	(1912),
Sydney	Pollack	(1934),
Twyla	Tharp	(1941),
William	Wyler	(1902).

1

1973: Passing the Aloha Tower in downtown Honolulu on this day, **John Gregory Dunne** turns to wife **Joan Didion** and says 16 words that make them a mint: "**James Taylor** and **Carly Simon** in a rock and roll version of *A Star Is Born*." The couple motivating this movie were *living it* and not interested in *filming it* so the Dunne-Didion script fell to two newly divorced divas: **Cher** and **Barbra Streisand**. When Streisand won the toss, Dunne and Didion exited (with screen credit, a $125,000 fee and 10% of the gross — all for 16 words).

1985: "Boy, I'm glad I saw *Rambo* last night," asides **President Reagan** at a press conference announcing the successful resolution to the TWA hijack in Beirut. "Now, I'll know what to do next time." That little Presidential plug sent the grosses of **Sylvester Stallone**'s war romp soaring.

1998: Barely visible beneath a 15-foot diaphanous veil, Barbra Brolin makes her entrance on this day as **Barbra Streisand** walks down the aisle of her Malibu living room to wed Groom No. 2, **James Brolin**. Said the *Post*'s **Cindy Adams**: "The wedding, due originally last year, was delayed because Streisand put the vows through 37 rewrites."

1998: *Nights of Cabiria*, the second Best Foreign Language Film Oscar winner in a row for director **Federico Fellini** and his actress-wife *Giulietta Masina* (after their *La Strada*), dawns again at New York's Lincoln Plaza Cinemas — with the seven-minute "man with the sack" sequence unseen since the 1957 Cannes Film Festival. Cabiria, translated into *Sweet Charity*, was the first of three Broadway musicals made from Fellini's four Oscar-winning films. It was followed by *La Strada* and *Nine* (nee *8½*).

1999: "They always had me ironing somebody's shirt," said **Sylvia Sidney** of her '30s reign as definitive tenement waif from *City Streets* to *Dead End*. Throat cancer claims her on this day at age 88.

THE WIND STOPS HERE: Olivia de Havilland, Leslie Howard, Laura Hope Crews, and Mary Young in *Gone With the Wind*. *CHARITY* BEGINS HERE: Giulietta Masina in *Nights of Cabiria*.

CATFISH ROW--*FRIED*: Dorothy Dandridge and Sammy Davis Jr. in *Porgy and Bess*.
THE HILLS ARE ALIVE—*AT LAST!*: Julie Andrews in *The Sound of Music*.
BACK FROM THE BOTTOM OF THE BIN: Jane Wyman and Lew Ayres in *Johnny Belinda*.

2

1947: "Who the hell wants to see a movie where the leading lady doesn't say a word?" grouses **Jack L. Warner** as he grudgingly agrees to film *Johnny Belinda* — and gets, on this day, **Jean Negulesco** to direct it. The movie made from **Elmer Harris'** play about a raped deaf-mute so enraged him he yanked Negulesco out of the editing room, fired him on the spot and let the picture settle to the bottom of Warners' film bin where the Warner brother in New York, **Harry Warner**, found it gathering dust for almost a year. Harry screened it, liked it and campaigned for a prestigious premiere which ultimately paid off in a dozen Oscar bids, including Best Picture, Best Direction and all four acting categories (**Lew Ayres, Jane Wyman, Charles Bickford** and **Agnes Moorehead**). "It's wonderful to be wrong," beamed Jack, who personally apologized to Negulesco, but the director never again set foot on Warners terra firma.

1958: Catfish Row — and the costumes therein — go up in $2.5 million flames on this day, hours before cameras are to begin rolling on *Porgy and Bess*. **Samuel Goldwyn** ordered everything replaced — including, 25 days later, **Rouben Mamoulian**, who'd directed both the original play *and* **Gershwin**'s "folk opera" and had already put in eight months steering the film through casting and prerecording. **Otto Preminger**, Mamoulian's replacement on *Laura*, took command (by virtue of having directed **Dorothy Dandridge, Pearl Bailey, Diahann Carroll** and **Brock Peters** before — in *Carmen Jones*), but he had no rapport with **Sammy Davis Jr.** and, at one point, refused to speak to him. Unintimidated by the director's ranting, Davis walked up to Preminger, twirling a cigarette slowly with his fingers, and uttered World War II's vilest movie threat: "Ve have vays of making you talk."

1964: Pressured by Fox to return to the backlot when location-lensing runs 26 days behind schedule and $740,000 over budget, director **Robert Wise** holds out for one last exterior shot — and, on this day, *gets it* after four frustrating days of rain: For a half-hour in mid-afternoon, weather relents long enough for an aerial photographer to swoop in and "discover" **Julie Andrews** swirling on a hilltop outside Salzburg, singing the title tune in *The Sound of Music*. The result was the most memorable opening-shot in movies since — well, since the slow-crawl across skyscrapers Wise devised for *West Side Story*. His two Best Director Oscars for these Best Picture musicals upstage a primarily tuneless, basically dramatic career that includes editing **Orson Welles'** masterworks (*Citizen Kane* and *The Magnificent Ambersons*) and directing heavy-duty opuses (*Odds Against Tomorrow, Executive Suite, The Set-Up, The Sand Pebbles, The Day the Earth Stood Still, Until They Sail* and *I Want To Live!*).

1942: Director **Michael Curtiz** is surprised on this day — in the middle of his Oscar-winning work on the Oscar-winning *Casablanca* — with a party to celebrate his 15 full years at Warners, tossed by his producer-of-the-moment, **Hal B. Wallis**.

1951: After some faulty film detours, **Alfred Hitchcock** gets back on the right track with *Strangers on a Train*, pulling into New York's Warner (nee Strand) on this day. His direction of this murder-swapping suspenser was widely praised by critics.

1958: Starting to reign over Manhattan on this day: *Kings Go Forth* at the Capitol (**Frank Sinatra** vs. **Tony Curtis** over a mulattoed **Natalie Wood**), and *King Creole* at the Loews State (**Elvis Presley** rising from Boubon Street busboy to nightclub headliner). Presley, who admired — indeed, emulated — the way Curtis combed his hair, nixed the role in *The Defiant Ones* that won Curtis his only Oscar nomination. (Actually, it was Presley's so-billed Technical Advisor, **Col. Tom Parker**, who turned it down for him — on the grounds the character, chained for the duration to **Sidney Poitier**, didn't have any songs!)

1965: The golden palomino that film-debuted carrying **Olivia de Havilland** through Sherwood Forest in *The Adventures of Robin Hood* and subsequently took **Roy Rogers** through 87 features and 101 TV shows — **Trigger** — dies of old age (33) on this day. "It was like losing one of the family," said The King of the Cowboys, who, sparing the feelings of the kids of the world, didn't announce the horse's death till March 30, 1966. Rogers had the animal stuffed and mounted for his Western museum at Apple Valley, CA.

1969: "Fill your hands, you son of a bitch!" roars the outraged Rooster Cogburn (**John Wayne**) — challenging Lucky Ned Pepper (**Robert Duvall**) to a shootout-on-horseback — in *True Grit*, which rides into Radio City Music Hall on this day. It being Wayne's best role (maybe his best moment in movies), he relaxed his cardinal rule and cussed on camera for the first — and only — time in his career.

1999: "When I die, I know the obits will first read 'one of Hollywood's Unfriendly 10,' not 'director of *The Caine Mutiny, The Young Lions, Raintree County* and other films,'" quotes *The New York Times* on this day in the last paragraph of its obituary on **Edward Dmytryk**, 90. Its *first* paragraph, sure enough, noted he was "jailed for refusing to tell a Congressional committee whether he was a Communist" and was "the only member of the 10 who recanted and named names." On the adjacent *Times* obituary page on this day, running the full eight columns: "**Mario Puzo**, Author Who Made 'The Godfather' a World Addiction, Is Dead at 78." Puzo won Oscars co-writing two of the three *Godfather* films.

1927: *Naughty But Nice*, bowing at New York's Strand on this Independence Day, brings to the fore **Mervyn LeRoy**'s first official (if accidental) discovery. In his capacity as assistant director at First National studios, he was paging **Polly Ann Young** to do a part in this picture, but the casting call was intercepted (and filled!) by her younger sister, 14-year-old Gretchen Young. Both LeRoy and the film's star, **Colleen Moore**, claimed credit for rechristening Gretchen with the more felicitous first-name of **Loretta**.

1927: The author of *Star Spangled Girl* is born on this day: **Neil Simon**.

1930: *The Unholy Three*, the first and last sound film of **Lon Chaney** (a remake of his 1925 silent hit of the same name), bows at NYC's Capitol on this day. This one-of-a-kind Man of a Thousand Faces died of cancer 53 days later.

1932: On this Independence Day, a truly independent spirit reaches Hollywood. **Katharine Hepburn** arrived by train to commence her RKO contract, and, when she alighted at the Pasadena station, her eye was almost swollen shut (infected, en route, by a piece of steel filing), eliciting a gasp from agent **Myron Selznick** — and a crack: "*This* is what they're paying $1,500 for?"

1952: "Hey, Gramps, I'll have a choc malt, heavy on the choc, plenty of milk, four spoons of malt, two scoops of vanilla ice cream, one mixed with the rest and one floating." Easy for you to say, but, for a guy trying to get his first line of movie dialogue on the screen, it proved a mouthful. **James Dean** required four takes to give that hi-cal command to **Charles Coburn**, a millionaire-turned-sodajerk, in 1952's *Has Anybody Seen My Gal?* bowing on this day at New York's Mayfair. "Only an ice cream freak could get that load of garbage right the first time," he figured after fluffing the line a third time. Dean also had a line at the end of 1951's *Fixed Bayonets* ("It's a rear guard coming back"), but it was cut. His first film job — barely a visible bit in 1951's **Dean Martin-Jerry Lewis** *Sailor Beware* — had no lines.

1985: MGM/UA releases on this day the first black-and-white feature color-converted by Color Systems Technology: *Yankee Doodle Dandy*, aptly enough.

1996: "I don't know if any of you have seen this new movie *Independence Day*," says **President Bill Clinton** on this Independence Day at a bicentennial celebration in Ohio, "but somebody said I was coming to Youngstown because this is the day the White House got blown away by space aliens. I hope it's there when I get back." He'd caught an advance screening and had no trouble giving the film a Presidential thumbs-up.

1942: Special 25, a spy-training school in Canada, cranks out its first graduate on this day — one **Ian Fleming**, who let none of that information go to waste when he later sat down and started contriving spy-scrapes for Agent 007.

1943: G.I. morale dips discernibly on this day as trumpeter **Harry James** weds World War II's reigning pin-up queen, **Betty Grable**. The union lasted 21 years. On this day 30 years later, funeral services were held for Grable, who succumbed to cancer — as did James, exactly ten years later, *again on this day*.

1956: For his second feature — his second opposite **Pier Angeli** and his second as a **James Dean** replacement — **Paul Newman** reaches stardom playing **Rocky Graziano** in *Somebody Up There Likes Me*, bowing on this day at NYC's Loews State. Between films, Newman stepped in for Dean a third time — for a TV-musical version of *Our Town* — and, at the time of Dean's fatal car-crash, the two Actors Studio alums were two and a half weeks away from co-starring in "The Battler," an autobiographical **Ernest Hemingway** yarn on live TV (NBC's "Pontiac Presents Playwrights 56"). **Dewey Martin** replaced Dean. The strong physical resemblance between Dean and Newman was duly noted by **Elia Kazan**, who screen-tested them to see if they could pass for twins ("Cal" and "Aron" in *East of Eden*). Newman was six years older so the part went to **Richard Davalos**.

1957: After less than two years of marriage and more than three years to sign the divorce papers, **Frank Sinatra** and **Ava Gardner** are, on this day, exes.

A GIANT LEAP, PERHAPS: David Gilliam and Ray Milland in *Frogs*.
WHICH TWO WILL WED?: Charlotte Greenwood, Jackie Gleason, Kitty Kallen, Harry James, Carmen Miranda, Betty Grable, John Payne and Cesar Romero in *Springtime in the Rockies*.
A ROCKY LIFE: Paul Newman, Robert Loggia and Dick Rich in *Somebody Up There Likes Me*.

1972: "TODAY the Pond! TOMORROW the World!" promise ads for *Frogs*, springing into Manhattan theaters on this day — and right out again, into richly deserved obscurity. For schlock copy, however, it's hard to top the stuff churned out for the short-and-sweet release of *Sweet and Savage* in 1983: "SEE rebel guerrillas torn apart by trucks! SEE corpses cut to pieces and fed to dogs and vultures! SEE the monkey trained to perform nursing duties for her paralyzed owner!"

1991: Ninety-year-old **Mildred Dunnock** dies on this day. None of the subsequent obituaries made note of her second most memorable role (after Linda Loman in *Death of a Salesman*): Barely recognizable, she played the wheelchaired little old lady who got shoved down a flight of stairs by the giggling, psychotic gangster in *Kiss of Death* (**Richard Widmark**, in his 1947 star-making film bow).

6

1948: On this day, **Lilli Palmer** rushes to L.A. from New York to stand by her spouse, **Rex Harrison**, during the media circus that follows the suicide of **Carole Landis**. Harrison had been filming *Unfaithfully Yours* — and living it off-camera with 29-year-old Landis, but on Independence Day he posted his own independence plans — to leave her, and Hollywood, and to do *Anne of the Thousand Days* on Broadway — driving her to OD on Seconal. The friend she always called during previous suicide attempts (the mother of **Dick Haymes**) was away holidaying on the Fourth and returned the call a day too late to save her. Harrison went on to win a Tony for *Anne of the Thousand Days*.

1960: "You didn't tell me about the sequel!" **Bette Davis** once yelled at writer-director **Joseph L. Mankiewicz** years after their *All About Eve* triumph, referring to the decade of hectic happily-ever-aftering her "Margo Channing" had with "Bill Sampson" (Davis' fourth husband, **Gary Merrill**) before they faded out on this day in a bitter divorce. She'd made her *Eve* entrance directly from *Payment on Demand* (then titled, aptly, *The Story of a Divorce*) and was speaking in a **Tallulah**-like rasp, having suffered a broken blood vessel in her larynx from screaming matches with No. 3, **William Grant Sherry**). Meeting Merrill, she mellowed and fell in love with him on the first day of filming in San Francisco. "We only played two love scenes before I said, 'Will you marry me?'" Merrill later remembered. She did on July 28, 1950 — but, instead of a happy ending, Davis entered what she called "my darkest decade." In April of 1960, while touring in *Sandburg*, they stayed at the same San Francisco hotel where their romance had begun. There was nothing left to be rekindled.

1964: With **Princess Margaret** in attendance, **The Beatles** put in *A Hard Day's Night* at the London Pavillion on this day, premiering their first flick. Not that the title ever made much sense — even *in English* — but, on its journey around the globe, it got some *very* loose translations: in Greece, *Let's Have Fun with the Beatles*; in Israel, *The 4 Magnificent*; in Brazil, *Kings of Ie, Ie, Ie*, and in Portugal, *The Four Haircuts of the After-Calypso*.

A RACE TO RICHES:Tom Hanks in *Forrest Gump* ; The Beatles in *A Hard Day's Night*.
MOVIE MARRIAGES: From left: Gary Merrill and Bette Davis in *All About Eve*. Rex Harrison and Lilli Palmer in *The Four Poster*.

1994: Paramount Pictures opens a box of chocolates, nationally, on this day: *Forrest Gump*, which jumps to the third rung (after *E.T.* and *Jurassic Park*) on the list of all-time top grossing feature films in the domestic market, taking in $329 million. Come March 27, it struck a mother lode of Oscar gold (six).

1998: Congestive heart failure claims The King of the Cowboys, 86, on this day.

1934: *Chained* completes shooting on this day. Among its distinctions: the first screen-sighting (sorta!) of **Keenan Wynn**, stunt-doubling in longshots for **Joan Crawford**. The film's director, **Clarence Brown**, was the same man who in 1928 used **Lou Costello** as **Dolores Del Rio**'s stunt-double for *The Trail of '98*.

1936: *The Garden of Allah* finishes principal photography on this day, officially ending **Joshua Logan**'s cinematic baptism-by-fire. Recruited from Broadway as a dialogue director, Logan had the Herculean chore of smoothing out **Dietrich's** Teutonic tangle and **Boyer**'s Gallic garble so that the "desert poetry" could be deciphered by movie audiences. (Marlene thought the "scwipt" was "twash" — a **Garbo** reject, like Dietrich's most recent lover, the late **John Gilbert**). Other Logan obstacles: convincing **Joseph Schildkraut** *not* to try a Russian-Jewish accent, and following the direction of Polish-born **Richard Boleslawski**. On his first day on location, Logan reported to Boleslawski for orders — and got a doozy of an assignment: "Direct the scene; I'm busy."

1980: On this day — 20 years to the day that his Tony-winning play on **FDR** (*Sunrise at Campobello*) finished filming — producer **Dore Schary**, 74, dies.

1991: Director **Robert Altman** and his cinematographer, **Jean Lepine**, spend the day wielding a camera all over Hollywood Center Studio (nee the old Zoetrope), introducing most of the star players in *The Player* in one fell swoop of a tracking shot that prowls the corridors of power in a functioning studio. As opening shots go, this one went on for eight minutes and six seconds — an industry record, save for **Hitchcock**'s 1948 *Rope* where continuous takes lasted as long as each film reel. Setting the tone of satiric self-analysis, Altman had studio security chief **Fred Ward** weaving in and out of the shot, rhapsodizing about good ol' pre-MTV days when **Orson Welles**' *Touch of Evil* pulled off just such an extravagantly complex shot.

1997: Hollywood's oldest guard files into the Beverly Hills Presbyterian Church on this day to salute a wonderful life, some 60 years of which was spent in cinema: **James Stewart**'s. The only co-star in attendance was his frequent screen wife, **June Allyson**. Also present: **Bob Hope** (at 94, the last of Stewart's generation of male movie royalty), **Esther Williams**, former First Lady **Nancy Reagan**, agent **Lew Wasserman** and **Carol Burnett** (who grew up idolizing the actor as a movie usherette). **Kelly Harcourt**, one of the actor's twin daughters, spoke for the family and invoked the closing sentiment of *It's a Wonderful Life*, that no man is a failure who has friends. "Here's to our father," she said, her voice catching and her hand moving over her heart, "the richest man in town."

A STAND-UP-AND-CHEER FINALE: Ralph Bellamy as FDR in *Sunrise at Campobello*. WHY IS THIS MAN SMILING? Robert Altman getting His Opening Shot for *The Player*. WHERE THE TONGUES OF MANY LANDS WAG: Marlene Dietrich and Charles Boyer in *The Garden of Allah*.

1932: Easily the most bizarre movie ever ground out of MGM's Dream Plant, **Tod Browning**'s *Freaks* gets to market on this day — over the strenuous objections of **Louis B. Mayer**, to be sure — and even *The New York Times* critic wondered whether it should be shown at the Rialto "or in, say, the Medical Centre." Public hue and cry soon got the film yanked from exhibition, but years later it surfaced and acquired a cult rep as one of the screen's authentic horrors.

1950: "On the long list of **Arthur Freed** productions, *Pagan Love Song* has a singular distinction: It is the only mediocre picture he ever made," admits Freed's Boswell, **Hugh Fordin**, about the rotten apple that wraps on this day. It was to have been **Stanley Donen**'s first shot at solo-directing, but **Esther Williams** wouldn't hear of it, feeling he and co-director **Gene Kelly** had treated her with disdain during the making of *Take Me Out to the Ball Game*. **Robert Alton** got the assignment instead, struggled through a weather-ruined Hawaiian shoot and never directed another movie. Donen, in happy contrast, was rerouted to *Royal Wedding* and put his best foot forward with **Fred Astaire**. "I've always felt I owe my career to Esther Williams," the director admits dry-eyed.

WET FOOT FORWARD: Esther Williams and Howard Keel in *Pagan Love Song*.
BATHHOUSE HORSEPLAY: Kim Novak, Susan Strasberg, William Holden and Cliff Robertson in *Picnic*.
A PLOT FATALITY: Ian Bannen, Peter Finch, Christian Marquand, Richard Attenborough, George Kennedy and James Stewart in *The Flight of the Phoenix*.

1955: Director **Joshua Logan** wraps *Picnic* on this day — Americana *con amore*.

1965: While executing the plot specifications for *The Flight of the Phoenix* on this day, **Paul Mantz** dies trying to make airborne a rickety crate put together with bailing wire and body parts taken from a downed airliner. The craft came apart in midair, and he was killed — but stuntman **Bobby Rose**, who was riding with him, survived and successfully performed the stunt Nov. 4. When the movie went into release three months later, the veteran daredevil who did some dazzling aviation-doubling (*Ceiling Zero, Twelve O'Clock High, Test Pilot, The Spirit of St. Louis*) received a stirring salute in the closing moments of screen credits: "It should be remembered . . . that Paul Mantz, a fine man and a brilliant flyer, gave his life in the making of this film."

1972: A guest of the North Vietnamese, **Jane Fonda** arrives in Hanoi on this day to inspect damage done by U.S. bombing. It was a visit she would later regret.

1985: On this day, principal photography begins on *She's Gotta Have It*, a street-smart sex-farce that starts writer-director-editor (and, occasionally, on-camera comedy-relief) **Spike Lee** making waves into the American mainstream.

1998: The stork is overburdened with star bundles on this day: **Ethan Hawke** and **Uma Thurman** greet daughter **Maya Ray** while **Will Smith** and **Jada Pinkett Smith** welcome son **Jaden Christopher Syre**.

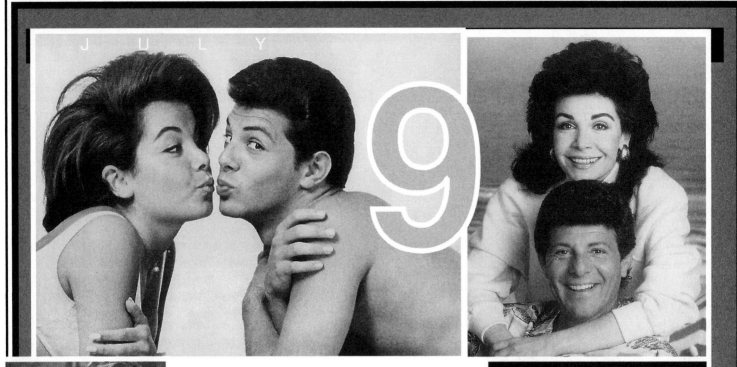

J U L Y

9

1932: The cameras start turning on **Katharine Hepburn**'s debut vehicle on this day. RKO wanted to bring her on as an untamed jungle girl, arising out of the backlot flora and fauna in *Three Came Unarmed*, but director George Cukor spotted star quality in her test and recast her in a civilized setting — as **John Barrymore**'s daughter in *A Bill of Divorcement*. She aroused more than fatherly feelings in Barrymore, and there was a pass (incomplete, of course). "Thank goodness I don't have to act with you any more," huffed Hepburn at filming's end. Shot back Barrymore: "I didn't know you ever had, darling."

1937: All of Fox's silent films — each one carefully labeled and preserved — go up in acrid smoke on this day as the summer sun causes its storage vault at Little Ferry, NJ, to explode. Pretty much destroyed in the blast (along with considerable property and one life) was the whole career of **Theda Bara**. Only two of her 39 Fox films are now known to exist: *A Fool There Was* and *East Lynne*.

1979: The star with the most Oscars (4) and most Oscar-nominations (12), **Katharine Hepburn**, made her only (1) appearance at the Oscars the day after April Fools Day in 1974 — and got upstaged by **Robert Opel**, whose 15 minutes of fame was more like 15 seconds. He shucked his shorts and "streaked" the Oscar show. **David Niven**, a presenter at the time, saw the spectacle in the TV monitor and managed a memorably urbane ad-lib: "Isn't it fascinating that probably the only laugh that man will ever get is by stripping off his clothes and showing his shortcomings?" Truth to tell: Opel got lots of laughs as a professional streaker — plus, Oscarcast director **Marty Pasetta** said his "shortcomings" weren't so short ("and he wasn't Jewish"). This line of "work" ended in late '74 when, after streaking the Los Angeles city council, he was convicted for public lewdness and put on four-year probation. Almost five years later, on this day, in a San Francisco sex-paraphernalia shop he owned called "Fey Way," two men with sawed-off shotguns burst in and blow him away for five dollars, a used camera and a new backpack.

1992: "Haven't you always felt I've had the perfect life?" **Annette Funicello**, 49, asks *USA Today* rhetorically on this day, heading off tabloid tales of public "drunkenness" by admitting she has multiple sclerosis. She opted to go public with it because her equilibrium was starting to fail her and she had to walk with a cane. "From the waist up, you'd never know anything was wrong," wryly added the **Elizabeth Taylor** of *Mickey Mouse Club* mouseketeers.

10.

1942: With much of its magnificence left on the cutting-room floor when reduced from 131 minutes to 88, *The Magnificent Ambersons* world-premieres on this day at two Los Angeles theaters, occupying the bottom half of a double bill with *Mexican Spitfire Sees a Ghost*, a 70-minute **Lupe Velez** vehicle — this, nine days after booting **Orson Welles**' Mercury Productions off of the RKO lot. Suddenly, the catch phrase of the moment became "All's well that ends Welles."

1944: Director **Alfred Hitchcock** starts shooting *Spellbound* with **Ingrid Bergman** on this day — the seventh anniversary of her less-than-spellbinding marriage to **Dr. Petter Lindstrom**. Two cakes marked the spot — but, significantly, no groom.

1953: "No mistake about it," cheers *New York Post* critic **Archer Winsten** on this day about *The Band Wagon* which has just rolled into Radio City Music Hall, a review of it "boils down to a collection of superlatives. It is the best musical of the month, the year, the decade, or, for all I know, of all time." A pair of rare cinematic "wild cards" (**Nanette Fabray**, momentarily defecting Broadway for movies, and **Jack Buchanan**, suavely stepping in at the suggestion of first-choice **Clifton Webb**) assisted **Fred Astaire, Cyd Charisse** and **Oscar Levant** in delivering an even-dozen of **Arthur Schwartz** and **Howard Dietz**' vintage ditties, plus their new one. Producer **Arthur Freed** merely put in his order for a no-business-like-show-business number and, in a half hour, had "That's Entertainment." There was no Oscar-nomination for this (!), but the song became the film industry's anthem.

1968: A month after the death of his stepson **Ron** in Vietnam, **James Stewart** starts drowning his sorrows in a comedy that commences filming on this day. *The Cheyenne Social Club* was the first Western that he ever attempted without Pie, his trusty steed since *Winchester '73* in 1950. The old horse couldn't cut the high altitude any more, and another one had to be used, but the animal did make it to the location and was a comfort to the grieving star. So, too, was co-star and longtime pal, **Henry Fonda**, a Sunday painter who did a watercolor rendering of the horse and presented it to Stewart shortly before Pie died.

1989: The voice of Bugs Bunny, Porky Pig, Sylvester, Tweety, Yosemite Sam, Pepe Le Pew, Foghorn Leghorn, Speedy Gonzales and Barney Rubble is suddenly stilled on this sad day: **Mel Blanc**, the **Laurence Olivier** of cartoon voices, dies at age 81 — just a few hours before Olivier himself dies at age 82. On his tombstone are the three little words he immortalized: "That's all, folks!"

11

1937: Five songs along into the score for *The Goldwyn Follies*, on this day 38-year-old **George Gershwin** succumbs to a brain tumor. His passing was mourned mightily by **Samuel Goldwyn**, who'd taken him off the payroll only the month before for not showing up at the studio because of a migraine. Of the last melodies Gershwin composed, one ("Just Another Rhumba") was not used, another ("Love Walked In") was overused, and the best — his last — was used too sparingly: "(Our) Love Is Here to Stay." The lyric Gershwin's brother, **Ira**, gave the latter was slightly ironic since George was on the emotional mend from an affair with **Charles Chaplin**'s third wife, **Paulette Goddard**.

1940: "I'd play **Wallace Beery**'s grandmother if it was a good part," cracked **Joan Crawford**, explaining why she pounced on a part **Norma Shearer** passed on — the former half of *Susan and God*, which bows at New York's Capitol on this day. Shearer didn't like the idea of playing the mother of a teenager — and rejected *Mrs. Miniver* for the same vain reason. And that's precisely the kind of role that got Crawford the Oscar five years later (namely, *Mildred Pierce*, which, not so incidentally, is said to have been turned down by **Bette Davis**).

1967: New Jersey Central railroad station in Jersey City passes for Baltimore's on this day as filming commences on *Funny Girl*, and right off — for the first scene of her first movie — **Barbra Streisand** "suggests" that director **William Wyler** have her emerge mystically from the train steam, like **Garbo**'s *Anna Karenina*, then go into a coughing spasm from all the smoke. Wyler, who directed more Oscar-winning performances than anyone (hers would be his 14th and last), took the suggestion under advisement and shot the scene his way — although she got off a little cough and he let it pass.

1973: With his last love (**Maureen O'Sullivan**) at his side, 64-year-old **Robert Ryan** dies of cancer on this day. His best performance went into release three months later: the inactive activist who was himself awaiting death in *The Iceman Cometh*. Critic **Charles Champlin** called it Ryan's "monument . . . his finest hour as a superb craftsman," and there *was* a poignancy about him uttering lines like "What's before me is the fact that death is a fine, long sleep — I'm damn tired — and it can't come too soon for me." The National Board of Review was moved to award him, posthumously, its Best Actor prize for this.

1991: Glowing with great expectation (daughter **Scout Willis**, born nine days later), a naked and pregnant **Demi Moore** adorns the cover of *Vanity Fair*, which hits newsstands in New York and Los Angeles on this day and quickly sells out.

12

1895: The only Oscar to win an Oscar is born on this day — **Oscar Hammerstein II** — and, again true to his name, he did it *twice*, writing words to the Best Songs of '41 and '45 — with different composers: **Jerome Kern** for the former ("The Last Time I Saw Paris" from *Lady Be Good*), and **Richard Rodgers** for the latter ("It Might As Well Be Spring" from *State Fair*).

1912: "This is my one chance for immortality," said stage star **Sarah Bernhardt** of her first film fling — the 40-minute *Queen Elizabeth*, premiering at New York's Lyceum on this day. The invited celebrities sat spellbound through its unprecedented four reels and applauded heartily at the end. Produced in France by **Louis Mercanton**, the film was imported by **Adolph Zukor**, who made enough to hire "famous players in famous plays" for Paramount Pictures. In the next 64 years, Zukor reached Paramount's peak — and beyond — and, when he died June 10, 1976, he was the oldest mogul of all: 103 years old!

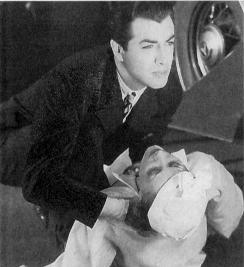

SPARKS ON—& OFF—CAMERA: Patricia Neal and Gary Cooper in *The Fountainhead*.
ROAD TO REDEMPTION — AND STARDOM: Robert Taylor and Irene Dunne in *Magnificent Obsession*.
ROB REMEMBERS MOM: Meg Ryan and Billy Crystal in *When Harry Met Sally . . .*

1935: MGM contractee **Robert Taylor** begins his tenth film on this day on loan-out to Universal, and it's the one that makes him a star (as it will for **Rock Hudson** when remade in 1954). *Magnificent Obsession*, **Lloyd C. Douglas**' inspirational schmaltz, told of a dapper young drunk turning doctor to restore the sight and win the heart of a widow he loves. When **Irene Dunne** blinked after the bandages had been removed and found him hovering over her, Taylor came into focus for a legion of fans.

1935: *The Murder Man*, a modest stop-the-presses saga, goes into general release on this day. Its only news was that it marked **Spencer Tracy**'s first film for MGM and **James Stewart**'s first feature ever. Both played reporters (the sixth-billed, six-feet-three Stewart was the one they called "Shorty").

1945: *The Story of G.I. Joe* has a memorial premiere on this day in Albuquerque, hometown of its central character: war correspondent **Ernie Pyle**, who was killed by a sniper's bullet less than three months earlier. **Burgess Meredith** played Pyle, and **Robert Mitchum** was an especially moving young officer.

1948: Howard Roark (**Gary Cooper**) and Dominique Francon (**Patricia Neal**) cross paths at a Fresno rock quarry on this day, igniting sparks that start the filming of *The Fountainhead* — and set off a long-running off-camera romance.

1989: Director **Rob Reiner** throws his mom a terrific catch-phrase for her one-line bit in *When Harry Met Sally . . .*, bowing on this day at New York's Beekman. To cap the scene where **Meg Ryan** simulated an orgasm in a public diner for **Billy Crystal**'s embarrassed enlightenment, **Estelle Reiner** turned to her waiter and hazily ordered: "I'll have what she's having."

13

END OF THE LINE FOR TECHNICOLOR: Jane Russell, Dan Duryea and Jeff Chandler in *Foxfire*.
KAZAN & 'KIDS': Director Elia Kazan, Marlon Brando, Julie Harris and James Dean during a late-night *East of Eden* shoot.
\$U\$PICIOU\$: Joel McCrea and Miriam Hopkins in *The Richest Girl in the World*.

1925: Lucille LeSueur and Myrna Williams make their film debuts together in the chorus of *Pretty Ladies* (premiering at New York's Capitol on this day). When they changed those names, they *really* got somewhere: Between the two of them, **Joan Crawford** and **Myrna Loy** put in a full century before the cameras (Crawford toiled till *Trog* in 1970, Loy till *Just Tell Me What You Want* in 1980).

1934: A comedy where **Miriam Hopkins** has cau\$e to question the depths of her lovers — *The Richest Girl in the World* — goes into production on this day. It brought its 22-year-old author, **Norman Krasna**, \$4,000 from RKO Radio and, seven months later, an Oscar nomination for Best Original Story of 1934.

1954: Taking in the backlot amusement-park set of *East of Eden* on this day, director **Elia Kazan**'s guest — his *On the Waterfront* star, **Marlon Brando** — sticks around till four a.m., checking out the work of acting rival **James Dean**.

1955: *Foxfire* — "the phosphorescent glow that comes from rotting timbers" — starts lighting up NYC's Globe Theater on this day. In addition to its feeble film firsts (**Jane Russell**'s entry on the Universal lot, **Jeff Chandler**'s crooning debut via the title tune he wrote with **Henry Mancini**), it also marked the quiet end of an era — the last time Technicolor's three-color cameras and process were used on an American film.

1962: Producer **Jerry Wald**, 49, dies of a heart attack on this day. The day before, he'd gone home ill from the set of his latest, *A Woman in July* (i.e., **William Inge**'s play, *A Loss of Roses*, bought for **Marilyn Monroe** but released as *The Stripper* with **Joanne Woodward**). *Hemingway's Adventures of a Young Man* was the last completed Wald. In the works: **James Joyce**'s *Ulysses* and **Robert F. Kennedy**'s *The Enemy Within*. The latter, which was never made, was being adapted by **Budd Schulberg**, one of Wald's pallbearers. Schulberg bothered to reiterate that the high-octane producer in his classic Hollywood novel, *What Makes Sammy Run?* — Sammy Glick — was *not* Jerry Wald but, rather, a filmland composite. Proof? "He wouldn't have hired me for *Enemy Within*. If I thought he was Glick, I'd never have put myself in his hands."

14

1936: A great Hollywood sex scandal ignites on this day when **Mary Astor** countersues her ex (**Dr. Franklyn Thorpe**) for custody of their four-year-old daughter, **Marylyn**, prompting Thorpe to play his unfit-mother card: a diary he'd swiped in which Astor detailed her affairs with the rich and famous — in particular, one euphoric off-the-charts relationship with playwright **George S. Kaufman**, maybe the world's least likely-looking lothario ("Once George lays down his glasses, he's quite a different man. . . . We shared our fourth climax at dawn"). Because pages had been removed from the diary, it couldn't be admitted in evidence, but it could be leaked to the press — and was. Outraged moguls then descended on **Samuel Goldwyn** to get him to fire Astor from the then-shooting *Dodsworth*. "A woman fighting for her child?" he shot back with mocked shock. "This is good." As it turned out, the notoriety *was* good, costing Astor neither her child nor her career. **Judge Goodwin Knight** awarded the actress Marylyn for nine months of the year, and Astor remained in movies till 1965. Years later when Marylyn came to visit her in a nursing home, Astor airily waved her away because she'd not made an appointment in advance.

1954: *Oklahoma!* begins lensing in Arizona on this day. Director **Fred Zinnemann** had Not-Just-Singers apply and consequently got a "sensational" test out of **James Dean**, doing Curly's "Pore Jud Is Dead" number with **Rod Steiger**. (Just imagine *that* road taken!) Steiger did get into the film at Zinnemann's insistence, but the director later thought the actor's conspicuous brilliance *unbalanced* the picture, making Jud seem even more isolated and, therefore, deserving of *some* sympathy.

1969: *Easy Rider*, the ultimate biker trip, takes off at New York's Beekman on this day. A countercultural phenomenon, it got the young-market vote and changed the face of film. Made for a measly $400,000, it amassed more than $50 million, won **Dennis Hopper** the Cannes prize for Best Director, put **Jack Nicholson** into the Oscar running for the first time and turned the film's "Captain America," producer **Peter Fonda**, into a poster-art icon of '60s rebellion. "The first thing I put down on paper was the image of the motorcycle," said Fonda. "I wanted to make it attractive to people, like a red-white-and-blue cock."

1998: Lung cancer claims helicopter pilot **J. David Jones**, 61, on this day. He coordinated, choreographed and masterminded some of the most memorable aerial moments in movies (for two: the "Flight of the Valkyries" 'copter invasion in *Apocalypse Now* and **Barbra Streisand**'s "Don't Rain on My Parade" race to the altar via tugboat and the Statue of Liberty in *Funny Girl*).

15

1937: Eight years and 36 films into his career, **Joel McCrea** finally goes West via *Wells Fargo* — which starts shootin' on this day — and finds a screen niche that sticks for the rest of his days — the heroic Westerner.

1964: The exes of the *Butterfield 8* stars (**Elizabeth Taylor** and **Laurence Harvey**) dial a more perfect union on this day. Indeed, the marriage of **Michael Wilding** and **Margaret Leighton** endured till her death Jan. 13, 1976.

1988: *A Fish Called Wanda* lands in Manhattan movie houses on this day, a pretty schizo display of Anglo-American goofiness that separates the Brits from the Yanks in terms of styles and senses of humor. Eight months later they separated again and made this the only movie to produce *two* Oscar-winning Best Supporting Actors: On March 19 the British Academy Award in that category went to **Michael Palin**. Ten days later the American chapter singled out one of *its* own for that honor — **Kevin Kline**.

1993: "Any number of actors can point to an Oscar on the shelf," notes **William Grimes** in *The New York Times* on this day. "Only **Conrad Brooks** can stand up and say that he appeared in virtually every film by **Edward Wood Jr.**, often acclaimed as the worst director in the history of the cinema, the anti-genius behind *Plan 9 From Outer Space*, a film that must be seen several times for full comprehension of its absolute ineptitude in every category of the filmmaking art." Like a dutiful disciple, Brooks came out of the, er, Woodwork to spread the word about The Master and perhaps drum up a little business for Film Forum's week-long Ed Wood retrospective that would be beginning the next day. "He wanted to make movies in the worst way," said Brooks. "And he did."

1997: *Carnegie Hall Celebrates the Glorious MGM Musical*, a two-day Some Singing! Some Dancing! Some Talking! card of primal movie-nostalgia, fills the great hall on this day, co-hosted by **Roddy McDowall** and **Michael Feinstein** and featuring a glittering procession of golden-oldie survivors: **Mickey Rooney**, **Ann Miller**, **Tony Martin**, **Cyd Charisse**, **Van Johnson**, **June Allyson**, **Donald O'Connor**, **Kathryn Grayson**, **Skitch Henderson**, **Betty Comden**, **Adolph Green**, **Gloria De Haven**, **Betty Garrett**, **Celeste Holm**, **Arlene Dahl** and **Julie Wilson**. Most conspicuous no-shows: **Jane Powell**, **Debbie Reynolds**, **Lena Horne**, **Dolores Gray** and **Esther Williams**. At least Williams got out of the pool and made the next MGM reunion at Carnegie May 25 and 26, 1999 — along with **Margaret O'Brien**, half of the dancing **Champions** (**Marge**), half of the **Nicholas** brothers (**Harold**) and **Nanette Fabray**.

1945: The forgotten father of film, **D.W. Griffith**, visits the *Duel in the Sun* set on this day to watch two of his old stars, **Lionel Barrymore** and **Lillian Gish**, work — and his presence so rattles them that director **King Vidor** has to ask him politely to scat, but The Master's influence lingered on: *Sun*'s Big Scene — "the gathering of the clans" where Barrymore rounds up all available horsemen to ride against the railroaders — was a shot-for-shot steal of the KKK calling in Griffith's 1915 *The Birth of a Nation*.

1948: *Key Largo* bows at New York's Strand on this day, and with it comes the cold gray light of "Gaye Dawn," the lush thrush **Claire Trevor** plays to perfection. "Moanin' Low," which she sang (for a drink), took her to memorable heights — and the Oscar podium.

1964: *The Unsinkable Molly Brown* — the Denver dowager who didn't go down with the *Titanic* — sails into Radio City Music Hall on this day in the sparkplug form of **Debbie Reynolds**, who won the role with a determination and tenacity in tune with her big song, "I Ain't Down Yet." While producer **Hal B. Wallis** toyed with MGM over loanout terms for **Shirley MacLaine**, Reynolds campaigned for the part, letting it be known she'd do it for nothing (well, practically). When MacLaine called her on the carpet for undercutting her [MacLaine's] price, Reynolds dragged out the soft soap — "Shirley, this might be my last film, and I'm sure you're going on to make many great films" — and it worked: MacLaine stepped aside, and Reynolds marched on to a renewed box-office life, her best-ever reviews and an Oscar nomination (her one and only). She was right about MacLaine, too: Many more great roles did await her — including *Postcards from the Edge*'s fictional facsimile of Debbie Reynolds.

1996: Retiring early on this day, **Robert Downey Jr.** strips to his boxer shorts and T-shirt, neatly folds his jeans over a chair and climbs into bed. Shortly after 9 p.m., a strange woman tried rousing him and finally phoned police to have him removed from the premises. It then gradually dawned on Downey he'd wandered, drug-dazed, into the home of neighbors and curled up in their son's bed. Although he claimed his limo driver had let him out at the wrong house and he hadn't noticed the difference, he was booked for trespassing — the second of three arrests in less than a month on drug-related charges. This one, known as The Goldilocks Incident in Hollywood's thickening chronicles of substance abuse, caused him to be court-ordered into a rehab program. Somehow, during this particular month of chaos, he finished two films — *Hugo Pool*, directed by his father, and *One Night Stand*, directed by **Mike Figgis** — without causing delays.

1999: *Eyes Wide Shut* opens wide on this day, running the gamut of reviews.

ARRIVING TO CHEERS: Giulietta Masina in *La Strada*.
DISNEY'S FIRST OSCAR: *Flowers and Trees*.
WHAT DOWNPOUR?: Gene Kelly in *Singin' in the Rain*.
WHILE *MOTHER* WAS AWAY: Monroe and Grable in *How To Marry a Millionaire*.

1913: *A Noise From the Deep* goes into general release on this day, introducing a new slapstick trick: **Mabel Normand**, ad libbing, hurls the screen's first custard pie — into the unsuspecting puss of **Roscoe "Fatty" Arbuckle**.

1932: *Flowers and Trees*, done in three-color Technicolor after an expensive false-start in black and white, takes root at Grauman's Chinese on this day. Not only was this 29th *Silly Symphony* cartoon the first film in three-color Technicolor, it was the first Oscared for Best Short Subject. With this color christening, **Walt Disney** began a two-year contract that granted him exclusive use of Technicolor's palate, giving him the edge over other animators.

1935: The news that country folks don't dig country films is spelled out in *Variety*ese across its front page on this day: "STICKS NIX HICK PIX."

1946: The gates of 20th Century-Fox part for the first time on this day for its once-and-future **Marilyn Monroe**, who makes her way to the set for **Betty Grable's** *Mother Wore Tights* where photographer **Leon Shamroy** shoots a 100-foot roll of silent color film stock — her screen test and, subsequently, her official entree into films.

1951: On this day **Gene Kelly** goes into his classic "Singin' in the Rain" dance on the "East Side Street" of MGM's Culver City backlot.

1951: The first Desilu production sees the light of day on this day — seven-pound, six-ounce **Lucie Desiree Arnaz**, measuring in at TV size (21 inches long) at Cedars of Lebanon Hospital — and it's followed by a legendary line of other Desilu productions. Since they were already "on a creative roll," **Desi Arnaz** and **Lucille Ball** chose to spend the first pregnancy of their decade-long marriage plotting a half-hour co-starring sitcom. The pilot was made before a live audience five months into the pregnancy, and the result — *I Love Lucy* — reached the airwaves Oct. 15, 1951, keeping the couple off the big screen till *The Long, Long Trailer* brought them back in 1954 as if they were small-screen royalty (which, by then, they indeed were). When the artifacts of '50s life finally fell into place, there were those who thought this classic series deserved to be called *The Greatest Show on Earth* more than DeMille's Oscar-winning circus epic which a pregnant Lucy had to pass on — to **Gloria Grahame**.

1956: *La Strada* (*The Road*) begins on this day for writer-director **Federico Fellini** and his actress-wife, **Giulietta Masina**, as the Manhattan critics start cheering their arrival on the film scene.

17

18

1939: *Babes in Arms*, **Arthur Freed**'s first production solo, wraps on this day a few hours before the Westwood sneak of his unofficial first effort, *The Wizard of Oz*. Freed's name didn't make a single frame of *Oz*, but, as assistant to producer **Mervyn LeRoy**, he was the project's prime-mover. The morning after the preview, he laid his new career on the line ("The song stays, or I go!"), waging a one-man war to keep "Over the Rainbow" in the picture. He won, the tune got an Oscar, and **Judy Garland** had a signature song for life.

ARTHUR FREED'S FIRST PRODUCTION & LAST DANCE FILM: From left: *Babes in Arms* with Mickey and Judy; *Silk Stockings* with Cyd and Fred. WHAT SALINGER SAW: Holden and Caulfield in *Dear Ruth*.

1947: *Dear Ruth*, a postwar diversion based on **Norman Krasna**'s play, goes into national release on this day, and, two days short of four years later (July 16, 1951), its literary illegitimate off-spring is born, published — *The Catcher in the Rye*. Its author, **J. D. Salinger**, supposedly saw the name of his main character in the ads for *Dear Ruth* ("starring **William HOLDEN** and **Joan CAULFIELD**"). Holden Caulfield's story is the most successful hold-out for cinemazation there is. Producer-adapter **Ernest Lehman** once proposed a film version of the book for Salinger only — and, if Salinger didn't like the result, the prints would be destroyed. Salinger's agent wrote Lehman his client was "used to such fantastic offers from Hollywood" and the answer was still a non-negotiable no.

1957: *Silk Stockings* bows at Radio City Music Hall on this day, ending an era of sorts. Just as the Broadway version was **Cole Porter**'s last stage musical and **George S. Kaufman**'s last produced play, the movie version became **Fred Astaire**'s and producer **Arthur Freed**'s last big dance feature, **Cyd Charisse**'s last made-in-Hollywood musical and the last film directed by **Rouben Mamoulian**. The very last thing Mamoulian directed was a cat drinking a saucer of milk on a balcony — a shot he got after principal photography ended. When asked if the shot was necessary to the film, Mamoulian exclaimed "Crucial!" (All 16 of his previous movies contained at least one shot of a cat. This was his signature, and he literally signed himself out of cinema with it.)

1989: Less than an hour before she's to meet **Francis Ford Coppola** about playing an innocent girl gunned down in *The Godfather Part III* (a role played by Coppola's own daughter, **Sofia**, when **Winona Ryder** pulled out) — **Rebecca Schaeffer**, 21, answers her doorbell and is shot dead by an obsessed stalker (**Robert Bardo**, 19) on this day. Prosecuted by L.A. deputy district attorney **Marcia Clark**, Bardo was convicted of first-degree murder and is now serving a life sentence without the possibility of parole. "I was a fan of hers, and I may have carried it too far," he conceded.

SPIELBERG SPECTACLE: The Mothership lands in *Close Encounters of the Third Kind.*
CONVINCING ENOUGH TO CAUSE A DIVORCE: Sarah Miles and Kris Kristofferson in *The Sailor Who Fell From Grace to the Sea.*
BULL'S-EYE CASTING: Errol Flynn in *The Adventures of Robin Hood.*

19

1935:
While serving as *Captain Blood*'s special visual consultant, **Dwight Franklin** on this day asks **Jack L. Warner**, "Don't you think that **Cagney** would make a swell Robin Hood?" Warner did indeed and announced James Cagney for the part, but the deal deflated when the actor walked off the lot after a contract dispute. In January — a month after *Captain Blood* hit the screen and proved popular — Robin of Locksley was properly cast with the Captain Blood that Franklin had somehow overlooked: **Errol Flynn**.

1955:
Kismet's "Night of My Nights" number commences shooting on MGM's backlot on this day, helmed by **Stanley Donen** — a superb substitute for designated director **Vincente Minnelli**, who'd departed for his *Lust for Life* locales in Europe. The sequence was the only scene adequately fitted to the film's CinemaScope frame, and it stood out against stilted shambles of the rest of the picture. Minnelli expert **Stephen Harvey** knew the difference but not who to thank when he wrote, "Just once, in the dusk of the Caliph's nuptial 'Night of My Nights,' Minnelli offers up the spangled spectacle Freed hoped would saturate every frame of *Kismet*."

1961:
TWA becomes the first airline to introduce regular in-flight movies on this day by treating the first-class section traveling from New York to Los Angeles to a churning tub of suds starring **Lana Turner**: *By Love Possessed.*

1966:
"*Ha!*" scoffs **Ava Gardner** on this day when she learns her ex (**Frank Sinatra**) has just married a flat-chested 21-year-old with close-cropped hair (**Mia Farrow**). "I always knew Frank would end up in bed with a boy."

1973:
Country singers **Kris Kristofferson** and **Rita Coolidge** start domestic harmonizing on this day. Dissonance came three years later in the form of a graphic *Playboy* pictorial between Kristofferson and **Sarah Miles**, supposedly plugging their just-finished flick *The Sailor Who Fell From Grace With the Sea* but in truth writing *fini* to the Kristofferson marriage.

1976:
Some 400 extras who've been standing around for days gawking at the ceiling of a defunct World War II dirigible hanger in Mobile, AL, now have something to look at: On this day, director **Steven Spielberg** begins lensing the landing of the huge, 20-ton Mothership in *Close Encounters of the Third Kind.*

1977:
On L.A.'s "Nine in the Morning Show," **Jacqueline Eastland** echoes the prediction another psychic, **Gloria James**, had made 50 days earlier in Boston — that **Elvis** will die soon. "Soon" would be less than a month (Aug. 16, 1977).

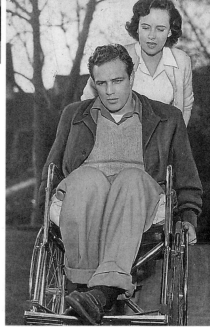

1950: *The Men* brings Broadway's **Marlon Brando** to Radio City Music Hall on this day — and the vehicle that got him there was a wheelchair. Playing a paraplegic war veteran was the socially responsible, calculatingly uncommercial move of a born rebel, but the truth is he accepted the project without reading the script. Bumming about Europe, he lost his passport in Paris and was running with Left Bank riffraff, begging for money, having a great time till MCA's **Lew Wasserman** promised him passage home and a new passport if he'd consider it.

1956: On this day — her 18th birthday — **Natalie Wood** has her first date with the man who'll co-star with her three times and marry her twice: **Robert Wagner**.

1957: *Island in the Sun*, **Alec Waugh**'s yarn about racial crisscrossing in the Caribbean (with **Joan Fontaine** and **Harry Belafonte** prominent among the participants), tippytoes into Wetumpka, AL, on this day. Trying not to inflame his clientele, the owner of the Dixie Drive-In (**Max Singleton**) did a tightrope-act in his ad: "This is the one that is banned all over the South. While we dare to show it, we do not indorse [sic] it. Make up your mind about seeing it." That warning had the effect of an engraved invitation to the KKK. Demonstrators cut the power line before Singleton could get off a single showing and chased him and his wife into a field. They emerged from the ordeal with a new statement: "We will not attempt the show again for our own protection."

1961: Floundering in the dregs of a career gone south, **Joan Fontaine** booked herself out of her class for **Irwin Allen**'s *Voyage to the Bottom of the Sea*, the theatrical dry-run for his TV series. "What Mr. Allen's huge, blinking and unwinking juke box of a sub really needs is a psychiatrist," prescribes *The New York Times*' **Howard Thompson** on this day. "And this it has in the svelte person and furrowed brow of Miss Fontaine, clicking around in high heels near the ocean floor. As a psychiatrist badly in need of one herself, Miss Fontaine meets a grisly fate. She will never make it back to Manderley now."

1973: The screen king of kung fu — **Bruce Lee**, 32 — dies of an acute brain edema in Hong Kong on this day. His first splash in Hollywood's mainstream — Warners' *Enter the Dragon* — hit Manhattan like a tidal wave 28 days later, and he became the most popular Chinese actor in the world.

1998: As it must to all men, birth comes to **Charles Foster** [*bleep!*] on this day, firstborn of twice-Oscared **Jodie Foster**, who declined to identify the father.

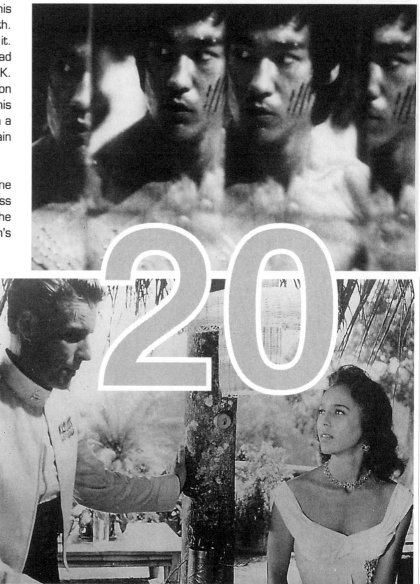

A FILM ENTRANCE & A FILM EXIT: From top: Marlon Brando (with Teresa Wright) in *The Men*; Bruce Lee in *Enter the Dragon*.
DIXIE ANGINA: John Justin and Dorothy Dandridge in *Island in the Sun*.

1919: On this day, ten days after burying **Norman Spencer Chaplin** (his three-day-old firstborn), **Charles Chaplin** starts filming *The Kid*, a classic tear-jerker in which he cast the title role with an impish four-year-old he found upstaging his parents' vaudeville act at L.A.'s Orpheum. For Chaplin, there was some-thing in **Jackie Coogan** that echoed either his recent loss or his distant past (Chaplin, too, had been a toddling stage-trouper). They toiled in perfect comedic harmony a year and nine days, creating a silent-screen classic. In 1972, during Chaplin's triumphant return to Hollywood, *The* (now-bald, pot-bellied, 57-year-old) *Kid* rushed up to meet him at a party and was barred by **Walter Matthau**, who was ferociously shielding Chaplin from harassment — but, when The Great Man saw who the insistent "crasher" was, he burst into tears, and they embraced. "I would rather see you than anybody," he whispered in Coogan's ear.

1932: Universal puts into general release on this day *Tom Brown of Culver*, a cadet-school flick in which the nominal stars (**Tom Brown**, **Richard Cromwell**, **Ben Alexander**, **Andy Devine**) don't entirely outshine a future one: **Tyrone Power** (then billed as **Jr.**). Even the picture's director was on the brink of better things: **William Wyler**.

1936: Shooting starts on this day for a Poverty-Row shoot-'em-up series that will ride out of Republic 58 times from 1936 to 1943: *The Three Mesquiteers*, starring **Robert Livingston**, **Ray Corrigan** and **Syd Saylor** in the title roles (i.e., Stony Brooke, Tucson Smith and Lullaby Joslin). The characters were introduced the previous year in Beacon's *The Law of 45's* and RKO Radio's *Powdersmoke Range*, but neither studio took the series to a second chapter.

1938: *Love Finds Andy Hardy* — and how! **Mickey Rooney** claimed in his 1991 "kiss-and-yell" autobiography that, during the filming of this Hardy boy installment (No. 4 of 16, bowing on this day at New York's Capitol), he and co-star **Lana Turner** had an affair — and, subsequently, an abortion. On hearing this news, however, Turner bolted out of near-seclusion to deny it in no uncertain terms.

A SON WHEN HE NEEDED ONE: Tom Wilson, Charles Chaplin and Jackie Coogan in *The Kid*. **THREE ON A SHOESTRING:** Robert Livingston, Syd Saylor and Ray Corrigan. **A [FUTURE] STAR LINEUP:** Tyrone Power, Richard Cromwell, Dick Winslow, Norman Phillips Jr., Marty Roubert, Tom Brown, Kit Wain and Ben Alexander in *Tom Brown of Culver*. **"KISS & YELL" — & YELL BACK:** Mickey Rooney and Lana Turner in *Love Finds Andy Hardy*.

22

1932: The battle of the **Barrymores** begins on this day as **Lionel, Ethel** and **John** start lensing their only feature-length team-effort, *Rasputin and the Empress* (or, as it was known in some quarters, *Disputin' and the Empress*). "You need not worry about Mrs. Colt," John said to the press when Ethel joined him and Lionel for *Rasputin*. "Our sister will be standing right before the camera — in front of us." Their sibling rivalry was pawned off as grand-scale scene-stealing, but in truth the threesome helped each other. The brothers were particularly good about toning their sister's broad stage-acting down to subtle screen level. In no time at all, she was "Empress of All the Rushes."

1934: Gangster-on-the-lam **John Dillinger**, a die-hard **Myrna Loy** fan, catches his last flick — her *Manhattan Melodrama* — on this day and *does* die hard, mowed down under the marquee of Chicago's Biograph Theater by a task force of G-men.

1941: "For **Carlotta**, on our 12th Wedding Anniversary," writes **Eugene O'Neill** on this day. "I give you the original script of this play of old sorrow, written in tears and blood. A sadly inappropriate gift, it would seem, for a day celebrating happiness. But you will understand. I mean it as a tribute to your love and tenderness which gave me the faith in love that enabled me to face my dead at last and write this play — write it with deep pity and understanding and forgiveness for *all* the four haunted Tyrones." When this just-completed *Long Day's Journey Into Night* premiered on Broadway 16 years later, it won O'Neill — posthumously — his first Tony and his fourth Pulitzer Prize. Its Tony-winning star, **Fredric March**, refused to do the film without his Tony-nominated co-star (Mrs. March: **Florence Eldridge**), so those roles went to **Spencer Tracy** and **Katharine Hepburn** — only Tracy couldn't quite see himself as a faded matinee idol so he passed the part along to **Ralph Richardson**.

1947: A couple of California lads who found their way to the motion picture cameras are born on this day: San Francisco's **Danny Glover** and Los Angeles' Albert Einstein. The latter, smartly, changed his name to **Albert Brooks**.

1957: On this day, **Lana Turner** makes an ex of **Lex Barker** (her fourth), and they rapidly become strangers. She supposedly fainted during their wedding service in Turin September 7, 1953 — but the balloon burst in a big way in less than four years. When she learned he'd sexually abused her 13-year-old **Cheryl**, Turner gave him 20 minutes to clear out. The former screen Tarzan collapsed and died of a heart attack on a New York street May 11, 1973, three days after his 54th birthday. Eulogized the dry-eyed Turner: "What took him so long?"

FAMILY SECRETS: Dean Stockwell, Ralph Richardson, Jason Robards and Katharine Hepburn in *Long Day's Journey Into Night*.
SIBLING REVELRY: Lionel and Ethel and John in *Rasputin and the Empress*.
BIRTHDAY BOYS: Danny Glover and Albert Brooks.

23

1954: "YOU HAVE NEVER DONE A MUSICAL. NEITHER HAVE I. WE NEVER DID SHAKESPEARE EITHER," wires *Julius Caesar* director **Joseph L. Mankiewicz** to his Marc Antony, **Marlon Brando**, on this day, somehow convincing him to do Sky Masterson in *Guys and Dolls*. **Gene Kelly** had been first choice, but MGM wouldn't loan him out, opening the role up to **Clark Gable**, **Bing Crosby**, **Frank Sinatra**, **Robert Mitchum**, **Burt Lancaster**, **Kirk Douglas** and **Tony Martin**. Until Mankiewicz put the kibosh on it, producer **Samuel Goldwyn** proposed turning it into a **Dean Martin-Jerry Lewis** romp. Sinatra, the only contender who could reach this Sky unaided, settled for second banana Nathan Detroit (originated by the utterly unmusical **Sam Levene**), but his quick-study approach to acting was run aground by Brando's prosaic Method. "Don't put me in the game, coach, until 'Mumbles' is through rehearsing," he told Mankiewicz. Brando's take on Sinatra: "He's the kind of guy that, when he dies, he's going up to Heaven and give God a hard time for making him bald."

1980: On this, the first day of filming *On Golden Pond* at Squam Lake, N.H., two certifiable legends meet at last: **Henry Fonda** and **Katharine Hepburn**. She presented him with a battered old hat that had been **Spencer Tracy**'s favorite (an exact replica of **John Ford**'s good-luck hat). Fonda cried on the spot, of course, and wore it for the film's first scene. "For luck," she said. That luck got them both Oscars, his after the longest wait between nominations in Academy history (41 years); hers was an unprecedented No. 4. Last-minute shoulder surgery almost forced her out of the film — **Barbara Stanwyck** was on standby — but she rallied. **Jane Fonda**, who produced the picture and gave an Oscar-nominated performance as their daughter, got clearance from Screen Actors Guild to shoot during a strike because her father's health was precarious. Indeed, this was his final feature. When filming finished, he thanked Hepburn for the hat by painting a still life of it between two of his own. **Ernest Thompson**, who struck Oscar gold too for writing *On Golden Pond*, eventually got the three-hatted painting when Hepburn realized "the picture made me sad — with Spencer gone and Hank gone."

1966: Two movie matinee-idols named Montgomery die on this day — **Douglass Montgomery**, 58, and **Montgomery Clift**, 45.

1982: One of Hollywood's most ghastly filming accidents occurs on this day during the shooting of *Twilight Zone — The Movie*. **Vic Morrow**, 53, and two Vietnamese children, seven-year-old **My-ca Dinh Lee** and six-year-old **Renee Shin-Yi**, were killed when a Bell C-205 helicopter crashed on top of them in the final shot of a nighttime location at the Indian Dunes Park, near Saugus, CA.

24

1929: A day of milestones for men named Peter: British director **Peter Yates** is born on this day, and British actor **Peter Sellers** dies on it 51 years later. In between, on this day in 1934, **Peter Lorre** reaches America from Germany.

1943: A publicist's nightmare begins on this day when **Greer Garson** finishes her day's work on *Madame Curie* and heads for the Santa Monica Presbyterian Church to marry **Richard Ney**, who'd played her baby-faced 19-year-old son, Vin, in her Oscar-winning vehicle, *Mrs. Miniver*. (**Montgomery Clift** rejected the role because it came with a longterm MGM contract). The film's Oscar-winning director, **William Wyler**, felt "very responsible" for the union, admitting privately he only picked Ney out of "a bunch of silly kids because he seemed the silliest." Garson and Ney had wanted to wed when romance first dawned between "mother" and "son," but **Louis B. Mayer** made them promise to hold off — at least until *Mrs. Miniver* had finished its first-run gigs. Their marriage began with a ten-year gap in ages, but, when they divorced four years later, this difference had curiously shrunk to two years.

WAY OUT WEST IN RIVERSIDE PARK: Charles Bronson in *Death Wish*. AWKWARDLY, ALL IN THE FAMILY: Christopher Severn, Greer Garson, Clare Sandars, Walter Pidgeon and Richard Ney in *Mrs. Miniver*. DIVORCE COURT: Hayward v. Barker.

1953: A divorce announcement on this day is **Susan Hayward**'s peculiar way of celebrating her ninth wedding anniversary to **Jess Barker**.

1965: A cerebral hemorrhage claims **Constance Bennett**, 59, on this day. The last of her 45 films arrived 10 months later. Producer **Ross Hunter** lured her out of a 12-year retirement to play the formidable mother-in-law of *Madame X* (**Lana Turner**), and it was a glamorous exit, swathed in a $50,000 sable (the most expensive garb in film history, according to *The Guinness Book of Records*).

1974: *Death Wish*, a paean to urban vigilantism that would go into extra innings (four sequels over the next decade), opens on this day at Loews Astor Plaza and Cine theaters in New York. A stunned **Brian Garfield**, who wrote the novel on which the movie was (de)based, later told *The Hollywood Reporter* his intent in the novel was the exact opposite of the film's, that director **Michael Winner** "made **Charles Bronson**, who was supposed to be evil, a knight on a white horse."

1998: The celebrity-hounding photographer who brought a new word into being via *La Dolce Vita* — **Tazio Secchiaroli**, 73 — dies of a heart attack on this day. The word: *paparazzi*, for the pesky packs of photographers running alongside of cafe society, constantly clicking away at its heels. Secchiaroli was the model for the most persistent of the lot in *La Dolce Vita*, played by **Walter Santesso** and named "Signor Paparazzo" for a boyhood pal of director **Federico Fellini**'s who "spoke very quickly without stopping and could imitate the sounds of insects, particularly mosquitoes."

1936: "A bout of pneumonia" is the euphemism *The Hollywood Reporter* uses on this day for why **John Barrymore** won't be playing Baron de Varville to **Greta Garbo**'s *Camille*. Truth was, director **George Cukor** visited him in a Culver City detox clinic and realized he wouldn't be up to it. That despairing visit became the basis for the sanitarium scene in *A Star Is Born* with Norman Maine (another role Barrymore was, at the time, too drunk to do). His brother **Lionel** got hastily assigned the baron role, then was shifted to the part of **Robert Taylor**'s disapproving father. **Henry Daniell** did bravado justice to the baron.

SERIES SISTERS: From left: Cecilia Parker from the Andy Hardy films (with Betty Ross Clarke, Lewis Stone, Mickey Rooney and Fay Holden) and Nan Grey from the *Three Smart Girls* films (with Binnie Barnes, Charles Winninger, Deanna Durbin and Barbara Read).
ENTER MR. BELVEDERE: Robert Young, Maureen O'Hara and Clifton Webb in *Sitting Pretty*.
BIOGRAPHY-BOUND BETTY: Hutton as Texas Guinan in *Incendiary Blonde*.

1945: *Incendiary Blonde* goes off at New York's Paramount on this day, a fictionalized film biography of Prohibition nightclub queen **Texas Guinan** that revealed, behind **Betty Hutton**'s knockaway comedy, a certain dramatic ability. Had a heart attack not forced her mentor, **B.G. DeSylva**, to retire as Paramount production chief, she felt she'd have "become a great dramatic actress because he was heading me toward that way." Keeping that course kept her in more movie "biographies" — of serial star **Pearl White** (*The Perils of Pauline*), vaudeville headliner **Blossom Seeley** (*Somebody Loves Me*) and especially, on a lucky loan-out to MGM, sharpshooter **Annie Oakley** (*Annie Get Your Gun*). At various times, she also considered playing **Theda Bara**, **Clara Bow**, **Sophie Tucker** and **Mabel Normand** — but none of these film projects came to fruition.

1947: In a story conference on this day, **Darryl F. Zanuck** assesses *Sitting Pretty* as a one-joke situation and suggests screenwriter **F. Hugh Herbert** hold back a few storytelling cards so the comedy can be strung out the feature-length distance — specifically, that the baby-sitting Lynn Belvedere (an imperious, Oscar-nominated **Clifton Webb**) not introduce himself as a writer to his suburban employers (**Robert Young** and **Maureen O'Hara**), just that he is a genius and requires eight hours sleep a day. The result became 20th Century-Fox's big hit of '48 and spilled over into sequels: *Mr. Belvedere Goes to College* (1949) and *Mr. Belvedere Rings the Bell* (1951).

1993: Two of the screen's big sisters pass away on this day: **Deanna Durbin**'s in the *Three Smart Girls* films (**Nan Grey**, 75) dies in San Diego, and **Mickey Rooney**'s in the Andy Hardy series (**Cecilia Parker**, 79) expires in Ventura.

25

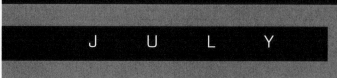

26

1938: Director **Henry King** and **Tyrone Power** board King's plane on this day and fly 1,550 miles from Hollywood to the Ozarks for a then-rare location shoot. Their *Jesse James* was the first Technicolor Western, and it was rough riding with the James gang — especially for horses crashing through plate-glass windows, riding tumultuously over the terrain, plunging off cliffs into rivers. Stuntman **Cliff Lyons** executed that last spectacular spill — twice! — and the horses he drove into that 75-foot drop were both killed hitting the water, causing the Missouri Humane Society to haul the studio into court. As a result, a stricter policing of movie stunts by SPCA stemmed from this "casual carnage."

1940: *They Drive by Night*, a truck-driving retread of 1935's *Bordertown*, pulls into New York's Strand on this day. In it, **Ida Lupino** committed murder to land **George Raft**, then went spectacularly to pieces on the witness stand — as did **Bette Davis** over **Paul Muni** before her. Lupino's last feature-film outing — 1972's meagerly released *Deadhead Miles* — reunited her with Raft for a cameo-gag that kidded *They Drive by Night*.

1971: Eve Harrington officially turns into Margo Channing on this day: **Anne Baxter** — who played that ultimate in underhanded understudies in *All About Eve* — begins her Broadway run in *Applause*, the stage musical version of that film, playing the Channing part she inherited from **Lauren Bacall** (when the first-choice replacement, **Rita Hayworth**, couldn't master the lines). Carried another dimension: Baxter's own swan song was a role meant for her movie Margo, **Bette Davis** (ailing at the time, unable to play the grande dame of TV's *Hotel*). Davis and Baxter's classic star-vs.-understudy clash was drawn from "The Wisdom of Eve," a 1946 Cosmopolitan short story by **Mary Orr**, who never knew who the real Eve was but based Channing on **Elisabeth Bergner**, the Austrian actress her then-fiance (**Reginald Denham**) had directed on Broadway in 1943's *The Two Mrs. Carrolls*. Bergner hired as an assistant a stagedoor fan so star-struck she knew Bergner's whole role and got to play it at a replacement audition — a deed that got her summarily sacked by a more jealous-than-flattered Bergner. This fan, who never got a dime out of the story that damned and maligned her, lives now in Venice, Italy, under the name of **Martina Lawrence** (the name, not accidentally, of "the good twin" Bergner played in 1939's *A Stolen Life*).

THE JAMES BROTHERS MAKE A COSTLY GET-AWAY: Tyrone Power and Henry Fonda in *Jesse James*.
"LITTLE MISS EVIL" CAUGHT IN THE ACT: Anne Baxter in *All About Eve*.
SEPARATED BY 32 YEARS: From left: George Raft and Ida Lupino in *Deadhead Miles* and *They Drive by Night*.

27

1936: "The Arkansas Traveler," **Bob Burns**, actually travels to Arkansas on this day to help the Little Rock launching of his *Rhythm on the Range.* **Martha Raye** feature-debuted, and **Bing Crosby** crooned the title tune. Its big hit had **Johnny Mercer** words and music: "I'm an Old Cowhand from the Rio Grande."

1940: Bugs Bunny is born on this day, as *A Wild Hare* scampers out of the Warners pen and into the marketplace. There had been three rough-draft dry-runs at stardom — in *Porky's Hare Hunt* (1938), *Hare-um Scare-um* (1939) and *Elmer's Candid Camera* (1940) — before the tough-hide hare we all know and love emerged in this Oscar-nominated short-subject. He started out as "Happy Rabbit," but the name and persona evolved into something else when **Mel Blanc** (who spoke for him) rechristened him after the artist who had drawn him, **Ben "Bugs" Hardaway**. Blanc gave the character a brassy Flatbush sound — tempered with **Gable**'s impertinence, **Bogie**'s coolness and **Cagney**'s street-smarts. All of that sauntered up to a befuddled Elmer Fudd, chomped into a carrot and asked casually, "Eh, what's up, Doc?" (That immortal line was a last minute ad-lib on Blanc's part, tossed out in an attempt to improve on the slightly old-hat signature phrase which had originally been suggested: "What's cookin'?")

1966: Most of Tokyo seems to turn out on this day for the arrival of **Sean Connery**, and the calamitous mobbing continues for six weeks of location lensing there, eventually convincing Connery that *You Only Live Twice* is more than enough of James Bond. When the filming concluded, he swore off the role, but that picture's title proved to be particularly prophetic: After successor **George Lazenby** dropped the ball with 1969's *On Her Majesty's Secret Service*, Connery lapsed back into 007 stride for 1971's *Diamonds Are Forever* and then, again, said never again. Turns out, he was only talking about The Official, Authorized Film Series put out by **Albert R. Broccoli** and **Harry Saltzman**. In 1983, a rival producer (**Jack Schwartzman**) talked him back into Bonding for a maverick remake of *Thunderball*, called (Connery's idea) *Never Say Never Again*.

1975: "I decided finally not to do *Antichrist*," **Charlton Heston** writes in his diary on this day. "You have to be skeptical — I do, anyway — of accepting an offer just to reassure yourself you're employable. I've only just finished *Midway*, but there are always the old doubts rising almost at once." **Gregory Peck**, who would pounce on the *MacArthur* part that Heston passed up two years later, eventually did *Antichrist*, which went into release as *The Omen*, rivaled *Midway* as a box-office success and produced two equally profitable sequels.

28

1934: On this day, 65-year-old **Marie Dressler** becomes the first Oscar-winning *performer* to die. The first *Oscar winner* to die was **Joseph Farnham**, who passed away two years after the first Oscar ceremony where he got the prize for Best Title Writing. His runner-up, **Gerald Duffy**, expired a few months *before* the event, and the category itself also died because sound suddenly made it passe.

1940: Warner Bros. pulls the plug on the prize-winning pair behind 1936's *The Story of Louis Pasteur*, 1937's *The Life of Emile Zola* and 1939's *Juarez* — director **William Dieterle** and title-player **Paul Muni** — dissolving their contracts on this day. The official company line was that the studio couldn't afford prestige pictures anymore, but, in truth, what it couldn't afford was Muni's diva-like demands for rewrites. The actor's insistence on having his *Juarez* role built up disfigured the drama, bloated the picture and doomed its box office. The final straw: Muni wanted *High Sierra* revised to eliminate all the gunplay, fearful it might tip his *Scarface* roots and sully the lofty rep as Warners' foremost waxwork impersonator. This was not the image Warners exec **Hal B. Wallis** was anxious to preserve. "Every time Paul Muni parts his beard and looks down a telescope," Wallis wailed, "this company loses $2 million."

1948: *Abbott and Costello Meet Frankenstein*, the A&C series' second-most popular entry (after *Buck Privates*), debuts on this day at New York's Loews Criterion — but not for **Boris Karloff**. The actor first to shuffle across the screen as the Frankenstein monster declined even to *view* the film, preferring not to see his creation parodied. (For a fee, however, he'd pose outside a theater playing the movie.) Two of the actors playing celebrity monsters here died of cancer in 1973: The Wolf Man (**Lon Chaney Jr.**, 67, on July 12) and the Frankenstein monster (**Glenn Strange**, 74, on Sept. 20). During filming, when Strange hurt his foot on studio cables, Chaney spent a day in monster makeup hurling a damsel out the window. A third monster was felled by a heart attack: Dracula (**Bela Lugosi**, 72, on Aug. 16, 1956).

KARLOFF LOOKED THE OTHER WAY: Lou Costello and Glenn Strange in *Abbott and Costello Meet Frankenstein*.
DRESSLER IN OSCAR-WINNING FORM: Battling Wallace Beery in *Min and Bill*.
GOOD QUEEN BESS: Bess Flowers.

1985: Hollywood's "Queen of the Extras" — **Bess Flowers**, 85, the perennial party-guest for backlot bashes — dies on this day in Woodland Hills, CA. The long-stemmed, silver-haired, Texas-born actress was a familiar fixture for any festive function thrown in films from the 1920s to the 1970s, lending class, tone and dignity to her surroundings by her mere presence. Bess' two best bits: congratulating **Anne Baxter** on winning the Sarah Siddons Award in *All About Eve* and sitting at **Judy Garland**'s Oscar-night table in *A Star Is Born*.

29

1940: Novelist-turned-screen hack **F. Scott Fitzgerald** writes wife **Zelda** on this day of his plan to salvage the floundering career of **Shirley Temple**: star her in his *Babylon Revisited* (a.k.a. *The Last Time I Saw Paris* when finally filmed in '54 with **Elizabeth Taylor**). There were worse ideas. Columbia suggested a Barnum & Bailey clown in *Jo-Jo*, a bride in *June Moon* and a melancholy maiden in *June Madness*. MGM offered *Topsy and Eva* with **Judy Garland** in blackface or *Babes on Broadway* with Garland and **Mickey Rooney** — but only filmed *Kathleen*, which flopped. So did her UA opus (*Miss Annie Rooney*). Then, producer **David O. Selznick** tossed her a life raft — a seven-year contract — and she set sail with *Since You Went Away*.

1954: The critical eruption for **Elia Kazan**'s *On the Waterfront* commences on this day. **Frank Sinatra** was to have starred, but, when producer **Sam Spiegel** could secure only half-financing on Sinatra's name and full-financing on **Marlon Brando**'s, suddenly Ol' Blue Eyes sported a shiner. Sinatra sued Spiegel for $500,000 — but, in 1961, settled for the installation of a Hi-Fi system.

1965: Of the star-packed *Ship of Fools* that just docked in New York, *Times* critic **Bosley Crowther** notes on this day "the actor who plays the key role is not a star" — **Oskar Werner** — "yet it is his fine performance as the ship's doctor . . . that pumps the main irony and pity into the troubled heart of this film." Werner made the Oscar running for Best Actor but lost to a fellow *Ship*mate in another film (*Cat Ballou*'s **Lee Marvin**). Werner also acted that year with another Best Actor contender (**Richard Burton** in *The Spy Who Came In From the Cold*).

1983: The first film co-produced by a studio and an insurance company, *Brainstorm*, reaches the marketplace on this day. When **Natalie Wood** drowned during filming, MGM shut down production and submitted an insurance claim of $15 million to Lloyd's of London, insisting the film couldn't be finished without her. **Douglas Trumbull**, its writer-director, begged to differ — and Lloyd's bet $2.75 million he could. Wood had completed all but two scenes when she died. One was eliminated, and the other redesigned so her plot function could be assigned to **Joe Dorsey**, playing a lab assistant of her scientist-husband (**Christopher Walken**). A canoe ride Wood filmed with Walken was cut to keep from echoing the actual tragedy — along with a fantasy sequence in which their son imagines he is drowning. When the 18 days of principal photography was completed, MGM balked at six more months of special-effects post-production, forcing Lloyd's to fork over another $3 million and become the first insurance company to own a percentage of a movie's profits.

WOW, VOYAGERS!: Vivien Leigh, Simone Signoret, Jose Ferrer, Lee Marvin, Oskar Werner, Elizabeth Ashley, George Segal, Jose Greco, Michael Dunn, Charles Korvin and Heinz Ruhmann in *Ship of Fools*.
WHAT SLIPPED THROUGH SINATRA'S FINGERS: Marlon Brando and Eva Marie Saint in *On the Waterfront*.
BRAINSTORMING *BRAINSTORM*: Natalie Wood and Christopher Walken in *Brainstorm*.

1933: Doctors let **Clark Gable** come to the set for two hours on this day and shoot his first scene for *Dancing Lady*. He'd been sidelined by a gum infection that caused a toxic condition in his body (and would cost him his teeth). A few hours after shooting the sequence, he was rushed to Cedars of Lebanon for an emergency appendectomy, delaying the film even longer. The gist of Gable's scene was to introduce **Joan Crawford** (the green kid he had plucked from the chorus to replace the star of the show) to the fabulous **Fred Astaire** (played by the actual and no-less-fabulous Fred, in his film bow) — and this was the last day the scene could be shot since, on Aug. 1, Astaire began his RKO contract, flying down to Rio with **Ginger** Somebody.

1951: After some creative editing successfully obscures the charges of anti-Semitism that have kept **David Lean's** *Oliver Twist* barred from this country (or, at least, at bay), the 1948 flick settles belatedly into New York's Park Avenue Theater on this day, *sans* seven-to-ten minutes of "offending footage" — primarily, closeups of Fagin (**Alec Guinness**, who was, true to **Charles Dickens'** description, unrecognizable behind the bushy beard and grotesque hooked-nose).

1965: Finally free of the no-motorcycling clause that kept him frustratingly wheel-less during the filming of *Tickle Me*, **Elvis Presley** goes on a bike-buying spree at a Harley dealership in Los Angeles on this day, treating himself and nine members of his "Memphis Mafia" to brand-new motorcycles. Then, the ten — dubbed "El's Angels" by The King himself — hit the open road.

1968: On this day, **The Beatles** close their Apple Boutique in London and, in hours, give away $25,000 worth of goods. First customer: **Michael J. Pollard**, *Bonnie and Clyde*'s driver, who made out like a bandit with some free shirts.

1993: *Rising Sun* reaches area theaters in New York on this day, ethnically altered by adapter-director **Philip Kaufman** so that **Michael Crichton's** polemic against the Japanese invasion of American economy rarely rises above the level of a slick whodunit — a *new* whodunit at that, since the killer of the Caucasian call-girl in the Japanese boardroom is *not* who it was in the book. When it became apparent after a diluted first-draft that Kaufman was muzzling what Crichton meant to be "a wake-up call" for U.S. business, the novelist took his money and walked off the film. Regardless, none of that mattered to the Media Action Network for Asian Americans (MANAA), which mobilized without seeing one frame of film and marched against this "Nineties version of the yellow peril."

31

1928: The trademark roar of Leo the Lion is heard for the first time on this day, heralding MGM's first sound film at New York's Astor Theater. *White Shadows in the South Seas* was finished in the Marquesas Islands of the South Pacific as a silent film, forcing **Douglas Shearer** (the company's sound chief and **Norma**'s brother) to trek to deepest, darkest New Jersey to sprinkle the soundtrack with a synchronized score and sound effects. The talk in this purported "talkie" consisted of only one word — "Hello" — uttered by **Monte Blue**.

1938: "I am convinced that the majority of fans who think I should not play this kind of character are right," **Norma Shearer** informs *The New York Times* on this day, masking her disappointment about the deluge of negative mail triggered by *The Times*' June 28th announcement that she'd play Scarlett O'Hara. Other turndowns: *Mrs. Miniver* and *Madame Curie*, either of which could have reversed her engines and saved her career — as could have the tempting offers Warner Bros. was waving at her: *Now, Voyager* and *Old Acquaintance* — but instead Shearer chose to self-destruct — fulfilling her contract on a steady diet of stale champagne (the strenuously artificial *We Were Dancing* and the well-named *Her Cardboard Lover*).

1961: Production Code seals of approval are finally granted to a pair of **Otto Preminger** pictures — 1953's *The Moon Is Blue* and 1955's *The Man With the Golden Arm* — on this day, better late than never. Among other "shocking" offenses, the pseudo-blue *Moon* introduced to the moviegoing public the word "virgin."

1987: A brand-new James Bond (No. 4 in the "official" series) springs into action on this day in 1,728 theaters in *The Living Daylights*: **Timothy Dalton**. Series producers, who'd been considering him for the part since **Sean Connery** made it available after 1971's *Diamonds Are Forever*, played that ancient hunch 15 years later when their first choice (**Pierce Brosnan**) suddenly fell out of the picture because of a television commitment. Dalton never really got out of the L's of the series. After *The Living Daylights* and *Licence To Kill* two years later, he lateraled the role back to Brosnan for 1995's *GoldenEye*.

1988: Writer-director **Spike Lee** returns to Bed-Stuy to his third week of filming *Do the Right Thing*, having spent the weekend in Atlanta where the First National Black Arts Festival unreeled his features, music videos, trailers and commercials. "Damn," gasped Spike, "a retrospective already!"

A CLEAN BILL OF HEALTH FOR A COUPLE OF PREMINGERS: From left: *The Moon Is Blue* (David Niven, Maggie McNamara and William Holden) and *The Man With the Golden Arm* (Arnold Stang and Frank Sinatra).
BOND 4: Timothy Dalton in *The Living Daylights*.
A RETROSPECTIVE *WAS* RUSHING IT: Spike Lee and Danny Aiello in *Do the Right Thing*.

1

CONVINCING WESTERN PRESENCE: John Dierkes, Jack Palance, Douglas Spencer and Elisha Cook Jr. in *Shane*. PLODDING POST-MORTEM: Jason Robards in *Raise the Titanic!* THOU SWELL: Dorothy McGuire and Gary Cooper in *Friendly Persuasion*.

1935: At RKO Radio, **Lily Pons** faces film cameras for the first time, debuting in *I Dream Too Much*. **Max Steiner**, head of the studio's music department, called it *I Ask Too Much* because (1) Pons insisted her arias be conducted by fiance **Andre Kostelanetz** and (2) **Jerome Kern** requested **Robert Russell Bennett** conduct the songs he and **Dorothy Fields** wrote.

1953: *Shane* goes into general release on this day, and **Jack Palance**'s stock soars. With minimal dialogue, he fashioned a vivid, Oscar-nominated villain: Wilson, the hired gun brought in to battle title-gunslinger **Alan Ladd**. Like any self-respecting New York actor, Palance lied that he could ride a horse — a handicap which director **George Stevens** creatively overcame by contriving a memorably unexpected entrance for him: *leading* his horse into town, walking in a deliberate cadence that set the rattler tone of his character. When the actor inadvertently managed a perfect dismount once, Stevens used that footage for both dismounting and (by reversing it) mounting. Ironically, the part that finally got Palance the Oscar — on his next nomination, *38 years later!* — was that of a grizzled trail-boss who nursemaided *City Slickers* (**Billy Crystal, Bruno Kirby, Daniel Stern**, et al) through the rigors of a modern cattle-drive. (You could say he understood their predicament.)

1955: Still out of favor with Hollywood for running off with director **Roberto Rossellini** (and *marrying him!*), **Ingrid Bergman** declines **William Wyler**'s *Friendly Persuasion* on this day — the third actress (after **Katharine Hepburn** and **Vivien Leigh**) to pass up the part of **Gary Cooper**'s Quaker-preacher spouse. **Jane Wyman, Maureen O'Hara, Teresa Wright, Martha Scott, Eleanor Parker** and **Mary Martin** rated consideration. At one point — to tease writer **Jessamyn West** — Wyler tossed in **Jane Russell**'s name ("She's a very pious girl, I understand. Goes to church, teaches Sunday school, sings hymns.") **Dorothy McGuire** eventually won the role — and 1956's Best Actress nod from the National Board of Review (one of the few film groups *not* to pick Ingrid Bergman's *Anastasia*).

1980: "Take the adventure out of an adventure movie, and what have you got?" asks **Janet Maslin** in *The New York Times* on this day. The answer, surfacing at the Ziegfeld unworthy of the punctuation, was *Raise the Titanic!* The sinking was something; the salvaging was, as another critic put it, "about as exciting as playing in your bath." This celluloid disaster swallowed up $36 million — and burped back $6.8 million. Most of the expense came from building a giant model of the ship before seeing if a tank existed large enough to hold it. (There wasn't, so one was built.) "Raise the Titanic?" exclaimed its producer, **Lord Lou Grade**. "It would have been cheaper to lower the Atlantic."

1935: In a cabaret set filled with 250 extras on this day — almost eight years after "you ain't heard nothin' yet" — **Chaplin** Sings! (or, more accurately, lifts his voice in song, and out comes gibberish). Was it hostile or ironic that the first time his voice is heard in films — in *Modern Times* — he speaks a language all his own? "When he found a voice to say what was on his mind," said **Billy Wilder**, "he was like a child of eight writing lyrics for Beethoven's Ninth."

1941: An exasperated **Darryl F. Zanuck** noodges associate producer **Len Hammond** on this day about the slow-mo progress of new-boy-on-the-lot **Jean Renoir**. The great French director thought he'd found a safe harbor from World War II in the backlot Okefenokee of 20th Century-Fox where, with a ripple of **Walter**s (**Brennan** and **Huston**) and virtually "nonexistent English" of his own, he made a murky masterpiece: *Swamp Water*. Unfortunately, Zanuck insisted on faster paddling. More memos followed, browbeating Renoir for his leisurely, improvisional shooting style. "Goodbye, Mr. Zanuck," the director said at film's end, hitting the door to make movies elsewhere. "It certainly has been a pleasure working for 16th Century-Fox."

A FOX-SWAMPED RENOIR: Mary Howard, Walter Huston and Dana Andrews in *Swamp Water*.
CONNIE COULD BE CATTY: Constance Bennett and Albert Dekker in *As Young As You Feel*.
A TIME TO SING: Charles Chaplin in *Modern Times*.

1951: The first **Paddy Chayefsky** story to reach the screen (*As Young As You Feel*) reaches the screen of NYC's Palace on this day. Its only distinction was a secretary bit by sixth-billed **Marilyn Monroe**, who later inspired Chayefsky to an unflattering film portrait (*The Goddess*). A sign that a goddess was then in the works: the fifth-billed, no-longer-young-feeling **Constance Bennett** was heard to purr with acerbic admiration as MM undulated through 20th Century-Fox's commissary one day, "Now, there's a broad with a future behind her."

1957: In typical Hollywood overstatement, "The Trial of a Hundred Stars" commences on this day — but, by actual count in court, only one shows: **Dorothy Dandridge**, who withdraws her $2 million suit against *Confidential* magazine about an alleged forest frolic she had with "naturalists" and settles handsomely out of court. Next case: **Maureen O'Hara**, who on Aug. 17 flashed a passport proving she was in Spain and not (as *Confidential* contended) in the loge of Grauman's Chinese carrying on a game of "Chinese Chest" with a swarthy South American. Witnesses stuck to their stories. Even O'Hara's Irish-nun sister couldn't unhang the hung jury, which had *Confidential* fork over $5,000 instead of the $5 million requested. But more stars filed suit, bankrupting the rag.

1998: After a two-year search for a domestic distributor, director **Adrian Lyne**'s *Lolita* finds on this day an outlet: Showtime. (The Samuel Goldwyn Company gave it a brief theatrical spin, sometimes playing in tandem with **Stanley Kubrick**'s 1962 version.)

AUGUST 3

1939: Her American *Intermezzo* over, **Ingrid Bergman** spends this day — her next-to-last in Hollywood before returning home to Sweden — in Rhett Butler's bedroom (Stage 3 on the *Gone With the Wind*), doing her first color test. Although the results were ravishing, she didn't turn to color till three years (and two days) later when she reported to work on *For Whom the Bell Tolls*.

1942: A 40-minute workday for **Paul Henreid** and **Ingrid Bergman**, milling about the black market outside The Blue Parrot, concludes the *Casablanca* filming on this day — and, while the two are doing publicity stills, word reaches Bergman that the role she thought had gotten away is hers. She'd slummed her way through *Casablanca* in blue funk, having lost the plum part of Maria in *For Whom the Bell Tolls* to **Vera Zorina**, but once the rushes started rolling in (showing Zorina gingerly bounding about the bolders of the Sierra Nevada highlands, betraying her balletic roots), Paramount was panicked into serious second thoughts. Two days later, Bergman was on location, being greeted by **Gary Cooper** with "Hello, Maria." She blushed, in character (and for real). Only in time did Bergman realize the film she did as a consolation prize would emerge the classic she thought the pseudo-prestigious *Bell* would be.

1967: On this day, **Charlton Heston** reaches the Statue of Liberty and films the shocker end of *Planet of the Apes*. Three different reactions were to be shot, but only one actually was — three little words Heston dreamed up: "God damn you!"

1976: On this day, **Martin Sheen** celebrates his 36th birthday — by getting authentically stinko for the opening drunk scene in *Apocalypse Now*. He also cut himself on a mirror, and director **Francis Ford Coppola** (unable to risk real blood) used the take.

DWARFED BY THE PLOT: Grant Williams as *The Incredible Shrinking Man*.
THE HEART THUMP OF DARKNESS: Martin Sheen in *Apocalypse Now*.
CHEST-THUMPER: Kim Hunter, Charlton Heston and Linda Harrison in *Planet of the Apes*.
THE ONE THAT GOT AWAY DIDN'T: From left: Bergman in *For Whom the Bell Tolls* with Cooper and in *Casablanca* with Henreid.

1985: At the V.A. in West L.A. on this day, **Grant Williams**, 54, dies of blood poisoning. His career never grew beyond *The Incredible Shrinking Man*. As he later realized, "When it was released, I wasn't even the star — the story was."

1936: *Daily Variety* more or less posts the epitaph for **Rowland Brown**'s directing career on this day by announcing almost all the scenes of an original story he and **Frank Fenton** developed for **Freddie Bartholomew**, **Jackie Cooper** and **Mickey Rooney** — *The Devil Is a Sissy* — have been reshot by **W.S. Van Dyke**. It was the fourth time another director was called in to finish a Brown film so he stuck to creating "original stories" for other directors to tell with the camera.

1939: On this day — her last in Hollywood before returning to Sweden — **Ingrid Bergman** goes down to the wire, retaking and retaking her entrance into U.S. movies. Perfectionist producer **David O. Selznick** — wanting audiences to "Ahhh" at first sight of her in his *Intermezzo* remake — flailed away at that effect. Bergman made it to the train station just as the *Super Chief* was pulling out.

1952: For what little good it does, film censors issue a warning to Columbia Pictures on this day that **Burt Lancaster** and **Deborah Kerr** are to remain clad in bathrobes when they hit Blowhole Beach in Oahu for their Big Love Scene. Director **Fred Zinnemann** originally staged the sequence standing up, but, when producer **Buddy Adler** objected to this at the rehearsal, Lancaster volunteered to show them a horizontal version he and Kerr had worked out earlier in the day. The resulting shot of ocean waves crashing around the lovers as they kiss passionately, lying on the sand in their bathing suits, required three days and 100 people to film — "a record in time, manpower and equipment for a single movie love scene," contended *Look* magazine — but one of the most famous romantic images of the repressed 1950s came from their labors.

1989: Wearing Cannes' Palme d'Or, *sex, lies and videotape* settles snugly into New York's Cinema Studio I and II on this day, and critics cheer the new cinematic voice behind it: writer-director **Steven Soderburgh**, who's all of 26.

1997: At 122, the oldest person whose age has been verified by official documents expires on this day in Arles, the southern French city where she began life Feb. 21, 1875 — one year before **Alexander Graham Bell** patented his telephone and 14 years before **Alexandre Gustave Eiffel** built his tower. **Jeanne Louise Calment** was also cited by *The Guinness Book of Movie Facts & Feats* as "the oldest performer to have played a speaking role on screen." She played herself, at age 114, in a 1990 French-Canadian film, *Vincent and Me*, recalling the **Vincent Van Gogh** she knew as a child of 12 or 13: She found the artist "very ugly, ungracious, impolite, sick — I forgive him, they called him loco."

ON FIRST SIGHT: Ingrid Bergman and Leslie Howard in *Intermezzo*.
ON THE BEACH: Deborah Kerr and Burt Lancaster in *From Here to Eternity*.
ON *TAPE*: Andie MacDowell in *sex, lies, & videotape*.

1929: The best-known couple of their time — **Mary Pickford** and **Douglas Fairbanks Sr.** — complete their first co-starring effort on this day, an early-talkie attempt at *The Taming of the Shrew* (remembered mostly for a notorious, oft-quoted and totally untrue credit-line: "By William Shakespeare, with additional dialogue by **Sam Taylor**"). At filming's end, Pickford realized the marriage too was also over — working together only underlined the differences in their temperaments, she thought. Another celebrated marriage didn't survive a brush with The Bard's battle of the sexes, either: **Elizabeth Taylor** and **Richard Burton**, the best-known couple of *their* time, divorced — twice — after the *Taming* they did for **Franco Zeffirelli** in 1967.

1952: "MARILYN INHERITS HARLOW'S MANTLE," trumpets a headline in *The New York World Telegram & Sun* on this day over an **Erskine Johnson** story that dubs **Marilyn Monroe** the new **Jean Harlow**. On this exact day a decade later, Monroe is found in her L.A. bedroom dead from an overdose of sleeping pills.

1987: Tooling a rented BMW through Northern Ireland on this day, with girlfriend **Jennifer Grey** beside him, **Matthew Broderick** crashes head-on into another car, killing a mother and daughter. He was hospitalized with a leg fracture, but Grey was only slightly bruised. On Feb. 15, 1988, Broderick pleaded guilty to "careless driving" and was fined $175.

1958: "You think I'm going to stick my head in a moose?" asks **Samuel Goldwyn**, turning down a business deal on this day in his inimitable way with words.

1996: "I don't know what it is, I'm going on vacation, I'm trying to get away, and then — boom — gotta make a rescue," said **Tom Cruise** after putting in a busy year of off-screen heroics. On March 4, in Santa Monica, he called EMS for an uninsured hit-and-run victim (**Heloisa Vinhas**, 22), accompanied her to the UCLA Medical Center and footed her $7,000 hospital bill there. On July 4, at the London launching of his *Mission: Impossible*, he prevented a surging mob of fans from crushing a young Brit (**Laurence Sadler**, 7) against a security fence. And, on this day, while vacationing aboard a yacht in the Tyrrhenian Sea, he helps save five people from a boat fire off Italy's island of Capri — "my latest recorded rescue," he shrugged lightly about this scrape.

1998: "I am the patron saint of Halloween. I never have to go out in costume. I just go as myself, and I get a lot of candy." Or so says **Jamie Lee Curtis**, who movie-debuted in 1978's *Halloween* and has returned to its bloody turf for a 20th-anniversary update, *Halloween: H20*, opening nationally on this day.

6 AUGUST

1959: *The 30-Foot Bride of Candy Rock*, the screen's only Budless Lou, slips unnoticed into release on this day. **Lou Costello**, in lieu of **Bud Abbott**, hired a *tall* straight-woman — **Dorothy Provine**. Critics practically threw rocks at the screen — an indignity Costello was spared, having died of a heart attack five months earlier (March 3, three days before his 53d birthday). Abbott heard of Costello's death from a TV bulletin.

1960: Something else **Gene Kelly** and **Stanley Donen** shared beyond screen credit for co-directing *On the Town*, *Singin' in the Rain* and *It's Always Fair Weather* was dancer **Jeanne Coyne**, who usually served as their choreographing assistant. She became the first Mrs. Donen in 1948, and, on this day, she becomes (after *Marty*'s **Betsy Blair**) the second Mrs. Kelly.

1979: On this day, **Warren Beatty** begins what'll be Oscar work — directing *Reds*.

1982: Dorothy Michaels does her "Famous Fashion Shoot" montage on this day for national magazines begging to put her puss on their covers. Not everyone recognized Dorothy: When she sidled up to **Jon Voight** at the Russian Tea Room, he had to be told Dorothy Michaels was **Dustin Hoffman**, his *Midnight Cowboy* sidekick, in drag as *Tootsie*.

1983: The ten-month marriage of **Margot Kidder** and French director **Philippe de Broca** begins on this day. She previously sprinted through marriages with New York actor **John Heard** (six weeks) and Canadian writer **Tom McGuane** (18 months).

1990: On this day, at an underattended mid-afternoon showing of *Young Guns II*, **Dustin Hoffman** slips discreetly into Manhattan's Gotham Theater to see how **Emilio Estevez** plays a wheezing, wizened Billy the Kid who supposedly survives to the 1950s. (Suffice to say, Little Big Man slept well *that* night.)

1992: The only person to get two Oscars for one performance — one an honorary award, the other for Best Supporting Actor of 1946 — becomes, on this day, the first person to sell an Oscar. With 1946's *The Best Years of Our Lives* now 46 years behind him, 78-year-old **Harold Russell** swapped his supporting-actor Oscar for some *real* support to pay for emergency expenses and his wife's cataract operation. Academy president **Karl Malden**, an Oscar winner in that same supporting category five years later, urged him not to go through with the sale, but the World War II veteran did — and, thus, earned the second distinction in his lifetime. The first Oscar to be auctioned off went for $60,500 to an anonymous recipient in New York City. Minus the commission, Russell netted $55,000. Exactly twice that — $110,000 — went to the *second* Oscar to be sold — two months later: the one **John Lennon** got for his contribution to the Best Original Song Score of 1970 (**The Beatles'** *Let It Be*).

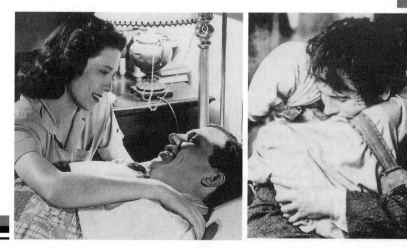

ABE LINCOLN IN ILLINOIS & BROOKLYN: Raymond Massey (with Ruth Gordon) as Honest Abe; then in *Arsenic and Old Lace* (with Peter Lorre), Josephine Hull, Cary Grant, Priscilla Lane and Jean Adair). **BARKERING UP THE RIGHT TREE:** Susan Hayward (with Brian Donlevy) in *Canyon Passage*.

1927: The Jazz Singer wraps on this day. It was to have starred Broadway's original title-player, **George Jessel**, but the money-haggling sent **Jack Warner** elsewhere (first to **Eddie Cantor**, then to Jessel's arch-rival, **Al Jolson**). "It is tempting to speculate that if Jessel had accepted," film historian **Arthur Knight** once observed, "we might still have silent movies."

1934: Anne of Green Gables, a little orphan Annie by **L. M. Montgomery**, begins its second screen telling on this day, with **Dawn O'Day** making her starring debut in the title role. At film's end, as a publicity gimmick, she permanently changed her professional name to the character's, so, when the sequel (*Anne of Windy Poplars*) rolled around in 1940, **Anne Shirley** played Anne Shirley.

1939: Abe Lincoln in Illinois goes before the cameras on this day, with **Raymond Massey** reprising to Oscar-nominated effect his stirring stage performance. Some say **Robert E. Sherwood** wrote the play, and the part, for **Gary Cooper** (who passed on it, intimidated); others contend Sherwood refused **Samuel Goldwyn**'s bid because the producer wanted it for Coop. In any event, America's 16th President became the role constantly associated with Massey — a Canadian. Even though he reprised it only once more on the big screen (a tableau cameo in *How the West Was Won*), the association stuck, often interfering with other performances: In *Arsenic and Old Lace*, when Massey was supposed to look like **Boris Karloff**, he looked alarmingly Lincolnesque. **George S. Kaufman** once quipped, "Massey won't be satisfied until he's assassinated."

1946: Universal contract player **Jess Barker** is not to be found in *Canyon Passage*, bowing if not wowing today at NYC's Loews Criterion, but the wife who'd accompanied him to his screen test is conspicuous in all her Technicolored glory. Titian-haired **Susan Hayward** plus fire proved a combustible combination for producer **Walter Wanger**. From the Indian-torched homesteads here, he sent her to other blazes: in her own home (*Smash-Up — The Story of a Woman*), in a Venice palace (*The Lost Moment*), in a Mississippi plantation (*Tap Roots*) and, most spectacularly of all, in an Oklahoma oil field (*Tulsa*). After cooling off for almost a decade, they reteamed in *I Want To Live!* This time he sent her to the gas chamber where she at least found her elusive, long-overdue Oscar.

1978: Star Trek, the NBC-TV series that died (despite the protests and outcries of "Trekkie" cultists) Sept. 2, 1969, comes back big time — big screen — on this day as director **Robert Wise** finishes the first scene for *Star Trek: The Motion Picture*. Miraculously, its television cast — **William Shatner, Leonard Nimoy, DeForest Kelley, George Takei, Nichelle Nichols, James Doohan, Walter Koenig**, et al — made the whole film-feature trek, one of the highest-grossing series in screen history.

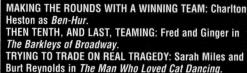

8

1948: After a decade apart, **Fred Astaire** and **Ginger Rogers** go into their last feature dance (No. 10) on this day — as *The Barkleys of Broadway*.

1958: "Charioteering is a hard-won and largely useless skill, but I can't help taking pride in it," **Charlton Heston** notes in his diary on this, his next-to-the-last-day at the races at Rome's Cinecitta. To the victor — his Ben-Hur — would go, 19 months later, an Oscar (one of a then-unprecedented 11).

1969: At the spellbinding bidding of **Charles Manson**, four of his cult followers (**Tex Watson, Patricia Krenwinkel, Susan Atkins** and **Linda Kasabian**) ride out of Spahn Movie Ranch and head for L.A.'s Benedict Canyon in a beat-up old Ford on this day. Just after midnight, they reach 10050 Cielo Drive and murder everybody on the premises — five in all, among them director **Roman Polanski**'s 26-year-old actress-wife, **Sharon Tate**, who was 8 1/2 months pregnant with their child. The last to die, she pleaded for her baby's life, but instead her killers scrawled "pig" on the door in her blood. It turned out to be the wrong house. Manson felt cheated by **Doris Day**'s record-producing son, **Terry Melcher**, and thought he still lived there with his then-girlfriend, **Candice Bergen**. In the 1971 *Macbeth* that marked Polanski's return to filmmaking, he injected an extravagantly violent mass-murder scene that mirrored the real-life rampage. Today, Manson and his "chosen four" are serving life sentences.

1973: "SEE BURT AND SARAH IN A TORRID LOVE STORY THAT SHOCKED THE COUNTRY!" cry the ads for *The Man Who Loved Cat Dancing* on this day, taking a tawdry tactic to drum up business for this **Burt Reynolds-Sarah Miles** Western by alluding to the Quaalude suicide of Miles' 26-year-old "personal assistant," **David A. Whiting**, six months earlier. Since Whiting had roughed her up a bit for staying too long in Reynolds' motel room, the tabloid press went into front-page euphoria. Only by threatening a lawsuit was Reynolds able to get MGM to revise the ad copy to read " . . . THAT SHOCKED THE OLD WEST."

1995: "In a scene that could have come from one of his horror flicks" [*Hell's Bloody Devils, Blood of Dracula's Castle*, et al], "Hollywood B-movie director **Al Adamson** was found murdered and buried in a grave where his indoor Jacuzzi once sat," reports the *Los Angeles Times* on this day. "The guy made some pretty gruesome movies, with bodies turning up all over the place, so finding his body where we did is a pretty ironic twist," noted investigating officer **Lt. Bruce Bower**. Charged with the killing was **Fred Fulford**, 46, an independent contractor who'd been living in the 66-year-old filmmaker's home while remodeling it.

9

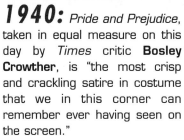

1940: *Pride and Prejudice*, taken in equal measure on this day by *Times* critic **Bosley Crowther**, is "the most crisp and crackling satire in costume that we in this corner can remember ever having seen on the screen."

1948: Writer-director **Joseph L. Mankiewicz** finishes *A Letter to Three Wives* on this day, dissatisfied with **Jeanne Crain**'s walk-through performance ("Talk about an actress who doesn't take the part home with her!"). Vowing never to work with her again, he squelched **Darry F. Zanuck**'s notion of Crain playing Eve Harrington to **Marlene Dietrich**'s Margo Channing in *All About Eve* but had to use her when pregnancy forced **Anne Baxter** out of *People Will Talk*. Asked why both Crain characters were called Deborah, Mankiewicz replied: "I don't like the name Deborah, and I don't like Jeanne Crain."

1949: For her last act at Warner Bros., **Bette Davis** on this day redubs dialogue so ironically apt she has to laugh: "I've *got* to get out of here. Let me out of *here*." Although *Beyond the Forest* was her nadir, it allowed her a line that became a camp classic when **Edward Albee** retrieved it and reprised it in *Who's Afraid of Virginia Woolf?*: Surveying the home **Joseph Cotten** had provided her, she sneered, "What a dump!"

1977: On this day — the eighth anniversary of his wife's murder — director **Roman Polanski** tries plea-bargaining his way out of the charge of raping a 13-year-old, pleading guilty to "unlawful sexual intercourse." That still earned him a 90-day stretch in Chino. On Jan. 27, he was released after 42 days for final sentencing on Feb. 1. Learning the judge would return him to jail for the additional 48 days — then limit that sentence *only* if Polanski deported himself voluntarily upon release — the director drove to Los Angeles airport, bought the last remaining seat out of the country, flew to London and began his post-Hollywood exile.

1984: On this day — as **Richard Burton** goes to his final resting place in Celigny, Switzerland — a single red rose accompanies his casket into the grave. Nobody knew whose rose that was, but the actor's brother, **Graham Jenkins**, believes it was from the second (and third) Mrs. Burton, **Elizabeth Taylor**, who was barred from the funeral by the fifth (and final) Mrs. Burton, **Sally Hay**. Unthwarted, Liz surfaced eight days later in Pontrhydyfen, Wales, extending her sympathies to Burton's seven surviving siblings — with full AP coverage.

MINDING JANE AUSTEN'S MANNERS: Heather Angel, Marsha Hunt, Edmund Gwenn, Mary Boland, Greer Garson, Ann Rutherford and Maureen O'Sullivan in *Pride and Prejudice*
BOLTING OUT OF WARNER BROS.: Bette Davis in *Beyond the Forest*.
SUFFERING FROM CRAIN-STRAIN: Jeanne Crain, Walter Slezak, Cary Grant and Sidney Blackmer in *People Will Talk*.

10

1932: *Horse Feathers* starts flying at NYC's Rialto on this day, extending **Marx Bros.** mayhem Round 4 at Paramount. After a fifth, they went into two years of R&R, bouncing back in MGM's *A Night at the Opera/A Day at the Races*.

1936: *Theodora Goes Wild* goes before the camera on this day with a reluctant **Irene Dunne** in the title role (a Sunday schoolteacher who authors a scandalous best-seller under a pseudonym). She resisted the film because it was a comedy, but Columbia held her to it contractually. The happy consequence: one of the screwiest of the then-voguish screwball comedies — and an Oscar shot for Dunne.

1945: Exhausted from **David O. Selznick**'s ego-exertions, director **King Vidor** hands his megaphone to the producer on this day and walks off *Duel in the Sun*. The film was finished by two bona fide directors (**William Dieterle** and **Josef von Sternberg**), a production designer (**William Cameron Menzies**), a film editor (**Hal Kern**) and four interim directors, including Selznick himself, but the sole directorial credit went (as per Screen Directors Guild ruling) to Vidor — much to Selznick's chagrin.

1950: Director **Billy Wilder** opens *A Can of Beans* at Radio City Music Hall on this day — under its real name. To keep this sardonic assessment of Hollywood a secret (for fear Paramount would scuttle the project), the director and his long-time writing partner, producer **Charles Brackett**, invented a bogus storyline for their bosses and called it *A Can of Beans*. The

WILDLY PHOTOGENIC: Irene Dunne, Frederick Burton, Harold Goodwin, Don Brodie and Billy Wayne in *Theodora Goes Wild*.
THE JETS TAKE OFF: Russ Tamblyn (center) and The Jets in *West Side Story*.
OUT-MARXED: Thelma Todd (with Chico and Harpo) in *Horse Feathers*.

result: cinema's most celebrated self-portrait, *Sunset Boulevard*. Critics then and now hail it "the best Hollywood movie ever made on Hollywood," but moguls weren't amused. When the film was first previewed for Hollywood's elite at Paramount's backlot studio, **Louis B. Mayer** came out fuming. "You bastard," he raged at Wilder, "you have disgraced the industry that made you and fed you. You should be tarred and feathered and run out of Hollywood." Wilder, a master of the riposte, settled for a simple "Fuck you!"

1960: Co-directors **Robert Wise** and **Jerome Robbins** commence lensing *West Side Story* on this day on the streets of NYC after more than a year of preparation (including an unprecedented two-and-a-half months of full cast rehearsals). Nineteen months later, both men marched to the Oscar podium to pick up the Best Director prize — the first, and only, time that award was shared — and significantly neither thanked or acknowledged the other.

LAST HURRAHS: From top, John Wayne (with James Stewart) in *The Shootist*; Anne Ramsey (with Danny DeVito) in *Throw Momma From the Train*. **HAIR TODAY, HERE TOMORROW:** Bette Davis and John Dall in *The Corn Is Green*.

1944: Queen-of-the-lot **Bette Davis** gets crowned on this day — most unceremoniously! — by the steel cover of an arc light, which mysteriously falls out of the flies above the soundstage and conks her on the head while she is administering a difficult exam to **John Dall** in *The Corn Is Green*. What spared her serious injury was the extra padding of a wig she belatedly decided on after filming began, necessitating 12 days of retakes.

1976: At New York's Loews Astor Plaza on this day, **John Wayne** comes out shooting as *The Shootist* — his 142nd and final leading role (more than any other actor) — a grizzled gunfighter battling what "Doc" **James Stewart** diagnosed as "a cancer." Parallels on both sides of the screen were inescapable.

1982: "The Boy Next Door" to **Judy Garland** in *Meet Me in St. Louis* succumbs to lung cancer on this day at age 63. **Tom Drake** inherited that label — and the winsome image which went with it — when the originally cast **Van Johnson** was upgraded to Star. Drake himself never soared far from the Culver City backlot because of a boozing problem, but he was liked by his MGM contemporaries. (**Elizabeth Taylor**'s generosity and clout got him into her *Raintree County* and *The Sandpiper*.) Attending his funeral: one of the girls of *Two Girls and a Sailor* (**Gloria DeHaven**) and a next-door neighbor from *St. Louis* (**Margaret O'Brien**).

1988: On this day, lung cancer claims **Anne Ramsey**, 59, who attained stardom — and a 1987 Oscar nomination (for *Throw Momma From the Train*) — at the tail-end of her 37-year career. She owed her last hurrah to actor-director **Danny DeVito**, who remembered her from **Jack Nicholson**'s 1978 *Goin' South* when both were buried in the credits (he was billed 8th, she 22d) and cast her as Momma.

1988: Like Nero's court (only, possibly, less decadent), Universal execs lounge around the fourth-floor balcony of the publicity office on this day, munching on sandwiches and drinking in the spectacle below them: a **DeMille**-sized multitude of Christian fundamentalists roiling in front of the studio, protesting its release of *The Last Temptation of Christ*, waving placards ("The Greatest Story Ever Distorted") and chanting "J-E-S-U-S" like cheerleaders. Some came by car and, at $3 a pop, used Universal Studio Tours parking lot, earning the company about $4,500 in hard-earned Christian cash.

12

FRESH FROM LONG BROADWAY RUNS: From left: William Powell and Irene Dunne in *Life With Father*; Mitzi Gaynor and Rossano Brazzi in *South Pacific*.
WHAT THOSE SPIES WERE AFTER: *The House on 92nd Street*.

1945: Now that it can be told, **Darryl F. Zanuck** tells the secret behind the movie he originally titled *Now It Can Be Told*: On this day — six days after Hiroshima is bombed and 45 days before *The House on 92nd Street* arrives at the Roxy — the 20th Century-Fox chief reveals that the cryptic "Process 97" sought by the film's homefront Nazis was, in reality, part of the A-bomb formula. **Leo G. Carroll**, **Gene Lockhart**, **Signe Hasso**, **William Eythe**, **Lloyd Nolan** and other professional actors were oblivious to this while they were acting it out, but some of the bit players (actual FBI agents) were knowing. Even **J. Edgar Hoover** got off a guest shot, having freely — gleefully! — turned over to Fox his top-secret FBI files and surveillance footage of Fifth Columnists at work.

1946: *Life With Father* finishes filming on this day. Not only did the play — which rang up 3,224 performances on Broadway — cost **Jack L. Warner** a bundle, he also had to hire free-lancers for the leads. **Bette Davis** tested for Vinnie Day to prove she could pass for a docile, demure housewife, but nobody bought it. Nor was anyone convinced by the three tests **Mary Pickford** came out of a 13-year retirement to do. The role eventually went to **Irene Dunne** from whom — bitter pill — Davis had snatched *Now, Voyager*. **Ronald Colman** consented to a Clarence Day test, but **William Powell** won the part with no test at all, saving his best shot for the cameras and earning the Best Actor prize from The New York Film Critics. Ironically, that year's Oscar went to Colman (for *A Double Life*), prompting 55-year-old Powell to wire 57-year-old Colman: "After all, it's a good thing you won instead of me, because you haven't many years left and I have so many ahead of me." The jest had a germ of truth: Colman died a decade later, but Powell retired in '55 and lived to be 91.

1957: At Lihue on the Hawaiian island of Kauai on this day, principal photography begins on *South Pacific* — and Somebody (namely, the original stage director: **Joshua Logan**) remembered to bring the gels. Years later, in his autobiography — in a chapter called "Inglorious Technicolor" — Logan confessed it'd been his idea to heighten the major musical moments with color filters, *but*, when he realized the disfiguring error of his ways and tried to remove them, 20th Century-Fox couldn't take the time for the three-months lab work required to bring *South Pacific* out of its self-inflicted fog. Lamented Logan: "I wanted to carry a sandwich board in front of every line at the box office, saying, 'I DIRECTED IT AND I DON'T LIKE THE COLOR EITHER!'"

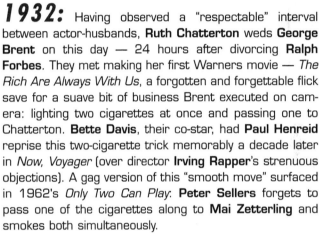

13

1932: Having observed a "respectable" interval between actor-husbands, **Ruth Chatterton** weds **George Brent** on this day — 24 hours after divorcing **Ralph Forbes**. They met making her first Warners movie — *The Rich Are Always With Us*, a forgotten and forgettable flick save for a suave bit of business Brent executed on camera: lighting two cigarettes at once and passing one to Chatterton. **Bette Davis**, their co-star, had **Paul Henreid** reprise this two-cigarette trick memorably a decade later in *Now, Voyager* (over director **Irving Rapper**'s strenuous objections). A gag version of this "smooth move" surfaced in 1962's *Only Two Can Play*: **Peter Sellers** forgets to pass one of the cigarettes along to **Mai Zetterling** and smokes both simultaneously.

1942: "Man in forest!" "Deer in theater!" After five years on the drawing board (1937-1942), **Walt Disney**'s gentlest creation — *Bambi* — wanders wobbly-legged into Radio City Music Hall on this day.

1961: The Berlin Wall starts going up on this day, creating all kinds of continuity problems for **Billy Wilder**, who's there directing *One, Two, Three* in the shadow of the Brandenburg Gate. Production designer **Alexander Trauner** was obliged to build a full-scale replica of the gate on the backlot of the Bavaria Studios in Munich, at a cost of $20,000. "It was like making a picture in Pompeii with all the lava coming down," said Wilder. "We had to make continual revisions to keep up with the headlines."

1967: *Bonnie and Clyde* comes out shooting on this day at New York's Forum and Murray Hill theaters, provoking more hot lead the next day from *The New York Times'* **Bosley Crowther**, who knocked the flick off earlier at the Montreal Film Festival and kept the bombardment up in scattergun attacks called "Sunday pieces." Eventually, *Bonnie and Clyde* bumped *him* off: Pressure was applied to *The Times* to put him out to pasture as a *passe* opinion-maker, and the paper obliged. A decade later, Crowther came around: *Bonnie and Clyde* was the only film featured on both the front *and* back of his book, *Reruns: 50 Memorable Films*. The weighted words inside

AN AMBUSH BY BOSLEY, PERHAPS?: Michael J. Pollard, Faye Dunaway and Warren Beatty in *Bonnie and Clyde*. THE OLD TWO-CIGARETTE ROUTINE: Bette Davis, Ruth Chatterton and George Brent in *The Rich Are Always With Us*. THE MARINES SAY THANKS: John Agar and John Wayne in *Sands of Iwo Jima*.

conceded, "No film turned out in the 1960s was more clever in registering the amoral restlessness of youth in those years. This is why it became so popular and is a landmark film today." Big man, Bos.

1973: The U.S. Marine Corps League's "Iron Mike Award," given for Americanism, goes on this day to **John Wayne** (a.k.a. Sergeant Stryker of *Sands of Iwo Jima*).

14

1935: Director **George Cukor**, **Katharine Hepburn** and **Cary Grant** begin their first — and worst — collaboration (*Sylvia Scarlett*) on this day, and on this day five years later they complete their last — and best: *The Philadelphia Story*.

1947: *The Pirate*, one of **Judy Garland**'s most problematic pictures, completes principal photography on this day — three days short of half a year. Much mopping-up and many retakes still had to be done. Of the 135 days of rehearsal, shooting and layoff, Garland was present for only three dozen. It was the last time she was directed by then-husband **Vincente Minnelli**. He was fired five days into her next film, *Easter Parade* — "for personal reasons."

1972: At Goldwater Memorial Hospital on Welfare Island, *The Exorcist* begins production on this day with a scene in which guilt-ridden Father Karras (**Jason Miller**) goes to a charity ward to visit his mother (**Vasiliki Maliaros**). Before the first shot, the film's Father Dyer (**The Reverend William O'Malley, S.J.**) recited a blessing that didn't entirely eliminate "negative energy" but may have brought it down a notch or two. During the nine-month shoot: the main Georgetown-home set, built at Ceco Studios in midtown Manhattan, was reduced to ashes by a Sunday morning fire; the film's $5-million budget reportedly doubled; **Ellen Burstyn** was laid up a week with a wrenched back; a lighting technician lost a toe in an on-set accident; Miller's five-year-old son was injured in a motorcycle mishap; **Max von Sydow**'s brother and **Linda Blair**'s grandfather died, and — two weeks after he played murder victim Burke Dennings — **Jack MacGowran**, 54, died.

1980: A **Monroe**-like blonde of 20 named **Dorothy Stratten** is shotgunned to death by her estranged spouse, **Paul Snider**, who then kills himself, on this day — two months after her Playboy Playmate-of-the-Year pictorial and one month after her star-making turn in **Peter Bogdanovich**'s *They All Laughed*. This tragedy was subsequently splashed across big screen and small (*Star 80*, **Bob Fosse**'s feature-length account with a surgically enhanced **Mariel Hemingway**, and *Death of a Centerfold*, **Gabrielle Beaumont**'s 1981 TV-movie with **Jamie Lee Curtis**) and in print (*The Killing of the Unicorn* by the infatuated Bogdanovich). Guilt and grief prompted the director to send Dorothy's younger sister, **Louise**, through private school and modeling classes, and, when *she* turned 20, he married her.

FROM WORST TO BEST IN EXACTLY FIVE YEARS: From left: Cary Grant and Katharine Hepburn in *Sylvia Scarlett* and *The Philadelphia Story*.
A LONG AND TOUGH SHOOT: Judy Garland and Gene Kelly in *The Pirate*.
TRAGEDY AFTER *THEY ALL LAUGHED*: Mariel Hemingway and Eric Roberts in *Star 80*.

15

1935: In New England filming **Eugene O'Neill**'s *Ah, Wilderness!* on this day, director **Clarence Brown** reads of the Alaskan plane-crash that claims **Will Rogers** — a flight Rogers would have missed had he accepted Brown's offer to be in the film. The actor passed because he was embarrassed by a scene in which his character (the father role **George M. Cohan** had done on stage) lectures his son on s-e-x.

1939: Mounted police and grandstand bleachers make their first Hollywood appearance on this day to accommodate the commotion accorded the premiere of *The Wizard of Oz* at the Grauman's Chinese — and the world is off to see the wizard! In 50 years time — thanks to TV — more people have seen the picture than any other movie (i.e., beyond a billion contented customers, and growing).

1969: A farmer in upstate New York named **Maxie Yasgur** throws open his gates to a generation on this day, and 600,000 blissed-out hippies fill his 600 acres outside Bethel for rock 'n' roll's last roar of the '60s — "three days of peace and music" called the Woodstock Music and Art Festival. The bill: **Crosby, Stills, Nash and Young, Janis Joplin, Jimi Hendrix, The Who, Joan Baez, John Sebastian, Joe Cocker, Santana, Canned Heat, Sha Na Na, Country Joe and the Fish, Sly and the Family Stone, Ten Years After, Arlo Guthrie, Richie Havens.** All that filmmaker **Michael Wadleigh** and his massive camera crew had to do was circulate to create a rockumentary with the epic sweep of social history. Edited by **Martin Scorsese** into the 184-minute *Woodstock*, the film caught the spirit of the thing — and the Oscar for 1970's Best Documentary.

1996: According to *USA Today* on this day, posthumous pitching from **John Wayne** has boosted Coors Light sales 10%. Doing commercials was something The Duke ducked in life, but in death some shrewd film-editing recycled a fraction of his 11-minute, six-scene cameo in 1966's *Cast a Giant Shadow* so it would pass for beer huckstering. Even from the grave, he could cast a giant shadow, putting a new spin on *Death of a Salesman!* (The true star of *Cast a Giant Shadow*, **Kirk Douglas**, didn't make the cut.) To use this clip, Coors coughed up seven figures for The John Wayne Cancer Institute.

WE'RRRRRE OFF . . . : Bert Lahr, Jack Haley, Judy Garland, Frank Morgan and Ray Bolger in *The Wizard of Oz*. *CASTING GIANTS*: Kirk Douglas and John Wayne in *Cast a Giant Shadow*. FLEEING THE BIRDS AND BEES: Blushing Will Rogers (inset) chose to skip the father-son talk that Lionel Barrymore and Eric Linden had in *Ah, Wilderness!*

16

1935: *Top Hat*, the quintessential **Fred Astaire-Ginger Rogers** outing, bows at Radio City Music Hall on this day and soon breaks all existing records at the showplace, taking in $134,800 the first week ($24,000 more than any other movie in the same time period) — all this with a Depression going on!

1947: Director **Nicholas Ray** completes principal photography on his first feature on this day, but he has to do two more (1948's *A Woman's Secret* and 1949's *Knock on Any Door*) — and they have to be successful — before RKO's eccentric new chief, **Howard Hughes**, will release it. **Edward Anderson**'s much-praised novel of wayward youth, *Thieves Like Us*, was the basis of Ray's debut film, and, although its title was somewhat established, studio execs nixed it because they heard "like" as a verb. *Your Red Wagon*, from the bebop song-of-the-moment, was seriously considered, then *The Twisted Road* (which it actually escaped to England as in 1948). What finally slipped into New York's Criterion on Nov. 3, 1949 — much admiration from *film noir* cultists but no business — was titled *They Live by Night*. When director **Robert Altman** remade the property in 1974, with **Keith Carradine** and **Shelley Duvall** in the roles originated by **Farley Granger** and **Cathy O'Donnell**, he insisted on sticking with the novel's title. (His *Thieves Like Us* was liked no better by the masses.)

1949: *Gone With the Wind* author **Margaret Mitchell**, 48, dies on this day in Atlanta from injuries she sustained when struck by a speeding cab as she crossed her beloved Peachtree Street. The cabbie, **Hugh D. Gravitt**, had 22 traffic violations on his record and was, at the time, free on $5,000 bond.

1964: "It won't be Buck Rogers," is all MGM is promising on this day as it announces the start of production on *Journey Beyond the Stars*. By the time the visualized results reached theatrical screens four years later, it is known — separately and collectively, now and forever — as *2001: A Space Odyssey*. Writer-producer-director **Stanley Kubrick**, who was involved on *all* levels of its production, personally created and filmed 205 special effects sequences for the movie — a feat which, a year later, won him his only Oscar: Best Achievement in Special Visual Effects of 1968.

1977: The King of Rock 'n' Roll, 42, dies at his Graceland home.

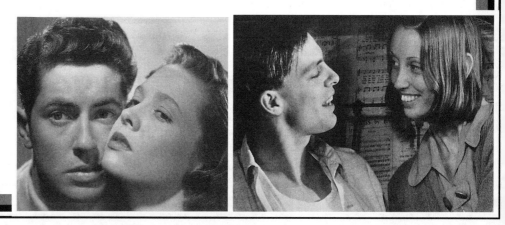

17

1934: A new chauffeur, **Manuel** (whose accent he'll approximate/appropriate) drives **Paul Muni** to work on a new film (*Bordertown*) on this day.

1939: On this day, **Vivien Leigh** sets sail with fiance **Laurence Olivier** from London for America — only to learn en route she won't be co-starring with him in *Rebecca*. **Joan Fontaine** will. Producer **David O. Selznick** had overheard Fontaine at a party insisting **Margaret Sullavan** should do the part, and it struck him that any actress who'd depreciate her own suitability for the role would be right for it. This part of the second Mrs. Maxim de Winter, the film's timid heroine and narrator, was so self-effacing she was identified only as "I" — never by name — and the fledgling Fontaine's tentative attack on the part was so perfect Olivier demanded she be replaced by Leigh — a rejection that only heightened Fontaine's insecurities and enhanced her work, which, like Olivier's, would be Oscar-nominated. She'd get her Oscar a year later for her next Hitchcock, *Suspicion*.

1979: *Raging Bull* finishes its New York lensing on this day and takes a two-month break so **Robert De Niro** can gain 55 pounds on pancakes, chocolate milk shakes and cheesecake.

1987: The man who directed **Garbo** and **Gable** more times than anyone — **Clarence Brown**, 97 — dies of kidney failure on this day, 34 years after his retirement from MGM. He is one of the few to make the Oscar running for Best Director as many times as six (*Anna Christie, Romance, A Free Soul, The Human Comedy, National Velvet* and *The Yearling*) without winning the award. *Intruder in the Dust*, generally regarded as his masterpiece, was totally unnominated.

"R" BEFORE "I": Joan Fontaine cases *Rebecca*.
CHAUFFEURED TO *BORDERTOWN*: Bette Davis and Paul Muni.
PASTA PERFORMANCE: Robert De Niro in ring — and 55 heavyweight pounds later — in *Raging Bull*.

1932: Looking and acting like an **Ernst Lubitsch** confection, *Love Me Tonight* lifts off at New York's Rivoli on this day. It was, in truth, the highly innovative work of **Rouben Mamoulian** — and a seminal step forward in the evolution of musical comedy as pure cinema. Director Mamoulian put **Richard Rodgers** and **Lorenz Hart**'s trunkload of instant evergreens to creative use — particularly "Isn't It Romantic?" which wafted like love fumes from one locale to another, connecting **Maurice Chevalier**'s tailor shop in Paris with **Jeanette MacDonald**'s chateau in the French countryside. Various subsidiary characters grabbed verses along the way, like a musical relay race, and one was still humming that song in 1980 when she ended her theatrical-film career. In the last scene of *Just Tell Me What You Want*, **Myrna Loy** left **Alan King** and **Ali MacGraw** smooching and walked down a hospital corridor humming "Isn't It Romantic?" Though shot, that ending was scrapped in favor of a conventional Ali-Alan clinch.

1939: On this day, **Preston Sturges** sells a six-year-old script, *The Vagrant*, to Paramount for peanuts, *provided* he directs it. (*The Guinness Book of Records* identified the peanuts as the lowest fee paid for the script of a major Hollywood feature — $10.) Shot as *Down Went McGinty* and redubbed more positively by Paramount's publicity department as *The Great McGinty*, it won the Oscar for 1940's Best Original Screenplay — and one of Hollywood's most original wits was on his way as a writer-director.

1983: The New York *Daily News* on this day reports that something less than an officer and a gentleman — identified as **Richard Gere** at the East Fifth Street police station — has been issued a summons, No. EO10857918, for urinating in the street in the early a.m. not far from his Greenwich Village apartment.

STILL *DANCING* TEN YEARS LATER: Patrick Swayze and Jennifer Grey in *Dirty Dancing*. THE SONG THAT HAUNTED HER: Charles Ruggles, Myrna Loy and C. Aubrey Smith in *Love Me Tonight*. SHELLEY'S CHOICE: Montgomery Clift and Shelley Winters in *A Place in the Sun*.

1997: Finally, on this day, **Patrick Swayze** rates a star on the Hollywood Walk of Fame. Two days later, he joins **Jennifer Grey** at Universal City's Citywalk Theater for the 10th anniversary gala re-premiere of their *Dirty Dancing* (an AIDS benefit in memory of the film's director, **Emile Ardolino**, who died of the disease in 1993). Their modest $5 million movie raked in $170 million worldwide and won the Oscar for Best Song: "(I've Had) The Time of My Life."

1998: "I just found out I was born the day women got the vote," says **Shelley Winters**, explaining why she restored the two years she'd subtracted, making her 78 on this day. Eight days earlier, she received a Lifetime Achievement award at the Hollywood Film Festival. "My God, I've been in movies for 50 years — but 50 years isn't as long as it used to be." The pick of her litter: *A Place in the Sun*.

1935: *A Tale of Two Cities*, not *A Tale of Two Colmans*, concludes filming on this day: Because of his difficulty doing a dual role two years before (*The Masquerader*), **Ronald Colman** took on "Sydney Carton" *only* if he didn't have to do "Charles Darnay" also (as per a certain plot requirement). When attempts failed to cast **Robert Donat** or **Brian Aherne** as the latter, director **Jack Conway** and producer **David O. Selznick** settled for **Donald Woods**, hardly a Colman clone. Just as well, Selznick came to believe (after, of course, he had talked Colman into doing a dual role again — for 1937's *The Prisoner of Zenda*): "I think a great deal of the illusion of the picture might have been lost," Selznick said about the Dickens *Tale*, "had Colman rescued Colman and had Colman gone to the guillotine so that Colman could go away with Lucie."

1949: At 8:30 p.m. on this day, while vacationing at St. Paul-de-Vence, **Simone Signoret** experiences the changing of the Yveses: Her four-year-marriage to director **Yves Allegret** recedes sharply as **Yves Montand** enters her life. The union was formalized in 1951 when she said yes to the latter Yves (then a singer, six and a half months her junior) in a ceremony at St. Paul-de-Vence witnessed by her daughter, **Catherine Allegret**, and **Mrs. Charles David** (a.k.a. **Deanna Durbin**). The marriage survived his dalliances during filming *Let's Make Love* (**Marilyn Monroe**) and *My Geisha* (**Shirley MacLaine**). "We have quarreled a lot," Signoret admitted, "but that is good. Otherwise, things would have been very sad." Her daughter's view was less rose-colored: "They played *Who's Afraid of Virginia Woolf?* 24 hours a day." Cancer claimed Signoret at 64, and, on Oct. 2, 1985, as she was buried in Paris' Pere Lachaise cemetery, Montand placed a red rose on her coffin, joining her there Nov. 13, 1991. He never remarried, but his companion, **Carole Amiel**, did make him a father for the first time at age 67. Their son, **Valentin**, was born the last day of 1988.

1976: The versatile **Alastair Sim**, 75, succumbs to cancer on this day. One of Britain's top character-comedians (*The Green Man*, *The Belles of St. Trinian's*), he is best-remembered for a dramatic turn as the screen's greatest Scrooge.

1977: The second most impersonated entertainer of the 20th century (after **Elvis Presley**) dies on this day (three days after Elvis Presley): **Groucho Marx**, 86.

1993: Well, whaddayaknow? He *IS* — on this day, anyway — *The Marrying Man*: **Alec Baldwin** weds the leading lady he met on that 1991 flick, **Kim Basinger**.

20

1936: Three weeks before his death, producer **Irving Thalberg** brings a dream to market: *Romeo and Juliet*, bowing at New York's Astor on this day. The original choice for Romeo, **Brian Aherne**, did a test of the balcony scene with Mrs. Thalberg (a.k.a. **Norma Shearer**) and felt age was not on his side. (At 34, he was two years younger than his Juliet.) After passing on the part, he learned Thalberg considered **Fredric March** (38) before signing **Leslie Howard** (46).

1938: "The Battling Bogarts" are born on this day as **Humphrey Bogart** takes a bride he found under the heading of *Marked Woman*. A last-minute replacement for **Jane Wyman** in that flick, **Mayo Methot** played what was politely called "a clip-joint hostess," and Bogie was a fictional facsimile of **Thomas A. Dewey** cracking the prostitute ring of **Eduardo Ciannelli**, a fictional facsimile of **Lucky Luciano**. He and Wife Three lived hectically ever after, till **Bacall** came along.

1989: British conservationist **George Adamson**, 83, is gunned down on this day in the Kora National Reserve by poachers. The Nairobi-born game warden had a more idyllic life in the movies (where he was portrayed by himself in 1971's *An Elephant Called Slowly*, by **Nigel Davenport** in 1972's *Living Free* and by **Bill Travers** in 1966's *Born Free*). In 1971, he and wife **Joy** (played by **Virginia McKenna** in the latter and by **Susan Hampshire** in the sequel) separated. She stayed at Meru to work with leopards and, on Jan. 3, 1980, was also murdered — stabbed to death by a park-staffer. Adamson settled in the Kora Reserve after his lion, Boy (the mate of Elsa, the *Born Free* lioness), mauled the son of the Meru Park warden and had to be put away. The same fate befell Elsie's last male cub, shot dead in 1991 for trespassing in a neighbor's yard.

1989: LIVE Entertainment chairman **Jose Menendez**, 43, and wife **Kitty**, 45, are shotgunned to death while watching TV in their glitzy Beverly Hills home on this day. Five years and seven months later, their sons — **Lyle**, 28, and **Erik**, 25 — are convicted of the crime and sentenced to life in prison without parole.

THE THIRD MRS. BOGART IS THIRD FROM THE LEFT: Lola Lane, Rosalind Marquis, Mayo Methot, Bette Davis, Jane Bryan and Isabel Jewell in *Marked Woman*.
THOSE CRAZY TEENAGE KIDS!: Leslie Howard and Norma Shearer in *Romeo and Juliet*.
REAL LIFE WAS MORE VIOLENT: Virginia McKenna, Elsa and Bill Travers in *Born Free*.

21

1927: The gangster genre begins on this day with the arrival of *Underworld* at New York's Paramount. Brash, movie-debuting **Ben Hecht** got off the first shot — and the first Oscar for Best Original Story (which, actually, was a recall of the Prohibition-spawned hoodlums he'd known first-hand as a Chicago newspaperman). One such tough customer became the screen's first King of the Underworld and was played —

antedating **Robinson, Cagney, Muni, Bogart, Garfield**, et al — by **George Bancroft**, whose acclaim for this mobster portrayal went straight to his head: By the time he and director **Josef von Sternberg** were sequeling themselves with *The Drag Net*, the actor was insisting on going out in a hail of bullets, reasoning unreasonably "One shot can't stop Bancroft!" Since von Sternberg had final cut, a solitary bang *did* bring down the mighty Bancroft.

1941: During her 17-year reign at Warners, **Bette Davis** was allowed off the lot twice — in 1934 to play Mildred Rogers in **W. Somerset Maugham**'s *Of Human Bondage*, and in 1941 to play Regina Giddens in **Lillian Hellman**'s *The Little Foxes*. The latter, premiering on this day at Radio City Music Hall, came to pass strictly as a star-swap arrangement among the moguls: **Jack Warner** let Davis play Regina for **Samuel Goldwyn** if Goldwyn let **Gary Cooper** play *Sergeant York* for Warner. The upshot of all this: two of 1941's best performances; Coop's was Oscared, and Davis' was nearly Oscared. Both stars hope to film *Ethan Frome* together, but this is as close as they came to any kind of deal, passing each other like ships in the night.

1942: "Louis, I might have known you'd mix your patriotism with a little larceny." No. "Louis, I begin to see a reason for your sudden attack of patriotism. While you defend your country, you also protect your investment." No. "If you ever die a hero's death, Heaven protect the angels!" No. On this day — a full 20 days after **Humphrey Bogart** finishes filming *Casablanca* — producer **Hal B. Wallis** finally picks the picture's famous last line (one he wrote): "Louis, I think this is the beginning of a beautiful friendship," Bogart returned to record it, and it's used for the overhead shot of him and **Claude Rains** strolling into a fog-bound tomorrow.

1947: Not knowing it can't be done, first-time director **Nicholas Ray** proceeds to do it on this day: use a helicopter for the first time in a feature film to shoot sequences from the air. Photographer **Paul Ivano** went aloft and caught two action scenes for *They Live by Night* — one depicting a car chase, the other showing escaped convicts fleeing through a wheatfield.

22

1922: Renowned for doing her own daredevilry, **Pearl White** acquiesces on this day and lets **John Stevenson** don a blonde wig to double for her in a difficult stunt for *Plunder* — leaping from the top of a double-decker bus to an elevated girder at the corner of 72d St. and Columbus in NYC. Unfortunately, Stevenson missed the swing, was thrown 25 feet before he fell to the ground and died the same day from a fractured skull. *Plunder* sped to completion, after which guilt-racked White went into permanent retirement in France.

1932: On this day, as *Night After Night* begins filming, **Mae West** hip-waves into movies — and "goodness," as the lady says, "has nothing to do with it." Settling for fourth billing (but never again!), Mae found movies much to her liking. "She stole everything but the cameras," cracked the easily topped, top-billed **George Raft** (who died Nov. 24, 1980, outliving West by two days).

1933: A splinter off the old block, *The Son of Kong* concludes five frantic months of filming on this day. The miracle was that it made it to market the same year as its old man, but, even with *King Kong*'s original creators at the wheel (directors **Ernest B. Schoedsack** and **Merian C. Cooper**, chief technician **Willis O'Brien**, scripter **Ruth Rose**, composer **Max Steiner**, actors **Robert Armstrong** and **Frank Reicher**, et al), no more than a puny postscript could be produced. Even **Fay Wray**'s recycled shrieks couldn't raise this deadweight.

1938: *Trade Winds*, which begins churning on this day, gives **Joan Bennett**'s career a second wind, changing her from blonde to brunette from that point on.

1956: Ready or not, **Vivien Leigh** sweeps onto the set of *The Prince and the Showgirl* on this day to see how her husband, **Laurence Olivier**, is faring as he directs and performs the movie version of their stage success (*The Sleeping Prince*). With **Marilyn Monroe** inheriting her role, Leigh knew only too well he was faring miserably in both departments. Yes, she'd wanted to do the part on film, "but Larry went and fell in love with Marilyn Monroe, silly boy" — pause, then a deliciously malicious postscript — "and a fat lot of good *that* did him!"

1972: The aptly named *And Now for Something Completely Different*, opening on this day at NYC's 68th Street Playhouse, dumps a clown-car load of British comics onto these apathetic shores. It took three more years before they (**Terry Jones**, **Eric Idle**, **Graham Chapman**, **Terry Gilliam**, **John Cleese** and **Michael Palin**) found the American funnybone — via *Monty Python and the Holy Grail* — following that with *Life of Brian* (1979) and *The Meaning of Life* (1983) before finally fragmenting into individual careers.

VANISHED AFTER THE *PLUNDER* BLUNDER: Pearl White. TAXING THE ACTING TITAN: Laurence Olivier and Marilyn Monroe in *The Prince and the Showgirl*. STEALING THE SCENE AS HIS EYES CLOSE: Mae West and George Raft in *Night After Night*.

1926: At ten minutes past noon on this day, 31-year-old heartthrob **Rudolph Valentino** dies from peritonitis, putting the world's women in widow's weeds.

1929: On this day in Boise City, OK, Vera Ralston is born. Since the Screen Actors Guild already had one of those, she assumed the name **Vera Miles**.

1938: *You Can't Take It With You*, which marked the movie debut of **Dub Taylor** and subsequently won **Frank Capra** his third and last Oscar for Best Director, is unveiled on this day by Columbia Pictures at a special international press preview. The verdict: cheers and laughter from the assemblage — and, 10 months later, the Academy Award for Best Picture of 1938. But tragedy ruled the day of its coming-out for Capra: His son John, 3, died of a cerebral hemorrhage.

1939: The Pulitzer Prize-winning playwright of *They Knew What They Wanted* — **Sidney Howard**, 58 — is killed on this day on his estate in Tyringham, MA., when a tractor he is cranking suddenly lunges forth and crushes him against his garage wall. His last work was his most famous — a lion's share of the *Gone With the Wind* screenplay. **David O. Selznick** engaged a dozen other writers on it also, each of them using a different colored paper. The finished script resembled a rainbow — and there was gold at the end of it: Howard, given solitary screen credit, became the first posthumous Oscar winner.

1942: The one brilliant flick **Henry Fonda** did on the 20th Century-Fox contract he had to sign to do *The Grapes of Wrath* wraps on this day: *The Ox-Bow Incident*. Fearing a flop, Fox mogul **Darryl F. Zanuck** fought it every foot of film — and was, of course, right about it bombing at the box office, but it developed a late-blooming cult that brought it up to moneymaking speed — and few films earned Fox more prestige.

1970: "You do not have to be a drug addict, pederast, sado-masochist or nitwit to enjoy *Performance*, but being one or more of those things would help," says **John Simon** on this day in a Sunday piece in *The New York Times* titled "The Most Loathsome Film of All?" There was no question about this in 1969 when Warners chief **Ken Hyman** chunked it into storage. It escaped into release only because Hyman's successor, **Ted Ashley**, reasoned any flick that featured **Mick Jagger** in the buff and in outrageous drag would at least have "camp value."

1919: During a publicity shoot on this day, a "papier-mache" bomb explodes violently in the hands of **Harold Lloyd**, knocking the comic out of commission for 10 months. It was feared he'd be disfigured and blind, but the only permanent damage was to his right hand: He lost the thumb and forefinger. Happily, a prosthetic device kept his secret and let him aggressively continue his daredevil slapstick.

1931: On this day, **Boris Karloff** starts shuffling into screen immortality as filming begins on *Frankenstein*, one of 18 (!) movies of his released in 1931. Universal offered the role to **Bela Lugosi**, who rejected it because he was proud of his voice and the role required only grunts. "Poor old Bela," Karloff sighed. "He was really a shy, sensitive, talented man who had a fine career on the classical stage in Europe, but he made a fatal mistake: He never took the trouble to learn our language."

1938: On this day, **Clark Gable** heeds the public outcry to play Rhett Butler and signs up for $4,500 a week plus a $16,666 bonus. For his services and $1.25 million, MGM got distribution dibs on *GWTW* for the first five years and 50% of the profits.

1942: The James Brothers, Frank and Jesse, join the World War II ranks on this day — **Henry Fonda** in the Navy, **Tyrone Power** in the Marines. "If this keeps up," meowed **Adolphe Menjou**, "the women stars in movies will be willing to work with men of their own age."

1944: *The Clock* stops ticking on this day, and MGM seriously considers cutting its losses ($200,000) and scrapping its attempt to turn **Judy Garland** into a songless dramatic wonder. She, however, told her *Meet Me in St. Louis* director **Vincente Minnelli** to meet her at *The Clock*, take command (from **Fred Zinnemann**) and press on. A wartime romance cast with fragile stars coming out of bad first-marriages (**Robert Walker** from **Jennifer Jones**, Garland from **David Rose**), *The Clock* proved affecting — and, by filming's end, Garland had stabilized. She and Minnelli married June 15, 1945.

1946: *Swamp Fire* sweeps into New York's Gotham on this day — a bland blaze at best, notable only for the slight fact it was the only non-series, non-cameo feature appearance in **Johnny Weissmuller**'s career. There was a croc to wrestle — just to keep his hand in — and ex-Tarzan **Buster Crabbe** co-starred.

1992: Director **Steven Spielberg** starts four months of principal photography on *Jurassic Park* on this day, not a day too soon: The first three weeks were spent on the island of Kauai, and the day before filming was completed there, Hurricane Iniki swept by, leveling this lush tropical paradise.

NO MUSICAL TROLLY OR TRAIN THIS TIME: Robert Walker and Judy Garland in *The Clock*.
GABLE GOES WITH THE *WIND*: David O. Selznick and Louis B. Mayer sign up the obvious Rhett Butler.
A LOCATION GONE WITH THE WIND: Ariana Richards, Sam Neill and Joseph Mazzello in *Jurassic Park*.

25

1937: "The show undoubtedly belongs to the six incomparable urchins imported from the stage production," finds *The New York Times* on this day about the dirty half-dozen film-debuting in *Dead End*, **William Wyler**'s cinemazation of **Sidney Kingsley**'s Broadway smash. **Leo Gorcey, Huntz Hall, Billy Halop, Gabriel Dell, Bobby Jordan** and **Bernard Punsly** were all promised contracts by **Samuel Goldwyn**, but he reneged on the deal — and they reacted in character, going on a backlot rampage and smashing a studio truck into a soundstage. Hastily, Goldwyn sold their contracts to Warners. *Angels With Dirty Faces* (which they played at the feet of **Cagney**) was as good as it got there. Then, the gang became staples of the low-budget plants and kept that bottom-of-the-bill ball in the air till 1958's *In the Money*, aging along the way from The Dead End Kids to Little Tough Guys to The East Side Kids to The Bowery Boys.

1941: "When I was a freshman at Hamilton, I was thrown into the college fount. In the early days of the last war, I had to take care of the bedpans in an Army hospital. But never have I been so humiliated as on my few appearances in the movies," critiqued critic **Alexander Woollcott** — but that didn't keep him completely out of camera range. On this day — for $5,000 flat — he lends his lofty presence to *Babes on Broadway*, his third and final foray into features.

1943: A theater in Huckstep about 15 miles from Cairo delivers a triple dose of **Jack Benny** on this day — two live shows for servicemen and a movie, *George Washington Slept Here*. **George S. Kaufman** and **Moss Hart**'s comedy about New York City-dwellers settling into a dilapidated (if historic) shack in Bucks County went through a conspicuous gender-switch turning to celluloid: All the bright, brittle lines **Jean Dixon** had bounced off **Ernest Truex** on stage wound up on Benny's court and screen wife **Ann Sheridan** became the straight-man. Her only good gag was not in the script but on a theater marquee in Glasgow, Scotland, in foot-high letters: GEORGE WASHINGTON SLEPT HERE WITH ANN SHERIDAN.

1990: *Pretty Woman*, which set **Julia Roberts**' star soaring and rescued **Richard Gere**'s, becomes on this day — five months into release — Disney's top grosser.

26

1940: Sweet revenge for the laughs she got campaigning to play Queen Elizabeth opposite **Katharine Hepburn**'s *Mary of Scotland* finally comes to **Ginger Rogers** on this day as she begins filming her Oscar-winning *Kitty Foyle*. Content with being The New York Film Critics' choice of Best Actress of 1940 (for *The Philadelphia Story*), Hepburn professed to be pleased by Oscar's pick: "I was offered *Kitty Foyle*, and I didn't want to play a soap opera about a shopgirl. Ginger was wonderful. She's enormously talented, and she deserved the Oscar. As for me, prizes are nothing. My prize is my work." Read like a lady who would land more Oscars (4) and more nominations (12) than anybody.

1940: *One Night in the Tropics* goes before the cameras on this day, bringing to the film fore (in supporting roles) **Bud Abbott** and **Lou Costello** as henchmen named Abbott and Costello, refereeing the romantic runarounds of **Allan Jones**, **Nancy Kelly**, **Robert Cummings** and **Peggy Moran**.

1946: The first of two exquisitive screen romances directed by **David Lean** — *Brief Encounter*, drawn from **Noel Coward**'s one-act *Still Life* — opens to acclaim at New York's Little Carnegie on this day. The other romance? *Summertime*. Ironically, women are next-to-nonexistent in Lean's big Oscar winners, *The Bridge on the River Kwai* and *Lawrence of Arabia*.

1948: After six years of flirting with film projects (a **Strindberg** drama in 1944, a **Bing Crosby** vehicle at Paramount in 1945, an **Alexander Korda** production at Columbia in 1947), **Greta Garbo** on this day inks a deal with producer **Walter Wanger** for a comeback flick and actually shows up in Rome ready to work exactly a year later on this day. The **George Sand** Story, scripted by Garbo pal **Salka Viertel**, and a movie of **Alphonse Daudet**'s 1884 *Sappho* both took backseats to a version of **Honore de Balzac**'s *La Duchesse de Langeais*. Retitled *Friend and Lover*, it was budgeted at $1 million and given a Cinecitta start-date of Oct. 10. Then, while the *paparazzi* kept Garbo tearfully popping from hotel to hotel, the deal died. Banker's Trust, already burned by the flop *Joan of Arc* Wanger did with **Ingrid Bergman**, got cold feet. Co-star **James Mason** bolted next, and Garbo nixed Wanger's idea of replacements (**Errol Flynn** or **Louis Jourdan**). In November, director **Max Ophuls** bailed out to helm *La Ronde*, leaving the Garbo film flapping in the wind another fruitless month. Said Viertel: "The display of dilettantism, inflated egos, incompetence, and a hypocritical, indecent disregard for the sensibilities of a great actress had been unsurpassed, even in the history of films. It made Garbo once and for all renounce the screen."

MORE BACK-BURNER THAN *FLAMES OF PASSION*: Celia Johnson and Trevor Howard in *Brief Encounter*.
SLIPPING INTO MOVIES: Lou Costello and Bud Abbott in *One Night in the Tropics*.
AN OSCAR IN HER FUTURE: Ginger Rogers in *Kitty Foyle*.

27

1941: On this day, **Ida Lupino** rejects a role **Bette Davis** supposedly *pleaded* to do — the deranged Cassandra of *Kings Row*. **Olivia de Havilland** also turned it down, leaving Warners with pretty slim pickings for the part (**Priscilla Lane, Susan Peters** and **Joan Leslie**). It eventually went to a gifted outsider on loan from Paramount: **Betty Field**.

1943: Born on this day — a Friday — is **Tuesday Weld** (real name: **Susan Ker Weld**).

1952: *The Crimson Pirate* swings into action — and New York's Paramount — on this day, with **Burt Lancaster** in the title role and a real-life childhood pal and circus partner as his mute sidekick, Ojo (**Nick Cravat**). "The best fun conjured up by these derring-do dramas since the days of the fabled **Douglas Fairbanks** the elder," cheered **Alton Cook** in the *New York World Telegram*. Thirty years later, director **Richard Brooks** tried to talk up a sequel, *The Son of the Crimson Pirate*, that would bring Lancaster and Cravat back for seconds but leave the derring-do to a younger set (**Mikhail Baryshnikov** and **Anthony Andrews** were mentioned as *Crimson* contenders).

1964: Alighting at Grauman's Chinese on this day amid much premiere commotion — the biggest Disney do since *Snow White and the Seven Dwarfs* — **Julie Andrews** arrives on the big screen as *Mary Poppins*.

1962: *It Happened at the World's Fair*, despite the title, starts filming on this day on MGM's Culver City backlot — but shifts production to Seattle on September 5 to take in the sights, starting with the monorail. When **Elvis Presley** wasn't on camera, he was knee-deep in (6) Pinkerton plainclothesmen. The 11-year-old boy who film-debuted here as "Boy Who Kicks Elvis" — **Kurt Russell** — grew up to play The King in the 1978 TV-movie, *Elvis*, winning the role over 700 others and the objections of **Colonel Parker** (who favored **Stallone**).

1986: "Billy Jack Beats Back Beer Bottle Basher," begins a story in the New York *Daily News* on this day — a clear-case of an actor taking his role home with him: Two nights earlier, while strolling on Broadway near 72d, **Tom Laughlin** broke up a barroom brawl that had spilled out onto the streets with a simple "Look, you touch him again and I'm going to rip your arm off." Knowing a Billy Jack when he saw one, the bottle-brandishing assailant hit the bricks.

1997: *Deconstructing Harry*, in which a neurotic novelist (**Woody Allen**) draws heavily on his private life for his "fictional" characters, is unveiled at the Venice Film Festival on this day — out of competition. Six months later when it entered competition — i.e., Oscar competition — it sent Allen straight to the head of the writers' class with his 13th Oscar nomination for screenplay. That lucky 13th bettered **Billy Wilder**'s long-standing record of an even dozen bids.

USING THE CIRCUS TRAINING: Burt Lancaster and Nick Cravat in *The Crimson Pirate*.
LANDING IN FILMS, VIA UMBRELLA: Julie Andrews as *Mary Poppins*.
THE CRAZED CASSANDRA: Betty Field (with Robert Cummings) in *Kings Row*.

28

1947: Nick and Nora Charles (**William Powell** and **Myrna Loy**) go into their sixth sleuthing assignment, *Song of the Thin Man* — and a swan song at that, arriving on this day at New York's Capitol. It was the third MGM series to grind to a halt in almost as many months: **Ann Sothern** hung her Maisie (Ravier) out to dry in May with Installment 10, *Undercover Maisie*, and the Dr. Kildare-Dr. Gillespie flicks signed off in June with its 16th episode, *Dark Delusion*.

1947: In a Hollywood Bowl concert on this day, **Mario Lanza** establishes his film beachhead, wowing not only **Kathryn Grayson** (co-star of his first two films, *That Midnight Kiss* and *The Toast of New Orleans*) but also **Louis B. Mayer** (who released all but one of the seven movies in his screen career).

1951: As two physicians try to revive him with sodium amytol after a drinking bout, 32-year-old **Robert Walker** dies on this day. At the time, he was nearing the end of his role as **Helen Hayes'** Communist son in *My Son John*. (Hayes, ironically, had just lost her daughter and took on the movie as therapy.) To finish the film, director **Leo McCarey** got outtakes of Walker in a phone booth from **Hitchcock**'s *Strangers on a Train*. Walker's first wife, **Jennifer Jones** (then Mrs. David O. Selznick), and their two sons didn't attend the funeral.

1978: On this day — what would have been **Charles Boyer**'s 79th birthday — Phoenix coroner **Thomas Jarvis** rules that the actor's death Aug. 26 was a suicide. Forever at odds with his "Great Lover" film image, the famous Frenchman was a one-woman man in real life. Two days after his wife of 44 years (British actress **Pat Paterson**) died of cancer, he followed her, ODing on Seconal. Their only son, **Michael**, died at age 21 from a self-inflicted gunshot wound in 1965.

1981: Director **James Bridges** vacates *The Verdict* on this day because **Robert Redford** keeps tinkering with **David Mamet**'s script, prompting producers **David Brown** and **Richard Zanuck** to rid themselves of Redford and pursue either **Jon Voight** or **Paul Newman** for the star spot. The latter eventually won the toss and, under the direction of **Sidney Lumet**, an Oscar nomination for Best Actor.

LYING [BIG TIME] TO MOM: Robert Walker and Helen Hayes in *My Son John*.
BUTCH FOLLOWS SUNDANCE: Newman replaces Redford in *The Verdict*.
CHEERS TO NICK AND NORA CHARLES: From left: William Powell and Myrna Loy in 1934's *The Thin Man* and in 1947's *Song of the Thin Man*.

29

1898: Born on this day is Edmond Preston Biden, who invented kiss-proof lipstick and introduced the club sandwich to Germany. He also grew up to become **Preston Sturges**, a one-man fun-factory in '40s films responsible for uncorking a procession of audacious, irreverent antics (*Hail the Conquering Hero, The Lady Eve, The Miracle of Morgan's Creek, The Palm Beach Story, Christmas in July*). As his movie-director hero in *Sullivan's Travels* says at trail's end: "There's a lot to be said for making people laugh. Did you know that's all some people have? It isn't much, but it's better than nothing in this cockeyed caravan. *Boy!*"

1945: The only movie musical by **Richard Rodgers** and **Oscar Hammerstein II**, *State Fair*, premieres on this day at the Paramount — not the one in New York, the one in downtown Des Moines, IA (as in the flick's big ditty, "All I Owe Ioway"). Catchy though that was, their Oscar — their *only* team-Oscar — was for "It Might As Well Be Spring."

1958: *The Fly* alights at 100-plus NYC theaters on this day, a fanciful sci-fi in which **Al** (later **David**) **Hedison** is molecularly confused with a common housefly — with horrific consequences. The hardest scene to film didn't involve special effects; it involved two grown-up actors (**Vincent Price** and **Herbert Marshall**) struggling to keep their hysterics in check while conversing with a miniaturized Hedison caught in a spider's web. "It took a whole day to film that scene," Price recalled. "We kept laughing ourselves sick. In the end we had to film it standing back to back — we just couldn't look each other in the face."

1982: Cancer claims **Ingrid Bergman** at her Chelsea home in London on this day — but not before a little birthday celebration (her 67th) and a last sip of champagne with a few old friends (including ex-husband **Lars Schmidt**).

1997: The self-professed "singularly heterosexual" **Tom Selleck** is back reiterating that stance, according to *USA Today* on this day, hoping to head off any speculation that might surface from his playing a gay journalist in the upcoming *In & Out*. Seconding this motion, Selleck said his big kissing scene with **Kevin Kline** took 30 takes — and once he missed Kline's mouth altogether!

SURGES OF STURGES: Joel McCrea, Mary Astor, Preston Sturges, Claudette Colbert and Rudy Vallee working on *The Palm Beach Story*. Inset: Joel McCrea and Veronica Lake in *Sullivan's Travels*. **KISSING, AND MISSING, KEVIN:** Kevin Kline and Tom Selleck in *In & Out*. **BAD BUZZ:** Charles Herbert and Vincent Price in *The Fly*.

1934: Donning disguises on this day, **Carole Lombard** and beau **Russ Columbo** sneak into a sneak of his *Wake Up and Dream*, and, as they exit, she trills, "You're going to be a star!" Sadly, when the film was released a few weeks later, the star was stillborn. Three days after the preview, Columbo and a friend were examining antique pistols when one discharged a bullet that ricocheted off a tabletop and caught Columbo above the left eye, taking his life two hours later. Because Columbo's near-blind mother, **Julia**, had just suffered a heart attack, she was not informed of the tragedy. Instead, Lombard and the Columbo clan concocted "a compassionate conspiracy," telling her he was on a world tour, reading "his" letters to her weekly. The lie outlived even Lombard, lasting till Mrs. Columbo died a decade later. "Tell Russ how happy and proud he has made me," were her dying words. She left part of her estate to him.

1935: After 42 weeks of *Modern Times*, **Chaplin** calls it a shoot on this day.

1936: *The Great Ziegfeld* premieres in Los Angeles on this day — the last movie launching attended by **Irving Thalberg**, 37, who would die 15 days later. **Virginia Bruce**, the blonde topping for the huge wedding cake in that film's spectacular "A Pretty Girl Is Like a Melody" production number, wound up almost 50 years later in the Motion Picture Country House "just down the hall" from Thalberg's widow, **Norma Shearer**. A stroke had left Shearer in such mental disarray she was forever asking strangers "Are you Irving?" Said Bruce to writer **Jim Watters**: "The biggest of them all, and here she is blind and dying, after all that, all that fame and riches, and now this. Maybe I haven't had it so tough." Shearer died of pneumonia (as did Thalberg) June 13, 1983, at 82.

1973: Granted, *Zabriskie Point* wasn't much of a picture to build a career on — it was **Michelangelo Antonioni**'s only one in America, and probably his worst anywhere — but its 25-year-old star, **Mark Frechette**, makes an extreme career move on this day: into armed bank robbery. Bungling it, he was arrested in Boston and sent to prison in Norfolk where he died Sept. 27, 1975, at age 27. Cause of death: "freak prison accident." (He was lying on a bench in the gym when the bar of a 160-pound weight which he was lifting fell on his throat.)

1974: The Telluride Film Festival debuts on this day in Telluride, CO — and not with a whimper, thanks to its salute to the controversial **Leni Riefenstahl**.

1948: On this day — one day before he is to address a National Youth Week gathering at Los Angeles City Hall — **Robert Mitchum** is arrested in a raid on the Laurel Canyon home of starlet **Lila Leeds** and charged with "conspiracy to possess marijuana." Moralists made much of this, but moviegoers stormed his latest release, *Rachel and the Stranger*. **Sid Rogell** and **Jack L. Gross**, producers of that surprise hit, quickly put the pre-trial Mitchum into work on *The Big Steal*. Despite its pregnant leading lady (**Jane Greer**) and the 150 co-workers thrown out of work, it had to shut down while he served his 60 days in the L.A. County Jail. Although set up by opportunistic parasites, Mitchum admitted his guilt, took his medicine and emerged from the ordeal a bigger star and a bigger man. The experience didn't diminish his wit, either: Prison farm, he told the waiting press, was "just like Palm Springs — without the riffraff, of course."

1950: Not a second too soon — on this day, at the end of summer — *Summer Stock* reaches New York's Capitol. One of **Judy Garland**'s most problem-plagued productions, it was lucky to get there at all. The best moments were the last in the film — and the last to be filmed. Two months after the principal photography ended, Garland reported back to work to give the film a fitting finale. Twenty pounds slimmer than she was in the rest of the picture, she slammed over a sensational "Get Happy" — the last thing she ever filmed at MGM.

1955: At Fourth and La Brea in L.A., a bus collides with an auto driven by **Bernard Gorcey**. The four-foot-ten comedian, who died of his injuries 12 days later, was famous for two long-running roles: on Broadway as Isaac Cohen in the original record-breaking five-and-a-half-year run (and subsequent movie version) of *Abie's Irish Rose*, and on screen from 1946's *In Fast Company* to 1956's *Dig That Uranium* as Louie Dumbrowski, the sputtering proprietor of Louie's Sweet Shop where two of his real-life sons always hung out as Bowery Boys — **Leo** ("Slip") **Gorcey** and **David** ("Chuck") **Gorcey**.

EVER-CHANGING GARLAND: From left: Judy chunky and sleek in *Summer Stock*.
A LONG-DISTANCE RUNNER: Bernard Gorcey gives his Bowery Boy Leo some acting lessons.
JAIL INTERRUPTED THE FILMING: Robert Mitchum, Jane Greer, Patric Knowles, John Qualen, and Frank Hagney in *The Big Steal*.

31

THE KING AS AUTHENTIC HERO:
Clark Gable and Myrna Loy in
Too Hot to Handle.

1929: Obstreperous even then, **Ward Bond** elbows his way onto the big screen, crashing the Sigma Chi clique of USC Trojans **John Wayne** lined up to play footballers in **John Ford**'s *Salute*, an Army-Navy clash going into national release on this day. He become Wayne's best friend and (after **Paul Fix** and **Yakima Canutt**) his third most frequent co-star. To Wayne's **Frank "Spig" Wead**, Bond even played John Ford (i.e., "John Dodge") in Ford's 1957 bio of the screenwriting aviator, *The Wings of Eagles*.

1938: While winning World War I with *The Dawn Patrol* on this day, **Errol Flynn** tries heading off at the pass his next picture—a Western—by having his agent tell **Jack L. Warner** the accent won't work out West. *Dodge City*, alas, was the first of eight Westerns for Warners, and he convinced in all (after it was established he was from "back East" or "Boston").

1954: At sea under the hot Midway sun on this day, a lone cloud lazily crosses the sky during the first take of the first shot of *Mister Roberts*, causing a light-change as **William Powell** and **Henry Fonda** play the long opening scene. Misreading this as a good omen and considering the cloud more important than the conversation, director **John Ford** printed the scene. (It was reshot four months later on Warners' Burbank backlot by another director.) Fonda and Ford quickly realized they were mismatched for the material, but it took an act of God to reverse the engines. When a gall-bladder operation sidelined Ford, **Mervyn LeRoy** took over and restored as much of the original play as possible. Then the play's co-author, **Joshua Logan**, stepped in and directed scenes blue-penciled by Ford (the scotch-making bit, the laundry-room explosion, etc.); what Ford footage survives consists mostly of exteriors: the nurses' ship-visit, the shirt-less-sailor episode and a classic slapstick stunt (which Fonda and producer **Leland Hayward** removed but which Warners restored): a drunken motorcyclist's high-speed plunge off the pier. The surprising upshot of these conflicting agendas: a beloved comedy much enjoyed by the masses. Ford and Fonda remained unconvinced and disavowed it.

LOVERS OF *H.M.S. TITANIC*: Leonardo DiCaprio and Kate Winslet.
OFFICERS OF THE *S.S. RELUC-TANT*: Jack Lemmon, James Cagney, Henry Fonda and William Powell in *Mister Roberts*.
HOPING TO DUCK DODGE: David Niven, Errol Flynn and Basil Rathbone in *The Dawn Patrol*.

1959: **Eddie Fisher** answers **Elizabeth Taylor**'s phone and hears the word that wrecks their marriage: *Cleopatra*. He blithely suggested she ask for $1 million to play the part, and she relayed this jokingly to the phoner, producer **Walter Wanger**, who took her seriously enough to talk 20th Century-Fox into forking over that fee — then, the highest ever offered an actress for a single film.

1998: *Titanic* begins its video voyage on this day, already the first film to gross $600 million in U.S. theaters—with a worldwide take that's nearing $1.8 billion.

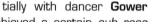

CRAWFORD, TWICE-*POSSESSED*: From left: with Gable in 1931's *Possessed* and with Massey in 1947's *Possessed*. *THE THIRD MAN*'S SECOND FUNERAL: Starring Joseph Cotten and Valli. BEFORE SHE WAS A CHAMPION: Marjorie Bell in *Honor of the West*.

1919: Born on this day is Marjorie Celeste Belcher, better known when paired musically and martially with dancer **Gower Champion** as **Marge Champion**. She achieved a certain *sub rosa* celebrity as well from Husband No. 1—Disney animator **Art Babbitt**—serving as the live-action model for the title heroine of *Snow White and the Seven Dwarfs*, the Blue Fairy of *Pinocchio* and the nimble-footed hippo in the gossamer tutu who blithely leapt and sprinted through "The Dance of the Hours" in *Fantasia*.

1931: Self-possessed **Joan Crawford** starts on this day the first of two films called *Possessed*. In this, she got **Clark Gable** (off screen as well); in the other—16 years later—she got a Best Actress nomination.

1938: *Daily Variety* on this day reports **David O. Selznick** has purchased **Daphne Du Maurier**'s novel, *Rebecca*, for $50,000 and plans to star **Ronald Colman** and **Carole Lombard**. He wound up with **Laurence Olivier** and **Joan Fontaine**, but it was a colorful scramble for those Oscar-nominated roles. Tested or considered: **Vivien Leigh**, **Leslie Howard**, **Olivia de Havilland**, **Anne Baxter**, **Margaret Sullavan**, **William Powell**, **Loretta Young**, **Anita Louise**.

1949: "I had paid my last farewell to Harry a week ago, when his coffin was lowered into the frozen February ground, so that it was with incredulity that I saw him pass by, without a sign of recognition, among the host of strangers in the Strand," wrote **Graham Greene** on the back of an envelope at a dull dinner party. He slipped it to producer **Alexander Korda** as a picture possibility, and the result debuts on this day at London's Plaza Theater: **Carol Reed**'s *The Third Man*, its single sentence stretched by Greene into a superb screenplay—save for the celebrated "cuckoo clock" spiel (which was dashed off by the elusive Harry Lime himself, title-player **Orson Welles**).

1986: On this day, **Cathy Evelyn Smith** gets three years for involuntary manslaughter in connection with the 1982 drug-overdose death of **John Belushi**.

2

3

1920: Filmed amid much wintry hardship at White River Junction, VT, *Way Down East* premieres on this day at New York's 44th Street Theater—and the dark clouds that plagued the production have not lifted: **Bobby Harron**, 26, the Biograph office-boy who became **D.W. Griffith**'s top juvenile actor but somehow got left out of this film (supplanted, pointedly, by **Richard Barthelmess**)—shot himself to death the night before the big launch. Then, there was the mysterious location death of **Clarine Seymour**, 21, who was playing Barthelmess' intended and had to be replaced by **Mary Hay**. Death was, however, breathlessly averted once—*and the cameras caught it*: the genuine heroics of Barthelmess, snatching **Lillian Gish** to safety just as the ice floe they were riding on went over a waterfall. Gish did not escape entirely unharmed, though. The hand she dangled so long in the icy river suffered permanent damage.

1936: *A Day at the Races* dawns on the backlot of MGM on this day. Even before filming began, 37 real-life doctors named Quackenbush had lined up, threatening legal action if their name was given to a horse doctor. Over **Groucho**'s objections, the studio changed his character's name to "Hackenbush."

1938: "Every day's a great day for a race," crows the Kentucky colonel archetype (**Walter Brennan**) in *Kentucky* as it commences lensing. Cast as the white-suited, Southern-fried "grand old man of the American turf," Brennan went into the film with the picture's tag-line—watching **Loretta Young** and **Richard Greene** go into the fade-out clinch, he was to tee-hee from the sidelines, "Well, it looks like Kentucky won't have to worry about thoroughbreds for a while!"—but, in the playing of the piece, his character emerged so vivid the filmmakers opted for an emotional finish and gave him a fatal heart attack after winning The Big Race. The film's new last lines went to rival horseracer **Moroni Olsen**, eulogizing Brennan's passing as the passing of an era. That shrewd maneuver won Brennan the Oscar race for Best Supporting Actor. Tee-hee, indeed!

1969: *The Valley of Gwangi*, a dinosaur opus, clomps unnoticed into New York theaters on this day. Its creator, **Ray Harryhausen**, credited its bad box office to "permissive" competition: "If you didn't have nudity in a picture, nobody wanted to know. A naked dinosaur just wasn't outrageous enough."

1998: A survey of 600 teenagers comparing their knowledge of the Constitution and pop culture, according to *USA Today* on this day, revealed "more teens know that **Leonard DiCaprio** starred in *Titanic* than know that **Al Gore** is vice president."

1911: Sweden becomes on this day the first country to establish a State Censorship Board. After Dec. 1, the Board had to certify any film shown there.

1934: *It's a Gift*, a **W.C. Fields** antic scripted under the *nom de plume* of Charles Bogle, begins production on this day, reuniting The Great Man with his tot co-star from *The Old Fashioned Way*, **Baby LeRoy**. One day, when the youngster's crying was holding up production, Fields diverted the boy's nurse and slipped a couple of noggins of gin in his milk bottle. That, unfortunately, put the little nipper out like a light and ended the day's shooting. Leaving the set, Fields yelled to director **Norman McLeod**, "I told you the kid was no trouper."

1937: A couple of short-lived Hollywood marriages start on this day: Director **Anatole Litvak** weds *The Woman I Love* (title player **Miriam Hopkins**)—for two years; **Alice Faye** and **Tony Martin**, who first harmonized in *Sing, Baby, Sing*, marry—for three. **Darryl F. Zanuck**'s wedding present to the latter couple had a catch: He'd give them a European honeymoon which would begin as soon as they give him another film. They did (*Sally, Irene and Mary*).

1939: On this day, "**Hitler** was taking Poland as **Marlene** was taking the San Fernando Valley," wrote her biographer **Steven Bach** of the *Destry Rides Again* start-up. When she set eyes on **James Stewart** that first day of filming, she was heard to moan, "That's for me!" He, however, was absorbed in Flash Gordon comics and didn't get her drift, so she had the art department make up a life-sized Flash Gordon doll, delivered it herself to his dressing room—and locked the door.

1955: *Oklahoma!* lovers **Gordon MacRae** and **Shirley Jones** are reunited on this day in Boothbay Harbor, ME, to begin their *Carousel* spin. She stepped in for **Judy Garland** early on, but he was a last-minute replacement for **Frank Sinatra**, who bolted from location when he learned each scene would be shot twice (in conventional 35mm CinemaScope and in the new, debuting 55mm version).

1964: *The Gospel According to St. Matthew*, the spartan antithesis of The Gospel According to **DeMille**, presents a starkly naturalistic, human Christ to the 24th International Film Festival in Venice on this day, bringing fame, acclaim and five prizes to **Pier Paolo Pasolini**. The Italian adapter-director cast nonactors throughout—even his own mother as the Virgin Mary—and created a kind of New Testament documentary. Two years before, his attempt to parody Hollywood's biblical epics—via *La Ricotta*, his quarter contribution to the four-part feature *Rogopag*—got him reviled at Venice and convicted of slandering church and state. (It also got him a Gold Medal from film critics.)

NEXT STOP — A MARRIAGE-GO-ROUND: Gordon MacRae and Shirley Jones in *Carousel*.
A "FLASH" OF REVELATION: James Stewart and Marlene Dietrich in *Destry Rides Again*.
SPIKING BABY'S MILK: W. C. Fields and Baby LeRoy.

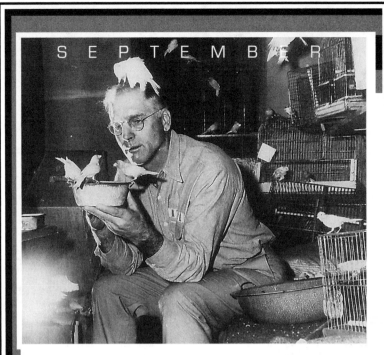

SEPTEMBER

1921: Starlet **Virginia Rappe**, 25, is rushed to the exclusive Pine Street Hospital on this day after a wild weekend party in San Francisco. Based on her dying words to a nurse ("He hurt me, Roscoe hurt me")—and this seconded by the damning testimony of Rappe's friend, **Bambina Maude Delmont**—manslaughter charges were leveled at "Roscoe" (a.k.a. 266-pound comedian **"Fatty" Arbuckle**), who endured two mistrials—the first 10-2 for acquittal, the second 10-2 for conviction—before being finally acquitted. But irreparable damage had been done: He was more or less banned from the screen. The repelled public boycotted his pictures, forcing Paramount to cancel his $3 million contract and junk what films he had done. In time, he came back—quietly, behind the camera, directing comedies as **William B. Goodrich** (long for **Will B. Good**).

1932: The nude corpse of MGM exec **Paul Bern** is discovered on this day—along with a message to his wife of two months, **Jean Harlow**. "Dearest dear," Bern had written on page 13 of his Morocco-bound guest book, "Unfortunately this is the only way to make good the frightful wrong I have done you and to wipe out my abject humiliation. I love you." There was also a cryptic postscript: "You understand last night was only a comedy." This note fanned the front-page scandal and made the actress a suspect till the death was officially ruled a suicide. Two days later, while *Red Dust* resumed shooting without Harlow, **Louis B. Mayer** paged **Tallulah Bankhead** to replace her, but Bankhead said no and called the offer "one of the shabbiest acts of all time." In two more days, Mayer had reverted to his paternal-saint pose and personally escorted Harlow to Bern's calamitous press-circus funeral. The following Monday—one week into the tragedy—Harlow returned to the set and plowed through gamely if glumly. "How are we going to get a sexy performance with *that* look in her eyes?" wondered director **Victor Fleming**, who somehow managed. Indeed, the film was a major Harlow hit. For once, a star not only survived a scandal but was strengthened by it.

1962: *Birdman of Alcatraz*—the film biography of **Robert Stroud**, a convicted killer who in 42 years of solitary confinement became a scholar and research scientist—is screened on this day at the Venice Film Festival. The lone U.S. entry this year, it won the Best Actor nod for title player **Burt Lancaster**.

1975: On this day—80 days into release at just-under-1,000 theaters—*Jaws* chaws its way to the top of the top-grosser heap, devouring *Godfather* and putting its director on the moviemaking map (new kid named **Steven Spielberg**).

BURT FOR THE BIRDS: Lancaster as *Birdman of Alcatraz*.
STAR-DINING: Robert and Roy and Richard in *Jaws*.
SCANDAL-SCARRED: "Fatty" Arbuckle.

1944: *Double Indemnity* reaches the screen of New York's Paramount on this day—without its last 20 minutes. **Billy Wilder** counted this gas-chamber scene—with **Fred MacMurray**'s boss, **Edward G. Robinson**, heartbreakingly in attendance—among his best work, but he canned it for a quicker, cleaner ending.

1951: On the Western street at Columbia's ranch on this day, cameras start turning at *High Noon*. In a role turned down by **Kirk Douglas**, **Marlon Brando** and **Gregory Peck**—the marshal who made a lonely stand against an outlaw gang—**Gary Cooper** strode unsteadily into film history. A troublesome hip triggering tension in Coop's face deepened his performance, producing a pathos in tune with the plaintive, periodic wails of **Tex Ritter**, pleading "Do Not Foresake Me, Oh My Darlin'." Next March 19, when it fell to **John Wayne** to collect the Best Actor Oscar for the absent Coop, he jokingly wondered why he didn't get the part. (Actually, he hated the film, and its latent politics, so much that he made a rebuttal—called *Rio Bravo*).

1959: "Oh, Teddy, it must be awfully hard," director **George Seaton** says to the dying **Edmund Gwenn**, 83, on this day. The actor who'd been Seaton's Oscar-winning Santa in *Miracle on 34th Street* shot back **Edmund Kean**'s famous last words, "Yes, but not as hard as playing comedy." They were Gwenn's last words as well. On this same day, the 50-years-younger **Kay Kendall** dies of leukemia in the London Clinic. A comedienne in the **Carole Lombard** class, she left her fans with a lovely last-gesture: Her final shot in *Once More, With Feeling*, released posthumously five months later, has her blowing a kiss to **Yul Brynner**—but it was aimed at the camera and, thus, the audience.

SHOOTING FROM THE HIP: Gary Cooper in *High Noon*. TIME TO PAY: Fred MacMurray and Edward G. Robinson in a cut scene from *Double Indemnity*. WHO'S STARRING:?: Rosanna and Madonna in *Desperately Seeking Susan*.

1985: *Desperately Seeking Susan* bows on this day in the U.K., with **Rosanna Arquette** top-billed and in the biggest role (a bored New Jersey housewife who crisscrosses identities with an East Village kook). Nevertheless, next March 3, Arquette somehow won the British Academy Award for Best *Supporting* Actress. Which happens when you share the screen with a movie-debuting **Madonna**. Later, when Madonna married **Sean Penn** and needed a maid of honor, Arquette declined. "I don't think so" she said (supposedly sweetly).

1998: Japan's master moviemaker—**Akira Kurosawa**, 88—succumbs to a stroke on this day. He could samuraize Shakespeare (transposed *Macbeth* into *Throne of Blood* and *King Lear* into *Ran*) and, in turn, have his own Eastern epics Westernized (*The Seven Samurai*, *Yojimbo* and *Rashomon* became *The Magnificent Seven*, *A Fistful of Dollars* and *The Outrage*). "The world has lost a rich treasure," eulogized **George Lucas**, who found in Kurosawa's 1958 *The Hidden Fortress* the seeds for Princess Leia and her trusty droids.

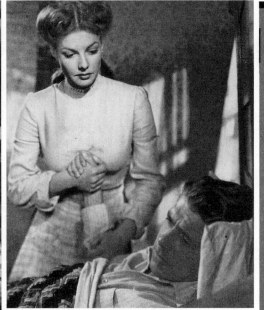

7

1932: Director **Mervyn LeRoy** wraps "the most important film I ever made" on this day: *I Am a Fugitive From a Chain Gang*. A set accident helped him achieve what critic **Pauline Kael** called "one of the great closing scenes in the history of films" when **Paul Muni** says goodbye to girl-friend **Helen Vinson** and she asks him how he lives. During a rehearsal of that ending, an arc light short-circuited, plunging the set into blackness just as Muni whispered the picture's last two words: "I steal."

1933: Shubert Alley apple vendor **Ellen McCarthy**, 73, is belle of the ball on this day, guest of Columbia's *Lady for a Day* launching at Radio City Music Hall. The studio treated her to a new wardrobe and an expensive hotel stay—a gimmick that got applause at the time because it paralleled the Cinderella fate of **May Robson**'s Oscar-nominated Apple Annie in the picture. About a year later, it backfired when McCarthy and her husband were found dead from gas in the tiny flat where they existed on home relief.

1941: After weeks of worrying and with no rehearsal (his own request), **Ronald Reagan** achieves his best moment in movies on this day—in one take: As Drake McHugh in *Kings Row*, he had to come from unconsciousness to the full realization that both his legs had been amputated (needlessly, by a vengeful doctor), and he had to express all this anguish in five words—the most famous words Reagan would speak in films: "Where's the rest of me?"

1950: To the tune of **Lerner** and **Lane**'s "You're All the World to Me" from *Royal Wedding*, **Fred Astaire** goes into orbit on this day with his most celebrated solo—a seven-shot, two-day shoot that gave the illusion he's dancing on the walls and ceiling of his bedroom. In truth, his feet never left the ground. Instead, twirling 360-degrees around him were the camera, its operator and the room itself (a cube-shaped "squirrel cage" built by Bethlehem Steel).

STARS & STRIPED: Paul Muni and Edward Ellis in *I Was a Fugitive From a Chain Gang*.
DAY OF THE ACTOR: Ann Sheridan and Ronald Reagan in *Kings Row*.
TURN TURN TURN: Fred Astaire in *Royal Wedding*.

THE MISTRESSES OF MANDERLEY: Judith Anderson and Joan Fontaine in *Rebecca*.
NOT A MARRIED KIND OF LOVE: Garbo and Gilbert in *Flesh and the Devil*.
FATED TO BE MATED TO HARPO: Oprah in *The Color Purple*.

8

1926: At **Marion Davies'** Beverly Hills hacienda on this day, actress **Eleanor Boardman** and director **King Vidor** marry. It was to have been a double wedding, but the star of Vidor's *The Big Parade*—**John Gilbert**—got stood up by the love of his life, **Greta Garbo**. Their relieved boss, **Louis B. Mayer**, almost gleefully slapped Gilbert on the back and asided, "What do you have to marry her for? Why don't you just fuck her and forget about it?" The actor responded instinctually—with fisticuffs that cost him his career. "You're finished, Gilbert," L.B. decreed from the floor. "I'll destroy you if it costs me a million dollars." It was widely suspected that Mayer—or his chief sound engineer (**Douglas Shearer**)—manipulated the knobs of Gilbert's first talkies so that a quite adequate speaking voice came out high-pitched. Whatever, shrill declarations of love in *His Glorious Night* drew gales of derisive snickers, and the days of the highest-paid matinee idol of the '20s were numbered. Thus robbed of his fans, Gilbert rushed into drunken decline and a decade later, at age 36, died after a last-ditch attempt to win back Garbo.

1939: On this day—as World War II clouds darken England—**Alfred Hitchcock** starts shooting *Rebecca*, activating his U.S. career. For his first scene on these shores, he had the camera trail **Joan Fontaine** around the formidable, maze-like corridors of Manderley till she got lost in her new home.

1979: Discovered dead of a barbiturate overdose in her car on a Paris street on this day is **Jean Seberg**, 40. It was her seventh suicide attempt, most of them occurring around the anniversary of the death of her two-day-old daughter nine years earlier. (The infant was born two months premature, hours after Seberg read in *Newsweek* the father was "a black activist." This fiction, previously published as a blind item by gossip columnist **Joyce Haber** and others, was later revealed to be a deliberate lie spread by the FBI to smear Seberg because of her Black Panthers involvement.) Like **Dorothy Dandridge** and **Maggie McNamara** before her, she was the third actress brought to stardom by **Otto Preminger** to end up a suicide.

1996: After two years at the top of the World's Highest-Paid Entertainer list, director **Steven Spielberg** slips to second place—according to the *Forbes* that hits the stands on this day—replaced by the woman he brought to the movies in an Oscar-nominated performance: talk-show queen **Oprah Winfrey**. In 1985, he paid her peanuts to play Sophia, wife of Harpo, in *The Color Purple*, but it was a role she was fated to do (Harpo, spelled backwards, is Oprah).

SEPTEMBER

9

A NEW PROP: Harold Lloyd.
THE LINDY LANDING: James Stewart in *The Spirit of St. Louis.*
WELL-TRAINED: Sylvester Stallone and Burgess Meredith in *Rocky.*
BEYOND (& BENEATH) BOVARY: Lana and Ann in *A Life of Her Own.*

1917: In *Over the Fence*, a baseball one-reeler released on this day, **Harold Lloyd** dons his trademark tortoise-shelled spectacles for the first time.

1947: *Madame Bovary*, announces MGM on this day, will return **Lana Turner** to the screen after her year off playing wife to tin-plate millionaire **Henry J. ("Bob") Topping**. When time came for the cameras to roll, however, pregnancy prevented that, and **Jennifer Jones** took the part. Turner toyed with the idea of doing the latter half of *The Reformer and the Redhead* (eventually done, in black and white, by **June Allyson**). Then, she considered a film of **Esther Forbes**' novel, *The Running of the Tide*, which **Charles Vidor** would direct with **Elizabeth Taylor** and **Margaret O'Brien**, but that too never happened. When Turner did return to the screen, two years had elapsed and it was in **George Cukor**'s *A Life of Her Own*—and she lost that to **Ann Dvorak**'s brilliant bit of an aging model.

1951: A *Batman*-to-be, **Michael Keaton**, is born on this day—as Michael Douglas.

1955: *The Spirit of St. Louis* takes off as a film with its historic touchdown at Le Bourget Airdrome (reconstructed at Guyancourt, outside Paris, according to a letter producer **Leland Hayward** wrote to Warners on this day). The first day's shooting was an all-night affair, with **Billy Wilder** directing 5,000 French extras back and forth across rain-soggy fields to greet the plane. In the director's cut, **Franz Waxman**'s heroic music came to a startlingly dramatic halt when the wheels of the plane came to a stop on French soil—and, in silence, one could see from under the belly of the plane the horde of welcomers charging forth, their cheers growing to a roar. Somehow, this ending didn't pack the preview punch **Jack L. Warner** desired, but, by that time, Wilder had moved on to another part of Paris and another story (*Love in the Afternoon*) so Hayward had director **John Sturges** reedit and reshoot the sequence which was then rescored (much more conventionally, by **Roy Webb**).

1997: An indispensable actor regardless of role or medium expires at his Malibu home on this day at age 89. "I truly feel without his participation in the film it would never have had its emotional core," said **Sylvester Stallone** of the man who played *Rocky*'s feisty trainer. "**Burgess Meredith** always was to me an irreplaceable legend." That performance and the one in *The Day of the Locust* earn him his only Oscar nominations in almost 60 years of screen acting—incredibly, in view of other great ones he left behind: George in *Of Mice and Men*, Mio in *Winterset*, Ernie Pyle in *The Story of G.I. Joe*, et al.

10

1963: The New York Film Festival flickers into existence via *The Exterminating Angel*, **Luis Bunuel**'s surreal satire about dinner guests who overstay their welcome (i.e., until they drop dead). If you missed this flick at its festival-inaugurating showing, then you had nearly a four-year wait—till Aug. 21, 1967—before it would go into a commercial release in New York.

1971: Polish-born **Bayla Wegier**, 44, opens the gas jets on her stove in her Monte Carlo home and ends her life. She had left France for Hollywood in 1952, searching more for a mealticket than for screen stardom, but the latter presented itself first when she settled into a much-whispered-about *menage a trios* with **Darryl F. Zanuck** and his wife, **Virginia**. Redubbed **Bella Darvi** (the surname, please note, was an amalgam of the first names of her hosts), she starred in *Hell and High Water*, *The Egyptian* and *The Racers* before daughter **Susan Zanuck** got wind of the whispers and had the wench removed. Zanuck himself soon followed, staying away from his wife 17 years. The girlfriends he subsequently gave feature-length screen-tests to (**Juliette Greco** and **Genevieve Gilles**) enjoyed the same conditional stardom that Darvi did, lasting exactly as long as Zanuck's interest in them lasted. The secret of Darvi's success with Zanuck was simple, in the view of **Nunnally Johnson**, a top Zanuck screen-scribe: "Bella made Darryl take her to bed. Until then, Darryl thought it was somethin' you did on a desk."

1976: A check for $10,000—made out to **Cliff Robertson**, bearing the actor's endorsement—is cashed at a branch in Wells Fargo Bank in L.A. Robertson discovered this the following February when asked to pay taxes on money he never saw. Investigating further, he learned his name was signed by Columbia Pictures president **David Begelman**, who pocketed the money. This simple act of forgery unraveled into one of modern Hollywood's great scandals, finally reaching the ugly glare of daylight Jan. 12, 1978, in a **Liz Smith** column in The New York *Daily News* headlined: "And now folks, Hollywoodgate."

1979: Filming begins in Chicago on **Steve McQueen**'s 28th, and last, movie—*The Hunter*.

1993: The Best Costume Designer of 1956 (for *The Solid Gold Cadillac*)—**Jean Louis**, 85—and the Best Actress of 1947 (for *The Farmer's Daughter*)—**Loretta Young**, 80 years young—become husband and wife in Beverly Hills, thus making them the oldest Academy Award-winning couple. The marriage lasted for three and a half years—till his death April 20, 1997. Prior to becoming Loretta Louis, the actress was Loretta Lewis, wife of producer **Tom Lewis**.

1934: *The Captain Hates the Sea*, **John Gilbert**'s last picture, stumbles to a stopping point, after rough weather and a rocky filming produced an impressive bar-bill—not only from the hard-drinking Gilbert but also from **Victor McLaglen, Walter Connolly, Walter Catlett, Leon Errol** and **Fred Keating**. "HURRY UP, THE COSTS ARE STAGGERING," cabled Columbia prexy **Harry Cohn**. Director **Lewis Milestone** wired back: "SO IS THE CAST."

1934: **Claudette Colbert** completes her *third* Oscar-contending Best Picture of 1934—*Imitation of Life*—which, like her *Cleopatra*, would lose to her first (*It Happened One Night*) five months later. She got nominated, and

THE COLBERT CONTENDERS: A winning ticket with Clark Gable (*It Happened One Night*, center), flanked by two also-rans with Warren William (from left: *Cleopatra* and *Imitation of Life*).
A GROGGY CROSSING: John Wray, Leon Errol, Walter Catlett, John Gilbert and Wynne Gibson in *The Captain Hates the Sea*.

the award, for the latter. All three movies were later remade. *Life*, the second time around, fared better in the nomination department. **Louise Beavers** as Colbert's maid and **Fredi Washington** as Beavers' mulatto (and passing) daughter went unnominated for the original film—supporting categories didn't come into existence till two years later—but **Juanita Moore** and **Susan Kohner** made the running for the remake.

1947: Hot on the hooves of **David O. Selznick**'s lust-in-the-dust Western (*Duel in the Sun*) comes its lame, lazy-legged forerunner—*The Outlaw*, a-pokin' into New York's Broadway Theater—hitching a reissue ride on *Duel*'s controversial coat-tails. Finished in '41, the film was bushwhacked by moralists and run out of towns in 1943. Its controversy was centrally located on **Jane Russell**, the amply endowed dental receptionist **Howard Hughes** discovered. This man who made planes and films applied his engineering skills to designing her a special brassiere. She claimed later she never wore it, but she stayed branded with that bust-first image beyond her film career, surfacing on TV as a bra spokesperson reviewing the options left open to "us full-figured girls."

1959: A heart attack kills **Paul Douglas**, 52, at his Hollywood Hills home, just before starting what became the **Fred MacMurray** role in *The Apartment*. A sports broadcaster, Douglas owed his whole acting career to a public display of domestic violence with his then-wife, actress **Virginia Field**. During a row in a NYC drugstore, he hauled off and knocked her off a stool. **Garson Kanin**, who witnessed this scene, was writing just such a brute—the loud, loutish "junk king," Harry Brock, in *Born Yesterday*—and got the announcer to turn actor for it. Douglas put in 1,024 Broadway performances, took one of **Judy Holliday**'s replacements to be the fourth and final Mrs. Douglas (**Jan Sterling**) and heeded the call to Hollywood. His first part was his best: Porter Hollingsway, the errant husband (and a chip off the old Brock) in *A Letter to Three Wives*.

DON'T FENCE ME IN: From left: Basil Rathbone with Errol Flynn in *The Adventures of Robin Hood* and with Tyrone Power in *The Mark of Zorro*. HEEDING THE CALL: Penny Singleton, Arthur Lake and Larry Simms in *Blondie!* AUDITIONS, NOT OSCARS, WON THE ROLE: Robert De Niro and Ruth Nelson in *Awakenings*.

1938: *Blondie!* The starting yelp is sounded for the longest-running non-Western screen series of 'em all — all 28 feature-length installments which populated the bottom of the berth double-bills from 1938 to 1950. The title role in this live-action extension of **Chic Young**'s comic strip — intended first for **Gloria Blondell**, then for **Una Merkel** — eventually went to **Shirley Deane**, who relinquished it at the last moment due to illness. A pert brunette, **Penny Singleton**, lightened her tresses and leapt into the filming, playing Blondie to **Arthur Lake**'s bumbling Dagwood Bumstead for the whole series.

1940: The first and finest of **Tyrone Power**'s four great swashbucklers finishes filming. It was called *The Californian* right up until the eve of its release when it was retitled *The Mark of Zorro*. "Power was the most agile man with a sword I've ever faced before a camera," admitted the movie's main adversary, **Basil Rathbone**, who had on a few memorable occasions crossed swords with **Errol Flynn**. "Tyrone could have fenced Errol Flynn into a cocked hat."

1992: At her Manhattan home, 87-year-old **Ruth Nelson** dies of cancer complicated by a stroke and pneumonia. Capping an acting career of almost 70 years was her best (and last) film performance — that of a woman whose son (**Robert De Niro**) comes out of a 30-year coma in 1990's *Awakenings* — and she auditioned repeatedly to win the part. Because of the delicate nature of this drama, casting director **Bonnie Timmerman** and director **Penny Marshall** insisted all applicants — no matter how seasoned their status — read for the role, a request that went against the grain of at least two Academy Award-winners: **Jo Van Fleet**, who'd lost her memorizing ability to booze by then, blew her last chance at a comeback with a burst of temperament; and, when **Shelley Winters** was asked to read, she whipped one of her two Oscars out of her bag, placed it on the table and said, "*Some* people think I can act."

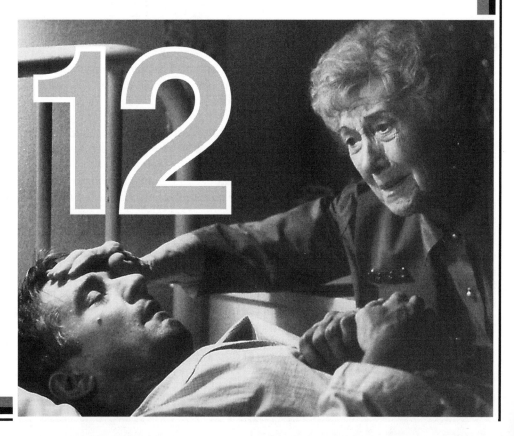

13

1918: In a trench freshly abandoned by **Kaiser Wilhelm**'s German infantry, a star is born on this day in Fleury, France—one of six pups born to a near-starving German shepherd that had been the sole survivor of a kennel bombing. **Lee Duncan**, a noncommissioned pilot who discovered the dogs, kept a female and a male for himself, naming them **Nanette** and **Rin Tin Tin** after the legend of the two French lovers who alone lived through the German bombing of a railway station. Nanette died of pneumonia three days before reaching the U.S., but "Rinty" was trained for movies and, with 1923's *Where the North Begins*, began a nine-year career that saved Warner Bros. from bankruptcy.

1932: Mortified to read he requires booze to loosen up for his love scenes—a line of ballyhoo(ey) slipped to columnist **Sidney Skolsky** by **Samuel Goldwyn**'s overzealous publicity chief, **Lynn Farnol**—the impeccably poised **Ronald Colman** loses his legendary cool and slaps the mogul with a $2-million defamation of character suit, according to the *Los Angeles Herald-Express* on this day. The case was settled out of court, but, after finishing the film he was then doing (*Cynara*) and another on the runway (*The Masquerader*), the actor did no more Goldwyn films, stopping at 18 and sitting out the last two years of his contract. Thereafter—for other employers—Colman went to some pains to prove he could, "unaided," pull off a helluvah drunk scene (as in *A Tale of Two Cities*).

1936: The annual MGM picnic, a cookout for studio employees and their families, is held on this date at the ranch of producer-director **Clarence Brown**. Its traditional climax—a tug of war with **Louis B. Mayer** and **Irving Thalberg** leading opposing teams—is played out without Thalberg in attendance. His wife, **Norma Shearer**, sent a telegram in his name: "ONLY ILLNESS KEEPS ME FROM BEING WITH YOU." The next morning The Boy Wonder of MGM, 37, dies of pneumonia—and his passing is an inestimable loss to movies, then and now.

1982: While driving home along a treacherous mountain road in the Cote d'Azur region on this day, **Grace Kelly** of Monaco and movies suffers a cerebral hemorrhage, sending her car plunging down a 110-foot embankment. She died a day later in Monaco's Princess Grace Hospital. Her first journey along that winding road in the hills above the Mediterranean was for the movie cameras filming **Alfred Hitchcock**'s *To Catch a Thief*, and then she negotiated those hairpin curves without her glasses—but with much wear-and-tear on her co-star. At a hometown tribute earlier in '82, the 52-year-old Philadelphian jokingly confessed that her driving "caused **Cary Grant** to turn dead white under his tan."

BORN IN FRANCE, DIED IN MONACO: From left: Rin Tin Tin, and Grace Kelly (with Cary Grant in *To Catch a Thief*).
A TITAN DETRAINS: Irving Thalberg (with wife Norma Shearer).
LEAVING GOLDWYN WITH A DOUBLE VISION: Ronald Colman and Ronald Colman in *The Masquerader*.

14

1932: Fishermen find the body of **Dorothy Millette** in a slough off the Sacramento River on this day. A week before, when her name was spelled out in national headlines, she jumped from the *Delta Queen* and was washed away by its paddle wheel, her death ruled a suicide—like that of her common-law husband, **Paul Bern**, nine days before. Bern had wed **Jean Harlow** two months earlier—hence, the headlines. To spare its star a bigamy battle, MGM contrived a massive cover-up that kept the truth at bay for years (maybe, forever). The likeliest scenario: Millette showed up on Bern's doorstep, and the two were discovered by Harlow, who left in a huff for her mother's. Planning to apologize with flowers to be delivered the next day to Harlow's dressing room ("the only way to make good the frightful wrong I have done you"), Bern had left the accompanying note in his guest book, calling the collision of wives "only a comedy," but his death gave the words a darker meaning. Only $38 was found in Millette's purse—barely enough for a pauper's grave in potter's fields—so Harlow herself footed the bill for "a decent burial."

1934: *The Good Fairy* begins filming —64 days of love and war for **William Wyler** and **Margaret Sullavan**. On days when they fought, Sullavan photographed badly; on days when they didn't, she was radiant. When cameraman **Norbert Brodine** pointed this out to Wyler, the director decided he'd ask her out. They got on so well he did it again. And again. On November 25, they up and married in Yuma. The divorce came in March of 1936.

1937: "Mr. Deeds" and his director—**Gary Cooper** and **Frank Capra**—turn up on this day in the same maternity halls of the Good Samaritan Hospital, pacing back and forth "like a Mutt and Jeff act" awaiting the births of their daughters. Coop's **Maria** came first, the next day; Capra's **Lucy** followed the day after.

1956: Two genuine World War II heroes make an improbable pair of sagebrush brothers (6'3" **James Stewart** and 5'5" **Audie Murphy**) in *Night Passage*, a not-overly-convincing Western which commences to shootin' today.

1998: In what will be her last public performance, **Peggy Cass** reprises her best—her Tony-nominated, Oscar-nominated Agnes Gooch—to **Charles Busch**'s *Auntie Mame* for an AIDS benefit at New York's American Place Theater. "Every single time she opened her mouth, there was an ovation," recalled Busch. "She really had no awareness people had such affection for her. It was such a shock to her. She felt like **Maria Callas**, she said. She'd been retired, and, afterward, she said, 'I'm ready to go back to work.'" Cass, 72, died of heart failure six months later.

15

1951: Splashed big in the tabloids on this day is a predawn slugfest between **Franchot Tone** and **Tom Neal** over **Barbara Payton**. Tone lost the fight (landing in the hospital with a concussion, a broken nose and a fractured cheekbone) but won the girl (wedding her two weeks later). Then, before he'd fully recovered, she took up with Neal again and divorced Tone in May. After that, unable to find acting assignments, Payton drifted into obscurity and prostitution, dying of natural causes May 10, 1967, at her parents' home. Tone's career continued undamaged by the scandal till his death of lung cancer Sept. 18, 1968. Neal abandoned acting, became a landscape gardener and died of congestive heart failure Aug. 7, 1972—only eight months after serving a seven-year sentence for the involuntary manslaughter of his third wife, **Gail Evatt**.

1954: A gust of wind from a NYC subway grating on Lexington, between 51st and 52d Sts., hoists **Marilyn Monroe**'s skirt skyward on this day during the location shoot for *The Seven Year Itch*—and a cinematic icon is born. That spectacle pleased the crowd but mortified **Joe DiMaggio**. The news their eight-month marriage was over came 19 days later, surprising all but **Oscar Levant**, who reasoned, "No man can excel at two national pastimes."

1974: Wearing ruby red slippers recreated by **Halston**, a wedding dress of bright yellow and a five-carat emerald ring, the daughter of Dorothy Gale (**Liza Minnelli**) skips down the aisle to wed the son of The Tin Man (**Jack Haley Jr.**) in Santa Barbara on this day. The happy ending: divorce in April of 1979.

1987: With **Pope John Paul II** on the premises, the HOLLYWOOD sign reads HOLYWOOD on this day. Less than two months earlier—on July 20, 1987—"environmental sculptors" laid siege to it and tinkered with it till it came out OLLYWOOD, saluting the big hero of the moment: **Oliver North**.

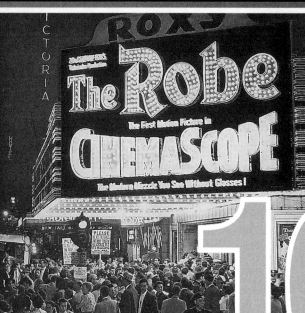

ROLL OUT THE LONG, NARROW CARPET!: The Roxy premieres *The Robe*.
FIRST DANCE, FOURTH PARTNER: Loretta Young and James Cagney in *Taxi!*
ONE EIGHTH OF A SCREEN COURTSHIP: Olivia de Havilland and Errol Flynn in *The Adventures of Robin Hood*.

16

1931: *Taxi!* moves up to the starting line on this day, and, along its melodramatic course, head hack **James Cagney** is allowed his first major screen dance. His leading lady evolved from **Dorothy Mackaill** to **Joan Blondell** to **Nancy Carroll** to—*eureka!*—**Loretta Young**.

1937: Studio exec **Hal B. Wallis** anoints **Olivia de Havilland** "Maid Marian" in *The Adventures of Robin Hood* on this day, but official word must wait till an underling tells **Anita Louise**, who's been counting on co-starring with **Errol Flynn** ever since de Havilland bumped her out of *The Charge of the Light Brigade*. As consolation prize, she was given *Green Light*, a minor Flynn flick. It was even less of a *Charge* to play his sister-in-law in *The Sisters*—so she left Warners to freelance. Unfettered, the box-office coupling of Flynn and de Havilland lasted six years and eight films.

1938: MGM sends *Too Hot To Handle* into general release on this day, the fifth and final pairing of **Clark Gable** and **Myrna Loy**. It came perilously close to being Loy's last, period. During a scene where Gable was to save her from a burning plane, the "controlled fire" got out of hand, and he rushed to the rescue anyway, cameras turning, making the next day's papers. When he emerged from the smoke carrying Loy in his arms, relieved fiancée **Carole Lombard** cracked, "You big ham!"

1940: *This Thing Called Love*, in which **Melvyn Douglas** and **Rosalind Russell** try launching their wedlock with three months of chastity so their personalities can adjust, goes into production on this day. Intended as innocuous fluff, it was received as anything but: The Legion of Decency banned the antic because it "militated against the Christian concept of marriage." And Columbia Pictures was threatened with a lawsuit by the film's third wheel, **Binnie Barnes**, for forcing her to disrobe. (Quaint, what?) Barnes didn't know it at the time, but she was married to Columbia's future president—**M.J. "Mike" Frankovich**.

1953: *The Robe*, premiering on this day at New York's Roxy, unveils 20th Century-Fox's Rx for TV: a low-slung screen-stretch process named CinemaScope. "A smashing display of spectacle," ruled *The New York Times*' **Bosley Crowther**, who admitted being underwhelmed by the *rest* of the picture.

1960: Director **Ingmar Bergman** on this day finishes what will be his *second* Oscar-winning Best Foreign Language Film in a row. His *first* won't happen until April 17, 1961; No. Two becomes official the next April 9. Then-president of the Motion Picture Association of America **Eric Johnston** announced both Bergman victories, cooing first "Oooooo, it's *The Virgin Spring*," then "Ooooooo, *Through a Dark Glass*—*Through a Glass Darkly!*"

1983: Austrian-born **Arnold Schwarzenegger** becomes a U.S. citizen.

17

LAST STOP--THE PARTY CRASHERS: Insert: Bobby Driscoll (with Connie Stevens); Below: in Oscar-winning form in *The Window* (with Ruth Roman and Paul Stewart).
INTERIM STOP--*CASABLANCA*: John Qualen (with Paul Henreid).
NEXT STOP--THE BIG KISS: James Lydon and Elizabeth Taylor in *Life With Father*.

1947: A fetching, 15-year-old **Elizabeth Taylor** racks up a couple of film firsts in *Cynthia*, an otherwise unnoteworthy teen thing bowing on this day at NYC's Loews State: her first top-billing, sealed with her first screen kiss. Administering the latter was **Jimmy Lydon**, her beau from *Life With Father* but a pretty thin reed for such work (the sort of suitor, said *Times* critic **Bosley Crowther** unkindly, who "will completely knock the props from under all those sentimental people who have got their ideas of teenage boys from Alcott books"). Taylor, with barely one real-life kiss of her own at that time (from fellow MGM actor **Marshall Thompson**), found Lydon's effort lightweight—"That buss was more like a handshake"—but it prompted some nightly practicing with her pillow. When her second screen kiss came along (from **Peter Lawford** in *Julia Misbehaves*), she found it a breeze.

1954: Between matinee and evening performances of *The Pajama Game* on this day, **Shirley MacLaine** weds **Steve Parker** at the Marble Collegiate Church, with none other than the apostle of *The Power of Positive Thinking* presiding: **Dr. Norman Vincent Peale**. The next day, the bride leaves Broadway for a movie career—via Vermont, debuting in **Hitchcock**'s *The Trouble With Harry*.

1958: *Variety*, on this day, reviews *The Party Crashers*, a low-budget teen flick from Paramount notable for the fact it was the last film stop for two particularly lost Hollywood souls trying for comebacks and failing: **Frances Farmer** and **Bobby Driscoll**, playing mother and son.

1987: Veteran character actor **John Qualen**, 79, dies of heart failure on this day in Torrance, CA. His legacy was a number of indelible performances, three in particular: the Caterpillar-crazed Muley in *The Grapes of Wrath*, Axel Swanson ("yumpin' yiminy") in *The Long Voyage Home* and the astonished, all-but-forgotten father of The Dionne Quintuplets in *The Country Doctor*.

1996: The front page of *The New York Times* on this day heralds the discovery and recovery of a film archivists believe to be the oldest complete American feature, preserved in near-mint condition in an Oregon basement—a 55-minute rendering of Shakespeare's *Richard III*, directed by **James Keane** and featuring in the title role **Frederick Warde**. After Dickens' *Oliver Twist* (released five months earlier and existing now with one reel missing), this *Richard III* was the second of eight features released in 1912, the first year features were made in the U.S. "It's like finding a Rembrandt that you didn't know existed, in somebody's closet," said **Jean Picker Firstenberg**, director of the American Film Institute, which received the print from **William Buffum**, 77, a retired Portland flour-mill manager and part-time movie projectionist.

18

1933: "I know it's trite," **Jean Harlow** tells reporters on this day after eloping with her *Red Dust* cameraman, **Hal Rosson**, "but I want to go on record that ours is one Hollywood marriage that will last!" (It lasted eight months.)

1935: Producer **Pandro S. Berman** apprises composer **Jerome Kern** on this day that their *Love Song* will be released as *I Dream Too Much* (after what Berman hopes to be the film's big hit). Kern earned $5,000 per week on this movie; **Dorothy Fields**, who wrote the lyrics (and, thus, the title) made a mere grand a week.

1940: Dallas and Fort Worth co-host the launching of *The Westerner* on this day. A natural for the title role, **Gary Cooper** fought tooth and nail against doing it and only caved in when producer **Samuel Goldwyn** screamed lawsuit. From the script, Coop saw he'd be participating only as a good-guy sidekick in what was essentially the story of "the law West of the Pecos," Texas' notorious **Judge Roy Bean**—and he realized he wouldn't stand a chance with this part being played by **Walter Brennan** (whom he'd known since they were both falling off horses together as cowboy extras). Brennan aggravated the situation by phoning up Cooper and, in his best Goldwyn impersonation, threatening to give top billing to Brennan. P.S.: Coop was right. Brennan made history with his performance, winning an unprecedented third Oscar (a record for a performer subsequently surpassed only by **Katharine Hepburn** and equaled only by **Ingrid Bergman** and **Jack Nicholson**).

1949: A heart attack kills *The Wizard of Oz*—**Frank Morgan**, 59—on this day, two days after finishing *Key to the City* with **Clark Gable** and **Loretta Young**. The performance he was in midst of (Buffalo Bill in *Annie Get Your Gun*) was scrapped—along with all the aborted **Judy Garland** footage—and **Louis Calhern** took over the part when filming resumed with **Betty Hutton** in the title role.

1975: Using the electric sign over Nathan's in NYC's Times Square, **Tom Laughlin** on this day shoots back for *Billy Jack*'s critical bushwhackings, telling the world in large glowing letters that **Paul Zimmerman** and **Joseph Morgenstern** flogged their own scripts to Hollywood while they reviewed movies for *Newsweek*. He also asked the rhetorical question "What is a **Pauline Kael**?" The choices were an actual entity or a figure of **Robert Altman**'s imagination.

19

1940: Eighteen-year-old **Judy Garland** completes her first "solo-starrer," her first title role, her first dual role and her first adult role all on this day. *Little Nellie Kelly* was also the only time she ever died on the screen, but MGM softened the blow by bringing her back as her own daughter.

1959: "The face of humanity is more beautiful than its backside," intones Soviet Premier **Nikita Khrushchev** on this day after he and his wife, **Nina**, inspect the cans of *Can-Can* on a visit to 20th Century-Fox studios. "Immoral," huffed the premier—an opinion roundly seconded by the bluenoses in the movie (but *their* excuse was the film was set in 1896). There were numerous Hollywood functions held for the Khrushchevs, but the once-left-now-wildly-right **Ronald Reagan** skipped them all, and **Natalie Wood** (the only star in town who could speak Russian) was never asked to any.

1989: The Library of Congress on this day posts a list of 25 American films to be placed on the National Film Registry as "culturally, historically or esthetically significant." Other lists of 25 in other years followed, but The First 25 out of the hopper were (in tactful alphabetical order): *The Best Years of Our Lives, Casablanca, Citizen Kane, The Crowd, Dr. Strangelove, The General, Gone With the Wind, The Grapes of Wrath, High Noon, Intolerance, The Learning Tree, The Maltese Falcon, Mr. Smith Goes to Washington, Modern Times, Nanook of the North, On the Waterfront, The Searchers, Singin' in the Rain, Snow White and the Seven Dwarfs, Some Like It Hot, Star Wars, Sunrise, Sunset Boulevard, Vertigo* and *The Wizard of Oz.*

1994: *My Fair Lady*, 30, re-premieres at New York's Ziegfeld Theater on this day, restored frame by frame to former glory by film conservators **James C. Katz** and **Robert A. Harris**—with a little extra bonus: Unearthed in forgotten film vaults in Van Nuys, CA, were two vocal tracks **Audrey Hepburn** did in pre-production ("Show Me" and "Wouldn't It Be Loverly") before it had been decided her singing would be dubbed by **Marni Nixon**. The "Loverly" number, allowing Hepburn to sing at last for herself, crowned the film's second-coming gala. La Nixon introduced the sequence. Also in attendance was **Theodore Bikel** (seventh billed as the Embassy Ball nuisance, Zoltan Karpathy), one of two principals from the picture still alive; the other—**Jeremy Brett** (Freddy Eynsford-Hill), 59—died of heart disease in London exactly 51 weeks later.

1998: Ten reels of *Town & Country* are taken from a courier van parked in Manhattan on this day, forcing **Warren Beatty** and **Goldie Hawn** to return to the cameras to reshoot scenes.

'BY GEORGE, SHE'S [FINALLY] GOT IT!': Rex Harrison, Audrey Hepburn and Wilfrid Hyde-White in *My Fair Lady.*
CAN IT, NIKITA!: Frank Sinatra, Shirley MacLaine and Maurice Chevalier in *Can-Can.*
A FESTIVAL OF GARLAND FIRSTS: George Murphy, Judy Garland and Charles Winninger in *Little Nellie Kelly.*

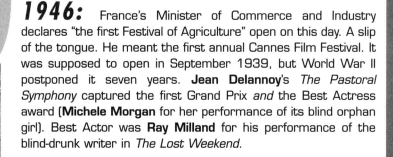

1946: France's Minister of Commerce and Industry declares "the first Festival of Agriculture" open on this day. A slip of the tongue. He meant the first annual Cannes Film Festival. It was supposed to open in September 1939, but World War II postponed it seven years. **Jean Delannoy**'s *The Pastoral Symphony* captured the first Grand Prix *and* the Best Actress award (**Michele Morgan** for her performance of its blind orphan girl). Best Actor was **Ray Milland** for his performance of the blind-drunk writer in *The Lost Weekend*.

1948: World War II-ravaged Vienna starts receiving one of the most vivid "atmosphere soaks" in screen history on this day as **Robert Krasker**'s Oscar-winning cinematography starts drinking in its vulnerable sights for *The Third Man*—from the giant Ferris wheel to the underground sewers. When **Orson Welles** was first pitched the title role of Harry Lime, he responded glibly—"I don't work sewers"—but he rose to the bait of having a hand in the writing.

1951: "In the Cool, Cool, Cool of the Evening," an Oscar-winning ditty **Hoagy Carmichael** and **Johnny Mercer** did for a never-made **Betty Hutton** film (*The Mack Sennett Girl*), is smartly pranced out by **Bing Crosby** and **Jane Wyman**—and director **Frank Capra** catches it all in one continuous take for *Here Comes the Groom*, bowing at the Astor on this day. When Capra returned to the screen eight years later via *A Hole in the Head*, another Oscar-winning song welcomed him back: **James Van Heusen** and **Sammy Cahn**'s "High Hopes." Two projects he canceled with his Paramount project—*Friendly Persuasion* with Crosby and **Jean Arthur**, and *Roman Holiday* with **Cary Grant** and **Elizabeth Taylor**—were made, with different stars, by **William Wyler**.

1954: As Juror #8, a voice of reason among **Reginald Rose**'s *12 Angry Men*, the lone dissenter who brings the 11 other jurors around to a "reasonable doubt," **Robert Cummings** delivers his best (and *only* award-winning) performance on live TV's *Studio One* on this day. **Henry Fonda** turned producer to recycle that role for the movies, and, if his performance fell short of Cummings' Emmy-winning level, his picture didn't. It made the Oscar running for Best Picture, Best Screenplay and Best Director (TV vet **Sidney Lumet** in a brilliant big-screen bow)—but, even with its the meager budget ($340,000, spent on a tight 17-day shoot), the film flopped. Fonda never saw a profit—much less his own deferred salary—yet it was one of three films (after *The Grapes of Wrath* and the also-profitless *The Ox-Bow Incident*) he considered his proudest achievements.

12--COUNT 'EM--12: Lee J. Cobb, George Voskovec, E.G. Marshall, Robert Webber, Jack Warden, Ed Begley, Jack Klugman, Joseph Sweeney, Henry Fonda, John Fiedler, Martin Balsam and Edward Binns in *12 Angry Men*.
PLAYING COOL: Jane Wyman and Bing Crosby in *Here Comes the Groom*.
HARRY THE RAT WITH SEWERS: Orson Welles in *The Third Man*.
RAY THE LUSH WITH PRIZES: Ray Milland in *The Lost Weekend*

21

1917: The first Technicolor film—indeed, the first full-length color feature produced in the US (and the third in the world)—premieres on this day at New York's Aeolian Hall: *The Gulf Between*, a five-reeler starring **Grace Darmond**.

1933: "Lips of Thunder on Lips of Fire! Love Swept Them to the Desperate Destiny of Those Who Play Against the Rules! A Combination the Devil Himself Couldn't Top! The Irresistible Woman Meets the Immovable Man! IMAGINE. . . . the Clash, the Drama, the EXPLOSION when she whispers at last that she loves him . . . AND MANY OTHER MEN!" All that for a movie called *I Loved a Woman*, opening on this day at New York's Strand. It turned out to be about a Chicago meat-packer (**Edward G. Robinson**) amassing a fortune by selling tainted meat.

> **Situation Wanted, Women**   **98**
> **Artists**
>
> MOTHER OF THREE - 10, 11 & 15 - DIVORCÉE. AMERICAN. THIRTY YEARS EXPERIENCE AS AN ACTRESS IN MOTION PICTURES. MOBILE STILL AND MORE AFFABLE THAN RUMOR WOULD HAVE IT. WANTS STEADY EMPLOYMENT IN HOLLYWOOD. (HAS HAD BROADWAY.)
> Bette Davis, c/o Martin Baum, G.A.C.
> REFERENCES UPON REQUEST.

1962: Under the "Situation Wanted, Women Artists" heading in the back pages of *The Hollywood Reporter* on this day, **Bette Davis** places a kidding-on-the-square ad for employment.

1968: A daughter is born to **Roger Vadim**, awkwardly, on the birthday of his ex. "WHAT A NICE GESTURE OF FRIENDSHIP," wired **Brigitte Bardot** to the mother, **Jane Fonda**, who named the child **Vanessa** (after a fellow activist and her future Oscar-winning *Julia*). "VV BORN ON BB'S BIRTHDAY" squealed the French papers.

1973: On this day—the day her last film, *Honeybaby, Honeybaby*, comes out of the labs in finished form—**Diana Sands**, 39, dies of cancer. Best-known as the sister, Beneatha, in **Lorraine Hansberry**'s milestone play and film, *A Raisin in the Sun*, Sands was forced by illness to withdraw from *Claudine*. **Diahann Carroll** took over that title role and took it to an Oscar nomination.

1974: The first person to win three Oscars for acting—**Walter Brennan**, the Best Supporting Actor of 1936 (*Come and Get It*), 1938 (*Kentucky*) and 1940 (*The Westerner*)—dies of emphysema on this day at the age of 80.

1984: *All of Me* and *Places in the Heart*, the pictures that produced the New York Film Critics' picks for Best Actor (**Steve Martin**) and Best Actress (**Sally Field**), both bow in New York on this day. Not all of them agreed about *All of Me*. "I'm still in shock over that one," wrote **Rex Reed** of Martin's win. The night of the awards banquet, Martin returned fire: "It's a great honor to have been given this award by so many distinguished critics—and Rex Reed."

22

SOMEDAY HER PRINCE WILL COME: Audrey Hepburn and William Holden in *Sabrina*.
DEAN'S LAST SCENE: James Dean in *Giant*.
ONCE MORE FOR THE MOVIE CAMERAS: Audie Murphy in *To Hell and Back*.

1949: *Kings Row* kingpin **Sam Wood**, 65, dies on this day. He directed the best of the **Marx Brothers** flicks (*A Night at the Opera*, *A Day at the Races*), the best of the baseball biographies (*The Pride of the Yankees*, *The Stratton Story*) and at least 32 uncredited minutes of *GWTW*.

1954: *Sabrina*, a Cinderella yarn tailored for **Audrey Hepburn**, is installed in New York's Criterion on this day—three days before she weds the Prince Charming she found opposite her in Broadway's *Ondine*, **Mel Ferrer**. During the *Sabrina* shoot, her top husband prospect was the married **William Holden**, but news of his vasectomy sent her spouse-shopping elsewhere.

1955: On this day, **James Dean** does his last work on film—the "last supper" scene in *Giant*. (It was later dubbed by **Nick Adams**.) Director **George Stevens** screened it with pride for studio execs five days later, but Dean arrived late and never saw it. Three days later, he was killed in a car crash.

1955: "I want this picture to be a success, and I'm not sure the public will accept me in the role. I don't think I'm the type—maybe **Tony Curtis** would do," **Audie Murphy** said of the war saga storming into NYC's Capitol on this day by way of his autobiography, *To Hell and Back*. It was the first time an actor ever recreated for the cameras his own war exploits, and the results brought Murphy his first (and last) set of raves. The influential British film magazine *Picturegoer* counted him among its best actors of the year along with **Laurence Olivier** for *Richard III*, **Yul Brynner** for *The King and I*, **Marlon Brando** for *Guys and Dolls* and **James Dean** for *Rebel Without a Cause*. (In 1961, Curtis played an authentic World War II hero—to less effect and fans—in 1961's *The Outsider*: **Ira Hamilton Hayes**.)

1966: During an action sequence for *You Only Live Twice* on this day, two copters collide over the Japanese village of Ebino, and the rotor blade of one smashes into the leg of aerial camera specialist **Johnny Jordan**. Reacting with a cameraman's mentality, he photographed his nearly severed foot, hoping this would help surgeons. Unfortunately, the leg had to be amputated three months later, but Jordan was back in the action fray for the next Bond, *On His Majesty's Secret Service*. On May 16, 1969, he was killed when he was thrown from the fuselage of a B-25 bomber while filming *Catch-22*.

1998: Re-creating for the *Man in the Moon* movie his 1982 brawl that put **Andy Kaufman** in a neck brace, wrestler **Jerry Lawler** does so well on this day he leaves **Jim Carrey** with neck trauma.

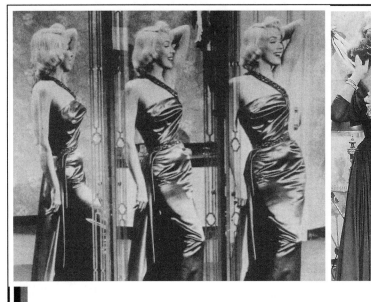

1931: On this day in India, **Chaplin** meets **Gandhi**. More than 50 years later, both would have their life stories filmed by director **Richard Attenborough**.

1961: NBC demonstrates how to start up a weekly movie series (*Saturday Night at the Movies*) on this day with *How To Marry a Millionaire*.

1963: *The Long Flight* commences on this day, following the 1878 trek that 300 Cheyenne Indians made from their barren Oklahoma reservation to their homeland in Wyoming. Before director **John Ford** began what would be his final film foray into Monument Valley, he shot a dissonant detour to Dodge City on the Warners backlot—a satiric 24-minute sequence which had nothing to do with the rest of the picture but did allow **James Stewart** a shot at Wyatt Earp. Ford was eventually persuaded to pare this intrusive episode down before the movie world-premiered in London 13 months later as *Cheyenne Autumn*. The title was changed because a studio custodian, sweeping up the droppings of 50 or so horses on the soundstage, asked Ford what the name of his film was. When Ford said *The Long Flight*, the fellow said, "That's funny—I don't see any airplanes."

24-KARAT GOLDDIGGERS: Marilyn Monroe and Lauren Bacall in *How To Marry a Millionaire.* **NUMBER 2 IRONS:** Jeremy Irons, Genevieve Bujold and Jeremy Irons in *Dead Ringers.* **BRITISH AND ATTENBOROUGH SUBJECTS:** Robert Downey Jr. as *Chaplin*; Ben Kingsley as *Gandhi.*

1988: In *Dead Ringers*, bowing at New York theaters on this day, **Jeremy Irons** delivers finely etched performance(s) of twin gynecologists teetering on madness. To achieve the subtle shadings in this dual portrayal, he insisted on having two different dressing trailers for the filming. Proof he was right in the request came at year's end when the New York Critics named him—both of him—1988's Best Actor.

1997: The MTV generation owes much to **Shirley Clarke**, who dies on this day at age 77. One of America's original independent filmmakers, she arrived in a whirl of controversy—a banned and praised adaptation of **Jack Gelber**'s drug-addict play, *The Connection*, which reprised the four-letter word junkies use for cocaine (the first time that expletive had been used on the screen). She applied her *cinema verite* style to Harlem street gangs (*The Cool World*), a black gay hustler (*Portrait of Jason*) and the Oscar-winning *Robert Frost: A Lover's Quarrel With the World.*

23

1942: *Tales of Manhattan*, the first film flight of **S.P. Eagle**, takes wing at Radio City Music Hall on this day. Eagle was really **Sam Spiegel**, who subsequently produced three Oscar-winning Best Pictures (*On the Waterfront, The Bridge on the River Kwai, Lawrence of Arabia*) and two also-rans (*The African Queen, Nicholas and Alexandra*). The pseudonym was necessary because he was an illegal immigrant with a criminal record and no work permit—"shortcomings" that still didn't stop him from outfitting Film One with **Charles Boyer**, **Rita Hayworth**, **Ginger Rogers**, **Henry Fonda**, **Charles Laughton**, **Edward G. Robinson**, **Paul Robeson** and **Ethel Waters**. The man had *charm*!

REUNION OF CONSPIRATORS: Joan Crawford, Norma Shearer and Rosalind Russell in *The Women*.
THOSE THE EAGLE HAS LANDED: Paul Robeson, Eddie "Rochester" Anderson and Ethel Waters in *Tales of Manhattan*.
GREAT BALLS O' FIRE: Howard da Silva, Gary Cooper and Paulette Goddard in *Unconquered*.

1947: The plight of indentured servants in colonial America (particularly, pretty **Paulette Goddard**) goes public on this day as *Unconquered*. **Cecil B. DeMille** had wanted **Deborah Kerr** but wouldn't cough up $72,000-plus-expenses so he made do with Goddard, a veteran DeMille campaigner (*North West Mounted Police, Reap the Wild Wind*)—for $100,000. A game actress (he thought), Goddard got subjected to all sorts of DeMillian excesses: the lash, the stake, the waterbarrel bubble-bath, the pesky barflies, the canoe ride over the waterfall—the movie was known as *The Perils of Paulette* during filming—but she *did* draw the line when the special-effects boys started lobbing unmanageable fireballs at her. DeMille called her a coward in front of the whole company, then tried threats. She responded by hopping the next flight to New York, forcing him to use a double (who, along with 30 others, *did* suffer minor burns doing the scene). He didn't speak to her for years and ignored her pleas to play the elephant girl in *The Greatest Show on Earth*. In his *Autobiography*, DeMille gave Goddard cursory mention but lavished praise on an unbilled extra, **Robert Baughman**, the little drummer boy who, during Fort Pitt's

fireballing, kept playing—*with flaming drumsticks* (he wore gloves)—till DeMille yelled "Cut!" In C.B.'s book, "that is what makes the difference between an actor and someone who comes to the studio to collect a certain number of dollars for standing in front of a camera a certain length of time."

1974: In the New York tabloids on this day, **Joan Crawford** gets a ghastly gander at what she's become (from photographs taken of her at a Rainbow Room party she hosted for her old co-conspirator in *The Women*, **Rosalind Russell**)—and decides a life of seclusion is the only way to go. It will be her final public appearance. She died May 10, 1977.

1939: Quasimodo delivers The Gettysburg Address on this day. In full regalia and makeup as *The Hunchback of Notre Dame*, **Charles Laughton** recited—for crew, not for camera—Lincoln's (and *Ruggles of Red Gap*'s) famous speech. Initially, Laughton passed on the bellringer role because MGM was paging him for *Cyrano de Bergerac*. **Orson Welles**, **Claude Rains**, **Robert Morley**, **Bela Lugosi** and **Lon Chaney Jr.** shuffled forth for hunchback consideration, then the *Cyrano* deal soured and Laughton sought sanctuary in RKO's Notre Dame.

1952: Two high-flying screen-series stalwarts of the '70s and '80s are born on this day: Luke Skywalker (**Mark Hamill**) and Superman (**Christopher Reeve**).

1962: *The Longest Day* (three hours of mortar shells) rates, on this day, the longest premiere (six hours of champagne and fireworks) at the 2,700-seat Palais de Chaillot in Paris. A local paper said the gala brought together "the two most celebrated Parisians, the longest and the shortest—the Eiffel Tower and **Edith Piaf**": Pyrotechnics rocketed from the Eiffel Tower, and Piaf provided a free concert. This commotion started a reversal of fortune for financially-strapped-and-sinking 20th Century-Fox, which didn't go under during the money-draining voyage of *Cleopatra* because of loot from *The Longest Day*.

1980: Guesting on **Tom Snyder**'s *Tomorrow* TV show on this day, **Chevy Chase**—in a glancing, jesting manner—characterizes **Cary Grant** as a "homo." Unamused, Grant sued the comic and subsequently collected six figures ($100,000) for that four-letter word.

1981: *Chariots of Fire* opens the 19th New York Film Festival on this day and goes on to become the festival's first film to win the Oscar for Best Picture.

1998: On the *starwars.com* website on this day, **George Lucas** officially dubs the start of his *Star Wars* sagas *Star Wars: Episode I—The Phantom Menace*.

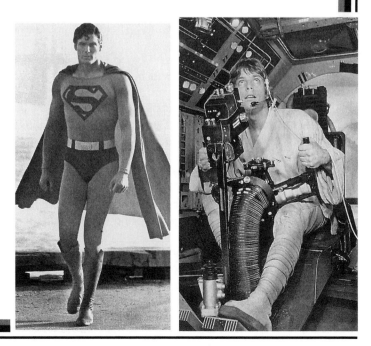

26

1945: Hollywood's version of Italy's neorealism—a documentary in story form—debuts on this day at New York's Roxy, initiating a postwar wave of life-sized reenactments on the screen. Although *The House on 92nd Street* was actually filmed at a house on 93rd Street (a no-longer-existing edifice at 53 East 93rd), this landmark semi-documentary about the spies who conspired there achieved remarkable realism with location photography, most of it at the actual NYC locales of its fact-based story. Producer **Louis de Rochemont**, who pioneered this no-frills style in *The March of Time* newsreel series, hired director **Henry Hathaway** to keep that illusion going the whole feature-length distance.

1951: While trying on costumes at MGM on this day, **Ava Gardner** collapses and is rushed to St. John's Hospital in Santa Monica. She stayed there almost three weeks, rethinking her scheduled remake of *Flesh and the Devil* with **Ricardo Montalban** and **Fernando Lamas**. (Thank God and **Garbo**, it wasn't made.)

1975: *The Rocky Horror Picture Show*, a shock-spoof musical, bows at L.A.'s Westwood Theater on this day, and a midnight-movie cult begins to foam/form.

1979: A pulmonary embolism on this day claims **John Cromwell**, 91, a director whose list of memorable female performances could make even **George Cukor** blanch: **Kim Stanley** in *The Goddess*, **Claudette Colbert** and **Jennifer Jones** in *Since You Went Away*, **Bette Davis** in *Of Human Bondage*, **Eleanor Parker** and **Hope Emerson** in *Caged*, **Irene Dunne** in *Anna and the King of Siam*, **Dorothy McGuire** in *The Enchanted Cottage*. Cromwell's last film work was as an actor in **Robert Altman** movies, playing the querulous bishop of *A Wedding* and a sexually active old-married in *3 Women*. With him in the latter was his wife (No. 4) of 33 years, **Ruth Nelson**, an original Group Theatre actress who turned down the role of a lifetime—Linda Loman in the original Broadway *Death of a Salesman*—to remain with Cromwell in L.A. during his blacklisting ordeal. She survived, along with his son, **James Cromwell** (*Babe*'s Oscar-nominated farmer).

1984: On this day, three days after his 87th birthday, **Walter Pidgeon** dies of a series of strokes. A contract player and proud of it, he always gloried in his days at the Dream Factory and coasted the rest of his career on the high profile he got there: "I was like a kept woman during my 21 years at MGM," he once said. "Hollywood was like an expensive, beautifully run club. You didn't need to carry money. Your face was your credit card—all over the world."

27

1934: *David Copperfield* begins filming on this day with ten-year-old **Freddie Bartholomew** missing a front tooth. After a hasty trip to the dentist for a false one, it's "Action!" Next stumble: **Charles Laughton** as Mr. Micawber. Editor **Hal Kern**, reviewing the first three days of footage, thought "Laughton looked as if he was going to molest the child." Casting noggins came together, and up came an inspired choice: **W.C. Fields**, at his blustering best.

1940: Populated with Warners' colorful contractees (**James Cagney**, **Ann Sheridan**, **Frank Craven**, **Donald Crisp**, **Frank McHugh**, **George Tobias**, **Jerome Cowan**, **Anthony Quinn** and two gifted newcomers, **Elia Kazan** and **Arthur Kennedy**), *City for Conquest* starts preaching to the converted on this day at Manhattan's Strand stand. "Best of the supporting players is Elia Kazan, a Group Theater boy who does a gangster that would scare **Eddie Robinson**," said **Bosley Crowther** in *The New York Times*. "We tremble to think what the Warners will coax out of this magnificent talent." Despite such a send-off, the studio came up with only one other film (*Blues in the Night*) before Kazan decided the actor's life was not for him. When a critic ridiculed his chest hair (!), Kazan took offense and took up directing. Nine years later he directed Kennedy to a Tony Award as Biff in **Arthur Miller**'s *Death of a Salesman*. (Counting that in with *All My Sons*, *The Crucible* and *The Price*, Kennedy originated more Miller roles on Broadway than any other actor.)

FIELDS' BEST DAY: As Mr. Micawber to Freddie Bartholomew's *David Copperfield*.
IN *NEVER . . . NEVER* LAND: Sean Connery in *Never Say Never Again*.
HAIL THE CONQUORING ACTOR: Frank McHugh, Elia Kazan and James Cagney in *City for Conquest*.

1955: MGM Publicity alerts the media on this day that over the weekend one of the studio's largest location units was dispatched to **George W. Vanderbilt**'s palatial Biltmore estate at Asheville, NC, to film *The Swan*. The South-bound included **Grace Kelly**, **Alec Guinness**, **Louis Jourdan**, **Jessie Royce Landis**, **Agnes Moorehead**, **Brian Aherne**, **Estelle Winwood** and **Leo G. Carroll**.

1965: While watching a telecast of 1929's *The Virginian*, directed by one of her ex-lovers (**Victor Fleming**) and starring another (**Gary Cooper**), 60-year-old **Clara Bow** dies of a heart attack at her home in West L.A. on this day. **Bruce Williamson** and **Shirley Sealy**'s *The Intimate Sex Lives of Famous People* credited the much-beauxed Bow with bedding **Gilbert Roland**, **Eddie Cantor**, **John Gilbert**, **Bela Lugosi** and the (eventually disproved) "entire USC football team." Talkies—or, more accurately, her abrasive Brooklynese—brought her screen days to a screeching halt. In her 32 years of retirement, she gave no interviews and only once emerged from the shadows: to supply the mystery voice for "Mrs. Hush" on radio's *Truth or Consequences*.

1982: After 11 straight years of saying never again, **Sean Connery** returns to his James Bond role on this day as filming begins on — *Never Say Never Again*.

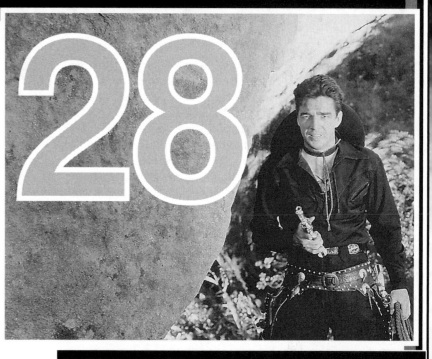

1934: *The Barretts of Wimpole Street* begins residence on this day at the Capitol in New York, with **Fredric March** playing **Robert Browning** to **Norma Shearer**'s **Elizabeth Barrett**. ("When poets love," trumpeted the opening-day ad, "Heaven and Earth fall back to watch.") The villain of the piece, Barrett's incestuously inclined father, was slyly slipped past the Hays Office by **Charles Laughton**, reasoning rightly, "They can't censor the gleam in my eye!"

1936: On this day, **Louise Platt** becomes the first actress to test for Scarlett O'Hara. No soap, but she did catch **John Ford**'s *Stagecoach* (as the pregnant Army wife). **Talullah**, three months later, was the second to test.

1960: Awakening with a cold on this day, **Elizabeth Taylor** cancels her first scheduled appearance as Queen of the Nile. The eight-acre outdoor set built at Pinewood for *Cleopatra* proved a drafty and hazardous place for its titular player, whose condition worsened to the point of a tracheotomy. "You've ruined us by having that girl in the picture," Fox chief **Spyros Skouras** groused to producer **Walter Wanger** when, two months and $6 million later, production halted without a single frame of usable film to show for it. "I wish to hell we'd done it with **Joanne Woodward** or **Susan Hayward**—we'd be making money now." (And, if *those* casting notions don't seem off the mark, consider his alternatives: **Audrey Hepburn** or **Marilyn Monroe**!)

IT DIDN'T PAY TO ADVERTISE: Lash La Rue.
ONCE MORE, WITH FEELING: Richard Burton, Rex Harrison and Elizabeth Taylor in *Cleopatra*.
. . . THEN, THE FIRST *STAGECOACH* OUT OF TOWN: Donald Meek, Louise Platt and John Carradine in *Stagecoach*.

1961: In true Finnegan Begin Again fashion, **Elizabeth Taylor** takes *Cleopatra* from the top again on this day—with a new location (sunny Cinecitta instead of chilly London), a new director (**Joseph L. Mankiewicz** instead of **Rouben Mamoulian**), a new Caesar (**Rex Harrison** instead of **Peter Finch**) and a new Antony (**Richard Burton** instead of **Stephen Boyd**). What could go wrong?

1964: Figuring if it worked for **Bette Davis** it would work for him, **Lash La Rue** takes out his own Help Wanted ad in *The Hollywood Reporter* on this day. It read: "Ready to work. Was box office when an irresponsible jerk. Now adult, worthy and well-qualified. Good health, small waistline, and a full head of hair. A better man makes a better actor. Let me prove it!" Alas, no takers—so he took up selling air-conditioners in L.A.

1981: On this day—for the first time in three and a half years (since, in fact, he blew the whistle on Columbia Pictures president **David Begelman** for forging his name to a $10,000 check)—**Cliff Robertson** begins acting in a Hollywood film, *Brainstorm*. In the interim, Begelman got convicted of forgery, had the felony reduced to a misdemeanor and became president of MGM where he found himself in the ironic position of okaying the Robertson casting.

29

1907: The only person with five stars on the Hollywood Walk of Fame (for films, TV, radio, records and live performances) is born on this day in Tioga, TX: **Gene Autry**.

1930: Director **Tod Browning** begins *Dracula* on this day, delaying to the last the casting of the title character. **Lon Chaney**'s death the month before had left the role wide open, so Browning cast around a lot (**Paul Muni, Joseph Schildkraut, John Wray, Victor Jory, William Courtenay, Ian Keith, Chester Morris**) before finally settling on the obvious: the eminently available **Bela Lugosi**, who had done the role on Broadway and abroad and who, swallowing hard, agreed to do the movie version for a mere $35,000 for seven weeks' work.

1954: As advertised, "the most eagerly awaited motion picture of our times" premieres at Hollywood's Pantages on this day: the **Judy Garland** *A Star Is Born*. "Can you imagine?" wrote **Hedda Hopper** rhetorically. "Five years ago, Judy lost *Annie Get Your Gun*, and she was so upset about it. Now, five years later, here we are at this amazing premiere, all of us cheering Judy on—and just yesterday **Betty Hutton** announced her retirement from show business."

1954: Meanwhile, on the *other* coast (at NYC's Capitol) on this day, another star is born: Maria Vargas (nee **Ava Gardner**, a.k.a. *The Barefoot Contessa*). "GOOD LUCK. HOPE YOU'RE NOT AS NERVOUS AS I," grammatically wired **Garland** in the West to Gardner in the East. A California neighbor of Garland's, **Humphrey Bogart** turned down a chance to play her husband in *Star* to play Gardner's director in *Contessa*.

1966: Finally, officially, on this day, **Jennifer Jones** turns into *The Country Girl* (if only for 22 performances and two previews at the New York City Center). Pregnancy prevented her from doing the movie version, so **Grace Kelly** got the part and the Oscar. Jones also had dibs on the Oscar-winning role of Aurora Greenway, optioning **Larry McMurtry**'s novel, *Terms of Endearment*, and hiring adapter-director **James L. Brooks**, who then turned it into a **Shirley MacLaine** showcase (but at least he remembered to thank Jones in his Oscar-acceptance speech). The film Jones did come out of retirement for, 1974's *The Towering Inferno*, called for her to take a fatal dive off a California high-rise — a spectacular death emulated May 11, 1976 (two days after Mother's Day) by the daughter whose birth had cost her the *Country Girl* film, **Mary Jennifer Selznick**.

1992: Following **Howard Ashman** (March 14, 1991) and **Peter Allen** (June 18, 1992), a third Oscar-winning songwriter succumbs to an AIDS-related illness on this day: **Paul Jabara**, 44, who struck Oscar gold with "Last Dance" from 1978's otherwise-forgettable *Thank God It's Friday*.

1936: Heatherden Hall—a 156-acre estate near Iver Heath, Buckinghamshire, some 25 miles west of London—on this day turns into Britain's biggest film studio—Pinewood, named presumably for the pine trees in the area and the "wood" of Hollywood. The first film completed there—**Herbert Wilcox**'s frothy *London Melody* which brought his future wife, **Anna Neagle**, to the screen—had been started at another studio. The first all-Pinewood piece of work—a **Carol Reed** thriller, *Man With My Voice*, with American imports **Ricardo Cortez** and **Sally Eilers** (plus **Margaret Rutherford**)—was released as *Talk of the Devil*.

1938: Snow White toils for *The Wizard of Oz* on this day. **Adriana Caselotti**, the voice for the Disney heroine, got $100 to sing a single line—"Wherefore art thou, Romeo?"—in the Tin Woodman's "If I Only Had a Heart."

1948: *Red River*, which would wind up being the last picture show in *The Last Picture Show*, rolls into NYC's Capitol in its original release on this day. A week before—after 450 prints had been struck for simultaneous launchings in Texas, New Mexico and Arizona—**Howard Hughes** wired **Howard Hawks** he was seeking an injunction against the film's opening because the showdown between **John Wayne** and **Montgomery Clift** was stolen from the showdown in *The Outlaw* where **Walter Huston** commanded **Jack Buetel** to draw, shot at him to make him draw and nicked his ears with those shots. Hughes forgot (or chose not to remember) that Hawks had written that scene in the first place before he passed the directorial reins of *The Outlaw* over to Hughes. Recalled Hawks: "I told Hughes I didn't think he made the scene very good in *The Outlaw*, and I said, 'Some day, I'll show you how to do it,' and I made it again. That made him mad, so he sued me to make me take out a line that said, 'Draw your gun.' Hughes sent down a battery of lawyers. We'd have won if we'd wanted to defend it, but finally I cut it out, and it played better without the line. I got some of the funniest telegrams from other directors—**Billy Wilder** sent me a telegram saying, 'I own the rights to say, "They went that-a-way."' And **Frank Capra** said, 'I own the rights to say, "I love you."' It was quite a collection."

1952: A spectacular new process for projecting films is world-premiered on this day at New York's Broadway Theater under the title of *This Is Cinerama*. With three 35mm projectors showing a composite picture on a massive screen with an arc of 146 degrees, it represented movie theaters' greatest challenge to TV.

1975: Home Box Office begins programming across the U.S. on this day.

MOST NOMINATED OSCAR LOSERS: *Becket*'s Oscar competitors Richard Burton and Peter O'Toole.
PRE-PERFECT WIFE: Ann Harding, Leslie Howard and Myrna Loy in *The Animal Kingdom*.
EAT MY CROPDUST: Cary Grant in *North by Northwest*.

1932: RKO starts turning *The Animal Kingdom*, **Philip Barry**'s play, into a film — *without* new-girl-on-the-lot **Katharine Hepburn**. After filling *A Bill of Divorcement* in her film debut, Hepburn tested for a role she was fired from on Broadway—the unsympathetic, cheated-on wife—but producer **David O. Selznick** instead picked an actress then only nine films and 18 months away from *The Thin Man* and her niche as The Perfect Wife: **Myrna Loy**. When Loy entered *The Animal Kingdom*, she rounded a corner, stepping out of a casting rut (evil exotics a specialty, a la **Boris Karloff**'s demonic daughter in *The Mask of Fu Manchu*) and onto a new level of screen sophistication which she never left. Attempts to reissue *The Animal Kingdom* in 1935 and 1937 were denied because the Production Code, then in place, took a dim view of Howard leaving home and hearth for Harding. The film was thought destroyed, but, on Jan. 15, 1985, it resurfaced completely reconstructed at a Carnegie Hall gala; occupying the seat of honor: Myrna Loy, Eternal Wife.

1958: On this day (and for most of the week), **Cary Grant** finds himself dashing along a desolate stretch of backroad near Bakersfield, ducking the machine-gun strafing of a crop-dusting plane, for **Alfred Hitchcock**'s *North by Northwest*.

1973: The only sequel to win the Best Picture Oscar starts filming on this day, under the direction of **Francis Ford Coppola**: *The Godfather Part II*.

1982: *My Favorite Year*, a movie that began as **Bat Masterson**'s boozy flight through Little Old New York and wound up as **Errol Flynn**'s first brush with live TV of the 1950s, starts a multi-theater run in New York on this day. In like Flynn was **Peter O'Toole**, making an unsuccessful seventh Oscar bid and matching **Richard Burton**'s long-standing record as Oscar's Most Nominated Non-Winner. When told of this dubious "distinction" after Burton's death, O'Toole reacted with bemused self-deprecation: "You mean I still have a chance at the title?"

1993: Opening the 31st New York Film Festival is *Short Cuts*, which has 22 all-stars for director **Robert Altman** to juggle a la *Nashville*. Among them, in his first major film role, is rocker **Huey Lewis** (*sans* The News), giving the distinct impression of being the first actor to be seen, in full view, urinating on camera. "It's actually a prosthetic," he said later, "a plastic dick with a tube running up my leg—a disgusting-looking thing." He used it, he said, because he "couldn't pee on command. This way, they pump water through it. You get as much pee as you want take after take after take."

1939: Exes mark the sport for *He Married His Wife*, a frenetic farce beginning production on this day at 20th Century-Fox. Because **Warner Baxter** and **Binnie Barnes** knew the moves (having been the "husband" and "friend" of *Wife, Husband and Friend*), they were first in line for these title roles—then replaced by **Joel McCrea** and **Nancy Kelly**. Presiding over the merry mixups was that underappreciated ditz, **Mary Boland**.

1951: Birth, where is thy **Sting**? In Wallsend, England, on this day, the rocker-actor is born—under the more conventional name of Gordon Sumner.

1957: *Raintree County*, a Yankee *Gone With the Wind* wannabe, premieres on this day in Louisville where it was made—at the Brown Theater—with **Elizabeth Taylor**, **Eva Marie Saint** and **Lee Marvin** attending. (**Montgomery Clift** relayed regrets.) The picture started Taylor on the path to the elusive Oscar, which she eventually won on her fourth consecutive bounce.

1967: *Bandolero!* begins lensing on this day in Brackettville, TX, on refurbished sets built for *The Alamo*. **Raquel Welch** saddled up with **James Stewart**, **Dean Martin** and **George Kennedy** for this stock shootout.

1978: *10* commences filming on this day, minus a leading man. **George Segal** stayed home—supposedly in a script-snit with director **Blake Edwards**—and was replaced with **Dudley Moore**, who became a sudden box-office force with it. Segal, in contrast, never quite recovered from this major career stumble.

1985: AIDS takes its first screen superstar on this day—59-year-old **Rock Hudson**—reducing the actor's six-foot-four frame to a skeleton-like 91 pounds.

1998: On this day, three months after the death of the King of the Cowboys (**Roy Rogers**), another singing cowboy heads for the last roundup—Rogers' predecessor and chief competitor, **Gene Autry**, 91—who rode a chestnut stallion named Champion out of the Poverty Row shoot-'em-ups into a multi-million-dollar business empire. Of his movie debut in **Ken Maynard**'s 1934 opus, *In Old Santa Fe*, Autry dirt-kicked, "I sang a song or two, and nobody got sick." A year later, his starring career got rolling with *Tumbling Tumbleweeds* and ran for 95 films (*Down Mexico Way*, *Melody Ranch*, *South of the Border*). He also cut 635 records ("That Silver-Haired Daddy of Mine," "Here Comes Santa Claus," his signature "Back in the Saddle Again") and wrote a good half of those songs himself; his biggest hit was a **Bing Crosby** reject, "Rudolph the Red-Nosed Reindeer," and became (after Crosby's "White Christmas") the second best-selling single in history.

LOUISVILLE LAUNCHING : Liz Taylor and Montgomery Clift in *Raintree County*.
MOORE THE MERRIER: *10*'s Dudley Moore and Bo Derek.
MARITAL MIX-UPS: Elisha Cook Jr., Mary Healy, Mary Boland, Barnett Parker and Joel McCrea in *He Married His Wife*.

2

1925: At MGM's "Circus Maximus" in Culver City, 48 horses and a dozen chariots driven by **Ramon Novarro**, **Francis X. Bushman** and 10 stuntmen begin the chariot race in *Ben-Hur.* **Douglas Fairbanks**, **Mary Pickford**, **Harold Lloyd**, **Lillian Gish** and the **Barrymore** brothers bopped by for the long-delayed event, lorded over by **Fred Niblo** and his 60 assistant directors. One toga-clad A.D. would command *Ben-Hur*'s next day at the races 33 years later: **William Wyler.** On his first day in the stadium built at Rome's Cinecitta, Wyler addressed the 6,000 extras in the stands and, indicating the dozens of A.D.s on the track, "Which one of these guys is going to direct the next *Ben-Hur*?" Of course, the crowd roared.

1929: A heroin overdose kills **Jeanne Eagels**, 35, on this day—and 28 days later she becomes the first posthumous Oscar nominee (for *The Letter*, which **Bette Davis** reprised 11 years later—also to Oscar-nominated effect; **Herbert Marshall** made both treks: doomed lover in 1929, and weak husband in 1940).

1976: A so-called "million dollar hour" occurs on this Sunday from eight to nine in the morning—the time the Nijmegen Town Council closes down the much-trafficked Nijmegen Bridge so director **Richard Attenborough** can reenact a battle that had taken place there in 1944 for his film, *A Bridge Too Far.* The same hour was set aside for several successive Sundays in case retakes were required. Since the sequence climaxed the action for **Robert Redford**'s character and since the actor was contracted to work only till Wednesday, another Sunday shoot would send his overtime tab alone to half a million dollars; the other half would go to the 250 *other* people working the scene. Happily for producer **Joseph E. Levine**, a last-minute break in the drizzle allowed Redford & Co. to do the scene in a single take.

1977: In *Julia*, opening at NYC's Cinema 1 on this day, two left-wing women of the '70s—**Jane Fonda** and **Vanessa Redgrave**—play two left-wing women of the '30s. Fonda, an Oscar-nominated **Lillian Hellman**, got Oscar-*winning* support—from Redgrave (the only actress to win a supporting Oscar in a title role) and from **Jason Robards** (the only person to win back-to-back Oscars in the supporting ranks—both times as real people: **Ben Bradlee** in *All the President's Men* and **Dashiell Hammett**, Hellman's lifelong love, in *Julia*).

1995: After 16 months of world scrutiny and four hours of jury deliberation, approximately 150 million gather around TV sets on this day and hear **O.J. Simpson** pronounced "not guilty" of killing his wife, **Nicole**, and **Ron Goldman**.

4

1937: An Austrian import acquired by **Louis B. Mayer** after one glance at *Ecstasy*—Hedwig Kiesler—checks into Chateau Marmont on this day, misspelling her brand-new MGM-issued name. **Hedy Lamar** she wrote.

1938: At last, Eliza Doolittle ends up with Henry Higgins on this day—*not* (as had previously been the case) with Freddie Eynsford-Hill. At a press screening of *Pygmalion*—two days before its London premiere and too late to do anything about it—**George Bernard Shaw** suddenly saw the romantic finish he'd resisted since he wrote the play in 1912. He scrupulously avoided responsibility or endorsement for the change, but the happy ending the world had been waiting for made him rich and put him in England's top tax bracket. "Another such stroke of luck would ruin me," he wrote a friend. Nor was his Oscar for Best Screenplay any better appreciated. "It's perfect nonsense," huffed The Bearded Wonder, then 82. "My position as a playwright is known throughout the world. To offer me an award of this sort is an insult, as if they had never heard of me before—and it's very likely they never had."

1944: The ridiculous meets the sublime head-on in *Gypsy Wildcat*, opening on this day at the Loews Criterion, with **Maria Montez** in the spotlight and **James M. Cain** on the script. After Cain's first draft, producer **George Waggner** took the famous writer aside and told him: "Jim, I'm delighted with what you've done, but she couldn't play your dialogue. It has to be translated into the kind of baby talk she can handle."

1966: On this day, director **Arthur Penn** starts shooting *Bonnie and Clyde* (because **Francois Truffaut** and **Jean-Luc Godard** were busy), and **Faye Dunaway** hits stardom stride as the disstaff side of the notorious bank-robbing act (because **Tuesday Weld**, **Jane Fonda** and **Sue Lyon** declined). Producer/co-star **Warren Beatty** got the idea for the film from his then-lover and *Promise Her Anything* co-star, **Leslie Caron**, and, when he didn't promise her the lead, their relationship sputtered and stopped. **Robert Towne** made his script-doctor reputation on this flick, working with the film's Oscar-nominated authors, **Robert Benton** and **David Newman**; one road wisely not taken: the homosexual tension between Beatty's character and **Michael J. Pollard**'s.

1970: "Tora-ble, Tora-ble, Tora-ble" moans the headline of **Vincent Canby**'s Sunday piece on this day about the terrible events of Dec. 7, 1941, depicted in the new road-show-in-town. "From the moment you read the ads for *Tora! Tora! Tora!* ('The Most Spectacular Film Ever Made!'), you are aware that you're in the presence of a film possessed by a lack of imagination so singular that it amounts to a death wish," began the *New York Times* critic's second blasting.

5

1932: Filming begins on *42nd Street* on this day—minus its scheduled director: Because **Mervyn LeRoy** was ailing, **Lloyd Bacon** got to be the forgotten-man-behind-the-megaphone—forgotten because he was upstaged every tap of the way by dance director **Busby Berkeley**, translating girls into geometric designs. Not everyone was awestruck. "Busby Berkeley," cynically summarized **Billy Wilder**, "shot musical numbers from the point of view of the electrician on the ceiling."

1938: It's obvious to all on this day—as *A Christmas Carol* begins filming *without* **Lionel Barrymore**—he'll do the rest of his acting from a wheelchair. He tripped over a sound cable filming *Saratoga*, aggravating an already-injured hip. He played *Test Pilot* half-standing/half-sitting and had *You Can't Take It With You* rewritten to accommodate his handicap, but Ebenezer Scrooge (his perennial radio role) couldn't be so easily fixed. **Louis B. Mayer** proposed postponing production, but Barrymore instead bit the bullet, gave the role to **Reginald Owen** and coached him from the sidelines. He turned his radio audience over to Owen that year (but returned "by popular demand" the next year and played it till the last year of his life). **David O. Selznick** wanted him for Doc Meade in *Gone With the Wind* but went with **Harry Davenport** because of the potentially ludicrous spectacle of Barrymore, in his wheelchair, tooling through acres of Confederate wounded at Atlanta's depot. When *A Family Affair* took off into a series, **Lewis Stone** took over the Judge Hardy part Barrymore had begun, and Barrymore was rerouted to a role he *could* play in a wheelchair: cranky Dr. Gillespie in the *Dr. Kildare* movies. According to Barrymore biographer **Hollis Alpert**, other actors considered that wheelchair "the best scene-stealing vehicle since the chariot in *Ben-Hur*."

1955: Batjac Productions (read: **John Wayne** and producer **Robert Fellows**) places in NYC's Paramount on this day its first production, *Blood Alley*, a Commie-clashing action romp for its co-producer—although it didn't start out that way. A week into filming, Wayne relieved **Robert Mitchum** of the lead (supposedly for "horseplay" on the set) and took command himself—this after examining the price tags of possible replacements (**Humphrey Bogart** and **Gregory Peck**, for two) and realizing he'd never get any "jack" back.

1990: *Henry & June*, a sensual and cerebral flick based on **Anais Nin**'s view of **Henry Miller**'s open marriage in randy Paree of 1931, bows on the open market on this day, wearing a brand-new movie rating for the customers to contend with: "NC-17" ("No Children Under 17 Admitted"), replacing the "X" of old. Comedians, as **Kathleen Carroll** noted in her *Daily News* review, are already saying the new nomenclature "sounds like a brand name for a new wart cream."

THE NEW SCROOGE: June Lockhart, Reginald Owen, Kathleen Lockhart and Terry Kilburn in *A Christmas Carol*. DUKE TAKES CHARGE: Lauren Bacall, John Wayne and Victor Sen Yung in *Blood Alley*. AXING THE X: Maria de Medeiros, Fred Ward and Uma Thurman in *Henry & June*.

6

GARBO REALLY JUST SMILED: Greta Garbo and Melvyn Douglas in *Ninotchka*.
YOU TELL 'EM, AL!: Al Jolson in *The Jazz Singer*.
HIS FIRST INTRO: Sean Connery in *Dr. No*.

1927: Two reels into the first talkie, **Al Jolson** gets off—between songs—a classic understatement. "You ain't heard nothin' yet," he assures folks as *The Jazz Singer* premieres at the Warner Theater in New York on this day, promptly revolutionizing the whole film industry. **The Brothers Warner**, who'd brought this to pass, were not to be found celebrating: The day before, on the eve of their greatest triumph, one of the quartet (39-year-old **Sam Warner**) died of a cerebral hemorrhage, and the whole clan returned West to go into mourning.

1939: In her next-to-last flick—*Ninotchka*, world-premiering on this day at Grauman's Chinese in Hollywood—**Greta Garbo** strikes some unexpected comic sparks in her reticent fashion. Ads echoing the historic ones for her first talkie, 1930's *Anna Christie* ("Garbo Talks"), promised "Garbo Laughs"—and she did with a little mechanical help. The peels of hysterical laughter pouring out of her mouth when **Melvyn Douglas** toppled over backwards in his chair were added later. "She was unable to articulate so much as a titter during the shooting of the restaurant scene," wrote Douglas in his autobiography, *See You at the Movies*. "I never learned whether the laughter, which must have been added in the dubbing room, was Garbo or not."

1949: Radio City Music Hall on this day becomes the first theater to display **Olivia de Havilland**'s soon-to-be-Oscared portrayal of *The Heiress*, an ugly duckling at the mercy of a fortune hunter (**Montgomery Clift**). Directed by the demanding **William Wyler**, it was not a performance easily reached. For the crucial "jilt scene" (which **Ruth** and **Augustus Goetz** invented for the play version of **Henry James**' novella, *Washington Square*), Wyler had de Havilland trudging up and down a long staircase for so many retakes she eventually threw the suitcase she was carrying at him. It was then he realized why the scene wasn't working: The suitcase was empty. He filled it with books and had her take it from the bottom again. Now barely able to lift the suitcase, her exhausted effort resonated with the despair and humiliation he was after.

1962: A world-premiere crowd at London's Pavilion on this day witnesses the first big-screen utterance of a future film icon: "I admire your courage—Miss?" This was said sexily, through a swirl of cigarette smoke, to a playgirl at a *chemin de fer* gaming table in London's Les Ambassadeurs. **Eunice Gayson** replied, "Trench. Sylvia Trench. Mr.?"—to which **Sean Connery** answered, "Bond. James Bond." And Agent 007 was off to the screen-series races with *Dr. No*.

1933: Boston, on this day, gets first peek at *The Private Life of Henry VIII*—five days before New York and 17 days before London. Director **Alexander Korda**'s courtesy to "the colonies" was quite calculating—and it paid off: His British flick became the first to Oscar-compete for Best Picture—and the first actually to win an Oscar: for **Charles Laughton**'s title(d) performance.

1943: The only MGM star to shed makes a solid Radio City Music Hall bow(wow) on this day in *Lassie Come Home*. **Roddy McDowall**'s double in the film grew up to be the original Tony of *West Side Story*: **Larry Kert**.

1953: *Sobbin' Women*, a musical based on **Stephen Vincent Benet**'s frontier retelling of *Rape of the Sabine Women*, is dubbed *Seven Brides for Seven Brothers* on this day by MGM publicity chief **Howard Dietz**.

1959: Death silences the screen's most charismatic tenor, **Mario Lanza**, 38, on this day when a bloodclot moves from his leg to his heart in a Rome clinic. It was widely suspected (but never proven) that **Lucky Luciano** had a heavy hand in this movement because Lanza had skipped a charity concert the crime czar gave.

1987: The ashes of **Lee Marvin**, who succumbed to a heart attack at age 63 on Aug. 29, are transferred to Arlington National Ceretery in Washington, D.C. on this day and buried there in a ceremony with full military honors. In real life, the leader of *The Dirty Dozen* was a Marine who received numerous medals for his World War II heroism, including the Purple Heart (having been wounded in South Pacific action). He's still the only Oscar winner to be buried there.

1993: The original nine-man stage-and-screen cast of *The Boys in the Band* loses its fifth member to AIDS on this day: **Kenneth Nelson**, 63, who played the venomous party-host, Michael. Two guests at that groundbreaking gay-gathering died of the disease in 1992: **Frederick Combs** (Donald), 57, on Sept. 19 and **Keith Prentice** (Larry), 52, eight days later. AIDS also claimed **Leonard Frey** (Harold, the birthday boy) and **Robert LaTourneaux** (Cowboy, his birthday gift).

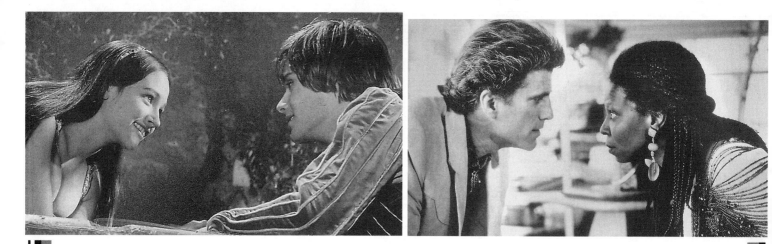

1929: On this day, Transcontinental Air Transport becomes the first airline to show in-flight movies. (They started *lite*: with a newsreel and two cartoons.)

1940: *They Knew What They Wanted*, a Napa Valley triangle (**Charles Laughton** vs. **William Gargan** over **Carole Lombard**), premieres on this day in San Francisco where the lead lovers in **Sidney Howard**'s play meet.

1956: *The Reno Brothers* reaches filming's end on this day—but, when the post-Civil War Western pulled into New York's Paramount 34 days later, it's called *Love Me Tender* after a ballad sung by the third-billed, film-bowing **Elvis Presley**. One of the last scenes filmed—an alternate ending letting him live—was not used. As it was, he won *Harvard Lampoon*'s Worst Supporting Actor of the Year award and never again taxed his fans by trying to act.

1968: The screen's sixth *Romeo and Juliet*—this one adapted and directed by **Franco Zeffirelli** to be commercially popular and teenage-friendly—bows at New York's Paris on this day with unknowns in the title roles: **Leonard Whiting** and **Olivia Hussey**. Mr. Z's first choice for Romeo was *very* known: **Paul McCartney**.

1981: The New York *Daily News*' **Larry Sutton** on this day reports the chaotic end of **Gloria Grahame** three days earlier. The 55-year-old actress had a row with her British doctors, bolted from the London hospital where she was being treated for breast cancer and hopped the first available flight for New York. En route, she went into shock and was met at Kennedy Airport by an ambulance, which sped her to St. Vincent's where she died three hours later. English actor **Peter Turner**, an ex-lover born the year Grahame gave her Oscar-winning performance in *The Bad and the Beautiful* (1952), cared for her when she collapsed in Lancaster and later wrote poignantly of her last days; his memoir was titled after a remark of Grahame's: *Film Stars Don't Die in Liverpool*.

1993: A relationship formed during the filming of *Made in America* begins unraveling in public on this day when **Ted Danson** dons blackface for a Friars Club roast of **Whoopi Goldberg**. The fallout following his offensive racial "humor" took the affair down for the count, and 24 days later the two mutually announced they were changing partners. In fairly short order, both were headed back down the aisle—Goldberg with film-union organizer **Lyle Trachtenberg**, and Danson with a subsequent co-star, **Mary Steenburgen**.

HELLO, YOUNG LOVERS: Olivia Hussey and Leonard Whiting in *Romeo and Juliet*.
GOODBYE, OLD LOVERS: Ted Danson and Whoopi Goldberg in *Made in America*.
WILL HE PULL THROUGH OR NOT?: Richard Egan, Debra Paget and Elvis Presley in *Love Me Tender*.

9

1935: In the San Bernardino Mountains, Hollywood starts its third trek down *The Trail of the Lonesome Pine*—the scenic route this time, it being Technicolor's first venture into the outdoors. Standing tallest, if stoop-shouldered, amid the beautiful commotion of a mountaineer blood-feud (Falins vs. Tollivers) was **Henry Fonda**, whose great American face resembled one created by **Al Capp** a year earlier: L'il Abner's.

1935: On this day, **Thelma Todd** begins her sixth film with **Stan Laurel** and **Oliver Hardy**—*The Bohemian Girl*—playing Queen of the Gypsies till filming's end Nov. 20. Twenty days later, the 30-year-old blonde died of carbon monoxide poisoning. Whether her death was suicide or murder was never determined, but producer **Hal Roach** ordered retakes to minimize her participation, lest he be accused of cashing in on the mounting notoriety. An older actress, **Zeffie Tilbury**, took over the Gypsy Queen duties, and Todd's affair with Devilshoof (**Antonio Moreno**) was assigned to Mrs. Hardy (**Mae Busch**). The remaking of the picture was a patchwork enterprise, incredibly unnecessary.

1947: *Nightmare Alley* hits New York's Mayfair screen on this day, and, as *Time* critic **James Agee** noted, "**Tyrone Power**, who asked to be cast in the picture, steps into a new class as an actor." The film, underattended at the time, acquired a cult following and introduced a new word to movie audiences: "geek" (for the carnival grotesque that conman Power became). It was always his favorite performance.

1995: A documentary feature on gay-bashing by Hollywood movies, *The Celluloid Closet* opens a crack on this day for a New York Film Festival press screening in Alice Tully Hall and reveals for the first time the lavender subtext of 1959's *Ben-Hur*. Interviewed in the film about his uncredited contribution to the script, **Gore Vidal** claimed he created a homosexual relationship between Messala (**Stephen Boyd**) and Judah Ben-Hur (**Charlton Heston**)—the two had had sex as youths, Messala assumes this relationship will resume when they are reunited as adults, and, when it doesn't, the rejection turns to a hatred that propels the rest of the story. Director **William Wyler** approved the premise but cautioned Vidal to tell only Boyd. Consequently, in the reunion scene while Boyd's eyes darted furiously, Heston flashed only a fixed, uninformed smile.

10

1930: Three New York stage actors reach the big screen for the first time on this day: **James Cagney** in *Sinner's Holiday* at the Strand; **Spencer Tracy** and **Humphrey Bogart** in *Up the River* at the Roxy. Tracy and Bogart struck up a friendship making this **John Ford** prison film and always hoped to co-star again. **William Wyler** gave them that chance with *The Desperate Hours*, but—friendship or not—neither would budge an inch about top billing so Tracy withdrew and Bogart co-starred instead with **Fredric March**.

1961: At NYC's Victoria on this day, *Splendor in the Grass* springs **Warren Beatty** on the unsuspecting moviegoing public as an innocent Kansas teenager. For this performance and the more worldly one that followed two months later (**Vivien Leigh**'s gigolo in *The Roman Spring of Mrs. Stone*), Warner Bros. Oscar-promoted him for Best Supporting Actor— but Beatty begged to differ. Considering himself (correctly) a Best Actor, he asked the Academy to strike his name from the ballot, and, when told he was too late, he vowed to decline the honor—rashly, since he got no nomination. It fell to **George C. Scott**, who *was* nominated as Best Supporting Actor of 1961 (for *The Hustler*), to become the first person to refuse an Oscar nomination.

1985: "As it must to all men, death came to Charles Foster Kane"—and The King: **Orson Welles**, 70, and **Yul Brynner**, 65, die hours apart on this day.

1994: The recently reattached **John Wayne Bobbitt** extends his 15 minutes of fame to 87 minutes on this day via the video release of *John Wayne Bobbitt Uncut*, a porn offering hope and how-tos for the penis-repaired. **Lorena** was played by **Veronica Brazil**, and, in a "screenplay" by **Boom Boom Anderson**, hers was not an overly sympathetic portrayal ("I told the police where I threw the penis. That was the least that I could do.").

BEATTY'S UNNOMINATED BEGINNINGS: Warren Beatty in *Splendor in the Grass* with Natalie Wood and in *The Roman Spring of Mrs. Stone* with Vivien Leigh.
PUZZLEMENT AND PUZZLES: Yul Brynner in *The King and I*; Orson Welles (with Dorothy Comingore) in *Citizen Kane*.

MOVIE MARRIEDS: From left: Franchot Tone and Joan Crawford in *Today We Live*, Lauren Bacall and Humphrey Bogart in *To Have and Have Not*, Richard Burton and Elizabeth Taylor in *The V.I.P.s*
BACK FROM A RASH DEMISE: Samuel L. Jackson in *The Long Kiss Goodnight*.

1935: "I'll never marry again as long as I live," insisted **Joan Crawford** when Marriage One (to **Douglas Fairbanks Jr.**) failed. "There is no such thing as honesty or true love. If anyone ever catches me believing in anything, I hope they give me a good sock in the jaw." On this day, La Crawford forgets all the above and elopes with **Franchot Tone**. "Thank God I'm in love again!" gushed Joan Tone, born-again romantic. "Now, I can do it for love—and not for my complexion."

1939: Two four-star marriages come apart in divorce court on this day: **Betty Grable** sheds **Jackie Coogan** as **Miriam Hopkins** divorces director **Anatole Litvak**.

1944: Bowing on this day at the Hollywood Theater in New York is the result of a bet: *To Have and Have Not*, made when director **Howard Hawks** told **Ernest Hemingway** he could make a movie out of Hemingway's worst yarn. Critically speaking, it's hard to say who collected, but something of permanence came out of it, slinking: **Lauren Bacall**. "I saw your test," said **Humphrey Bogart** on meeting his new co-star. "We're going to have a lotta fun together." (Their marriage—his fourth, last and longest—endured to his death Jan. 14, 1957.)

1957: On this day, **Marlon Brando** marries what he believes to be a Darjeeling-born Buddhist named **Anna Kashfi** (an actress who starred in *The Mountain*, *Battle Hymn* and *Cowboy*), but the London tabs soon reveal her to be **Joanne O'Callaghan**, Calcutta-born of Welsh parentage. The deception doomed the union. The two legally separated Sept. 25, 1958, and were divorced Aug. 22, 1959.

1975: "Sturm has remarried Drang, and all is right with the world," declares *The Boston Globe* on this day; translation: **Richard Burton** and **Elizabeth Taylor** have gone back for connubial seconds, remarrying in Botswana, South Africa. Burton fell off the wagon on the spot and, by Christmas, had spied his next ex while riding a ski lift outside Gstaad: **Susan Hunt**. In February, during his Broadway run of *Equus*, he finally asked Taylor for a divorce that would stick.

1989: A heart attack claims film historian **Whitney Stine**, 59, on this day—five days after the death of a friend and favorite subject (*Mother Goddam* and the just-finished *"I'd Love To Kiss You...": Conversations with* **Bette Davis***"*).

1996: *The Long Kiss Goodnight* opens nationally on this day, and (contrary to the original script) **Samuel L. Jackson** manages to live all the way through this nonstop melee. Test audiences' reactions were so vociferously against his death scene that new footage was shot to return him to the living on *Larry King Live*.

12

LETTING GEORGE DO IT: From left: George Stevens directing Rock Hudson, Elizabeth Taylor and James Dean in *Giant*; George Cukor directing Judy Garland in *A Star Is Born*.
A DEATH IN THE WEST: Tom Mix.
THE *GIFT* OF LAUGHTER: W.C. Fields in *It's a Gift*.

1932: *Rain* comes to the Rivoli on this day, with **Joan Crawford** as **W. Somerset Maugham**'s famous shady-lady making a godly man (**Walter Huston**) forgetful. Under **Lewis Milestone**'s direction, Crawford proved she could act, outpointing **Gloria Swanson**'s *Sadie Thompson* before her (1928) and **Rita Hayworth**'s *Miss Sadie Thompson* after her (1953).

1934: It's a wrap for *It's a Gift* on this day—arguably **W.C. Fields**' funniest.

1940: Zipping along Route 80 on this day in his custom-built Cord roadster at a breakneck pace greater than he rode Old Blue and Tony in movie Westerns, **Tom Mix**, 60, goes off the road just outside Florence, AZ, and sails full-throttle to his death. The statue of a riderless pony was erected at the site.

1953: Producer **Sid Luft** gives his star/wife a bracelet inscribed: "Columbus discovered America on October 12, 1492. **Judy Garland** began principal photography on *A Star Is Born* on October 12, 1953. With all my love—Sid." Director **George Cukor** let her wear it for luck in the first scene—Esther Blodgett's stand-in stint, waving from a train in a snowstorm. (One day short of 15 years earlier, Garland had found herself beginning *The Wizard of Oz*.)

1955: One of the most gigantically long shooting schedules in screen history—certainly, B.C. (before the '63 *Cleopatra*)—ends on this (115th) day: *Giant*.

1959: "Darling, what's an Alamo?" English actress **Margaret Leighton** is supposed to have innocently asked when her husband, **Laurence Harvey**, informed her he'd signed for *The Alamo*—and now, on this day, she finds herself *in* a film facsimile of one at Brackettville, TX, visiting him there on location.

1991: Veteran character actress **Sheila** (*Mad Max*, *The Tale of Ruby Rose*) **Florance**, 75, dies of cancer in Melbourne on this day—nine days after winning the Australian Film Institutes's award for Best Actress for her first starring performance: that of a woman dying of cancer in **Paul Cox**'s *A Woman's Tale*.

1994: A new studio soon to be dubbed DreamWorks is formed by **Steven Spielberg**, **Jeffrey Katzenberg** and **David Geffen** on this day—with their own $100 million.

1937: The once and future "King of the Cowboys"—**Roy Rogers**—hits the trail into movies on this day, signing up as a lowly Republic Pictures contract player.

1939: Two months and two days before its Atlanta launching, the opening sequence of *Gone With the Wind* is filmed for the fifth, and absolutely last, time. It was the same troublesome scene—Scarlett and the Tarleton boys on the steps of Tara—that started principal photography Jan. 26. In the interim, **George Bessolo** (who played one of the Tarletons) changed his name to **George Reeves**, but, in making this switch in the film's credits, he is incorrectly listed as playing Brent, instead of Stuart, Tarleton. (Reeves, of course, later took to changing his clothes in telephone booths—as TV's Superman.)

1950: Fasten your seat belts: *All About Eve* bows at NYC's Roxy on this day.

1958: A chess game between Death (**Bengt Ekerot**) and a knight (**Max von Sydow**) puts Sweden's **Ingmar Bergman** on the moviemaking map, as *The Seventh Seal* is opened at New York's Paris Theater on this day. More masterworks to come.

1994: After hearing **Gwyneth Paltrow** read the title role, Miramax executive **Harvey Weinstein** decides on this day to give neophyte adapter-director **Douglas McGrath** the green light to make a feature film out of **Jane Austen**'s *Emma*.

SCARLETT BEAUX: Fred Crane, Vivien Leigh and George Reeves in *Gone With the Wind*.
A PERSUASIVE PALTROW: Ewan McGregor and Gwyneth Paltrow in *Emma*.
AN ARM-IN-ARM ARRIVAL: Gary Merrill, Bette Davis, George Sanders, Anne Baxter, Hugh Marlowe and Celeste Holm in *All About Eve*.

13

14

1932: Hell hath no fury like a sorority sister scorned, according to *Thirteen Women* arriving at the Roxy on this day. **Myrna Loy** played a half-caste case-in-point, killing off the snooty dozen who dissed her in college. One critic said she moved through the movie "like a young woman suffering from insomnia and a desire to become an actress," but Loy lasted longest of all the title players, putting in 55 years on the big screen and earning an honorary Oscar at the end. Her victims fared less well: **Irene Dunne** enjoyed a long career too but never collected on five Oscar nominations. Four co-stars (**Jill Esmond, Florence Eldridge, Kay Johnson** and **Julie Haydon**) got lost in the shadows of their higher-profiled spouses (**Laurence Olivier, Fredric March, John Cromwell** and **George Jean Nathan**). The unluckiest, and most legendary, of the 13 was the Theater Guild grad film-debuting as "Hazel." **Peg Entwistle** changed coasts and mediums to escape an unbroken run of nine flop plays. When this didn't do it for her—and RKO dumped her—she climbed the five-story-tall H in the HOLLYWOODLAND sign on Mt. Lee and leapt spectacularly to her death, becoming a classic metaphor to the dashed dreams that abound in Tinseltown.

1941: *Babes on Broadway* finishes filming on this day—*minus* new-kid-on-the-MGM-block **Shirley Temple**, who bowed out and was replaced with **Virginia Weidler**—but MGM's true facsimile of Temple *is* in the film, briefly, as a tenement babe benefiting from **Mickey & Judy**'s "big show": **Margaret O'Brien**, 4.

1954: VistaVision, Paramount's contribution to the big-screen war against TV, hits the biggest screen possible on this day—Radio City Music Hall's—with *White Christmas*, an **Irving Berlin** songfest destined to become a seasonal perennial, on TV.

1959: "I'll live this half of my life—I don't care about the other half," says **Errol Flynn**, who calls it 50/50 and checks out on this day at age 50.

1987: *The Whales of August* makes its New York splash on this day, boasting a star cast with a collective age of 325 (**Lillian Gish**, 93; **Bette Davis**, 78; **Ann Sothern**, 78; **Vincent Price**, 76).

1996: As of 4:01 p.m. on this day, it's **Madonna** and child (**Lourdes Maria Ciccone Leon**). Four days later, the kid made her first list, placing 101.5 on *Entertainment Weekly*'s list of The 101 Most Powerful People in Entertainment.

SEASONAL: Bette Davis, Vincent Price, Lillian Gish and Ann Sothern in *The Whales of August.*
SEASONABLE: Bing Crosby, Rosemary Clooney, Danny Kaye and Vera-Ellen in *White Christmas.*

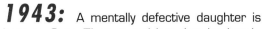

15

1943: A mentally defective daughter is born to **Gene Tierney** and her then-husband, designer **Oleg Cassini**, on this day. The illness was traced to the actress contracting German measles during her pregnancy. Eventually, a lady Marine came forth and boasted to Tierney she was such a fan she had once broken quarantine to meet her during a Hollywood Canteen hostessing stint—information that caused the actress to have a nervous breakdown. (This factual incident provided a plot twist for **Agatha Christie**'s *The Mirror Crack'd*.)

1946: *Summer Holiday* concludes on this day on the MGM backlot. It was **Mickey Rooney**'s second stint as a member of this Miller clan—he played the younger son in the songless original film of 1935, **Eugene O'Neill**'s *Ah, Wilderness!*—and the set was the same old Hardy home-and-hearth he normally occupied as Andy Hardy.

1960: Cast and crew assemble at Papeete, Tahiti, for the second screen coming of *Mutiny on the Bounty* and officially go on salary on this day. Foreshadowing trouble ahead, neither the ship nor the script arrived with them. Budgeted at $8.5 million, the movie was brought in almost a year later for $26 million because of stormy weather and stormier temperaments. **John Sturges, Sir Carol Reed, Lewis Milestone** and **George Seaton** all had a directorial hand in the film's steerage—as did **Marlon Brando**. Given his choice of Captain Bligh or Mister Christian, Brando picked the latter role, but by December (averred MGM) he felt he should be playing John Adams, lone survivor of the mutiny.

1980: On this day—nine days after he and **Anne Byrne** divorce—**Dustin Hoffman** marries their babysitter, **Lisa Gottsegen**. In *Rain Man*, he gave his in-laws a measure of film immortality by memorizing the phonebook up to "Gottsegen."

THE OPEN ROAD: From left: Dustin Hoffman and Tom Cruise in *Rain Man*; Agnes Moorehead, Mickey Rooney, Walter Huston, Jackie "Butch" Jenkins, Gloria DeHaven and Selena Royle in *Summer Holiday*. BRANDO PICKS: Marlon Brando in *Mutiny on the Bounty* FACTUAL GRIST FOR AGATHA'S MILL: Kim Novak, Rock Hudson and Elizabeth Taylor in *The Mirror Crack'd*.

1939: "Mr. Smith Day" in Washington is declared on this day, and denizens converge on Constitution Hall the next night to see director **Frank Capra**'s latest. Greeting them on their way out was a special edition of the Washington *Times Herald* (put out by the National Press Club), proclaiming across the front page "4,000 WELCOME 'MR. SMITH' TO WASHINGTON." Well, WELCOME wasn't the word for Washington's reaction. Senators resented being portrayed as crooks, reporters resented being portrayed as drunks—even the Boy Scouts of America objected, forcing Capra to redub them Boy Rangers. **Jimmy Fidler** reported some studios offering Columbia $2 million to shelve the film "as an appeasement gesture to Congress, lest it inflict punitive legislation on the industry." Fast-forward to Sept. 19, 1989, one month short of a half-century later: *Mr. Smith Goes to Washington* was among the first 25 American films the Library of Congress placed on the National Film Registry as "culturally, historically or esthetically significant."

1943: Film-debuting as the tartish maid in *Gaslight*, **Angela Lansbury** is obliged by law to wait until this day—her 18th birthday—before she can shoot her cigarette-smoking scene. After a party on the set, she puffed away like a well-practiced pro. Her performance got her Oscar-nominated for Best Supporting Actress, making her the youngest contender in that category since **Bonita Granville** (14, at the time of her *These Three* bid).

1984: On this day in Woodland Hills, CA, **Peggy Ann Garner** dies of cancer at 53. At 15, she nosed out *National Velvet* (**Elizabeth Taylor**) to win the honorary Oscar for the outstanding juvenile performance of 1945—as the tomboy Francie Nolan of *A Tree Grows in Brooklyn*—but she wasn't as lucky as Liz at clearing the "awkward age" hurdle that stopped most child stars. Her attempts at adult roles were negligible, and she gradually drifted out of the business.

1992: The Australian Film Institute Awards come out, on this day, strictly *Strictly Ballroom*. This high-octane antic about ballroom dancing fox-trotted off with prizes for Best Film, Best Supporting Actor (**Barry Otto**), Best Supporting Actress (the late **Pat Thomson**), Best Director (**Baz Luhrmann**) and Best Screenplay (Luhrmann and **Craig Pearce**), then turned right around on March 26, 1993, and repeated the feat with the Australian Film Critics' Circle.

16

1932: Despite her pedigree (Russian-Jewish-American), **Sylvia Sidney** on this day takes on a title role that will bring her strange fame in the Far East: *Madame Butterfly*. Her Cho-Cho San made her recognizable in the Orient—so much so that she soon decorated, courtesy of a stolen still from *Merrily We Go to Hell*, packets of prophylactics sold there. For a whole generation of users, the name "Sylvia Sidney" was the Eastern euphemism for condoms.

1939: On this day, **George Raft** flings back a perfectly good script for *The Roaring Twenties*, sternly reminding studio chief **Jack L. Warner** of their verbal agreement that Warners wouldn't ask him to play any more villains. The screenplay for *The Sea Wolf* came boomeranging back, too; even though his role, ultimately played by **John Garfield**, was the (relative) hero and *did* get the girl, Raft thought that the role was "a bit" beside **Edward G. Robinson**'s Wolf Larsen. When Raft and Robinson finally did cross paths in the same picture (*Manpower*), they came to some unscripted blows.

1944: One of the most haunting of movies (and melodies), *Laura* goes into national release on this day, quite changed from its original conception. **Jennifer Jones, John Hodiak, Monty Woolley** and **Reginald Gardiner** were first choices for the roles played by **Gene Tierney, Dana Andrews, Clifton Webb** and **Vincent Price**. Most crucial change of all was **Otto Preminger**'s switch from producer to director, replacing **Rouben Mamoulian**, who seemed to be shooting blanks. With Mamoulian went the Tierney portrait his wife had done; Preminger, instead, had a photographic blowup retouched to look as if it were a painting.

1957: "CLOSED FOR A LITTLE PRIVATE PARTY TONIGHT," understates the marquee outside Madison Square Garden on this day. Inside milled 18,000 of producer **Mike Todd**'s nearest and dearest (including 5,000 fourth-estaters and all manner of fun-lovers, freeloaders and looters). CBS-TV extended the guest-list another 35 million, all transfixed before their TVs watching the party-hardies pushed the bash into a primetime brawl. The occasion was the first year anniversary of Todd's one and only movie, the Oscar-winning Best Picture of 1956: *Around the World in 80 Days*. Todd left the roiling disaster in a huff, threw a set of keys at an underling and told him to lock up—vowing never to throw another party for more than eight guests.

PORTRAIT OF GENE: Clifton Webb, Gene Tierney and Dana Andrews in *Laura*.
THE GRIPES OF RAFT: From left: Frank McHugh, James Cagney and Humphrey Bogart in *The Roaring Twenties*; John Garfield, Ida Lupino and Edward G. Robinson in *The Sea Wolf*.

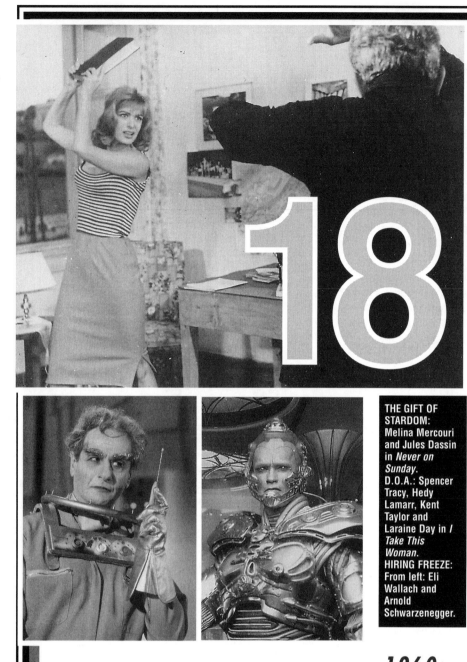

18

THE GIFT OF STARDOM: Melina Mercouri and Jules Dassin in *Never on Sunday*.
D.O.A.: Spencer Tracy, Hedy Lamarr, Kent Taylor and Laraine Day in *I Take This Woman*.
HIRING FREEZE: From left: Eli Wallach and Arnold Schwarzenegger.

1938: Some formula schmaltz about a dedicated doctor (**Spencer Tracy**) and his flighty wife (**Hedy Lamarr**) begins its bumpy journey to the screen on this day. It set out as *A New York Cinderella* (after an unpublished **Charles MacArthur** yarn) but soon became known as *I Take This Woman*. The wags tagged it *I Retake This Woman*—and with reason: **Josef von Sternberg** shot the first 18 days of it before the script shot back. Then, **Frank Borzage** rushed in and finished it. A year later, all *that* was scrapped as **W.S. Van Dyke** gamely took it from the top *again*—with a new supporting cast. "*I Take This Woman* will go down in history as the most extensively operated-on film of 1938-39-40," predicted **Frank S. Nugent** in his *New York Times* pan. "Unfortunately, the patient died."

1960: For her 35th birthday, **Melina Mercouri** is given international stardom via *Never on Sunday*, the $125,000 cinematic diamond-in-the-rough put on display at New York's Plaza Theater on this day—a gift from **Jules Dassin**, her then-fiance/later-husband who wrote, produced, directed and co-performed this amiable fable about an American abroad playing Pygmalion to a Greek prostitute ("a Grecian earner," as it were). **Manos Hadjidakis'** Oscar-winning title-tune paved the way for more Greek imports—among them, Zorba.

1981: As the Panhellenic Socialist Movement sweeps to power in Greece on this day—a Sunday, and her 56th birthday—*Never on Sunday*'s **Melina Mercouri** is tapped to become that country's Minister of Culture, the first woman in Greek government to hold a senior cabinet post. She served in the position for eight years, spending much of her time and energy crusading (unsuccessfully) to get the British Museum to return the Elgin Marbles to Greece. She was serving in that capacity again when she died—of cancer—on March 6, 1994, also a Sunday.

1996: On this day, **Arnold Schwarzenegger** puts in his first day of dirty work as "Mr. Freeze," the arch-foe of *Batman & Robin*—at a salary considerably higher than title players **George Clooney** and **Chris O'Donnell**. Some sources said $20 million, others said $25 million—but the truth was lower than that "in return for a share of the *Batman & Robin* merchandising tie-ins, which could earn him tens of millions." None of these numbers sat well with **Eli Wallach**, who originated the role of "Mr. Freeze" in the *Batman* TV series, but only his wife (actress **Anne Jackson**) saw his fury. "I get more mail from all over the world for having played 'Mr. Freeze' on *Batman*," he once admitted. "I did one episode for $350. Arnold Schwarzenegger did it for $25 million. I said to Anne, 'You see! You see!' And she said, 'Why didn't you lift weights?'"

1938: *Gunga Din* grinds to its 104th, and final, day of production on this day—at $1,909,669.28, then the most expensive film in RKO Radio's history. **Sabu**, who was just arriving on the movie scene with *Drums* and *Elephant Boy*, was perfect for the title role, but producer **Alexander Korda** was readying *The Thief of Bagdad* for him and wouldn't lend him out; the part went to **Sam Jaffe**, who was 30 years older and Jewish but could, upon request, do a terrific Sabu.

1954: True to his hit single in which she anonymously finishes his sentence—"A Man Chases a Girl (until she catches him)"—**Eddie Fisher** and **Debbie Reynolds** post their engagement announcement via MGM's publicity department on this day, but the movie the studio got to go with this news was the opposite of the high-styled comedy it threw when **Elizabeth Taylor** first walked down the aisle (**Vincente Minnelli**'s *Father of the Bride*). **Richard Brooks**' *The Catered Affair* came from **Paddy Chayefsky**'s small-screen, ring-around-the-kitchen-sink school of dramaturgy. Also, Brooks wouldn't hear of Fisher befouling his film and hired **Rod Taylor** for the groom-to-be. He would barely hear of Reynolds but badgered a believable, unDebbie-like performance out of her that impressed not a few (including The National Board of Review, which called her the Best Supporting Actress of 1956).

1957: "One of the biggest surprises to hit Hollywood in a long time came yesterday," writes columnist **Louella O. Parsons** on this day, "when **Rock Hudson** moved into the Hotel Beverly Hills under an assumed name." Meaning: Three weeks short of Anniversary Two, his marriage to **Phyllis Gates** is on the rocks.

A SABU SUB & HIS THREE COMRADES: Sam Jaffe, left, and Cary Grant, Victor McLaglen and Douglas Fairbanks Jr. in *Gunga Din*.
BROOKS LOOKS AT PRE-MARITAL MESSES: From left: Bette Davis and Debbie Reynolds in *The Catered Affair*, Richard Gere and Diane Keaton in *Looking for Mr. Goodbar*.

1977: New York and Los Angeles on this day get first look at *Looking for Mr. Goodbar*, a true and cautionary tale for the free-love/post-pill/pre-AIDS '70s. Directed and adapted by **Richard Brooks** from **Judith Rossner**'s bestseller, the film starred the Oscar-bound Annie Hall, **Diane Keaton**, in a radical change-of-pace as a sexual wanton who brings home a homicidal one-night-stand. Among her Stars-of-Tomorrow pickups: **Richard Gere** (in his third film—and first screen butt-baring) and **Tom Berenger**. "People got us both mixed up," the latter later lamented to the *Los Angeles Times*, "maybe because it was lit so darkly."

20

1936: The Thin Man and his missus leave footprints and handprints in the forecourt of (**Sid**) **Grauman**'s Chinese Theater on this day. As a gag on Grauman, **William Powell** and **Myrna Loy** arrived in outsized clown's shoes!

1937: *You're Only Young Once*, which starts Andy Hardy off on Installment 2 of his 16-film series on this day, also starts **Mickey Rooney** off with a fresh slate of parents: In the eight months since the first film chapter (*A Family Affair*), **Lionel Barrymore**'s crippling condition had grown so severe he had to relinquish to **Lewis Stone** his Judge Hardy role; **Spring Byington** jumped ship as well, leaving Mother Hardy to **Fay Holden**. The Hardy series stretched to 15 innings, from 1937 to 1946—plus a feature-length 1958 postscript where Rooney actually *did* fall heir to Stone's bench in hometown Carvel. In 1942, an Oscar certificate went to "MGM Studio for its achievement in representing the American Way of Life in the production of the *Andy Hardy* series." The films were **Louis B. Mayer**'s pride and joy. "Don't make these pictures any better," he'd caution their creators. "Just keep 'em the way they are."

1951: Director **Ida Lupino** divorces her producer (**Collier Young**) on this day so she can, on the next, wed her co-star (**Howard Duff**). It too was a bumpy ride.

1990: A heart attack claims **Joel McCrea**, 84, on this day—his 57th wedding anniversary. He and **Frances Dee** met co-starring as young marrieds in 1933's *The Silver Cord*. It seemed such a good idea they soon became just that.

1991: Although *Billy Jack Goes to Washington* didn't go beyond three city bookings 14 years earlier, title-player **Tom Laughlin** decides to go back for seconds on this day, announcing—*for real!*—his candidacy for the President of the United States. The *Village Voice* labeled Laughlin "**Jack Webb** of the Left" when he first arrived on the scene as 1971's *Billy Jack* (a bigot-bashing pacifist/half-Native American/former Green Beret). Still flickering with unrest and reform at age 60, the old firebrand subjected himself to a little reality-testing called the New Hampshire primary where he easily gave the best performance by a stump orator ("The second American Revolution is about to happen," etc.), but, at his "victory" party, a blues band broke into "Born Under a Bad Sign" as the results started rolling in. Bottom line: almost 3,000 votes, just under the 2% of the total. Still, that looked like up to Laughlin, who declared, "We have realized the dream!" By spring, the dream had died.

1949: In The Gospel According to **Cecil B. DeMille** released nationally on this day, **Victor Mature** and **Hedy Lamarr** pass for *Samson and Delilah*. A biblical epic of the old school, the film was what the wags call "a movie for de Millions"—but not, evidently, for de **Marx**: "First picture I've ever seen," groused **Groucho**, "in which the male lead has bigger tits than the female."

1954: James Bond materializes for the first time—on the small screen—in an hour-long television adaptation of *Casino Royale* on this day. "Americanized" for this occasion (redubbed "Jimmy Bond" and reassigned to the CIA), 007 was played by the undauntedly dapper **Barry Nelson** in a shawl-collared tuxedo and what looked suspiciously like a clip-on bow tie. **Peter Lorre**, **Linda Christian** and **Michael Pate** co-starred. CBS-TV, which aired the piece as the third entry in its *Climax Mystery Theater* anthology series, shelled out a measly $1,000 for the TV rights to **Ian Fleming**'s first (1953) Bond yarn. **Charles Feldman** secured its film rights from **Gregory Ratoff** for $75,000 and refused to sell them into the "authorized" series for $500,000, instead producing his own cluttered, chaotically uncomical *Casino Royale*. This rumored spoof required (but wasted) the services of five directors, eight writers, two second-unit directors and a galaxy of stars.

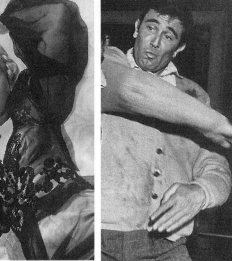

OTTO-MATIC STARDOM: Director Preminger and Jean Seberg.
HEDY & HUNK: Lamarr and Mature as DeMille's *Samson and Delilah*.
BODY & BOND: From left: Marie McDonald and George Lazenby.

1956: On this day (in the afternoon), **Otto Preminger** announces his *Saint Joan* will be a 17-year-old unknown he plucked from Marshalltown, IA—**Jean Seberg**—and (in the evening) he has her perform her audition scene before 60 million Americans watching *The Ed Sullivan Show*. Despite all that huff 'n' puff, the movie that resulted was a shallow **Shaw** show. "My most distinguished flop," Preminger later allowed. "I've had much less distinguished ones."

1965: "The Body" dies on this day: **Marie McDonald**, 42. Husband No. 6 discovered her dead from a pill overdose in their Calabasas, CA, home. **Neil Simon** based *The Marrying Man*—after a fictional fashion—on the rush she got from shoe magnate **Harry Karl**, whom **Debbie Reynolds** later married (and divorced).

1968: At 7:45 a.m. on this day—surrounded by ten gorgeous women at the mountaintop Piz Gloria restaurant in Switzerland—a star is stillborn: **George Lazenby**, presuming to assume the James Bond role **Sean Connery** vacated. *On Her Majesty's Secret Service* allowed him more screen time than any Bond before or since (140 minutes)—as well as a wife (**Diana Rigg**, till death rather quickly did them part)—but critics complained that the Australian model with no previous acting experience couldn't hold a candle to Connery. (In all fairness, who could—or has?) Lazenby likely would have continued in the role, however, had he not come down with an acute and unmanageable case of "star-itis."

22

1947: *Forever Amber* opens to a new house record at NYC's Roxy on this day. Of the $5 million squandered on **Kathleen Winsor**'s best-selling bodice-ripper about an upwardly mobile tart bed-hopping through the court of Charles II, $2 million never saw the light of release: British newcomer **Peggy Cummins** and director **John Stahl** bailed out after a stumbling start, deferring to director **Otto Preminger**, who, ignoring the homelot campaign of **Maureen O'Hara**, petitioned that **Lana Turner** be brought over from MGM and finally settled for the Fox contractee who'd once been the heavenly vision **Jennifer Jones** saw in *The Song of Bernadette*: **Linda Darnell**. No match made in Heaven, this: Two years later, while filming *A Letter to Three Wives*, Darnell was to glance with glacial hatred at the photo of a romantic rival—a feat director **Joseph L. Mankiewicz** achieved by substituting a shot of Preminger.

GOTTA DANCE: Leonide Massine, Moira Shearer and Robert Helpmann in *The Red Shoes*.
THE FIRM, TEUTONIC TOUCH OF OTTO: Cornel Wilde, director Preminger and Linda Darnell working on *Forever Amber*.
THUMBS UP FROM PREVIEWERS: Sylvester Stallone in *First Blood*.

1948: *The Red Shoes* begins its two years and seven weeks at New York's Bijou Cinema on this day, becoming the first (and, for years, only) British opus to crack *Variety*'s list of top-grossing "Golden Fifty" films. The definitive gotta-dance flick, it made an instant icon of an auburn-haired movie unknown, **Moira Shearer**, who actively fought against doing the film for fear she'd lose her prized place with the Sadler's Wells Ballet. Money, unidealistically, brought her around, and she started generations of impressionable teenage girls twirling toward ballet. Shearer danced again for director **Michael Powell** (1951's *The Tales of Hoffman*), passed on two others (*The Tempest* and *The Loving Eye*) and got "conned" into a third collaboration (as a murder victim in 1960's cultish *Peeping Tom*).

1950: Control of the Screen Directors Guild hangs precariously in the balance on this day as Guild president **Joseph L. Mankiewicz** arm-wrestles with **Cecil B. DeMille** over a motion DeMille is trying to railroad through at the height of Hollywood's Red scare—one imposing a loyalty oath on Guild members. An emergency meeting was called in the Crystal Room of the Beverly Hills Hotel, and, when the smoke cleared at 2 a.m., Mankiewicz was still Guild prexy and DeMille was forced to resign from the board (along with 14 of his cohorts). Writer-director **Richard Brooks**—an eye witness to that legendary session—had inspected the original transcripts and was planning to make a movie of the event at the time of his death (March 3, 1992).

1982: The Customer-Is-Always-Right Department: *First Blood* bows in New York on this day—with a new ending dictated by previewers who had reacted badly to **Sylvester Stallone**'s screen death. Thus, John Rambo was spared and lived to fight another day and another day. His two sequels grossed more than $500-mil.

1941: Patrons at the Broadway Theater on this day see an elephant fly: *Dumbo*.

1951: When he memos **Darryl F. Zanuck** on this day to suggest a film biography of **George S. Patton**, a retired brigadier general-turned-movie producer named **Frank McCarthy** sets himself up for a Best Picture Oscar almost 20 years later. Denied Pentagon assistance for 13 years, McCarthy got the ball rolling in the spring of 1965 by hiring a 26-year-old film student to do the first screenplay draft. That job got **Francis Ford Coppola** $50,000 (which jump-started his own directing career via *You're a Big Boy Now*)—and an Oscar six years later. The night he started writing *Patton*, Coppola conceived its stunning prologue—a bemedaled general addressing his troops/the audience before an immense American flag—and that was the last scene filmed. **George C. Scott** got it right on Take One—and later won, like it or not, the Oscar.

1958: *The Last Hurrah*, bowing on this day at New York's Roxy, marks just that for three venerable character actors in their final feature outing: **James Gleason**, **Ricardo Cortez** and, in a particularly winning and impish exit, **Edward Brophy**. Director **John Ford** packed this political comedy to capacity with seasoned scene-stealers of that stripe (**Donald Crisp**, **Jane Darwell**, **Pat O'Brien**, **Basil Rathbone**, **John Carradine**, **Wallace Ford**, **Frank McHugh** and other charter members of his stock company), but the film was still dominated by **Spencer Tracy**'s fine portrayal of an old war-horse running for mayor one last time.

1983: On this day—33 years to the day after **Al Jolson** died—the actress who played his mother in *The Jolson Story* and *Jolson Sings Again* dies. **Tamara Shayne**, 80, always considered that role "the most wonderful professional experience of my life." (Jolson had personally picked her for the part.)

1992: With a bite as ferocious as its bark, *Reservoir Dogs* from first-time director **Quentin Tarantino** sets critics cheering in NYC and L.A. on this day.

1995: In Westwood on this day at an industry screening of *Powder*—the film meant to pull him out of the low-budget amateur league and into the big-time mainstream—director **Victor Salva** is confronted by a placard-brandishing **Nathan Winters**, whom he was convicted of molesting in 1987 while directing the boy (then 12) in a horror film called *Clownhouse*. Execs at Disney, where family entertainment is synonymous, were startled and embarrassed by the incident but insisted Salva had paid his debt when he was paroled from California Training Facility in Soledad after serving 15 months of his three-year sentence.

24

1929: On this day—"Black Thursday"—while Wall Street crumbles on one coast, **Jean Harlow**'s stock soars on the other: She signs up with **Howard Hughes** and spends her next eight weeks replacing **Greta Nissen** in *Hell's Angels*. When Hughes turned it into a talkie, the Swedish actress couldn't make the switch to sound. **Ann Harding**, **Carole Lombard**, **June Collyer**, **Marion Marsh** and **Thelma Todd** were considered for the part before Hughes decided to create his own star. Okay, maybe Harlow *didn't* convince as a British socialite, but she was persuasive as a woman—and that factor overcame her stilted line-reading of the classic come-hither, "Would you be shocked if I put on something more comfortable?"

1930: "And now, ladies and gentlemen," says California governor **James Rolph**, raising the curtain at Grauman's Chinese on A New Screen Epic on this day, "let us sit back in our chairs and watch the most spectacular motion picture ever made in this country of ours—*The Big Parade*." What then trudged across **Sid Grauman**'s massive screen was *not* a World War I classic with **John Gilbert** but a Western with **John Wayne**—the first, in fact: *The Big Trail*. Not till this showing did Wayne's name see the light of the silver screen. Director **Raoul Walsh** had hoped to have **Gary Cooper** or **Tom Mix** head up this westward trek from Missouri to Oregon, but, what with the Movietone sound and the Grandeur photography, little was left of its $2-million budget, prompting Walsh to pick **John Ford**'s prop boy, a strapping unknown of 22. Marion Michael Morrison didn't sound like the man of the West he had in mind so Walsh renamed him for a Revolutionary War hero. Production chief **Winfield Sheehan**, however, thought Anthony Wayne "too Italian" and Tony Wayne too feminine so he made it John Wayne. The bad omen in the guv's goof came true soon enough: Theaters couldn't afford to outfit themselves for Grandeur photography, and *The Big Trail* became The Big Flop, sentencing Wayne to nine years of Poverty Row Westerns—till Ford's model *Stagecoach* rolled along and took him to The Big Time.

1942: On this day, **Vincente Minnelli** finishes the first of his 33 MGM films—*and* the first of 13 musicals he'd do there. *Cabin in the Sky* was, as directorial debuts go, a baptism-by-fire because of battling between the nominal star (**Ethel Waters**) and the sexy one (**Lena Horne**). When the latter broke her leg during filming, she had to do "Honey in the Honeycomb" sitting on a bar. "**Rochester** was so bad," Lena later laughed. "He came up and told me, 'Ethel made a sign on the floor where you slipped.'"

25

1937: *Mannequin*, which *The New York Times* found "glib, implausible and smartly gowned . . . as typically Metro-Goldwyn-Mayer as Leo himself," finishes filming on this day. In it, **Joan Crawford** married *both* of her leading men (**Alan Curtis** *and* **Spencer Tracy**), but the guy who *really* caught her eye was buried way down in the credits as "the man at stage door," and he became—from 1942 to 1946—the third of her four husbands: **Philip Terry**. His most notable portrayal came in Crawford's Oscar year (1945), as **Ray Milland**'s brother in *The Lost Weekend*.

1954: A modestly played 14-line item in *Variety* on this day announces major surgery ahead for the **Judy Garland** *A Star Is Born* because the film was clocking in at three hours and two minutes and Warners' New York office wanted to get in an extra showing every day. (Today's exhibiting practice of permitting ushers an hour to pick up popcorn droppings between shows would have driven the old moguls mad.) Critic **Bosley Crowther** did a war dance in *The New York Times* about the injustice—"A Star Is Shorn"—but, in the name of commerce over art, 27 minutes of a musical masterpiece vanished from human gaze (not forever but for almost 30 years).

1969: *Paint Your Wagon* pulls itself to market (New York City's Loews State II) on this day—a pretty hefty ($20-million, 166-minute) load for its three nonsinging stars to carry. **Lee Marvin, Clint Eastwood** and **Jean Seberg** had their way with **Lerner**-and-**Loewe** songs when they formed the Gold Rush triangle concocted by **Paddy Chayefsky** to replace the wobbly original Broadway book.

1973: Playwright **Neil Simon** weds actress **Marsha Mason** on this day—three weeks after meeting at the first rehearsal of their Broadway-bound *The Good Doctor*. They divorced right before their tenth anniversary, but, during that decade, three of Mason's four Oscar-nominated performances were created—if not custom-fitted for her—by hubby: *The Goodbye Girl* in 1977 (an original for the movies), *Chapter Two* in 1979 (from his stage antic about a widower starting over, based loosely on their own love story, with Mason playing essentially herself) and *Only When I Laugh* (a massive rewrite for her of a role that had won **Maureen Stapleton** a Tony: *The Gingerbread Lady*). The fourth nomination was her first—the noticeably less halo-lit bar tart in 1973's *Cinderella Liberty*.

26

MARCHING TO THE O.K. CORRAL: From left: Kirk Douglas, Burt Lancaster, John Hudson and DeForest Kelley in *Gunfight at the O.K. Corral*; Sam Melville, Frank Converse, Jason Robards and James Garner in *Hour of the Gun*.
NO FORD IN HIS FUTURE: Walter Brennan (with Henry Fonda) in *My Darling Clementine*.
MILK SHAKES WEREN'T THE PROBLEM: W.C. Fields in *Never Give a Sucker an Even Break*.

1881: In an exchange of hot lead lasting a little more than a minute, the **Earps** and the **Clantons** shoot it out on this day. Movies have made much of that gunfight. **John Sturges** directed the long, and the short, of it: His grandiose 1957 *Gunfight at the O.K. Corral* weighed in at seven and a quarter minutes; when he restaged it a decade later for a no-frills, new-stars sequel, *Hour of the Gun*, he brought it in just under 15 ugly seconds. The best version of this pistol-play came in 1946's *My Darling Clementine* from **John Ford**, who did his major damage in 45 seconds but spent another minute finishing off **Old Man Clanton** (brilliantly dispatched by **Walter Brennan**). In executing Clanton's sidewindin' exit, the four-time Oscar-winning director and the three-time Oscar-winning character actor locked horns and vowed never to work together again. (They didn't, either.) Although Brennan's character actually died months before the showdown and **Doc Holliday** died well after it (in a tuberculosis sanitarium), Ford contended his account was precisely the way the real **Wyatt Earp** had described it to him when Ford was a prop-boy apprentice in silent films at Universal. "They didn't just walk up the street and start banging away at each other," Ford told **Peter Bogdanovich**. "It was a clever military maneuver."

1935: The *New York Evening Journal* declares on this day, "**JACKIE COOGAN** GETS MILLION ESTATE TODAY AS HE COMES OF AGE"—erroneously: When the 21-year-old former child-star had his father's will probated, he found no trust fund left for him. His millions had gone to his mother and **Arthur Bernstein**, the family's business manager she'd married. In 1938 Coogan sued both for $4 million but, after months of angst and acrimony, settled for $126,307.50. The strain of the trial also cost him his marriage to starlet **Betty Grable**. A year later—too late to remedy this injustice—California's state legislature passed the Child Actor's Bill, commonly called The Coogan Act, assuring half a child actor's income be set aside in an irrevocable trust fund for the child to claim at maturity. Blackballed in showbiz, Bernstein floundered about in fly-by-night enterprises till his death in 1947. At the funeral, Coogan noticed his stepfather was decked out in a pair of the exploited actor's best slacks.

1941: In his last starring vehicle—*Never Give a Sucker an Even Break*, bowing on this day at New York's Rialto—**W.C. Fields** goes out in character: diving out of an airplane after a bottle of booze. It was a symbolic exit since his alcoholism was so excessive studios wouldn't hire him for anything longer than cameos. Like the film's Esoteric Studios, Universal fired Fields, ending his budget-bloating benders.

27

GRIEF & GUILT: Greta Garbo and Robert Taylor in *Camille*.
THE OSCAR CLAUSE: Paul Muni and David Wayne in *The Last Angry Man*.
ANOTHER RICH DITZ: Billie Burke, Tom Brown, Constance Bennett and Bonita Granville in *Merrily We Live*.

1936: The Best Actress of 1937 (according to The National Board of Review and The New York Film Critics) concludes principal photography on her doomed *Camille* on this day. The sudden death of **Irving Thalberg**, 37, midway through the shoot not only deepened the grief of **Greta Garbo**'s classic portrayal, it deepened her guilt as well: Days before his death, she'd ordered The Boy Wonder off the set because he made her nervous. On Nov. 7, she followed *his* orders and, without any argument, began the retakes he had requested. (Oscar's choice of Best Actress of 1937 was also produced by Thalberg: **Luise Rainer** in *The Good Earth*.)

1937: *Merrily We Live*, a *My Man Godfrey* imitation about rich eccentrics rehabilitating hobos, begins filming on this day, giving the terminally dithering **Billie Burke** a shot at proving **Alice Brady** hadn't cornered the market on bird-brained matriarchs. Burke, like Brady, got Oscar-nominated.

1947: The House Un-American Activities Committee starts on this day amassing its list of witnesses held in contempt for not answering "Are you now or have you ever been a member of the Communist Party?" **John Howard Lawson** led off that "pinko parade," The Unfriendly Ten (followed by **Dalton Trumbo**, **Albert Maltz** and **Alvah Bessie** the next day, **Samuel Ornitz**, **Herbert Biberman**, **Edward Dmytryk** and **Adrian Scott** on the 29th, **Ring Lardner Jr.** and **Lester Cole** on the 30th). Leave it to **Billy Wilder** to lighten the situation: "Of The Unfriendly Ten," he said, "only two have talent. The other eight are just unfriendly."

1959: *The Last Angry Man*, **Paul Muni**'s last film, bows in New York on this day. It was written into the actor's contract that he would receive a bonus from Columbia if he got Oscar-nominated (which he *was*, the following Feb. 22).

1962: A private screening of *Roman Holiday* on this day, requested by **President John F. Kennedy** while he awaits Russia's response to his blockade ultimatum, relieves some of the mounting tension at the peak of the Cuban missile crisis. (The next day, the Soviets agreed to dismantle their Cuban-based missiles.)

28

1937: "Her admirers—middle-aged men and clergymen—respond to her dubious coquetry, to the sight of her well-shaped and desirable little body, packed with enormous vitality, only because the safety curtain of story and dialogue drops between their intelligence and their desires," writes **Graham Greene** on this day in the British magazine *Night and Day*, going erotically off the track in his critique of **Shirley Temple**'s *Wee Willie Winkie*. The 9-year-old, who *still* considers this her best flick, successfully sued Greene over the review, winning 2,000 pounds for herself and 1,500 pounds for her studio—money "recycled immediately into five percent British War Bonds," she said in her autobiography. "I kept on my bathroom wall, until a bomb removed the wall," Greene wrote later, "the statement of claim—that I had accused 20th Century-Fox of 'procuring' Miss Temple for 'immoral purposes.'"

1939: Cancer claims one of the most memorable of movie moms on this day, six days before her 47th birthday. **Alice Brady** tended to be a scatterbrained ditz when mothering daughters (a la her Oscar-nominated work in *My Man Godfrey*) and a rock-solid matriarch when rearing sons. Two vivid examples of the latter illuminated her last two years in films: She upstaged the stars and fires of *In Old Chicago*, turning the cow-owning Mrs. O'Leary into a northwestern Mother Courage and earning an Oscar for it as 1937's Best Supporting Actress. An even better portrayal was the one she went out on: the frontier woman whose two sons are defended of murder charges by the *Young Mr. Lincoln* (**Henry Fonda**).

1941: Adapter-director **Orson Welles** begins principal photography on Screen Masterpiece No. Two, *The Magnificent Ambersons*, on this day—one day short of two years since **Walter Huston** and wife **Nan Sunderland** co-starred with him in the Mercury Theater radio version of **Booth Tarkington**'s novel. In the film, **Joseph Cotten** and **Dolores Costello** took the roles originated by the Hustons, and Welles passed his along to **Tim Holt**—ultimately, the film's Achilles' heel.

1976: Believing the bill of goods that **Eve Arden** sold her in *Mildred Pierce* ("Personally, Veda's convinced me that alligators have the right idea: They eat their young!"), **Joan Crawford** signs her will on this day, stipulating in italics "it is my intention to make no provision herein for my son **Christopher** or my daughter **Christina** for reasons which are well known to them." That final act of meanness prompted Christina to pen her *Mommie Dearest* bestseller, exposing the actress as an abusive adoptive mother—sweet vengeance indeed!

MORE MAGNIFICENCE: Tim Holt and Dolores Costello in *The Magnificent Ambersons*.
ABE TO THE DEFENSE: Henry Fonda and Alice Brady in *Young Mr. Lincoln*.
GREENE MADE HER SEE RED: Shirley Temple and Victor McLaglen in *Wee Willie Winkie*.
DAY OF THE DISINHERITANCE: Joan Crawford with Christina and Christopher.

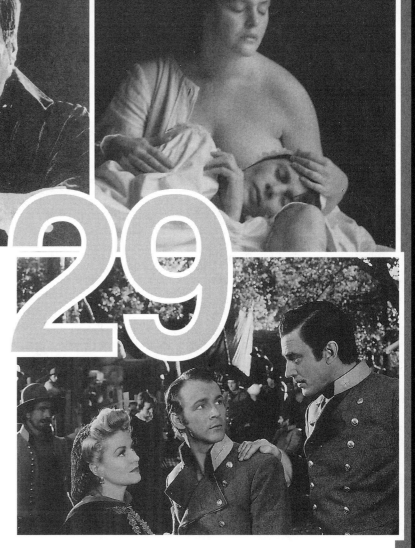

29

1924: Although he has already struck Metro-Goldwyn-Mayer gold (a creative association that will run, for six years and 18 films, till his death), **Lon Chaney** returns on this day to Universal—the scene of his *Hunchback of Notre Dame* triumph—for one last film, his best: *Phantom of the Opera*.

1939: As ludicrous as it may sound, **Roy Rogers** starts riding with **Walter Pidgeon**'s vigilantes (by any other name: Quantrill's raiders) on this day as filming commences on *The Dark Command*. In a rare, wild, ill-advised swing at acting, Rogers tried to stretch to "Fletch McCloud," hotheaded sibling to the heroine, **Claire Trevor**.

1952: On this day, **Attorney General James P. McGranery** announces he has revoked the reentry permit of British-born **Charles Chaplin**—on a world tour with his family at the time—and, to be readmitted to the U.S., the actor "must prove his worth" (read: pay several decades of back taxes). Instead, Chaplin and clan settled in Switzerland, and, when he did come back to America 20 years later, it was as a conquering hero, raking in awards on both coasts: one from The Film Society of Lincoln Center, the other an honorary Oscar.

1953: Via a bulletin by *her* studio (MGM) on this day—ten days shy of a second anniversary—**Frank Sinatra** learns his marriage to **Ava Gardner** is over. Deejays were dry-eyed ("And now, here's Ava Gardner's new release: Frank Sinatra.")

1956: Following the Royal Film Performance of *The Battle of the River Plate* (in the U.S.: *Pursuit of the Graf Spee*) on this day, **Queen Elizabeth II** meets an American commoner only 42 days her junior: **Marilyn Monroe**, playing hookey from the filming of *The Prince and the Showgirl* to partake of The Real Thing.

1957: MGM's founding father, **Louis B. Mayer**, dies of leukemia on this day at the age of 72. His funeral was SRO, prompting **Billy Wilder** to quip a classic epitaph: "It just goes to show, give the public what it wants and they'll show up." (**Red Skelton** supposedly reprised the same line four months later at the also-well-attended service for Columbia's much-disliked kingpin, **Harry Cohn**.)

1971: An intimate struggle with eminent death, waged by three sisters (**Harriet Andersson**, **Liv Ullmann**, **Ingrid Thulin**) and their maid (**Kari Sylwan**), comes to filming's end on this day as **Ingmar Bergman** wraps his first major work in years—*Cries and Whispers*—the only Bergman film to crack the language barrier and compete for the Best Picture Oscar. He was Oscar-nominated in three major categories (producer, director, screenwriter), and cameraman **Sven Nykvist** took the cinematography Oscar as he would for Bergman's last, *Fanny and Alexander*.

1929: *Variety* reports the stock-market crash on this day with a legendary headline stretched across Page One: "WALL STREET LAYS AN EGG."

1942: Through the image-shattering generosity of **Jack Benny**, movies gains a crackerjack comedian on this day as *George Washington Slept Here* hits New York's Strand: **Percy Kilbride**, who'd done the laconic caretaker in **Kaufman** and **Hart**'s play. When **Jack Warner** objected to screen-testing Kilbride, Benny footed the bills himself—but neither he nor **Ann Sheridan** ever got through the test without cracking up so Warner wound up hiring him untested anyway. The new recruit took so well to movies he never returned to the stage where he'd done some 800 roles from 1928 to 1942. A bachelor all 76 years, he was best-known as lackadaisical Pa Kettle, a part he created in 1947's *The Egg and I* and perpetuated seven more times on the screen in a series that got Universal out of hock.

1946: "It's wonderful to be associated with people who listen to my ideas," said **Hedy Lamarr**, turning producer with *The Strange Woman*—but *Variety*'s critic voices a contrary opinion on this day when he reviews the results: "Hedy bit off more than she can chew, so the chewing was done by the rest of the cast, and what was chewed was the scenery."

1947: "When I cry, do you want the tears to run all the way, or should I stop them halfway down?" **Margaret O'Brien** asked **Henry Koster**, her director for *The Unfinished Dance*, which bows on this day at New York's Capitol. "She's the only actress, besides **Ethel**, who's made me take out my handkerchief in 30 years," rhapsodized **Lionel Barrymore**. "If that child had been born in the Middle Ages, she'd have been burned as a witch."

1977: The two most famous **Bergman**s in cinema—**Ingrid** and **Ingmar**—conclude *Autumn Sonata*, their one and only collaboration, on this day. The actress never made another feature, but this one got her within nomination range of equalling **Katharine Hepburn**'s record of four Oscars. Ill with cancer, she rallied for one last great hurrah four years later—for TV: *A Woman Called Golda*, which paid off with a (posthumous) Emmy.

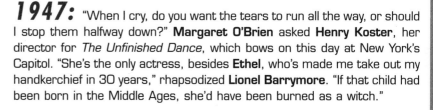

1997: Iconoclastic writer-producer-director **Samuel Fuller**, 85, who created a gallery of cult films out of no budget to speak of, dies on this day at his Hollywood Hills home. A darling with critics abroad and a late-blooming success here, Fuller turned director in 1948 by fulfilling the assignment of B-movie mogul **Robert L. Lippert** to do an assassination movie with a cowboy in it. Hence: *I Shot Jesse James*, done in 10 days for $118,000, with **John Ireland** as *I* (**Bob Ford**) and **Reed Hadley** as J.J.

31

1963: "Miss Doolittle, mum," says **Henry Daniell** on this day, introducing The Queen of Transylvania (**Baroness Rothschild**) to Eliza Doolittle (**Audrey Hepburn**) after a stately walk down a corridor lined with extras leading to *My Fair Lady*'s Embassy Ball. Before cameras could be set up for the next shot, Daniell, 69, died of a heart attack on the set. By ten the next morning **Alan Napier** was in Daniell's gray beard finishing the performance. **George Cukor** opted not to reshoot the scene—more for sentiment than expense. Daniell was, after **Katharine Hepburn**, the director's second-most used actor—a kind of lucky charm—and, although their last encounter was brief and tragic—it brought Cukor the Oscar that had too-long eluded him.

1968: The *Ben-Hur* who preferred hims—**Ramon Novarro**, 69—is murdered on this day by two Chicago hustlers he lets into his $125,000 Hollywood Hills home. **Paul Ferguson**, 23, and his 17-year-old brother, **Tom**, were acting on rumors that Novarro had $5,000 stashed on the premises. All they could find was $45, so they savagely bludgeoned the actor, who strangled on his own blood. Promptly arrested, the brothers were convicted of the murder and sentenced to life—but were paroled seven years later.

1988: Producer (*The Bad and the Beautiful*) and late-blooming actor (*The Paper Chase*) **John Houseman**, 86, lives long enough to mark the 50th anniversary of Mercury Theater of the Air's historic Halloween Eve broadcast of *The War of the Worlds* — the nationwide fright he and **Orson Welles** produced — then a day later, on this day, dies of spinal cancer at his Malibu home.

1993: On this day—the day after his 50th wedding anniversary — **Federico Fellini** dies at age 73. Director of four Oscar-winning Best Foreign Language Films, he became the third person in a row connected with the Lifetime Achievement Oscar to die within the year. **Satyajit Ray**, the Fellini of India, survived a month after receiving his from **Audrey Hepburn**, who passed away herself the following January and got a posthumous Jean Hersholt Humanitarian Award in March the night Fellini was cited; **Giulietta Masina**, Fellini's widow, succumbed to cancer before another Lifetime Achievement Oscar could awarded.

DEATHS THE DAY AFTER A 50TH ANNIVERSARY: From left: John Houseman; Federico Fellini (with Giulietta Massina). **DEATHS DURING FILMING:** From left: River Phoenix, and Henry Daniell.

1993: Outside **Johnny Depp**'s Viper Room nightclub **River Phoenix** collapses and dies (from speedballing cocaine and heroin) while brother **Leaf** phones 911 and sister **Rainbow** attempts mouth-to-mouth resuscitation. The film the 23-year-old actor was a month away from finishing, *Dark Blood,* with **Judy Davis** and **Jonathan Pryce**, was junked, and his upcoming role of the reporter conducting the *Interview With the Vampire* went to **Christian Slater**, who did it for free, donating his $250,000 salary to Phoenix's favorite eco-charities.

TWO SWAN SONGS: Producer Frank Taylor, Montgomery Cliff, Eli Wallach, writer Arthur Miller, Marilyn Monroe, director John Huston and Clark Gable working on *The Misfits*.

1934: *We Live Again* bows at Radio City Music Hall on this day, and **Anna Sten** dies again at the box office—despite the desperate ad: "The directorial skill of **Mamoulian**, the radiance of Anna Sten and the genius of **Goldwyn** have united to make the world's greatest entertainment." Producer Goldwyn scrutinized the copy that had produced no customers and declared admiringly: "That's what I like: Facts. No exaggeration."

1934: Production begins on *Clive of India* on this day, *without* **Ronald Colman**'s trademark matinee-idol mustache. The only other film in which he was seen without it was the one which he made after this one: *A Tale of Two Cities*.

1946: *A Matter of Life and Death* unreels as Britain's first Royal Command Performance on this day at the Empire Theater in Leicester Square. The **David Niven-Raymond Massey** fantasy was rechristened *Stairway to Heaven* for these shores. Apparently, sniffed co-director **Michael Powell**, "it was only the United States that had to be protected from the realities of life and death." Interestingly, Niven and Massey both died on July 29, 1983.

1948: *Scott of the Antarctic*, starring **John Mills** as the British explorer, rates a Royal Command Film Performance on this day in London. The then-princess, then-pregnant **Elizabeth** didn't attend, but her mother, sister and husband did, and the "supporting" starlight included **Laurence Olivier, Virginia Mayo, Alan Ladd, Vivien Leigh, Ronald Reagan, Patricia Neal** and **Michael O'Shea**. Depleted by the demands of Olivier's stage *Antigone*, Leigh nodded off—and, worse, her breast slipped out of her dress. Ladd and O'Shea spent most of the screening debating who'd tell her or, indeed, if either should. (They let the matter droop.)

1968: To stave off censorship and stay self-regulating, The Motion Picture Association of America starts serving alphabet soup on this day, classifying films according to their recommended audience—be it "G," "M," "R" or "X."

1986: *The Wails of August* (as **Vincent Price** tagged it) starts subsiding on this day as *The Whales of August* finishes filming. Not a happy shoot, this—due to **Bette Davis**' chronic crankiness over the TLC accorded co-star **Lillian Gish**. When director **Lindsay Anderson** complimented Gish on "a lovely closeup," Davis was heard crabbing, "She *ought* to know about closeups. Jesus, she was around when they *invented* them!" Indeed, Gish was. For this swan song performance, *The Guinness Book of Movie Facts & Feats* calls Gish "the oldest actress to have played a major role in a movie." The movie bowed in New York on Gish's 93rd birthday, which could explain Davis' absence. Davis skipped the L.A. launch because she learned the gala sponsors, Women in Film, were giving her its newly established Lillian Gish award.

2

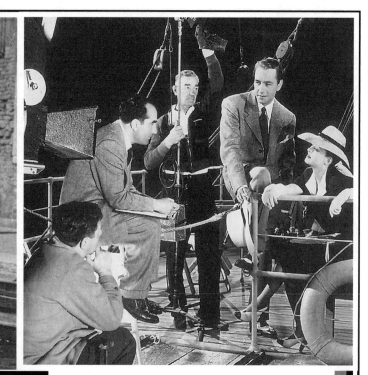

A SPLASH THAT LASTS: Gaitano Audiero and Katharine Hepburn in *Summertime*. *NOW* [AGAIN], *VOYAGER*: Cinematographer Sol Polito, director Irving Rapper, a prop-man, Paul Henreid and Bette Davis making *Now, Voyager*. PASOLINI ENDS WHERE HE BEGAN: Franco Citti and Franca Pasut in *Accattone!*

1954: *Look* magazine on this day devotes seven pictures to the classic sight of **Katharine Hepburn** toppling backward into Venice's Grand Canal. *Summertime* was the movie in which the audience fell in love with Venice as Hepburn fell head over heels for **Rossano Brazzi**—and into the Grand Canal (which was scenic—but a sewer). Hepburn took the fall herself. Although she was covered with lotions and disinfectants, her eyes became instantly inflamed. "When I got out," she said, "my eyes were running. They've been running ever since. I have the most ghastly infection—I'll never lose it till the day I die. When people ask me why I cry such a lot in pictures, I say, mysteriously, 'Canal in Venice.'"

1975: "In the end he was the victim of his own characters—a perfect tragedy foreseen in its own aspects—without knowing that one day it would end up overcoming him," remarked **Michelangelo Antonioni** on learning of the murder of fellow Italian filmmaker **Pier Paolo Pasolini**. The 53-year-old novelist-essayist-poet and late-blooming movie director dies on this day on a deserted field outside Rome—his thorax crushed by the wheels of his own Alfa Romeo sportscar as it is being stolen by a 17-year-old homosexual prostitute. **Giuseppe Pelusi** pleaded self-defense, but many believed the crime was politically motivated. The setting and circumstances of Pasolini's violent death oddly echoed those in *Una Vita Violenta* (*A Violent Life*), his 1959 novel which he translated into his first film, 1961's *Accattone!*

1989: "Fasten your seat belts — it's going to be a bumpy eternity," eulogizes **James Woods** on this day at a memorial for **Bette Davis** held at Burbank Studios on Warners' Soundstage 18 where 47 years before she had sailed forth "to seek and find" in *Now, Voyager*. Attending: **Kim Carnes**, **Julius J. Epstein**, **Glenn Ford**, **Angela Lansbury**, **Clint Eastwood**, **David Hartman**, **Ann-Margret**, **Roddy McDowall**, **Linda Gray**, **Vincent Price** and **Robert Wagner**. "It was no accident," observed columnist **Robert Osborne**, "that [Bette] chose as her final resting place a plot of Forest Lawn that overlooks the Burbank Studios and all those soundstages where she churned out the good work for 18 years."

1993: On this day, **Federico Fellini** makes his final trip to Cinecitta's cavernous Studio No. 5 where he made his films and his name, lying in state against the sky-blue backdrop he used in 1987's *Intervista* while thousands of Romans file by his coffin to pay respects. "What he gave Italy," said *The New York Times*, "was the sum of their dreams and fantasies and sins, encased in an artistry that helped define the nation's self-image, at home and abroad."

1931: A brash, breezy actor-comedian with a bright future in films (after only four of them his first year out)—**Robert Williams**, 31—dies on this day following operations for appendicitis and peritonitis. He never saw his last—*Platinum Blonde*, in which he was torn between **Loretta Young** and **Jean Harlow**—but its director, **Frank Capra**, believed he would have been "a great star."

1953: On this day, the premiere installment of *Playboy* magazine hits the stands, and the flash-of-flesh featured inside—**Marilyn Monroe**'s famous nude-calendar pose—hits the fan. Publisher **Hugh Hefner** was so doubtful there'd be Issue Two that he didn't give the first one off the presses an issue date.

1970: "Do you think with all the natural stuff we're doing that maybe no one will know it's a movie?" asks **Shirley MacLaine** on this day of the screenwriter and first-time director of her *Desperate Characters*, **Frank D. Gilroy**. Said he: "Now that you've dumped that load on me, you should feel untroubled and be able to devote complete attention to your work." It got laughs from all hands.

1971: *Play Misty for Me*, bowing at the New York nabes on this day, earns **Clint Eastwood** his directing spurs. Not a few critics confessed he had a certain . . . flair for violent action. "All you need to get into the Director's Guild is for someone to give you a job," said Eastwood after the fact, "so I gave myself a job. I said, 'Kid, you got the job.'" Twenty-one years and 16 directorial efforts later, he knocked off two Oscars in a single shot, producing as well as directing the Best Picture of 1992: *Unforgiven*.

1993: On this day, **Duncan Gibbins**, a 41-year-old British director-screenwriter in Hollywood, dies from burns sustained in a Malibu wildfire trying to rescue a stray cat near the guest house he rented. His three screen credits ranged from the 1986 feature, *Fire With Fire*, to HBO's 1989 movie, *Third Degree Burn*.

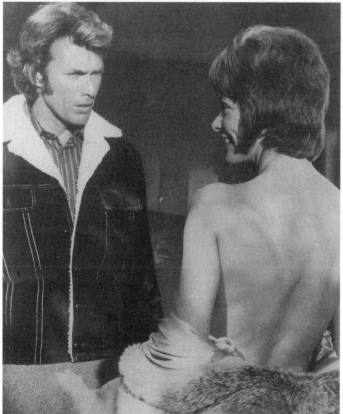

FEMMES, FORWARD & FATALE: From top: Jean Harlow and Robert Williams in *Platinum Blonde*; Clint Eastwood and Jessica Walter in *Play Misty for Me*.

THEIR LAST SCENE: Monroe and Gable in *The Misfits*.
HER HOLLYWOOD "TEST": Marlene Dietrich (with Rosa Valetti) in *The Blue Angel*.
HER LAST ROLE: Margaret Lockwood in *The Slipper and the Rose*.

4

1929: One of the screen's great director-star collaborations begins bilingually on this day as *Der blaue Engel* (*The Blue Angel*) goes before the cameras at UFA's Neubabelsberg Studios—in both English and German. Ostensibly the cautionary tale of how lust leveled the life of a milquetoast school-teacher (**Emil Jannings**), it became instead—under the calculating steerage of **Josef von Sternberg**—a deification of the hussy who took him to the cleaners. The resulting footage won **Marlene Dietrich** a contract with Paramount and a place in the Hollywood sun.

1938: After two weeks of ineffectual filming on *The Wizard of Oz* by **Richard Thorpe**, director **Victor Fleming** takes it from the top again on this day—and he, too, stumbles down The Yellow Brick Road: His first shot called for Dorothy and Toto to come upon The Scarecrow, who has a raven on his shoulder. The latter was played by "Jim" (billed as "the world's only trained raven"), but—on the first take, despite his billing—the bird soared to the rafters of Stage 26 and roosted there till he was retrieved in the early a.m.

1958: Producer **Sam Zimbalist**, 54, suffers a fatal heart attack on location in Rome on this day, trying to top his *Quo Vadis* with *Ben-Hur*. For the record, he succeeded—*in spades*: The spectacle raced off with a chariot-load of Oscars (11 out of 12 nominations—a record unmatched until 1997's *Titanic*).

1960: On this day, **Marilyn Monroe** and **Clark Gable** ride off into the sunset in a station wagon for what's not only the last scene in *The Misfits* but also the last scene of both their careers. "How do you find your way back in the dark?" she asks, snuggling up beside him. "Just head for that big star straight on," he tells her. "The highway's under it. It'll take us right home." It was the only scene in the picture director **John Huston** got on the first take.

1976: *The Slipper and the Rose*, a Cinderella musical by the **Sherman** brothers (**Robert B.** and **Richard M.**), makes a glittery entrance at Radio City Music Hall on this day—and, with it, two grand ladies of English cinema (**Edith Evans** and **Margaret Lockwood**) make graceful exits from the screen, providing refined cameo support to **Richard Chamberlain**'s Prince Charming and **Gemma Craven**'s Cinderella.

1980: On this Election Day, **Ronald Reagan** learns *Where's the Rest of Me?*—the title of his 1965 autobiography and his most famous movie line (uttered in *Kings Row* on realizing sadistic Dr. **Charles Coburn** has removed his legs): He is the first (and only) actor—and divorced person—to be elected President. At age 69, he was also the oldest President—and he went the whole two terms.

1930: In his real-life role of Academy founder-emcee, **Conrad Nagel** presents the Oscar to **Norma Shearer** for *The Divorcee* on this day. (Ironically, he was the only suitor she spurned in that film.)

1947: The first film resulting from an annual $200,000 Novel Award initiated by MGM to secure screen rights before publication—**Elizabeth Goudge**'s *Green Dolphin Street*—goes into national release on this day. (The only other Novel Award winner filmed was *Raintree County*.) Goudge certainly gave the studio its money's worth: exotic locales (the Channel Islands and New Zealand in the 1840s), a Maori uprising, a clipper-ship wreck (shot but shelved for plot brevity), an Oscar-winning earthquake—all set in **Rube Goldberg** motion by "a mere slip of the pen": A drunken sailor (**Richard Hart**) proposes marriage by mail to his beloved Marguerite (**Donna Reed**) but writes the name of her sister, Marianne (**Lana Turner**). Had censors allowed a *menage a trois*, all that could have been avoided because the sisters slept on plainly marked pillowcases.

1955: "What's the fuss?" shrugs **Don "Red" Barry** over the star-versus-starlet donnybrook reported in the papers on this day. "I just happened to invite both girls to drop in for coffee some time." When **Jil** (*The Twinkle in God's Eye*) **Jarmyn** took him up on it at 11 a.m. the day before, she found a pajama-clad **Susan Hayward**. Fists and epiteths were flung, followed by rattling rounds with lawyers. ("That Red Barry must make *some* cup of coffee!" cracked **Marlene Dietrich** on the sidelines.) Barry of B-grade Western fame met Hayward doing a bit in *I'll Cry Tomorrow*—an A.A. worker who—yes, offers her coffee. Because that line drew laughs at previews, it was cut.

1960: Heart attacks claim two Tinseltown fixtures on this day: slapstick pioneer **Mack Sennett**, 80, and sagebrush reliable **Ward Bond**, 55. *Chicago Tribune* critic **Michael Wilmington** noted that Bond appeared seven times on the American Film Institute's list of the 100 Greatest American Movies, more than any other actor (*It Happened One Night*, *Bringing Up Baby*, *Gone With the Wind*, *The Grapes of Wrath*, *The Maltese Falcon*, *It's a Wonderful Life* and *The Searchers*).

1972: The only actor to play Sherlock Holmes (1933's *A Study in Scarlet*) AND Dr. Watson (1932's *Sherlock Holmes*) in feature films dies on this day: **Reginald Owen**, 85, a Brit in Hollywood from 1929 to 1968 (*A Christmas Carol*, *Mrs. Miniver*, *Random Harvest*, *Pride and Prejudice*, et al). In other mediums, another Brit took on both roles: **Jeremy Brett** was Watson to **Charlton Heston**'s Holmes in an L.A. stage production of *The Crucifer of Blood* before taking up the deerstalker himself to play Holmes more than 40 times in TV's *Mystery!* series.

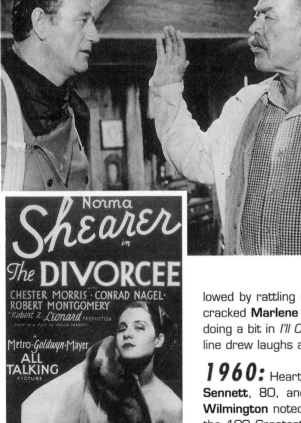

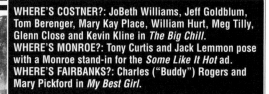

1927: United Artists unleashes a shocking sight at New York's Rialto: the first screen kiss of "Little **Mary**" Pickford, 35-playing-18, in her final silent, *My Best Girl*. **Charles ("Buddy") Rogers** came down out of the clouds of *Wings* to do the honors. Hand-picked by Pickford, 11 years her junior and plainly smitten with her, he'd become a decade later her third and last husband. Her *second*—**Douglas Fairbanks**—"just dropped by" the set the day the kiss was shot, then scurried away in a funk. "It's more than jealousy," he later said. "I suddenly felt afraid." No atonement was required, but Pickford contributed a becalming cameo to *The Gaucho*, appearing to Fairbanks as a vision of the Virgin Mary. Save for unbilled bits, it was the first time they acted together. Ahead: their talkie *Taming of the Shrew*, then divorce.

1958: *Some Like It Hot* wraps, $500,000 over budget and many weeks behind schedule because of the no-shows of **Marilyn Monroe**. "I'm the only director who ever made two pictures with Monroe," sighed **Billy Wilder** (inaccurately). "It behooves the Screen Directors Guild to award me a Purple Heart." Does that mean he'd never do another picture with her? "I have discussed this project with my doctor and my psychiatrist," responded Wilder, "and they tell me I'm too old and too rich to go through this again."

1960: An ambulance rushes **Clark Gable**, 59, to Hollywood Presbyterian Hospital suffering from a coronary thrombosis—his second tension-free day after wrapping *The Misfits* with the chronically tardy **Marilyn Monroe**. It was also the 25th birthday of **Judy Lewis Tinney**, the daughter he and **Loretta Young** had out of wedlock and the one he met only once. Ten days later, on Nov. 16, The King died of a second heart attack; ironically, this was the first birthday of **Maria Tinney**, the granddaughter he never knew he had. Both daughter and granddaughter have Gable's trademark—big ears—as do his great-grandsons, **Michael** and **Gregory Dagit**. All his life Gable wanted a male heir; his widow, **Kay**, gave him one—posthumously—March 20, 1961: **John Clark Gable**.

1998: "One of the funkier ironies of recent Hollywood history is that the actor most often mentioned in connection with **Lawrence Kasdan**'s 1983 hit, *The Big Chill*, never showed his face," *Newsday* critic **Jack Mathews** notes on the occasion of the film's 15th anniversary re-issue. "**Kevin Costner** played the corpse being dressed for his funeral in the opening scene." (For the record, Kasdan decided against a flashback scene that did feature Costner.)

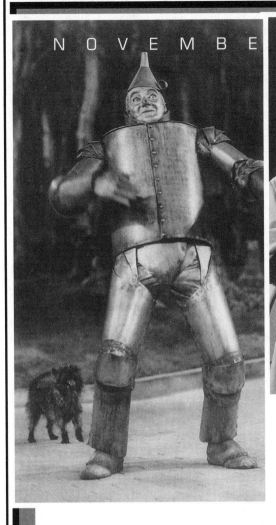

1938: On this day, **Jack Haley** is officially off to see The Wizard of Oz, hitting the yellow bricks late when **Buddy Ebsen** is suddenly sidelined by an allergic reaction to the aluminum powder in his Tin Woodman makeup—a fine how-do-you-do for being a good sport and swapping his Scarecrow role for **Ray Bolger**'s tin type (after much nudging by Bolger). Ebsen's star didn't rise again for 17 years—when **Walt Disney** got him to sidekick with **Fess Parker**'s *Davy Crockett* on TV.

1956: Crossing paths at Pinewood on this day, **Laurence Olivier** and **Katharine Hepburn** pipedream about doing a picture together—they did, nearly 20 years later, and got Emmys for it (*Love Among the Ruins*, a TV movie directed by **George Cukor**)—but, for the unhappy present, both are sinking in their own oil-and-water juices: If a couple was more mismatched than Olivier with **Marilyn Monroe** in *The Prince and the Showgirl*, it was the couple-next-soundstage in *The Iron Petticoat*: Hepburn and **Bob Hope**!

1974: "You don't have to be **W.C. Fields** to want to swat it," decreed *The New York Times*' **Vincent Canby** of *The Little Prince*, bowing on this day at Radio City Music Hall. The first musical since 1958 for both director **Stanley Donen** and tunesmiths **Alan Jay Lerner** and **Frederick Loewe**, it marked the last L&L score and the last on-screen dancing of **Bob Fosse**, slithering through the Sahara as a sssssnake. When *Prince* was released, Fosse was hospitalized for nearly working himself into a heart attack editing *Lenny* and prepping Broadway's *Chicago*, and, during a Donen visit, Fosse suggested turning on the TV to catch **Pat Collins**' *Prince* review. It was a devastating notice, which, like clockwork, pushed Fosse into a coronary. Later, when he was filming his quasi-autobiographical *All That Jazz*, Fosse recreated this incident, with **Chris Chase** playing the coronary-causing critic.

1980: Fast-track **Steve McQueen**, 50, comes to the end of the line on this day, suffering from mesothelioma (a rare form of lung cancer, unresponsive to chemotherapy and radiotherapy, often caused by exposure to asbestos). In a desperate bid for life, McQueen checked into a controversial Juarez clinic run by a Texas dentist with no medical degree and subjected himself to a rigorous regimen of coffee enemas, animal-cell injections, Laetrile and hundreds of pills a day. He improved—then doctors discovered a huge tumor in his right lung and, in a three-and-a-half hour operation, removed it—but the ordeal put so much pressure on his heart he suffered a fatal heart attack.

1951: MGM requires NYC's Astor *and* Capitol on this day to launch the fourth film version of **Henryk Sienkiewicz'** *Quo Vadis*—this, directed by **Mervyn LeRoy** and starring **Robert Taylor** and **Deborah Kerr**. Two years earlier **Gregory Peck, Elizabeth Taylor** and director **John Huston** dove into all this S.P.Q.R. spectacle and drowned. Only the Nero of **Peter Ustinov** s u r v i v e d — a n d , between filmings, that was almost recast with **Robert Morley** because the studio thought Ustinov too young. "If you wait much longer, I shall be too old. Nero died at 31," Ustinov quickly wired California. MGM replied: "Historical research has proved you correct. The part is yours." Not only did Ustinov play the part, he played to an Oscar-nominated hilt.

1956: Poolside at the Beverly Hills Hotel on this day, **Norma Shearer** spots a stranger who reminds her of her late husband and invites him to play **Irving Thalberg** in the **Lon Chaney** biography **James Cagney** is doing at Universal, *Man of a Thousand Faces*. The studio wanted one of its contractees (**John Saxon** or **John Gavin**) for the part, but Shearer had casting approval—so **Robert Evans** left the women's clothing business for show business. She then wanted him to do Monroe Stahr—the thinly veiled Thalberg in **F. Scott Fitzgerald**'s *The Last Tycoon*, under **George Cukor**'s direction—but, after his bullfighter bit in *The Sun Also Rises* with **Tyrone Power** (Shearer's first Stahr choice), her enthusiasm cooled. **Elia Kazan** eventually (1976) did that film with a more unlikely **Robert** Stahrred: **De Niro**. Possibly what Shearer saw in Evans was his filmmaking acumen: He produced *The Godfather*, *Love Story*, *The Great Gatsby*, et al. "Later, when I became head of production at Paramount," said Evans, "it made Norma seem almost psychic. If the Academy ever presents me with the Thalberg award, life will imitate art all the way."

1965: Following a *To Tell the Truth* telecast on this day, CBS's **Douglas Edwards** reports: "**Dorothy Kilgallen**, just seen on the preceding prerecorded program, was found dead in her home today." The next day, The Great Eastern Seaboard Blackout occurred, and a booze-blurred **Joan Crawford** (who'd taped that TV game-show with Kilgallen six days earlier) was heard to sob at the blackened Manhattan skyline: "What a wonderful tribute to Dorothy!" On that blackout's fourth anniversary, Crawford starred in the NBC movie pilot for **Rod Serling**'s *Night Gallery*, playing a blind heiress whose sight is restored the night of that blackout. Making his directing bow six weeks shy of his 21st birthday was **Steven Spielberg**!

1998: The Beast in **Jean Cocteau**'s *Beauty and the Beast* and the man in his life for most of his life—**Jean Marais**, 84—dies of pulmonary disease on this day.

9

1942: A crone of a character comedienne well-placed in period-piece pictures like *Little Women*, *Drums Along the Mohawk*, *David Copperfield* and *Cimarron*, **Edna May Oliver** dies of an intestinal disorder on this day, her 59th birthday.

1950: *Devil's Doorway*, opening at New York's Capitol on this day, seconds the sympathetic pro-Indian stance *Broken Arrow* took four months before—and marked the first Mann-of-the-West vision: Director **Anthony Mann**'s debut Western called for a second, this with Taylor's then-wife, **Barbara Stanwyck**—*The Furies*. Mann's way with the West impressed *Broken Arrow*'s **James Stewart**, who waved him over to Universal to take *Winchester '73* away from **Fritz Lang**. *That* success led to seven other Mann-Stewart collaborations, mostly Westerns (*Bend of the River*, *The Naked Spur*, *The Far Country*, *The Man From Laramie*) but not always (*Thunder Bay*, *The Glenn Miller Story*, *Strategic Air Command*).

1955: Columnist **Cal York** reported on this day—**Rock Hudson**'s wedding day—"even his mother" was surprised by the sudden turn of events. The marriage—to his agent's secretary, **Phyllis Gates**—held together less than two years.

1984: Director **Wes Craven** on this day cranks up Freddie Krueger (**Robert Englund**, flambé into a frightful sight) and points him toward theaters playing *A Nightmare on Elm Street*. More *Nightmare*s follow, hiking the box office and body count.

1989: At 11:17 p.m. on this day, as the heavily guarded borders separating East and West Germany come toppling down, the whole *raison d'etre* of a Cold War spy thriller on location there with **Gene Hackman** and **Mikhail Baryshnikov**

abruptly evaporates. As celebrants danced on the Berlin Wall and chipped away at its hated concrete barrier—for 28 years, the grim symbol of a divided Europe—writer-director **Nicholas Meyer** toiled desperately over his instantly dated plot. "At that point, the movie was called *Dinosaurs*," recalled co-star **Howard McGillin**. "It was supposed to be a movie about two relics from the past—from a Cold War which was no more because of *glasnost*. No one anticipated the wall falling. Suddenly, the dramatic tension of a spy film was rendered obsolete. Nick tried to take all that into account, but he couldn't because it was changing daily. Checkpoint Charlie was carted away on a flatbed truck three days after we shot there. In fact, they had to arrange the shooting schedule to get Checkpoint Charlie in before they hauled it away." Paramount wanted to pull the plug on the movie immediately and *did* abandon it, throwing it to MGM to distribute. The murky mishmash that resulted—titled first *Russian Roulette*, then *Company Business*—limped lamely to market, mortally wounded, and died there, unnoted.

1938: On this day, **Fred Astaire** and **Ginger Rogers** go into their last dance for a decade—their last ever at RKO—as they start spinning *The Story of Vernon and Irene Castle*. The results hit Radio City Music Hall's screen in March, and Astaire attended—for a while. A notorious perfectionist, he jumped out of his seat during one dance number and ran to the nearest phone. "Get someone out here right away," he told the studio. "The film is five frames out of sync!"

1939: *The Roaring Twenties* comes roaring into NYC's Strand on this day. A gat-blasting battle of bootleggers, it ended poignantly, with **James Cagney** expiring from his third (and last) gun-battle with **Bogart** in the arms of a heart-of-gold hussy (**Gladys George**, who replaced **Ann Sheridan**, who replaced **Lee Patrick**, who replaced **Glenda Farrell**). What they let George do was to eulogize him with the film's eloquent last line: "He used to be a big shot."

1941: *Time*'s cover girl on this day, identified as **Fred Astaire**'s "best" dance partner, is the once-and-future *Cover Girl*, **Rita Hayworth**—not, as you might imagine, the one who has completed nine film dances with him: **Ginger Rogers**. "Best" wasn't the best word, but Hayworth was one of the few Astaire invited back for a second screen twirl—*You Were Never Lovelier* after *You'll Never Get Rich*; in between those two musicals, she and Rogers came as close to co-starring as they ever did (doing neighboring episodes in the multi-storied *Tales of Manhattan*). In real life, the two were second cousins by marriage.

1958: *A Hole in the Head*—and director **Frank Capra**'s feature comeback after eight years on the bench—gets rolling on this day, starring (as brothers) a pair of actors born on Dec. 12: 1893's **Edward G. Robinson** and 1915's **Frank Sinatra**. The result wasn't up to the movie's song, "High Hopes."

1928: "The most beautiful woman in Hollywood" (in the well-considered opinion of **Florenz Ziegfeld**) hits the screen at NYC's Colony in *The Good-Bye Kiss* on this day. **Sally Eilers** was spotted by **Mack Sennett** at the studio commissary with drama-school classmate **Carole Lombard**. After a few bits and comedy shorts, she went straight to the star-spot of *The Good-Bye Kiss*. Hello Sally!

1941: A gift from **Greer Garson** greets her director on this day when he reaches the set to begin filming *Mrs. Miniver*: a pair of black velvet gloves. The accompanying note said, "For the iron hand of **William Wyler**." The film won them both Oscars and nabbed 1942's Best Picture prize as well, but Wyler quickly found its sunlit flag-waving embarrassing when he entered real combat and never truly felt redeemed until his second Oscar-winning Best Picture: 1946's *The Best Years of Our Lives*.

1942: Miffed his campaign for the *Casablanca* lead came to naught (even with **Jack L. Warner** going to bat for him!), **George Raft** buys up his contract and exits Warners for good on this day. The Bros., frankly, bore up rather well.

1942: "Like Webster's Dictionary," **Bing Crosby**, **Bob Hope** and **Dorothy Lamour** are Moroccan bound on this day as their *Road to Morocco* pulls into New York's Paramount slightly ahead of schedule (hitching a free ride on the publicity generated by the Allied invasion of North Africa four days before). This third of their seven *Road*shows remains the pick of the litter.

1948: Columbia commences a second chorus of **Al Jolson**'s life story on this day. Although the real Jolson auditioned twice for the part, it still went to **Larry Parks**—resuming in *Jolson Sings Again* the title role he'd begun in *The Jolson Story*—but the original gave the imitation a run for the money on the soundtrack: "He sang every song as if he were going to drop dead at the end of it," said Parks, who had to keep up visually what Jolson did vocally. The sequel did so well there was talk of a *third* installment—tentatively titled *GI Jolson*—but that stopped abruptly when Jolson, 64, died of a heart attack Oct. 23, 1950—one day short of five years when cameras started turning on the first biopic that returned him to prominence.

1964: "Er, how come they call this place a tea house, dear?"—inquiring bodies want to know. **Raquel Welch** uttered that—her first line on screen—entering an espresso bar early on in *Roustabout*, which goes into national release on this day. This was the flick in which **Elvis Presley** almost met **Mae West**, but West went thataway and **Barbara Stanwyck** (in her next-to-the-last feature) stepped in.

1935: Because **Fredric March** picks *Anthony Adverse* over *The Prisoner of Shark Island*, producer **Darryl F. Zanuck** and director **John Ford** face production on this day with **Warner Baxter** in the title role of the man whose "name is Mudd" (**Dr. Samuel A. Mudd**, who was imprisoned for medically attending **Lincoln**'s assassin, **John Wilkes Booth**). Baxter's hokey Southern accent had Zanuck and Ford going round after round.

1939: On this day, filming begins on *My Little Chickadee*, a spoofy shoot-'em-up scripted and performed by that improbable pair, **Mae West** and **W.C. Fields**. The title was a phrase **Joseph L. Mankiewicz** invented for a routine he wrote for Fields and **Alison Skipworth** in 1932's *If I Had a Million*.

1951: Although **Audrey Hepburn**'s screen test has been received with hosannas in Hollywood—and will be enough to win her *Roman Holiday*—director **William Wyler** orders Paramount in London on this day to have a backup test done of **Suzanne Cloutier**, directed by the same man (**Thorold Dickinson**) in the same manner (to keep the cameras rolling after the scene is finished to check the actress' spontaneity and natural deportment). Cloutier, of course, didn't get the brass ring (although she did get a wedding ring from **Peter Ustinov**). Fame came and went for her in 1955—as **Kenneth More**'s fiancee in *Doctor in the House* and as Desdemona to **Orson Welles**' *Othello*.

1986: Colorized *film noir*, indeed! Turner Broadcasting System airs that odd contradiction in terms—a colorcast of 1941's *The Maltese Falcon*—on this day. The next day director **John Huston**, 80 years old and ill with emphysema, held a press conference to gasp out his eloquent objections to his film's "new look."

1995: *The Evening Star* starts shining in Houston on this day, as production begins on the sequel to *Terms of Endearment*. **Shirley MacLaine**, reprising her Oscar-winning portrayal of Aurora Greenway, carried the character deeper into grandmotherhood and eventually to the grave. The also-Oscared **Jack Nicholson** bopped by for a cameo, but, otherwise, residing next door was a different Oscar winner—**Ben Johnson**, in his last film outing (the 75-year-old actor suffered a fatal heart attack five months later, on April 8, visiting his mother in Mesa, AZ.

13

1940: A casual conversation between animator **Walt Disney** and conductor **Leopold Stokowski** creates the best of both of their worlds on this day: *Fantasia*, world-premiering at New York's Broadway Theater. Their original discussion concerned casting Mickey Mouse as "The Sorcerer's Apprentice" in a 1938 short—an idea Stokowski embraced so enthusiastically he promised to conduct the score himself if Disney would carry that concept to feature length. Neither instigator lived to see their shared dream soar to box-office heights, but it *did* happen—in the 1970s, when the film was viewed as a psychedelic experience—and an adjunct to pot-smoking.

1945: On this day, **William Boyd** buys the rights to the role with which he has become synonymous—a career move that made him a mint when Hopalong Cassidy hit TV land. Actor and character fused with the first Hopalong feature in 1935—only the two weren't in sync at the starting gate: Boyd had the part of Buck Peters, the clean-living Bar 20 ranch foreman, and comedian **James Gleason** was cast as Cassidy (who, in the books of **Clarence E. Mulford**, was a hell-raising, hard-drinking, ill-kempt galoot). Reinventing himself *and* the character, Boyd talked producer **Harry "Pop" Sherman** into implanting Peters' sanitized qualities in Hoppy. In this radically revised disguise, Boyd's Cassidy embarked on the longest series of features ever made—66 features in all (41 at Paramount, 25 at United Artists)—plus a 52-episode run on TV. Nearing 40 and barely able to sit a horse in '35, Boyd let stuntman **Cliff Lyons** do the riding till he became a flashy horseman himself. **Cecil B. DeMille**, who gave Boyd his first movie job (a bit in 1919's *Why Change Your Wife?*), gave him his last (a Hopalong "ride-on" in 1952's *The Greatest Show on Earth*).

1957: *Kind Sir*, the flop romanticomedy that engaged **Charles Boyer** and **Mary Martin** briefly on Broadway in 1953, is rechristened *Indiscreet* on this day—five days before **Cary Grant** and **Ingrid Bergman** begin filming it at Elstree Studios. Other handles fondled and discarded: *They're Not Married*, *Irresistible*, *Better Than Married*, *As Good As Married* and *Mister and Mistress*.

1970: Sweden's **Ingmar Bergman** puts the finishing touches to *The Touch*, his first English-speaking film, on this day. In an attempt to broaden his box office, he employed his first American movie star. **Dustin Hoffman** passed, but **Elliott Gould** pounced, at the chance to play the man disrupting the marriage of **Bibi Andersson** and **Max von Sydow** (Bergman regulars, both). Given that miscasting, the title could be pronounced *The Tetched*.

1996: On this day, **Daniel Day-Lewis** takes a bride, **Rebecca Miller**, daughter of the **Arthur** who had sent him to the gallows (via *The Crucible*).

CASSIDY, SCRUBBED UP & SQUEAKY-CLEAN: William Boyd as Hopalong.
GRANT TAKES BERGMAN: Cary and Ingrid in *Indiscret*.
BERGMAN TAKES GOULD: Elliot and Ingmar working on *The Touch* with Bibi Andersson.

HENIE HITS THE ICE: Sonia Henie in *One in a Million*.
THEY DID: Lew Ayres and Ginger Rogers in *Don't Bet on Love*.
"MAD AS HELL": Peter Finch in *Network*.

1934: Ignoring the title of the movie that brought them together (*Don't Bet on Love*), **Ginger Rogers** on this day weds the favorite of her five husbands: **Lew Ayres**. In 1936 they separated and, five years later, divorced. Their lingering estrangement was one reason she passed on playing his (and **Katharine Hepburn**'s) sister in 1938's *Holiday*.

1936: The gold-medal figure-skating champ at the 1928, 1932 and 1936 Olympics—**Sonia Henie**—goes for the Oscar gold (missing it by a country mile) via *One in a Million*, her debut film which finishes principal photography on this day. There were retakes, of course—mostly to overcome her thick Norwegian accent. "I caution you against giving Sonia Henie too many lines," **Darryl F. Zanuck** warned the writers of her next vehicle, *Thin Ice* (a better, and more critically accurate, handle than its original title, *Her Majesty's Car*). "You should work it like we did in *One in a Million*, where we get the impression that she is carrying the whole thing, whereas if you analyze it, you will see that everything is happening around her, and only occasionally does she speak a line. And, when she does, it is always a very effective one."

1976: *Network*, a savage satire of television from director **Sidney Lumet**, bows on this day at New York's Sutton Theater. **Paddy Chayefsky**'s Oscar-winning screenplay provoked three Oscar-winning performances: from **Peter Finch**, **Faye Dunaway** and Lumet's ex-cousin-in-law, **Beatrice Straight**. The only other film to win three (of the four) Oscars for acting is *A Streetcar Named Desire* 25 years earlier.

1991: AIDS claims **Tony Richardson**, 63, on this day. The British director came to cinema by repeating a couple of stage successes he'd had with **John Osborne** plays (1959's *Look Back in Anger* and 1960's *The Entertainer*); soon, he was sprinkling impressive new stars on the screen: **Rita Tushingham** and **Murray Melvin** in *A Taste of Honey* and **Tom Courtenay** and **James Fox** in *The Loneliness of the Long Distance Runner*). He got his Best Director Oscar for helming the Oscar-winning Best Picture of 1963 (*Tom Jones*), and his last film (*Blue Sky*) struck Oscar gold 40 months *after* his death, winning **Jessica Lange** the prize for Best Actress of 1994. (The picture had been stashed in a Manhattan bank vault after its studio, Orion, went bankrupt and bellied-up.) **Natasha Richardson** and **Joely Richardson**—his two actress-daughters by **Vanessa Redgrave**—and a third daughter from another marriage were his survivors.

15

FIGHTING SULLAVAN: Katharine Hepburn, Ginger Rogers and Eve Arden in *Stage Door*.
FIGHTING MORAL CLAUSES: William Haines and Leila Hyams in *Alias Jimmy Valentine*.
FIGHTING HEART DISEASE: Tyrone Power in *Solomon and Sheba*.

1928: MGM sacrifices its first star to the vagaries of sound on this day as *Alias Jimmy Valentine* bows at the Astor, and—surprise, surprise—**William Haines** passes the talkie test with flying colors ("Irrepressible," ruled *The New York Times*' **Mordaunt Hall**). It was the moral clause in his contract that tripped him up and ended his days as an actor. Openly homosexual with a particular predilection for men in uniform, the actor was arrested with a Naval pickup in a vice-squad raid on a San Diego YMCA, and an incensed **Louis B. Mayer** booted him off the lot, vowing he'd never again work for the majors. And he didn't. Haines exited the screen in a quickie for Mascot called, unfortunately, *The Marines Are Coming*—then went into interior decorating with his lover and stand-in, **Jimmy Shields**. Together, they became—with the help of co-star pals like **Joan Crawford** and **Marion Davies**—stylish trend-setters in Hollywood. Haines died of cancer in 1973, followed shortly by Shields' suicide, but rumors of his flamboyant affairs died hard. (One supposedly changed the direction of *Gone With the Wind*.)

1936: The **Katharine Hepburn**-**Margaret Sullavan** rivalry gets intense on this day when Sullavan weds their mutual agent (and lover), **Leland Hayward**. Hepburn broke down sobbing in the middle of filming *Quality Street* but rallied to wire her "warmest" congratulations to the couple and immediately started plotting to do the movie version of the star part in *Stage Door* Sullavan was then doing on Broadway. **Edna Ferber** had written the role for Hepburn, but Hayward had channeled it to Sullavan. Similarly, he'd advised Hepburn to turn down the female lead in *The Little Minister*, a role she didn't want—*till* she heard Sullavan wanted it. "Then, of course, it became the most important thing in the world for me that I should get it," Hepburn admitted. "Several of my parts in those days I fought for just to take them from someone who needed them."

1958: Irked that a promised perk hadn't materialized, **Gina Lollobrigida** hits the Madrid soundstage of *Solomon and Sheba* on this day like a diva-in-heat. "Don't upset yourself," counseled her Solomon, **Tyrone Power**. "Life goes on." A few hours later, life stopped for Power, 44, stricken with a fatal heart attack *on camera* while dueling with **George Sanders**. The whole picture had to be done over with **Yul Brynner**. Officially, Power's last *finished* film was a volunteer bit for the American Heart Association: "For all of us, the most precious element we have is time. But time runs out all too soon for many millions of us, because of an enemy that takes more lives than all other diseases combined: the heart."

16

SPRING ETERNAL: Katharine Hepburn, Jean Parker,
Spring Byington, Frances Dee, Joan Bennett and
Mabel Colcord in *Little Women*.
BLACK IN THE RED: Claire Forlani and Brad Pitt in
Meet Joe Black.
ALONE AT THE TOP: Macaulay Culkin in *Home Alone*.

1930: At New York's Rivoli on this day, **Marlene Dietrich**'s "after picture" reaches the U.S. screen 19 days before her "before picture": Between her first Hollywood film (*Morocco*) and her last Berlin film (an English-speaking version of *The Blue Angel*) is a world of difference—from the plump chanteuse of the second to the sleek siren of the first. By surrendering to a Tinseltown makeover, she totally reinvented herself, creating a glamorous image that lasted 60 years!

1933: *Little Women* premieres at Radio City Music Hall on this day, setting the house record of $100,000 (one-eighth of the picture's total gross). **Katharine Hepburn**, **Joan Bennett**, **Frances Dee** and **Jean Parker** had the title roles—Jo, Amy, Meg and Beth, respectively—and film-debuting as their mother, Marmee March (winning the role over **Billie Burke**, **Ann Shoemaker** and **Phoebe Foster**), was the "born middle-aged" **Spring Byington**.

1935: *Jumbo* bows at Broadway's Hippodrome on this day, starring **Jimmy Durante** as publicist for a mangy circus whose star attraction is a performing pachyderm. Happily, the actor lived long enough to do the movie version in 1962. (Who else could get away with a line like "*What* elephant?") The reason for the 27-year delay was the red tape of *Jumbo*'s producer, **Billy Rose**, who scuttled *two* versions proposed by producer **Arthur Freed** (one with **Judy Garland** and **Frank Sinatra**; another, right after *Singin' in the Rain*, with **Debbie Reynolds** and **Donald O'Connor**). What eventually got to the screen was with **Doris Day** and **Stephen Boyd** and had an aerial trapeze ballet that marked the final film extravagance of **Busby Berkeley**.

1990: The battle of the box office beginning on this day (*Rocky V* vs. **Macaulay Culkin**, 10) is won by the bantamweight tyke, whose *Home Alone* outgrossed The Italian Stallion's last round by $3 million and went on to earn $286 million in theaters—the only comedy to crack the list of 10 all-time top-grossing films. That statistic made Culkin the highest-paid child star in screen history—until he abdicated in 1996, refusing to do another movie till his bitterly estranged parents resolved their custody dispute. A year later **Christopher "Kit" Culkin** relinquished control to **Patricia Brentrup**, but the actor is still sitting out his career. With an estimated $17 million, he can well afford to leave the acting to four of his six siblings.

1998: CEO **Frank Biondi Jr.** topples from the top on this day for turning *Death Takes a Holiday* into *Universal Takes a Bath* (a.k.a. *Meet Joe Black*). This **Brad Pitt** splat weighed in at exactly three hours and a rumored $90 million and covered the same turf which, in 1934, took 101 minutes less and a finite fraction of that cost.

1933: In the final frames of *The Invisible Man* on this day at New York's Roxy, **Claude Rains** makes his first appearance in talkies. Director **James Whale** chose an unknown for the title role over **Boris Karloff**, **Chester Morris** and **Paul Lukas**—and the debut was so inconspicuous the *Variety* review didn't mention Rains at all. It was, literally, a performance he could have phoned in.

1936: A despondent actor who went out when talkies came in—**John Bowers**, 36—rents a sailboat on this day to (as he told a friend) "sail into the sunset" at Malibu. The next day, along Huntington Beach, the second unit for *A Star Is Born* caught a spectacular sunset effect for Norman Maine's suicidal walk into the ocean. The day after that, Bowers' body washed ashore about a mile from where the movie crew had been filming.

1936: At RCA studios on this day, **Jeanette MacDonald** and **Nelson Eddy** performed their first commercial recording: "Indian Love Call" from *Rose Marie*, backed by their first on-screen duet, "Ah, Sweet Mystery of Life" from *Naughty Marietta*. An immediate hit, the record remained among the company's "101 Best Sellers" for years—but 25 years passed before the two stars got their gold record. "That sure was a mighty slow Indian," cracked Eddy on its arrival. These two recordings—plus three others they did four days later ("Will You Remember" and "A Farewell to Dreams" from *Maytime* and "Song of Love" from *Blossom Time*)—were their only commercial recordings at the height of their careers.

1959: Some glossy schmaltz installed in New York's Paramount on this day—*Beloved Infidel*—presents **Deborah Kerr** and **Gregory Peck** as that improbable pair of literary lovers, gossip columnist **Sheilah Graham** and acclaimed novelist **F. Scott Fitzgerald**. It fell to Peck, playing the frazzled Fitzgerald in his final days as a Hollywood hack, to be the first person to utter the word "bitch" on screen (as in "You silly bitch!" to a pretty stewardess who'd not read his books). Graham wasn't granted her "wish list" for the leads: She felt **Marilyn Monroe** and **Bing Crosby** were "emotionally closest" to the real-life counterparts. Interestingly, the columnist died on this day 29 years later—of congestive heart failure, at 84.

1997: Arriving on red crutches (from a taxi mishap), **Liza Minnelli** joins fellow Oscar winner **Joel Grey**, co-star **Marisa Berenson** and **Gwen Verdon** (widow of the film's Oscar-winning director, **Bob Fosse**) on this day for a New York charity gala marking the 25th anniversary of *Cabaret*. Grey confided that, despite his Tony as *Cabaret* emcee, he wasn't first choice for the movie: Incredibly, "they wanted **Ruth Gordon** or **Anthony Newley**." The Oscar-winning role Grey *did* lose? **Linda Hunt**'s.

A SHOW OF HANDS FOR POPS WHO ADOPT: From left: Wallace Beery (with Jackie Cooper) in *The Champ*, and Fredric March (*really!*) in *Dr. Jekyll and Mr. Hyde*.
GATE OPENS TO HELL: Isabelle Huppert and Kris Kristofferson in *Heaven's Gate*.

18

1915: Mutual Film Corporation brings *Inspiration* to the screen on this day—and, with it, what *The Guinness Book of Records* calls "the first leading lady to appear nude on screen": **Audrey Munson**. An artist's model in real life, she played an innocent country maid who became a "life model" for a sculptor. By the time she appeared nude again on the screen a year later in *Purity*, she had *au naturel* competition from 1) **June Caprice**, 16, romping through the woods in the altogether in *The Ragged Princess* and 2) the "Million Dollar Mermaid" herself, Australian swimming star **Annette Kellerman**, in *Daughter of the Gods*.

1928: The first synchronized sound cartoon goes into release on this day—*Steamboat Willie*—introducing audiences to Mickey Mouse. His name originally was Mortimer, but **Lillian Disney** talked her husband out of that and into a more audience-friendly moniker. **Walt Disney** not only drew the character (with **Ub Iwerks**) but supplied his voice as well—until 1947.

1932: By one vote, **Fredric March** wins one Oscar for two performances (*Dr. Jekyll and Mr. Hyde*) on this day—but **Louis B. Mayer** pressures Academy officials into calling it a tie and divvying up another Oscar to *The Champ* (MGM's Best Actor contender, **Wallace Beery**). Both stars had recently adopted children, prompting March to remark naughtily, "It seems a little odd that Wally and I were given awards for Best Male Performance of the year."

1965: On this day, **Tommy Sands** strides into the *L.A. Times* and punches out critic **Kevin Thomas** for calling him "hopelessly hammy" in *None But the Brave* nine months before. "He must be a slow reader," figured Thomas.

1980: Tinkering down to the wire, director **Michael Cimino** completes cutting *Heaven's Gate*, hops the "red-eye" for New York and delivers his "wet print" to Cinema I for the press unveiling on this day. The screening played so disastrously that, at intermission, United Artists broke out the bubbly in the remote hope of making the second half seem less painful. Afterward, critics bolted for their respective typewriters to bang out the bad news for the next day's paper. **Vincent Canby** of *The New York Times*, true grace under pressure, felt the film "fails so completely that you might suspect Mr. Cimino sold his soul to the Devil to obtain the success of *The Deer Hunter*, and the Devil has just come around to collect."

TALL & TALENT-FREE: Rock Hudson, Robert Stack, Don Phillips and Edmond O'Brien in *Fighter Squadron*.
THE BEST FOR LAST: Lee Tracy in *The Best Man*.
ANOTHER PATH OF GLORY: Kirk Douglas and director Stanley Kubrick on the *Spartacus* set.
BELOW THE BORDER & BELOW THE BELT: Lee Tracy dressed for *Viva Villa!*

1933: On this day, **Lee Tracy** effectively pisses away his screen career. The morning after some wild Mexico City carousing, he awoke to a parade outside his hotel, staggered naked to the balcony and urinated on a corps of Mexican cadets below. Since Mexico was already incensed that Pancho Villa was being played by MGM's clown oaf, **Wallace Beery**, the incident triggered national turmoil. Not only was Tracy kicked off *Viva Villa!* and replaced by **Stuart Erwin**, his contract with the studio was instantly canceled. The fact a plane carrying footage of Tracy's last three weeks of shooting crashed and burned that same weekend convinced MGM to do the right thing. Tracy stayed in B-films till his last hurrah: the **Truman**-like ex-President in *The Best Man*; that got him Broadway acclaim and an Oscar-nominated screen exit.

1948: Among the *Fighter Squadron* bailing out at New York's Strand on this day is a six-foot-four, 22-year-old, newly named **Rock Hudson**, getting his baptism-by-film from veteran director **Raoul Walsh**. Hudson stood out—or, at least, tallest—in group shots of World War II flyboys and delivered four lines of dialogue (one took dozens of retakes and eventual rewriting to get right). Seeing some screen seasoning was in order, Walsh footed the bills for acting lessons—which Hudson paid for by chauffeuring the director around town and painting his house—and arranged for screen-tests at five different studios. The one Hudson did for 20th Century-Fox is *still* shown as an example of how a terrible test can't stop a true star. Eventually, Walsh enrolled him in Universal's star-making program, class of '49 (**Jeff Chandler**, **Piper Laurie**, **Tony Curtis**, **Lori Nelson**, **Richard Long**, **Julia Adams**, **Rod McKuen**, **Meg Randall**), and the studio remained homebase his whole career.

1958: After half a year of haggling preproduction on *One Eyed Jacks*, **Marlon Brando** and **Stanley Kubrick** reach an impasse on this day. Kubrick wanted **Spencer Tracy** to play Brando's two-faced partner, but Brando had promised the part to **Karl Malden** so, for $100,000, the director left the picture (immediately heeding the S.O.S. of another producer-star, **Kirk Douglas**, to rush to Madrid and take up the megaphone abandoned by **Anthony Mann** three days into *Spartacus*). As for *One Eyed Jacks*, Brando hired himself to helm the film—a self-inflicted miscalculation he lived to regret.

1960: Police find **Phyllis Haver** dead at her home in Falls Village, CT, on this day, a suicide at 60. She began her screen career with custard-pie pummelings as a **Mack Sennett** bathing beauty and finished it seducing an Oscar-winning **Emil Jannings** in *The Way of All Flesh*. Cosmetic technology helped her make that transition: It was for her **Max Factor** invented false eyelashes.

REACHING STARDOM BY CAMEL: Omar Sharif and Peter O'Toole in *Lawrence of Arabia*.
SOPHIE IS CHOICE: Herbert Marshall, Gene Tierney, Tyrone Power and Anne Baxter in *The Razor's Edge*.
QUESTIONABLE WESTERNERS: From left: Joan Crawford in *Johnny Guitar*, Ronald Reagan and Barbara Stanwyck in *Cattle Queen of Montana*.

1946: *The Razor's Edge*, going into general release on this day, cuts little ice with critics—but for **Tyrone Power**, returning to the screen after World War II, it proves a high-minded homecoming, *hugely* popular with the masses. **Darryl F. Zanuck** ladled on the all-stars: **Gene Tierney**, **John Payne**, **Anne Baxter**, **Clifton Webb**, **Lucile Watson**, **Herbert Marshall** and **Elsa Lanchester**. Webb, at his waspish best, was Oscar-nominated, and Baxter won the award in the surefire role of Power's dipso darling, Sophie—a part coveted, and campaigned for, by **Alice Faye** and **Judy Garland** (both, evidently, craving a complete change of image).

1953: As if being reduced to a Republic Western (*Johnny Guitar*) isn't enough crow to choke on, **Joan Crawford** also has to contend with cheers from cast and crew for **Mercedes McCambridge**'s skilled execution of a difficult scene—and that ignites a celebrated catfight, which a phony Photo Op on this day tries to counteract with a rather steely kiss-and-make-up pose by the two stars. "Poor old rotten-egg Joan," McCambridge later said. "I kept my mouth shut about her for nearly a quarter of a century, but she was a mean, tipsy, powerful, rotten-egg lady. I'm still not going to tell what she did to me. Other people have written some of it, but they don't know it all, and they never will because I am a very nice person and I don't like to talk about the dead even if they were rotten eggs."

1960: After toying with **Marlon Brando** and testing **Albert Finney**, producer **Sam Spiegel** announces on this day **Peter O'Toole**, 28, an Irish stage actor with three small film roles to his credit, will play *Lawrence of Arabia*. His hopes for the other roles—**Cary Grant**, **Jack Hawkins**, **Horst Buchholz**, **Laurence Olivier**—were filled by Hawkins, **Anthony Quayle**, **Omar Sharif**, **Alec Guinness**. O'Toole's finely etched performance of the enigmatic adventurer established him as a major international star. **Noel Coward**, for one, thought if O'Toole were any more beautiful they'd have to call the film *Florence of Arabia*.

1966: At the annual Screen Actors Guild membership meeting on this day, Governor-elect **Ronald Reagan** shows up to bestow the SAG award on **Barbara Stanwyck**, who only a dozen years before was his *Cattle Queen of Montana*.

21

1961: Director **Sam Peckinpah** concludes principal photography on this day on *Ride the High Country*, and **Randolph Scott** concludes a career—as does (save for a couple of inconsequential programmers) **Joel McCrea**. This sleeper started out with Scott as the goodguy and McCrea as the badguy, but they switched roles on the first day of filming. Either way, both had a wonderful movie to ride out on. Even when MGM dumped it on the lower half of a double bill, it *still* won a Venice Film Festival prize and a place on *Newsweek*'s and *Film Quarterly*'s Ten Best lists.

1969: Even with *his* anguished history of aborted film projects (*The Clock*, *Custer*, **Mike Todd**'s *War and Peace*, *The Old Man and the Sea*, *Hawaii*), director **Fred Zinnemann** is devastated by the cruel fate that befalls **Andre Malraux**'s *Man's Fate* on this day: After almost three years of pre-production, MGM president **James T. Aubrey** shelves the $10 million movie three days before cameras start turning. **Liv Ullmann**, **David Niven**, **Peter Finch** and the rest of the cast played the whole hand anyway, spending their last three days on salary working with Zinnemann until the script was completely rehearsed scene by scene. Then, they had a wistful wrap-party on the fully-dressed sets—as if the movie *had* happened—and scattered to the four winds, never knowing but always wondering what might have been.

1983: On this day—the day before her 71st birthday—**Lee Patrick** dies of a heart seizure in her Laguna Hills home. Her flibbertigibbet appearances littered four decades of films, and she's in *The Guinness Book of Records* as the person with the longest interval between playing the same part: Effie Perine, girl Friday to Sam Spade (**Humphrey Bogart** in 1941's *The Maltese Falcon*) and Sam Spade Jr. (**George Segal** in 1975's *The Black Bird*). Her best-known role: Mrs. *Topper* on TV.

1997: A 44-year-old feud triggered by one of the most famous scenes of all time—the taxi-cab ride in *On the Waterfront*—has ended, according to Page Six's **Richard Johnson** in the *New York Post* on this day. **Marlon Brando** was so annoyed that his "coulda been a contender" speech brought real tears from **Rod Steiger** he walked off the set, leaving poor Steiger to do his close-ups alone. The latter fumed all those years—only to be quickly defused when Brando sent him a flowery telegram after the two had crossed paths in Montreal.

22

1955: In *The New York Times* on this day, critic **Bosley Crowther** applauds "a pip of a murder thriller, ghost story and character play rolled into one" (translation: *Diabolique*), a French shocker from **Henri-Georges Clouzot** which set the high watermark for screen terror at that time and sent **Alfred Hitchcock** not only to the shower (for *Psycho*) but also to the library to get another taut yarn (*Vertigo*) by the same writer, **Pierre Boileau**—who also did *The Bridge on the River Kwai* and *Planet of the Apes* as Pierre Boulle. *Diabolique*'s big hair-raising scene found a sadistic school-headmaster (**Paul Meurisse**)—drowned by his wife (**Vera Clouzot**) and mistress (**Simone Signoret**)—rising from his bathwater and driving the wife into a fatal, fear-induced heart attack. In real life, heart attacks killed Meurisse, 66, in 1979; director Clouzot, 69, in 1977, and Clouzot's actress-wife, Vera, 48, in 1960.

1963: After three days off to rest from overwork, a relatively refreshed **Audrey Hepburn** resumes *My Fair Lady* on this day, one of the darkest in modern history. She and **Jeremy Brett** were in a carriage filming Eliza's return to Covent Garden with Freddy when someone rushed up with the news that **John F. Kennedy** had been killed in Dallas. The two stayed in the carriage with the blinds drawn, held each other and wept. Director **George Cukor** was too upset to break the news to the company so Hepburn stoically volunteered to do it.

1965: On this day, **Steve McQueen** starts filming his one and only Oscar-nominated performance, arriving in the great Shanghai Bund of 1926 (actually, the seaport of Keelung in North Taiwan) for the opening scene of *The Sand Pebbles*. He arrived by rickshaw—but it had to be specially built, since that vehicle had long ago been outlawed by contemporary Chinese as "demeaning."

1967: When she refuses to walk out on the behind-schedule *Rosemary's Baby* in California and join him in front of the cameras in New York for *The Detective*, **Frank Sinatra** "fires" Wife No. 3 (**Mia Farrow**) on this day. While his publicist (**Jim Mahoney**) gently broke the news of a "trial separation" to the public, she got the word from a hireling (his attorney, **Mickey Rudin**) who interrupted the filming of a party scene on the Paramount backlot to tell her a divorce was indeed in the works. Farrow resumed the party-scene-in-progress and "used" her new-found hysteria. The resulting performance was a revelation—and, from that film on, she was taken seriously as an actress. **Jacqueline Bisset** filled the vacancy in *The Detective*, and nearly a decade later **Barbara Marx** stepped into the wife role.

1944: "Whatever it was that this actress never had, she still hasn't got," snaps one of **Loretta Young**'s sterner critics (**Bosley Crowther** of *The New York Times*) on this day about her efforts in *And Now Tomorrow*. "Miss Young gives a performance which may best and most graphically be compared to a **Fanny Brice** imitation of a glamorous movie queen." Okay, Bos, no Christmas card this year.

1960: *G.I. Blues* goes into general release on this day, returning newly discharged (March 4) Army sergeant **Elvis Presley** to his waiting fans.

1963: A bugler sounds taps, the flag is lowered to half-staff and an elegiac service worthy of a **John Ford** movie is conducted in Monument Valley—for real—on this day, the day of national mourning following **President Kennedy**'s assassination. Like Captain Nathan Brittles addressing the troops, director Ford confronted the cast and crew of *Cheyenne Autumn* at Goulding's Lodge, said America had lost a great leader but the republic would survive and led the assemblage in a reading of the Lord's Prayer. Then, after **Harry Carey Jr.** sang "The Battle Hymn of the Republic," the company was dismissed for the day.

1973: Two legends of the silent screen succumb to pneumonia on this day—**Constance Talmadge**, 73, in Los Angeles and **Sessue Hayakawa**, 83, in Tokyo.

FOREVER YOUNG: Grant Mitchell, Beulah Bondi, Susan Hayward, Loretta Young and Barry Sullivan in *And Now Tomorrow*.
OBERON'S SCREEN EXIT: Robert Wolders and Merle Oberon in *Interval*.
POST-ARMY PRESLEY: Elvis in *G.I. Blues*.

1979: One of the screen's most enduring beauties—**Merle Oberon**, 68—dies of a stroke at her Malibu home on this day. She almost got to the grave with her Great Secret intact (i.e., that she was an Anglo-Indian mix and not the Tasmanian aristocrat she pretended to be), but days before her death, while in hospital mending from open-heart surgery, she got a comp copy of *Charmed Lives* about a family she'd been a part of, from 1939 to 1945, when married to the first of her four husbands, London Films magnate **Alexander Korda**. The book was by the family Boswell, nephew **Michael Korda**, who sent it to her with the warmest of regards and, therefore, was stunned when she phoned him up in the middle of the night to disinherit him. "I'd say I used kid gloves on Merle, but apparently, not kid enough." He made up for her disinheritance (and then some) by writing the best-selling *Queenie*, a plainly-marked fiction in which he paraded the Auntie Merle stories he'd considerably muted the first time out. (At the time she entered the kingdom of Korda, Oberon went under the name of Queenie Thompson.) Her last husband—a Dutch actor a quarter of a century her junior, **Robert Wolders**—subsequently became **Audrey Hepburn**'s last companion.

24

1954: Member of the wedding, kinda: on this day, a-straddle his motorcycle, **James Dean** watches ex-girlfriend **Pier Angeli** emerge from St. Timothy's as Mrs. **Vic Damone**—then he disappears for ten days. Toward the end of her life, she admitted, "I was only in love once in my life, and that was with Jimmy Dean."

1974: **Sidney Lumet**'s star-packed *Murder on the Orient Express* pulls into New York's Coronet Theater—with one Oscar-winning performance on board: **Ingrid Bergman** actually *apologized* for winning her Best Supporting Actress award—an Academy first!—over competition she thought more deserving (**Valentina Cortese** for **Truffaut**'s *Day for Night*). "Please forgive me, Valentina—I didn't mean to," she said, accepting Oscar No. 3. (Inevitably, the other three nominees in this category took umbrage at the slighting.)

1980: Leukemia claims **George Raft**, 85, on this day. Almost 12 years later, he *finally* got in an Oscar-winning film (excluding non-star parts in *Around the World in 80 Days* and *Some Like It Hot*): The actor was a *character*, played—overanimated—by **Joe Mantegna** in *Bugsy*, the **"Bugsy" Siegel** bio which won two Oscars out of 10 nominations: for Best Art Direction (**Dennis Gassner** and **Nancy Haigh**) and for Best Costume Design (**Albert Wolsky**).

1990: *The Alamo* rises again—in all its original 192-minute glory—in a confirmation screening on this day at Toronto's Eglinton Theater. A half-hour of footage unseen since the film was roadshown 30 years before was intact, miraculously (thanks to the fact that it had been mislabeled as the 161-minute version that commonly survived). This discovery prompted MGM/UA Home Video to use the print to replace the version in release.

1998: The *New York Post* reports a rarity on this day: "Skinhead-flick director sues for getting too *much* credit." Claiming his "professional standing and reputation in the cinema community" has been sullied by being associated with *American History X*, **Tony Kaye** sued New Line Cinema and Directors Guild of America for $275 million for not crediting his direction to one Humpty Dumpty. (Kaye didn't OK **Edward Norton** beefing up his own screen time—and the studio sided with the actor.) It did not argue well for Kaye's case that the film's lone Oscar nomination was Norton's sleeper bid for Best Actor.

EYEING THE ENEMY: Richard Widmark, Laurence Harvey and John Wayne in *The Alamo*.
THE LONELY NOMINEE: Edward Norton in *American History X*.
THE LOVE THAT GOT AWAY: James Dean and Pier Angeli on the Warners backlot.
A RELUCTANT OSCAR WINNER IS ABOARD: Anthony Perkins, Vanessa Redgrave, Sean Connery, Ingrid Bergman, George Coulouris, John Gielgud, Albert Finney, Rachel Roberts, Wendy Hiller, Denis Quilley, Michael York, Jacqueline Bisset, Lauren Bacall and Martin Balsam in *Murder on the Orient Express*.

1937: Illuminating New York's Rialto today is the first **Mickey & Judy** movie—*Thoroughbreds Don't Cry*—Film #3 on her resumé and her first with top billing (and cooing).

1940: "Guess who? Ha-ha-ha-*ha*-ha." Woody Woodpecker makes his screen entrance (through Andy Panda's roof) in a cartoon aptly called *Knock Knock*, going into release on this day. **Walter Lantz** always claimed he got the idea for Woody from a pesky woodpecker pounding away outside his honeymoon cottage—but he didn't marry **Grace Stafford** till the year *after* Woody's debut. **Mel Blanc** first supplied Woody's voice, then storyman **Ben "Bugs" Hardaway**; eventually—after auditioning 50 actors for the part—Lantz unwittingly selected the speeded-up voice of his own wife. She bowed as Woody in 1948's *Banquet Busters* and continued the characterization till the series' demise in 1972 two dozen years later, keeping her identity a secret until 1952 because she feared children would be disillusioned to know a woman provided the voice. In all, Woody racked up 193 theatrical short subjects.

1952: "I want you to be sure and see my *Hans Christian Andersen*," producer **Samuel Goldwyn** tells a friend on this day after the picture premieres at the Paris and Criterion in New York. "It's full of charmth and warmth," said Sam.

1955: *The Big Knife* lands in Los Angeles theaters on this day, its savage caricature of a studio kingpin intact from **Clifford Odets'** play and italicized by **Rod Steiger's** emphatic performance. The role's inspiration, Columbia chief **Harry Cohn**, hated the film—especially that it had come from **Robert Aldrich**, who'd just started a three-pix deal at Columbia with **Joan Crawford's** weeper, *Autumn Leaves*. This timing kept the mogul and the director forever at a distance. "I had an across-the-room relationship with Cohn," recalled Aldrich. "He wanted me to come there; I didn't want to come there."

1976: At San Francisco's Winterland, **The Band** goes into *The Last Waltz*, a signoff concert dutifully and beautifully covered by the documentary cameras of **Martin Scorsese** for a worldwide theatrical replay two years later.

WELL, *SOMETIMES* THEY CRY: From left: Mickey & Judy in *Babes on Broadway* and *Girl Crazy*.
THE MOVIE WAS MILES FROM SMILES: Ida Lupino, Jack Palance, Jean Hagen, Wendell Corey, Ilka Chase, Everett Sloane and Rod Steiger in *The Big Knife*.
A SHOW OF HANS: Danny Kaye in *Hans Christian Andersen*.

26

1936: Director **George Stevens** reaches the end of *Quality Street* on this day. His heart, set on filming *Winterset*, had been elsewhere during the shooting—and it showed in **Katharine Hepburn**'s artificial emoting. He got better work from her—Oscar-nominated work—as *Alice Adams* and *Woman of the Year*. As for *Winterset*, director **Alfred Santell** brought it—and its film-debuting **Burgess Meredith**—to the screen in a dark, stagebound, thoroughly mediocre production.

1940: *Come Live With Me*, a modest comedy-drama **James Stewart** completes on this day, didn't change the face of cinema, but 13 years later he discovered its true value: "It's a funny thing the things people remember you for," he said. "A guy came up to me one time. I was making *The Far Country* up in Canada some place, and this fella nodded to me, and he said how much he'd liked this scene I'd done *years before*. It was a little thing—a poem I did in *Come Live with Me*—and he remembered it, and he said that it was good. He didn't remember the Indians I'd killed or the bridges I'd taken or the bad men I'd run outta town. He just remembered this one little thing. He said, 'I doubt if it *means* much to you . . .' Well, when he told me that, it was the most *moving*—I tell you, it was better than getting a fistful of fine notices. Did it *mean* anything? Why, it means *everything* to me. When they get around to writing my epitaph, I'll settle for, I'll be happy with, 'He sure gave us a lot of pleasure over the years.' I wouldn't mind that at all, to die knowing—knowing you've given people just a little piece of—a small piece of *time* they'll never forget."

1952: Los Angeles on this day gets the first look-see—a double look-see, with specially prepared glasses, at the downtown Paramount and Hollywood theaters—at a picture that will bring the industry a new dimension: *Bwana Devil*, in Natural Vision 3-D. It didn't actually deliver "A Lion in your lap! A Lover in your arms!" as advertised, but it *did* provide pokes in the eye from natives' spears, and it *did* revolutionize the film business. Briefly.

1980: Hours before he opens in *My Fair Lady* at Los Angeles' Pantages on this day, **Rex Harrison** learns his fourth ex (**Rachel Roberts**, 53) was found dead in the backyard garden of her West L.A. home. Police said it was a heart attack, but Harrison called it suicide, recanting that in later editions, saying he repeated misinformation he'd been given. On Nov. 30, the coroner ruled him right the first time: Death had come from swallowing a lethal fluid like lye alkali or a toxic acid.

FARCE HERE, TRAGEDY LATER: Rachel Roberts , Louis Jourdan, Rex Harrison and Rosemary Harris in *A Flea in Her Ear*.
SHADOWS & FOG: Margo, Burgess Meredith and Myron McCormick in *Winterset*.
A LITTLE POEM WITH A DELAYED PUNCH: Hedy Lamarr and James Stewart in *Come Live With Me*.
THE FIRST 3-D FEATURE: Robert Stack and Barbara Britton in *Bwana Devil*.

27

1950: On this day, **Lucille Ball** boards *The Magic Carpet* **Harry Cohn** spitefully assigned her when she requested her last Columbia film be delayed so she could play the wisecracking elephant-trainer in **Cecil B. DeMille**'s *The Greatest Show on Earth*. Cohn figured she'd jump ship and run off to the circus, breaking her contract and sacrificing the $85,000 Columbia still owed her for one more film. Instead, Ball took the fast five-day *Carpet* ride—each day letting out her flimsy harem outfits a bit more—and, when filming finished, she phoned Cohn and informed him of her pregnancy. "Congratulations," a resigned C.B. said to **Desi**, "you're the only man in history who screwed Lucille Ball, Columbia Pictures, Paramount Pictures, Harry Cohn and Cecil B. DeMille all at the same time."

A HEAVILY VEILED SECRET: Lucille Ball and John Agar in *The Magic Carpet*.
RIGHT-THINKING: Lee Aaker, Geraldine Page, John Wayne and Ward Bond in *Hondo*.
AUTHOR *ARTHUR*: Steve Gordon and Dudley Moore.
CALLING IT: John Carradine.

1953: *Hondo* rides into national release on this day, returning **John Wayne** to the Western for the first time in three years—and with an added dimension (also three). The first 3-D Western, *The Charge at Feather River*, had come four months earlier, but *Hondo* was the best of that admittedly rare breed. Intending only to co-produce the film with **Robert Fellows**, Wayne hired **Glenn Ford** to play Hondo, but, when Ford flatly refused to make another film with director **John Farrow** after their mutual *Plunder of the Sun* debacle, Wayne stuck by Farrow, fired Ford and hired himself. "A man ought to do what he thinks is right," as Hondo non-politically put it. Aside from **Thomas Mitchell**'s Oscar-winning *Stagecoach* support and Wayne's own Oscar-winning work in *True Grit*, this was the only other John Wayne Western to win an Oscar nomination for acting. **Geraldine Page** earned that distinction—and, because she tipped her liberal leanings to right-wing co-star **Ward Bond**, she didn't do films again till the early '60s when she reprised (also to Oscar-nominated effect) her acclaimed stage performances in two **Tennessee Williams** plays, *Summer and Smoke* and *Sweet Bird of Youth*.

1982: *Arthur* author **Steve Gordon**, 44, dies of a heart attack in New York on this day, just as the doors of Hollywood are swinging open for him. *Arthur* was just his second screenplay (*The One and Only* was the other), but he held out for a shot at directing it—and got it. With a domestic gross of around $40 million, his was one of the most commercially notable directorial debuts in modern times. Also, he reactivated **Dudley Moore** as the inebriated millionaire of the title and provided **John Gielgud** with long-overdue Oscar work.

1988: "Milan! What a beautiful place to die!" sighed **John Carradine**, after climbing 328 steps to the top of the town's famed Gothic cathedral, the Duomo, moments before he collapsed. Three days later—on this day—the 82-year-old actor does indeed die there, in a hospital, of heart and kidney failure.

28

1942: Almost 1,000 merrymakers pack Boston's Cocoanut Grove on this day—400 over its official seating capacity—to pay tribute to cowboy star **Buck Jones**, 53. They were standing around three and four deep at the nightclub's basement bar shortly after 10 p.m. when a tiny blaze appeared around an imitation cocoanut tree and suddenly spread into the worst fire tragedy in the nation's history. The honoree expired two days later "from smoke inhalation and burned lungs and from third and second degree burns on the face and neck." He was the 481st person (out of 492, eventually) to perish in that disaster.

1955: Fearing she's too old to play opposite **William Holden** (11 years her junior), **Katharine Hepburn** on this day relinquishes the role of the susceptible spinster who's wooed by a traveling con-man in *The Rainmaker*. When the title part eventually scared off Holden, **Burt Lancaster** applied since he already owed producer **Hal B. Wallis** a picture (plus, he promised to stick around for Wallis' *Gunfight at the O.K. Corral*). Then the producer pulled Hepburn back into the picture by screening for her a film he'd just done with Lancaster, *The Rose Tattoo*; the bravado of that performance and the fact that Lancaster was four years older than Holden cinched the deal. Both stars wound up perfectly cast: Hepburn got Oscar-nominated for *The Rainmaker*, and Lancaster tapped into that braggadocio-masking-vulnerability vein which would bring him the Oscar as 1960's *Elmer Gantry*.

1956: Critics come with carving knives to an exclusive showing of a new movie at the Cinema Normandie on the Champs-Elysees on this day. "The best thing about this film is that it will forever end the career of that annoying little starlet," wrote one; "what a terrible image this film will give of France as portrayed by the vulgarity of Mlle Bardot," wrote another. *Au contraire*, gentlemen. **Brigitte Bardot**, as presented here by her then-husband and director **Roger Vadim**, entered international stardom assuredly with . . . *And God Created Woman*—make that: *And Vadim Creates Bardot*—becoming not only the most famous French woman of her time but also "the symbol of France" on stamps.

1976: The *Auntie Mame* who preached, "Life is a banquet, and most poor suckers are starving to death!"—**Rosalind Russell**, 65—succumbs to cancer on this day.

HAPPILY, SHE HAD SECOND THOUGHTS: Lloyd Bridges, Cameron Prud'homme, Wendell Corey, Earl Holliman, Katharine Hepburn and Burt Lancaster in *The Rainmaker*.
A FIERY FINISH: Buck Jones.
DENNIS, ANYONE?: Rosalind Russell in *Auntie Mame*.
A CRITIC-PROOF CREATION: Curt Jurgens and Brigitte Bardot in . . . *And God Created Woman*.

29

1940: "Mahatma Kane Jeeves should receive the writer of the year award," wrote **William Saroyan** about the author of *The Bank Dick*, which goes into general release on this day. The name was a pseudonym for the film's star, **W. C. Fields**, who created it out of a cliche in old English drawing-room dramas (i.e., the scene in which the stuffy English aristocrat leaves his mansion and says to his butler, inevitably named Jeeves: "My hat, my cane, Jeeves"). At the end of *The Bank Dick*, just such a set-up confronted Fields' character—Egbert Souse' ("accent grave over the 'e'")—as he left his manse. Instead, Fields picked up a pith helmet, causing the Jeeves-on-duty to offer a hat-and-cane alternative with: "I think, sir, this is the more appropriate."

1944: Producer **Arthur Freed** is splendidly vindicated on this day when critical raves greet *Meet Me in St. Louis*, a nostalgic musical with instant evergreens ("The Trolley Song," "The Boy Next Door," "Have Yourself a Merry Little Christmas"). Getting it to such acclaim was a long studio fight. "Finally," Freed recalled, "we had a meeting, and Mayer said: 'Arthur's record has been so good—either he'll learn a lesson, or we'll learn a lesson—so go make the picture.' And it was the biggest-grossing picture they had for five years."

1954: Driving to work in a torrent of rain on this day— his first day as a director—**Roger Corman** pulls his car over to the side of the road, throws up, then presses on to Iverson's Ranch on the far edge of the San Fernando Valley where, for nine days and $60,000, he makes *Five Guns West*. **John Lund**, **Dorothy Malone**, **Touch** (later **Mike**) **Connors**, **Paul Birch** and **Jonathan Haze** starred, imaginatively surrounded by a cast of thousands that Corman acquired in stock shots of Indian raids. The future "King of the B's" was, indeed, in business!

1981: A slightly intoxicated **Natalie Wood**, 43, missteps trying to get from her yacht into a rubber dinghy, falls into the waters off Santa Catalina Island 22 miles from the California coast and drowns shortly after midnight on this day. Her husband, **Robert Wagner**, and her current (*Brainstorm*) co-star, **Christopher Walken**, were aboard the yacht at the time but did not hear her cries for help.

1986: The man who made it all look so easy—screen stylist **Cary Grant**—dies on this day, a decade and a day after the death of **Rosalind Russell**, *His Girl Friday*. (The expendable component in that triangle—**Ralph Bellamy**, always the also-ran in romantic rivalries with Grant—died on this day five years later.)

30

1935: *The Petrified Forest* finishes filming on this day, with alternate endings: the happy one where **Leslie Howard** survives a **Humphrey Bogart** gunning vs. the original Broadway one where he doesn't. Wisely, Warners went with the latter. Bogie always said Howard was his best victim: "One shot, and he dies."

> **EASY TARGET:** Leslie Howard in *The Petrified Forest*.
> **SOMETIMES, THE TOUCH WAS A SPANK:** Ernst Lubitsch (right) directing Gary Cooper and Claudette Colbert in *Bluebeard's Eighth Wife*.
> **FRENCH SNUBBING:** Pierce Brosnan in *GoldenEye*.

1940: *Citizen Kane* is completed on this day by the camera crew **Gregg Toland** left behind to join **Howard Hughes** on *The Outlaw*. The last word of Charles Foster Kane—"Rosebud"—is the last to be lensed. **Orson Welles** constantly contended that *Kane* had nothing to do with **William Randolph Hearst**, but Hearst knew better: "Rosebud" was Hearst's pet expression for the clitoris of his movie-star mistress, **Marion Davies**.

1947: The screen master of naughty froth, **Ernst Lubitsch**, leaves behind one last "Lubitsch touch" on this day when he has a heart attack showering after sex. The director died before the doctor arrived — also before he could pay the prostitute, who began weeping *loudly* over being so emphatically stiffed. Only when Lubitsch's chauffeur cleared the account did she clear out.

1990: Early reports on the stroke **Burt Lancaster** suffers while visiting a friend at the John Douglas French Center for Alzheimer's Disease identify the friend: **Dana Andrews**. The robust Lancaster never recovered, living almost four years with difficulty speaking and moving his right side, avoiding industry well-wishers (even **Kirk Douglas**).

1994: In the lobby of a mid-Manhattan recording studio on this day, "gangsta" rapper-turned-actor **Tupac Shakur** is shot five times by thieves. Three cops who rushed to his aid were among those who busted him a year before for luring a woman to his hotel room for a gang-rape. The jury on *that* case came in the day after the shooting with a verdict: guilty of sex abuse. On Feb. 7 a sobbing Shakur was sentenced to up 4 1/2 years. On April 1, he became the first rapper to debut at No. 1 on the charts (*Me Against the World*) while in jail. Eight months into his sentence, on Oct. 12, he was bailed out with $1.4 million from Death Row Records and was in a car with that company's president, **Marion "Suge" Knight**, Sept. 7 when it was sprayed by a hail of bullets. Shakur, 25, died six days later.

1995: *GoldenEye* gets a black eye from the French on this day when they call off its gala launching because the new 007 (**Pierce Brosnan**) has Greenpeace ties.

1935: Writer-director-actor **Woody Allen** is born, exactly one decade to the day before his screen wife in *Scenes From a Mall*: **Bette Midler.**

1937: *Test Pilot*, a picture of painful transition for **Lionel Barrymore**, starts two and a half months of filming on this day — and the pain is visible: He began playing his aviation mogul from a standing position, aided by a cane, but a hip injury worsened during the shoot to such an extent that when **Clark Gable** told him off at the end, he had to take it all sitting down. He spent the rest of his career in a wheelchair.

1948: *Three Godfathers* goes into general release, "introducing" **Harry Carey Jr.** and dedicated to the memory of his dad, "Bright Star of the early Western sky." **John Ford** had directed the first version of this yarn with Sr. (as 1919's *Marked Men*) and was filming this remake with **John Wayne** when Carey passed away Sept. 24, 1947. Another homage to him occurred in the closing shot of a later, greater Ford-Wayne Western, 1956's *The Searchers*: Instead of entering a homestead presided over by Carey's widow (**Olive Carey**), Wayne places his hand on his elbow — a favorite mannerism of Harry Carey's — and moseys off into Monument Valley while the door of the homestead slowly closes. Off-camera, Mrs. Carey quietly dissolved into tears.

1960: Two teen idols — Walden Robert Cassotto, 24, and Alexandra Zuck, 18 — take 10 minutes to tie the knot at the Camden, NJ, home of music publisher **Don Kirshner** on this day. Better known as **Bobby Darin** and **Sandra Dee**, they met three months earlier when romantically paired in *Come September*, and it felt real to them. Turns out, they only photographed like dream lovers (twice more: *If a Man Answers* and *That Funny Feeling*); in real life, a whirl of speed, booze and careerism brought the marriage to a halt in seven years. Darin, whose "Mack the Knife" resides at No. 7 on Billboard's all-time Hot 100, died of heart failure at 37 in 1973; Dee retreated into eating disorders and drink before their only child, **Todd Darin**, helped her round the bend to recovery.

1977: NYC critics have a hearty hello on this day for *The Goodbye Girl*, apparently the only picture to put three left-handed performers into the Oscar running: **Marsha Mason**, young **Quinn Cummings** and the winnah, **Richard Dreyfuss**.

1994: On this day, some six months after taking out a full-page $30,000 ad in *The Times* of London declaring their heterosexuality and denying divorce rumors, **Richard Gere** and **Cindy Crawford** fess up to the press they've hit Splitsville.

1936: Director **Rex Ingram** and his actress-wife, **Alice Terry** — fugitives from *The Garden of Allah* (MGM's 1927 version) — watch bemused across the street from Grauman's Chinese on this day as customers leave the premiere of director **Richard Boleslawski**'s remake with **Marlene Dietrich**. Its (re)launching got the full nine yards of klieg-lit glamour — such a festive sight that newsreel footage of it found its way into the opening of 1952's *Singin' in the Rain* and the closing of 1937's *A Star Is Born*.

1937: Under her real name of Edith Marrener, **Susan Hayward** puts in the first of two unsuccessful tests for Scarlett O'Hara on this day. Glimpses of what could have been came 11 years later with *Tap Roots*, an upfront GWTW counterfeit letting her apply shades of Scarlett to Morna Dabney, a Mississippi miss whose plantation also got torched by Yankees.

ON POINTE IN PARIS: Leslie Caron and Gene Kelly in *An American in Paris*.
METHOD DIRECTING: Marlon Brando in *One Eyed Jacks*.
TAPPING TARA: Van Heflin, Susan Hayward and Whitfield Connor in *Tap Roots*.

1950: Prerecording is completed on this day for the then-longest ballet scene in a mainstream movie — the 18-minute capper to *An American in Paris*, in which **Gene Kelly** and **Leslie Caron** cavort to Gershwin against backdrop imitations of Dufy, Manet, Utrillo, Rousseau, Van Gogh and Toulouse-Lautrec. Director **Vincente Minnelli** lavished time (Dec. 6 – Jan. 2) and producer **Arthur Freed** lavished money ($542,000 of the film's $2,723,903 total cost) to get the scene right, and their gamble paid off — at the box office (grossing $8,005,000-plus) and in Oscar gold (winning the Best Picture prize).

1958: "A greater opportunity for expression" gets rolling on this day as **Marlon Brando** begins directing *One Eyed Jacks*, with a shooting schedule of 60 days and a budget of $1.8 million. Six months and $6 million later, production ended, with more than a million feet of exposed film (a record, then). Brando turned in four hours and 42 minutes of that which Paramount pared to 141 minutes and brightened (by sparing the lives of the hero and heroine in the reediting). The remains were released March 30, 1961 — to mixed reviews and mild box office. Brando disavowed this black-eyed Jacks and never directed again.

1996: Hollywood's No. 1 box-office champ from 1978 to 1982, **Burt Reynolds**, enters a new chapter on this day — Chapter 11 — declaring himself bankrupt with assets of $6.65 million and a debt of $11.2 million. Poor career choices sped his downfall, like turning down a role **James L. Brooks** wrote specifically for him: the astronaut-next-door to Shirley MacLaine in *Terms of Endearment* (Oscar work for **Jack Nicholson**); Reynolds also let **Kevin Kline**'s part in *Soapdish* slip through his fingers because then-wife **Loni Anderson** feared he'd rekindle old flame **Sally Field**. Marriage to Anderson and other bad investments sapped Reynolds' wealth — as did, tweaked *Entertainment Weekly*, Edward Katz Hair Design (to which he owed $121,797).

3

1927: The first official **Laurel & Hardy** team-effort — *Putting Pants on Philip* — rolls off Hal Roach's assembly line on this day and into the marketplace.

1928: Movietone News begins issuing weekly installments on this day, less than six weeks after it bowed at NYC's Roxy as the first regular sound newsreel.

1934: On this day, **Spencer Tracy** begins what will be the last release on his Fox contract, *Dante's Inferno* — "one of the worst pictures ever made anywhere, anytime," in his well-considered opinion — but it launched into films a lovely Latin who signed up for seven years as Margerita Cansino (a name soon altered to the more accessible **Rita Hayworth**).

1949: Diminutive, deep-voiced **Maria Ouspenskaya**, 73, dies on this day at the Motion Picture Country Home from a stroke and the burns she suffered three days earlier while smoking in bed. The Russian-born actress specialized in making much of little. Broadway's *Dodsworth* allotted her 21 lines of dialogue, but she used them to illuminate a world beyond her character — the proud, doomed Old World aristocracy — and she repeated that trick on screen, earning an Oscar nomination for her U.S. movie bow; another nomination came three years later as **Charles Boyer's** grandmother in *Love Affair*. Hailing from the Moscow Art Theater, she taught acting between her 20 films, and she did Teacher to the italic hilt in films, too — of piano (*I've Always Loved You, A Kiss in the Dark*), ballet (*Waterloo Bridge, Dance, Girl, Dance*) and gypsy lore (*The Wolf Man, Frankenstein Meets the Wolf Man*); even when patently miscast in *Tarzan and the Amazons* as queen of the latter litter, all 90 pounds of her lorded majestically over them.

1964: From 6 p.m. to 12 midnight on this day, director **Sam Peckinpah** labors diligently over a throwaway scene from *The Cincinnati Kid*, in which gambler **Rip Torn** sets up a big poker game over the phone while fondling a half-clad cutie, who lies stretched across the bed reading a book called *The Power of Surrender*. By the time he got the take he wanted, the girl was stark naked beneath a fur coat. Although the nudity was more sensed than seen, producer **Martin Ransohoff** was shocked enough to fire Peckinpah and replace him with **Norman Jewison**. Reporting this change in directors, trade journals compounded Ransohoff's misinterpretation by giving the impression that Peckinpah was spending MGM money to film his own private pornography — a damaging falsehood that kept Peckinpah away from directing features until *The Wild Bunch* brought him back with a bang four years later.

MARIA TO THE MAX: Irene Dunne, Maria Ouspenskaya and Charles Boyer in *Love Affair*.
OFF AND RUNNING: Oliver Hardy and Stan Laurel in *Putting Pants on Philip*.
DEBUTING ON A DANCE FLOOR: Rita Cansino (Hayworth) and Gary Leon in *Dante's Inferno*.

NEWT TOWN: Spencer Tracy and Mickey Rooney in *Boys Town*.
DEMILLE'S FIRST TEN: Theodore Roberts in *The Ten Commandments*.
LAHR'S LAST NIGHT: Britt Ekland and Bert Lahr in *The Night They Raided Minsky's*.

1923: In a premiere at Grauman's Egyptian Theater in Hollywood on this day, **Cecil B. DeMille** issues his first set of *The Ten Commandments*. It took the producer-director 45 films to find his first Bible story, and even then the public had to show him the way: The *Los Angeles Times* held a contest in which the entrant with the best movie idea would get $1000; eight suggested the story of Moses and The Ten Commandments so director DeMille dutifully doled out a grand to each of the eight.

1932: "Quite the disappointment of the year," laments **Philip K. Scheuer** on this day in the *Los Angeles Times*, "is the news of **Erich von Stroheim**'s failure as director of *Walking Down Broadway*. Ballyhooed as potentially great, touted sky-high to exhibitors, it goes back for a complete remake at Fox studios." When it came out of that mix, it was unrecognizably revised, stripped of von Stroheim, and — worse, still — called *Hello, Sister!* This first brush with sound was his second incomplete film in a (very slow) row — following at a respectable distance his 1928 debacle of *Queen Kelly* — but those two strikes were enough to put him out of the directing ballgame. His lifetime total: seven completed films that got to market, maimed and mangled by the meat-grinding studio system. He never ran out of ideas, just studios.

1967: The Cowardly Lion (a.k.a. **Bert Lahr**, 72) dies on this day of cancer, a disease he never knew he had. His obituaries reported the cause of death as pneumonia, developed shortly after starting *The Night They Raided Minsky's*. That movie was subsequently rewritten, and edited, to utilize all of his footage — a fond farewell which was warmly applauded by the critics when the film came out.

1988: A motorcycle mishap in Culver City on this day sends **Gary Busey** flying head-first and unhelmeted into a curb, and two hours of surgery are required to save his life. An outspoken opponent of mandatory helmets for bikers, Busey remained unregenerated, but in time the near-tragedy did turn his head around.

1994: Returning fire to the First Lady for labeling as "unbelievable and absurd" his proposal to use orphanages to reduce welfare rolls, House Speaker-elect **Newt Gingrich** uses an appearance on NBC-TV's *Meet the Press* on this day to tell **Hillary Rodham Clinton** where to go: i.e., "to Blockbuster and rent the **Mickey Rooney** movie about Boys Town." The remark got him headlines and the invitation of Turner Broadcasting System boss **Ted Turner** to host a showing of 1938's *Boys Town* on TNT's *Our Favorite Movies*. The Republican congressman jumped at the chance and taped an appearance that aired on Dec. 29.

5

1939: Director **Ernst Lubitsch** closes *The Shop Around the Corner* after a month or so of filming. **Margaret Sullavan** and **James Stewart** starred as antagonistic storeclerks who become, unwittingly, amorous penpals. So well constructed was this featherweight fluff that it was musically remade for films (1949's *In the Good Old Summertime* with **Judy Garland** and **Van Johnson**) *and* for Broadway (1963's *She Loves Me* with **Barbara Cook** and **Daniel Massey**) and again, for films, *sans* songs (1998's *You've Got Mail* with **Meg Ryan** and **Tom Hanks**).

1939: Composer **Max Steiner** completes his *Gone With the Wind* score, 16 weeks after starting it and 10 days before the film's Atlanta launching. A magnificent work, it ran longer than any other score (three hours and 45 minutes), had 16 individual themes and was divided into 282 separate musical segments—but this wasn't enough for an Academy Award. The Oscar for 1939's Best Original Score went to an *orchestrator* (!), **Herbert Stothart**, who merely *arranged* the song score **Harold Arlen** had *composed* for *The Wizard of Oz*.

1963: The performer who holds the Guinness record for performing in the most movies—**Tom London**—dies at age 81. He was a locomotive driver who was asked to play one in *The Great Train Robbery* of '03, the first of more than 2,000 appearances he racked up during almost 60 years on the screen. By 1919 he was starring in Universal films under his real name (Leonard Clapham), which he changed in 1924. When he grew too old for leads, he took on character roles. Sheriffs in B-Westerns (and lower) were a specialty.

1963: Radio City Music Hall opens its Christmas picture—the stylish and unseasonably violent *Charade*—only two weeks after **JFK**'s death in Dallas. The word "assassinate" was the first to go—**Cary Grant** and **Audrey Hepburn** hastily redubbed "eliminate" in its place—but a certain stigma stayed. "[*New York Times* critic] **Bosley Crowther** was still upset and blamed us for the Kennedy assassination," said scripter **Peter Stone**, overreacting a bit.

1984: The first movie to hit 2,000 screens simultaneously—*Beverly Hills Cop*—makes **Eddie Murphy** a Star. **Sylvester Stallone** had nixed the flick.

A STAR SHOT: Eddie Murphy in *Beverly Hills Cop*.
HE STAYED ON THE TRAIN: Tom London, Katy Jurado and Grace Kelly in *High Noon*.
SHOPWORN: From bottom to top: James Stewart and Margaret Sullavan in *The Shop Around the Corner*; Van Johnson and Judy Garland in *In the Good Old Summertime*, and Meg Ryan and Tom Hanks in *You've Got Mail*.

1935: The opening title card for *A Night at the Opera*, hitting the screen of New York's Capitol on this day, proclaims — to a highly appropriate tune from **Ruggerio Leoncavallo**'s opera *I Pagliacci* (*The Clowns*) — Metro-Goldwyn-Mayer presents the **Marx** Brothers **Groucho Chico Harpo**. Somehow, **Zeppo** got lost in the two-year shuffle from Paramount to MGM — but not to the detriment of the trio remaining. Divided, they conquered: "The loudest and funniest screen comedy of the Winter season," ruled *The New York Times'* **Andre Sennwald**.

1948: On this day, *Life* magazine pitches its cover to **Montgomery Clift**, predicting stardom for him on the basis of his performances in *Red River* and *The Search*. The latter, which made the Oscar running two months later, was directed by **Fred Zinnemann**, who five years later picked Clift (over **Brando**) for *From Here to Eternity*; the results returned both to the Oscar running.

1962: At 3:30 p.m. on this day, in Kramer Park (a back-lot square block at Revue Studios), **Spencer Tracy** is hurled into a pet shop, and a half-dozen dogs rush over with warm licks — that's the way *It's a Mad, Mad, Mad, Mad World* ends, after 636,000 feet of exposed film (approximately 125 miles). Only 21,938 feet were released to the public, and that dwindled after roadshows — but the video got the length back up there and threw in cut footage as well.

1986: The stars of *Wisdom*, **Emilio Estevez** and **Demi Moore**, display some on this day. Calling their cold feet scheduling conflicts, they decided not to wed. In less than a year (Nov. 21, 1987), Moore the marrier headed back down the aisle and, this time, got there, tying the knot with **Bruce Willis**.

1992: Seasoned sagebrusher **Hank Worden**, 91, dies of natural causes on this day in Los Angeles. In 1930 he and his rodeo roommate, **Tex Ritter**, made a sharp right turn into show business when they were tapped to play cowhands in Broadway's *Green Grow the Lilacs* (later musicalized into *Oklahoma!*). Worden film-debuted supporting DeMille's Wild Bill (a.k.a. **Gary Cooper**'s *The Plainsman*) and stayed in the movie West for most of his career, almost always at the side of **John Wayne** (*The Fighting Kentuckian*, *Chisum*, *Rio Lobo*, *Fort Apache*, *Three Godfathers*, *Angel and the Badman*). He played Wayne's sidekick off-camera too, standing watch outside the hospital room during The Duke's last rounds with cancer. His best bit: Old Mose Harper, who loved his rocking chair, in Wayne's (and **John Ford**'s) great Western, *The Searchers*.

MUSICAL MARX: Harpo, Chico and Groucho in *A Night at the Opera*.
IN THE SHADOW OF THE DUKE: Hank Worden, Frankie Avalon and John Wayne in *The Alamo*.
WISE DUO: Demi Moore and Emilio Estevez in *Wisdom*.

1931: With the bold stroke of a pen — as Archibald Alexander Leach (then 27 years, 11 months and one week old) signs up for his first five years in films at $450 a week — **Cary Grant** is officially born on this day. The studio insisted on the name change, and Archie Leach was summarily retired, surfacing only as inside jokes for Grant in *Gunga*

Din and *His Girl Friday* and as the name of the character **John Cleese** played as an homage in *A Fish Called Wanda*. **Fay Wray** and her play-writing husband, **John Monk Saunders**, suggested he take the name of the character he'd just played on Broadway in their fast-to-fold flop, *Nikki* — Cary Lockwood — and Paramount prexy B.P. Schulberg refined that with the right surname plucked from a typewritten list of alternatives. Cary Grant not only invited instant confusion with **Gary Cooper**, it also carried the same box-office punch as **Clark Gable**'s initials. (Grant and Gable used to get together every Christmas to swap any monogrammed presents which the other didn't want.)

1941: Japan attacks Pearl Harbor on this day, necessitating a production shutdown and rewrite on **John Huston**'s *Across the Pacific*, an action adventure about Japan attacking Pearl Harbor (!) already before the cameras at Warners!

1944: On this day, **Joan Crawford** does The Studio Switch — from MGM to Warners — and gets busy on what'll be her Oscar-winning performance: *Mildred Pierce*.

PEARL HARBOR ANTICIPATORS: Sydney Greenstreet, Humphrey Bogart, Victor Sen Yung and Mary Astor in *Across the Pacific*.
CARY-IN ON: John Cleese in *A Fish Called Wanda*.
O CHRISTMAS THREE: John Payne, Natalie Wood and Edmund Gwenn in *Miracle on 34th Street*.

1968: On this day — the 27th anniversary of the Day of Infamy — the most famous name in Japanese cinema, **Akira Kurosawa**, begins filming his country's side of the story for 20th Century-Fox. Seventeen days later, on Christmas Eve, the director was removed from *Tora! Tora! Tora!* because Fox believed him ill — just because he was demanding protection from assassins and insisting the national anthem be played, with all standing at attention, when he arrived on the set.

1989: Hours after *Miracle on 34th Street* flickered by on his bedroom TV set and he was too sick to watch it, 77-year-old **John Payne** dies of congestive heart failure at his Malibu home. That was the flick where Payne played the lawyer who proved in a court of law there really *is* a Santa Claus.

1997: "Baby and Moses" — **Lauren Bacall** and **Charlton Heston** — wind up on this day among the 20th set of recipients for the Kennedy Center Honors in Washington.

BOMBS AWAY: From left: Slim Pickens replacing Peter Sellers in *Dr. Strangelove*.
COALHOUSE ONE: Howard E. Rollins Jr. in *Ragtime*.

1938: Rendering the results of a readership poll, columnist **Ed Sullivan** presents The King and Queen of Hollywood with velvet and tin crowns at Hollywood's El Capitan Theater. As expected, **Clark Gable** was The King, remaining so the rest of his days, but few recall his Queen — which was okay with **Myrna Loy**. "Gable remembered," she'd say with pride in her eyes. "He always called me Queenie." Gable's raucous fiancée, **Carole Lombard**, behaved herself during the coronation broadcast — but later quipped, "If Clark had an inch less, he'd be Queen of Hollywood!"

1941: "Now, boys and girls, we . . . have had bad news, but we have a wonderful story to tell the world, so let's put away sad things and begin," director **Michael Curtiz** tells his cast on this day, after **President Roosevelt**'s radio broadcast declaring war on Germany and Japan. Thus, filming started — the day after Pearl Harbor — on the ultimate cinematic flag-waver, *Yankee Doodle Dandy*. **James Cagney** originally turned the title role down but took it on when **George M. Cohan** (terminally ill with cancer) insisted. It earned Cagney the first Oscar ever accorded a musical performance and remains the work for which he is most remembered — this, despite his imposing gallery of killers, kooks, cons and crooks.

1950: A routine cops-and-robbers flick with **Steve Cochran** screeches into New York's Strand on this day, leaving behind a winding trail of movie-title roadkill — from *The Two-Million-Dollar Bank Robbery* to *Road Block* to *The Million Dollar Bank Robbery* to *The Tri-State Gang* — ultimately arriving (D.O.A.) as *Highway 301*.

1983: Despite a cowpoke past as rodeo star and B-Western sidekick, when **Slim Pickens** dies of pneumonia on this day, the image he leaves behind is more bomb-riding than bronc-riding: Major T.J. King Kong in **Stanley Kubrick**'s *Dr. Strangelove, Or How I Learned To Stop Worrying and Love the Bomb*, coming out of the bomb-bay doors of his B-52, straddling an atomic bomb and riding it all the way down to Doomsday. The part was initially on **Peter Sellers**' plate, but a broken ankle during filming forced him to relinquish it to Pickens. Critics loved the cry of triumph that turned to bloodcurdling terror in Pickens' final free-fall shot — the result, he said, of doing his own stunt.

1996: *Ragtime*'s firebrand, Coalhouse Walker Jr., flickers anew on this day — brought back to life by **Brian Stokes Mitchell** in a stage musicalization remake bowing in Toronto — only two hours after the role's Oscar-nominated originator (**Howard E. Rollins Jr.**, 46) expires of cancer in New York. The promise in Rollins' *Ragtime* arrival went unrealized, leading only to another film (1984's *A Soldier's Story*) and a TV series based on 1967's Oscar-winning *In the Heat of the Night*.

1941: Fresh from escorting **Greta Garbo** into permanent screen retirement (via *Two-Faced Woman*), **Melvyn Douglas** goes into *We Were Dancing*, **Norma Shearer**'s next-to-last film outing. Attention strayed only once, for seconds, to Something Spectacular in slacks and a silk blouse crossing the hotel lobby (**Ava Gardner** in her first screen slink-on).

1944: On this day, a heart attack kills **Laird Cregar**, 28, the portly menace of *I Wake Up Screaming* and *The Lodger*, dieting for his first heterosexual affair.

1954: The five-month, two-film stardom of model-turned-actress **Doe Avedon**, which started as the stewardess serving *The High and the Mighty*, finishes as **Mrs. Sigmund Romberg** on this day when *Deep in My Heart* bows at Radio City Music Hall. Her own marriage — to photographer **Richard Avedon** — came first, but it was kaput by the time writer **Leonard Gershe** got a fictional facsimile of it onto the screen. **Fred Astaire** put on hold (permanently, it turned out) *Papa's Delicate Condition* to play Avedon, but the leading lady proved more elusive. **Carol Haney**, in *The Pajama Game* on Broadway, was first choice; then, **Cyd Charisse**. Eventually, Gershe came across a quote from **Audrey Hepburn** in a film magazine, longing to do musicals — and the result was *Funny Face*.

1981: Newly Oscared **Timothy Hutton** is topped by **Sean Penn** and **Tom Cruise** in *Taps*, a cadet drama parading New Faces of 1982 into theaters on this day.

1983: "Go ahead, make my day," **Clint Eastwood** invites the survivor of a holdup quartet who is going for his gun — in an otherwise unmemorable fourth Dirty Harry film opening in New York. *Sudden Impact* was not only the name of that picture, it was also how that particular catch-phrase caught on.

1991: For all we know, suggests *Variety*, the **Bette**-versus-**Barbra** battle may have a fleck of truth to it — a rumor prompted by the fact that both **Midler** and **Streisand** have films racing for the same awards and audiences at year's end: *The Prince of Tides* originally ended with Streisand singing "For All We Know" over the closing credits, but she (as director) yanked it suddenly, she said, because she didn't want to divert attention from **Nick Nolte** (but some suspected it was because Midler got to market six weeks earlier with that song in *For the Boys*). Midler lost the money race but made the Oscar one for Best Actress; Streisand missed that nomination as well as the one for Best Director but made the one for Best Picture (as producer) and drew Oscar-nominated work from six others (notably, Nolte and **Kate Nelligan**).

10

1934: Broadway tap star **Eleanor Powell** goes into her screen career on this day as *George White's 1935 Scandals* goes into production. From that guest shot, she stepped up to the star spot of *Broadway Melody of 1936*; of the 11 flicks that followed, only *Sensations of 1945* was not at MGM.

1936: Wrapping today is *Top of the Town*, a musical revue that introduces a new Universal logo: Instead of a plane circling a globe, it's the world that turns and glitters. Another feature bow: **Peggy Ryan**, 12, reprising a pint-sized **Eleanor Powell** routine she had done at an Actors' Fund Benefit. (She and **Donald O'Connor** were happy tappers at Universal during World War II.)

1938: Just after the torch is put to his backlot sets, **David O. Selznick** meets **Vivien Leigh** — and, in the amber glow of Atlanta in flames, the producer sees his Scarlett O'Hara. She screen-tested on Dec. 21–22, and, three days later when she asked director **George Cukor** at his Christmas party who'd play the part, he told her: "I guess we're stuck with you." The official announcement came Jan. 13, causing one of the other finalists (**Jean Arthur**, **Joan Bennett** or **Paulette Goddard**) to burn her screen test in a fit of anger.

1960: The man who would be **Laurence Olivier** is born on this day: **Kenneth Branagh**, who, 29 years later, made the same audacious film-directing debut Olivier did at 36: directing himself as Henry V. Whereas Olivier's opus netted nominations for Best Actor and Best Picture and an honorary Oscar, Branagh's nabbed nominations for Best Actor and Best Director and an actual Oscar (for **Phyllis Dalton**'s costumes). In other acting-directing efforts, Branagh has (1) been made up in *Dead Again* to resemble Olivier's Maxim de Winter in *Rebecca*, (2) taken up Olivier's torch for bringing Shakespeare to the screen (*Much Ado About Nothing*) and (3) even taken on Olivier's Oscar-winning role (Hamlet).

1978: Never fully mindful of the depths of his fame, the man hailed (with a certain universality) as the worst director of all time — **Ed Wood Jr.**, 56 — dies of a heart attack on this day. His rotten roster of films — *Plan 9 From Outer Space* and *Glen or Glenda?* arguably reek the worst — was awful enough to earn him a cult following and a posthumous film biography by the equally kinky but infinitely more talented **Tim Burton**. The Oscar that had eluded him in life (by several light years!) finally went to *Ed Wood* in 1995 — not to **Johnny Depp**'s commendably clueless title performance but to **Martin Landau**'s brilliant supporting one of Wood's star attraction: **Bela Lugosi**, in spectacular decline.

11

1905: In Juarez, Mexico, is born Luis Antonio Damaso De Alonso. Paramount prexy **B.P. Schulberg** tried to change that name to John Adams, but the actor who later played in *Juarez* (the movie) opted for **Gilbert Roland**.

1940: *A Dispatch from Reuters*, opening at New York's Globe and following *Dr. Ehrlich's Magic Bullet*, ends a patch of Pauls (and facial hair) for **Edward G. Robinson** — namely: **Paul Julius Reuter**, who founded the news service, and **Paul Ehrlich**, who developed the cure for venereal disease. It also ended the Warner Bros. days of **William Dieterle**, who directed both bios.

1944: When **Otto Preminger** was making *Laura* and **Gypsy Rose Lee** was making *Belle of the Yukon*, their paths crossed in Hollywood — amorously — resulting in a son, born out of wedlock on this day in New York Hospital. At her insistence, his paternity was kept secret until after her death in 1970. The following March 10, the director claimed him and named him **Erik Lee Preminger**, officially adopting him and later employing him as the screenwriter of his 1975 *Rosebud*.

1984: The Motion Picture Academy acknowledges two blacklisted scripters — **Carl Foreman** and **Michael Wilson** — as the actual screenwriters of *The Bridge on the River Kwai* and move that the Academy Awards that were denied them 27 years earlier be sent to their widows. Foreman, who never got an Oscar but was up for five (*High Noon*, *Champion*, *The Men*, *The Guns of Navarone* and *Young Winston*), learned the award was on the way hours before his death of cancer June 26, 1984. **Pierre Boulle**, who wrote the French novel from which the *Kwai* film came, had been given the Best Screenplay prize — despite the slight fact that he could neither read nor write English.

1991: Nine months after winning 1990's Best Picture Oscar (for *Dances With Wolves*) and three months before winning 1991's (for *The Silence of the Lambs*), Orion Pictures files on this day for Chapter 11 bankruptcy protection. Four years later, Orion is still winning Oscars with what it already has in the can: **Jessica Lange** plucks a 1994 Best Actress Oscar out of 1991's *Blue Sky*.

1992: With launchings in more than 50 nations around the world, *A Few Good Men* garners the Guinness nod for most simultaneous world premieres.

A PAUL-ING TIME: From left: Edward G. Robinson in *A Dispatch From Reuters* and *Dr. Ehrlich's Magic Bullet*.
MILITARY MEN: From left: Donald Crisp and Gilbert Roland in *Juarez*; Jack Nicholson and Tom Cruise in *A Few Good Men*.

THREE EIGHTHS: From left: Charles Laughton in *The Private Life of Henry VIII*, Robert Shaw in *A Man for All Seasons* and Richard Burton in *Anne of the Thousand Days*.
JUDGE FOR YOURSELF: Sylvester Stallone in *Judge Dredd*.
ROMAN ERUPTION: Mario Vitale and Ingrid Bergman in *Stromboli*.

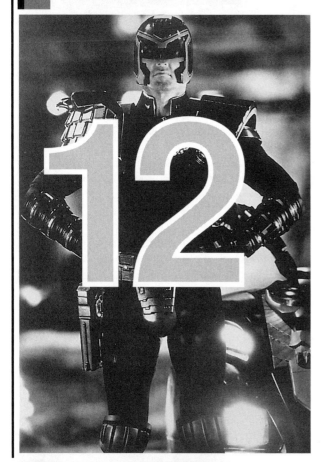

12

1928: With the oldest Episcopalian minister in Virginia officiating (her own grandfather, **Rev. Sewell Stavely Hepburn**, 83), **Katharine Hepburn** begins her brush with matrimony — a union of less than two months — by marrying **Ludlow Ogden Smith** in her parents' West Hartford home. She accepted his proposal when he changed his name to Ogden Ludlow (she didn't want to be called Mrs. Smith or, worse, Kate Smith). They didn't divorce till 1934, but the marriage was over when Hepburn asked for the job back she'd given up to get married: understudying **Hope Williams** in Broadway's *Holiday* (a part Hepburn did in films a decade later).

1939: One era of Hollywood history ends as another begins: **Douglas Fairbanks Sr.**, 56, dies of a heart attack the same day *Gone With the Wind* is press-previewed. Its director, **Victor Fleming**, ducked the film's Atlanta launch to be pallbearer for the star who'd given him his start in films. Fairbanks' widow, **Lady Sylvia Ashley**, married Rhett Butler a decade and five days later (Dec. 17, 1949), becoming the fourth of **Clark Gable**'s five wives.

1949: The Los Angeles *Examiner* hits the stands with **INGRID BERGMAN** BABY DUE IN THREE MONTHS AT ROME. Tipped off by **Howard Hughes** that the actress and **Roberto Rossellini** were more than movie-making, **Louella O. Parsons** played her scoop grandly: "Few women in history, or men either, have made the sacrifice the Swedish star has made for love." Bergman wasn't impressed: "She said she cried over her typewriter when she had to write the news that I was delivering a son! I think they were tears of joy."

1969: Universal telegraphs **Richard Burton** that the press response in NYC and L.A. to *Anne of the Thousand Days* was nothing short of sensational — or, at least, superior to *A Man for All Seasons* and *The Lion in Winter* — but the actor is unconvinced, having gone into overtime making this mediocre rubbish credible. "We shall see," he writes in his diary. What he sees Feb. 16 is that he is the third Henry VIII to make the Oscar race. No other role produced so many acting nominations — but his was only a nomination (as in **Robert Shaw** for *A Man for All Seasons*), not the award (as in **Charles Laughton** for *The Private Life of Henry VIII*); Laughton won the hard way: His Oscar for Best Actor of 1932–33 was the first Oscar awarded to a non-Hollywood picture.

1995: *Judge Dredd* (i.e., **Sylvester Stallone** as a futuristic comic-strip crimefighter) hits video stores on this day. Cracked a self-deprecating Stallone about the video cover: "Why didn't someone tell me I looked like a Buick?"

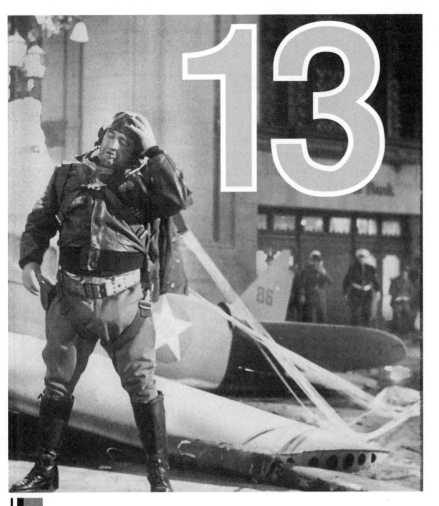

13

1940: Two noted American novelists reduced to Hollywood hacks — **Nathanael West**, 37, and **F. Scott Fitzgerald**, 44 — commiserate over dinner at West's North Hollywood abode on this day with West's bride of eight months (**Eileen McKenney**) and Fitzgerald's gossip-columnist girlfriend (**Sheilah Graham**). In nine days' time, three of the four would be dead. Fitzgerald succumbed to a heart attack in Los Angeles on Dec. 21, and the next day the Wests were killed in a car crash near El Centro, California. Many were surprised that West was driving; a suicidally bad driver, he usually left the driving outside the city limits to his wife. (Inside the city limits, his male vanity dictated that he take the wheel.) One week after the accident, a play inspired by Mrs. West — *My Sister Eileen* — bowed at the Biltmore on Broadway, to raves and a long run.

1951: Suspecting that wife **Joan Bennett** is cuckolding him with agent **Jennings Lang**, producer **Walter Wanger** surprises them in the MCA parking lot, whips out a .38-caliber pistol and fires twice, one bullet hitting the agent in the groin. Lang lived, and Wanger did some time (albeit, 98 days).

1958: *The Inn of the Sixth Happiness* opens in New York — over the protests of its subject, China missionary **Gladys Aylward**: "I understand the film contains a love scene. I never had a love scene in my life." Nor did she like being played by **Ingrid Bergman**, despite critical raves to the contrary (London's *Daily Sketch* called it "the finest performance of her life — the most beautiful, indeed, since **Garbo**'s peak"). A decade later, Bergman traveled to Formosa to meet Aylward finally — but arrived ten days after Aylward's death.

1979: Director **Steven Spielberg**, who was born in 1947, unveils his *1941* at New York's Rivoli on the day, not accidentally, that just happens to be the 38th anniversary of the day depicted in his film — six days after Pearl Harbor when comic pandemonium was supposedly rampant up and down California's coast. This $27.5-million "one-man's opinion" didn't quite jive with the view held by *The New York Times*' film critic, **Vincent Canby**, who contended that all this chaos was as much fun as a 40-pound wristwatch. Even with the pre-*Blues Brothers* duo of **Dan Aykroyd** and **John Belushi** on board, the film bombed badly, prompting *Saturday Night Live* pal, **Michael O'Donoghue**, to print up special birthday buttons for Belushi proclaiming "John Belushi: Born 1950, Died 1941."

GROGGY LANDING: John Belushi in *1941*. AYLWARD AND ONWARD: Ingrid Bergman and Curt Jurgens in *The Inn of the Sixth Happiness*. AN AFFAIR TO REMEMBER: Joan Bennett.

6-18

1944: "Mexican Spitfire" **Lupe Velez** commits suicide on this day in the Beverly Hills hacienda she called "Casa Felicitas" — Happy House — leaving behind a damning note to the father of her unborn child (French actor **Harald Ramond**).

1968: The first X rating ever handed down by the freshly formed Motion Picture Association of America greets *Greetings* (its X was later reduced to an R). An anti-Establishment antic preaching to the converted draft-age set, the film depicted the libidinous limbo of three guys waiting for word from Uncle Sam. "The trio of beatniks are **Jonathan Warden**, **Gerritt Graham** and **Robert Di Niro**," noted *Variety*'s "**Japa**," who had better luck spelling the name of the film's director and co-writer, **Brian De Palma**. De Niro and De Palma had film-debuted together five years earlier with *The Wedding Party* but lacked the funds to get the film to market; in the credits of that, the actor's name was spelled "Robert De Nero."

1985: Members of the Los Angeles Film Critics Association show up for a showdown on this day — in a back room of the Beverly Hills Gun Club, aptly enough — and emerged from their voting huddle with *Brazil* as Best Picture and its director-writer (Monty Python's **Terry Gilliam**) doubly honored for Best Direction and Best Screenplay (co-written with **Tom Stoppard** and **Charles McKeown**). They'd seen the movie only the week before in clandestine screenings in the basement of the Irving Thalberg Building at MGM — clandestine because the company that made it (Universal) abandoned it, deeming it interminable (MCA/Universal president **Sidney Sheinberg**) and unreleasable (MCA chairman **Lew Wasserman**). The honors persuaded them to think again.

1998: *Titanic* is launched at L.A.'s Mann's Chinese Theater on this day. The fact this occurred on the 14th of the month was not lost on **David Hochman**, who knitted an elaborate little riff for *Entertainment Weekly* about the significance of that number to the ship, starting with the day it struck the iceberg (April 14, 1912) and the coordinates where it sank (41 degrees 16' N 50 degrees 14' W). Mann's Chinese Theater has 1,492 seats (and 1492 was the year Columbus crossed the Atlantic). The film had 14 separate opening credits, ran three hours and 14 minutes and won 14 Oscar nominations. Thanks to the patronage of millions of 14-year-olds, it set the record for consecutive weekends as No. 1 in its 14th week, scored its biggest one-day take on Feb. 14 ($13,048,711), hit the $500 million mark at the end of its 14th week (its gross that day: $1.4 million) and surpassed *Star Wars* as the top-grossing film in history on March 14.

UNLUCKY 13 PLUS ONE: A scene from *Titanic*. SAD END AT HAPPY HOUSE: Lupe Velez. BARELY REFLECTED GLORY: Jonathan Pryce in *Brazil*.

15

1936: The millionth copy of *Gone With the Wind* is published, and publisher Macmillan presents it to author **Margaret Mitchell**, who'd given all her personal copies away.

1939: *Gone With the Wind* world-premieres in **Margaret Mitchell**'s backyard of Atlanta. Hollywood's elite planed in for the event and were greeted at the airport by a band playing "Dixie." "Listen, **David**," simpered the very British **Vivien Leigh** to producer **Selznick**, "they're playing the theme from the picture!" The film's other Oscar-winning actress, **Hattie McDaniel**, was already in Atlanta visiting friends, waiting in vain to be invited to the festivities. The next day, an unidentified woman offered a princely sum for **Clark Gable**'s hotel suite—provided the sheets hadn't been changed.

1957: A heart attack claims **Alfonso Bedoya**, 53. The Mexican character-actor, who'd just played the ranch hand assisting **Gregory Peck**'s bronc-taming in *The Big Country*, created a comic style from the frustrations accompanying his faulty English. Its most memorable application: Gold Hat, the bandido leader menacing **Humphrey Bogart** in *The Treasure of the Sierra Madre*—a bravado performance director **John Huston** badgered out of him with retakes ("Badges? We ain't got no badges. We don't need no badges. I don't have to show you any stinking badges!")

1993: Scarlett turns green on the 54th anniversary of the *Gone With the Wind* launching—when an anonymous telephone bidder shells out $510,000 to Sotheby's in New York for the Academy Award **Vivien Leigh** earned as Katie Scarlett O'Hara Hamilton Kennedy Butler. The actress was only paid a paltry $15,000 for the performance—plus, it came with a contract which kept her shackled to producer **David O. Selznick** for the next seven years.

1996: Scarlett sees red when the only Oscar accorded her Rhett Butler—**Clark Gable**, for 1934's *It Happened One Night*—fetches more cash at Christie's than was paid for **Viven Leigh**'s Scarlett O'Hara Oscar: $550,000 from an anonymous bidder, who turned out to be an Oscar winner himself and who returned the award to the Academy with a noble note attached: "The Oscar statuette is the most personal recognition of good work our industry can ever bestow, and it strikes me as a sad sign of our times that this icon could be confused with a commercial treasure." (**Steven Spielberg**, however, kept the other memento he picked up at the auction for $244,500—Gable's *Gone With the Wind* script—stashing it beside his $61,000 "Rosebud" sled from *Citizen Kane*.) The $1.5 million **Michael Jackson** paid June 12, 1999, for **David O. Selznick**'s Best Picture Oscar for *GWTW* set the record not only for an Oscar sale but for any single piece of movie memorabilia.

1943: Radium is discovered at Radio City Music Hall on this day by **Greer Garson**'s *Madame Curie*. It was a role **Garbo** left behind when she left movies.

1956: At the 10 a.m. mass on this Sunday, **Francis Cardinal Spellman** enters the pulpit of St. Patrick's Cathedral — the first time the Archbishop of New York has personally mounted the pulpit since February 1949 when he condemned the Communist jailing of **Joseph Cardinal Mindszenty** of Hungary — and warns Roman Catholics that it is a sin to see *Baby Doll*.

1960: Two months after the demise of **Clifton Webb**'s mother, **Noel Coward** records in his diary his dread of Webb's holiday visit and the accompanying wailing and sobbing over Maybelle's death. "As she was well over 90, gaga, and had driven him mad for years, this seems excessive and over-indulgent. He arrives here on Monday, and I'm dreaming of a wet Christmas." Indeed, the weepy Webb was unrelenting — till Coward finally made him dry up with: "It must be tough to be orphaned at 71."

1970: *Love Story* is launched at Loews State I in New York bringing two things new to movies — a cinematic catch phrase ("Love means never having to say you're sorry") and a future Oscar winner (billed 10th as **Tom Lee Jones**, who played **Ryan O'Neal**'s Harvard roommate and had been, in real life, **Al Gore**'s Harvard roommate).

1989: Heart attacks on this day claim a couple of key players in Italian cinema: **Silvana** (*Anna*, *Bitter Rice*) **Mangano**, 59, the actress-wife of producer **Dino De Laurentiis**, and **Lee** (*For a Few Dollars More*, *The Good, the Bad and the Ugly*) **Van Cleef**, 64, the Hollywood heavy-turned-Spaghetti Western hero.

1998: The most bizarre of the 1998 Best choices made by The New York Film Critics Circle is their Best Actress candidate: **Cameron Diaz** for *There's Something About Mary*, a fourth-ballot upset which *People* magazine's **Leah Rozen** characterized as "a groinswell." Neither Diaz nor the critics' supporting picks — **Bill Murray** for *Rushmore* or **Lisa Kudrow** for *The Opposite of Sex* — made the Oscar running. In fact, only in one category did the critics' choice coincide with Oscar's selection: *Shakespeare in Love* for Best Screenplay.

CURIE-O: Walter Pidgeon and Greer Garson in *Madame Curie*.
MUCH A 'DO: Cameron Diaz in *There's Something About Mary*.
BABY BASHING: Carroll Baker in *Baby Doll*.

1936: *Waikiki Wedding*, which **Bing Crosby** had initially nixed as not right for him, gets underway on the Paramount backlot (process photography to come), and The Groaner is indeed in that number, thanks to a fast rewrite. No doubt sweetening the deal: **Harry Owens**' "Sweet Leilani" — the first of four Oscar-winning songs Crosby introduced (more than anyone else).

1942: "Between the two of them," said director **Mervyn LeRoy** of his *Random Harvest* stars, **Ronald Colman** and **Greer Garson**, "the English language was never spoken more beautifully on film." On this day, their only screen teaming begins one of Radio City Music Hall's longest runs ever — and no thanks to the recommendation of critic **James Agee**: "I would like to recommend this film to those who can stay interested in Ronald Colman's amnesia for two hours and who could with pleasure eat a bowl of Yardley's shaving cream for breakfast."

1959: *On the Beach*, **Stanley Kramer's** 134-minute think piece on world peace (by depicting the Doomsday alternative) becomes the first film to bow simultaneously on both sides of the Iron Curtain in 18 world cities.

1975: *The Man Who Would Be King*, a Kipling romp that had long gnawed on adapter-director **John Huston**, finally premieres in New York, with **Sean Connery** and **Michael Caine** in the roles he had originally designed for **Gable** and **Bogart**. When the project was reactivated in the mid 70s, Huston saw it as sort of a *Butch Cassidy and the Sundance Kid Go to India* reunion for **Paul Newman** and **Robert Redford**, but Newman sent the script boomeranging back with the right idea: "For Christ's sake, John, get Connery and Caine!"

1987: A beautifully filmed short story from **James Joyce**'s *Dubliners* collection reaches New York's Cinema I D.O.A. (i.e., under its defiantly uncommercial original title: *The Dead*). Sadly, the same state applied to the film's great director, **John Huston**, who didn't live to see this last triumph, having died in his sleep of complications from emphysema four months earlier.

1993: Christie's in London fetches 55,000 pounds for a hat and cane — once wielded on the screen, with art and grace, by **Charles Chaplin**.

HAIL, BRITANNIA! Greer Garson and Ronald Colman in *Random Harvest*.
SIDEKICK & *KING*: Michael Caine and Sean Connery in *The Man Who Would Be King*.
SWEET LEILANIS: Martha Raye, Bing Crosby and Shirley Ross in *Waikiki Wedding*.

18

1913: The director-general of **Jesse L. Lasky**'s Feature Play Company, **Cecil B. DeMille**, steps off the train at Flagstaff, AZ, on this bright, hopeful, sunshiny day — and doesn't like what he sees: The scenery was not at all the Wyoming he and Oscar Apfel had envisioned on the ride out, scripting the movie they'd co-direct, *The Squaw Man* — so, before the train could leave the station, he herded his star (**Dustin Farnum**), the star's dresser (**Fred Kley**) and the cameraman (**Al Gandolfi**) back on board, and all pressed on to L.A., the end of the line — in several senses of the phrase — and the beginning of Hollywood.

1957: The Bridge on the River Kwai opens for business at Broadway's Palace. To play a role that didn't exist in the novel (and was invented wholly to give the film an American reference point), **William Holden** got $300,000 plus ten percent of the profits — making him the highest paid film star in the world — and he was fourth choice for the role, too! (**Humphrey Bogart**, **Cary Grant** and **Montgomery Clift** couldn't, or wouldn't, do it.) **Alec Guinness** got much less but won every major Best Actor award of the year — for a part he turned down initially. **Noel Coward**, **Ralph Richardson**, **Laurence Olivier**, **Spencer Tracy**, **Anthony Quayle**, **Ray Milland**, **Douglas Fairbanks Jr.**, **James Mason** and **Ronald Colman** were considered till Guinness came around — a decision he tried to rescind when director **David Lean** greeted him on location in Ceylon with "They sent me you, and I wanted **Charles Laughton**." Ironically, Laughton — in his last great performance (in *Witness for the Prosecution*) — was one of the stars Guinness beat out of the Oscar.

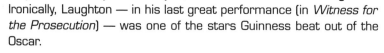

1959: With guards posted outside Universal's Stage 18-A, **Janet Leigh** starts spending the week in the shower, filming her slash-and-splash *Psycho* demise. Her killer, **Anthony Perkins**, was actually on the other coast, rehearsing *Greenwillow* for Broadway when the actual shooting/stabbing took place (a double did the dirty work). After the scene, Leigh swore off showers forever.

1974: The second movie **Billy Wilder** got out of **Jennings Lang** bows at two Manhattan theaters. For this one — a third filming of *The Front Page*, with **Jack Lemmon** and **Walter Matthau** — Lang was executive producer. For the other, he was the unofficial inspiration: Rumor was, when Lang was wounded by the cuckolded **Walter Wanger**, the trysts were held in the pad of an unmarried subordinate at Lang's agency. Wilder coupled this notion of professional advancement with a character who caught his interest in *Brief Encounter* (the barely seen stranger who obligingly supplied the adultery space for **Celia Johnson** and **Trevor Howard**) — and *voila!* he was off to winning three Oscars for producing, directing and co-writing *The Apartment*.

19

RUINING RAIN: Malcolm McDowell in *A Clockwork Orange*.
OFF TO THE FRONT: Jennifer Jones and Rock Hudson in *A Farewell to Arms*.
IN LIEU OF MARIO AND MARLON: From left: Edmund Purdom (with Ann Blyth) in *The Student Prince* and in *The Egyptian*.

1924: One of the Ready-Or-Not New Faces of 1954 is born: **Edmund Purdom**. The dashing Brit stepped from 14th billing aboard 1953's *Titanic* (as the ship underling who sounded the iceberg alert) to the title roles of *The Student Prince* and *The Egyptian*, both freshly vacated by demanding stars: In the first, he pretended **Mario Lanza**'s glorious tenor streamed from his tentative lips; in the second, he uttered the diseased dialogue **Marlon Brando** couldn't stomach. These two strikes were followed by two more title roles — these earmarked for the also-temperamental **Stewart Granger** (*The Prodigal* and *The King's Thief*). Then, the pooped Purdom went abroad and tapered off into a line of B films.

1957: *A Farewell to Arms*, **David O. Selznick**'s last lush effort as a movie producer, debuts on this day at Grauman's Chinese. Top-billed was the man who, in order to do it, turned down an Oscar-nominated role (**Marlon Brando**'s in *Sayonara*), an Oscar-winning role (**Charlton Heston**'s in *Ben-Hur*) and a star-making role (**John Gavin**'s in *A Time To Love and a Time To Die*) — the same man who, in his truck-driving days a decade before, loitered near the back gates of Selznick's studio, hoping to be noticed by some star-spotter: **Rock Hudson**.

1971: Going into orbit at New York's Cinema I, *A Clockwork Orange* touches off controversy over a bit of the old ultra-violence, not the least of which is reprising *Singin' in the Rain* as music-to-rape-by. **Malcolm McDowell**, the singing rapist in question, plucked that song out of his own head ("it's the only song I know") while shooting the sequence, and clearance was secured later — but sore feelings followed: When he later crossed paths with **Gene Kelly** (whose jubilant rendition of the tune — his signature song — accompanies *Clockwork*'s credit-crawl), the unamused Kelly cold-shouldered him.

1996: Rome's famed Trevi Fountain where **Marcello Mastroianni** once cavorted with curvy **Anita Ekberg** in *La Dolce Vita* is shut off and draped in black cloth on this day to mark the passing, in Paris, of the screen's most celebrated Latin lover since Rudolph Valentino. The next day's *New York Post* headline said it all: LA DOLCE VITA IS OVER FOR MASTROIANNI. The 72-year-old Italian star died of pancreatic cancer, flanked by an old flame (**Catherine Deneuve**) and their 25-year-old daughter (**Chiara**, his last co-star — in *Three Lives and Only One Death*). His body was flown home to Rome where it laid in state on the Campidoglio, the town hall square, prior to a secular funeral arranged by **Flora Carabella**, whom he married in 1948, and their daughter, **Barbara**. Seated with the grieving family was **Sophia Loren**, his playing partner in a dozen films.

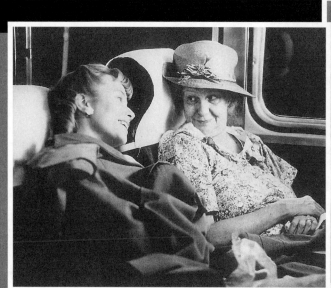

1938: *Plane No. 4* takes off into production, its working title flapping in the wind, eventually getting to market as *Only Angels Have Wings*. **Howard Hawks** directed (as only Howard Hawks could) this manly adventure romp about a tinny air-freight service in the banana port of Barranca running mail across the Andes. Most people, if they remember the movie at all, remember it incorrectly as the one in which **Cary Grant** said to **Rita Hayworth** "Judy, Judy, Judy." Although he was constantly saying things like "Come on, Judy" and "Hello, Judy" and "Now, Judy," the triple configuration didn't come in that film. His most imitated line of dialogue simply never existed — unless, he once allowed, he said it doing a Lux Radio Theater commercial with **Judy Garland**.

1950: **Stewart Granger** and **Jean Simmons** (who met among the rabble supporting Shaw's *Caesar and Cleopatra* and made a convincing romantic couple in *Adam and Evalyn*) wed in Tucson, with **Michael Wilding** serving as best man. That was the fadeout **Michael Powell** anticipated when he directed her as the native-girl siren in *Black Narcissus* and Granger saw her in costume, eating a squishy fruit with a ring through her nose. Powell always said it was the baggy umbrella she carried that, he felt, "was the final erotic touch."

1957: Columbia Pictures shuts its short shop officially on this day with the completion of *Sappy Bullfighters*, the final featurette of **The Three Stooges**. A few weeks later, when head Stooge **Moe Howard** made a sentimental journey back to the studio to say goodbye to some execs, the guard at the front gate wouldn't allow him on the very lot where the Stooges had reigned for 24 years.

1985: *The Trip to Bountiful*, opening at New York's Cinema II, proves soon enough to be a trip to the Oscar podium for the great **Geraldine Page**, who had been stopped short of victory seven previous times. The man who wrote her Oscar-winning ticket — Pulitzer Prize winner **Horton Foote** — also did the same for **Gregory Peck** (*To Kill a Mockingbird*) and **Robert Duvall** (*Tender Mercies*).

1996: **Albert Brooks**' *Mother* arrives for a multi-run in New York — **Debbie Reynolds**' first starring performance in pictures in 25 years and one she pounced on after a couple of her MGM cohorts passed it up: **Nancy [Davis] Reagan** and **Esther Williams**. It came close to getting into the Oscar running.

21

1925: *The Big Parade*, **King Vidor**'s World War I saga with **John Gilbert**, marches into the East Room of the White House for a special viewing by **President** and **Mrs. Calvin Coolidge** and son **John** — the first time any President had seen a film there.

1925: Director **Sergei Eisenstein**'s landmark masterpiece, *Battleship Potemkin*, is launched in Russia — and, somehow, cinema is never the same.

1933: *Flying Down to Rio*, the first film pairing of **Fred Astaire** and **Ginger Rogers**, touches down at Radio City Music Hall. He was billed fifth and she was billed fourth, and they were allowed only one dance — The Carioca — but it was enough to show the world what true stars are made of.

1937: Bolting to the other coast in the middle of supporting **Bette Davis**'s second Oscar-winning performance (*Jezebel*), **Henry Fonda** arrives just in time for the birth of his first-born, herself a future two-time Oscar winner. In 1977, when **Jane Fonda** hosted Davis's salute from the American Film Institute, she used the occasion to apologize for her dad's absence. Actually, the strain of rearranging the shooting schedule to oblige a baby-on-the-way charged Davis's performance (albeit not without colorful side-effects that prolonged production: a red swelling on her face, a "charley horse," bronchitis, exhaustion). The day before Henry's departure and Jane's arrival ended with Davis collapsing in hysterics after 11 consecutive hours of lensing. An easier birth also was achieved on this day: *Snow White and the Seven Dwarfs*, the first full-length animation feature, bowed at Hollywood's Carthay Circle Theater, putting **Walt Disney** on the map; on Feb. 23, 1939, the Motion Picture Academy acknowledged this accomplishment — a significant screen innovation — with one regular-sized honorary Oscar and seven miniature ones.

SEASONAL GREETINGS: Thomas Mitchell, Carol Coomes, Donna Reed, Jimmy Hawkins, James Stewart, Karolyn Grimes, Sarah Edwards, Edward Keane, Larry Sims and Beulah Bondi in *It's a Wonderful Life.* **SNOW WHITE AND THE SEVEN OSCARS:** A scene from *Snow White and the Seven Dwarfs.*

1946: Because the Technicolor prints of *Sinbad the Sailor* won't be ready for the holidays, RKO Radio decides to court the family trade by rushing into release *It's a Wonderful Life* — which is how the quintessential Christmas flick happened to premiere on this day, with a charity event, at New York's Globe.

1967: **Barbra Streisand** finishes her first film — *Funny Girl* — and at the subsequent wrap party director **William Wyler** pointedly presents her with a megaphone bearing the Directors Guild of America insignia. (Intended as a joke, it came in handy when she started *officially* directing her own performances.) Wyler, notorious for numerous retakes, had finally met his match in Streisand, who outdid even him on that score. "I wish Willie wouldn't be so rough on Barbra," quipped a crony on the set. "It's only the first film she's directed."

22

1943: "The Lady in the Tutti-Fruitti Hat," a **Harry Warren–Leo Robin** ditty cued by a headgear of bananas and strawberries concocted by designer **Yvonne Wood**, undulates onto the screen of New York's Roxy in *The Gang's All Here*, and a camp-cult following quickly forms from this colorful (!) collision of director **Busby Berkeley** and The Brazilian Bombshell, **Carmen Miranda**. The number's Freudian finale — when Miranda's banana headdress faded into a painted backdrop of bananas stretching to infinity — got Berkeley so euphoric he rode his camera boom right into her elaborately outsized hat, sending giant bananas and strawberries crashing down around her. She had to be coddled into another take ("Thees time, make weeth the careful! Knock one banana off my head, and I will make of you the flat pancake!"). The phallic overtone of the scene was not lost on her country's censors, and South America took it away.

1946: *The Wicked Lady*, the Restoration romp that brought **Margaret Lockwood** to the peak of her popularity in Britain, gallops into New York's Winter Garden a year later. Reason for the delay: Lockwood, as a high-born lady in low-cut costumes, displayed such daring decolletage retakes were required before the film was allowed on these shores! *The New York Times* found her "hardly convincing as the Jezebel of the tale," but it wound up being her most famous role. In 1983, adapter-director **Michael Winner** offered to write Lockwood into his **Faye Dunaway** remake of *The Wicked Lady*, but the original wouldn't budge out of retirement.

1967: The newsreel as we knew it in weekly theatrical installments is officially history with the final issue of Universal Newsreel.

1988: The niece of **Diana** (*Too Much Too Soon*) **Barrymore** — 13-year-old **Drew Barrymore** — has gone into rehab for alcoholism, according to her spokesperson. The whole sorry mess was later relayed in Drew's autobiography, *Little Girl Lost*, written at age 15 with **Todd Gold**.

1995: The squeaky-voiced slavey, "Prissy," who knew all there was to know about "birthin' babies" (*NOT!*) and who rode a buckboard through a blazing Atlanta to safety in her first and most famous film (*Gone With the Wind*) — **Thelma Butterfly McQueen**, 84 — expires from critical burns she suffered when a kerosene heater caught fire in her home near Augusta, GA.

BANANA MIRANDA: Carmen Miranda in *The Gang's All Here*.
A COVER-UP JOB: Margaret Lockwood in *The Wicked Lady*.
DOUBTING DR. PRISSY: Vivien Leigh and Butterfly McQueen in *Gone With the Wind*.

23

1932: *Rasputin and the Empress*, bowing at NYC's Astor, "achieves one feat which is not inconsiderate," said the *New York Herald-Tribune* critic: "It manages to libel even the despised **Rasputin**." Actually, the cry of libel came from Rasputin's known killer and his wife, **Prince Felix Youssoupoff** and **Princess Irina Alexandrovna** (in the film: **John Barrymore** and **Diana Wynyard**). They sued — he because he was called Chegodieff and not credited for his deed, she because she was depicted as raped by Rasputin — and they *won*, as did a real Prince Chegodieff. Ever since, no Hollywood film has gone into release without the line "The events and characters in this film are fictional and any resemblance to persons living or dead is purely coincidental."

1938: The Wicked Witch of the West comes perilously close to going up in smoke when a fire effect goes off too soon as **Margaret Hamilton** takes off from Munchkinland. She suffered first-degree burns on her face and second-degree burns on her hand. No amount of cajoling could coax her back on her broom when she resumed work Feb. 11 so stunt double **Betty Danko** did it for her — and landed in the hospital with an identical mishap.

1957: Sweeping into New York's Sutton very out of season is *Smiles of a Summer Night*, a sex farce very out of character for Sweden's **Ingmar Bergman**, possibly softening up the market for the intellectual big-guns — *The Seventh Seal* and *Wild Strawberries* — he already has in the can, ready to roll out and establish his rep as a world-class filmmaker.

1975: Composer **Bernard Herrmann** completes the background score for *Taxi Driver* — and dies the following day of a heart attack. When the film went into release, it was dedicated to Herrmann. Critic **John Simon** was less kind: "I don't know what Herrmann died of," he said of the composer's next-to-last opus (*Obsession*), "but I wouldn't rule out shame as a possibility." All the same, those last two scores comprised two-fifths of the nominees for Best Original Score of 1976. **Martin Scorsese**, who directed *Taxi Driver*, so enjoyed Herrmann's music for 1962's *Cape Fear* he remade the movie in 1991 just to give it posthumous replay.

MILES FROM A SUMMER NIGHT: Gunnar Bjornstrand, Eva Dahlbeck and Ulla Jacobsson in *Smiles of a Summer Night*.
MENACE FOR THE MENACE: Margaret Hamilton and Judy Garland in *The Wizard of Oz*.
RASPUTIN DISPUTIN': Diana Wynyard and John Barrymore in *Rasputin and the Empress*.

ON JOAN'S TERMS: Joan Crawford, Henry Fonda and Dana Andrews in *Daisy Kenyon*.
HELLO, SARONG: Dorothy Lamour and Ray Milland in *The Jungle Princess*.
A MAN FOR ALL SEAS: James Mason, Peter Lorre, Kirk Douglas and Paul Lukas in *20,000 Leagues Under the Sea*.

1906: *The Story of the Kelly Gang*, the world's first full-length feature film, emerges Down Under on this day — at the Melbourne Town Hall — recounting in 60 to 70 minutes the life of Irish bushranger/Australian outlaw Ned Kelly.

1925: A two-reeler co-directed by **Stan Laurel** and featuring future partner **Oliver Hardy** in a ship's-captain bit, *Madame Mystery* finishes filming on this day — and, with it, ends the screen career of **Theda Bara**. She got $15,000 for the title role — a haughty **Margaret Dumont**-like figure around whom swirled ocean-liner thieves and spies — but the results so dismayed her she never went near a camera again, leaving screen seduction to new-vamp-in-town **Greta Garbo**. Considering her notoriety as film temptress from 1915 to 1919, Bara turned out alarmingly well, marrying one of her directors (**Charles Brabin**) and settling down to 34 years of happily-ever-aftering as a Hollywood social hostess. But the dream died hard: Until her death, she advertised in the Hollywood casting directory as being "at liberty."

1936: A sarong is born, just in time for the Christmas holidays, as **Dorothy Lamour**'s *The Jungle Princess* debuts at New York's Rialto. Her revealing wraparound triggered a fad for tropical fabrics that lasted a decade. "I would never say that the sarong made Dorothy Lamour a star," designer **Edith Head** later clarified. "If someone else had worn it, chances are that neither the girl nor the sarong would have been heard of again — but, when Dottie filled out that piece of cloth, it was magic." Lamour was *toujour* grateful: "I thank God for that little strip of cloth." Of her 60 or so flicks, she wore the sarong in no more than six, but it did become a kind of trademark — "and it did hinder me. They expect you to always be the young girl leaning against the palm tree. Why should you want me to act?"

1947: "I'll do it if I can have **Henry Fonda** and **Dana Andrews**," says **Joan Crawford**, consenting to *Daisy Kenyon*, which the Roxy opens on Christmas Eve. She was being literal, too: When ordinary approaches didn't get through to shy-guy Fonda, she had the wardrobe person create a jockstrap of rhinestones, gold sequins and red beads and presented it to him one morning, gift-wrapped.

1954: Last seen nobly walking into the Pacific Ocean at the end of *A Star Is Born*, **James Mason** suddenly surfaces with a snarl at New York's Astor Theater, skippering **Jules Verne**'s super-sub, *The Nautilus*, through *20,000 Leagues Under the Sea*.

1946:
On a day he professed to loathe: *Christmas!* — **W.C. Fields**, 67, dies at a Pasadena sanatorium. He woke from a coma, found his secretary and a nurse keeping vigil, raised his forefinger to his lips to signal silence, winked and died. A few weeks earlier, friends visiting him discovered him reading the Bible. "Just looking for loopholes," he explained.

1949:
The star who film-debuted last Dec. 23 in *Every Girl Should Be Married*, **Betsy Drake**, lands the leading man, **Cary Grant**, on this Xmas.

1954:
With the arrival of *The Silver Chalice* at NYC's Paramount, **Paul Newman**'s film career gets off to a running stop. "The worst film made in the entirety of the 1950s," wailed the actor who began his $1,000-a-week Warners contract with it, woefully miscast as a Greek silversmith spouting overripe dialogue and displaying knobby knees. After that, Newman declared costume movies off limits ("I wore a cocktail dress once, in *The Silver Chalice* — never again," he said, nixing *Ben-Hur*). When *Chalice* hit L.A. TV for a week's run, he bought a *Times* ad proclaiming "Paul Newman Apologizes Every Night This Week" — a gesture that only sent the film's TV ratings soaring.

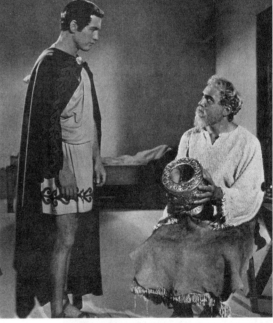

1957:
"Also, merely as a footnote — what a picture to open on Christmas Day!" exclaimed critic **Bosley Crowther**, at the conclusion of his *Times* review of *Paths of Glory*, which marched into New York's Victoria. Director **Stanley Kubrick**'s first authentic masterpiece tackled a novel that had tempted Hollywood for 22 years: **Humphrey Cobb**'s account of an actual World War I incident in which three innocent French soldiers were executed for cowardice as a face-saving measure for a general whose whole regiment retreated. The anti-war epic that premiered one week earlier — *The Bridge on the River Kwai* — took most of the year's awards, leaving *Paths of Glory* completely out in the cold. Unnominated, but hardly unnoticed, was the performance of producer **Kirk Douglas**, who defended the doomed trio (**Timothy Carey**, **Ralph Meeker**, **Joseph Turkel**) and railed against the military leaders who dictated their deaths (**George Macready**, **Wayne Morris**, **Adolphe Menjou**). The film's lone female, **Susanne Christian**, appears at the end as the German girl who hushed a tavern-ful of rowdy French soldiers with a halting, haunting rendition of the universally known "Soldier Boy" song. The following April, she became Mrs. Kubrick.

PRESCRIPTION MARRIAGE: Cary Grant and Betsy Drake in *Every Girl Should Be Married.*
NO ABSENCE OF CHALICE MALICE: Paul Newman and Lorne Greene in *The Silver Chalice.*
A KUBRICK CHRISTMAS: Kirk Douglas in *Paths of Glory.*

1933: "The calla lilies are in bloom again," **Katharine Hepburn** utters for the first time on this day as *The Lake* bows on Broadway. The line didn't become a catch phrase until a revamped scene from that play was used four years later as the play-within-the-play scene in her *Stage Door* flick. The second most memorable line involving *The Lake* came from critic **Dorothy Parker**, who was of the opinion that "Miss Hepburn ran the gamut of emotions from A to B." Hepburn couldn't have agreed more. "Hell," she cracked years later, "I didn't even make it to B."

1940: *The Philadelphia Story* premieres at Radio City Music Hall on this day. Basically a **Katharine Hepburn** vehicle as it was on stage, it wound up winning the Oscar for one of her beaus: third-billed **James Stewart**. Four days short of 53 years later, a film titled only *Philadelphia* opened in NYC, producing an Oscar-winning Best Actor as well: the latter-day James Stewart, **Tom Hanks**.

1956: Playing the driven Vincent Van Gogh in *Lust for Life*, **Kirk Douglas** wins the Best Actor prize from The New York Film Critics Circle on this day. Director **Vincente Minnelli** always counted this his favorite film — and it wasn't even a musical! — but he was blackmailed into it: MGM exec **Dore Schary** would only green-light the Van Gogh project if Minnelli would agree to direct *Kismet.*

1974: The dream of a big-screen comeback dies with **Jack Benny**, 80, on this day. **Bing Crosby** and **Bob Hope** had put in a big bid to do *The Sunshine Boys* on film, but **Neil Simon** instead tested Benny and **Red Skelton** — with sensational results, he has said; Skelton soon chickened out, but Benny fully believed he'd be back starring in movies for the first time since *The Horn Blows at Midnight* 30 years earlier. Benny's best pal, **George Burns**, making his first feature in 36 years, replaced him and became the oldest performer ever to win the Oscar (80 years, 2 months at the time he was named Best Supporting Actor of 1975). When he died 49 days after his 100th birthday, Burns was the oldest Oscar-winning performer of all — but **Jessica Tandy** (80 years, 9 months when she was cited Best Actress of 1989 for *Driving Miss Daisy*) had inherited, by mere months, his distinction of being the older performer to win the Oscar. The oldest Best Actor Oscar winner: **Henry Fonda** (76 years, 317 days when *On Golden Pond* got him the prize). The oldest Best Supporting Actress Oscar winner: **Dame Peggy Ashcroft** (77, when cited for *A Passage to India*). The oldest performer to receive an Oscar: **Groucho Marx** (83, at the time of his 1973 honorary).

26

27

1933: "Despite this morning's review in The [*Hollywood*] *Reporter*, I believe *Jezebel* contains an excellent foundation for a picture," director **William Wyler** memoes to Universal chief **Carl Laemmle Jr.** on this day after a dizzy Broadway bender of 14 plays. He thought it a swell vehicle for the studio's **Margaret Sullavan**, but Junior was apathetic. As fate would have it, Wyler wedded Sullavan 11 months later and filmed *Jezebel* four years later (for Warners — with **Bette Davis**, who called him the great love of her life).

1934: *In Caliente* is off and filming, with **Lloyd Bacon** in the director's chair and **Busby Berkeley** in charge of the dance numbers. Between the two of them, they crossed the color barrier: Contrary to the title of Mort Dixon and Allie Wrubel's big song, costumes for "The Lady in Red" were really a shade of blue that looked red when photographed on black-and-white film.

1944: **Tallulah Bankhead**'s depiction of the war-correspondent diva aboard *Lifeboat* outshines **Ingrid Bergman**'s *Gaslight* for Best Actress honors from The New York Film Critics Circle. Movies weren't her medium; she did only 11. "The talkies," she once groused, "makes me sound as if I'd been castrated."

1954: "The scenery might look pretty if the fuzziness of Superscope and the blobbiness of the color were not offensive to the eye," decries critic **Bosley Crowther** in *The New York Times* about the first film to be made in Superscope, *Vera Cruz*, a below-par below-the-border shoot-'em-up with **Gary Cooper** and **Burt Lancaster**. Nevertheless, it made so much money Hecht-Lancaster Productions had to make the Oscar-winning *Marty* as a tax loss.

1963: As *Time*'s film critic figures it, the remake of a remake — **Doris Day**'s salvaging (*Move Over, Darling*) of **Marilyn Monroe**'s aborted redoing (*Something's Got To Give*) of **Irene Dunne**'s original (*My Favorite Wife*) — "doesn't half make it. It has been tailored for Doris Day, who just can't bring herself to attempt MM's celebrated nude bathing scene. DD just drives a Chrysler convertible through an automatic car wash and lets it go at that."

BANKHEAD BETTERS BERGMAN: Tallulah in *Lifeboat*.
LESS-THAN-SUPERSCOPE: Gary Cooper, Denise Darcel and Burt Lancaster in *Vera Cruz*.
OSCAR'S OLDSTERS: Jessica Tandy in Fried Green Tomatoes, Gloria Stuart in *Titanic*.

1991: NYC's Baronet starts serving *Fried Green Tomatoes* — a rare "chick flick" delicacy which, in less than two months, brings **Jessica Tandy** another Oscar distinction: On Feb. 19, 1992, the 82-year-old actress became the oldest Oscar-nominated performer, besting (by mere months) the distinction **Eva LeGallienne** earned in 1981 for *Resurrection*. Seven years later Tandy was topped by **Gloria Stuart**, 87, up for Best Supporting Actress via *Titanic*.

28

1895: France's **Lumiere** brothers — **Auguste, Marie, Louis, Nicholas** and **Louis-Jean** — give the first screening for a paying audience on this day at the Grand Cafe on the Boulevard des Capucines in Paris, charging one franc entrance fee for images projected through the cinematographe (a movie camera and projector) they invented — an occasion that qualifies as the cornerstone for commercial movie exhibition.

1921: *Orphans of the Storm* (or The **Gish** Girls Get Through the French Revolution) bows in Boston on this day, five days before it opens at New York's Apollo. It was **Lillian**'s last for her mentor, director **D.W. Griffith**.

1934: *Becky Sharp*, another film twirl of Thackeray's *Vanity Fair*, comes to a sudden stop on this day when director **Lowell Sherman**, 49, dies of double pneumonia. **Rouben Mamoulian** stepped in, scrapped all of Sherman's hard work and started from scratch. Before taking up directing full-time, Sherman was an actor whose best-known portrayal was that of a hard-driving, heavy-boozing, death-embracing director not unlike himself in the first film telling of *A Star Is Born*: 1932's *What Price Hollywood?*

1940: Being wife to The World's Greatest Entertainer is not the easiest of roles, and on this day **Rudy Keeler** relinquishes the part in divorce action against **Al Jolson**. Ducking his jealousy over her most frequent co-star (**Dick Powell**), she simply charged that he humiliated her in public and called her stupid. Six years later he had to call her Julie Benson because Keeler declined to lend her name to *The Jolson Story*. **Evelyn Keyes** played her — er, Julie.

1943: *The Hard Way*, on this day, earns **Ida Lupino** — who somehow never made the Oscar running — The New York Film Critics Circle's nod as Best Actress of 1943.

29

REACHING HEIGHTS:
Laurence Olivier and
Merle Oberon in
Wuthering Heights.
FATAL BLOW: Jack Nance
in *Eraserhead.*
FRIGHT AT FIRST SIGHT:
Fay Wray in *King Kong.*

1913: The first movie serial with cliffhanger plotting designed to scare audiences into returning — *The Adventures of Kathlyn*, starring **Kathlyn Williams** and **Tom Santschi** — begins unreeling in Chicago the first of 13 chapters. It was co-produced by The Selig Company (which released it) and The Chicago *Tribune* (which ran the story serially on its pages).

1932: *King Kong* starts stirring with sound and ferocious music on this day, as recording begins for **Fay Wray**'s over-the-top-and-off-the-charts shrieks and **Max Steiner**'s heart-thumping score. Ignoring RKO's instructions to recycle already existing scores — when producer **Merian C. Cooper** personally promised to pay for an original — Steiner composed (in eight weeks) the absolute corker in early-talkie soundtrack excitement. Then, at a cost of $50,000, 46 musicians recorded it.

1938: Producer **Samuel Goldwyn** and director **William Wyler** confer/collide on this day about whether they should continue filming *Wuthering Heights*. Goldwyn lost the toss but won the battle: A year later (less two days), the producer learned that the finally finished result was considered by The New York Film Critics Circle— in a year blindingly gone with the wind — the Best Picture of 1939.

1964: "My advisers all thought it would destroy my image, but there's a lot of good image in **John Wayne** licking cancer," trumpets the actor over drinks in his Encino home on this day in an exclusive with columnist **James Bacon**. "I had the Big C, but I've beaten the son of a bitch. Maybe I can give some poor bastard a little hope by being honest. I want people to know cancer can be licked." When *Life* reprised the story, Wayne was on the cover under the classic caption, "I licked the Big C!" To close friends, he called cancer the Red Witch (after the ship he skippered in *Wake of the Red Witch* — and the one that ultimately carried him to a watery grave). When he went for check-ups, it was "Well, I'm going down to La Jolla to see if the Red Witch is waiting for me." When he returned, it was "Well, the bitch wasn't there this time." The most famous cancer out-patient in America kept the bitch at bay for 15 years and 18 films before she finally caught up with him June 11, 1979.

1996: A blow to the head of "Eraserhead" during a doughnut-shop altercation proves fatal the next day for **Jack Nance**, 53, who played that title role (the electric-haired Henry Spencer) in director **David Lynch**'s 1978 cult classic. When Lynch moved into the movie mainstream, Nance moved with him — in smaller roles (*Dune*, *Blue Velvet*, *Wild at Heart*, *Lost Highway* and TV's *Twin Peaks*).

1930: Lensing begins on *Bad Sister*, the movie that brought **Bette Davis** to the movies — blushing. As good sister to **Sidney Fox**'s bad, she had a scene where she was to bathe her baby. "It was the first time I ever saw a naked male," the actress later recalled — and her beet-red embarrassment was not lost on the black-and-white camerawork: "My face goes gray. You can see the blush right there on the film."

1932: An unsung, generally unpraised *Madame Butterfly* takes flight nationally on this day — Film No. 7 for **Cary Grant** his first year on screen — and a lucky No. 7 it is: The dazzling sight of Grant in Lieutenant Pinkerton's Navy whites strolling out of the studio commissary crossed **Mae West**'s ever-roving eye. Her heavy lids actually lifted a little, and she asked after him. When told he was making *Madame Butterfly*, she said, "I don't care if he's making Little Nell! If he can talk, I'll take him" (i.e., for leading man in her first starring vehicle, *She Done Him Wrong*). In truth, she done him right: Major stardom quickly followed.

1937: A painstaking craftsman with impeccable credits as a director (*The Guardsman*, *The Good Earth*, *Reunion in Vienna*), **Sidney Franklin** finally puts into production — after four years of pre-production — *Marie Antoinette* and is promptly relieved of command by **W.S.** (One Take) **Van Dyke**. Rather rough handling of The Widow Thalberg, some thought — and a heavy-handed indication that **Louis B. Mayer**'s enthusiasm for this lavish **Norma Shearer** vehicle had dimmed since the death of his first-lieuenant and her husband, exec **Irving Thalberg**. What ultimately went into release opened with a deep (though not nearly deep enough) bow: "To Sidney Franklin . . . for his contribution in the preparation of this production . . . grateful acknowledgement." It was also a graceful exit for a company man who came back to direct only one more time (two decades later to remake his 1934 *Barretts*). That L.B. was all heart.

WINNING OSCARS WITH BERGMAN REJECTS: From left: Olivia de Havilland in *To Each His Own*; Loretta Young in *The Farmer's Daughter*.
SIDNEY SAT THIS ONE OUT: Joseph Schildkraut and Norma Shearer in *Marie Antoinette*.
AN OFFER HE COULDN'T REFUSE: Cary Grant and Mae West in *She Done Him Wrong*.

1945: Effective on this day, **Ingrid Bergman** is contract-free of producer **David O. Selznick**. Wanting one last film out of her, he had pitched her parts that would win the next two Best Actress Oscars — 1946's *To Each His Own* (**Olivia de Havilland**) and 1947's *The Farmer's Daughter* (**Loretta Young**) — but she turned them both down.

ANOTHER PART IN THE FOREST: Lita Baron and Johnny Weissmuller in *Jungle Jim.*
A CASE OF CLASS: Alfred Hitchcock, Joan Tetzel, Louis Jourdan, David O. Selznick, Ann Todd, Charles Laughton, Charles Coburn, Ethel Barrymore and Gregory Peck.
CHEERS FOR THE CHARIOTEER: Ramon Novarro in *Ben-Hur.*

1925: "WELL KID," wires **Nicholas Schenck** to an ailing **Irving Thalberg** about the tumultuous launching he had just witnessed at New York's George M. Cohan Theater, "YOU WERE REPAID LAST NIGHT FOR ALL THE HARD WORK YOU PUT IN ON *BEN HUR.* IT WAS THE MOST MAGNIFICENT OPENING I HAVE EVER WITNESSED. THE ONLY TIME I REMEMBER GETTING AS BIG A THRILL AS I DID DURING THE CHARIOT RACE WAS AT THE **DEMPSEY-FIRPO** FIGHT AND THE ENTIRE AUDIENCE WAS AS EXCITED AS I WAS."

1941: Producer **Hal Wallis'** final inter-office memo of the year is a single sentence dispatched to All Departments: "The story that we recently purchased entitled *Everybody Comes to Rick's* will hereafter be known as *Casablanca.*"

1947: Showman-with-not-much-to-show **David O. Selznick** hires two theaters in the Westwood section of L.A. on this day to launch his last **Hitchcock**, *The Paradine Case.* Unable to lure **Garbo** out of retirement to play the enigmatic did-she-or-didn't-she accused murderess — and he'd bought the yarn for her 14 years before, back in their old MGM days — Selznick settled for Italian actress **Alida Valli** (rechristened simply Valli for these shores). Garbo was right.

1948: Having reigned longest as Tarzan, Lord of the Jungle (a dozen films from 1932 to 1948), **Johnny Weissmuller** turns in his loincloth and dons a safari suit to work another part of the backlot jungle as *Jungle Jim,* just arriving at New York's Ambassador. Fifteen feature-length outings followed for the next seven years — plus a 26-episode half-hour television series in 1956.

1955: After sending two mechanical whales to Davy Jones' locker off the Canary Islands — and faced with the prospect of losing a third, **John Huston** grabs a bottle of Scotch on this day and gamely climbs into his metal-wood-latex white whale to get the concluding shots he needs for *Moby Dick,* shouting, "Lose this whale, and you lose me!" The crew came through, a Happy New Year was had by all, and Huston lived to direct even greater films.